Saint Thomas Aquinas

Commentary on the Letters of Saint Paul to the Galatians and Ephesians

Biblical Commentaries

Volume 39
Latin/English Edition of the Works of St. Thomas Aquinas

AQUINAS INSTITUTE | EMMAUS ACADEMIC
GREEN BAY, WI | STEUBENVILLE, OH

This printing was funded in part by donations made in memory of Marcus Berquist and Rose Johanna Trumbull.

Published with the ecclesiastical approval of
The Most Reverend Paul D. Etienne, DD, STL
Bishop of Cheyenne
Given on August 27, 2012

Copyright © 2012
Aquinas Institute, Inc.
Green Bay, Wisconsin
www.aquinasinstitute.org

Printed in the United States of America

Second Printing 2021

PUBLISHER'S CATALOGING-IN-PUBLICATION DATA

Aquinas, St. Thomas.
 Commentary on the Letters of Saint Paul to the Galatians and Ephesians / Saint Thomas Aquinas.
 p. 360 cm.
 ISBN 978-1-62340-003-3

1. Bible. N.T. Galatians -- Commentaries -- Early works to 1800.   2. Bible. N.T. Ephesians -- Commentaries -- Early works to 1800.   I. Title.   II. Series

BS2685.T4612 2012
227'.4'07--dc23   2012945236

Notes on the Text

Scripture

The text of Sacred Scripture presented at the beginning of each lecture is given in Latin, English, and Greek. Since St. Thomas appears to be familiar with more than one translation, quotes from memory, and often enough paraphrases, it has proven difficult to reconstruct the version of scripture with which St. Thomas was working. However, the closest available version of Scripture to St. Thomas's text was found to be the Clementine Vulgate of 1598, and this version of the Vulgate is the one found at the beginning of each lecture. The choice of an English version of Scripture to parallel to the Vulgate was therefore the Douay-Rheims. Both of these versions have been slightly modified to fit the text of St. Thomas. The Greek text is from the Nestle-Aland, Novum Testamentum Graece, 27th Revised Edition, edited by Barbara Aland, Kurt Aland, Johannes Karavidopoulos, Carlo M. Martini, and Bruce M. Metzger in cooperation with the Institute for New Testament Textual Research, Münster/Westphalia, © 1993 Deutsche Bibelgesellschaft, Stuttgart. Used with permission. The numbering of Scripture in the lecture headings and the English translation of the commentary is taken from the Nestle-Aland 27th Revised Edition and the RSV, while the numbering St. Thomas uses in the Latin text has been kept intact.

Latin Text of St. Thomas

The Latin texts of the commentaries on Galatians and Ephesians are based on the Corpus Thomisticum texts of the Fundación Tomás de Aquino <www.corpusthomisticum.org>. These texts are based on the Marietti 1953 edition, prepared by Fr. Raffaele Cai OP, transcribed by Fr. Roberto Busa SJ, and revised by Dr. Enrique Alarcón and other editors and collaborators of this bilingual edition. © 2012 Fundación Tomás de Aquino, Pamplona. Used with permission.

English Translation of St. Thomas

The English translation of the commentary on Galatians was prepared by Fr. Fabian Richard Larcher, O.P., who left it in draft form at the time of his death in 1991. The manuscript came into the hands of Matthew Levering, who had the permission of Fr. Larcher's superiors to utilize the translation for scholarly purposes. Dr. Levering's colleague, Dr. Jeremy Holmes, spearheaded a team of graduate students at Ave Maria University who transcribed the entire document. A thorough correction of the text has been made by the editorial team at The Aquinas Institute for the Study of Sacred Doctrine in Lander, Wyoming.

The English translation of the commentary on Ephesians is by Fr. Matthew L. Lamb of Ave Maria University. No critical Latin edition of the commentary on Ephesians has been published. Fr. Lamb's translation is based on the Parma edition of the complete works of Thomas Aquinas. He also consulted the Piana edition as used by Raphael Cai, O.P., in the eighth revised Marietti edition of *Super Epistolas S. Pauli Lectura* volume II (Rome, 1953).

The Aquinas Institute requests your assistance in the continued perfection of these texts.
If you discover any errors, please send a note to us by e-mail: admin@theaquinasinstitute.org.

Dedicated with love to
Our Lady of Mt. Carmel

Contents

Commentary on the Letter of Saint Paul to the Galatians

Prologue 1

Chapter 1
Lecture 1 - Gal 1:1–5 3
Lecture 2 - Gal 1:6–10 9
Lecture 3 - Gal 1:11–14 15
Lecture 4 - Gal 1:15–17 19
Lecture 5 - Gal 1:18–24 22

Chapter 2
Lecture 1 - Gal 2:1–5 27
Lecture 2 - Gal 2:6–10 33
Lecture 3 - Gal 2:11–14 38
Lecture 4 - Gal 2:15–16 44
Lecture 5 - Gal 2:17–18 47
Lecture 6 - Gal 2:19–21 49

Chapter 3
Lecture 1 - Gal 3:1 55
Lecture 2 - Gal 3:2–5 59
Lecture 3 - Gal 3:6–9 63
Lecture 4 - Gal 3:10–12 66
Lecture 5 - Gal 3:13–14 71
Lecture 6 - Gal 3:15–18 74
Lecture 7 - Gal 3:19–20 78
Lecture 8 - Gal 3:21–25 81
Lecture 9 - Gal 3:26–29 84

Chapter 4
Lecture 1 - Gal 4:1–3 89
Lecture 2 - Gal 4:4–5 92
Lecture 3 - Gal 4:6–7 96
Lecture 4 - Gal 4:8–11 99
Lecture 5 - Gal 4:12–18 103
Lecture 6 - Gal 4:19–20 108
Lecture 7 - Gal 4:21–23 110
Lecture 8 - Gal 4:24–27 114
Lecture 9 - Gal 4:28–31 120

Chapter 5
Lecture 1 - Gal 5:1–4 123
Lecture 2 - Gal 5:5–12 127
Lecture 3 - Gal 5:13–15 133
Lecture 4 - Gal 5:16–17 136
Lecture 5 - Gal 5:18–21 140
Lecture 6 - Gal 5:22 144
Lecture 7 - Gal 5:23–26 149

Chapter 6

Lecture 1 - Gal 6:1–5 153
Lecture 2 - Gal 6:6–10 158
Lecture 3 - Gal 6:11–13 163
Lecture 4 - Gal 6:14–15 166
Lecture 5 - Gal 6:16–18 169

Commentary on the Letter of Saint Paul to the Ephesians

Introduction 173
Prologue 177

Chapter 1

Lecture 1 - Eph 1:1–5 181
Lecture 2 - Eph 1:6–7 188
Lecture 3 - Eph 1:8–10 191
Lecture 4 - Eph 1:11–12 195
Lecture 5 - Eph 1:13–14 198
Lecture 6 - Eph 1:15–18 202
Lecture 7 - Eph 1:19–21 206
Lecture 8 - Eph 1:22–23 211

Chapter 2

Lecture 1 - Eph 2:1–3 215
Lecture 2 - Eph 2:4–7 220
Lecture 3 - Eph 2:8–10 224
Lecture 4 - Eph 2:11–13 227
Lecture 5 - Eph 2:14–18 230
Lecture 6 - Eph 2:19–22 236

Chapter 3

Lecture 1 - Eph 3:1–6 241
Lecture 2 - Eph 3:7–9 246
Lecture 3 - Eph 3:10–12 250
Lecture 4 - Eph 3:13–17 255
Lecture 5 - Eph 3:18–21 259

Chapter 4

Lecture 1 - Eph 4:1–4 265
Lecture 2 - Eph 4:5–6 269
Lecture 3 - Eph 4:7–10 272
Lecture 4 - Eph 4:11–13 276
Lecture 5 - Eph 4:14–16 280
Lecture 6 - Eph 4:17–19 284
Lecture 7 - Eph 4:20–24 288
Lecture 8 - Eph 4:25–27 292
Lecture 9 - Eph 4:28–29 295
Lecture 10 - Eph 4:30–32 298

Chapter 5

- Lecture 1 - Eph 5:1–2 301
- Lecture 2 - Eph 5:3–4 303
- Lecture 3 - Eph 5:5–7 305
- Lecture 4 - Eph 5:8–11 308
- Lecture 5 - Eph 5:12–14 311
- Lecture 6 - Eph 5:15–17 313
- Lecture 7 - Eph 5:18–21 315
- Lecture 8 - Eph 5:22–27 318
- Lecture 9 - Eph 5:28–30 322
- Lecture 10 - Eph 5:31–33 325

Chapter 6

- Lecture 1 - Eph 6:1–4 329
- Lecture 2 - Eph 6:5–9 332
- Lecture 3 - Eph 6:10–12 335
- Lecture 4 - Eph 6:13–17 339
- Lecture 5 - Eph 6:18–24 343

Commentary on the Letter of Saint Paul to the Galatians

Commentary on the Letter of Saint Paul to the Galatians

Prologue

Leviticus 26:10

Comedetis vetustissima veterum, et vetera novis supervenientibus proiicietis.	καὶ φάγεσθε παλαιὰ καὶ παλαιὰ παλαιῶν καὶ παλαιὰ ἐκ προσώπου νέων ἐξοίσετε.	You shall eat the oldest of the old store, and, new coming on, you shall cast away the old.

1. Haec verba competunt praesenti epistolae, in qua Apostolus redarguit Galatas, qui intantum seducti fuerant a pseudo, ut simul servarent legalia et Evangelium, quod Apostolus improperat eis in verbis praemissis, dicens *vetera, novis supervenientibus, proiicietis*.

In quibus verbis innuit Dominus quadruplicem vetustatem. Prima vetustas est erroris, de qua Is. XXVI, 3: *vetus error abiit*, et haec remota est per novitatem doctrinae Christi. Mc. I, 27: *quae est haec nova doctrina?*

Secunda vetustas est figurae, de qua Hebr. c. VIII, 8: *consummabo super domum David, et super Iuda testamentum novum, non secundum testamentum quod feci patribus eorum*. Ubi primo ostendit primum testamentum esse vetustum, et hoc renovari per novitatem gratiae, seu veritatis praesentiae Christi. Ier. XXXI, 22: *novum faciet Dominus super terram*, et cetera.

Tertia est vetustas culpae, de qua Ps. XXXI, v. 3: *quoniam tacui* (confitendo scilicet peccata mea), *inveteraverunt*, et cetera. Et haec renovatur per novitatem iustitiae. Rom. VI, 4: *in novitate vitae ambulemus*, et cetera.

Quarta est vetustas poenae. Thren. III, 4: *vetustam feci pellem meam*. Et haec renovabitur per novitatem gloriae, de qua novitate Is. ult.: *ecce ego creo caelum novum*, etc.; Apoc. XXI, 21: *dixit, qui sedebat in throno: ecce nova facio omnia*.

1. These words befit the present epistle in which the Apostle reproves the Galatians who had been so deceived by false teachers as to observe at once the rites of the law and those of the Gospel. For this the Apostle rebukes them with the above words: *the new coming on, you shall cast away the old*.

In these words the Lord suggests a fourfold oldness. First, the oldness of error: *the old error is passed away* (Isa 26:3). This is removed by the newness of the doctrine of Christ. *What is this new doctrine?* (Mark 1:27).

The second oldness is that of figure: *behold, the days shall come, says the Lord: and I will perfect, unto the house of Israel and unto the house of Judah, a new testament not according to the testament which I made to their fathers* (Heb 8:8). Here he shows first of all that the first testament is old and that it is made new by the newness of grace or of the reality of Christ's presence. *The Lord has created a new thing upon the earth* (Jer 31:22).

The third is the oldness of guilt: *because I was silent* (not confessing my sins), *my bones grew old* (Ps 31:3). And this is made new by the newness of justice. *So we may walk in newness of life* (Rom 6:4).

The fourth is the oldness of punishment. *My skin he has made old* (Lam 3:4). And this will be made new by the newness of glory, of which newness it is said: *behold I will create a new heaven and a new earth* (Isa 66:22). And he who sat on the throne said: *behold, I make all things new* (Rev 21:5).

Chapter 1

Lecture 1

1:1 Paulus, apostolus non ab hominibus, neque per hominem, sed per Jesum Christum, et Deum Patrem, qui suscitavit eum a mortuis: [n. 2]

1:2 et qui mecum sunt omnes fratres, ecclesiis Galatiae.

1:3 Gratia vobis, et pax a Deo Patre, et Domino nostro Jesu Christo, [n. 10]

1:4 qui dedit semetipsum pro peccatis nostris, ut eriperet nos de praesenti saeculo nequam, secundum voluntatem Dei et Patris nostri, [n. 14]

1:5 cui est gloria in saecula saeculorum. Amen. [n. 15]

1:1 Παῦλος ἀπόστολος, οὐκ ἀπ' ἀνθρώπων οὐδὲ δι' ἀνθρώπου ἀλλὰ διὰ Ἰησοῦ Χριστοῦ καὶ θεοῦ πατρὸς τοῦ ἐγείραντος αὐτὸν ἐκ νεκρῶν,

1:2 καὶ οἱ σὺν ἐμοὶ πάντες ἀδελφοί, ταῖς ἐκκλησίαις τῆς Γαλατίας:

1:3 χάρις ὑμῖν καὶ εἰρήνη ἀπὸ θεοῦ πατρὸς ἡμῶν καὶ κυρίου Ἰησοῦ Χριστοῦ,

1:4 τοῦ δόντος ἑαυτὸν ὑπὲρ τῶν ἁμαρτιῶν ἡμῶν ὅπως ἐξέληται ἡμᾶς ἐκ τοῦ αἰῶνος τοῦ ἐνεστῶτος πονηροῦ κατὰ τὸ θέλημα τοῦ θεοῦ καὶ πατρὸς ἡμῶν,

1:5 ᾧ ἡ δόξα εἰς τοὺς αἰῶνας τῶν αἰώνων: ἀμήν.

1:1 Paul, an apostle, not of men, neither by man, but by Jesus Christ and God the Father, who raised him from the dead: [n. 2]

1:2 And all the brethren who are with me: to the churches of Galatia.

1:3 Grace be to you, and peace from God the Father and from our Lord Jesus Christ, [n. 10]

1:4 Who gave himself for our sins, that he might deliver us from this present wicked world, according to the will of God and our Father: [n. 14]

1:5 To whom is glory forever and ever. Amen. [n. 15]

---

2. Scribit ergo Apostolus Galatis hanc epistolam, in qua ostendit, quod, veniente gratia Novi Testamenti, debet proiici Vetus Testamentum, ut impleta veritate deseratur figura, quibus duabus, scilicet gratia et veritate, adeptis, perveniatur ad veritatem iustitiae et gloriae. Acquiruntur autem illa duo, si observantia legalium dimissa, observantiae Evangelii Christi ferventer insistamus.

Ordo autem huius epistolae congruus est, ut post duas epistolas ad Corinthios, in quarum prima agitur de sacramentis Ecclesiae, in secunda de ministris horum sacramentorum, necessarie sequatur epistola ad Galatas, in qua agitur de cessatione sacramentorum Veteris Testamenti.

Dividitur autem haec epistola in duas partes, in salutationem, et epistolarem narrationem, ibi ***miror quod***, et cetera.

In salutatione autem

primo ponitur persona salutantis;

secundo ponuntur personae salutatae, ibi ***ecclesiis Galatiae***, etc.;

tertio bonum optatum, ibi ***gratia vobis***, et cetera.

Circa primum, primo, ponitur persona salutans principaliter, quae describitur ex nomine et ex auctoritate.

3. Ex nomine quidem cum dicit ***Paulus***, quod congruit humilitati suae, quia interpretatur humilis. Unde

2. The Apostle therefore writes the Galatians this epistle in which he shows that with the coming of the grace of the New Testament, the Old Testament should be cast out, so that with the fulfillment of the truth, the figure may be abandoned, and with the attainment of these two, namely, grace and truth, one may arrive at the truth of justice and glory. And these two are acquired, if, abandoning the observance of the *legalia*, we concentrate fervently on observing the Gospel of Christ.

The order of this epistle is fitting in that, after the two epistles to the Corinthians, in the first of which it is a question of the sacraments of the Church, and in the second, of the ministers of these sacraments, there should necessarily follow the epistle to the Galatians, treating of the termination of the sacraments of the Old Testament.

This epistle is divided into two parts: namely, into a greeting, and the setting forth of the epistle, at ***I wonder that you are so soon removed*** (Gal 1:6).

In the greeting, however:

first, the person who sends the greeting is mentioned;

second, the persons greeted are mentioned, at ***to the churches of Galatia***;

third, the good he wishes them, at ***grace be to you***.

As to the first, mention is made first of the person principally sending the greeting; and he is described by his name and his authority.

3. By his name, indeed, when he says ***Paul*** which, because it means 'humble', accords with his humility. Hence it

dicitur I Cor. XVI, 9: *ego sum minimus apostolorum*, et cetera.

Item congruit officio suo, quia secundum alium modum interpretatur os tubae, in quo specialiter est officium praedicationis significatum. Is. LVIII, 1: *quasi tuba exalta vocem tuam*, et cetera.

4. Ex auctoritate autem describitur, cum dicitur **apostolus**. Ubi duo ponuntur, scilicet eius auctoritas, et auctoritatis origo.

Auctoritas, quia **apostolus**, qui idem est quod missus.

Sciendum est autem, quod Apostolus in quibusdam epistolis scribit se *servum*, ostendens nomen humilitatis, ut in Epistola ad Romanos; in quibusdam vero scribit se **apostolum**, ostendens auctoritatem suam. Cuius ratio est, quia Romani superbi erant, et ideo Apostolus, ut inducat eos ad humilitatem, scribit se servum, in exemplum humilitatis. Galatis vero, quia stulti erant et superbi, ut frangat eos, nominat se **apostolum**; et ideo hic ponit auctoritatem suam.

5. Originem autem auctoritatis suae describit, cum dicit **non ab hominibus**, et cetera. Et

primo removet originem aestimatam;

secundo assignat veram, ibi **sed per Iesum Christum**, et cetera.

6. Origo autem aestimata erat, quia intantum Galatae seducti erant a pseudo, quod crederent Apostolum non esse eiusdem auctoritatis qua alii apostoli erant, quia non fuit doctus a Christo vel conversatus cum eo, sed esset missus ab eis, quasi minister eorum. Opinionem ergo istam removet, cum dicit **non ab hominibus**, et cetera.

Quidam enim mittebantur a toto collegio apostolorum et discipulorum. Et ideo ostendens se non esse ab eis missum, dicit **non ab hominibus**. Quidam enim mittebantur ab aliquo apostolorum speciali, sicut Paulus aliquando mittebat Lucam et Titum. Et ideo ostendens, quod nec sic missus sit, dicit **neque per hominem**, id est, per aliquem apostolorum in speciali, sed per Spiritum Sanctum, qui dicit, Act. XIII, 2: *segregate mihi*, et cetera.

7. Causa autem originis huius auctoritatis vera est Christus Iesus, et ideo dicit **sed per Iesum Christum, et Deum Patrem**.

Haec autem distinctio, cum dicit **per Iesum Christum et Deum Patrem**, potest accipi, vel quantum ad personam Patris, et personam Filii, et tunc alius est in persona Deus Pater, et alius Iesus Christus. Ab utroque autem missus est Beatus Apostolus Paulus ad praedicandum, et a tota Trinitate, quia inseparabilia sunt opera Trinitatis. Non fit autem mentio de persona Spiritus Sancti, quia cum sit unio et nexus duorum, positis

is said: *I am the least of the apostles, who am not worthy to be called an apostle* (1 Cor 15:9).

Furthermore, it accords with his office, because in another sense it means 'the mouth of the trumpet', in which the office of preaching is specially signified. *Lift up your voice like a trumpet* (Isa 58:1).

4. He is described by his authority, when he says, **an apostle**. Here two things are mentioned, namely, his authority and its source.

Authority, because he says **apostle**, which is the same as 'sent'.

Now it should be noted that the Apostle in some epistles calls himself *servant*, thereby showing a spirit of humility, as in the Epistle to the Romans; in others he calls himself **apostle**, thereby showing his authority. The reason for this is that the Romans were proud, and so the Apostle, in order to induce them to humility, calls himself a servant as an example of humility. But to the Galatians, who were stupid and proud, he calls himself an **apostle** in order to break them down; hence he here sets forth his authority.

5. He describes the source of his authority when he says, **not of men**.

First, he removes what is, according to their opinion, the source;

second, he presents the true source, at **but by Jesus Christ**.

6. The source in their opinion was in keeping with the fact that the Galatians had been so deceived by false teachers as to believe that the Apostle did not enjoy the same authority as the other apostles, as having neither been taught by Christ nor lived with him, but sent by them as their minister. He therefore removes this opinion when he says, **not of men, neither by man**.

For some had been sent by the whole college of apostles and disciples; hence, to show that he had not been sent by them, he says, **not of men**. Others had been sent by some particular apostle, as Paul sometimes sent Luke and Titus. Therefore, to show that he had not been sent in that manner, he says, **neither by man**, i.e., not by any apostle in particular, but by the Holy Spirit, who says: *separate for me Saul and Barnabas, for the work to which I have taken them* (Acts 13:2).

7. But because the true cause of the origin of this authority is Christ Jesus, he says, **but by Jesus Christ and God the Father**.

Now the distinction expressed when he says, **by Jesus Christ and God the Father**, can be taken with respect to the person of the Father and the person of the Son; and then God the Father is one person and Jesus Christ another. For the Blessed Apostle Paul was sent to preach by both, and indeed, by the whole Trinity, because the works of the Trinity are inseparable. Yet no mention is made of the person of the Holy Spirit, because, since he is the union and joining

personis duabus, scilicet Patris et Filii, intelligitur etiam Spiritus Sanctus.

Vel potest sumi distinctio praedicta quantum ad naturam assumptam, scilicet humanam, quia secundum naturam divinam non est distinctio inter Deum Patrem et Iesum Christum. Et tunc missus est Paulus per Deum Patrem, sicut per auctorem, et per Iesum Christum, sicut per ministrum. Rom. c. XV, 8: *dico Iesum Christum ministrum fuisse*, et cetera.

Quia vero Galatae derogabant Apostolo, quod non fuisset conversatus cum Christo sicut alii, nec missus ab eo, ideo in hoc specialiter magnificat se, quia illi fuerunt missi per Christum adhuc viventem in carne mortali, ipse vero a Christo iam glorificato missus est, ideo dicit **qui**, scilicet Deus Pater, **suscitavit eum**, scilicet Iesum Christum, inquantum hominem, **a mortuis**. Quasi dicat: apostolus sum, **non ab hominibus**, scilicet collegio apostolorum, **nec per hominem**, scilicet Christum in mortali carne viventem, sed sum apostolus per Christum iam suscitatum et glorificatum. Rom. VI, 9: *Christus resurgens a mortuis*, et cetera.

Et quia praesens vita significatur per sinistram, futura vero per dexteram, inquantum ista est caelestis et spiritualis, illa vero temporalis, ideo Petrus, qui vocatus fuit a Christo adhuc in carne mortali posito, ponitur in bulla Papae in sinistra parte; Paulus vero, qui vocatus fuit a Christo iam glorificato, ponitur in parte dextera.

8. Consequenter cum dicit *et qui mecum sunt*, etc., ponuntur personae adiunctae salutantes, quas describit a dulci familiaritate, quia *mecum sunt*, scilicet ad solatium et adiutorium. Prov. XVIII, 19: *frater qui iuvatur a fratre*, et cetera. Ps. CXXXII, 1: *ecce quam bonum*, et cetera.

Item ab inseparabili caritate, cum dicit **fratres**, Io. XIII, 35: *in hoc cognoscent omnes*, et cetera.

Item ab universalitate, cum dicit **omnes**; quod ideo addit, quia isti forte erant intantum seducti, quod dictum Pauli non reputarent.

Et ideo dicit **omnes qui mecum sunt**, ut ostendat eos testes esse veritatis suae, et facile intelligant se errare, dum ab omnibus reprehenduntur. II Cor. II, 6: *sufficit illi qui eiusmodi est obiurgatio haec, quae fit a pluribus*, et cetera.

9. Personas autem salutatas ponit, cum dicit **ecclesiis Galatiae**, et cetera.

Ubi sciendum quod sicut in Glossa tangitur, Brennus dux Senonum olim congregato exercitu intravit Italiam, qua pertransita, venit in Graeciam ante tempus Alexandri Magni, ubi cum essent aliqui de gente sua remanentes, in una parte Graeciae miscuerunt se Graecis; unde illa provincia Gallograecia dicta est; deinde illi Galatae

of the two, by mentioning two persons, namely, Father and Son, the Holy Spirit too is understood.

Or, the aforesaid distinction can be taken with respect to the assumed nature, i.e., the human, because according to the divine nature there is not a distinction between God the Father and Jesus Christ. In this sense, then, Paul was sent by God the Father as by the chief sender, and by Jesus Christ as by a minister. *For I say that Christ Jesus was minister of the circumcision* (Rom 15:8).

But because the Galatians belittled the Apostle for neither having lived with Christ, as did the others, nor having been sent by him, he extols himself on this very point, because they had been sent by Christ yet living in mortal flesh, whereas he had been sent by Christ now glorified. This is why he says, **who**, namely, God the Father, **raised him**, namely, Jesus Christ as man, **from the dead**. As though to say: I am an apostle **not of men**, i.e., not by the college of apostles, **neither by man**, namely, Christ living in mortal flesh, but I am an apostle through Christ now risen and glorified. *Christ rising again from the dead, dies now no more* (Rom 6:9).

And because the present life is signified by the left side and the future life by the right, inasmuch as the latter is heavenly and spiritual, and the former temporal, Peter, who was called while Christ was yet in mortal flesh, appears in papal bulls on the left side, but Paul, who was called by Christ now glorified, is set on the right side.

8. Then when he says, **and all the brethren who are with me**, he refers to the persons who join with him in sending the greeting. These he describes in terms of sweet familiarity, because they **are with me**, namely, for consolation and help. *A brother that is helped by his brother is like a strong city* (Prov 18:19). *Behold how good and how pleasant it is for brethren to dwell together in unity* (Ps 133:1).

And in terms of inseparable charity, when he says, **brethren**. *By this shall all men know that you are my disciples, if you have love one for another* (John 13:35).

And in terms of universality, when he says, **all**. He adds this because they might be so deceived as not to respect the words of Paul.

Hence he says, **all who are with me**, to show them as witnesses to his truthfulness and make it easy for them to understand that they are wrong, when they are rebuked by everyone else. *To him who is such a one, this rebuke is sufficient which is given by many* (2 Cor 2:6).

9. He mentions the persons greeted when he says, **to the churches of Galatia**.

Here it should be noted that, as is mentioned in a Gloss, Brennus, leader of the Senones, once gathered an army, and having entered Italy through which he passed, came into Greece before the time of Alexander the Great. There some of the invaders remained in a certain district of Greece and intermarried with the Greeks. For this reason that province

sunt appellati, quasi albi. Et licet Graeci sint acuti ingenii, tamen illi Galatae stulti erant et instabiles et ad intelligendum tardiores, sicut et indociles Galli, unde originem traxerunt. Et ideo infra dicit eis: *o insensati Galatae*, et cetera. Istis ergo scribit epistolam hanc et isti sunt personae salutatae.

10. Consequenter cum dicit *gratia vobis*, etc., ponit bona quae eis optat. Et

primo ponit ipsa bona optata;

secundo ipsorum bonorum auctorem, ibi *a Deo Patre*, et cetera.

11. Bona autem quae eis optat sunt duo, in quibus omnia spiritualia includuntur. Primum est *gratia*, quae est principium vitae spiritualis, cui in Glossa adscribitur remissio peccatorum, quae est primum in vita spirituali. Nullus enim potest esse in vera vita spirituali, nisi prius moriatur peccato.

Secundum est *pax*, quae est quietatio mentis in fine, quae in Glossa dicitur esse reconciliatio ad Deum.

Et sic, dum optat principium et finem omnium bonorum spiritualium, includit Apostolus tamquam inter duo extrema desiderium omnis boni eis proveniendum. Ps. LXXXIII, v. 12: *gratiam et gloriam dabit Dominus*. II Cor. ult.: *gratia Domini nostri*, et cetera.

12. Bonorum autem ipsorum auctor est Deus Pater, et ideo dicit *a Deo Patre*, et cetera. Ubi

primo ponitur bonorum causa;

secundo causandi modus, ibi *qui dedit*;

tertio gratiarum actio pro ipsis bonis, ibi *cui est honor*, et cetera.

13. Causa autem et auctoritas bonorum est Deus Pater tamquam auctor, inquantum Deus, et tota Trinitas, quae dicitur Deus omnium per creationem. Sap. XIV, 3: *tu autem, Pater, gubernas*, et cetera. Et ideo dicit *a Deo Patre*, et cetera.

Item auctor est Dominus Iesus Christus, sicut minister, et hoc inquantum homo. Rom. c. XV, 8: *dico Iesum Christum ministrum*, et cetera. Et quod per Christum sit nobis gratia, patet Io. I, 17: *gratia et veritas per Iesum Christum facta est*, et cetera. Rom. V: *iustificati gratis*, et cetera. Pax etiam est nobis per ipsum. Io. XIV, 27: *pacem meam do vobis*, et cetera.

14. Modus autem causandi huiusmodi bona ponitur, cum dicit *qui tradidit*, et cetera.

Ubi primo ponitur causa efficiens, quae est mors Christi. Et quantum ad hoc dicit *qui dedit semetipsum*, etc., quasi dicat: ideo Christus est auctor gratiae et pacis, quia ipse morti dedit se et sustinuit crucem. Unde ipsa mors Christi est causa efficiens gratiae. Rom. c. V: *iustificati gratis*, etc., et Col. c. I, 20: *pacificans quae in caelis*,

came to be called Gallic Greece and the inhabitants Galatians, as it were, 'white'. But whereas the Greeks are natively intelligent, those Galatians were stupid and inconstant and slow to understand, as the indocile Gauls from whom they descended. This is why he later says, *O senseless Galatians* (Gal 3:1). To these people, therefore, he writes this epistle, and they are the ones greeted.

10. Then when he says, *grace be to you and peace*, he mentions the good things he wishes them.

First, he mentions the goods he wishes;

second, the author of these goods, at *from God the Father and our Lord*.

11. The goods he wishes them are twofold, but in them are included all spiritual goods. The first is *grace*, which is the beginning of the spiritual life, and to it is ascribed in a Gloss the remission of sins, which is first in the spiritual life. For no one can be in the true spiritual life, unless he first die to sin.

The second is *peace*, which is the settling down of the mind in its end, and which in a Gloss is said to be reconciliation with God.

Thus in wishing them the beginning and the end of all spiritual goods, the Apostle includes, as it were, between the two extremes, the wish that every good come to them. *The Lord will give grace and glory* (Ps 84:12). *The grace of our Lord Jesus Christ and the charity of God and the communication of the Holy Spirit be with you all* (2 Cor 13:13).

12. The author of these goods is God the Father, and so he says, *from God the Father*. Here are mentioned

first, the cause of the goods;

second, the manner of causing, at *who gave himself*;

third, thanksgiving for these goods, at *to whom is glory*.

13. The cause and source of good things is God the Father as originator, precisely as God, and the entire Trinity, the God of all through creation. *But you, O Father, govern it* (Wis 14:3). Hence he says, *from God the Father*.

Again, the originator is the Lord Jesus Christ as minister; and this insofar as he is man. *For I say that Jesus Christ was a minister* (Rom 15:8). But that grace comes to us through Christ is plain: *grace and truth came by Jesus Christ* (John 1:17). *Being justified freely by his grace* (Rom 3:24). Peace, too, comes to us through him: *my peace I give unto you* (John 14:27).

14. The manner in which these goods are caused is also mentioned when he says, *who gave himself for our sins*.

Here is mentioned, first of all, the efficient cause, which is the death of Christ. Referring to this, he says *who gave himself for our sins*. As if to say: Christ is the author of grace and peace, because he gave himself to death and endured the cross. Hence the very death of Christ is the efficient cause of grace: *you have been justified freely by his*

et cetera. Et dicit primo **qui dedit**, etc., id est, sponte se obtulit. Eph. V, 2: *dilexit nos Christus, et tradidit*, et cetera. Hebr. II, 9: *ut pro omnibus nobis gustaret mortem*. Tit. II, 14: *qui dedit semetipsum*, et cetera.

Ex quo manifeste Apostolus arguit contra eos, quod si mors Christi est sufficiens causa salutis nostrae, et in sacramentis Novi Testamenti, quae efficaciam habent ex passione Christi, confertur gratia, quod sit superfluum simul cum Novo Testamento servari legalia, in quibus gratia non confertur, nec salus acquiritur, quia *neminem ad perfectum adduxit lex*, ut habetur Hebr. VII, 19.

Secundo ponitur finis et utilitas ipsorum bonorum quae est causa finalis. Et est duplex: unus est ut liberemur a peccatis praeteritis, et quantum ad hoc dicit **pro peccatis nostris**, scilicet praeteritis delendis et expiandis, quod est initium nostrae salvationis. Apoc. I, 5: *dilexit nos*, et cetera. Alius finis est, ut liberaret nos a potestate mortis, et quantum ad hoc dicit **ut eriperet nos de praesenti**, et cetera. Col. I, 13: *eripuit nos a potestate*, et cetera.

Et ponit tria, scilicet **ut eriperet**, inquit, **de praesenti**, et **saeculo**, et **nequam**.

Ut eriperet de praesenti, trahendo nos ad aeterna, per desiderium et spem. De **saeculo**, id est, de conformitate huius mundi qui nos allicit, ut non ei conformemur. Rom. XII, 2: *nolite conformari huic saeculo*, et cetera. **Nequam**, reducens nos ad veritatem iustitiae.

Et dicitur **saeculum nequam**, non propter sui naturam, cum bonum sit creatum a Deo, sed propter mala quae in eo fiunt, sicut illud Ephes. V, 16: *dies mali sunt*, et cetera. Gen. c. XLVII, 9, dixit Iacob: *dies peregrinationis vitae meae centum triginta annorum sunt, parvi et mali*, et cetera.

Et licet haec sint nobis per Christum, non tamen excluditur Deus Pater. Et ideo ponitur, tertio, acceptatio divinae voluntatis. Unde dicit **secundum voluntatem Dei, et Patris**. **Patris**, inquam, Christi per naturam, qua ab aeterno procedit, ut Verbum. Ps. II, 7: *ego hodie genui te*. Io. I, 1: *in principio erat Verbum*, et cetera. Item **Patris nostri** per adoptionem. Io. I, 12: *dedit eis potestatem*, et cetera. Primo modo ly **Deus Pater**, accipitur pro sola persona Patris; secundo modo pro tota Trinitate.

15. Et quia a Deo Patre nostro, scilicet a tota Trinitate, haec omnia proveniunt nobis per Christum, ideo ipsi, scilicet toti Trinitati, **gloria**, in se honor aliis sit vel est, **in saecula saeculorum**, id est semper. **Amen**, est nota confirmationis.

grace (Rom 3:24); *making peace as to the things that are in heaven* (Col 1:20). And he says, first of all, **who gave himself**, i.e., offered himself voluntarily. *Christ also has loved us and has delivered himself for us* (Eph 5:2); *that he might taste death for all* (Heb 2:9); *who gave himself for us* (Titus 2:14).

From this, the Apostle plainly is arguing against them that if the death of Christ is the sufficient cause of our salvation, and if grace is conferred in the sacraments of the New Testament, which have their efficacy from the passion of Christ, then it is superfluous to observe, along with the New Testament, the rituals of the old law in which grace is not conferred nor salvation acquired, because *the law brought nothing to perfection* (Heb 7:19).

Second, the end and utility of those goods, or the final cause, is mentioned. And it is twofold: one is that we be set free of past sins; and as to this he says, **for our sins**, namely, that past sins be removed and atoned for, which is the beginning of our salvation. *He loved us and washed us from our sins in his own blood* (Rev 1:5). The other end is that he might free us from the power of death; and as to this he says, **that he might deliver us from this present wicked world**. *He delivered us from the power of darkness* (Col 1:13).

Herein he mentions three things, namely **that he might deliver us from**: **this present**, and **world**, and **wicked**.

That he might deliver us from this present by drawing us to eternal things through desire and hope; from the **world**, i.e., from being conformed to this world which allures us, so that we do not conform to it: *and do not be conformed to this world* (Rom 12:2); **wicked**, leading us back to the truth of justice.

And it is called a **wicked world**, not because of its nature, for it was created good by God, but because of the evils perpetrated in it: *the days are evil* (Eph 5:16). And Jacob said: *the days of my pilgrimage are a hundred and thirty years, few and evil* (Gen 47:9).

Now although these things come to us through Christ, God the Father is not excluded. Hence there is mentioned in the third place, acceptance of the divine will. Therefore he says, *according to the will of God and our Father*. Of the **Father**, I say, of Christ, by nature, who proceeds from eternity as the Word: *this day have I begotten you* (Ps 2:7); *in the beginning was the Word, and the Word was with God, and the Word was God* (John 1:1). Also of **our Father** by adoption: *he gave them power to be made the sons of God* (John 1:12). In the first rendering, **God the Father** is taken for the sole person of the Father; in the second, for the whole Trinity.

15. And because it is from God our Father, namely, from the whole Trinity, that all things come to us through Christ, therefore to it, i.e., to the whole Trinity, **glory** in itself, honor from others, be or is, **forever and ever**, i.e., always. **Amen**. This is a mark of corroboration.

Habes ergo, in summa, in salutatione praedicta auctoritatem Apostoli, qua eorum superbiam frangit; virtutem gratiae, qua eos ad observantiam Evangelii provocat; et insufficientiam legalium, ut ab eis eos revocet.

You have therefore, in summary, in the above greeting, the Apostle's authority by which he breaks their pride; the power of the grace by which he exhorts them to observe the Gospel; and the insufficiency of the ceremonies of the law, in order to call them away from them.

Lecture 2

1:6 Miror quod sic tam cito transferimini ab eo qui vos vocavit in gratiam Christi in aliud evangelium: [n. 16]

1:7 quod non est aliud, nisi sunt aliqui qui vos conturbant, et volunt convertere Evangelium Christi. [n. 20]

1:8 Sed licet nos aut angelus de caelo evangelizet vobis praeterquam quod evangelizavimus vobis, anathema sit. [n. 22]

1:9 Sicut praediximus, et nunc iterum dico: si quis vobis evangelizaverit praeter id quod accepistis, anathema sit. [n. 28]

1:10 Modo enim hominibus suadeo, an Deo? an quaero hominibus placere? si adhuc hominibus placerem, Christi servus non essem. [n. 29]

1:6 Θαυμάζω ὅτι οὕτως ταχέως μετατίθεσθε ἀπὸ τοῦ καλέσαντος ὑμᾶς ἐν χάριτι [Χριστοῦ] εἰς ἕτερον εὐαγγέλιον,

1:7 ὃ οὐκ ἔστιν ἄλλο· εἰ μή τινές εἰσιν οἱ ταράσσοντες ὑμᾶς καὶ θέλοντες μεταστρέψαι τὸ εὐαγγέλιον τοῦ Χριστοῦ.

1:8 ἀλλὰ καὶ ἐὰν ἡμεῖς ἢ ἄγγελος ἐξ οὐρανοῦ εὐαγγελίζηται [ὑμῖν] παρ' ὃ εὐηγγελισάμεθα ὑμῖν, ἀνάθεμα ἔστω.

1:9 ὡς προειρήκαμεν, καὶ ἄρτι πάλιν λέγω, εἴ τις ὑμᾶς εὐαγγελίζεται παρ' ὃ παρελάβετε, ἀνάθεμα ἔστω.

1:10 Ἄρτι γὰρ ἀνθρώπους πείθω ἢ τὸν θεόν; ἢ ζητῶ ἀνθρώποις ἀρέσκειν; εἰ ἔτι ἀνθρώποις ἤρεσκον, Χριστοῦ δοῦλος οὐκ ἂν ἤμην.

1:6 I wonder that you are so soon removed from him who called you into the grace of Christ, unto another gospel. [n. 16]

1:7 Which is not another: only there are some who trouble you and would pervert the Gospel of Christ. [n. 20]

1:8 But though we, or an angel from heaven, preach a gospel to you besides that which we have preached to you, let him be anathema. [n. 22]

1:9 As we said before, so now I say again: if any one preach to you a gospel, besides that which you have received, let him be anathema. [n. 28]

1:10 For do I now persuade men, or God? Or do I seek to please men? If I yet pleased men, I should not be the servant of Christ. [n. 29]

---

16. In superioribus praecessit salutatio, sequitur in sequentibus epistolaris narratio, in qua arguit Apostolus eorum errorem; secundo eos monet ad correctionem, V cap., ibi *state ergo*, et cetera.

Errorem autem eorum arguit dupliciter, et per auctoritatem Evangelici documenti, et per rationem Veteris Testamenti, III cap., ibi *o insensati*, et cetera.

Arguit autem errorem ipsorum, ostendendo auctoritatem Evangelicae doctrinae.

Primo ostendendo ipsorum levitatem quantum ad levem dimissionem Evangelicae doctrinae;

secundo commendando auctoritatem ipsius doctrinae Evangelicae: ut sic quanto dignius est quod dimittunt, tanto eorum error appareat maior, ibi *notum enim vobis facio*, et cetera.

Circa primum duo facit.
Primo enim exaggerat culpam;
secundo infligit poenam, ibi *sed licet nos*, et cetera.
Culpam autem exaggerat et seductorum et seducentium, ibi *nisi sunt*, et cetera.

17. Circa primum tria facit. Primo enim aggravat culpam seductorum ex animi levitate.

Unde dicit *miror*, quasi dicat: cum sciatis tot bona quae dicta sunt provenire vobis per Christum, et quod cum fueritis ita bene instructi per me, tamen *sic*, id est, intantum et tam vehementer, ut videamini iam obliti,

16. The greeting given, it is followed by the epistle message, in which the Apostle refutes their error; second, he admonishes them with a view to their correction, at *stand fast* (Gal 5:1).

He refutes their error two ways: namely, on the authority of the Gospel teaching; and by reason of the Old Testament, at *O senseless Galatians* (Gal 3:1).

He refutes their error by showing the authority of the Gospel teaching.

First, by showing their fickleness in lightly dismissing the Gospel teaching;

second, by commending the authority of the Gospel teaching, as he intimates that in view of the precious value of that which they so lightly regard, their error is seen to be so much the greater, at *for I give you to understand* (Gal 1:11).

Regarding the first he does two things.
First, he enlarges upon their guilt;
second, he inflicts a punishment, at *but though we*.
Concerning the first, he enlarges upon the guilt both of the seduced and of those who seduced them, at *only there are some that trouble you*.

17. As to the first he does three things. First, he enlarges upon the guilt of those who were misled for their fickleness of mind.

Hence he says, *I wonder*. As if to say: although you are aware of the many good things already mentioned that come to you through Christ, and although I instructed you well, nevertheless you are thus, i.e., so far and so completely

tam cito, id est, in tam brevi tempore, *transferimini*, ut alludat nomini. Galatia enim translato dicitur. Quasi dicat: vos estis Galatae, quia tam cito transferimini. Eccli. XIX, 4: *qui cito credit, levis est corde*.

18. Secundo aggravat eorum culpam ex eo quod dimiserunt.

Si enim ratio recedit et transfertur a malo, commendabilis est et bene facit, sed quando recedit a bono, tunc est culpabilis. Et sic isti a bono translati erant. Et ideo dicit eis: et si mirandum sit quod tam cito et sic transferimini, addit tamen materiam admirationis, quod scilicet transferimini *ab eo*, scilicet a Deo, et fide eius, *qui vos vocavit in gratiam Christi*, id est, in participationem aeterni boni, quam habemus per Christum. I Petr. II, v. 9: *gratias agentes Deo, qui vos vocavit in admirabile lumen suum*. Item II Petr. II, 21: *melius erat eis viam veritatis non agnoscere, quam*, et cetera.

19. Tertio aggravat eorum culpam ex eo ad quod conversi sunt, quia non sunt conversi ad bonum, sed ad malum.

Unde dicit *in aliud evangelium*, id est, veteris legis, quae Annuntiatio bona est inquantum annuntiat quaedam bona, scilicet temporalia et carnalia. Is. I, 9: *si volueritis et audieritis me*, et cetera. Sed tamen non est perfecta et simpliciter, sicut Evangelium; quia non annuntiat perfecta et maxima bona, sed parva et minima. Sed lex nova est perfecte et simpliciter Evangelium, id est, bona annuntiatio, quia annuntiat maxima bona, scilicet caelestia, spiritualia et aeterna. Et licet sit aliud Evangelium secundum traditionem pseudo, tamen secundum meam praedicationem non.

Est enim aliud in promissis, sed non est aliud in figura, quia idem continetur in Veteri Testamento et in Novo: in Veteri quidem ut in figura, in Novo vero ut in re et expresse. Et sic est aliud evangelium quantum ad ea quae exterius apparent, sed quantum ad ea quae interius sunt et continentur, non est aliud.

20. Licet autem non sit aliud in se, tamen potest esse aliud ex culpa aliorum, scilicet seducentium. Et ideo eorum culpam exaggerans, dicit *nisi sunt aliqui*, scilicet seductores, *qui vos conturbant*, id est, puritatem sensus vestri, qua imbuti fuistis per fidei veritatem, obfuscant. Quia, licet idem contineatur quantum ad interiorem intellectum per vetus et novum testamentum, ut dictum est, tamen si post susceptionem Novi Testamenti reiteratur Vetus, videtur ostendi quod Novum non sit perfectum, et quod illud sit aliud ab isto. Et ideo dicit

removed, that you seem already to have forgotten; *so soon*, i.e., in such a short time, *you are removed*. With this word he alludes to their name, for Galatia means 'transferred'. As if to say: you are Galatians, because you are so quickly transferred. *He that is hasty to give credit is light of heart* (Sir 19:4).

18. Second, he amplifies their guilt on the part of that which they have abandoned.

For if reason withdraws and is removed from evil, it is worthy of praise and does well; but when it departs from the good, it is culpable. And this is how they were removed from good. So he says to them: although it is amazing that you are so quickly and so far removed, there is additional reason for wonder, namely, because you have removed yourselves *from him*, i.e., from God, and from faith in him *who called you into the grace of Christ*, i.e., into the sharing of the eternal good which we have through Christ: *giving thanks to God who has called you into his marvelous light* (1 Pet 2:9). Again: *for it had been better for them not to have known the way of justice than, after they have known it, to turn back from that holy commandment which was delivered to them* (2 Pet 2:21).

19. Third, he amplifies their guilt on the part of that to which they have turned, because they have been turned not to good but to evil.

Hence he says, *unto another gospel*, i.e., of the old law, which is a good message only insofar as it does announce some good things, namely, temporal and carnal: *if you be willing and will hearken to me, you shall eat the good things of the land* (Isa 1:19). Yet it is not completely perfect as is the Gospel, because it does not announce the perfect and loftiest goods, but small and slight ones. But the new law is perfectly and in the full sense a Gospel, i.e., a good message, because it announces the greatest goods, namely, heavenly, spiritual and eternal. And although it is another gospel according to the tradition of the deceivers, yet according to my preaching it is not.

For it is different in the promises, but not in the figure, because the same thing is contained in the Old Testament and in the New: in the Old, indeed, as in a figure, but in the New as in reality and expressly. Therefore it is another gospel if you consider the outward appearances; but as to the things that are contained and exist within, it is not another gospel.

20. Yet though it is not in itself another gospel, it can be another, if you consider the guilt of the others, i.e., of the deceivers. Hence in enlarging upon the guilt of the latter he says, *only there are some*, namely, the seducers, *who trouble you*, i.e., sully the purity of your understanding with which you were imbued with the truth of faith. Because although the same thing is contained, so far as the inward understanding is concerned, in the Old and New Testament, as has been said, yet if the Old is embraced after accepting the New, that seems to show that the New is

quod non est aliud, nisi sunt, etc., quia isti pseudo post fidei Evangelicae susceptionem cogebant eos circumcidi, ostendendo per hoc, quod circumcisio est aliquid aliud quam baptismus et efficit aliquid quod baptismus non potest efficere, et ideo isti conturbant vos. Infra V, 12: *utinam abscindantur qui vos conturbant*, et cetera.

21. Et vere conturbant, quia **volunt convertere Evangelium Christi**, id est, veritatem Evangelicae doctrinae in figuram legis, quod est absurdum et turbatio maxima.

In illud enim debet aliquid converti ad quod ordinatur; Novum autem Testamentum et Evangelium Christi non ordinatur ad Vetus, sed potius e contrario lex vetus ordinatur ad legem novam, sicut figura ad veritatem; et ideo figura converti debet ad veritatem, et lex vetus in Evangelium Christi, non autem veritas in figuram, neque Evangelium Christi in legem veterem: quod patet ex ipso usu loquendi. Non enim dicimus quod homo sit similis imagini hominis, sed potius e converso, imago est similis homini. Ier. XV, 9: *ipsi convertentur ad te*, etc.; et Lev. XXVI, 10: *novis supervenientibus*, et cetera.

22. Consequenter post exaggerationem culpae ponitur inflictio poenae, cum dicit **sed licet**, et cetera.

Et circa hoc duo facit.

Primo promulgat sententiam;

secundo rationem sententiae assignat, ibi **modo enim hominibus**, et cetera.

Circa primum duo facit.

Primo ostendit auctoritatem suae sententiae;

secundo profert eam, ibi **sicut praedixi**, et cetera.

23. Ostendit autem auctoritatem suae sententiae multam esse, eo quod non solum in perversores et in seductores subditos, sed etiam in pares, sicut sunt alii apostoli, et etiam in superiores, sicut sunt angeli, si huius criminis, scilicet conversionis Evangelii in veterem legem, rei essent, efficaciam haberet.

Et ideo dicit: quia nostrae sententiae auctoritas quam ego promulgo (quae est excommunicatio), non solum in illos qui talia intendunt, efficaciam habet, **sed licet nos**, scilicet apostoli, **aut angelus**, bonus vel malus, **de caelo veniens evangelizet, praeter quam quod evangelizatum est a nobis, anathema sit**, id est, reus erit huius sententiae, quam promulgamus.

24. Ad evidentiam autem dictorum tria inquirere oportet. Primo quid significat hoc nomen, **anathema**.

Circa quod sciendum est, quod *anathema* est nomen Graecum, et componitur ab *ana*, quod est sursum, et *thesis*, positio, quasi sursum positio. Et est ortum ex quadam antiqua consuetudine. Antiqui enim quando pugnabant, capiebant aliquando aliquam praedam ab

not perfect, and that the one is different from the other. Hence he says, **which is not another, only there are some who trouble you**, because those deceivers were compelling them to be circumcised after professing faith in the Gospel, showing thereby that circumcision is something different from baptism and does something that baptism cannot do, and for that reason they are troubling you. **Would that even those who trouble you were cut off** (Gal 5:12).

21. And they do indeed bring you trouble, because they **would pervert the Gospel of Christ**, i.e., the truth of the Gospel teaching, into the figure of the law—which is absurd and the greatest of troubles.

For a thing ought to be converted into that to which it is ordained. But the New Testament and the Gospel of Christ are not ordained to the Old, but contrariwise, the old law is ordained to the new law, as a figure to the truth. Consequently the figure ought to be converted into the truth, and the old law to the Gospel of Christ, not the truth into the figure, or the Gospel of Christ into the old law. This is plain from the way we ordinarily speak; for we do not say that a man resembles the image of a man, but contrariwise, that the image resembles the man: *they shall be turned to you and you shall not be turned to them* (Jer 15:19); *the new coming on, you shall cast away the old* (Lev 26:10).

22. Then after enlarging upon their guilt, the inflicting of the penalty is set forth when he ways, **but though we**.

And with respect to this he does two things.

First, he promulgates the sentence;

second, he gives a reason for the sentence, at **for do I now persuade**.

As to the first he does two things.

First, he presents authority for his sentence;

second, he passes sentence, at **as we said before**.

23. He shows that his authority for passing sentence is great on the ground that it would affect not only the perverters and seducers, who are subject to him, but also his own equals, as the other apostles, and even those above him, as the angels, were they guilty of this crime, namely, of turning the Gospel into the old law.

Hence he says: because the authority behind the sentence which we pass (which is excommunication) has efficacy, not only over those who are doing these things, then **though we**, namely, the apostles, **or an angel**, good or evil, coming **from heaven, preach a gospel besides that which we have preached, let him be anathema**, i.e., subject to this sentence that we pass.

24. To elucidate the foregoing, three things should be investigated. First, the meaning of this word, **anathema**.

Apropos of this it should be noted that *anathema* is a Greek word composed of *ana*, which means 'above,' and *thesis*, which means, 'a placing'; hence 'a placing above.' The word arose from an old custom. For the ancients, when they waged war, sometimes took from their enemies certain

hostibus, quam nolebant convertere in usum proprium, sed suspendebant illam in templis, vel in aliquo loco publico civitatis, quasi separatam a communi usu hominum, et omne tale sic suspensum nominabant Graeci anathema; et ex hoc inolevit consuetudo, quod omne illud quod excludebatur ab usu communi, diceretur anathematizatum. Unde dicitur Iosue VI, 17 de Iericho et omnibus quae in ea sunt, quod Iosue mox anathematizavit ea. Et ideo etiam hoc in Ecclesia inolevit, ut illi qui excluduntur a communi societate Ecclesiae, et a participatione sacramentorum Ecclesiae, dicantur anathematizati.

25. Secundo inquirenda est ratio eorum, quae dicit *licet nos aut angelus*, et cetera.

Ubi sciendum est, quod est triplex doctrina. Prima est philosophorum, qui ex ductu rationis propriae in cognitionem suae doctrinae devenerunt. Quaedam alia doctrina est, quae est tradita per angelos, sicut lex vetus. Lex enim non est allata voluntate humana (sicut dicitur ad Gal. III, 19), sed per angelos in manu mediatoris, ut dicitur infra III, v. 19. Quaedam vero doctrina tradita est a Deo immediate, sicut doctrina Evangelii. Io. c. I, 18: *Deum nemo vidit unquam*, et cetera. Ad Hebr. I, 2: *novissime diebus istis locutus est nobis in Filio*. Et post: *quae cum initium accepisset*, et cetera.

Doctrina ergo quae traditur per hominem potest mutari et revocari per alium hominem qui melius novit, sicut unus philosophus reprobat dicta alterius; item per angelum qui perspicacius videt veritatem. Doctrina etiam quae traditur per angelum posset forte removeri per alium angelum superiorem, seu per Deum. Sed contra doctrina quae immediate a Deo traditur, non potest neque per hominem, neque per angelum irritari. Et ideo si contingat quod homo vel angelus diceret contrarium illi quae per Deum tradita est, dictum suum non est contra doctrinam, ut per hoc irritetur et repellatur, sed potius doctrina est contra eum, quia ipse qui dicit, debet excludi et repelli a communione illius doctrinae.

Et ideo dicit Apostolus quod dignitas doctrinae Evangelicae, quae est immediate a Deo tradita, est tantae dignitatis, quod sive homo, sive angelus evangelizet aliud praeter id, quod in ea evangelizatum est, est anathema, id est, abiiciendus et repellendus est.

26. Tertio solvere oportet obiectiones quae circa hoc occurrunt. Quarum una est, cum par in parem non habeat imperium, et multo magis non habeat in superiorem, videtur quod Apostolus non potuit excommunicare apostolos qui erant sibi pares, et minus angelos qui sunt superiores. Matth. XI, v. 11: *qui minor est in regno caelorum, maior est illo*. Non est ergo anathema per hoc.

booty which they were unwilling to turn to their own use, but hung it in the temple or other public place of the city, as though to separate it from the common use of men. Everything so hung up, the Greeks called *anathema*. And from this arose the custom of declaring anathematized anything excluded from common use. Hence it is said of Jericho and of everything in it, that Joshua once anathematized it (Josh 6:17). Consequently, even in the Church the practice arose of declaring anathema those who are excluded from the common society of the Church and from partaking of the sacraments of the Church.

25. Second, we must look for an explanation of his statement, *though we, or an angel from heaven, preach a gospel to you besides that which we have preached to you, let him be anathema*.

Here it should be noted that there are three kinds of teachings: the first is that of the philosophers who have arrived at a knowledge of their doctrine with their own reason guiding them. Another is that which has been delivered by angels, as the old law. For the old law was not issued by a human will but by angels in the hand of a mediator (Gal 3:19). But the third teaching was given immediately by God himself, as the teaching of the Gospel: *no man has seen God at any time; the only begotten Son who is in the bosom of the Father, he has declared him* (John 1:18); *in these days he has spoken to us by his Son* (Heb 1:2); *which, having begun to be declared by the Lord, was confirmed unto us by them that heard him* (Heb 2:3).

Now, a teaching passed on by a man can be changed and revoked by another man who knows better, as one philosopher refutes the sayings of another, or by an angel who has a more penetrating knowledge of the truth. Even a teaching handed down by one angel could be supplanted by that of a higher angel or by God. But a teaching that comes directly from God can be nullified neither by man nor angel. Hence if a man or an angel were to state anything contrary to what has been taught by God, such a statement would not contradict God's teaching, so as to void or destroy it; rather, God's teaching would be against him, because one who speaks thus should be expelled and prevented from sharing his teaching.

Hence the Apostle says that the dignity of the Gospel teaching, which has come directly from God, is so great that if a man or even an angel preached another gospel besides that which he has preached among them, he is anathema, i.e., must be rejected and expelled.

26. Third, we must solve the objections which arise on this point. The first is that, since an equal has no authority over his peers and much less over his superiors, it seems that the Apostle has no power to excommunicate the apostles, who are his peers, and less so, angels who are superior. *He who is the lesser in the kingdom of heaven is greater than he* (Matt 11:11). Therefore the anathema is invalid.

Ad hoc dicendum est, quod Apostolus hanc protulit sententiam, non propria auctoritate, sed auctoritate Evangelicae doctrinae, cuius minister erat, cuius doctrinae auctoritas habet, ut quicumque contra illam dicunt, excludendi et repellendi sint. Io. X: *sermo quem locutus sum, ille iudicabit eum in novissimo die*, et cetera.

27. Alia quaestio est, quia ipse dicit, **praeterquam quod evangelizatum est**. Ergo non debet aliquis docere, neque praedicare, nisi quod scribitur in Epistolis et in Evangelio. Sed hoc est falsum, quia I Thess. III, 10 dicitur: *ut compleamus ea quae desunt fidei nostrae*, et cetera.

Respondeo. Dicendum quod nihil aliud evangelizandum est, quam illud quod continetur in Evangeliis, et in Epistolis, et in Sacra Scriptura implicite vel explicite. Nam Sacra Scriptura et Evangelium evangelizat esse credendum Christo explicite. Unde quidquid continetur in eis implicite, quod facit ad doctrinam eius, et ad fidem Christi, evangelizari et doceri potest. Et ideo cum dicit *praeter id*, etc., id est, omnino alienum addendo. Apoc. ult.: *si quis apposuerit ad haec, aut addiderit*, scilicet omnino alienum, *apponat Deus super illum plagas scriptas in libro isto*. Et Deut. IV: *non addetis quidquam*, etc., scilicet contrarium seu alienum, *nec minuetis*, et cetera.

28. Consequenter cum dicit *sicut praedixi*, etc., sententiam suam profert in malo, dicens: sicut praedixi de angelis et apostolis, idem dico de seductoribus. *Si quis* seductor *evangelizaverit praeter id quod accepistis* a me, *anathema sit*, id est, excommunicatus. Et haec est sententia quam profert.

Sed numquid ex hoc sunt excommunicati omnes haeretici? Videtur quod non, quia dicitur Tit. III, 10: *haereticum hominem post primam et secundam correctionem devita*, et cetera.

Respondeo. Dicendum est, quod haereticus potest dici aliquis, vel quia simpliciter errat ex ignorantia, et ex hoc non est excommunicatus; vel quia errat ex pertinacia et alios nititur pervertere, et tunc incurrit in canonem latae sententiae.

Utrum autem ex tunc his verbis sententiam in haereticos protulerit, dubium est. Cum tamen sententia iam lata sit contra haereticos in Conciliis. Potest tamen dici quod forte hic ostenduntur excommunicatione digni.

29. Consequenter cum dicit **modo enim hominibus**, etc., ostendit rationem sententiae. Ubi

primo ponit rationem ipsius sententiae;

secundo manifestat hic propositum, ibi **an quaero**, et cetera.

30. Posset enim aliquis dicere: quare sic excommunicas? *Forte aliqui sunt amici, vel alicuius auctoritatis, non ergo sic faciendum est*. Ideo respondens Apostolus, dicit: immo sic faciendum est, quia ea quae modo dico, non

The answer to this is that the Apostle passed this sentence not on his own authority, but on the authority of the Gospel teaching, of which he was the minister, and the authority of which teaches that whoever says anything contrary to it must be expelled and cast out. *The word that I have spoken, the same shall judge him in the last day* (John 12:48).

27. A second question arises from the words, **a gospel besides that which we have preached to you**. Therefore no one may teach or preach anything but what is written in the Epistles and Gospels. But this is false, because it is said: *praying that we may accomplish those things that are wanting to your faith* (1 Thess 3:10).

I answer that nothing is to be taught except what is contained, either implicitly or explicitly, in the Gospels and Epistles and Sacred Scripture. For Sacred Scripture and the Gospels announce that Christ must be believed explicitly. Hence whatever is contained therein implicitly and fosters its teaching and faith in Christ can be preached and taught. Therefore, when he says, **besides that which you have received**, he means by adding something completely alien: *if any man shall add to these things, God shall add unto him the plagues written in this book* (Rev 22:18). And *neither add anything*, i.e., contrary or alien, *nor diminish* (Deut 12:32).

28. Then when he says, **as we said before**, he pronounces his sentence on the evil person and says: as I have said of angels and apostles, so I say of the seducers. **If any** seducer **shall preach a gospel besides that which you have received** from me, **let him be anathema**, i.e., excommunicated. And this is the sentence he passes.

Now it may be asked whether all heretics are thereby excommunicated. And it seems not, because it is said: *a man that is a heretic, after the first and second admonition, avoid* (Titus 3:10).

I answer that a person might be called a heretic either because he errs solely from ignorance, and then he is not on that account excommunicated; or because he errs through obstinacy and tries to subvert others, and then he falls under the canon of the sentence passed.

But whether he was then and there passing sentence on heretics by these words is open to question, since sentence was later passed against heretics in the Councils. Yet it can be said that perhaps he was showing that they deserved to be excommunicated.

29. Then when he says, **for do I now persuade men**, he gives the reason for his sentence.

First, he gives the reason for his sentence;

second, he discloses here his purpose, at **or do I seek to please men?**

30. For someone might say: why do you excommunicate in this manner? Perhaps some are your friends or men of some authority. Therefore you ought not act in this way. But the Apostle says in answer: indeed, one should act in

sunt ad favorem hominum, sed ut placeam Deo, et hoc est quod dicit *modo enim*, id est, post conversionem, vel in ista epistola, *suadeo hominibus*, id est, tendit ad hoc appetitus meus, ut placeam hominibus, *an Deo?* Quasi dicat: haec quae facio, ideo facio, ut complaceam soli Deo. I Thess. II, 4: *loquimur non quasi hominibus placentes, sed Deo*, et cetera. Nec etiam loquimur auctoritate hominum, sed divina.

31. Quod autem non intendam placere hominibus, patet ex intentione et ex proposito meo. Nam ego non *quaero hominibus placere*, id est, non est intentionis meae homines convertere, ut placeam hominibus tantum, sed propter honorem Dei.

Et hoc patet, quia *si adhuc* intenderem *placere hominibus*, ut olim placui, *non essem servus Christi*. Cuius ratio est, quia haec sunt contraria. Ita dumtaxat, ut scilicet velim placere hominibus propter homines, non referendo illud in Deum. Si enim ideo intendam aliquando placere hominibus, ut eos traham ad Deum, non pecco. Sed si primo modo, non sum servus Christi. Is. XXVIII, 20: *coangustatum est stratum, ita ut alter decidat*, et cetera. Matth. VI, 24: *nemo potest duobus dominis servire*, et cetera. Ps. LII, 6: *confusi sunt qui hominibus placent*.

this way, because the things I say now are not to gain the favor of men but to please God, and this is what he means by *do I now*, i.e., after my conversion, or in this epistle, *persuade men*, i.e., is it my intention to please men, *or God?* As if to say: the things I do, I do to please God alone: *we speak, not as pleasing men, but God* (1 Thess 2:4); nor do we speak on the authority of men, but of God.

31. That I do not seek to please men is plain from my intention and purpose. For I do not *seek to please men*, i.e., it is not my intention in converting men to please men alone, but for the honor of God.

And this is plain, because *if I yet* sought to *please men*, as I formerly pleased them, *I should not be the servant of Christ*. The reason is that the two are opposed, more precisely, if I were to please men for the sake of men without referring it to God. For if I intend now and then to please men so that I might draw them to God, I do not sin. But if in the first way, I am not the servant of Christ: *for the bed is straitened, so that one must fall out, and a short covering cannot cover both* (Isa 28:20); *no man can serve two masters. For either he will hate the one and love the other; or he will sustain the one and despise the other* (Matt 6:24); *they who please men have been confounded* (Ps 53:5).

Lecture 3

1:11 Notum enim vobis facio, fratres, Evangelium, quod evangelizatum est a me, quia non est secundum hominem: [n. 32]

1:12 neque enim ego ab homine accepi illud, neque didici, sed per revelationem Jesu Christi. [n. 34]

1:13 Audistis enim conversationem meam aliquando in Judaismo: quoniam supra modum persequebar Ecclesiam Dei, et expugnabam illam, [n. 35]

1:14 et proficiebam in Judaismo supra multos coaetaneos meos in genere meo, abundantius aemulator existens paternarum mearum traditionum. [n. 37]

1:11 Γνωρίζω γὰρ ὑμῖν, ἀδελφοί, τὸ εὐαγγέλιον τὸ εὐαγγελισθὲν ὑπ' ἐμοῦ ὅτι οὐκ ἔστιν κατὰ ἄνθρωπον·

1:12 οὐδὲ γὰρ ἐγὼ παρὰ ἀνθρώπου παρέλαβον αὐτό, οὔτε ἐδιδάχθην, ἀλλὰ δι' ἀποκαλύψεως Ἰησοῦ Χριστοῦ.

1:13 Ἠκούσατε γὰρ τὴν ἐμὴν ἀναστροφήν ποτε ἐν τῷ Ἰουδαϊσμῷ, ὅτι καθ' ὑπερβολὴν ἐδίωκον τὴν ἐκκλησίαν τοῦ θεοῦ καὶ ἐπόρθουν αὐτήν,

1:14 καὶ προέκοπτον ἐν τῷ Ἰουδαϊσμῷ ὑπὲρ πολλοὺς συνηλικιώτας ἐν τῷ γένει μου, περισσοτέρως ζηλωτὴς ὑπάρχων τῶν πατρικῶν μου παραδόσεων.

1:11 For I give you to understand, brethren, that the Gospel which was preached by me is not according to man. [n. 32]

1:12 For neither did I receive it of man: nor did I learn it but by the revelation of Jesus Christ. [n. 34]

1:13 For you have heard of my behavior in time past in the Jews' religion: how that, beyond measure, I persecuted the Church of God and wasted it. [n. 35]

1:14 And I made progress in the Jews' religion above many of my equals in my own nation, being more abundantly zealous for the traditions of my fathers. [n. 37]

---

32. Supra Apostolus redarguit Galatas de levitate animi, eo quod sic cito dimiserant doctrinam Evangelii, hic vero ipsius Evangelicae doctrinae dignitatem ostendit. Et

circa hoc duo facit. Quia

primo commendat auctoritatem doctrinae Evangelicae secundum seipsam;

secundo ex parte aliorum apostolorum, et sua simul, cap. II, ibi **deinde post annos quatuordecim**, et cetera.

Iterum prima pars dividitur in duas, quia

primo proponit intentum;

secundo manifestat propositum, ibi **audistis enim**, et cetera.

Circa primum duo facit.

Primo proponit quod intendit;

secundo probat quod proponit, ibi **neque enim**, et cetera.

33. Intendens ergo commendare veritatem Evangelicae doctrinae, dicit **notum vobis**, etc., quasi dicat: ita sum certus de auctoritate Evangelii, quod non solum hominibus, immo etiam angelis contrarium non crederem; sed eos si contrarii essent, anathematizarem. Quam quidem certitudinem ex hoc habeo, quia magis credendum est Deo quam hominibus, seu angelis. Et ideo cum ego habuerim illud Evangelium a Deo, maximam certitudinem habere debeo et habeo.

Et ideo dicit **notum enim vobis facio, fratres, Evangelium, quod evangelizatum est a me** vobis et aliis ecclesiis, **quia non est secundum hominem**, id est, secundum humanam naturam discordantem a regula seu revelatione divina.

32. In the foregoing the Apostle rebuked the Galatians for their fickleness of mind in so quickly setting aside the Gospel teaching; now he shows the dignity of the Gospel teaching.

And concerning this he does two things:

first, he commends the authority of the Gospel teaching according to itself;

second on the part both of the other apostles and himself, at **then, after fourteen years** (Gal 2:1).

The first part is further divided into two others, because first, he presents his intention;

second, he manifests his purpose, at **for you have heard**.

Regarding the first he does two things.

First, he proposes what he intends;

second, he proves what he proposes, at **for neither**.

33. Intending, therefore, to commend the truth of the Gospel teaching, he says, **for I give you to understand, brethren**. As if to say: so certain am I of the Gospel's authority, that I would disbelieve not only men but even angels saying the contrary; so that if they were contrary, I would say anathema to them. And I have this certainty, because one must believe God rather than men or angels. Therefore, since I have this Gospel from God, I should and do have the greatest of certainty.

Hence he says, **for I give you to understand, brethren, that the Gospel which was preached by me** to you and to the other churches **is not according to man**, i.e., not according to human nature that is at variance with the divine rule or divine revelation.

Et sic ly *secundum hominem*, sonat in vitium. I Cor. III, 3: *cum enim sit inter vos zelus et contentio*, et cetera. Et sic accipit hic Apostolus. Et ideo dicit *non secundum hominem* docentem me vel mittentem: quasi dicat: nullo modo potest hoc Evangelium haberi ab homine, sed a Deo.

34. Et ideo subdit *neque enim ego ab homine*, etc., ubi duplicem modum acceptionis excludit. Primo quod non habuit ab homine auctoritatem evangelizandi, et quantum ad hoc dicit *neque ab homine*, scilicet puro, *accepi illud*, id est, auctoritatem evangelizandi Evangelium, sed a Christo. Rom. c. X, 15: *quomodo praedicabunt, nisi mittantur?* Is. XLII, 6: *dedi te in lucem gentium*, et cetera. Act. IX, 15: *vas electionis est mihi iste*, et cetera.

Secundo, quod non accepit scientiam evangelizandi ab homine. Et ideo dicit *neque didici*, scilicet Evangelium per hominem purum, *sed per revelationem Iesu Christi*, id est, per Iesum Christum omnia clare ostendentem. I Cor. II, 10: *nobis autem revelavit Deus*, etc., Is. l, 5: *Dominus Deus aperuit mihi aurem*, et cetera. Et ibid., 4: *Dominus dedit mihi linguam eruditam, ut sciam*, et cetera.

Haec autem revelatio facta fuit Apostolo, cum raptus fuit in paradisum, ubi *audivit arcana verba quae non licet homini loqui*, II Cor. XII, 4.

35. Consequenter cum dicit *audistis enim*, etc., probat propositum, scilicet quod non accepit ab homine Evangelium, neque ante conversionem, neque post conversionem ad Christum, ibi *cum enim placuit*, et cetera.

Quod autem non acceperit ab homine ante conversionem suam, ostendit et per odium quod habebat ad fidem Christi et ad Christianos, et per fervorem quem habebat ad Iudaismum, ibi *et proficiebam*, et cetera.

36. Dicit ergo: dico quod non accepi ab homine, et hoc ante conversionem meam, quod patet ex factis illius temporis, et ex odio quod habebam ad fidem. Nam vos ipsi *audistis*, infra eodem, *tantum autem auditum habebant*, etc., *conversationem meam aliquando*, dum infidelis eram, *in Iudaismo*, quo Iudaice vivebam. Et dicit, *meam*, quia hoc quod male facimus ex nobis est, ex Deo autem quidquid boni facimus. Os. XIII, 9: *ex te perditio tua, Israel, tantummodo in me auxilium tuum*.

Istud scilicet audistis, *quoniam supra modum*, scilicet aliorum, quia non solum per se, sed provocabat principes ad hoc. Alii enim forte a principibus inducti persequebantur, sed iste eos inducebat. Act. IX, 1: *Saulus adhuc spirans minarum*, etc., *accessit*, et cetera. Et quia non solum in Ierusalem, sed etiam per totam regionem. Unde *accepit litteras in Damascum*, et cetera. Unde de eo potest intelligi illud quod dicitur Gen. XLIX, 27:

In this sense, *according to man* implies something evil: *for whereas there is among you envying and contention, are you not carnal, and walk according to man?* (1 Cor 3:3). And this is the sense the Apostle takes here. Hence he says, *not according to man* teaching me or sending me, as if to say: this Gospel can in no way be had from men, but only from God.

34. That is why he adds, *for neither did I receive it of man*, whereby he precludes two ways of receiving. First, that he did not receive from man the authority to preach. As to this he says, *nor of man*, i.e., purely man, *did I receive it*, i.e., the authority to preach the Gospel, but of Christ: *and how shall they preach unless they be sent?* (Rom 10:15); *I have given you for a light of the gentiles* (Isa 42:6); *this man is to me a vessel of election* (Acts 9:15).

Second, that he did not receive the knowledge of what is to be preached from man. Hence he says, *nor did I learn it*, namely, the Gospel, from mere man, *but by the revelation of Jesus Christ*, i.e., by Jesus Christ showing everything clearly. *But to us, God has revealed them* (1 Cor 2:10); *the Lord has opened my ear, and I do not resist* (Isa 50:5), and *the Lord has given me a learned tongue* (Isa 50:4).

Now this revelation was made to the Apostle when he was rapt into paradise, where *he heard secret words which it is not granted to man to utter* (2 Cor 12:4).

35. Then when he says, *for you have heard of my behavior in time past*, he shows that he did not receive the Gospel from men, either before his conversion or after his conversion to Christ, at *but when it pleased him* (Gal 1:15).

That he did not receive it from man before his conversion he shows both by the hatred he bore toward the faith of Christ and toward Christians, and by the zeal he had for Judaism, at *and I made progress*.

36. He says therefore: I say that I did not receive it of man, and this is true of the time before my conversion. This, indeed, is obvious from my actions at that time and from the hatred I bore toward the faith. *For you yourselves have heard*, and below to the same purpose: *but they had heard only: he who persecuted us in times past now preaches the faith which once he impugned* (Gal 1:23), *of my behavior in time past*, when I was an unbeliever, *in the Jews' religion*, when I lived as a Jew. And he says, *my*, because the evil we do is from ourselves, but whatever good we do is from God: *destruction is your own, O Israel: your help is only in me* (Hos 13:9).

This you have heard, *how that, beyond measure*, i.e., more than others, because he bestirred not only himself to this but rulers as well. For others, when they persecuted, were led to it by the rulers, but he urged even them: *Saul, as yet breathing out threatenings and slaughter against the disciples of the Lord, went to the high priest* (Acts 9:1). Also because he did this not only in Jerusalem but in the entire region. Hence *he received letters to Damascus* (Acts 9:2).

Beniamin lupus rapax, et cetera. ***Persecutus sum Ecclesiam Dei***, scilicet inquirendo Christianos et fugando. I Cor. XV, 9: *non sum dignus vocari apostolus*, et cetera. ***Et expugnabam illam***, non quidem spiritualiter, quia corda fidelium non poteram a fide avertere, sed corporaliter affligendo eos poenis corporalibus, et ponendo in carcere. Act. IX, 21: *nonne hic est qui*, etc., Ps. CXXVIII, 1: *saepe expugnaverunt me*, et cetera.

Sic ergo patet, per odium quod habebat ad fidem Christi ante conversionem, quod non accepit Evangelium ab homine.

37. Patet hoc etiam per amorem et fervorem zeli, quem habuit ad Iudaismum, et hoc quantum ad profectum exteriorem. Unde dicit ***et proficiebam***, etc., ubi tria ponit quae exprimunt profectus magnitudinem, quia ***supra multos***, non supra paucos proficiebat, non supra senes ineptos ad profectum scientiae, sed ***coaetaneos***, scilicet adolescentes acutos et aptos ad profectum. Thren. III, 27: *bonum est viro, cum portaverit iugum ab adolescentia sua*.

Item non supra coaetaneos extraneos, quasi ignotae linguae, sed illos qui sunt ***in genere meo***, scilicet Iudaeorum. Act. XXII, 3: *ego sum vir Iudaeus, secus pedes Gamalielis eruditus*, et cetera.

Item quantum ad zelum interiorem quem habebat ad legem. Et ideo dicit ***abundantius prae aliis aemulator existens***, non solum legis, sed ***paternarum mearum traditionum***, scilicet quas habent Iudaei licitas, *quas boni patres addiderunt*, ut dicitur in Glossa, quas quidem traditiones vocat suas, quia ita reputabat eas, ac si suae fuissent. Phil. III, 5: *secundum legem Pharisaeus, secundum aemulationem persequens*, et cetera.

38. Sed quaestio est super hoc quod dicit Glossa: *boni patres addiderunt*. Videtur quod non fuerint boni, quia Deut. IV, 2 dicitur: *non addetis ad verbum quod ego loquor vobis*, et cetera. Ergo fecerunt contra mandatum domini, addentes traditiones, et sic non fuerunt boni.

Dicendum est quod *verbum* illud Domini intelligendum est sic: non addetis aliquid contrarium, seu extraneum verbis quae ego loquor, et cetera. Addere autem aliqua quae non sunt contraria, licuit eis, scilicet aliquos dies solemnes et alia similia, sicut factum est tempore Mardochaei, et tempore Iudith, in memoriam beneficiorum quae a Deo recipiebant.

Contra, Matth. XV, 6, Dominus reprehendit eos, dicens: *irritum fecistis mandatum Domini propter traditiones hominum*. Non ergo sunt licitae traditiones.

Therefore what is said in Genesis can be understood as applying to him: *Benjamin a ravenous wolf* (Gen 49:27). ***I persecuted the Church of God***, i.e., by hunting down Christians and discomfiting them: *I am not worthy to be called an apostle* (1 Cor 15:9); ***and I wasted it***, not indeed spiritually, because I was unable to turn the hearts of the faithful from their faith, but physically by inflicting bodily punishment on them and casting them into prison: *is not this he who persecuted in Jerusalem?* (Acts 9:21) *often have they fought against me* (Ps 129:1).

It is plain, therefore, from the hatred he bore toward the faith of Christ before his conversion, that he did not receive the Gospel from man.

37. It is plain also from the love and burning zeal he had for Judaism, as to outward progress. Hence he says, ***and I made progress in the Jews' religion above many of my equals in my own nation***: wherein he mentions three things that indicate how great was his progress. For he progressed not above a few but ***above many***, not above old men incapable of progress in learning, but ***my equals***, i.e., young men who were intelligent and capable of progress: *it is good for a man, when he has borne the yoke from his youth* (Lam 3:27).

Furthermore, not above equals who were foreigners and ignorant of the language, but equals ***in my own nation***, i.e., Jews: *I am a Jew, brought up at the feet of Gamaliel* (Acts 22:3).

Finally, as to the inward zeal he had for the law. Hence he says, ***being more abundantly zealous***, not only for the law, but ***for the traditions of my fathers***, namely, those traditions which the Jews lawfully kept and *which the good fathers added*, as is said in a Gloss. He calls these traditions his own because he treasured them as though they were his: *according to the law, a Pharisee; according to zeal, persecuting the Church of God* (Phil 3:5).

38. But a question arises from the fact that the aforesaid Gloss says: *the good fathers added*. For it seems that they were not good, because, it is said: *you shall not add to the word I speak to you* (Deut 4:2). Hence in adding traditions they acted against the command of God and so were not good.

To this one may answer that this *word* of the Lord is taken to mean that you shall not add anything contrary or alien to the words which I shall speak. But to add certain things not contrary was lawful for them, namely, certain solemn days and the like, as was done in the time of Mordochai and of Judith, in memory of the blessings they received from God.

But against this is the rebuke addressed to them by our Lord, when he says: *you have made void the command of the Lord for the traditions of men* (Matt 15:16). Hence those traditions were not lawful.

Respondeo. Dicendum est, quod non arguuntur, quod tenent traditiones hominum, sed quia propter traditiones hominum dimittunt mandata Dei.

I answer that they are not rebuked for holding the traditions of men, but because for the sake of the traditions of men, they neglect the commands of God.

Lecture 4

1:15Cum autem placuit ei, qui me segregavit ex utero matris meae, et vocavit per gratiam suam, [n. 39]

1:16ut revelaret Filium suum in me, ut evangelizarem illum in gentibus: continuo non acquievi carni et sanguini, [n. 43]

1:17neque veni Jerosolymam ad antecessores meos apostolos: sed abii in Arabiam, et iterum reversus sum Damascum: [n. 45]

1:15ὅτε δὲ εὐδόκησεν [ὁ θεὸς] ὁ ἀφορίσας με ἐκ κοιλίας μητρός μου καὶ καλέσας διὰ τῆς χάριτος αὐτοῦ

1:16ἀποκαλύψαι τὸν υἱὸν αὐτοῦ ἐν ἐμοὶ ἵνα εὐαγγελίζωμαι αὐτὸν ἐν τοῖς ἔθνεσιν, εὐθέως οὐ προσανεθέμην σαρκὶ καὶ αἵματι,

1:17οὐδὲ ἀνῆλθον εἰς Ἱεροσόλυμα πρὸς τοὺς πρὸ ἐμοῦ ἀποστόλους, ἀλλὰ ἀπῆλθον εἰς Ἀραβίαν, καὶ πάλιν ὑπέστρεψα εἰς Δαμασκόν.

1:15But when it pleased him who separated me from my mother's womb and called me by his grace, [n. 39]

1:16To reveal his Son in me, that I might preach him among the gentiles: immediately I did not condescend to flesh and blood. [n. 43]

1:17Neither did I go to Jerusalem, to the apostles who were before me: but I went into Arabia, and again I returned to Damascus. [n. 45]

---

39. Postquam autem Apostolus ostendit quod ipse non accepit ab homine Evangelium ante suam conversionem, nunc hic probat quod non accepit ipsum ab homine post conversionem suam. Et

circa hoc duo facit.

Primo ostendit quod non recepit Evangelium ab homine tempore conversionis suae;

secundo quod nec etiam post conversionem suam, ibi **deinde post annos tres**, et cetera.

Circa primum duo facit.

Quia primo ostendit quod non accepit Evangelium ab apostolis, neque didicit;

secundo quod non ab aliis fidelibus, ibi **sed abii in Arabiam**, et cetera.

Circa primum tria facit.

Primo ostendit causam efficientem suae conversionis;

secundo finem, ibi **ut revelaret**, etc.;

tertio modum, ibi **continuo non acquievi**, et cetera.

40. Circa primum notat causam suae conversionis, quae duplex est, scilicet beneplacitum Dei, quod est divina electio, et convertentis vocatio. Quantum ad primum dicit **cum autem placuit**, scilicet Deo, non quando volui ego, sed quando placitum fuit sibi, quia *non est volentis neque currentis*, etc., ut dicitur Rom. IX, 16. Ps. CXLVI, 11: *beneplacitum est Domino*, et cetera. Phil. II, 13: *Deus est qui operatur in nobis*, et cetera.

Qui, scilicet Deus, **me**, scilicet rebellem I Cor. XV, 9: *ego sum minimus apostolorum*, etc., *quoniam persecutus sum*, et cetera. Act. c. IX, 1: *Saulus adhuc spirans minarum*, et cetera. Persecutorem: *Saule, Saule, quid me persequeris*, etc. blasphemum I Tim. I, v. 13: *qui fui blasphemus*, et cetera.

Me, talem, inquam, **segregavit ex utero matris meae**. Vel ad litteram: qui fecit me nasci ex ventre matris meae.

41. Et vere dicitur Deus segregare ex utero, licet sit opus naturae, quae est quasi instrumentum Dei, quia

39. After showing that he did not receive the Gospel from man before his conversion, the Apostle now proves that he did not receive it from man after his conversion.

About this he does two things.

First, he shows that he did not receive the Gospel from man at the time of his conversion;

second, that neither did he receive it after his conversion, at **then, after three years** (Gal 1:18).

Regarding the first he does two things.

First, he shows that he did not receive or learn the Gospel from the apostles;

second, nor from any other believer, at **I went into Arabia**.

As to the first he does three things.

First, he shows the efficient cause of his conversion;

second, the end, at **to reveal his Son**;

third, the manner, at **immediately I did not condescend**.

40. In regard to the first point, he notes the twofold cause of his conversion, namely, the good pleasure of God, which is divine election, and the call of the one converting. Regarding the first he says, **when it pleased him**, namely, God: not when I willed, but when it pleased him, because *it is not of him who wills, nor of him who runs* (Rom 9:16); *the Lord takes pleasure in those who fear him* (Ps 147:11); *for it is God who works in us* (Phil 2:13).

Who, namely, God, **separated me**, namely, a rebel: *I am the least of the apostles, who am not worthy to be called an apostle, because I persecuted the Church of God* (1 Cor 15:9); *Saul, as yet breathing out threatenings* (Acts 9:1); and a persecutor: *Saul, Saul, why do you persecute you me?* (Acts 9:4); and a blasphemer: *who before was a blasphemer* (1 Tim 1:13).

Me, and such a one, I say, he **separated from my mother's womb**. Or, literally: who made me to be born from my mother's womb.

41. It is indeed true to say that God separates one from the womb, even though it is a work of nature, which is, as it

opera etiam nostra attribuuntur Deo, sicut principali auctori, Is. c. XXVI, 12: *omnia enim opera nostra operatus es in nobis*, etc., sicut et effectus principali agenti attribuuntur. Ideo dicitur Iob X, v. 11: *pelle et carnibus vestisti me*, et cetera. Et ab hoc utero segregatus est ad iustificationem, quia eiusdem est iustificare, cuius est condere. Ps. XXI, 11: *de ventre matris meae*, et cetera.

Vel: ***ex utero matris meae***, scilicet synagogae, cuius uterus est collegium Pharisaeorum, qui nutriebant alios in Iudaismo. Matth. XXIII, v. 15: *circuitis mare et aridam, ut faciatis*, et cetera. Sic ergo mater sua fuit synagoga. Cant. c. I, 5: *filii matris meae pugnaverunt contra me*, et cetera. Uterus eius sunt Pharisaei. Ex hoc ergo utero est segregatus per Spiritum Sanctum ad fidem Evangelii. Rom. I, 1: *segregatus in Evangelium Dei*.

Vel mater sua est Ecclesia Christi; uterus eius, collegium apostolorum. Segregavit ergo Deus ipsum ab utero Ecclesiae, id est, a collegio apostolorum in officium apostolatus et praedicationis ad gentes, quando dixit apostolis, Act. XIII, 2: *segregate mihi Barnabam et Paulum*, et cetera.

Vocat autem synagogam matrem suam, quia Pharisaeus erat, quasi magnus in ea, dum dicitur Pharisaeus, et ex Pharisaeis, quia zelator legis erat. Supra: ***abundantius autem aemulator***, et cetera.

42. Quantum autem ad aliam causam dicit ***et vocavit***, et cetera. Est autem duplex vocatio. Una est exterior, et sic dicit: ***vocavit*** me caelesti voce. Act. IX, 4: *Saule, Saule, quid me persequeris?* et cetera. *Vade in civitatem*, et cetera. Sic etiam alios apostolos vocavit.

Alia est interior, et sic vocavit per quemdam instinctum interiorem, quo Deus per gratiam tangit cor, ut convertatur ad ipsum, et sic ***vocavit*** a mala via in bonam, et hoc ***per gratiam suam***, non nostris meritis. Rom. VIII, 30: *quos praedestinavit, hos et vocavit*, et cetera. Is. XLV, 13: *suscitavit eum ad iustitiam*, et cetera. Amos, V, 8: *qui vocat aquas maris*, et cetera.

43. Finis autem conversionis ponitur, cum dicit ***ut revelaret filium***, etc., qui quidem finis est Christus.

Ordinatur autem conversio sua ad Christum dupliciter, scilicet facto, et sic dicit ***ut revelaret Filium suum***, id est, in eo quod circa me fecit, convertendo me et dimittendo peccata mihi, revelaret quanta sit mihi facta misericordia. I Tim. I, 15 s.: *Christus Iesus venit in hunc mundum peccatores salvos facere*, et cetera. *Sed ideo misericordiam Dei consecutus sum, quia ignorans*, et cetera. Sic ergo revelavit in eius conversione Filium suum, et hoc inquantum Filius dicitur gratia Dei. Item revelavit eum in eius operatione; unde dicebat ipse, Rom. XV, 18: *non enim audeo aliquid loqui eorum, quae per me non*

were, an instrument of God, because even our own works are attributed to God as to their principal author: *for you have wrought all our works for us* (Isa 26:12), as any effect is attributed to the principal agent: *you have clothed me with skin and flesh* (Job 10:11). And he was separated from this womb to be justified, for the same one justifies who makes: *from my mother's womb you are my God* (Ps 22:10).

Or: ***from my mother's womb***, i.e., the synagogue, whose womb is the college of Pharisees who trained him in Judaism: *you go round about the sea and the land to make one proselyte* (Matt 23:15). Thus, therefore, was the synagogue his mother: *the sons of my mother have fought against me* (Song 1:5). The Pharisees are its womb. And from this womb he was separated by the Holy Spirit unto faith in the Gospel: *separated unto the Gospel of God* (Rom 1:1).

Or his mother is the Church of Christ, and the womb, the college of apostles. Hence God separated him from the womb of the Church, i.e., from the college of apostles, for the office of apostleship and preacher to the gentiles, when he said to the apostles: *separate for me Saul and Barnabas* (Acts 13:2).

Again, he calls the synagogue his mother, because he was a Pharisee and an outstanding one, for which reason he is called a Pharisee and of the Pharisees, because he was zealous for the law: ***being more abundantly zealous for the traditions of my fathers*** (Gal 1:14).

42. Now as regards the other cause, he says, ***and called me by his grace***. But there are two kinds of call. One is exterior, and so he says: he ***called me*** with a voice from heaven. *Saul, Saul, why do you persecute you me . . . go into the city, and there it shall be told you what you must do* (Acts 9:4, 6). In a similar fashion he called the other apostles.

The other call is interior, and in this way he calls through a certain interior instinct, whereby God touches the heart to be turned to him, as when ***he calls*** one from the path of evil to good; and this ***by his grace*** and not our own merits: *and whom he predestined, them he also called* (Rom 8:30); *I have raised him up to justice* (Isa 45:13); *that calls the waters of the sea and pours them out upon the face of the earth: the Lord is his name* (Amos 5:8).

43. The end of his conversion is stated when he says, ***to reveal his Son in me***. Hence Christ is the end.

Now his conversion is ordained to Christ in two ways: first of all, by his works. Hence he says, ***to reveal his Son***, i.e., by what he did in my regard, by converting me and forgiving my sins, he revealed what a great act of mercy was bestowed on me: *Jesus Christ came into this world to save sinners, of whom I am the chief* (1 Tim 1:15); *but I obtained the mercy of God, because I did it ignorantly in unbelief* (1 Tim 1:13). Thus, therefore, in his conversion he revealed his Son in the sense that the Son is called the grace of God. Likewise, he revealed him in his action; hence he says: *for I dare not speak of any of those things which Christ*

effecit Christus in obedientiam gentium, in verbo, in factis, et virtute, et cetera. Et hoc inquantum Filius virtus est Dei. Item revelavit eum in eius praedicatione; unde ipse dicebat, I Cor. I, 23: *nos praedicamus*, etc., usque *et Dei sapientiam*. Et hoc inquantum Filius eius dicitur Dei sapientia.

Item ordinatur ad Christum sua conversio verbo, et sic dicit **ut evangelizarem illum in gentibus**, quia, aliis apostolis evangelizantibus Christum Iudaeis, Paulus de mandato Domini ivit ad gentes convertendas. Is. c. XLIX, 6: *parum enim est mihi, ut sis mihi servus*, etc., *dedi te in lucem*, et cetera. Act. XIII, v. 47: *sic enim praecepit*, et cetera. Infra: *ecce testem populis dedi eum, ducem ac praeceptorem gentibus*.

44. Modus autem suae conversionis est perfectus, et quantum ad effectum; unde dicit **continuo non acquievi carni et sanguini**, id est, statim ita perfecte fui conversus, quod omnis carnalis affectus recessit a me. Eccli. c. XI, 23: *facile est enim in oculis domini subito honestare pauperem*.

Et accipitur hic caro et sanguis pro vitiis carnalibus. I Cor. XV, 50: *caro et sanguis regnum Dei non possidebunt*, et cetera. Infra V, 17: **caro concupiscit**, et cetera. Vel pro affectu et amore ad carnaliter sibi coniunctos. Matth. c. XVI, 17: *caro et sanguis non revelavit tibi*, et cetera. Sic Apostolus et vitia sua superavit, et suos Iudaeos contempsit.

Item quantum ad intellectum; quia ita fuit instructus a Christo, quod non fuit ei necesse instrui ab apostolis. Et idco dicit **ncc vcni Icrosolymam**, ut scilicet ab eis instruerer.

45. Item non fuit necesse instrui ab aliis fidelibus. Et ideo dicit **sed abii in Arabiam**, etc., quasi dicat: non ivi ad loca ubi erant alii fideles, ut me instruerent, sed ivi in Arabiam, ubi non erant edocti in fide, sed infideles. **Et iterum reversus sum Damascum**, scilicet ad parentes. Iob XXXVIII, 25: *quis dedit vehementissimo imbri cursum*, et cetera.

Sed contra dicitur Act. IX, 25 quod *demiserunt eum de muro per sportam*, et cetera. *Cum autem venisset Ierusalem, tentabat se iungere discipulis*. Venit ergo Ierusalem.

Dicendum est quod venit, sed non ut instrueretur. Vel, melius, dicendum est quod non statim venit, sed post aliquod tempus, et ideo sequitur **deinde post annos**, et cetera.

works not by me, for the obedience of the gentiles by word and deed, by virtue of signs and wonders (Rom 15:18). And this inasmuch as the Son is the power of God. Furthermore, he revealed him in his preaching. Hence he said: *we preach Christ crucified . . . and the wisdom of God* (1 Cor 1:23). And this inasmuch as the Son is called the wisdom of God.

Second, his conversion is ordained to Christ by his words. Hence he says, **that I might preach him among the gentiles**, because, whereas the other apostles preached the Gospel of Christ to the Jews, Paul, on the Lord's command, went to convert the gentiles: *it is a small thing that you should be my servant . . . I have given you to be the light of the gentiles* (Isa 49:6); *for so the Lord has commanded us* (Acts 13:47); *behold, I have given him for a witness to the people, for a leader and a master to the gentiles* (Isa 55:4).

44. The manner of his conversion is perfect, and this with regard to its effect; hence he says, **immediately I did not condescend to flesh and blood**, i.e., at once I was so completely converted that all carnal affection left me: *it is easy in the eyes of God on a sudden to make the poor man rich* (Sir 11:23).

Flesh and blood are here taken for vices of the flesh: *flesh and blood cannot possess the kingdom of God* (1 Cor 15:50); *for the flesh lusts against the spirit* (Gal 5:17). Or they are taken for the affection and love borne toward blood relatives. *Flesh and blood has not revealed it to you* (Matt 16:17). Thus the Apostle overcame his own vices and scorned his fellow Jews.

Furthermore, his conversion was perfect with respect to his understanding, because he was so instructed by Christ that there was no need to be instructed by the apostles; hence he says, **neither did I go to Jerusalem**, i.e., to be instructed by them.

45. Again, it was not necessary for him to be instructed by any other of the faithful; hence he says, **but I went into Arabia**. As if to say: I did not go to places where there were believers who might instruct me, but I went to Arabia where they were not instructed in the faith but were unbelievers. **And again I returned to Damascus**, i.e., to his parents: *who gave a course to violent showers, or a way for noisy thunder?* (Job 38:25).

But someone might object that it is said: *in Damascus they let him down in a basket . . . and when he was come into Jerusalem, he essayed to join himself to the disciples* (Acts 9:25–26). Therefore, according to this, he went to Jerusalem.

To this I answer that he did go, but not to be instructed. Or, better still, he did not go at once but after some time. Hence he says in the next verse, **then, after three years I went to Jerusalem** (Gal 1:18).

Lecture 5

1:18 deinde post annos tres veni Jerosolymam videre Petrum, et mansi apud eum diebus quindecim: [n. 46]

1:19 alium autem apostolorum vidi neminem, nisi Jacobum fratrem Domini. [n. 48]

1:20 Quae autem scribo vobis, ecce coram Deo, quia non mentior. [n. 49]

1:21 Deinde veni in partes Syriae, et Ciliciae. [n. 50]

1:22 Eram autem ignotus facie ecclesiis Judaeae, quae erant in Christo:

1:23 tantum autem auditum habebant quoniam qui persequebatur nos aliquando, nunc evangelizat fidem, quam aliquando expugnabat:

1:24 et in me clarificabant Deum.

1:18 Ἔπειτα μετὰ ἔτη τρία ἀνῆλθον εἰς Ἱεροσόλυμα ἱστορῆσαι Κηφᾶν, καὶ ἐπέμεινα πρὸς αὐτὸν ἡμέρας δεκαπέντε·

1:19 ἕτερον δὲ τῶν ἀποστόλων οὐκ εἶδον, εἰ μὴ Ἰάκωβον τὸν ἀδελφὸν τοῦ κυρίου.

1:20 ἃ δὲ γράφω ὑμῖν, ἰδοὺ ἐνώπιον τοῦ θεοῦ ὅτι οὐ ψεύδομαι.

1:21 ἔπειτα ἦλθον εἰς τὰ κλίματα τῆς Συρίας καὶ τῆς Κιλικίας.

1:22 ἤμην δὲ ἀγνοούμενος τῷ προσώπῳ ταῖς ἐκκλησίαις τῆς Ἰουδαίας ταῖς ἐν Χριστῷ,

1:23 μόνον δὲ ἀκούοντες ἦσαν ὅτι Ὁ διώκων ἡμᾶς ποτε νῦν εὐαγγελίζεται τὴν πίστιν ἥν ποτε ἐπόρθει,

1:24 καὶ ἐδόξαζον ἐν ἐμοὶ τὸν θεόν.

1:18 Then, after three years, I went to Jerusalem to see Peter: and I tarried with him fifteen days. [n. 46]

1:19 But I saw none of the other apostles, except James the brother of the Lord. [n. 48]

1:20 Now the things which I write to you, behold, before God, I do not lie. [n. 49]

1:21 Afterwards, I came into the regions of Syria and Cilicia. [n. 50]

1:22 And I was unknown by face to the churches of Judea, which were in Christ:

1:23 But they had heard only: he, who persecuted us in times past now preaches the faith which once he impugned.

1:24 And they glorified God in me.

---

46. Postquam superius Apostolus ostendit se non accepisse Evangelium ab homine ante conversionem suam, nec tempore suae conversionis, hic probat quod nec etiam post conversionem accepit ipsum ab homine; sed potius hic ostendit quomodo doctrina sua fuit ab hominibus approbata. Et

circa hoc duo facit.

Primo enim manifestat quomodo doctrina sua fuit ab apostolis approbata;

secundo ostendit qualiter fuit approbata ab aliis fidelibus, ibi **deinde veni in partes**, et cetera.

Et primo narrat factum;

secundo confirmat veritatem dicti, ibi **ecce coram Deo**, et cetera.

47. Dicit ergo: licet non iverim ad apostolos, ut instruerer ab eis circa principium meae conversionis, quia iam eram instructus a Christo, tamen ex affectu caritatis compulsus, **post annos tres**, scilicet conversionis meae, **veni Ierosolymam**, quoniam iamdiu desideravi **videre Petrum**, non ut discerem ab eo, sed ut visitarem eum. Iob c. V, 24: *visitans speciem tuam*, et cetera. **Et mansi apud eum diebus quindecim**, repertus ab eo, ut verax apostolus.

Et dicit **diebus quindecim**, quia numerus iste componitur ex octo et septem. Octonarius autem est numerus Novi Testamenti, in quo expectatur octava resurgentium; septenarius autem, numerus Veteris Testamenti, quia celebrat septimam diem. Mansit autem apud

46. After showing above that he did not receive the Gospel from man before his conversion nor at the time of his conversion, the Apostle now proves that neither after his conversion did he receive it from man; but he shows, rather, how his teaching was approved by men.

About this he does two things.

First, he shows how his teaching was approved by the apostles;

second, he shows how it was approved by the rest of the faithful, at **afterwards, I came into the regions**.

First, he states the fact;

second, he confirms the truth of his statement, at **before God, I do not lie**.

47. He says therefore: although I did not go to the apostles to be instructed by them in the beginning of my conversion, because I had already been instructed by Christ, yet, being moved by a feeling of charity, **after three years**, i.e., after my conversion, **I went to Jerusalem**, because I had long desired **to see Peter**, not to be taught by him but to visit him; *and visiting your beauty you shall not sin* (Job 5:24). **And I tarried with him fifteen days**, and I was discovered by him to be a true apostle.

And he says **fifteen days**, because that number is the sum of eight and seven. Eight is the number of the New Testament, in which the eighth day of those who will rise is awaited; but seven is the number of the Old Testament, because it celebrates the seventh day. And so he stayed with

Petrum diebus quindecim, conferens cum eo de mysteriis Veteris Testamenti et Novi.

48. Et ne credatur quod licet non sit instructus a Petro, esset tamen etiam instructus ab aliis, subdit quod nec ab aliis fuit instructus. Unde dicit **alium autem apostolorum**, a quo instruerer, **vidi neminem**, id est nullum, **nisi Iacobum fratrem Domini**. Illum enim vidit in Ierusalem.

Circa istum Iacobum sciendum est, quod iste fuit episcopus Ierosolymorum, et fuit vocatus Iacobus Minor, eo quod vocatus fuerat post Iacobum alium. Dicuntur autem multa de isto Act. XV, 13 ss. Ipse etiam fecit epistolam canonicam.

Quare autem dicatur frater Domini, a diversis diversimode dicitur. Elvidius enim dicit, quod ideo dicitur frater Domini, quia fuit filius Beatae Virginis. Dicit enim quod Beata Virgo Christum concepit et peperit, et post partum Christi concepit de Ioseph, et peperit alios filios. Sed hic error est damnatus et reprobatus. Item patet esse falsum, quia Iacobus non fuit filius Ioseph, sed Alphaei.

Alii vero dicunt, quod Ioseph ante Beatam Virginem habuit aliam uxorem, de qua habuit filium Iacobum et alios, qua mortua, accepit in uxorem Beatam Virginem, de qua natus est Christus, non tamen cognita a Ioseph, sed per Spiritum Sanctum, ut in Evangelio dicitur. Quia ergo ex patre nominantur cognationes, et Ioseph putabatur pater Christi, ideo iste Iacobus, licet non fuit filius Virginis, tamen vocabatur frater Domini. Sed hoc est falsum, quia si Dominus matrem virginem noluit nisi virgini commendare custodiendam, quomodo sustinuisset sponsum eius, virginem non fuisse, et sic perstitisse?

Ideo alii dicunt, et in Glossa tangitur, quod Iacobus iste fuit filius Mariae Cleophae, quae fuit soror Virginis. Dicunt enim quod Anna mater Beatae Virginis nupsit primo Ioachim, ex quo peperit Mariam, matrem Domini, quo mortuo, nupsit Cleophae fratri Ioachim, ex quo peperit Mariam Cleophae, et ex hac natus est Iacobus Minor, Iudas et Simon, quo mortuo, dicitur quod nupsit adhuc cuidam tertio, qui vocatus est Salome, ex quo concepit et peperit aliam Mariam, quae dicta est Salome, et de hac natus est Iacobus Maior, et Ioannes, frater eius.

Sed huic opinioni dupliciter contradicit Hieronymus. Primo quia Salome non est nomen viri, ut etiam in Graeco apparet, sed est nomen mulieris, quae fuit soror Beatae Virginis, et ex Zebedaeo genuit Iacobum Maiorem et Ioannem, sicut Maria Cleophae ex Alphaeo genuit Iacobum Minorem, Iudam et Simonem. Dicitur autem frater Domini iste Iacobus, specialiter inter alios suos consobrinos, et hoc propter duo, primo propter similitudinem effigiei, quia similis erat Christo in facie; et

Peter fifteen days, conversing with him on the mysteries of the Old and New Testament.

48. But lest anyone suppose that, although he was not instructed by Peter, he might have been instructed by others, he adds that he was not instructed by others. Hence he says, **but of the other apostles**, by whom I might be instructed, **I saw none**, i.e., no one, **except James, the brother of the Lord**, for he saw him in Jerusalem.

Regarding James, it should be known that he was the bishop of Jerusalem and named James the Lesser, because he had been called after another James. Many things are recorded of him (Acts 15:13ff). He also wrote a canonical epistle.

Now there are various explanations why he is called the brother of the Lord. Elvidius says that it was because he was the son of the Blessed Virgin. For according to him, the Blessed Virgin conceived and gave birth to Christ, and after the birth of Christ she conceived of Joseph and brought forth other sons. But this error is condemned and refuted. Furthermore, it is clearly false, because James was not the son of Joseph but of Alpheus.

Others say that before the Blessed Virgin, Joseph had another wife of whom he had James and other children, and that after she died, he took as a wife the Blessed Virgin, from whom Christ was born, although she was not known by Joseph, but, as it is said in the Gospel, he was conceived by the Holy Spirit. But because progeny are named after their father, and Joseph was considered the father of Christ, for that reason, James, too, although he was not the son of the Virgin, was nevertheless called the brother of the Lord. But this is false, because if the Lord did not want as mother anyone but a virgin entrusted to the care of a virgin, how would he have allowed her husband not to be a virgin and still endure it?

Therefore others say, and this is mentioned in a Gloss, that James was the son of Mary of Cleophas, who was a sister of the Virgin. For they say that Anne, the mother of the Blessed Virgin, first married Joachim, of whom was born Mary, the mother of the Lord; but when Joachim died, she married Joachim's brother, Cleophas, from whom she bore Mary of Cleophas, and from her were born James the Lesser, Jude and Simon. Then after Cleophas died, she married a third man who was called Salome, of whom she conceived and bore another Mary, called Salome, from whom were born James the Greater and his brother John.

But this opinion is denied on two counts by Jerome: first of all, because Salome is not a man's name, as is plain in Greek, but the name of the woman who was the sister of the Blessed Virgin and who begot James the Greater and John, of Zebedee, just as Mary Cleophas begot James the Lesser, Jude and Simon, of Alpheus. Now this James is singled out from his other brothers and called the brother of the Lord for two reasons: first, because of a likeness in appearance, for he had a facial resemblance to Christ; and

propter similitudinem vitae, quia imitabatur Christum in moribus. Vel quia Alphaeus pater eius fuit de cognatione Ioseph. Et ideo quia Iudaei cognationis lineam texere solent a maribus, et *Christus putabatur filius Ioseph*, ut dicitur Lc. III, 23, ideo specialiter dictus est frater Domini, et non alii, qui solum ex matre coniuncti erant ei. Accipitur autem hic *frater* cognatione.

Nam in Scriptura fratres aliquando dicuntur natura. Matth. I, 2: *Iacob autem genuit Iudam et fratres eius*. Cognatione, sicut omnes consanguinei sunt fratres. Gen. XIII, 8: *ne, quaeso, sit iurgium inter te et me, fratres enim sumus*. gente, et sic omnes unius linguae dicuntur fratres. Deut. XVII, 15: *non poteris alterius gentis hominem regem facere, qui non sit frater tuus*. Affectione, et sic omnes amici, et qui habent eumdem affectum dicuntur fratres. II Cor. II, 13: *eo quod non invenerim Titum fratrem meum*, et cetera. Religione, et sic omnes Christiani qui habent unam regulam vitae, dicuntur fratres. Matth. XXIII, v. 8: *fratres estis*, et cetera. Ps. CXXXII, 1: *ecce quam bonum et quam iucundum habitare fratres in unum*, et cetera. Communiter autem omnes homines dicuntur fratres, quia ab uno Deo gubernati et educati. Mal. II, 10: *numquid non unus est Pater omnium nostrum*, et cetera.

49. Consequenter cum dicit *quae autem scribo vobis*, etc., confirmat per iuramentum quod dixerat, quasi dicat: ea *quae* nunc *scribo vobis* de me, *ecce* in manifesto sunt, ita quod satis constat *quia non mentior*. Et hoc dico, *coram Deo*, id est, teste Deo.

Iurat autem hic Apostolus non ex levitate, sed ex necessitate istorum, quibus necessarium erat, ut crederent. Nisi enim hoc faceret, non crederent ei. II Cor. II, 17: *coram Deo in Christo loquimur*. Rom. I, 9: *testis est mihi Deus*, et cetera.

Quid ergo dicit Dominus: *sit sermo vester, est, est; non, non; quod amplius est, a malo est*?

Dicendum est, quod est a malo eius qui non credit, vel a malo poenae quo cogitur quis iurare.

50. Consequenter cum dicit *deinde veni*, etc., ostendit quomodo fuit approbatus ab aliis ecclesiis Iudaeae. Ubi tria facit. Primo ostendit ubi fuit conversatus, quia in Cilicia. Unde dicit *deinde veni in partes Syriae et Ciliciae*, scilicet patriae; unde etiam fuit raptus, quia dicitur Act. XXII, 3: *erat autem Paulus a Tharso Ciliciae*, et cetera.

Secundo quomodo fuit cognitus ab eis, quia non facie, sed auditu tantum et fama. Unde dicit *eram enim ignotus facie ecclesiis Iudaeae quae erant in Christo*, id est, in fide Christi. II Cor. VI, 8: *sicut qui ignoti et cogniti*.

because of a likeness in their lives, for he imitated the manners of Christ. Or he is called the brother of Christ, because Alpheus, his father, was related to Joseph. Accordingly, because the Jews were accustomed to draw up the lines of ancestry on the father's side, and *Christ was considered the son of Joseph* (Luke 3:23), he, rather than the others, was called the brother of the Lord, because they were related to him only on his mother's side. Furthermore, **brother** is taken here in the sense of kinsman.

For in the Scriptures some are called brothers, who are so by nature: *Jacob begot Judas and his brothers* (Matt 1:2). Others, who are kinsmen, such as blood relations, are brothers: *let there be no quarrel, I beseech you, between me and you . . . for we are brothers* (Gen 13:8). Others, who are so by race; hence all who speak the same tongue are called brothers: *you may not make a man of another nation king, that is not your brother* (Deut 17:15). Others, who are so by affection; hence all who are friends and who have the same love are called brothers: *because I found not Titus my brother* (2 Cor 2:13). Others who are so by religion; hence all Christians who have one rule of life are called brothers: *for one is your master; and all you are brothers* (Matt 23:8); *behold how good and how pleasant it is for brothers to dwell together in unity* (Ps 133:1). And in general, all men are called brothers, because they are ruled and protected by one God: *have we not all one Father?* (Mal 2:10).

49. Then when he says, *now the things which I write to you, behold, before God I do not lie*, he confirms his statements with an oath. As if to say: *the things I now write to you* about myself, *behold*, are so well known that it is obvious *I do not lie*. And this I say *before God*, i.e., with God as my witness.

The Apostle here takes an oath not for a slight reason, but for the sake of those for whom it was necessary, that they might believe. For had he not sworn, they would not have believed him. *Before God, in Christ we speak* (2 Cor 2:17); *God is my witness* (Rom 1:9).

But what does the Lord say? *Let your speech be: yes, yes; no, no. And that which is over and above these is of evil* (Matt 5:37).

The answer to this is that it is of the evil of him who does not believe, or of the evil of punishment which compels one to swear.

50. Then when he says, *afterwards, I came into the regions of Syria and Cilicia*, he shows how he was approved by the other churches of Judea. Here he does three things: first he shows where he lived, namely in Cilicia. Hence he says, *then I came into the regions of Syria and Cilicia*, i.e., his native land, where he was caught up into paradise: because it is said: *Paul was born at Tarsus in Cilicia* (Acts 22:3).

Second, how he was known by the others, namely, not by sight but by report and reputation. Hence he says, *I was unknown by face to the churches of Judea, which were in Christ*, i.e., in the faith of Christ: *as unknown and yet*

Unde patet quod ecclesiae Iudaeae non docuerunt me. ***Tantum*** enim ***auditum habebant***, scilicet de me per famam, ***quoniam qui persequebatur***, et cetera.

Tertio quomodo approbatus est ab eis, quia ***in me glorificabant Deum***, id est, in mea conversione magnificum probabant, qui gratia sua me convertit. Is. XLIII, 20: *glorificabit me bestia*, et cetera.

known (2 Cor 6:8). Hence it is evident that the churches of Judea did not teach me. ***But they had heard only***, i.e., of me, from reports that ***he who persecuted us in times past, now preaches the faith which once he impugned***.

Third, how he was approved by them, because ***they glorified God in me***, i.e., in my conversion they glorified him who converted me by his grace: *the beast of the field shall glorify me* (Isa 43:20).

Chapter 2

Lecture 1

²:¹Deinde post annos quatuordecim, iterum ascendi Jerosolymam cum Barnaba, assumpto et Tito. [n. 51]

²:²Ascendi autem secundum revelationem: et contuli cum illis Evangelium, quod praedico in gentibus, seorsum autem iis qui videbantur aliquid esse: ne forte in vacuum currerem, aut cucurrissem. [n. 56]

²:³Sed neque Titus, qui mecum erat, cum esset gentilis, compulsus est circumcidi: [n. 60]

²:⁴sed propter subintroductos falsos fratres, qui subintroierunt explorare libertatem nostram, quam habemus in Christo Jesu, ut nos in servitutem redigerent. [n. 62]

²:⁵Quibus neque ad horam cessimus subjectione, ut veritas Evangelii permaneat apud vos:

²:¹Ἔπειτα διὰ δεκατεσσάρων ἐτῶν πάλιν ἀνέβην εἰς Ἱεροσόλυμα μετὰ Βαρναβᾶ, συμπαραλαβὼν καὶ Τίτον·

²:²ἀνέβην δὲ κατὰ ἀποκάλυψιν· καὶ ἀνεθέμην αὐτοῖς τὸ εὐαγγέλιον ὃ κηρύσσω ἐν τοῖς ἔθνεσιν, κατ' ἰδίαν δὲ τοῖς δοκοῦσιν, μή πως εἰς κενὸν τρέχω ἢ ἔδραμον.

²:³ἀλλ' οὐδὲ Τίτος ὁ σὺν ἐμοί, Ἕλλην ὤν, ἠναγκάσθη περιτμηθῆναι·

²:⁴διὰ δὲ τοὺς παρεισάκτους ψευδαδέλφους, οἵτινες παρεισῆλθον κατασκοπῆσαι τὴν ἐλευθερίαν ἡμῶν ἣν ἔχομεν ἐν Χριστῷ Ἰησοῦ, ἵνα ἡμᾶς καταδουλώσουσιν·

²:⁵οἷς οὐδὲ πρὸς ὥραν εἴξαμεν τῇ ὑποταγῇ, ἵνα ἡ ἀλήθεια τοῦ εὐαγγελίου διαμείνῃ πρὸς ὑμᾶς.

²:¹Then, after fourteen years, I went up again to Jerusalem with Barnabas, taking Titus also with me. [n. 51]

²:²And I went up according to revelation and communicated to them the Gospel which I preach among the gentiles: but separately to them who seemed to be something: lest perhaps I should run or had run in vain. [n. 56]

²:³But neither was Titus, who was with me, being a gentile, compelled to be circumcised, [n. 60]

²:⁴But because of false brethren brought in unawares, who came in privately to spy on our liberty which we have in Christ Jesus, that they might bring us into servitude. [n. 62]

²:⁵To whom we yielded not by subjection: no, not for an hour: that the truth of the Gospel might continue with you.

---

51. Postquam Apostolus in praecedenti cap., commendavit auctoritatem Evangelicae doctrinae secundum seipsam, nunc in isto cap. commendat ipsam ex parte aliorum apostolorum et sua simul. Et

circa hoc duo facit.

Primo commendat auctoritatem suae doctrinae ex approbatione aliorum apostolorum;

secundo ex exemplo sui et aliorum apostolorum, ibi *nos natura Iudaei, non ex gentibus*, et cetera.

Circa primum duo facit.

Primo ostendit quod alii apostoli approbaverunt suam doctrinam;

secundo ostendit quod libere reprehendit alios apostolos in his quae contraria suae doctrinae dicebant, ibi *cum venisset Petrus*, et cetera.

Circa primum duo facit.

Primo agit de collatione quam habuit cum apostolis;

secundo insinuat quid inde secutum sit, ibi *sed neque Titus*, et cetera.

51. After commending the authority of the Gospel teaching according to itself in the preceding chapter, the Apostle now in this chapter commends it on the part both of the other apostles and of himself.

About this he does two things.

First, he commends the authority of his teaching because of its approval by the other apostles;

second, from the example both of himself and of the other apostles, at *we by nature are Jews: and not of the gentiles* (Gal 2:15).

Concerning the first he does two things.

First, he shows that the other apostles approved his teaching;

second, that he fearlessly rebuked the other apostles in matters where they opposed his teaching, at *but when Cephas was come* (Gal 2:11).

As to the first he does two things.

First, he treats of the discussion he had with the apostles;

second, he narrates the consequences of that discussion, at *but neither was Titus*.

Circa primum duo facit.

Primo ponit circumstantias ipsius collationis;

secundo ponit ipsam collationem, ibi *et contuli cum illis*, et cetera.

Quantum ad primum tangit quatuor circumstantias, scilicet tempus, locum, testes, et motivum ipsius.

52. Describit autem tempus, cum dicit *deinde post annos quatuordecim*.

Sed contra est, quia Apostolus fuit conversus primo anno post passionem Christi, et post tres ivit in Ierusalem, et sic sunt quatuor, et hic dicit *post annos quatuordecim*, iterum ivit in Ierusalem, et sic fiunt decem et octo; et tunc invenit Petrum in Ierusalem. Et hoc non potest esse, quia Petrus sedit in Antiochia septem annis; in Roma vero viginti quinque annis. Et sic essent duo de viginti, et septem (qui sunt viginti quinque anni) antequam iret Romam, et Romae moratus est viginti quinque annis; ergo vixisset Petrus post passionem Christi quinquaginta annis, quod est falsum: quia quadragesimo anno a passione Christi passus est Petrus Romae, ut in historia habetur, quod fuit tempore Neronis.

Respondeo. Dicendum, quod cum dicitur *deinde*, etc., non est intelligendum quod post tres annos iterum elapsi sint quatuordecim anni, antequam iret in Ierusalem, sed quod anno quartodecimo suae conversionis iterum ascendit. Nec sunt addendi supra istos quatuordecim, septem anni, quibus Petrus rexit Ecclesiam Antiochenam, quia ante istos annos incepit regere. Et cum Antiochia sit prope Ierusalem, potuit esse ut aliquando Petrus ivisset in Ierusalem, et tunc Paulus invenerit eum ibi. Et sic colligitur ex historia, quod post annos quatuordecim Petrus venit Romam tempore Claudii imperatoris, et existens ibi viginti quinque annis, complevit numerum triginta novem annorum, et mortuus est quadragesimo anno post passionem Domini.

Dicit autem signanter, *quatuordecim*, ut ostendat, quod non indigebat apostolorum instructione, si quatuordecim annis fuit sine eis.

53. Locum vero describit, cum dicit *Ierosolymam*. Et dicit *ascendi*, quia in alto posita est. Ascendit autem Ierosolymam, ut ostenderet se concordare cum prophetia quae dicit Is. II, 3: *de Sion exibit lex*, et cetera.

54. Testes describit, cum dicit *cum Barnaba, assumpto et Tito*. Barnabas Iudaeus erat, Titus vero gentilis. Cum eis ergo ascendit, ut haberet testes suae doctrinae, et ut in nullam partem, sive Iudaeorum, sive gentilium, ostendat se declinare. Deut. XVII: *in ore duorum vel trium stat omne verbum*.

55. Motivum autem describit, cum dicit *secundum revelationem Dei*, id est, Deo revelante et praecipiente sibi quod ascenderet in Ierusalem. Ex hoc colligi potest

Regarding the first he does two things.

First, he gives the circumstances of that discussion;

second, what they discussed, at *and communicated to them the Gospel*.

With respect to the first he touches upon four things, namely the time, the place, the witnesses, and the motive.

52. He mentions the time when he says, *then, after fourteen years*.

Here some might object that if the Apostle was converted in the first year after the passion of Christ, and went to Jerusalem three years later, that makes four years. But he says, *after fourteen years* I went once more to Jerusalem, which makes a total of eighteen years, at which time he found Peter in Jerusalem. But this cannot be, because Peter had his See at Antioch seven years, and then at Rome for twenty-five years. So that makes eighteen plus seven, i.e., twenty-five years, before he went to Rome, and twenty-five years more he remained there. Hence Peter would have lived for fifty years after the passion of Christ, which is false, for in the fortieth year after the passion of Christ, Peter was martyred at Rome in the reign of Nero, as is recorded in history.

I answer that when he says, *then, after fourteen years*, it is not to be understood that after three years there was another lapse of fourteen years before he went to Jerusalem, but that he went again in the fourteenth year of his conversion. Nor should the seven years that Peter ruled the Church at Antioch be added to those fourteen years, because he began his rule before those years. Furthermore, since Antioch is near Jerusalem, Peter could at times have come to Jerusalem and Paul found him there then. Consequently, what is gathered from history is that after fourteen years Peter went to Rome in the reign of Claudius the Emperor and lived there for twenty-five years, making a total of thirty-nine years, and he died in the fortieth year after the passion of Our Lord.

Yet he purposely said *fourteen* in order to show that he did not need instructions from the apostles, if he went for fourteen years without them.

53. He gives the place when he says, *Jerusalem*. And he says, *I went up*, because it is built on a height. He went up to Jerusalem in order to show that he was in accord with the prophecy: *for the law shall come forth from Zion: and the word of the Lord from Jerusalem* (Isa 2:3).

54. He gives the witnesses when he says, *with Barnabas, taking Titus also with me*. Now Barnabas was a Jew, but Titus a gentile. He went up with them, therefore, in order to have witnesses to his teaching and to show that he leaned neither to the side of the Jews nor the gentiles: *in the mouth of two or three witnesses every word shall stand* (Deut 19:15).

55. He gives his motive when he says, *according to a revelation from God*, i.e., because God revealed and commanded him to go up to Jerusalem. From this can be

quod omnes actus apostolorum et motus fuerunt secundum instinctum Spiritus Sancti. Iob c. XXXVII, 11: *nubes spargunt lumen suum*, et cetera.

56. Consequenter cum dicit *et contuli*, etc., agit de ipsa collatione, ubi tria facit.

Primo manifestat materiam super quam contulit; secundo personas cum quibus contulit; et tertio causam propter quam contulit.

Materia de qua contulit, fuit Evangelium. Et ideo dicit *contuli cum illis Evangelium Dei*, et cetera. Personae cum quibus contulit sunt maiores et excellentiores inter apostolos *seorsum autem* cum *his*, et cetera. Sed causa utilis et necessaria *ne* scilicet *in vacuum*, et cetera.

57. Quantum ad primum dicit *ascendi Ierosolymam*, ubi *contuli cum illis*, tamquam cum amicis et paribus, *Evangelium* quod praedicavi *in gentibus*, non ut addiscerem, quia iam doctus eram a Christo, non ut certificarer, quia sic certus sum quod si angelus diceret contrarium, non crederem, ut patet supra I cap.

Sed contuli propter duo, scilicet ad insinuandam unitatem doctrinae meae cum doctrina aliorum Apostolorum. I Cor. I, 10: *idipsum dicatis omnes*, et cetera. Contulit ergo cum eis quasi idem verbum cum eis, sed non pares habuit. Item ad vitandum calumniam aliorum. Apostolus enim quia non fuerat conversatus cum Christo, nec edoctus ab apostolis, sed statim post conversionem suam incepit praedicare quae erant odiosa Iudaeis, et specialiter de vocatione gentium, et quod non debebant servari legalia.

Sic ergo contulit Evangelium.

58. Sed cum quibus hoc fecerit, ostendit subdens *seorsum autem his*, etc., quasi dicat: non cum omnibus, sed cum his qui erant inter alios alicuius auctoritatis et momenti, scilicet cum Petro, Iacobo et Ioanne et aliis magnis. Eccli. IX, 21: *cum sapientibus et prudentibus tracta*, et cetera. Sed *seorsum*, etc., non quod turpia vel falsa cum eis tractaret vel conferret, sicut haeretici faciunt, sed quia sciebat ibi esse Iudaeos calumniantes, propterea quia de legalibus docuerat. Et ideo ne veritas pateret calumniae, cum illis seorsum contulit, qui non calumniarentur. Prov. XXV, 9: *causam tuam tracta cum amico tuo, et secretum extraneo ne reveles*, et cetera. Eccli. VIII, 21: *coram extraneo ne facias consilium*, et cetera.

Sic ergo patet et materia collationis et personae.

59. Sequitur causa, quae fuit scilicet *ne in vacuum currerem, aut cucurrissem*, id est, ne reputarer

gathered that all the acts and movements of the apostles were according to an instinct of the Holy Spirit: *the clouds spread their light which go round about* (Job 37:11).

56. Then when he says, **and communicated to them**, he describes the conversation. About this he does three things.

First, he mentions the subject of their conversation; second, the persons with whom he conferred; third, the reason why he conferred with them.

The subject about which he conferred was the Gospel; hence he says, **I communicated to them the Gospel**; the persons with whom he conferred were the senior and more outstanding apostles; hence he says, **but separately to them who seemed to be something**. But the reason, both useful and necessary, was **lest I should run or had run in vain**.

57. Regarding the first, he says, **I went up to Jerusalem** where **I communicated to them**, as to friends and equals, **the Gospel which I preach among the gentiles**, not in order to learn, because I had already been taught by Christ, nor in order to be reassured, because I am so certain, that if an angel were to say the contrary, I would not believe him, as is plain above (Gal 1:8).

But I conferred for two reasons: namely, to show the unity of my teaching with that of the other apostles: *that you all speak the same thing and that there be no schisms among you* (1 Cor 1:10). Hence he conferred with them as one having the same word as they, and not as an adversary. Also, to avoid false accusation from others. For the Apostle had not lived with Christ or been taught by the apostles, but immediately after his conversion began to preach things odious to the Jews, especially the vocation of the gentiles and that they should not observe the justifications of the law.

In this way, then, he conferred about the Gospel.

58. But he indicates the ones with whom he did this, when he adds, **but separately to them who seemed to be something**. As though to say: not with all, but with those who were of some authority and importance among them, namely, with Peter, James and John and the other great ones: *treat with the wise and prudent* (Sir 9:21). **But separately**, not to talk or treat with them about ignoble or false things, as heretics do, but because he was aware of the presence there of Jews who brought false charges against him for his teachings about the law. Hence, in order that the truth might prevail over false charges, he spoke separately with those who would not bring false charges against him: *treat your cause with your friend, and discover not the secret to a stranger* (Prov 25:9); *before a stranger do no matter of counsel: for you do not know what he will bring forth* (Sir 8:21).

Thus the subject of the discussion as well as the persons are made known.

59. Then follows the cause, which was **lest perhaps I should run or had run in vain**, i.e., lest I be thought

praedicasse inutiliter. Vocat autem praedicationem suam, cursum, propter velocitatem suae doctrinae, quia in modico tempore a Ierusalem usque in Illyricum, et usque in Hispaniam praedicavit Evangelium. Unde posset dici de eo illud Ps. CXLVII, 15: *velociter currit sermo eius*, etc.; II Thess. III, 1: *fratres, orate pro nobis, ut sermo domini currat*, et cetera.

Sed numquid dubitabat quod in vacuum curreret? Dicendum est quod sibi non dubitabat, sed illis quibus praedicaverat, quia nisi ab illis firmiter teneretur sua doctrina, quantum ad illos in vacuum cucurrisset; et ideo voluit conferre cum eis, ut dum scirent auditores, quod doctrina sua concordaret cum doctrina aliorum apostolorum, et approbaretur ab eis, firmius eius doctrinam tenerent, et sic quantum ad eos non in vanum curreret. I Cor. IX, 26: *ego sic curro non quasi in incertum*.

60. Consequenter cum dicit **sed neque Titus**, etc., ostendit quid secutum sit ex collatione cum apostolis habita. Et ponit tria quae inde secuta sunt, scilicet

quod a sua sententia non recessit,

et quod suae doctrinae nihil superadditum fuit, ibi **ab his autem qui videbantur**, et cetera.

Tertio quod sua doctrina approbata est, ibi **sed contra cum vidissent**, et cetera.

Circa primum duo facit.

Primo ostendit quod non recessit a sua sententia in quodam particulari;

secundo ostendit quod etiam in nullo alio recessit ab ea, ibi **sed propter subintroductos**, et cetera.

61. Dicit ergo: dico quod ita contuli cum eis de doctrina Evangelii, quod ex hoc secutum est, quod doctrina mea et sententia firma permansit, scilicet de legalibus non observandis, sic quod gentiles non cogerentur ad servandum legalia, intantum quod **neque Titus, qui mecum erat, cum esset** etiam **gentilis, compulsus est**, rationibus eorum, **circumcidi**, sed susceptus est ab apostolis in societatem incircumcisus. Unde tunc data est sententia ab apostolis de legalibus non observandis, sicut habetur Act. XV, 28.

Ratio autem quare post passionem Christi non debent servari legalia, assignatur a Chrysostomo talis: *manifestum est enim quod instrumentum quod fit de aliqua promissione seu foedere tenet tantum quousque compleatur foedus et promissio, quibus completis, instrumentum praedictum in hoc non tenet. Circumcisio autem est quoddam instrumentum promissionis et foederis inter Deum et fideles homines; unde et Abraham accepit circumcisionem in signum promissionis, ut dicitur Gen. XVII. Et quia Christi peracta passione, soluta fuit promissio et completum foedus, ideo post passionem non tenet, nec valet circumcisio.*

to have preached to no purpose. He calls his preaching a 'running' on account of the rapidity of his teaching, for in a short time he preached the Gospel from Jerusalem to Illyricum and even as far as Spain. Hence the word can be said of him: *his word runs swiftly* (Ps 147:15); *pray, brethren, that the word of God may run and may be glorified, even as among you* (2 Thess 3:1).

But did he really wonder whether he was running in vain? I answer that he did not wonder for himself, but for those to whom he had preached, because if his teaching was not firmly held by them, he would have run in vain as far as they were concerned. So he wanted to confer with them, in order that when his hearers heard that his teaching was in agreement with that of the other apostles and approved by them, they would hold to it more firmly, and then he would not be running in vain with respect to them: *Therefore I so run, not as at an uncertainty* (1 Cor 9:26).

60. Then when he says, **but neither Titus who was with me**, he shows what resulted from the discussion held with the apostles. And he mentions three results:

that he did not depart from his opinion;

that nothing was added to his teaching, at **but of them who seemed** (Gal 2:6).

Third, that his teaching was approved, at **but contrariwise, when they had seen** (Gal 2:7).

Concerning the first he does two things.

First, he shows with respect to one definite point that he did not depart from his teaching;

second, that on no other point did he depart from it, at **but because of false brethren**.

61. He says, therefore: I say that the result of my discussion with them about the teaching of the Gospel was that my teaching and opinion remained unaltered concerning the non-observance of legalism, i.e., the gentiles would not be compelled to observe the rites of the law so that **neither was Titus who with me, being a gentile, was compelled to be circumcised**, but was admitted uncircumcised into their fellowship by the apostles. This discussion occasioned the decree handed down by the apostles on not observing the rites of the law, as is had in Acts (Acts 15:28).

The reason why these rites were not to be observed after the passion of Christ is assigned in the following way by Chrysostom: *for it is evident that the instrument drawn up for any promise or pact binds only until the pact and promise are fulfilled; but when fulfilled, the instrument no longer binds on that point*. Now circumcision is an instrument of the promise and pact between God and believing men. Hence it was that Abraham underwent circumcision as a sign of the promise, as is said in Genesis (Gen 11:26). And because the promise was fulfilled and the pact completed by the passion of Christ, neither the pact holds after the passion nor is circumcision of any value.

Sic ergo patet quod non recessit a sententia sua in hoc quod non permitteret circumcidi Titum.

62. Consequenter ostendit quod in nullo alio etiam recessit ab ea, cum dicit **sed propter subintroductos**, et cetera.

Littera autem ista est diversa in diversis et obscura, et legitur sic: tu dicis quod non permisisti circumcidi Titum, sed quare non permisisti? Nonne alibi permisisti Timotheum, sicut legitur Act. XVI, 3?

Ad hoc potest sic respondere Apostolus, quia tunc temporis, quando Timotheus fuit circumcisus, indifferens erat circumcisio, utrum scilicet servaretur vel non; sed modo cum ageretur de Tito, erat specialis quaestio de circumcisione, quam ego dicebam non debere servari. Unde si permisissem eum circumcidi, cum egomet diffinivissem quaestionem, fuisset factum in contrarium, nec licebat ultra de hoc movere quaestionem, vel facere difficultatem, utpote iam determinatam.

Et ideo dicit: dico quod non solum non permisi ipsum circumcidi ab illis, **quibus neque ad horam cessimus subiectione**, scilicet ut gentes subderentur legi. Et hoc **propter subintroductos**, a diabolo vel a Pharisaeis, **falsos fratres**, qui se fingunt amicos. II Cor. c. XII: *periculum in falsis fratribus*.

Qui, scilicet fratres falsi, **subintroierunt** in locum ubi erant apostoli, latenter **explorare**, id est ad explorandam, **libertatem nostram** a peccato et lege. II Cor. III, 17: *ubi Spiritus Domini, ibi libertas*. Rom. VIII, 15: *non enim accepistis spiritum servitutis*, et cetera. Infra IV, 5: **ut eos qui sub lege erant redimeret**.

Quam, scilicet libertatem, **habemus in Christo Iesu**, id est per fidem Christi. Infra IV, v. 31: **non estis ancillae filii, sed liberae**. Et ad hoc subintroierunt **ut in servitutem**, legis et carnalium observantiarum, **redigerent**, sicut ante passionem Christi, quod non est faciendum, quia *fundamentum aliud nemo potest ponere*, etc., I Cor. III, 11.

Et hoc **ut veritas Evangelii permaneat apud vos**, quasi dicat: in nullo cessimus eis propter hoc, ne scilicet occasionem daremus eis qui sine circumcisione dicebant vos non posse salvari, quod est contra veritatem Evangelii quod praedicavi vobis.

63. Ambrosius autem aliter legit. Secundum praemissa enim habetur, quod ideo ad horam non cessit propter subintroductos. Ex quo sequitur quod nisi fuissent subintroducti falsi fratres, cessisset eis de legalium observatione. Et ideo propter hoc non fuit, quia propter hoc non cessisset eis, sed propter ipsam veritatem.

Thus, therefore, his refusal to permit Titus to be circumcised makes it plain that he did not depart from his teaching.

62. Then when he says, **but because of false brethren brought in unawares**, he shows that he did not change on any other point.

This passage is obscure and variant readings are found. It should be read thus: you say that you did not permit Titus to be circumcised; but why? In another case did you not permit Timothy, as is read in Acts (Acts 16:3)?

To this the Apostle can respond: when Timothy was circumcised, it was an indifferent matter whether circumcision was observed or not; but later on, when it came to Titus, circumcision became a matter of paramount importance and I said that it is not to be observed. Hence, if I had allowed him to be circumcised, whereas I had already settled the question definitively myself, I would have been acting to the contrary. Furthermore, it was not lawful to raise this question again or to make difficulties about a matter now settled.

He says therefore: I say that I did not permit him to be circumcised by them, **to whom we yielded not by subjection, no, not for an hour**, i.e., that the gentiles be subject to the law; and this **because of false brethren brought in unawares** by the devil or by the Pharisees: **false brethren**, because they pretended to be friends: *in perils from false brethren* (2 Cor 11:26).

Who, namely the false brethren, **came in** to the place where the apostles were gathered, **in order to spy on our liberty** from sin and the law: *where the Spirit of the Lord is, there is liberty* (2 Cor 3:17); *you have not received the spirit of bondage again in fear; but you have received the Spirit of the adoption of sons* (Rom 8:15); **that he might redeem them who were under the law** (Gal 4:5).

Which liberty **we have in Christ Jesus**, i.e., through faith in Christ: **you are not children of the bondwoman but of the free** (Gal 4:31). And to this end were they brought in, **that they might bring us into servitude** of the law and the observances of the flesh, as before the passion of Christ. But this is not permissible, *for other foundation no man can lay, but that which is laid; which is Christ Jesus* (1 Cor 3:11).

And this, **that the truth of the Gospel might continue with you**. As if to say: we did not yield to them an iota, lest we give an occasion to those who said that you cannot be saved without circumcision, which is contrary to the truth of the Gospel I have preached to you.

63. Ambrose, however, reads it another way. According to the foregoing the reason he did not yield for the moment was on account of those brought in. From this it follows that if they had not been brought in, he would have yielded in the matter of observing legalism. Therefore it was not on that account, because on that account he would not have yielded to them, but on account of the truth itself.

Ideo dicit Ambrosius quod littera est falsa, et superfluit ibi *neque*. Unde vult quod non sit ibi *neque*. Et tunc est sensus: non permisi circumcidi Titum, sed Timotheum permisi circumcidi **propter subintroductos falsos fratres**, in loco ubi eram cum Timotheo et aliis, **qui subintroierunt**, et cetera. Quod cum facere nequivissent, populum in seditionem contra nos incitare moliebantur. **Quibus**, scilicet falsis fratribus, propter hoc **cessimus ad horam subiectionis**, in facto circumcisionis, circumcidendo Timotheum ibi ut veritas Evangelii permaneat, etc., quae habet quod nec circumcisio aliquid confert, neque praeputium, sed fides.

Fuit autem specialis causa quare Timotheus circumcisus fuit, et non Titus, quia Timotheus fuit ex patre gentili et matre Iudaea, Titus vero ex utroque parente gentili. Et sententia Apostoli erat quod qui ex aliquo parente Iudaeo nati fuerant, circumciderentur; qui vero totaliter ex gentilibus parentibus nati essent, nullo modo debeant circumcidi.

Therefore, says Ambrose, the text is faulty and the words, *no not even*, are superfluous. Hence he would have it that those words should not be there. And then the sense is: I did not permit Titus to be circumcised, but Timothy I did, **because of false brethren brought in unawares**, i.e., to the place where I was with Timothy and the others **who came in to spy on our liberty**. But when they failed in this, they tried to incite the people to rise up against us. **To whom**, i.e., to the false brethren, therefore **we yielded in the hour of subjection** in the matter of circumcision by circumcising Timothy, in order that the truth of the Gospel might continue with you, i.e., the Gospel which teaches that neither circumcision nor uncircumcision profits anything, but the faith.

But the special reason why Timothy was circumcised and Titus not, was that Timothy was born of a gentile father and Jewish mother, whereas Titus's parents were both gentiles. And the opinion of the Apostle was that those born of a Jewish parent on either side should be circumcised, but those born entirely of gentile parents should on no account be circumcised.

Lecture 2

2:6ab iis autem, qui videbantur esse aliquid (quales aliquando fuerint, nihil mea interest: Deus personam hominis non accipit): mihi enim qui videbantur esse aliquid, nihil contulerunt. [n. 64]

2:7 Sed e contra cum vidissent quod creditum est mihi Evangelium praeputii, sicut et Petro circumcisionis [n. 70]

2:8(qui enim operatus est Petro in apostolatum circumcisionis, operatus est et mihi inter gentes): [n. 72]

2:9et cum cognovissent gratiam, quae data est mihi, Jacobus, et Cephas, et Joannes, qui videbantur columnae esse, dextras dederunt mihi, et Barnabae societatis: ut nos in gentes, ipsi autem in circumcisionem: [n. 73]

2:10tantum ut pauperum memores essemus, quod etiam sollicitus fui hoc ipsum facere. [n. 75]

2:6ἀπὸ δὲ τῶν δοκούντων εἶναί τι ὁποῖοί ποτε ἦσαν οὐδέν μοι διαφέρει· πρόσωπον [ὁ] θεὸς ἀνθρώπου οὐ λαμβάνει ἐμοὶ γὰρ οἱ δοκοῦντες οὐδὲν προσανέθεντο,

2:7ἀλλὰ τοὐναντίον ἰδόντες ὅτι πεπίστευμαι τὸ εὐαγγέλιον τῆς ἀκροβυστίας καθὼς Πέτρος τῆς περιτομῆς,

2:8ὁ γὰρ ἐνεργήσας Πέτρῳ εἰς ἀποστολὴν τῆς περιτομῆς ἐνήργησεν καὶ ἐμοὶ εἰς τὰ ἔθνη,

2:9καὶ γνόντες τὴν χάριν τὴν δοθεῖσάν μοι, Ἰάκωβος καὶ Κηφᾶς καὶ Ἰωάννης, οἱ δοκοῦντες στῦλοι εἶναι, δεξιὰς ἔδωκαν ἐμοὶ καὶ Βαρναβᾷ κοινωνίας, ἵνα ἡμεῖς εἰς τὰ ἔθνη, αὐτοὶ δὲ εἰς τὴν περιτομήν·

2:10μόνον τῶν πτωχῶν ἵνα μνημονεύωμεν, ὃ καὶ ἐσπούδασα αὐτὸ τοῦτο ποιῆσαι.

2:6 But of them who seemed to be something, (what they were at one time is nothing to me: God does not accept the person of man): for to me they that seemed to be something added nothing. [n. 64]

2:7 But contrariwise, when they had seen that to me was committed the Gospel of the uncircumcision, as to Peter was that of the circumcision. [n. 70]

2:8(For he who wrought in Peter to the apostleship of the circumcision wrought in me also among the gentiles.) [n. 72]

2:9 And when they had known the grace that was given to me, James and Cephas and John, who seemed to be pillars, gave to me and Barnabas the right hands of fellowship: that we should go unto the gentiles, and they unto the circumcision: [n. 73]

2:10 Only that we should be mindful of the poor: which same thing also I was careful to do. [n. 75]

---

64. Ostenso quod Apostolus in nullo recessit a sententia sua in collatione praedicta, hic consequenter ostendit quod nihil suae doctrinae per alios apostolos superadditum fuit. Et

circa hoc duo facit.

Primo enim describit conditionem apostolorum, nihil ei addere valentium;

secundo prosequitur propositum, ibi **mihi enim qui**, et cetera.

Conditionem autem illorum describit ex tribus.

65. Primo ex auctoritate quam habebant in Ecclesia, quae est magna. Et quantum ad hoc dicit **ab his autem**, et cetera.

Littera defectiva est, unde debet suppleri sic **ab his autem**, scilicet Petro et Ioanne; quasi dicat: licet ad horam cesserim eis, nihil tamen accepi ab eis potestatis vel doctrinae. Et si ab his nihil accepi, multo minus ab aliis.

Sed notandum est quod hoc quod dicit **qui videbantur aliquid esse**, si hoc intelligatur secundum gratiam Dei quae in ipsis erat, sic verum est quod secundum hanc magni erant, quia *quos iustificavit, hos et magnificavit*, ut dicitur Rom. VIII, 30. Si vero intelligantur aliquid

64. Having shown that the Apostle did not depart from his opinion on any point in the conference mentioned above, he now shows that nothing was added to his teaching by the other apostles.

About this he does two things.

First, he describes the status of the apostles who were unable to add anything;

second, he proves his proposition, at **for to me**.

Their status he describes from three standpoints.

65. First from the authority they held in the Church, for it was great. Regarding it he says, **but of them**.

The text is deficient and should be amended to read, **but of them**, namely, Peter and John. As if to say: although I would have yielded to them at the time, yet I received from them no new power or teaching. And if I received nothing from them, much less so from others.

But it is to be noted that if his statement, **who seemed to be something**, is understood with reference to the grace of God that was in them, it is true that in this respect they were great, because *whom he justified, them he also glorified* (Rom 8:30). However, if it is understood that they were

esse secundum seipsos, sic falsum est, quia secundum hoc nihil erant. Nam si secundum se aliquid esse viderentur, semper fuissent magni; quia quod per se inest, semper inest. Unde cum non fuerint semper magni, non secundum se videbantur aliquid esse.

66. Secundo describit eorum conditionem ex statu eorum ante conversionem, quam habuerunt in synagoga. Et hunc statum caute ostendit fuisse abiectum et vilem. Unde dicit ***quales aliquando fuerint***, quia rustici, pauperes, idiotae, et sine litteris erant. I Cor. I, 26: *non multi sapientes secundum carnem*, et cetera. Sed ***quales fuerint nihil***, id est non, ***mea interest***, scilicet referre.

Et hoc forte introducit, ut considerantes statum quem illi habuerunt in synagoga (qui nullus fuit) et statum Pauli (qui magnus fuit), manifeste cognoscant quod Paulus in sententia quantum ad legalia sit eis praeferendus, et praesertim cum Paulus in statu Ecclesiae Christi eis aequaretur, ita quod Paulus eos in statu synagogae ante conversionem praecedebat, in statu post conversionem eis aequalis erat. Unde cum agebatur de synagoga, magis erat standum sententiae Pauli, quam aliorum; sed cum de Evangelio agereture, standum erat sententiae suae sicut sententiae aliorum. Et sicut alii non erant magni per legalia, sed per Christum, sic et Apostolus per Christum magnus erat in fide, et non per legalia.

67. Tertio describit eorum conditionem ex divina electione, et quantum ad hoc dicit ***Deus enim personam***, etc., quasi dicat: ideo magni sunt, quia Deus eos magnificavit, non attendens ad merita vel demerita eorum, sed ad ipsum quod facere intendit. Et ideo dicit ***Deus personam hominis non accipit***, id est, non considerat magnam vel parvam. Sap. VI, 8: *pusillum et magnum ipse fecit*, et cetera. Sed sine personarum acceptione ad salutem omnes vocat, non imputans illis delicta eorum, et hoc quia transierunt. II Cor. V, 17: *vetera transierunt*, et cetera. Ps. XV, 4: *nec memor ero nominum eorum*, et cetera. Et ideo dicit Petrus, Act. X, 34: *in veritate comperi, quod non est personarum acceptio*, et cetera.

68. Circa hoc sciendum est, quod accipere personam proprie est in aliquo negotio attendere, quasi regulam ipsius negotii, conditionem personae nihil facientem ad negotium, puta, cum ideo do beneficium alicui, quia est nobilis, sive pulcher. Nobilitas enim seu pulchritudo, nil facit ad hoc, quod habeat beneficium. Si vero conditio personae facit ad negotium, sic considerando illam conditionem in facto illo, non accipio personam; sicut si ideo do beneficium alicui, quia bonus est, et bene deserviet Ecclesiae, quia bene litteratus et honestus, non

something according to themselves, then it is false, because in that respect they were nothing. For if they seemed to be some thing according to themselves, they would always have been great, because whatever belongs to a thing according to itself is always present. Hence, since they were not always great, it was not according to themselves that they were seen to be something.

66. Second, he describes their status on the side of what they were before their conversion, i.e., the status they had in the synagogue. This status, he hints gently, was mean and lowly. Hence he says, ***what they were at one time***, for they had been coarse, poor, ignorant and unlettered: *there are not many wise according to the flesh, not many mighty, not many noble* (1 Cor 1:26). ***But what they were is nothing to me***, i.e., it is not my concern to mention.

Perhaps his reason for introducing this was that by considering the status they had in the synagogue, which was nothing, and the status of Paul, which was great, they might see that Paul's opinion on legalism should be preferred to theirs, particularly since Paul has an equal status with them in the Church; so that Paul had a higher rank in the synagogue before their conversion, but after the conversion, he had a rank equal to theirs. Hence when matters concerning the synagogue were discussed, the opinion of Paul deserved to prevail over the others, but when it came to the Gospel, his opinion was as good as theirs. And just as the others were not made great through things pertaining to the law but through Christ, so too in the faith the Apostle was great through Christ and not through things pertaining to the law.

67. Third, he describes their condition by reason of their election by God. Regarding this he says, ***God does not accept the person***. As if to say: they are great because God made them great, not by regarding their merits or demerits, but by regarding what he intended to accomplish. Hence he says: ***God does not accept the person of man***, i.e., he does not consider whether the person is great or little: *for he made the little and the great* (Wis 6:8). Furthermore, without regard to person, he calls everyone to salvation, no longer charging them with their sins for they have passed away: *the old things are passed away* (2 Cor 5:17); *nor will I be mindful of their name* (Ps 16:4). Therefore Peter says: *in very deed I perceive that God is not a respecter of persons* (Acts 10:34).

68. On this point it should be noted that accepting of persons in any transaction is, properly speaking, to take as a deciding factor in that transaction some aspect of the person that has nothing to do with the matter; for example, when I give a benefice to a person just because he is a noble or is handsome. For nobility or beauty have nothing to do with the question of getting a benefice. But if some aspect of the person does have something to do with the matter, then if I consider that aspect in settling the matter, I do not accept the person; for example, if I give a benefice to a person

sum acceptor personae. Nihil ergo est proprie accipere personam, quam considerare conditionem personae, nil facientem ad negotium.

Cum ergo Deus in operibus suis et beneficiis nihil praeexistens ex parte creaturae respiciat, quia ipsum, quod est creaturae, est effectus suae electionis, sed respiciat solum quasi pro regula beneplacitum voluntatis suae secundum quam omnia operatur, et non secundum aliquam conditionem personae, ut dicitur Ephes. IV, 7, manifestum est quod non accipit personam hominis.

69. Consequenter descripta conditione eorum, ostendit propositum, scilicet quod nil ei addere potuerunt. Et ideo dicit *mihi enim qui videbantur aliquid esse, nihil contulerunt*, quasi dicat: licet essent magnae auctoritatis, tamen nil addiderunt doctrinae meae nec potestati, quia, sicut supra dictum est neque ab homine accepi Evangelium, neque per hominem didici.

Glossa autem aliter legit *quales aliquando fuerunt*, etc., quasi dicat: non pertinet ad me referre statum eorum ante conversionem, quales scilicet fuerunt, quia et hoc nihil refert, cum et ego fuerim ipsius Ecclesiae etiam persecutor, et tamen Deus suae beneplacito voluntatis elegit me et magnificavit, et hoc quia Dominus personam hominis non acceptat.

70. Consequenter cum dicit *sed e contra cum vidissent*, etc., ostendit quomodo eius sententia sit approbata ab apostolis. Et

circa hoc tria facit.

Primo ponit causam approbationis;

secundo insinuat ipsam approbationem, ibi *Iacobus et Cephas*, et cetera.

Tertio addit quamdam conditionem approbationi interpositam, ibi *tantum ut pauperes*, et cetera.

Causam autem approbationis (quae movit Apostolos approbare sententiam Apostoli) ponit duplicem, scilicet praedicationis officium Apostolo iniunctum a Christo, et effectum iniuncti officii, ibi *et cum cognovissent*, et cetera.

Circa primum, primo ponit officium iniunctum quod movit eos ad approbandum;

secundo officii manifestationem, ibi *qui enim operatus est*, et cetera.

71. Dicit ergo: dico quod illi *qui videbantur aliquid esse, nihil mihi contulerunt*, sed potius, contra opinionem adversariorum, qui ascenderant contra me in Ierusalem ad apostolos pro ipsa quaestione, me ipsi apostoli approbaverunt, et hoc *cum vidissent quod creditum est mihi Evangelium*, id est, officium praedicationis, *praeputii*, id est, iniunctum praedicare incircumcisis, scilicet

because he is good and will serve the Church well, or because he is well-educated and honorable, I am not an acceptor of persons. Therefore to accept the person is nothing other than to consider some aspect of the person that has no relation to the business.

Hence, since God in his works and benefits regards nothing that pre-exists on the side of the creature, for that which pertains to the creature is an effect of his election, but takes as his measure merely what pleases his will, according to which he effects all things, and not the condition of their person, as is said in Ephesians (Eph 1:11), it is evident that he does not regard the person of man.

69. Then, having described their condition, he proves his proposition, namely, that they were unable to add anything to him. Hence he says, *for to me they that seemed to be something added nothing*. As if to say: although they had great authority, they added nothing to my teaching or to my power, because, as was said above, I neither received the Gospel from man nor learned it by man.

However, a certain Gloss has a different reading, namely, *what they were at one time is nothing to me*. As if to say: it is not my concern to recount their status before their conversion, i.e., what they were, because this too makes no difference, since I myself had even been a persecutor of that Church; yet God by the pleasure of his will chose and glorified me—and this because the Lord does not regard the person of man.

70. Then when he says, *but contrariwise, when they had seen*, he shows how his opinion was approved by the apostles.

About this he does three things.

First, he gives the reason for this approbation;

second, he mentions the approbation, at *James and Cephas*;

third, he adds a condition that was placed on the approbation, at *only that we should be mindful*.

He cites the two causes of the approbation (which moved the apostles to approve the opinion of the Apostle) namely, the office of teaching enjoined by Christ on the Apostle, and the effect of this appointment, at *and when they had known*.

As to the first, he does two things: first, he mentions the office to which he was appointed which moved them to approve him;

second, the manifestation of this office, at *for he who wrought*.

71. He says therefore: I say that those *who seemed to be something, added nothing to me*; but rather, contrary to the opinion of the adversaries who came up to Jerusalem to oppose me in this matter, it was I that the apostles approved, and this *when they had seen that to me was committed the Gospel*, i.e., the office of the preaching, *of the uncircumcision*, i.e., the injunction to preach to the uncircumcised,

gentibus. Ier. IX, 26: *omnes gentes habent praeputium, omnis autem domus*, et cetera. Sicut Petro commissa est auctoritas, ut praedicaret Iudaeis tantum, et Paulo gentibus; sed postmodum et Petrus praedicavit gentibus, et Paulus Iudaeis.

72. Sed quia aliquis posset dicere: unde constat nobis quod tibi sit commissum Evangelium in gentibus? Ideo interponens dicit, quod per operationes Christi. Sicut enim patet quod Petrus accepit Evangelium a Christo propter mirabilia quae Christus fecit per eum, ita patet quod ego ab ipso accepi propter miracula quae Christus operatus est, et operatur in me.

Et ideo dicit *qui operatus est Petro*, etc., id est, qui Petrum fecit apostolum in Iudaea, scilicet Christus, ipse me fecit apostolum in gentibus. Et haec est causa quae movet eos.

73. Sed quia non sufficit iniunctio et auctoritas praedicandi, nisi homo per bonam scientiam et discretam eloquentiam ipsam exequatur, et per bonam vitam commendet, ideo addit usum suae auctoritatis seu officii effectum, dicens *et cum cognovissent gratiam Dei*, et cetera. Et est littera suspensiva, id est, cum vidissent quod gratiosa et fructuosa esset praedicatio mea, tunc *Iacobus, et Cephas, et Ioannes*, et cetera.

74. In quo notatur approbatio seu societas facta cum eis et Paulo. Et primo ponuntur personae inter quas facta est societas, quae sunt *Iacobus, et Cephas*, id est Petrus, et *Ioannes*. Et praemittitur Iacobus, quia erat episcopus Ierosolymorum, ubi haec facta sunt. Ioannes autem iste fuit Ioannes Evangelista, qui non deseruit Iudaeam usque ad tempus Vespasiani.

Qui videbantur columnae esse. Metaphorice dicitur hoc, id est sustentatio totius Ecclesiae. Sicut enim totum aedificium sustentatur per columnas, ita per istos tota Ecclesia Iudaeorum sustentabatur et regebatur. Et de istis columnis dicitur in Ps. LXXIV, 4: *ego confirmavi columnas eius*, id est, apostolos Ecclesiae; Can. V, 15: *crura illius columnae marmoreae, quae fundatae sunt super bases aureas*.

Isti, scilicet ex una parte, *dederunt dextras societatis*, id est, consenserunt in societatem, *mihi et Barnabae*, in quo designantur personae ex alia parte. Per hoc autem quod dederunt sibi dexteras, significatur quod per manus se acceperunt in signum coniunctionis et unitatem opinionis.

Secundo ostenditur societatis tenor seu conditio, cum dicitur *ut nos in gentes, ipsi autem in circumcisionem*, scilicet praedicarent; quasi dicat: facta fuit inter nos coniunctio et unio, ita tamen quod sicut omnes fideles obediunt Petro in circumcisione, id est, in Ecclesia

namely, the gentiles: *for all the nations are uncircumcised in the flesh, but all the house of Israel are uncircumcised in the heart* (Jer 9:26). Just as to Peter was entrusted the authority to preach to the Jews alone, so to Paul to the gentiles; but later, Peter, too, preached to the gentiles and Paul to the Jews.

72. But because someone might say: what evidence have you that the commission to preach the Gospel to the gentiles was given you, he interjects that it was through certain works of Christ. For just as it is evident that Peter received the Gospel from Christ because of the marvels Christ wrought through him, so it is evident that I received it because of the miracles Christ worked and does work in me.

Therefore he says, *he who wrought in Peter to the apostleship*, i.e., made Peter an apostle in Judea, namely Christ, also made me an apostle among the gentiles. And this is the reason which moves them.

73. But because one's appointment and authority to preach are not enough, unless he carries it out through good understanding and discreet eloquence and commends it by a good life, he adds how he used his authority or the effect of his office, saying, *and, when they had known the grace of God*. This is a dependent clause, i.e., when they saw that my preaching enjoyed favor and was fruitful, then *James and Cephas and John, who seemed to be pillars, gave to me and Barnabas the right hands of fellowship*.

74. In this passage is mentioned the approval or fellowship entered into by them and Paul. First, the persons are mentioned with whom the fellowship was formed, namely, *James and Cephas*, i.e., Peter, *and John*. James is mentioned first, as being the bishop of Jerusalem where these events took place. The John mentioned was John the Evangelist who did not leave Judea until the time of Vespasian.

Who seem to be pillars. This is a metaphor standing for the support of the entire Church. For just as a whole edifice is supported by the pillars, so the whole Church of the Jews was supported and governed by these men. Of those pillars it is said: *I have established the pillars thereof* (Ps 74:4), i.e., the apostles of the Church; *his legs as pillars of marble, that are set upon bases of gold* (Song 5:15).

They, on the one side, *gave the right hands of fellowship*, i.e., consented to the fellowship, *to me and Barnabas*, the persons on the other side. By giving them their right hands they signified that they accepted them into their hands as a sign of union and unity of opinion.

Second, the intent or condition of the fellowship is shown when it is said, *that we should go unto the gentiles, and the unto the circumcision*, i.e., to preach. As if to say: a bond and union was made among us to the effect that just as the faithful obey Peter among the circumcision,

Iudaeorum fidelium: ita omnes gentiles qui conversi fuerunt ad Christum, obedirent Barnabae et Paulo.

75. Hoc tamen apposito, *ut nos essemus memores pauperum Christi*, qui scilicet vendiderant omnia bona sua, et pretium eorum ad pedes apostolorum posuerant, propter Christum pauperes effecti. *Quod* quidem *sollicitus fui hoc idem facere*, non minus affectus, quam ipsi qui ordinaverunt, sicut apparet Rom. XV, et I Cor. VI, et II Cor. c. VIII et IX.

Ratio autem quare consuetudo primitivae Ecclesiae de venditione possessionum servabatur in Ecclesia ex circumcisione, et non in Ecclesia ex gentibus, haec est, quia fideles Iudaei congregati erant in Ierusalem, et in Iudaea quae destruenda in brevi a Romanis erat, ut postmodum rei probavit eventus; et ideo voluit Dominus ut ibi possessiones non reservarentur ubi permansuri non erant. Ecclesia vero gentilium firmanda erat et augenda, et ideo consilio Spiritus Sancti factum est, ut in ea possessiones non venderentur.

i.e., in the Church of the Jewish believers, so all the gentiles converted to Christ should obey Paul and Barnabas.

75. But they added the condition that we should be mindful of the poor of Christ, i.e., of those who had sold all their goods and laid the price at the feet of the apostles and became poor for the sake of Christ. **Which same thing**, indeed, *also I was careful to do*, being no less moved than those commanding me, as is plain (Rom 15), (1 Cor 6) and (2 Cor 8, 9).

Now the reason why the custom prevailed in the early Church for those in the Church of the circumcision to sell their goods and not those in the Church of the gentiles was that the believing Jews were congregated in Jerusalem and in Judea, which was soon to be destroyed by the Romans, as later events proved. Hence the Lord willed that no possessions were to be kept in a place not destined to endure. But the Church of the gentiles was destined to grow strong and increase, and therefore, by the inspiration of the Holy Spirit, it came about that the possessions in it were not to be sold.

Lecture 3

²:¹¹Cum autem venisset Cephas Antiochiam, in faciem ei restiti, quia reprehensibilis erat. [n. 76]

²:¹²Prius enim quam venirent quidam a Jacobo, cum gentibus edebat: cum autem venissent, subtrahebat, et segregabat se, timens eos qui ex circumcisione erant. [n. 78]

²:¹³Et simulationi ejus consenserunt ceteri Judaei, ita ut et Barnabas duceretur ab eis in illam simulationem. [n. 81]

²:¹⁴Sed cum vidissem quod non recte ambularent ad veritatem Evangelii, dixi Cephae coram omnibus: si tu, cum Judaeus sis, gentiliter vivis, et non judaice: quomodo gentes cogis judaizare? [n. 82]

²:¹¹Ὅτε δὲ ἦλθεν Κηφᾶς εἰς Ἀντιόχειαν, κατὰ πρόσωπον αὐτῷ ἀντέστην, ὅτι κατεγνωσμένος ἦν.

²:¹²πρὸ τοῦ γὰρ ἐλθεῖν τινας ἀπὸ Ἰακώβου μετὰ τῶν ἐθνῶν συνήσθιεν· ὅτε δὲ ἦλθον, ὑπέστελλεν καὶ ἀφώριζεν ἑαυτόν, φοβούμενος τοὺς ἐκ περιτομῆς.

²:¹³καὶ συνυπεκρίθησαν αὐτῷ [καὶ] οἱ λοιποὶ Ἰουδαῖοι, ὥστε καὶ Βαρναβᾶς συναπήχθη αὐτῶν τῇ ὑποκρίσει.

²:¹⁴ἀλλ' ὅτε εἶδον ὅτι οὐκ ὀρθοποδοῦσιν πρὸς τὴν ἀλήθειαν τοῦ εὐαγγελίου, εἶπον τῷ Κηφᾷ ἔμπροσθεν πάντων, Εἰ σὺ Ἰουδαῖος ὑπάρχων ἐθνικῶς καὶ οὐχὶ Ἰουδαϊκῶς ζῇς, πῶς τὰ ἔθνη ἀναγκάζεις Ἰουδαΐζειν;

²:¹¹But when Cephas had come to Antioch, I withstood him to the face, because he was to be blamed. [n. 76]

²:¹²For before some came from James, he ate with the gentiles: but when they had come, he withdrew and separated himself, fearing them who were of the circumcision. [n. 78]

²:¹³And to his dissimulation the rest of the Jews consented: so that Barnabas also was led by them into that dissimulation. [n. 81]

²:¹⁴But when I saw that they did not walk uprightly unto the truth of the Gospel, I said to Cephas before them all: if you, being a Jew, live after the manner of the gentiles and not as the Jews do, how do you compel the gentiles to live as the Jews do? [n. 82]

---

76. Supra Apostolus ostendit quod ipse nil utilitatis accepit ex collatione habita cum dictis apostolis, hic vero ostendit quod ipse aliis profuit. Et

primo ostendit quomodo profuit Petro in corrigendo eum;

secundo manifestat ea quae dixit, ibi *prius enim quam venirent*, et cetera.

77. Dicit ergo: vere ipsi mihi nihil contulerunt, sed ego potius contuli eis, et specialiter Petro; quia *cum venisset Petrus Antiochiam*, ubi erat ecclesia gentium, ego *restiti ei in faciem*, id est, manifeste. Eccli. c. IV, 27: *ne reverearis proximum in casu suo, nec retineas verbum*, et cetera. Vel *in faciem*, id est non in occulto, tamquam detrahens et timens, sed publice, et ut par ei. Lev. XIX, 17: *non oderis fratrem tuum in corde tuo, sed publice argue eum*, et cetera. Et hoc ideo, *quia reprehensibilis erat*.

Sed contra: quia hoc fuit post acceptam gratiam Spiritus Sancti; sed post gratiam Spiritus Sancti nullo modo peccaverunt apostoli.

Respondeo. Dicendum quod post gratiam Spiritus Sancti nullo modo peccaverunt mortaliter apostoli, et hoc donum habuerunt per potentiam divinam, quae eos confirmaverat. Ps. LXXIV, 4: *ego confirmavi columnas eius*, et cetera. Peccaverunt tamen venialiter, et hoc fuit eis ex fragilitate humana. I Io. I, 8: *si dixerimus, quia peccatum non habemus*, scilicet veniale, *ipsi nos seducimus*, et cetera.

76. The Apostle showed above that he received nothing useful from the discussion held with the apostles; now he shows that he benefitted them:

first, he shows how he helped Peter by correcting him;

second, he tells what he said, at *for before some came*.

77. He says, therefore: indeed, they advantaged me nothing; rather I conferred something upon them, and especially upon Peter, because *when Cephas had come to Antioch*, where there was a church of the gentiles, *I withstood him to the face*, i.e., openly: *do not reverence your neighbor in his fall and do not refrain to speak in the time of salvation* (Sir 4:27). Or: *to the face*, i.e., not in secret as though detracting and fearing him, but publicly and as his equal: *you shall not hate your brother in your heart: but reprove him openly* (Lev 19:17). This he did, *because he was to be blamed*.

But it might be objected: this took place after they received the grace of the Holy Spirit; but after the grace of the Holy Spirit the apostles did not sin in any way.

I answer that after the grace of the Holy Spirit the apostles did not sin mortally, and this gift they had through the divine power that had strengthened them: *I have established the pillars thereof* (Ps 74:4). Yet they sinned venially because of human frailty: *if we say that we have no sin*, i.e., venial, *we deceive ourselves* (1 John 1:8).

Quod vero dicitur in Glossa: *restiti ei tamquam par*, dicendum est quod Apostolus fuit pro Petro in executione auctoritatis, non in auctoritate regiminis.

Ex praedictis ergo habemus exemplum: praelati quidem humilitatis, ut non dedignentur a minoribus et subditis corrigi; subditi vero exemplum zeli et libertatis, ut non vereantur praelatos corrigere, praesertim si crimen est publicum et in periculum multitudinis vergat.

78. Consequenter cum dicit **priusquam venirent**, etc., manifestat ea quae dixit. Et
primo hoc quod dixit eum reprehensibilem esse;
secundo vero hoc, quod dixit Petrum reprehendisse, ibi **sed cum vidissem**, et cetera.

Circa primum tria facit.
Primo ostendit quid Petrus sentiebat;
secundo quid faciebat, ibi **cum autem venisset**, etc.;
tertio quid inde sequebatur, ibi **et simulationi eius**, et cetera.

79. Dicit ergo circa primum, quod Petrus sentiebat legalia non esse servanda. Et hoc facto ostendebat, quia **priusquam venirent quidam**, Iudaei scilicet zelantes pro legalibus, **a Iacobo**, Ierosolymitanae ecclesiae episcopo, **edebat**, scilicet Petrus, **cum gentibus**, id est, indifferenter utebatur cibis gentilium; et hoc faciebat ex instinctu Spiritus Sancti, qui dixerat ei *quod Deus sanctificavit, tu ne commune dixeris*, ut habetur Act. X, 15, ut ipse ibidem sequenti cap. dixit Iudaeis, qui contra eum insurrexerunt, quia cum incircumcisis comedisset, quasi rationem reddens.

80. Quid autem faciebat, ostendit hic Paulus dicens, quod cum erat cum Iudaeis, **subtrahebat** se a consortio fidelium qui fuerant ex gentibus, adhaerens Iudaeis tantum, et congregans se cum eis.

Et ideo dicit **cum autem venisset**, scilicet a Iudaea, **subtrahebat se** Petrus a gentibus conversis, **et segregabat se** ab eis. Et hoc ideo, quia erat **timens eos, qui ex circumcisione erant**, id est, Iudaeos, non quidem timore humano sive mundano, sed timore caritatis, ne scilicet scandalizarentur, sicut dicitur in Glossa. Et ideo factus est Iudaeis tamquam Iudaeus, simulans se cum infirmis idem sentire; sed tamen inordinate timebat, quia veritas numquam dimittenda est propter timorem scandali.

81. Quid autem ex hac simulatione sequebatur, subdit dicens, quod **simulationi eius**, scilicet Petri, **consenserunt caeteri Iudaei**, qui erant Antiochiae discernentes cibos, et segregantes se a gentibus, cum tamen ante simulationem huiusmodi hoc non fecissent.

Et non solum illi consenserunt Petro, sed **ita** fuit illa simulatio in cordibus fidelium, **ut etiam Barnabas**, qui

Concerning what is said in a certain Gloss, namely, that *I withstood him* as an adversary, the answer is that the Apostle opposed Peter in the exercise of authority, not in his authority of ruling.

Therefore from the foregoing we have an example: to prelates, indeed, an example of humility, that they not disdain corrections from those who are lower and subject to them; to subjects, an example of zeal and freedom, that they fear not to correct their prelates, particularly if their crime is public and verges upon danger to the multitude.

78. Then when he says, **for before some came**, he manifests what he has said.
First, that he said he was to be blamed;
second, that he rebuked Peter, at **but when I saw**.

As to the first he does three things.
First, he shows what Peter's opinion was;
second, what he did, at **but when Cephas had come**;
third, what resulted from it, at **and to his dissimulation**.

79. He says therefore, as to the first point, that Peter felt that legalism ought not be observed. This he showed by the fact that **before some came**, namely, Jews zealous for the law, **from James**, bishop of the church at Jerusalem, **he ate**, namely, Peter did, **with the gentiles**, i.e., without compunction he ate the food of gentiles. He did this through the inspiration of the Holy Spirit who had said to him: *that which God has cleansed, do not call common* (Acts 10:15), and as he himself in the following chapter said in answer to the Jews who rose up against him, because he had eaten with the uncircumcised.

80. What Peter did Paul now shows, saying that when he was with the Jews, **he withdrew** from the company of the faithful who had been converted from the gentiles and adhered to the Jews alone and mingled among them.

Therefore he says, **but when they had come**, namely, from Judea, Peter **withdrew** from the converted gentiles **and separated himself from them**. This he did because he was **fearing them who were of the circumcision**, i.e., the Jews, not with a human or worldly fear but a fear inspired by charity, namely, lest they be scandalized, as is said in a Gloss. Hence he became to the Jews as a Jew, pretending that he felt the same as they did in their weakness. Yet he feared unreasonably, because the truth must never be set aside through fear of scandal.

81. What resulted from this dissimulation he mentions when he says that **to his dissimulation**, i.e., Peter's, **the rest of the Jews consented** who were at Antioch, discriminating between food and separating themselves from the gentiles, although prior to this act of dissimulation they would not have done this.

And not only did they consent to Peter, but such was the effect of that dissimulation upon the hearts of the faithful

mecum erat doctor gentium, et contrarium fecerat et docuerat, *duceretur ab eis in illam simulationem*, subtrahens se ab eis, scilicet gentibus. Et hoc ideo, quia, secundum quod dicitur Eccli. X, v. 2: *qualis est rector civitatis*, et cetera. Et ibidem: *secundum iudicem populi*, et cetera.

82. Consequenter cum dicit *sed cum vidissem*, etc., manifestat ea quae dixerat de reprehensione sua, qua Petrum reprehendit.

Et circa hoc tria facit.

Primo ponit causam reprehensionis;

secundo reprehendendi modum;

tertio reprehensionis verba.

83. Occasio autem reprehensionis est non levis, sed iusta et utilis, scilicet periculum Evangelicae veritatis. Et ideo dicit: sic Petrus reprehensibilis erat, sed ego solus, *cum vidissem quod non recte ambularent* illi qui sic faciebant *ad veritatem Evangelii*, quia per hoc peribat veritas, si cogerentur gentes servare legalia, ut infra patebit.

Quod autem recte non ambularent, ideo est quia veritas, maxime ubi periculum imminet, debet publice praedicari, nec fieri contrarium propter scandalum aliquorum. Matth. X, 27: *quod dico vobis in tenebris, dicite in lumine*. Is. XXVI, 7: *semita iusti recta est, rectus callis iusti ad ambulandum*.

84. Modus autem reprehendendi fuit conveniens, quia publicus et manifestus. Unde dicit *dixi Cephae*, id est, Petro, *coram omnibus*, quia simulatio illa in periculo omnium erat. Tim. V, 20: *peccantem coram omnibus argue*. Quod intelligendum est de peccatis manifestis, et non de occultis, in quibus debet servari ordo fraternae correctionis.

85. Cuiusmodi autem verba Apostolus dixerit Petro, cum eum reprehenderet, subdit dicens *si tu Iudaeus cum sis*, etc., quasi dicat: o Petre, *si tu cum Iudaeus sis*, natione et genere, *gentiliter et non Iudaice vivis*, id est, gentium et non Iudaeorum ritum servas, cum scias et sentias discretionem ciborum nihil conferre, *quomodo cogis gentes*, non quidem imperio, sed tuae conversationis exemplo, *iudaizare?*

Et dicit *cogis*, quia secundum quod Leo Papa dicit *validiora sunt exempla quam verba*. In hoc ergo Paulus reprehendit Petrum, quod cum ipse esset instructus a Deo, cum Iudaice prius viveret, ne postea amplius cibos discerneret Act. X, 15: *quod Deus sanctificavit, tu ne commune dixeris*, ipse contrarium simulabat.

86. Sciendum est autem quod occasione istorum verborum, non parva controversia est orta inter Hieronymum et Augustinum. Et secundum quod ex eorum verbis aperte colligitur, in quatuor discordare videntur.

that Barnabas also, who along with me was a teacher of the gentiles and had done and taught the contrary, *was led by them into that dissimulation* and withdrew from them, namely, from the gentiles. And this on account of what is said: *what manner of man the ruler of a city is, such also are they that dwell therein*, and, *as the judge of the people is himself, so also are his ministers* (Sir 10:2).

82. Then when he says, *but, when I saw*, he explains what he had said concerning the rebuke with which he rebuked Peter.

As to this he does three things.

First, he gives the reason for the rebuke;

second, the manner of rebuking;

third, the words of the rebuke.

83. The occasion of the rebuke was not slight, but just and useful, namely, the danger to the Gospel teaching. Hence he says: thus was Peter reprehensible, but I alone, *when I saw that they*, who were doing these things, *did not walk uprightly unto the truth of the Gospel*, because its truth was being undone, if the gentiles were compelled to observe the legal justifications, as will be plain below.

That, they were not walking uprightly is so, because in cases where danger is imminent, the truth must be preached openly and the opposite never condoned through fear of scandalizing others: *that which I tell you in the dark, speak in the light* (Matt 10:27); *the way of the just is right: the path of the just is right to walk in* (Isa 26:7).

84. The manner of the rebuke was fitting, i.e., public and plain. Hence he says, *I said to Cephas*, i.e., to Peter, *before them all*, because that dissimulation posed a danger to all: *them that sin, reprove before all* (1 Tim 5:20). This is to be understood of public sins and not of private ones, in which the procedures of fraternal charity ought to be observed.

85. The words the Apostle spoke to Peter when he rebuked him, he adds, saying, *if you, being a Jew*, by nature and race, *live after the manner of the gentiles and not as the Jews do*, i.e., if you observe the customs of gentiles and not of Jews, since you know and feel that discriminating among foods is of no importance, *how do you compel the gentiles*, not indeed by command, but by example of your behavior, *to live as the Jews do?*

He says, *compel*, because as Pope Leo says, *example has more force than words*. Hence Paul rebukes Peter precisely because he had been instructed by God that although he had previously lived as the Jews do, he should no longer discriminate among foods: *that which God has cleansed, do not call common* (Acts 10:15). But now Peter was dissembling the opposite.

86. It should be noted that these words occasioned no small controversy between Jerome and Augustine and, as their writings clearly show, they are seen to disagree on four points.

Et primo in tempore legalium, quando scilicet servari debuerunt. Nam Hieronymus duo tempora distinguit, unum ante passionem Christi, aliud post passionem. Vult ergo Hieronymus quod legalia ante passionem Christi viva essent, id est, habentia virtutem suam, in quantum scilicet per circumcisionem tollebatur peccatum originale, et per sacrificia et hostias placabatur Deus. Sed post passionem non solum dicit ea non fuisse viva vel mortua, sed, quod plus est, ea fuisse mortifera, et quod quicumque post passionem Christi ea servavit, peccavit mortaliter.

Augustinus vero distinguit tria tempora. Unum tempus ante passionem Christi, et concordans cum Hieronymo, dicit, isto tempore legalia viva fuisse. Aliud tempus est post passionem Christi immediate, ante gratiam divulgatam (sicut tempus apostolorum in principio), in quo tempore dicit Augustinus legalia mortua fuisse, sed tamen non mortifera Iudaeis conversis, dummodo ipsa servantes, spem in eis non ponerent, ita quod etiam ipsi Iudaei ea servantes tunc non peccarent. Si vero in eis spem posuissent, quicumque conversi ea servantes, peccassent mortaliter, quia si posuissent in eis spem, quasi essent necessaria ad salutem, quantum in eis erat, evacuassent gratiam Christi. Aliud tempus dicit esse post veritatem et gratiam Christi divulgatam, et in isto tempore dicit ea mortua et mortifera omnibus ea servantibus.

Ratio autem dictorum est, quia si Iudaei statim post conversionem fuissent prohibiti ab observantiis legalium, visum fuisset eos pari passu ambulare cum idololatris, qui statim ab idolorum cultura prohibebantur, et legalia non fuisse bona, sicut nec idololatriam. Et ideo instinctu Spiritus Sancti permissum est, ut legalia modico tempore servarentur ea intentione quae dicta est, ut per hoc ostenderetur legalia tunc bona fuisse. Unde dicit Augustinus quod per hoc ostendebatur quod mater synagoga cum honore deducenda ad tumulum erat, dum non statim post passionem Christi legalia prohibita sunt. Quicumque vero non eo modo ipsa servaret, non honoraret matrem synagogam, sed eam extumularet.

87. Secundo discordant praedicti Hieronymus et Augustinus de observatione legalium quantum ad ipsos apostolos.

Hieronymus enim dicit quod apostoli numquam secundum veritatem servabant legalia, sed simulaverunt se servare, ut vitarent scandalum fidelium qui fuerant ex circumcisione. Et hoc quidem modo dicit simulasse Paulum, quando persolvit votum in Templo Ierosolymitano, ut habetur Act. XXI, 26; et quando

First, as to the time of the legal justifications, namely, when they should have been observed. For Jerome distinguishes two periods, one before the passion of Christ and one after. Jerome's opinion is that the legal justifications were living before the passion of Christ, i.e., had validity, inasmuch as original sin was removed through circumcision, and God was pleased with sacrifices and victims. But after the passion they were, according to him, not only not living i.e., dead, but what is more, they were deadly, so that whoever observed them after the passion of Christ sinned mortally.

Augustine, on the other hand, distinguishes three periods. One period was before the passion of Christ and, in agreement with Jerome, he says that during that period the legal justifications were living. Another was the period immediately following the passion of Christ, before grace was promulgated (as the time of the apostles in the beginning); during this period, says Augustine, the legal justifications were dead but not yet deadly to the converted Jews, so long as the ones observing them placed no hope in them. Hence the Jews observed them during that period without sinning. But had they placed their trust in them when observing them after their conversion, they would have sinned mortally; because if they placed their trust in them so as to believe that they were necessary for salvation, then, as far as they were concerned, they would have been voiding the grace of Christ. Finally, he posits a third period, after the truth and grace of Christ had been proclaimed. It was during that period, he says, that they were both dead and deadly to all who observed them.

The reasoning that underlies these statements is that if the Jews had been forbidden the legal observances right after their conversion, it might have seemed that they had previously been on an equal footing with idolaters, who were immediately forbidden to worship idols, and that just as idolatry had never been good, so too the legal observances. Therefore, under the inspiration of the Holy Spirit, the legal observances were condoned for a short time for the reason given, namely, to show that the legal observances had been good in the past. Hence, says Augustine, the fact that the legal justifications were not forbidden right after the passion of Christ showed that the mother, the synagogue, was destined to be brought in honor to the grave. But whoever did not observe them in that manner would not be honoring the mother, the synagogue, but disturbing her grave.

87. Second, the aforesaid Jerome and Augustine disagree on the observance of the legal justifications with respect to the apostles.

For Jerome says that the apostles never really observed them but pretended to do so, in order to avoid scandalizing the believers who had been of the circumcision. He says that even Paul made this pretense when he fulfilled a vow in the Temple at Jerusalem (Acts 21:26), and when he circumcised Timothy (Acts 16:3), and when on advice from

circumcidit Timotheum, ut habetur Act. XVI, v. 3; et quando a Iacobo monitus quaedam legalia suscepit, ut habetur Act. XV, 20. Et hoc quidem facientes non deludebant alios, quia faciebant hoc, non intendentes legalia servare, sed propter aliquas causas, sicut quod quiescebant in sabbato non propter observantiam legis, sed propter quietem. Item abstinebant ab immundis secundum legem, non propter observantiam legis, sed propter alias causas, utpote propter abominationem et aliquid huiusmodi.

Augustinus vero dicit quod apostoli servabant ipsa legalia, et hoc intendentes, sed tamen non ponentes in eis spem, quasi essent necessaria ad salutem. Et hoc quidem licebat eis, quia fuerunt ex Iudaeis. Ita tamen quod haec servarent ante gratiam divulgatam; unde sicut eo tempore alii Iudaei conversi sine periculo servare poterant, absque eo quod in eis spem ponerent, ita et ipsi.

88. Tertio discordant de peccato Petri. Nam Hieronymus dicit in simulatione praedicta Petrum non peccasse, quia hoc ex caritate fecit, et non ex aliquo timore mundano, ut dictum est.

Augustinus vero dicit eum peccasse, venialiter tamen, et hoc propter indiscretionem quam habuit, nimis inhaerendo huic parti (scilicet Iudaeorum) ad vitandum eorum scandalum. Et validius argumentum Augustini contra Hieronymum est, quia Hieronymus adducit pro se septem doctores, quorum quatuor, scilicet Laudicensem, et Alexandrinum, Origenem et Didymum excludit Augustinus, utpote de haeresi infames. Aliis vero tribus opponit tres, quos pro se et pro sua opinione habet, scilicet Ambrosium, Cyprianum, et ipsum Paulum, qui manifeste dicit, quod reprehensibilis erat Petrus. Si ergo nefas est dicere in Scriptura Sacra aliquod falsum contineri, non erit fas dicere Petrum reprehensibilem non fuisse.

Et propter hoc verior est opinio et sententia Augustini, quia cum dictis Apostoli magis concordat.

89. Quarto discordant in reprehensione Pauli. Nam Hieronymus dicit, quod Paulus vere non reprehendit Petrum, sed simulatorie, sicut et Petrus simulatorie legalia servabat, ut scilicet sicut Petrus nolens scandalizare Iudaeos simulabat se legalia servare, ita Paulus ut non scandalizaret gentes, ostendit sibi displicere quod Petrus faciebat, et simulatorie reprehendit, faciebantque hoc quasi ex condicto, ut utrisque fidelibus sibi subditis providerent.

Augustinus vero sicut dicit Petrum vere servasse legalia, ita dicit Paulum eum vere reprehendisse, et non simulatorie. Sed et Petrus quidem servando peccavit, quia inde erat scandalum apud gentiles, a quibus se

James he observed some of the justifications (Acts 20:20). But in so doing the apostles were not misleading the faithful, because they did not act with the intention of observing the justifications but for other reasons; for example, they rested on the sabbath, not because it was a legal observance, but for the sake of rest. Likewise, they abstained from food legally unclean, not for the sake of observing the legal justifications but for other reasons; for example, on account of an abhorrence or something of that nature.

But Augustine says that the apostles observed the legal justifications and intended to do so, but without putting their trust in them as though they were necessary for salvation. Furthermore, this was lawful for them to do, because they had been Jews. Nevertheless, they observed them before grace was proclaimed. Hence just as certain other Jews could safely observe them at that time without putting any trust in them, so too could the apostles.

88. Third, they disagree on the sin of Peter. For Jerome says that in the dissimulation previously mentioned, Peter did not sin, because he did this from charity and, as has been said, not from mundane fear.

Augustine, on the other hand, says, that he did sin, although venially, on account of the lack of discretion he had by adhering overmuch to one side, namely, to the Jews, in order to avoid scandalizing them. But the stronger of Augustine's arguments against Jerome is that Jerome adduces on his own behalf seven doctors, four of whom, namely, Laudicens, Alexander, Origen, and Didymus, Augustine rejects as known heretics. To the other three he opposes three of his own, who held with him and his opinion, namely, Ambrose, Cyprian, and Paul himself, who plainly teaches that Peter was deserving of rebuke. Therefore, if it is unlawful to say that anything false is contained in Sacred Scripture, it will not be lawful to say that Peter was not deserving of rebuke.

For this reason the opinion and statement of Augustine is the truer, because it is more in accord with the words of the Apostle.

89. Fourth, they disagree on Paul's rebuke. For Jerome says that Paul did not really rebuke Peter but pretended to do so, just as Peter pretended to observe the legal justifications, i.e., just as Peter in his unwillingness to scandalize the Jews pretended to observe the justifications, so Paul, in order not to scandalize the gentiles, feigned displeasure at Peter's action and pretended to rebuke him. This was done, as it were, by mutual consent, so that each might exercise his care over the believers subject to them.

Augustine, however, just as he says that Peter really did observe the justifications, says that Paul truly rebuked him without pretense. Furthermore, Peter really sinned by observing them, because his action was a source of scandal to

subtrahebat. Paulus vero non peccavit reprehendendo, quia ex eius reprehensione nullum scandalum sequebatur.

the gentiles from whom he separated himself. But Paul did not sin in rebuking him, because no scandal followed from his rebuke.

Lecture 4

2:15 Nos natura Judaei, et non ex gentibus peccatores. [n. 90]

2:16 Scientes autem quod non justificatur homo ex operibus legis, nisi per fidem Jesu Christi: et nos in Christo Jesu credimus, ut justificemur ex fide Christi, et non ex operibus legis: propter quod ex operibus legis non justificabitur omnis caro. [n. 93]

2:13 Ἡμεῖς φύσει Ἰουδαῖοι καὶ οὐκ ἐξ ἐθνῶν ἁμαρτωλοί,

2:16 εἰδότες [δὲ] ὅτι οὐ δικαιοῦται ἄνθρωπος ἐξ ἔργων νόμου ἐὰν μὴ διὰ πίστεως Ἰησοῦ Χριστοῦ, καὶ ἡμεῖς εἰς Χριστὸν Ἰησοῦν ἐπιστεύσαμεν, ἵνα δικαιωθῶμεν ἐκ πίστεως Χριστοῦ καὶ οὐκ ἐξ ἔργων νόμου, ὅτι ἐξ ἔργων νόμου οὐ δικαιωθήσεται πᾶσα σάρξ.

2:15 We by nature are Jews: and not of the gentiles, sinners. [n. 90]

2:16 But knowing that man is not justified by the works of the law, but by the faith of Jesus Christ, we also believe in Christ Jesus, that we may be justified by the faith of Christ and not by the works of the law: because by the works of the law no flesh shall be justified. [n. 93]

---

90. Supra ostendit veritatem doctrinae apostolicae praedicatae per eum ex auctoritate aliorum apostolorum, hic ostendit idem ex eorum conversatione et exemplo. Et

circa hoc duo facit.

Primo ostendit propositum per apostolorum conversationem;

secundo adversantium obiectionem *quod si quaerentes iustificari*, et cetera.

Circa primum tria facit.

Primo praemittit apostolorum conditionem;

secundo insinuat eorum conversationem, ibi *scientes autem quod non iustificatur*, etc.;

tertio intentam conditionem, ibi *propter quod ex operibus legis*, et cetera.

91. Conditio autem apostolorum et etiam ipsius Pauli haec est, quod secundum naturalem originem ex Iudaeis processerunt. Et hoc est quod dicit *nos*, scilicet ego et apostoli alii, sumus *natura*, id est naturali origine, *Iudaei*, non proselyti. II Cor. XI, v. 22: *Hebraei sunt, et ego*, et cetera. Et haec est magna laus, quia, ut dicitur Io. IV, 22, *salus ex Iudaeis est*.

Et non ex gentibus peccatores, id est, non sumus peccatores, ut gentes idololatrae et immundae.

92. Sed contra est quod dicitur I Io. I, v. 8: *si dixerimus quoniam peccatum non habemus*, etc., ergo Iudaei sunt peccatores.

Respondeo. Dicendum est, quod aliud est peccantem esse, aliud peccatorem. Nam primum denominat actum, secundum vero promptitudinem, sive habitum ad peccandum. Unde Scriptura iniquos et gravibus peccatorum sarcinis oneratos peccatores appellare consuevit. Iudaei ergo propter legem superbientes, quasi per eam coerciti a peccatis, gentes quae sine fraeno legis erant, et ad peccandum pronae, peccatores vocabant. Eph. IV, 14: *non circumferamur omni vento doctrinae*, et cetera.

Cum ergo dicat Apostolus *non ex gentibus peccatores*, exponitur, id est, non sumus de numero peccatorum qui sunt inter gentiles, et cetera.

90. Having manifested the truth of the apostolic doctrine preached by him because of the authority of the other apostles, he now shows the same thing from their manner of life and example.

About this he does two things.

First, he proves his proposition from the manner of life of the apostles;

second, he raises an objection posed by his adversaries, at *but if, while we seek to be justified* (Gal 2:17).

As to the first he does three things.

First, he sets forth the status of the apostles;

second, their manner of life, at *but knowing that man is not justified*;

third, the intended conclusion, at *because by the works of the law no flesh shall be justified*.

91. The status of the apostles and even of Paul is that according to natural origin they were born Jews. That is why he says, *we*, namely, I and the other apostles, are *by nature*, i.e., by natural origin, *Jews*, not proselytes: *they are Hebrews: so am I* (2 Cor 11:22). And this is a great compliment, because, as it is said: *salvation is of the Jews* (John 4:22).

And not of the gentiles, sinners, i.e., we are not sinners as are the gentiles, idolatrous and unclean.

92. But against this can be set this word: *if we say that we have no sin, we deceive ourselves* (1 John 1:8). Therefore, the Jews were sinners.

I answer that it is one thing to sin and another to be a sinner. For the first names an act, but the second a readiness or habit of sinning. Hence Scripture is wont to call the impious and those loaded down with the heavy burden of sin, sinners. The Jews therefore, being haughty on account of the law, and as it were, restrained from sin by it, called the gentiles sinners, living as they were without the laws' restraint and being prone to sin: *be no more carried about with every wind of doctrine* (Eph 4:14).

When, therefore, the Apostle says, *not of the gentiles, sinners*, he means we are not of that number of sinners that exist among the gentiles.

93. Consequenter cum dicit *scientes autem quod non iustificatur homo*, etc., ponit apostolorum conversationem, quae quidem non est in legalibus, sed in fide Christi. Et

circa hoc duo facit.

Primo exprimit rationem apostolicae conversationis; secundo ponit ipsam apostolicam conversationem, ibi *et nos in Christo*, et cetera.

94. Erat ergo apostolica conversatio in fide, et non in legalibus. Cuius ratio est, quia licet fuerimus Iudaei natura et in legalibus nutriti, tamen *scientes* pro certo, *quod non iustificatur homo ex operibus legis*, id est, per opera legalia, nisi *per fidem Iesu Christi*, ideo deserentes illa conversamur in praeceptis fidei. Rom. III, 28: *arbitramur enim hominem iustificari per fidem sine operibus legis*. Act. IV, 12: *non est aliud nomen*, et cetera.

Sed contra, Rom. enim II, 13 dicitur: *non enim auditores legis iusti sunt apud Deum, sed factores legis iustificabuntur*, et cetera. Videtur ergo quod ex operibus legis iustificetur homo.

Respondeo. Dicendum est, quod iustificari potest dupliciter accipi, scilicet iustitiam exequi, et iustum fieri. Primo autem modo homo iustificatur, qui opera iustitiae facit. Non autem iustus fit aliquis nisi a Deo, per gratiam.

Sciendum est ergo, quod opera legis quaedam erant moralia, quaedam vero caeremonialia. Moralia autem licet continerentur in lege, non tamen poterant proprie dici opera legis, cum ex naturali instinctu, et ex lege naturali homo inducatur ad illa. Sed caeremonialia dicuntur proprie opera legis. Quantumcumque ergo homo quoad executionem iustitiae ex moralibus iustificetur, et etiam ex caeremonialibus, inquantum servare ea est opus obedientiae, ut ad sacramenta pertineant, et sic accipitur secundum dictum Apostoli ad Rom. II, 13.

Quantum tamen ad iustum fieri, ex operibus legis non iustificari homo per haec videtur, quia sacramenta veteris legis non conferebant gratiam. Infra IV, 9: *conversi estis ad egena elementa*, id est, gratiam non conferentia, neque gratiam in se continentia. Sacramenta vero novae legis, licet sint elementa materialia, non tamen sunt elementa egena, quia in se gratiam continent, unde et iustificare possunt. Si qui autem in veteri lege iusti erant, non erant iusti ex operibus legis, sed solum ex fide Christi, quem Deus proposuit propitiatorem per fidem, ut dicitur Rom. III, 20. Unde et ipsa sacramenta veteris legis non fuerunt nisi quaedam protestationes fidei Christi, sicut et nostra sacramenta, sed differenter, quia illa sacramenta gratiam Christi configurabant quasi

93. Then when he says, *but knowing that man is not justified by the works*, he sets forth the apostles' manner of life, which consists not in the works of the law but in the faith of Christ.

About this he does two things.

First, he gives the reason for the apostles' manner of life; second, he sets forth their manner of life, at *we also believe in Christ*.

94. Therefore the apostolic life rested on the faith of Christ and not on the works of the law. The reason for this is that although we were Jews by nature and were nourished in the works of the law, yet *knowing* for certain that man is *not justified by the works of the law*, i.e., through the works of the law, but *by the faith of Jesus Christ*, for that reason we have left the law and are living according to the precepts of the faith: *for we account a man to be justified by faith, without the works of the law* (Rom 3:28); *for there is no other name under heaven given to men whereby we must be saved* (Acts 4:12).

However, it is said: *for the hearers of the law are not just before God; but the doers of the law shall be justified* (Rom 2:13). Therefore, it seems that a man would be justified by the works of the law.

I answer that 'to be justified' can be taken in two senses, namely, doing what is just, and being made just. In the first sense, one is justified when he does the works of justice. But, in the second sense, no one is made just save by God through grace.

It should be known, therefore, that some works of the law were moral and some ceremonial. The moral, although they were contained in the law, could not, strictly speaking, be called works of the law, for man is induced to them by natural instinct and by the natural law. But the ceremonial works are properly called the works of the law. Therefore, to that extent is man justified by the moral laws, so far as the execution of justice is concerned, and also by the ceremonial laws that pertain to the sacraments, as their observance is a work of obedience. And this is the way it is taken in the word of the Apostle to the Romans (Rom 2:13).

But with respect to being made just by the works of the law, a man does not seem to be justified by them, because the sacraments of the old law did not confer grace. *How do you turn again to the weak and needy elements?* (Gal 4:9) i.e., that neither confer grace nor contain grace in themselves. The sacraments of the new law however, although they are material elements, are not needy elements; hence they can justify. Again, if there were any in the old law who were just, they were not made just by the works of the law but only by the faith of Christ *whom God has proposed to be a propitiation through faith* (Rom 3:25). Hence the sacraments of the old law were certain protestations of the faith of Christ, just as our sacraments are, but not in the same way, because those sacraments were configured to the grace

futuram; nostra autem sacramenta protestantur quasi continentia gratiam praesentem. Et ideo signanter dicit, quod *ex operibus legis non iustificatur homo, nisi per fidem Iesu Christi*, quia etsi olim aliqui servantes opera legis iustificarentur, non tamen hoc erat nisi per fidem Iesu Christi.

95. Ex hac autem scientia apostolorum quam habebant, quod iustificatio non est per operationem legis, sed per fidem Christi, concludit conversationem apostolorum eligentium fidem Christi et dimittentium opera legis. Unde sequitur *et nos in Christo Iesu credimus*, quia, ut dicitur Act. IV, 12, *non est aliud nomen datum*, et cetera. Unde sequitur *ut iustificemur ex fide Christi*. Rom. V, 1: *iustificati ergo ex fide*, et cetera.

96. Et ne aliquis credat quod simul cum lege Christi opera legis iustificent, subiungit *et non ex operibus legis*. Rom. III, 28: *arbitramur enim iustificari hominem per fidem*, et cetera.

Ex hoc concludit principale intentum, dicens quod si apostoli, qui sunt naturaliter Iudaei, non quaerunt iustificari per opera legis, sed per fidem, quod *non iustificatur omnis caro ex operibus legis*, nec homo quicumque potest iustificari per opera legis. Sumitur enim hic *caro* pro homine, scilicet pars pro toto, sicut Is. XL: *videbit omnis caro salutare Dei nostri*.

Dicens autem *propter quod*, etc., concludit quasi a maiori. Magis enim videtur naturale vel rationabile de Iudaeis, quod per opera legis, non per fidem, iustificarentur, quam alii; sed hoc non est: quare, et cetera.

of Christ as to something that lay in the future; our sacraments, however, testify as things containing a grace that is present. Therefore, he says significantly, that *it is not by the works of the law that we are justified, but by the faith of Christ*, because, although some who observed the works of the law in times past were made just, nevertheless, this was effected only by the faith of Jesus Christ.

95. From this knowledge which the apostles had, namely, that justification is not by the works of the law but by the faith of Christ, he concludes to their manner of life, in which they chose the faith of Christ and gave up the works of the law. Hence he adds, *we also believe in Christ Jesus*, because as it is said: *there is no other name under heaven given to men, whereby we must be saved* (Acts 4:12). Therefore he continued, that we may be justified by the faith of Christ. *Being justified, therefore, by faith, let us have peace with God* (Rom 5:1).

96. But lest anyone suppose that the works of the law along with the faith of Christ justify, he adds, *and not by the works of the law*: *for we account a man to be justified by faith, without the works of the law* (Rom 3:28).

From this he derives his main proposition, saying that if the apostles, who are Jews by nature, do not seek to be justified by the works of the law but by faith, then *by the works of the law no flesh shall be justified*, i.e., no man whatsoever can be justified by the works of the law. For *flesh* is taken here to stand for man, i.e., the part for the whole, as does *all flesh shall see the salvation of the Lord* (Isa 40:5).

Then by saying, *because by the works of the law no flesh shall be justified*, he concludes, as it were, *a fortiori*. For it seems more natural or reasonable for the Jews, more than anyone else, to be justified by the works of the law rather than by faith. But this is not the case. Therefore, etc.

Lecture 5

2:17 Quod si quaerentes justificari in Christo, inventi sumus et ipsi peccatores, numquid Christus peccati minister est? Absit. [n. 97]

2:18 Si enim quae destruxi, iterum haec aedifico: praevaricatorem me constituo.

2:17εἰ δὲ ζητοῦντες δικαιωθῆναι ἐν Χριστῷ εὑρέθημεν καὶ αὐτοὶ ἁμαρτωλοί, ἆρα Χριστὸς ἁμαρτίας διάκονος; μὴ γένοιτο.

2:18εἰ γὰρ ἃ κατέλυσα ταῦτα πάλιν οἰκοδομῶ, παραβάτην ἐμαυτὸν συνιστάνω.

2:17 But if, while we seek to be justified in Christ, we ourselves also are found sinners, is Christ then the minister of sin? God forbid! [n. 97]

2:18 For if I build up again the things which I have destroyed, I make myself a prevaricator.

---

97. Postquam Apostolus ostendit per conversationem apostolorum legalia non esse observanda, quod ipse dicebat, hic movet quaestionem in contrarium.

Et circa hoc tria facit.

Primo movet quaestionem;

secundo solvit eam, ibi *absit*, etc.;

tertio solutionem eius manifestat, ibi *ego enim per legem*, et cetera.

98. Primum dupliciter potest exponi secundum Glossam. Primo sic: posset enim aliquis dicere quod apostoli deserentes legem, veniendo ad fidem Christi peccassent. Sed ex hoc Apostolus introducit quasi quoddam inconveniens, scilicet Christum esse auctorem peccati, eo quod homines ad suam fidem vocat. Et hoc est quod dicit *quod*, id est sed, *si* nos apostoli *quaerentes iustificari* in ipso, id est, per ipsum, scilicet Christum, *inventi sumus*, id est, manifeste comprobemur, *et ipsi* Apostoli *peccatores* propter legis dimissionem, *numquid Christus est minister peccati?* Id est, inducens nos ad peccandum qui nos a statu legis ad suam fidem vocavit? Infra IV, 4: *factum sub lege, ut eos qui sub lege erant redimeret*, scilicet ab onere legis.

Respondet Apostolus *absit*, quia magis est minister iustitiae. Rom. V, 19: *per unius obedientiam iusti constituuntur multi*. I Petr. II, 22: *qui peccatum non fecit*, et cetera.

Et quod Christus non sit minister peccati abstrahens a lege veteri, patet, quia si ego ipse *quae destruxi*, scilicet superbiam gloriantem de lege, *iterum reaedifico*, volens redire ad gloriandum de lege, *praevaricatorem meipsum constituo*, resumens quae destruxi. II Petr. II, 22: *canis reversus ad vomitum*, et cetera. Ios. II: *maledictus homo qui reaedificaverit Iericho*.

Dicit autem *quae destruxi*, non ipsam legem, ut Manichaei volunt, quia lex sancta est, Rom. VII, 12, sed superbiam de lege, de qua dicitur Rom. X, 3: *quaerentes suam iustitiam statuere*, et cetera.

Si quis autem obiiciat quod cum ipse olim destruxerit fidem Christi, praevaricatorem se faciebat eam aedificans, patet responsio, quia fidem Christi conatus fuit quidem destruere, sed non praevaluit propter veritatem. Act. IX, v. 4: *quid me persequeris? Durum est tibi*, et

---

97. After proving by the apostles' manner of life that the works of the law ought not to be observed, the Apostle raises a question to the contrary.

About this he does three things.

First, he raises the question;

second, he solves it, at *God forbid*;

third, he explains his solution, at *for I, through the law* (Gal 2:19).

98. The first point can be developed in two ways according to a Gloss. First, thus: someone could say that the apostles sinned by abandoning the law and turning to the faith of Christ. But the Apostle shows that this would lead to the following unwelcome conclusion, namely, that Christ is the author of sin in calling men to his faith. This is what he means when he says, *but if, we apostles, while we seek to be justified* in him, i.e., through him, namely, Christ, *are found*, i.e., plainly proven to be, *sinners* for leaving the law, *is Christ then the minister of sin?* i.e., is he inducing us to sin, who called us from the slavery of the law to his faith? *Made under the law that he might redeem them that were under the law* (Gal 4:4), namely, from the burden of the law.

The Apostle answers, *God forbid*, because he is rather the minister of justice; *by the obedience of one, many shall be made just* (Rom 5:19); *who committed no sin, neither was guile found in his mouth* (1 Pet 2:22).

That Christ is not the minister of sin in leading one from the old law is plain, because *if I* myself, by wanting to glory once more in the law, *build up again the things I have destroyed*, namely, my pride taking glory in the law, *I make myself a prevaricator* in taking up what I destroyed: *the dog is returned to his vomit* (2 Pet 2:22); *cursed be the man that shall raise up and build the city of Jericho* (Josh 6:26).

He says, *which I have destroyed*, i.e., not the law itself, as the Manicheans would have it, because the law is holy (Rom 7:12), but pride in the law: *for they, seeking to establish their own justice have not submitted themselves to the justice of God* (Rom 10:3).

Now if someone were to object that since he formerly had wasted the faith of Christ, he makes himself a prevaricator by trying to build it up, the plain answer is that he did indeed try to destroy the faith of Christ, yet because of the truth he did not persist: *why do you persecute you me? It is*

cetera. Sed superbia legis vana erat, et ideo destrui poterat, et reaedificanda non erat.

99. Secundo modo potest exponi, ut quod dicit *inventi sumus et ipsi peccatores*, referatur non ad dimissionem legis, sicut nunc expositum est, sed magis ad ipsam legis observantiam. Manifestum enim est quod quicumque quaerit iustificari, profitetur se non esse iustum, sed peccatorem.

Est ergo sensus: *si* nos *quaerentes iustificari in Christo*, ex hoc ipso quod quaerimus nos iustificari, *inventi sumus*, id est, ratione comprobamur *et ipsi peccatores* fuisse, propter hoc quod legem observabamus, *numquid Iesus Christus minister peccati est?* Ut scilicet mandaverit homines post suam passionem legalia observare, quod sine peccato fieri non potest.

Et attendendum est, quod haec expositio procedit secundum opinionem Hieronymi, qui ponebat statim post passionem Christi legalia fuisse mortifera.

100. Tertio modo potest exponi, ut quod dicit *inventi sumus et ipsi peccatores*, pertineat quidem ad statum quo lex observabatur, non tamen quod ipsi offenderent propter legis observantiam, sed propter legis defectum, quae peccatum auferre non poterat, ut sit sensus: si quaerentes iustificari in ipso, inventi sumus et ipsi peccatores, id est, peccatum habentes, lege peccatum non auferente, secundum illud Rom. III, 9: *causati sumus Iudaeos et Graecos omnes sub peccato esse*, **numquid Iesus Christus peccati minister est**, ut reducat nos ad observantiam legis, in qua sub peccato eramus?

Et haec expositio procedit secundum expositionem Augustini.

Et respondet, secundum utramque expositionem, *absit*, quia ego destruxi legem carnaliter intellectam, spiritualiter iudicando et docendo. Unde si iterum vellem aedificare carnalis legis observantias, essem praevaricator legis spiritualis.

101. Potest et quarto modo sic exponi. Dixeram, hominem non iustificari ex operibus legis. Posset aliquis dicere, quod *nec etiam per fidem Christi*, quia multi post fidem Christi acceptam, peccant. Et hoc est quod dicit: *si quaerentes iustificari in Christo*, id est, per fidem Christi, *inventi sumus* post fidem Christi susceptam *etiam ipsi* nos fideles *peccatores*, id est, in peccatis viventes, *numquid Iesus Christus minister peccati est* et damnationis, sicut minister veteris legis est minister peccati et damnationis? Non quod lex induceret ad peccatum, sed occasionaliter, quia prohibebat peccatum, et non conferebat gratiam adiuvantem ad resistendum peccato. Unde dicitur Rom. VII, 8: *occasione accepta, peccatum per mandatum*, et cetera. Sed Christus dat gratiam adiuvantem. Io. I, v. 17: *gratia et veritas per Iesum Christum facta est*. Unde nullo modo est minister peccati, nec directe, nec occasionaliter.

hard for you to kick against the goad (Acts 9:4). But pride in the law was vain and this pride could be destroyed, never again to be re-established.

99. The second way in which it can be developed is to refer his statement, *we ourselves also are found sinners*, not to their abandoning the law, as in the first explanation, but to the observance of the law. For it is plain that anyone who seeks to be made just does not profess himself to be just but a sinner.

The sense, therefore, is this: *if, while we seek to be justified in Christ, we are* by the very fact of seeking to be justified *found*, i.e., reasonably proved, to have been *sinners*, because we observed the law, *is Jesus Christ then the minister of sin?* That is, does he command men to observe the works of the law after his passion, which is something that cannot be done without sin?

Note that this explanation harmonizes with Jerome's opinion which posited that the legal justifications were deadly immediately after the passion of Christ.

100. It is possible to explain, *we ourselves also are found to be sinners*, in a third way as referring, indeed, to the state in which the law was observed; not that they offended by observing the law, but that the law is deficient and cannot remove sin. Hence the meaning is this: if in seeking to be justified in it, we ourselves are found to be sinners, i.e., still in our sins, because the law does not remove sin: *for we have charged both Jews and Greeks, that they are all under sin* (Rom 3:9), *is Christ then the minister of sin*, so as to bring us back to observing the law in which we are under sin?

This explanation accords with Augustine's exposition.

And Paul answers to either explanation, *God forbid*, because I destroyed the law understood carnally by judging and teaching it spiritually. Hence, if I should desire to re-establish the observances of the carnal law, I would be a prevaricator of the spiritual law.

101. Furthermore, it can be explained in a fourth way, thus: I had said that man is not justified by the works of the law. But someone might say, *nor by the faith of Christ either*, because many sin after embracing the faith of Christ. And this is what he says: *if, while we week to be justified in Christ*, i.e., by the faith of Christ, *we ourselves*, who have become believers by embracing the faith of Christ, *also are found sinners*, i.e., living in sin, *is Christ then the minister of sin* and of damnation, as the minister of the old law is a minister of sin and damnation? Not that the law led one into sin, but was its occasion, because it forbade sin and conferred no grace to help one resist sin. Hence it is said: *but sin, taking occasion by the commandment, wrought in me all manner of concupiscence* (Rom 7:8). But Christ gives a helping grace: *grace and truth came by Jesus Christ* (John 1:17). Hence in no way is he the minister of sin, either directly or as its occasion.

Lecture 6

²:¹⁹Ego enim per legem, legi mortuus sum, ut Deo vivam: Christo confixus sum cruci. [n. 102]

²:²⁰Vivo autem, jam non ego: vivit vero in me Christus. Quod autem nunc vivo in carne: in fide vivo Filii Dei, qui dilexit me, et tradidit semetipsum pro me. [n. 108]

²:²¹Non abjicio gratiam Dei. Si enim per legem justitia, ergo gratis Christus mortuus est. [n. 111]

²:¹⁹ἐγὼ γὰρ διὰ νόμου νόμῳ ἀπέθανον ἵνα θεῷ ζήσω. Χριστῷ συνεσταύρωμαι·

²:²⁰ζῶ δὲ οὐκέτι ἐγώ, ζῇ δὲ ἐν ἐμοὶ Χριστός· ὃ δὲ νῦν ζῶ ἐν σαρκί, ἐν πίστει ζῶ τῇ τοῦ υἱοῦ τοῦ θεοῦ τοῦ ἀγαπήσαντός με καὶ παραδόντος ἑαυτὸν ὑπὲρ ἐμοῦ.

²:²¹οὐκ ἀθετῶ τὴν χάριν τοῦ θεοῦ· εἰ γὰρ διὰ νόμου δικαιοσύνη, ἄρα Χριστὸς δωρεὰν ἀπέθανεν.

²:¹⁹For I, through the law, am dead to the law, that I may live to God; with Christ I am nailed to the cross. [n. 102]

²:²⁰But I do not live now: but Christ lives in me. But that I live now in the flesh: I live in the faith of the Son of God, who loved me and delivered himself for me. [n. 108]

²:²¹I do not cast away the grace of God. For if justice be by the law, then Christ died in vain. [n. 111]

---

102. Hic Apostolus solutionem superius assignatam manifestat. Et

primo ponit solutionis manifestationem;

secundo concludit principale intentum, ibi **non abiicio gratiam Dei**, et cetera.

Sed attendendum est, quod Apostolus inquirendo procedens, nullum dubium indiscussum relinquit. Et ideo verba eius licet videantur intricata, tamen si diligenter advertantur, nihil sine causa dicit, et hoc apparet in verbis propositis. Ubi tria facit:

primo manifestat solutionem;

secundo explicat solutionis manifestationem, ibi **Christo confixus sum cruci**, etc.;

tertio removet dubitationem, ibi **quod autem vivo**, et cetera.

103. Quia ergo Apostolus dixerat **si enim quae destruxi**, etc., quod intelligitur de veteri lege, posset enim ab aliquo reputari legis destructor, et per consequens iniquus, secundum illud Ps. CXVIII, 126: *dissipaverunt iniqui legem tuam*, ideo Apostolus vult ostendere quomodo legem destruat, et tamen non est iniquus, dicens **ego enim per legem**, et cetera.

Ubi sciendum est, quod quando aliquis dissipat legem per ipsam legem, talis est praevaricator legis, non iniquus. Dissipatur autem lex per legem, quando in lege datur aliquod praeceptum locale seu temporale, ut scilicet lex illa tali tempore, seu tali loco servetur, et non alio, et hoc ipsum exprimatur in lege. Si quis tunc in illo tempore, seu in illo loco lege non utitur, destruit legem per ipsam legem, et hoc modo Apostolus destruxit legem. Unde destruxi, inquit, quodammodo legem, tamen per legem, quia ego **mortuus sum legi per legem**, id est, per auctoritatem legis ipsam dimisi, quasi legi mortuus.

102. Here the Apostle amplifies the solution given above.

First, he explains the solution.

Second, he concludes to his principal proposition, at **I do not cast away the grace of God**.

It should be noted that the Apostle proceeds in a very thorough manner, leaving no doubt unexamined. Hence his words, although they seem involved, nevertheless, if they are carefully considered, say nothing without a purpose. This is plain from the words he uses. Therefore, he does three things:

first, he manifests the solution;

second, he explains his manifestation of the solution, at **with Christ I am nailed to the cross**;

third, he settles the question, at **that I live now in the flesh**.

103. Therefore, because the Apostle had said, *for, if I build up again the things which I have destroyed* (Gal 2:18), which is understood to refer to the old law, for one might regard him as a destroyer of the law and consequently impious: *they have dissipated your law* (Ps 119:126), for that reason the Apostle wishes to show how he destroys the law without being impious, saying, **for I, through the law, am dead to the law**.

Here it should be noted that when anyone destroys a law by means of the law itself, he is indeed a prevaricator of the law, but not impious. For a law is destroyed by means of the law when the law itself contains some local or temporary precept, such that the law should be observed for such a time or in such a place and no other, and this fact is expressed in the law. If someone, therefore, after that time or outside that place, does not use the law, he destroys the law by means of the law itself, and in this way the Apostle destroyed the law. Hence he says: I somehow destroyed the law, but by means of the law; because **through the law I am dead to the law**, i.e., by the authority of the law I have rejected the law, as being dead to the law.

For the authority of the law, through which he is dead to the law, is cited in many places in Sacred Scripture. For example, although not in so many words, it is had: *I will make a new covenant with the house of Israel* (Jer 31:31); *the Lord will raise up to you a prophet of your brethren like unto me* (Deut 18:15), and in many other places. Therefore the Apostle is not a destroyer of the law in the sense of a transgressor of the law.

104. Or else, **I, through the** spiritual **law, am dead to the** carnal **law**. For he dies to the law when, being freed by the law, he casts it aside: *if her husband be dead, she is loosed from the law of her husband* (Rom 7:2). Now inasmuch as the Apostle was subject to the spiritual law, he says that he is dead to the law, i.e., loosed from the observances of the law: *for the law of the Spirit of life, in Christ Jesus, has delivered me from the law of sin and of death* (Rom 8:2).

105. Again there is another possible way of setting the law aside without prevarication, namely, because, a law, when it is written on a scroll, is called a dead law, and when it is in the mind of the lawgiver it is called a living law. Now it is plain that if someone were to act according to the word of the lawgiver against the written law and break the law, he would both be set free of the dead law and be acting according to the command of the lawgiver.

He says, therefore, along these lines, **I am dead to the law**, which is written and dead, i.e., I am loosed from it *that I may live to God*, i.e., that I may guide my movements according to his precepts and be ordained to his honor. For a law that has been passed does, indeed, hand down something in writing on account of those outside and of those who cannot hear the words spoken by the lawgiver; but for those in his presence he does not lay it down in writing but in words alone. For in the beginning, men were weak and unable to approach unto God; hence it was necessary for the precepts of the law to be given to them in writing, so that by the law, as by a pedagogue, they might be led by the hand to the point where they might hear the things he commands, according to the words given below: ***the law was our pedagogue in Christ, that we might be justified by faith*** (Gal 3:24). But after we have access to the Father through Christ (Rom 5:2), we are not instructed about the commands of God through the law, but by God himself. Hence he says: through the law leading me by the hand I have died to the written law, **in order that I may live unto God**, i.e., to the maker of the law, i.e., to be instructed and directed by him.

106. Then when he says, **with Christ I am nailed to the cross**, he amplifies what he said.

Now he had said that he died to the law and lives to God. Hence he explains these two things: first, that he died to the law, he explains by saying that **with Christ I am nailed to the cross**; second, that he lives to God, when he says: **but I do not live now, but Christ lives in me**.

The first point can be explained in two ways.

Uno modo sicut in Glossa, sic: quilibet homo secundum carnalem originem nascitur filius irae, Eph. II, 3: *eramus enim natura filii irae*, et cetera. Nascitur etiam in vetustate peccati, Bar. III, 11: *inveterasti in terra aliena*, et cetera. Quae quidem vetustas peccati tollitur per crucem Christi, et confertur novitas vitae spiritualis.

Dicit ergo Apostolus **Christo confixus sum cruci**, id est, concupiscentia seu fomes peccati, et omne huiusmodi, mortuum est in me per crucem Christi. Rom. VI, 6: *vetus homo noster simul crucifixus est*, et cetera. Item ex quo cum Christo confixus sum cruci, et mortuus sum peccato, et Christus resurrexit, cum resurgente etiam resurrexi. Rom. IV, 25: *traditus est*, et cetera. Sic ergo Christus in nobis renovat vitam novam, destructa vetustate peccati. Et ideo dicit **vivo autem**, id est, quia **Christo confixus sum cruci**, vigorem bene operandi habeo, **iam non ego** secundum carnem, quia iam non habeo vetustatem quam prius habui, **sed vivit in me Christus**, id est, novitas, quae per Christum nobis data est.

107. Vel aliter: homo quantum ad illud dicitur vivere, in quo principaliter firmat suum affectum, et in quo maxime delectatur. Unde et homines qui in studio seu in venationibus maxime delectantur, dicunt hoc eorum vitam esse. Quilibet autem homo habet quemdam privatum affectum, quo quaerit quod suum est; dum ergo aliquis vivit quaerens tantum quod suum est, soli sibi vivit, cum vero quaerit bona aliorum, dicitur etiam illis vivere.

Quia ergo Apostolus proprium affectum deposuerat per crucem Christi, dicebat se mortuum proprio affectui, dicens **Christo confixus sum cruci**, id est, per crucem Christi remotus est a me proprius affectus sive privatus. Unde dicebat infra ult.: *mihi absit gloriari nisi in cruce Domini nostri*, etc., II Cor. V, 14 s.: *si unus pro omnibus mortuus est, ergo omnes mortui sunt. Et pro omnibus mortuus est Christus, ut et qui vivunt iam non sibi vivant, sed ei*, et cetera. Vivo autem, id est, **iam non vivo ego**, quasi in affectu habens proprium bonum, **sed vivit in me Christus**, id est tantum Christum habeo in affectu, et ipse Christus est vita mea. Phil. I, 21: *mihi vivere Christus est, et mori lucrum*.

108. Consequenter autem cum dicit **quod autem nunc vivo**, etc., respondet dubitationi quae poterat esse duplex ex praemisso verbo. Una est quomodo ipse vivit, et non est ille, scilicet qui vivit; secunda quomodo confixus est cruci. Et ideo haec duo aperit.

109. Et primo primum, quomodo scilicet vivit, et non ipse vivit, dicens **quod autem nunc vivo**, et cetera.

In one way, as in a Gloss, thus: every man according to carnal origin is born a child of wrath: *by nature we were children of wrath, even as the rest* (Eph 2:3). He is also born in the oldness of sin: *you are grown old in a strange country* (Bar 3:11). This oldness of sin is removed by the cross of Christ, and the newness of spiritual life is conferred.

Therefore the Apostle says, **with Christ I am nailed to the cross**, i.e., concupiscence or the inclination to sin, and all such have been put to death in me through the cross of Christ: *our old man is crucified with him, that the body of sin may be destroyed* (Rom 6:6). Also from the fact that I am crucified with Christ and have died to sin; and because Christ rose again, I, too, have risen with him rising: *who was delivered up for our sins, and rose again for our justification* (Rom 4:25). Thus, therefore, does Christ beget a new life in us, after the oldness of sin has been destroyed. Hence he says, **but I do not live**, i.e., because I am nailed to the cross of Christ, I have the strength to act well, **now** according to the flesh, because I no longer have the oldness which I formerly had, **but Christ lives in me**, i.e., the newness which has been given to us through Christ.

107. Or, in another way: a man is said to live according to that in which he chiefly puts his affection and in which he is mainly delighted. Hence men who take their greatest pleasure in study or in hunting say that this is their life. However, each man has his own private interest by which he seeks that which is his own. Therefore, when someone lives seeking only what is his own, he lives only unto himself; but when he seeks the good of others, he is said to live for them.

Accordingly, because the Apostle had set aside his love of self through the cross of Christ, he said that he was dead so far as love of self was concerned, declaring that **with Christ I am nailed to the cross**, i.e., through the cross of Christ my own private love has been removed from me. Hence he says **God forbid that I should glory save in the cross of our Lord Jesus Christ** (Gal 6:14): *if one died for all, then all were dead. And Christ died for all, that they also who live may not now live to themselves, but unto him who died for them* (2 Cor 5:14). And I live, **now I do not live**, i.e., I no longer live as though having any interest in my own good, **but Christ lives in me**, i.e., I have Christ alone in my affection and Christ himself is my life: *to me, to live is Christ; and to die is gain* (Phil 1:21).

108. Then when he says, **but that I live now in the flesh**, he answers a twofold difficulty that might arise from his words. One is how he lives and yet it is not he who lives; the second is how he is nailed to the cross. Therefore he clears up these two points.

109. First of all, the first one, namely, how he lives and yet it is not he who lives. He answers this when he says **but that I live now in the flesh: I live in the faith of the Son of God**.

Here it should be noted that, strictly speaking, those things are said to live which are moved by an inner principle. Now the soul of Paul was set between his body and God; the body, indeed, was vivified and moved by the soul of Paul, but his soul by Christ. Hence as to the life of the flesh, Paul himself lived and this is what he says, namely, **but that I live now in the flesh**, i.e., by the life of the flesh; but as to his relation to God, Christ lived in Paul. Therefore he says, **I live in the faith of the Son of God** through which he dwells in me and moves me: *but the just shall live in his faith* (Hab 2:4).

And note that he says **in the flesh**, not *by the flesh*, because this is evil.

110. Second, he shows that he is nailed to the cross, saying: because the love of Christ, which he showed to me in dying on the cross for me, brings it about that I am always nailed with him. And this is what he says, **who loved me**: *he first loved us* (I John 4:10). And he loved me to the extent that **he delivered himself** and not some other sacrifice *for me*: *he loved us and washed us from our sins in his own blood* (Rev 1:5); *as Christ loved the Church and delivered himself up for it* (Eph 5:25).

But it should be noted that the Son delivered himself, and the Father delivered his Son: *he spared not even his own Son, but delivered him up for us* (Rom 8:32). Judas, too, delivered him up (Matt 26:48). It is all one event, but the intention is not the same, because the Father did so out of love, the Son out of obedience along with love, but Judas out of avarice and treachery.

111. Then when he says, **I do not cast away the grace of God**, he draws the principal conclusion. First, he draws the conclusion; second, he explains it.

He says, therefore: because I have received from God so great a grace that he delivered himself, and I live in the faith of the Son of God, **I do not cast away the grace of God**, i.e., I do not repudiate it or show myself ungrateful: *the grace of God in me has not been void, but I have labored more abundantly than all they* (1 Cor 15:10).

Hence another version has, **I am not ungrateful for the grace of God**. *Looking diligently lest any man be wanting to the grace of God* (Heb 12:15), i.e., by showing myself unworthy because of ingratitude.

112. A form of repudiation and of ingratitude would exist, if I were to say that the law is necessary in order to be justified. Hence he says, **for if justice be by the law, then Christ died in vain**, i.e., if the law is sufficient, i.e., if the works of the law suffice to justify a man, Christ died to no purpose and in vain, because he died in order to make us just: *Christ also died once for our sins, the just for the unjust, that he might offer us to God* (1 Pet 3:18).

Now if this could have been done through the law, the death of Christ would have been superfluous. But he did not die in vain or labor to no purpose (Isa 49:4), because through him alone came justifying grace and truth

qui ante passionem Christi iusti fuerunt, hoc etiam fuit per fidem Christi venturi, in quem credebant, et in cuius fide salvabantur.

(John 1:17). Therefore, if any were just before the passion of Christ, this too was through the faith of Christ to come, in whom they believed and in whose faith they were saved.

Chapter 3

Lecture 1

3:1 O insensati Galatae, quis vos fascinavit non obedire veritati, ante quorum oculos Jesus Christus praescriptus est, in vobis crucifixus? [n. 113]

3:1 Ὦ ἀνόητοι Γαλάται, τίς ὑμᾶς ἐβάσκανεν, οἷς κατ' ὀφθαλμοὺς Ἰησοῦς Χριστὸς προεγράφη ἐσταυρωμένος;

3:1 O senseless Galatians, who has bewitched you that you should not obey the truth? before whose eyes has Jesus Christ been set forth, crucified among you? [n. 113]

113. Supra confutavit Apostolus vanitatem et mutabilitatem Galatarum per auctoritatem Evangelicae doctrinae, ostendens suam doctrinam authenticam fuisse ab aliis apostolis, hic vero per rationem et auctoritatem ostendit hoc idem, scilicet quod legalia non sunt servanda. Et hoc dupliciter.

Primo ex insufficientia legis;

secundo ex dignitate eorum qui ad Christum conversi sunt; et hoc IV cap., ibi *dico autem: quanto tempore*, et cetera.

Circa primum duo facit.

Primo praemittit obiurgationem;

secundo prosequitur suam probationem, ibi *hoc solum a vobis volo*, et cetera.

Circa primum duo facit:

primo obiurgat eos, ostendens eorum fatuitatem;

secundo rationem obiurgationis assignat, ibi *ante quorum oculos*, et cetera.

114. Primo ergo eos de fatuitate obiurgat, vocans eos insensatos. Unde dicit *o insensati*, et cetera. Insensatus autem proprie dicitur qui sensu caret. Sensus autem spiritualis est cognitio veritatis; qui ergo veritate caret, proprie insensatus dicitur. Matth. V: *et vos sine intellectu estis*. Sap. V, 4: *nos insensati vitam istorum*, et cetera.

Sed contra, Matth. V, 22 dicitur: *qui dixerit fratri suo: fatue*, etc.; sed fatuus idem est quod insensatus; ergo Apostolus reus est Gehennae ignis.

Sed dicendum est, ut Augustinus dicit, quod intelligendum est si dixerit sine causa, et animo vituperandi; sed Apostolus ex causa dixit, et animo corrigendi. Unde dicitur in Glossa *hoc dolendo dicit*.

115. Secundo cum dicit *quis vos fascinavit*, etc., ostendit modum quo insensati erant effecti.

Ubi primo notandum est, quod insensatus fit aliquis multis modis. Vel quia non proponitur sibi aliqua veritas quam cognoscere possit; vel quia etsi proponatur sibi, tamen numquam eam acceptat; vel quia veritatem

113. Above, the Apostle reproved the Galatians for their vanity and fickleness on the authority of the Gospel teaching by showing that his doctrine was approved by the other apostles. Now through reason and authority he proves the same thing, namely, that the works of the law must not be observed. This he does in two ways.

First, from the insufficiency of the law;

second, from the dignity of those who have been converted to Christ, at *as long as the heir* (Gal 4:1).

Concerning the first he does two things.

First, he utters the rebuke;

second, he begins his proof, at *this only would I learn* (Gal 3:2).

As to the first, he does two things:

first, he rebukes them by showing that they are foolish;

second, he gives the reason for his rebuke, at *before whose eyes*.

114. First, therefore, he chides them for their folly, calling them senseless. Hence he says, *O senseless Galatians*. Now 'senseless' is properly said of one who lacks sense. But the spiritual sense is knowledge of the truth. Hence anyone who lacks the truth is appropriately called senseless: *are you also yet without understanding?* (Matt 15:16); *we fools esteemed their life madness* (Wis 5:4).

But against this, it is said: *whoever shall say to his brother, 'you fool', shall be in danger of hell-fire* (Matt 5:22). Now a fool is the same as one who is senseless. Therefore, the Apostle was in danger of hell-fire.

But it must be said, as Augustine suggests, that this applies if it is said without reason and with the intention to disparage. But the Apostle said it with reason and with an intention to correct. Hence a Gloss says: *he says this in sorrow*.

115. Second, when he says, *who has bewitched you*, he shows how they had become senseless.

Here it is to be noted, first of all, that someone becomes senseless in a number of ways: either because some truth he could know is not proposed to him; or because he departs from a truth that had been proposed and accepted, as when

propositam et acceptam deserit, a via veritatis recedens; et tales erant isti Galatae, qui veritatem fidei quam acceperant deserentes, veritatem propositam renuerunt. Supra I, 6: *miror quod sic tam cito*, et cetera. Et ideo istum gradum insensationis in eis reprehendit, dicens *quis vos fascinavit*, et cetera.

116. Ad sciendum autem quid sit fascinatio, sciendum est, quod secundum Glossam fascinatio proprie dicitur ludificatio sensus, quae per artes magicas fieri consuevit; puta cum hominem facit aspectibus aliorum apparere leonem vel cornutum, et huiusmodi. Et hoc etiam per Daemones potest fieri, qui habent potestatem movendi phantasmata, et reducendi ad principia sensuum, ipsos sensus immutando.

Et secundum hanc acceptionem satis proprie dicit Apostolus *quis vos fascinavit?* Quasi dicat: vos estis sicut homo ludificatus, qui res manifestas aliter accipit, quam sint in rei veritate: quia scilicet vos estis ludificati per deceptiones et sophismata, *veritati non obedire*, id est, veritatem manifestam, et a vobis receptam non videtis, nec obediendo recipitis. Sap. IV, 12: *fascinatio nugacitatis obscurat bona*. Is. V, 20: *vae qui dicunt bonum malum*, et cetera.

117. Alio modo accipitur fascinatio secundum quod aliquis ex aspectu malevolo laeditur, et hoc maxime in vetulis quae visu urenti et aspectu invido fascinant pueros, qui ex hoc infirmantur et vomunt cibum.

Huius causam volens assignare Avicenna in libro suo *de Anima* dicit, quod materia corporalis obedit substantiae intellectuali, magis quam qualitatibus activis et passivis in natura. Et ideo ponit quod ad apprehensionem substantiarum intellectualium (quas vocat animas seu motores orbium) multa fiunt praeter ordinem motus caeli et omnium corporalium agentium. Eodem modo dicit, quod quando anima sancta depurata est ab affectibus terrenorum, et a carnalibus vitiis, accedit ad similitudinem substantiarum dictarum, et obedit ei natura. Et hinc est quod aliqui sancti viri operantur quaedam mira praeter naturae cursum; et similiter quia anima alicuius foedata passionibus carnalibus, habet fortem apprehensionem in malitia, obedit ei natura ad transmutationem materiae, in illis maxime in quibus materia habilis est: sicut in pueris teneris contingit. Et sic contingit, secundum eum, quod ex forti apprehensione vetularum, in malitiam immutatur puer et fascinatur.

Haec autem positio satis videtur vera secundum opinionem Avicennae. Nam ipse posuit formas omnes corporales in istis inferioribus influi a substantiis incorporalibus separatis, et quod agentia naturalia non habent se ad hoc nisi ut disponentia tantum.

he abandons the way of truth. Such were these Galatians who rejected the truth proposed to them and abandoned the truth of the faith they had accepted: ***I wonder that you are so soon removed from him that called you into the grace of Christ, unto another gospel*** (Gal 1:6). This, therefore, is the type of senselessness for which he chides them when he says: ***who has bewitched you that you should not obey the truth?***

116. To understand what bewitchment is, it should be noted that according to a Gloss, bewitchment is, properly speaking, a sense delusion usually produced by magical arts; for example, to make a man appear to onlookers as a lion or as having horns. This can also be brought about by demons who have the power to set phantasms in motion as well as to produce in the senses the very alterations that real objects are wont to produce.

According to this acceptation the Apostle asks, appropriately enough, ***who has bewitched you?*** As if to say: you are as deluded men who take obvious things to be other than they are in very fact, namely, because you are deluded by artifices and sophisms, ***not to obey the truth***, i.e., you neither see the obvious truth received by you nor embrace it by obeying it: *for the bewitching of vanity obscures good things* (Wis 4:12); *woe to you that call evil good, and good evil* (Isa 5:20).

117. In another way bewitchment is taken to mean that someone is harmed by an evil look, particularly when cast by sorcerers whose inflamed eyes and hostile glance cast a spell on boys who grow faint from it and vomit their food.

Avicenna, attempting to explain this phenomenon in his book *On the Soul*, says that corporeal matter obeys an intellectual substance more than it obeys the active and passive qualities at work in nature. Accordingly, he supposes that through the mental activity of intellectual substance (which he calls the souls or movers of the heavenly spheres) many things occur outside the order of heavenly movements and of all corporeal forces. Along the same lines he says that when a holy soul is purged of all earthly affection and carnal vice, it acquires a likeness to the aforesaid substances, so that nature obeys it. This is why certain holy men achieve marvels that transcend the course of nature. In like manner, because the soul of someone defiled by carnal passions has a vigorous apprehension of malice, nature obeys it to the point of affecting matter, particularly in those in whom the matter is pliant, as in the case of tender children. Thus does it happen, according to him, that from the vigorous apprehension exercised by sorcerers, a child can be evilly affected and bewitched.

This position seems to be true enough according to Avicenna's tenets. For he postulates that all material forms in sublunar bodies are influenced by the separated incorporeal substances and that natural agents can be no more than dispositive causes in such matter.

Sed hoc quidem improbatur a Philosopho. Agens enim oportet esse simile subiecto. Non fit autem forma tantum, nec materia, sed compositum ex materia et forma. Id ergo quod agit ad esse corporalium, oportet quod habeat materiam et formam. Unde dicit quod transmutare materiam et formam non potest, nisi id quod habet materiam et formam, et hoc quidem vel virtute, sicut Deus, qui actor est formae et materiae: vel actu, sicut agens corporeum. Et ideo materia corporalis quantum ad huiusmodi formas, nec angelis, nec alicui purae creaturae obedit ad nutum, sed soli Deo, ut Augustinus dicit. Unde non est verum quod Avicenna dicit de huiusmodi fascinatione.

Et ideo dicendum, quod ad imaginationem seu apprehensionem hominis, quando fortis est, immutatur sensus, seu appetitus sensitivus: quae quidem immutatio non est sine alteratione corporis et spirituum corporis, sicut nos videmus quod ad apprehensionem delectabilis movetur appetitus sensitivus ad concupiscentiam, et exinde corpus calefit. Similiter ex apprehensione timendi, frigescit.

Immutatio autem spirituum maxime inficit oculos, qui infecti rem per aspectum inficiunt, sicut patet in speculo mundo, quod ex aspectu menstruatae inficitur. Sic ergo quia vetulae obstinatae in malitia et durae sunt, ex forti apprehensione immutatur appetitus sensitivus, et ex hoc, sicut dictum est, infectio maxime fit a venis ad oculos, et ex oculis ad rem perspectam. Unde quia caro pueri mollis est, ad earum invidum aspectum inficitur et fascinatur. Et quandoque quidem ad hunc effectum Daemones operantur.

Dicit ergo *quis vos fascinavit veritati non obedire?* Quasi dicat: vos aliquando obedistis veritati fidei, sed modo non; ergo estis sicut pueri, qui ex aliquo invido aspectu infecti, cibum receptum vomitis.

118. Rationem autem obiurgationis assignat, dicens *ante quorum oculos*, et cetera. Quod potest tripliciter legi.

Uno modo, secundum Hieronymum, ut respondeat primae acceptioni fascinationis; quasi dicat: dico vos fascinatos, quia *ante quorum oculos*, etc., id est proscriptio Christi, qui damnatus est in mortem, adeo vobis manifesta fuit, ac si ante oculos vestros fuisset, *et in vobis crucifixus*, id est, in intellectibus vestris erat crucifixio Iesu Christi, ita ut sciretis qualiter facta esset; unde si eam non videtis modo, nec obeditis, hoc contingit, quia

However, this is disproved by the Philosopher. For an agent should be similar to what is subject to it. Now what comes into existence is not a form alone or matter alone but the composite of matter and form. Consequently, that which acts to produce the existence of corporeal things ought to have matter and form. Therefore he says that the only thing which can cause changes of matter and form is something that itself has matter and form either virtually, as God, who is the maker of form and matter, or actually, as a bodily agent. Therefore with respect to forms of this kind, corporeal matter obeys the nod neither of angels nor of any mere creature but of God alone, as Augustine says. Hence what Avicenna says about this matter of bewitchment is not true.

Therefore it is better to say that when a man's act of imagining or apprehending is strong, the sense is affected or at least the sense appetite is now such as affection does not occur without some alteration taking place in the body and the bodily spirits; as, for example, we see that when something pleasant is apprehended, the sense appetite is moved to desire and as a result the body becomes warm. Similarly, as a result of apprehending something horrible, the body grows cold.

When the spirits are thus moved they mainly infect the eyes, which in turn infect certain things through their glance, as is plain in the case of a clean mirror that becomes defiled when looked into by a woman in her monthly purification. Therefore because sorcerers are obstinate and hardened in evil, their sense appetite is affected by the vigor of their apprehension; as a result, as has been said, the infection moves from the veins to the eyes and thence to the object upon which they look. Accordingly, because the flesh of children is soft, it is influenced and charmed by their hostile glance. And demons, too, can sometimes produce this effect.

He says, therefore, *who has bewitched you that you should not obey the truth?* As if to say: you once obeyed the truth of the faith, but now you do not. Therefore, you are as children infected by some hostile glance who vomit the food they have eaten.

118. Then he tells why he rebukes them, when he says, *before whose eyes Jesus Christ has been set forth, crucified among you*. This can be interpreted in three ways.

One way, which is according to Jerome, corresponds to the first meaning of bewitchment; as if he says: I say that you are bewitched, because *before your eyes Jesus Christ has been set forth*, i.e., the outlawing of Christ, who was condemned to death, is as vivid to your eyes as if it were being enacted before your eyes and he was being *crucified among you*, i.e., the crucifixion of Christ was as clear in your understanding as though it were taking place there.

estis ludificati et fascinati. Contra quod dicitur Cant. ult.: *pone me ut signaculum super cor tuum*, et cetera.

119. Alio modo secundum Augustinum; quasi dicat: recte fascinati estis, quia veritatem quam recepistis, scilicet Christum, per fidem, in cordibus vestris evomitis sicut pueri. Et hoc quia **ante oculos vestros**, id est, in vestra praesentia, **Iesus Christus proscriptus est**, id est, expellitur et eiicitur de haereditate sua, quod molestum deberet esse vobis; quia quem non deberetis pati quod ab aliis proscriberetur, et expelleretur, in vobis proscriptus est, id est, haereditatem suam amisit in vobis, id est, vosipsos.

Et tunc hoc quod sequitur, scilicet **crucifixus**, legi debet *cum pondere et ostensione doloris*, quia hoc addidit, ut considerarent quo pretio Christus emerit possessionem, quam in eis amittebat, et ex hoc moverentur magis. Quasi dicat: Christus proscriptus est in vobis, scilicet qui crucifixus, id est, qui cruce sua et sanguine proprio acquisivit hanc haereditatem. I Cor. VI, 20: *empti enim estis pretio magno*, et cetera. I Petr. I, 18: *non corruptibilibus auro vel argento*, et cetera.

120. Tertio modo secundum Ambrosium, quasi dicat: vere fascinati estis, **ante quorum oculos**, id est, in quorum reputatione, scilicet secundum iudicium vestrum, **Iesus Christus proscriptus est**, id est, damnatus, non alios salvans. **Et in vobis**, id est, secundum quod vos intelligitis, **crucifixus** est, id est, mortuus tantum, non autem alios iustificans, cum tamen de eo dicatur, II Cor. c. ult., quod *si mortuus est ex infirmitate nostra, vivit tamen ex virtute Dei*.

121. Potest, et quarto modo, exponi secundum Glossam, ut per hoc designet Apostolus gravitatem culpae eorum, quia in hoc quod Christum deserunt legem observantes, aequaliter quodammodo peccabant Pilato, qui Christum proscripsit, id est, damnavit. Ut dum insufficientem Christum credunt ad salvandum, similes in peccando crucifixoribus Christi sint, qui ipsum in ligno suspenderunt, morte turpissima condemnantes et afficientes. Aequalitas tamen est accipienda ex parte eius, in quem peccatur, quia in Christum Galatae peccabant, sicut Pilatus et crucifixores Christi.

Hence, if you no longer see it, it is because you have been deluded and bewitched. Against such a change of heart, it is said: *put me as a seal upon your heart, as a seal upon your arm* (Song 8:6).

119. Another way, which is according to Augustine, is as if he said: you are justifiably bewitched, because as children, you vomit out the truth you have received, namely, Christ by faith in your hearts. And you do this because **before your eyes**, i.e., in your presence, **Jesus Christ has been set forth**, i.e., expelled and refused his inheritance. This should trouble you, because the very one whom you should not allow to be outlawed and expelled by others has been outlawed among you, i.e., has lost his inheritance, namely, yourselves, among you.

Then that which follows, namely, **crucified**, should be read as *with a heavy burden and obvious pain*, because he adds this to make them consider the great price Christ paid for the inheritance he lost among them, and thus move them more deeply. As if to say: Christ has been outlawed among you, he who was crucified, i.e., who with his cross and his own blood purchased this inheritance: *you are bought with a great price* (1 Cor 6:20); *knowing that you were not redeemed with corruptible things, as gold or silver . . . but with the precious blood of Christ* (1 Pet 1:18).

120. The third way, which is according to Ambrose, is as though he says: yes, you are bewitched, you, **before whose eyes**, i.e., in whose opinion, namely, according to your judgment, **Jesus Christ has been set forth**, i.e., condemned without saving others. **And among you**, i.e., so far as you understand, he was **crucified**, i.e., merely died, but justified no one in spite of the fact that it is said of him, *although he was crucified through weakness, yet he lives by the power of God* (2 Cor 13:4).

121. It can be explained also in a fourth way according to a Gloss to the effect that by these words the Apostle proclaims the gravity of their guilt, because in deserting Christ by observing the law, they sin somewhat on a par with Pilate who set forth Christ, i.e., condemned him. For in believing that Christ does not suffice to save them, they are made to be sinners similar to Christ's executioners who hung him on the cross, condemning him to a most shameful death and killing him. The parity is taken on the side of the one against whom they sinned, because the Galatians sinned against Christ Jesus as did Pilate and those who crucified Christ.

Lecture 2

³:²Hoc solum a vobis volo discere: ex operibus legis Spiritum accepistis, an ex auditu fidei? [n. 122]

³:³sic stulti estis, ut cum Spiritu coeperitis, nunc carne consummemini? [n. 124]

³:⁴tanta passi estis sine causa? si tamen sine causa. [n. 125]

³:⁵Qui ergo tribuit vobis Spiritum, et operatur virtutes in vobis: ex operibus legis, an ex auditu fidei? [n. 126]

³:²τοῦτο μόνον θέλω μαθεῖν ἀφ' ὑμῶν, ἐξ ἔργων νόμου τὸ πνεῦμα ἐλάβετε ἢ ἐξ ἀκοῆς πίστεως;

³:³οὕτως ἀνόητοί ἐστε; ἐναρξάμενοι πνεύματι νῦν σαρκὶ ἐπιτελεῖσθε;

³:⁴τοσαῦτα ἐπάθετε εἰκῇ; εἴ γε καὶ εἰκῇ.

³:⁵ὁ οὖν ἐπιχορηγῶν ὑμῖν τὸ πνεῦμα καὶ ἐνεργῶν δυνάμεις ἐν ὑμῖν ἐξ ἔργων νόμου ἢ ἐξ ἀκοῆς πίστεως;

³:²This only would I learn of you: did you receive the Spirit by the works of the law or by the hearing of faith? [n. 122]

³:³Are you so foolish that, whereas you began in the Spirit, you would now be made perfect by the flesh? [n. 124]

³:⁴Have you suffered such great things in vain? If it be yet in vain. [n. 125]

³:⁵He therefore who gives to you the Spirit and works miracles among you: does he do it by the works of the law or by the hearing of the faith? [n. 126]

---

122. Posita obiurgatione, consequenter Apostolus procedit ad insufficientiam legis et virtutem fidei ostendendam. Et

primo ostendit insufficientiam legis;

secundo movet quaestionem et solvit, ibi *quid igitur lex*, et cetera.

Et circa primum duo facit.

Primo probat defectum legis et insufficientiam per ea quae ipsi experti sunt;

secundo per auctoritates et rationes, ibi *sicut scriptum est*.

Circa primum duo facit, quia

primo probat propositum, experimento sumpto ex parte ipsorum;

secundo probat idem, experimento sumpto ex parte ipsius apostoli, ibi *qui ergo tribuit vobis*, et cetera.

Circa primum duo facit.

Primo ostendit donum quod receperunt;

secundo defectum in quem inciderunt, ibi *sic stulti estis*, et cetera.

123. Donum autem quod receperunt ostendit, quaerendo ab eis unde illud receperunt. Unde susceptum donum supponens, interrogans, quaerit ab eis, dicens: quamvis fascinati et stulti sitis, tamen non tantum estis ludificati quin unum quod valde manifestum est, me docere possitis. Et ideo *solum hoc volo a vobis discere*, quia hoc solum sufficit ad probandum quod intendo: hoc, inquam, est, quia constat, quod Spiritum Sanctum accepistis; quaero ergo an accepistis illum *ex operibus legis, an ex auditu fidei?*

Ad quod sciendum est, quod in primitiva Ecclesia, ex divina dispositione, ut fides Christi promoveretur et cresceret, statim post praedicationem fidei ab apostolis

122. Having given his rebuke, the Apostle goes on to show the insufficiency of the law, and the power of the faith.

First, he proves the insufficiency of the law;

second, he raises a question and answers it, at *why then was the law?* (Gal 3:19).

Concerning the first, he does two things.

First, he proves the deficiency and insufficiency of the law by appealing to what they experienced;

second, by authority and reasons, at *as it is written* (Gal 3:6).

As to the first, he does two things:

first, he proves his proposition by appealing to something they experienced;

second, by using something he himself experienced, at *he therefore who gives to you*.

With respect to the first, he does two things.

First, he discusses the gift they have received;

second, the defect into which they have fallen, at *are you so foolish*.

123. He discusses the gift they received by asking them from whom they received it. Hence, presupposing that they accepted the gift, he interrogates them and asks: although you have been bewitched and are foolish, nevertheless you are not so deluded that you cannot explain to me something very obvious. Hence he says, *this only would I learn of you*, because this by itself is enough to prove my point; namely, it is evident that you have received the Holy Spirit. I ask, therefore, *did you receive the Spirit by the works of the law or by the hearing of faith?*

To elucidate this, it should be noted that in the early Church, by God's providence, in order that the faith of Christ might prosper and grow, manifest signs of the Holy

manifesta signa Spiritus Sancti fiebant super audientes. Unde de Petro dicitur Act. X, 44: *adhuc loquente Petro verba haec, cecidit Spiritus Sanctus*, et cetera. Ipsi etiam Galatae ad praedicationem Pauli manifeste Spiritum Sanctum acceperant.

Quaerit ergo Apostolus ab eis, unde habuerunt Spiritum Sanctum. Constat autem quod non per opera legis, quia cum essent gentiles, ante receptionem Spiritus Sancti legem non habebant; ergo habuerunt Spiritum Sanctum, id est, dona Spiritus Sancti ex auditu fidei. Rom. VIII, 15: *non accepistis spiritum servitutis iterum in timore*, qui scilicet dabatur in lege (unde et cum tremore lex data est), *sed accepistis Spiritum filiorum*, qui datur per fidem, quae est *ex auditu*, ut dicitur Rom. X, 17.

Si ergo hoc potuit fidei virtus, frustra quaeritur aliud per quod salvemur, quia multo difficilius est de iniusto facere iustum, quam iustum in iustitia conservare. Si ergo fides de iniustis Galatis sine lege iustos fecerat, non est dubium, quod sine lege poterat eos in iustitia conservare. Magnum ergo erat donum, quod per fidem acceperant.

124. Consequenter cum dicit **sic stulti estis**, etc., ostendit defectum in quem prolapsi sunt. Et exaggerat duplicem defectum in eis apostolus, scilicet quantum ad dona quae a Christo acceperant, et quantum ad mala quae pro ipso pertulerunt, ibi **tanta passi estis**, et cetera.

Circa primum sciendum est quod isti Galatae deserentes quod magnum erat, scilicet Spiritum Sanctum, adhaeserunt minori, scilicet carnali observantiae legis, et hoc stultum est. Et ideo dicit **sic stulti estis**, adeo **ut cum coeperitis** instinctu **Sancti Spiritus**, id est, initium perfectionis vestrae habueritis a Spiritu Sancto, **nunc**, dum perfectiores estis, **consummamini carne**, id est, quaeratis conservari per carnales observantias legis, a qua nec initium iustitiae potest haberi? Io. VI, v. 64: *caro non prodest quicquam*, et cetera. Et sic ordinem pervertitis, quia via perfectionis est ab imperfecto tendere ad perfectum. Vos autem, quia e converso facitis, stulti estis. Eccli. XXVII, 12: *homo sanctus permanet in sapientia sicut sol, stultus ut luna mutatur*.

Similes isti sunt his, qui incipiunt servire Deo cum fervore spiritus, postmodum deficiunt in carne; qui etiam assimilantur statuae Nabuchodonosor, cuius caput aureum, et pedes lutei, Dan. II, 32. Et ideo dicitur Rom. c. VIII, 8: *qui in carne sunt, Deo placere non possunt*. Et infra VI, 8: **qui seminat in carne, de carne metet corruptionem**.

125. Consequenter cum dicit **tanta passi estis**, etc., exaggerat eorum defectum quantum ad mala quae pro Christo pertulerunt.

Spirit took place in the hearers immediately after the apostles preached the faith. Accordingly, it is said of Peter: *while Peter was yet speaking these words, the Holy Spirit fell on all them that heard the word* (Acts 10:44). The Galatians, too, openly received the Holy Spirit at Paul's preaching.

The Apostle therefore asks them: whence did they obtain the Holy Spirit? For it is obvious that it was not through the works of the law, because, since they were gentiles, they did not have the law before they received the Holy Spirit. Therefore they had the Holy Spirit, i.e., the gifts of the Holy Spirit, by the hearing of faith: *for you have not received the spirit of bondage again in fear*, which was given in the law (for the law was given amid tremors), *but you have received the Spirit of adoption of sons* (Rom 8:15), which is given through faith, which *comes by hearing* (Rom 10:17).

Therefore, if the power of the faith could do this, it is vain to seek something else by which we are saved, because it is more difficult to make the unjust just than to preserve the just in their justice. Hence if the faith had made the unjust Galatians just without the law, no doubt it could without the law keep them just. Great, therefore, was the gift they had received through faith.

124. Then when he says, **are you so foolish**, he shows the defect into which they have fallen. And he amplifies a twofold defect, touching, namely, the gifts they had received from Christ and the evils they endured for him: **have you suffered such great things in vain?**

Concerning the first, it should be noted that the Galatians, after they left what was great, namely, the Holy Spirit, adhered to something less, namely, the carnal observances of the law, and this is foolish. Hence he says, **are you so foolish that, whereas you began in** the inspiration of the **Holy Spirit**, i.e., obtained the beginning of your perfection from the Holy Spirit, **you would now**, while you are more perfect, **be made perfect by the flesh**, i.e., do you seek to be preserved by the carnal observances of the law from which you could acquire not even the beginning of justice? *The flesh profits nothing* (John 6:64). Thus do you pervert right order, because the path of perfection consists in going from the imperfect to the perfect. But you, because you are doing the opposite, are foolish: *a holy man continues in wisdom as the sun; but a fool is changed as the moon* (Sir 27:12).

They are as those who begin to serve God with fervor of spirit but afterwards desert to the flesh. Again, they are as Nabuchodonosor's statute with head of gold and feet of clay (Dan 11:32). Hence it is said: *they who are in the flesh cannot please God* (Rom 8:8); **he who sows in his flesh, of the flesh also shall reap corruption** (Gal 6:8).

125. Then when he says, **have you suffered such great things**, he amplifies their desertion by considering the evils they endured for Christ.

Qui enim aliquid sine labore recipiunt, illud minus chare custodiunt; sed illud quod cum labore acquiritur vilipendere et non custodire stultum est. Isti autem cum labore et tribulatione magna, quam passi sunt a contribulibus suis propter fidem, receperunt Spiritum Sanctum. Et ideo dicit *tanta passi estis sine causa*, quasi dicat: non contemnatis tantum donum quod cum labore accepistis, alias illa, *sine causa*, id est sine utilitate, *passi estis*, quia haec sustinuistis ut perveniretis ad vitam aeternam. Rom. V, 3: *tribulatio patientiam operatur, patientia autem probationem, probatio vero spem*, et cetera. Unde si praecluditis vobis aditum vitae aeternae, deserentes fidem, quaerentes conservari carnalibus observantiis, *sine causa*, id est inutiliter, *passi estis*.

Et hoc dico, *si tamen sine causa*. Quod ideo dicit, quia in eorum potestate erat poenitere si vellent, quamdiu viverent. Ex hoc autem habetur, quod opera mortificata reviviscunt. Sap. III, 11: *labores eorum sine fructu*, et cetera. Gal. IV, 11: *timeo autem ne sine causa laboraverim*, et cetera. Si vero accipiatur de malis qui non poenitent, potest dici quod patiuntur sine causa conferente, scilicet vitam aeternam.

126. Consequenter cum dicit *qui ergo tribuit vobis*, etc., probat propositum, experimento sumpto ex parte apostoli.

Possent enim dicere quod verum est nos recepisse Spiritum Sanctum ex auditu fidei, tamen propter devotionem quam ad legem habuimus, accepimus fidem quam praedicabas. Et ideo dicit: non curo quicquid sit ex parte vestra, tamen illud quod ego feci, tribuens vobis ministerio meo Spiritum Sanctum, qui *operatur in vobis virtutes*, id est inter vos miracula, sed numquid facio hoc sic, *ex operibus legis, an ex operibus fidei?* Non utique ex operibus legis, sed ex fide.

127. Sed numquid aliquis potest dare Spiritum Sanctum? Augustinus enim, XV *de Trinitate*, dicit, quod nullus homo purus Spiritum Sanctum dare potest, nec ipsi apostoli dabant, sed imponebant manus super homines, et accipiebant Spiritum Sanctum. Quid ergo est quod hic dicit Apostolus de se loquens *qui tribuit vobis Spiritum Sanctum*?

Respondeo. Dicendum est quod in datione Spiritus Sancti tria per ordinem se habentia occurrunt, scilicet Spiritus Sanctus inhabitans, donum gratiae et caritatis cum caeteris habitibus, et sacramentum novae legis, cuius ministerio datur. Et sic potest ab aliquibus tripliciter dari.

Ab aliquo enim datur sicut auctoritatem habente quantum ad tria praedicta, scilicet respectu Spiritus Sancti inhabitantis, respectu doni, et respectu sacramenti; et hoc modo Spiritus Sanctus datur a solo Patre

For anyone who receives something without labor does not guard it as something precious; but that which is obtained by great effort, it is foolish to esteem lightly and not guard it. Now it was with labor and tribulation suffered at the hands of their fellow citizens that they had received the Holy Spirit. That is why he says, **have you suffered such great things in vain?** As if to say: you ought not to despise so great a gift received with labor; else **you have suffered in vain**, i.e., to no purpose, because you endured these things in order to attain to eternal life: *tribulation works patience, and patience trial, and trial hope; and hope does not confound* (Rom 5:3). Hence, if you shut yourselves out from the door to eternal life by deserting the faith and seeking to be preserved by carnal observances, it is **in vain**, i.e., uselessly, that **you have suffered**.

And I say, **if it be yet in vain**. He says this because it was still in their power to repent, if they willed, as long as they were alive. This shows that certain deadened works are revived: *their labors are without fruit, and their works unprofitable* (Wis 3:11); *I am afraid lest perhaps I have labored in vain among you* (Gal 4:11). If this is applied to evil men who do not repent, it can be said that they suffered without cause, i.e., a cause that can confer eternal life.

126. Then when he says, **he therefore who gives to you the Spirit**, he proves his proposition by appealing to his own experience.

For they might say that although it is true that we received the Holy Spirit by the hearing of faith, nevertheless it was because of the devotion he had to the law that we received the faith he preached. Hence he says: but even considering the matter not from your side but from what I have done in giving you through my ministration the Holy Spirit who **works miracles among you**, do I do this **by the works of the law or by the hearing of the faith?** In truth, not by the works of the law, but by faith.

127. But can anyone give the Holy Spirit? For Augustine in *On The Trinity* XV says that no mere man can give the Holy Spirit, for the apostles did not give the Holy Spirit but imposed hands on men, who then received the Holy Spirit. What then does the Apostle mean when he says of himself: **who gives to you the Holy Spirit**?

I answer that in the giving of the Holy Spirit three things conspire in a certain order, namely, the indwelling Holy Spirit, the gift of grace and charity along with the other habits, and the sacrament of the new law by whose administering he is given. Hence he can be given by someone in three ways.

For he can be given by someone as having authority with respect to all three, namely, in respect to the Holy Spirit's indwelling, in respect to the gift, and in respect to the sacrament. And in this way the Holy Spirit is given by

et Filio secundum quod eius auctoritatem habent, non quidem dominii sed originis, quia ab utroque procedit.

Sed quantum ad gratiam seu donum, et quantum ad sacramenta Spiritus Sanctus dat etiam se, secundum quod datio importat causalitatem Spiritus Sancti respectu donorum ipsius; quia, ut dicit Apostolus I Cor. XII, v. 11, *ipse dividit singulis prout vult*. Secundum autem quod in datione importatur auctoritas, non potest proprie dici Spiritum Sanctum seipsum dare.

Quantum vero ad sacramentum quod ministerio ministrorum Ecclesiae datur, potest dici quod sancti per ministerium sacramentorum dant Spiritum Sanctum.

Et hoc modo hic loquitur Apostolus secundum quod tangitur in Glossa, tamen huiusmodi modus non est consuetus neque extendendus.

128. Dicit etiam Glossa quod facere miracula attribuitur fidei, quia ex hoc quod credit quae supra naturam sunt, supra naturam operatur, et quia apostoli praedicabant fidem, quae quaedam rationem excedentia continebat, ideo oportebat ad eorum credulitatem aliqua testimonia adducere quod missi essent a Deo: quod rationem excedit. Unde Christus dedit eis signum suum ad hoc ostendendum.

Est autem duplex signum Christi. Unum est quod est Dominus omnium; unde dicitur in Ps. CXLIV, 13: *regnum tuum, regnum omnium saeculorum*, et cetera. Aliud est quod est Iustificator et Salvator, secundum illud Act. IV, v. 12: *non est aliud nomen sub caelo datum hominibus*, et cetera. Dedit ergo eis duo signa: unum est quod facerent miracula, per quod ostenderent quod missi sunt a Deo Domino creaturae omnis. Lc. X: *dedit eis potestatem et virtutem super omnia daemonia*, et cetera. Aliud quod darent Spiritum Sanctum ministerio, per quod ostenderent, quod missi sunt ab omnium Salvatore. Act. VIII, 17: *tunc imponebant manus super eos*, etc., et tunc *cum imposuisset illis manus Paulus, Spiritus Sanctus venit super illos*, et cetera. Et de his duobus modis dicitur Hebr. II, 4: *contestante Deo signis, et portentis, et variis virtutibus, et Spiritus Sancti distributionibus, secundum suam voluntatem*.

the Father and Son alone, inasmuch as they have the authority not of dominion but of origin, because he proceeds from both.

But as to the grace or gift and as to the sacraments, the Holy Spirit even gives himself in the sense that the giving implies the causality of the Holy Spirit with respect to his gifts, because, as the Apostle says: *he divides to everyone according as he wills* (1 Cor 12:11). But as far as the author of the giving is concerned, it is not appropriate to say that the Holy Spirit gives himself.

But concerning the sacrament which is given by the ministry of the Church's ministers, it can be said that holy men by administering the sacraments give the Holy Spirit.

And this is the way the Apostle had in mind: the way mentioned in a Gloss. Nevertheless, this is not the usual way of putting it, and it ought not be exaggerated.

128. Again, a Gloss says that the performing of miracles is attributed to faith, which, because it believes in things that are above nature, operates above nature. Hence because the apostles preached the faith which contained things above reason, they should have adduced in support of their credibility some testimony that they had been sent by God: a fact which surpasses reason. Hence Christ gave them his own sign to prove this.

Now there is a twofold sign of Christ. One is that he is the Lord of all; hence it is said: *your kingdom is a kingdom of all ages: and your dominion endures throughout all generations* (Ps 144:13). The other is that he is Sanctifier and Savior: *there is no other name under heaven given to men, whereby we must be saved* (Acts 4:12). Accordingly, he gave them two signs: one was the power to perform miracles, so that they could show they were sent by God, the Lord of all creatures: *he gave them power and authority over all devils and to cure diseases* (Luke 9:1). The other was that by their ministry they might give the Holy Spirit, in order to show that they had been sent by the Savior of all: *they laid their hands upon them, and they received the Holy Spirit* (Acts 8:17). Of these two ways it is said: *God also bearing them witness by signs and wonders and diverse miracles and distributions of the Holy Spirit, according to his own will* (Heb 2:4).

Lecture 3

3:6 Sicut scriptum est: Abraham credidit Deo, et reputatum est illi ad justitiam: [n. 129]

3:7 cognoscite ergo quia qui ex fide sunt, ii sunt filii Abrahae. [n. 131]

3:8 Providens autem Scriptura quia ex fide justificat gentes Deus, praenuntiavit Abrahae: quia *benedicentur in te omnes gentes*. [n. 132]

3:9 Igitur qui ex fide sunt, benedicentur cum fideli Abraham. [n. 133]

3:6 καθὼς Ἀβραὰμ ἐπίστευσεν τῷ θεῷ, καὶ ἐλογίσθη αὐτῷ εἰς δικαιοσύνην.

3:7 Γινώσκετε ἄρα ὅτι οἱ ἐκ πίστεως, οὗτοι υἱοί εἰσιν Ἀβραάμ.

3:8 προϊδοῦσα δὲ ἡ γραφὴ ὅτι ἐκ πίστεως δικαιοῖ τὰ ἔθνη ὁ θεὸς προευηγγελίσατο τῷ Ἀβραὰμ ὅτι Ἐνευλογηθήσονται ἐν σοὶ πάντα τὰ ἔθνη.

3:9 ὥστε οἱ ἐκ πίστεως εὐλογοῦνται σὺν τῷ πιστῷ Ἀβραάμ.

3:6 As it is written: Abraham believed God: and it was reputed to him unto justice. [n. 129]

3:7 Know, therefore, that they who are of faith are the children of Abraham. [n. 131]

3:8 And the Scripture, foreseeing that God justifies the gentiles by faith, told unto Abraham before: *in you shall all nations be blessed*. [n. 132]

3:9 Therefore, they who are of faith shall be blessed with faithful Abraham. [n. 133]

---

129. Supra probavit Apostolus experimento virtutem fidei et insufficientiam legis, hic vero probat idem per auctoritates et rationes. Et

primo probat virtutem fidei in iustificando;

secundo in hoc ostendit legis defectum, ibi **quicumque enim ex operibus legis**, et cetera.

Primum autem probat utens quodam syllogismo. Unde circa hoc tria facit.

Primo ostendit minorem;

secundo maiorem, ibi **providens autem Scriptura**, etc.;

tertio infert conclusionem, ibi **igitur qui ex fide**, et cetera.

Circa primum duo facit.

Primo proponit quamdam auctoritatem, ex qua elicit minorem;

secundo concludit eam, ibi **cognoscite ergo**, et cetera.

130. Dicit ergo: vere iustitia et Spiritus Sanctus est ex fide, **sicut scriptum est**, Gen. XV, 6, et introducitur Rom. IV, 3, quod *credidit Abraham Deo*, et cetera.

Ubi notandum est quod iustitia consistit in redditione debiti, homo autem debet aliquid Deo, et aliquid sibi, et aliquid proximo. Sed quod aliquid debeat sibi et proximo, hoc est propter Deum. Ergo summa iustitia est reddere Deo quod suum est. Nam si reddas tibi vel proximo quod debes, et hoc non facis propter Deum, magis es perversus quam iustus, cum ponas finem in homine. Dei autem est quidquid est in homine, et intellectus et voluntas et ipsum corpus; sed tamen quodam ordine, quia inferiora ordinantur ad superiora, et exteriora ad interiora, scilicet ad bonum animae; supremum autem in homine est mens. Et ideo primum in iustitia hominis est, quod mens hominis Deo subdatur, et hoc fit per

129. Having proved by experience the power of the faith and the insufficiency of the law, the Apostle now proves the same things by authority and by reasons.

First, he proves the power of the faith to justify;

second, in this he proves the insufficiency of the law, at *for as many as are of the works of the law* (Gal 3:10).

The first he proves by using a syllogism. Hence with respect to this he does three things.

First, he proves the minor premise;

second, the major premise, at **and the Scripture, foreseeing**;

third, he draws the conclusion, at **therefore, that they who are of faith**.

Concerning the first, he does two things.

First, he proposes a certain authority from which he takes the minor;

second, he concludes the minor, at **know, therefore**.

130. He says therefore: truly, justice and the Holy Spirit come from faith, **as it is written** in Genesis and mentioned again in Romans: *Abraham believed God and it was reputed to him unto justice* (Gen 15:6, Rom 4:3).

Here it should be noted that justice consists in paying a debt. Now man is indebted to God and to himself and his neighbor. But it is on account of God that he owes something to himself and his neighbor. Therefore the highest form of justice is to render to God what is God's. For if you render to yourself or your neighbor what you owe and do not do this for the sake of God, you are more perverse than just, since you are putting your end in man. Now, whatever is in man is from God, namely, intellect and will and the body itself, albeit according to a certain order; because the lower is ordained to the higher, and external things to internal, namely, to the good of the soul. Furthermore, the highest thing in man is his mind. Therefore the

fidem. II Cor. X, 3: *in captivitatem redigentes omnem intellectum in obsequium Christi.*

Sic ergo dicendum est in omnibus, quod Deus est primum principium in iustitia, et qui Deo dat, scilicet summum quod in se est, mentem ei subdendo, perfecte est iustus. Rom. VIII, 14: *qui Spiritu Dei aguntur, hi filii sunt Dei.*

Et ideo dicit **credidit Abraham Deo**, id est, mentem suam Deo per fidem subdidit. Eccli. II, 6: *crede Deo, et recuperabit te*, etc., et infra *qui timetis Dominum, credite illi*, et cetera. **Et reputatum est ei ad iustitiam**, id est, ipsum credere et ipsa fides fuit ei et est omnibus aliis sufficiens causa iustitiae, et quod ad iustitiam reputetur ei exterius ab hominibus, sed interius datur a Deo, qui eos qui habent fidem, per caritatem operantem iustificat, eis peccata remittendo.

131. Ex hac autem auctoritate concludit minorem propositionem, dicens **cognoscite ergo**, etc., quasi dicat: ex hoc aliquis dicitur filius alicuius, quod imitatur opera eius; *si ergo vos estis filii Abrahae, opera Abrahae facite*, Io. VIII, 39. Abraham autem non quaesivit iustificari per circumcisionem, sed per fidem; ergo et illi qui quaerunt iustificari per fidem, sunt filii Abrahae.

Et hoc est quod dicit: quia Abraham iustus est ex fide, per hoc quod Deo **credidit, et reputatum est ei ad iustitiam, ergo cognoscite**, quod illi **qui ex fide sunt**, id est, qui ex fide credunt se iustificari et salvari, **hi sunt filii Abrahae**, scilicet imitatione et instructione. Rom. IX, 8: *qui filii sunt promissionis aestimantur in semine*, et cetera. Lc. c. XIX, 9 dicitur Zachaeo: *hodie huic domui salus a Deo facta est, eo quod et ipse sit filius Abrahae*, et cetera. Et Matth. III, 9: *potens est Deus de lapidibus istis*, id est, de gentibus, *suscitare filios Abrahae*, inquantum scilicet facit eos credentes.

132. Consequenter cum dicit **providens autem Scriptura**, etc., ponit maiorem, quae scilicet est, quod Abrahae praenuntiatum est quod in semine suo benedicerentur omnes gentes.

Et hoc est quod dicit **providens autem Scriptura**, inducens Deum loquentem Abrahae dicit Gen. XII, 3, quod **Deus praenuntiavit Abrahae** quod **in te**, id est, in his qui ad similitudinem tuam filii tui erunt imitatione fidei, **benedicentur omnes gentes**. Matth. VIII, 11: *multi venient ab oriente et occidente*, et cetera.

133. Consequenter cum dicit **ergo qui ex fide**, etc., infert conclusionem ex praemissis.

Unde sic potest formari argumentum: Deus Pater nuntiavit Abrahae, quod in semine suo benedicerentur omnes gentes; sed illi qui quaerunt iustificari per fidem, sunt filii Abrahae; **ergo qui ex fide sunt**, id est, qui

first element of justice in a man is that a man's mind be subjected to God, and this is done by faith: *bringing into captivity every understanding unto the obedience of Christ* (2 Cor 10:5).

Therefore in all things it must be said that God is the first principle in justice and that whoever gives to God, namely, the greatest thing that lies in him by submitting the mind to him, such a one is fully just: *whoever are led by the Spirit of God, they are the sons of God* (Rom 8:14).

And hence he says, **Abraham believed God**, i.e., submitted his mind to God by faith: *believe God, and he will recover you* (Sir 2:6); and further on: *you who fear the Lord, believe him* (Sir 2:8), **and it was reputed to him unto justice**, i.e., the act of faith and faith itself were for him, as for everyone else, the sufficient cause of justice. It is reputed to him unto justice by men exteriorly, but interiorly it is wrought by God, who justifies them that have the faith. This he does by remitting their sins through charity working in them.

131. From this authority he draws the minor proposition, saying **know, therefore, that they who are of faith are the children of Abraham**. As if to say: someone is called the son of another because he imitates his works; therefore, *if you be the children of Abraham, do the works of Abraham* (John 8:39). But Abraham did not seek to be justified through circumcision but through faith. Therefore the sons of Abraham are they who seek to be justified by faith.

And this is what he says: because Abraham is just through faith, in that he believed God and it was reputed to him unto justice; **therefore, know that they who are of faith**, i.e., who believe that they are justified and saved by faith, **are the children of Abraham**, namely, by imitation and instruction: *they that are the children of the promise are accounted for the seed* (Rom 9:8); *this day is salvation come to this house, because he also is the son of Abraham* (Luke 19:9); *God is able of these stones*, i.e., of the gentiles, *to raise up children to Abraham* (Matt 3:9), inasmuch as he makes them believers.

132. Then when he says, **the Scripture, foreseeing that God justifies the gentiles by faith**, he sets down the major premise, namely, that Abraham was told beforehand that in his seed all nations would be blessed.

Hence when he says, **the Scripture, foreseeing**, he introduces God speaking to Abraham (Gen 12:3). Therefore he says, God **told unto Abraham before** that **in you**, i.e., in those who in your likeness will be your sons by imitating your faith, **shall all nations be blessed**: *many will come from the east and from the west, and shall sit down with Abraham, and Isaac, and Jacob in the kingdom of heaven* (Matt 8:11).

133. Then when he says, **therefore, they who are of faith**, he draws the conclusion from the premises.

Accordingly, the argument can be formulated thus: God the Father announced to Abraham that in his seed all nations would be blessed. But those who seek to be justified by faith are the children of Abraham. **Therefore, they who**

quaerunt iustificari per fidem, ***benedicentur cum fideli***, id est credente, **Abraham**.

are of faith, i.e., who seek to be justified through faith, ***shall be blessed with faithful***, i.e., with believing, **Abraham**.

Lecture 4

3:10 Quicumque enim ex operibus legis sunt, sub maledicto sunt. Scriptum est enim: *maledictus omnis qui non permanserit in omnibus quae scripta sunt in libro legis ut faciat ea.* [n. 134]

3:11 Quoniam autem in lege nemo justificatur apud Deum, manifestum est: quia justus ex fide vivit. [n. 140]

3:12 Lex autem non est ex fide, sed: qui fecerit ea, vivet in illis. [n. 143]

3:10 ὅσοι γὰρ ἐξ ἔργων νόμου εἰσὶν ὑπὸ κατάραν εἰσίν· γέγραπται γὰρ ὅτι Ἐπικατάρατος πᾶς ὃς οὐκ ἐμμένει πᾶσιν τοῖς γεγραμμένοις ἐν τῷ βιβλίῳ τοῦ νόμου τοῦ ποιῆσαι αὐτά.

3:11 ὅτι δὲ ἐν νόμῳ οὐδεὶς δικαιοῦται παρὰ τῷ θεῷ δῆλον, ὅτι Ὁ δίκαιος ἐκ πίστεως ζήσεται·

3:12 ὁ δὲ νόμος οὐκ ἔστιν ἐκ πίστεως, ἀλλ' Ὁ ποιήσας αὐτὰ ζήσεται ἐν αὐτοῖς.

3:10 **For as many as are of the works of the law are under a curse. For it is written:** *cursed is everyone who does not abide in all things which are written in the book of the law to do them.* [n. 134]

3:11 **But that in the law no man is justified with God, it is manifest: because the just man lives by faith.** [n. 140]

3:12 **But the law is not of faith: but he who does those things shall live in them.** [n. 143]

---

134. Supra ostendit Apostolus virtutem fidei, hic consequenter ostendit defectum legis. Et

primo per auctoritatem legis;

secundo per humanam consuetudinem, ibi *fratres, secundum hominem dico*, et cetera.

Circa primum tria facit.

Primo ostendit damnum occasionaliter ex lege consecutum;

secundo legis insufficientiam ad ipsum damnum removendum, ibi *quoniam autem in lege*, etc.;

tertio Christi sufficientiam, qua ipsum damnum est remotum, ibi *Christus autem nos redemit*, et cetera.

Circa primum duo facit.

Primo proponit intentum;

secundo probat propositum, ibi *scriptum est enim: maledictus*, et cetera.

135. Dicit ergo: *quicumque enim*, et cetera. Nam quia dixerat quod qui ex fide sunt benedicentur, cum sint filii Abrahae, posset quis dicere quod propter opera legis et propter fidem benedicuntur, et ideo, hoc excludens, dicit *quicumque ex operibus legis sunt, sub maledicto sunt*.

Sed contra. Antiqui patres fuerunt in operibus legis, ergo sunt maledicti, et per consequens damnati, quod est error Manichaei. Ideoque hoc est sane intelligendum.

Et attendendum est quod Apostolus non dicit: *quicumque* servant opera *legis sub maledicto sunt*, quia hoc est falsum pro tempore legis, sed dicit *quicumque ex operibus legis*, etc., id est, quicumque in operibus legis confidunt, et putant se iustificari per ea, *sub maledicto sunt*.

Aliud enim est esse in operibus legis, et aliud est servare legem; nam hoc est legem implere, et qui eam implet, non est sub maledicto. Esse vero in operibus legis

134. Above, the Apostle proved the power of faith; now he shows the shortcoming of the law.

First, through the authority of the law;

second, through a human custom, at **brethren (I speak after the manner of a man)** (Gal 3:15).

Concerning the first, he does three things.

First, he shows the curse brought on by the law;

second, the law's inability to remove that curse, at **but that in the law**;

third, the sufficiency of Christ by whom that curse has been removed, at **Christ has redeemed us** (Gal 3:13).

In regard to the first he does two things.

First, he sets forth his intended proposition;

second, he proves the proposition, at **for it is written**.

135. He says therefore: **for as many as are of the works of the law**. For since he had said that they who are of faith will be blessed through being sons of Abraham, someone might say that they are blessed both on account of the works of the law and on account of faith. Hence to exclude this he says: **as many as are of the works of the law are under a curse**.

But against this it can be said that the ancient fathers were of the works of the law. Therefore they are under a curse and, consequently, damned, which is a Manichean error. Hence it is necessary to understand this correctly.

And it should be noted that the Apostle does not say, **as many as** observe **the works of the law are under a curse**, because this is false when applied to the time of the law. He says rather: **as many as are of the works of the law**, i.e., whoever trusts in the works of the law and believes that they are made just by them **are under a curse**.

For it is one thing to be of the works of the law and another to observe the law. The latter consists in fulfilling the law, so that one who fulfills it is not under a curse. But to

est in eis confidere et spem ponere. Et qui in eis hoc modo sunt, **sub maledicto sunt**, scilicet transgressionis, quod quidem non facit lex, quia concupiscentia non venit ex lege, sed cognitio peccati, ad quod proni sumus per concupiscentiam per legem prohibitam. Inquantum ergo lex cognitionem peccati facit, et non praebet auxilium contra peccatum, dicuntur esse sub maledicto, cum nequeant illud per ipsa opera evadere.

136. Sunt autem quaedam opera legis caeremonialia, quae in observationibus fiebant. Alia sunt opera quae pertinent ad mores, de quibus sunt mandata moralia. Unde secundum Glossam hoc quod hic dicitur **quicumque ex operibus legis**, etc., intelligendum est de operibus caeremonialibus, et non de moralibus.

Vel dicendum quod loquitur hic Apostolus de omnibus operibus tam caeremonialibus quam moralibus. Opera enim non sunt causa quod aliquis sit iustus apud Deum, sed potius sunt executiones et manifestationes iustitiae. Nam nullus per opera iustificatur apud Deum, sed per habitum fidei, non quidem acquisitum, sed infusum. Et ideo quicumque ex operibus iustificari quaerunt, sub maledicto sunt, quia per ea peccata non removentur, nec aliquis quoad Deum iustificatur, sed per habitum fidei caritate informatum. Hebr. XI, 39: *hi omnes testimonio fidei*, et cetera.

137. Consequenter cum dicit **scriptum est enim**, etc., probat propositum, et hoc primo quidem secundum Glossam ostenditur per hoc quod nullus potest legem servare hoc modo, quo lex praecipit Deut. XXVIII, 15, quod *omnis qui non permanserit in omnibus quae scripta sunt in libro legis, ut faciat ea*, id est, qui non impleverit totam legem, *sit maledictus*. Sed implere totam legem est impossibile, ut dicitur Act. XV, 10: *ut quid tentatis imponere iugum, quod neque nos, neque patres nostri portare potuimus?* Ergo nullus est ex operibus legis, quin sit maledictus.

138. Potest etiam accipi hoc quod dicitur **scriptum est enim**, etc., non ut probatio propositi, sed ut ostendatur eius expositio; quasi dicat: dico quod sunt sub maledicto, sub illo scilicet de quo dicit lex **scriptum est enim: maledictus est omnis**, etc.: ut intelligatur de peccato, id est, de maledicto. Nam lex imperat bona facienda seu mala vitanda, et imperando obligat, sed non dat virtutem obediendi. Et ideo dicit **maledictus**, quasi malo adiectus, **omnis**, nullum excipiendo, quia, ut dicitur Act. X, 34, *non est personarum acceptio apud Deum*. *Qui non permanserit* usque in finem. Matth. XXIV, 13: *qui perseveraverit usque in finem*. **In omnibus**, non in quibusdam tantum, quia, ut dicitur Iac. II, 10, *quicumque totam legem servaverit, offendat autem in uno, factus est omnium reus*. **Quae scripta sunt in libro legis, ut faciat ea**, non solum ut credat seu velit tantum, sed ut opere

be of the works of the law is to trust in them and place one's hope in them. And they that are of the law in this way **are under a curse**, namely, of transgression; not that the law produces the curse, for concupiscence does not come from the law, but the knowledge of sin does, to which we are prone through concupiscence banned by the law. Therefore, inasmuch as the law begets a knowledge of sin and offers no help against sin, they are said to be under a curse, since they are powerless to escape it by those works.

136. Furthermore, some works of the law are ceremonies carried out in the observances; others are works that pertain to morals, with which the moral precepts deal. Hence, according to a Gloss, that which is said here, namely, **as many as are of the works of the law, are under a curse**, is to be understood of ceremonial works and not of moral works.

Or it should be said that the Apostle is speaking here of all works, both ceremonial and moral. For the works are not the cause making one to be just before God; rather they are the carrying out and manifestation of justice. For no one is made just before God by works but by the habit of faith, not acquired but infused. And therefore, as many as seek to be justified by works are under a curse, because sin is not removed nor anyone justified in the sight of God by them, but by the habit of faith vivified by charity: *and all these being approved by the testimony of faith, received not the promise* (Heb 11:39).

137. Then when he says, **for it is written**, he proves the proposition which, according to a Gloss, is proved by the fact that no one can keep the law in the way in which the law prescribed: *as many as do not keep and do all that is written in the book of the law*, i.e., who do not fulfill the whole law, *they shall be cursed* (Deut 28:15). But it is impossible to fulfill the whole law, as it is said: *why do you tempt God to put a yoke upon the necks of the disciples which neither our fathers nor we have been able to bear?* (Acts 15:10). Therefore by the works of the law no one is anything but cursed.

138. In another way the passage, **for it is written**, can be taken not as a proof of the proposition but as an exposition of the proof. As if to say: I say that they are under a curse, i.e., under that one of which the law says, **for it is written: 'cursed is every one'**, where the curse is understood to refer to sin. For the law commands that good be done and evils avoided, and by commanding it puts one under the obligation without giving the virtue to obey. And hence he says, **cursed**, as though placed in contact with evil, **is everyone**, without exception; because, as it is said: *God is not a respecter of persons; that does not abide* to the end (Acts 10:34): *he that shall persevere to the end* (Matt 24:13); **in all things**, not in some only, because as it is said: *whosoever shall keep the whole law, but offend in one point, is become guilty of all* (Jas 2:10); **which are written in the book of the law to do them**, not only to believe or will but actually to fulfill

impleat. Ps. CX, v. 10: *intellectus bonus omnibus facientibus eum.*

Sancti autem patres etsi in operibus legis erant, salvabantur tamen in fide venturi, confidentes in eius gratia, et saltem spiritualiter legem implentes. *Moyses enim*, ut in Glossa dicitur, *multa quidem praecepit, quae nullus implere potuit ad domandam Iudaeorum superbiam dicentium: non deest qui impleat, sed deest qui iubeat.*

139. Sed hic est quaestio de hoc quod dicitur **maledictus omnis**, et cetera. Dicitur enim Rom. XII, 14: *benedicite, et nolite maledicere.*

Respondeo. Dicendum est quod maledicere nihil aliud est quam malum dicere; possum ergo dicere bonum esse malum, et malum esse bonum, et rursum bonum esse bonum, et malum esse malum. Et primum quidem prohibet Apostolus, dicens: *nolite maledicere*, id est, nolite dicere bonum esse malum, et e contra; sed secundum licet, et ideo cum vituperamus peccatum, maledicimus quidem, sed non dicendo bonum malum, sed dicimus malum esse malum. Et ideo licet peccatorem maledicere, id est, dicere eum esse malo addictum vel esse malum.

140. Consequenter cum dicit **quoniam autem in lege**, etc., ostendit insufficientiam legis non valentis ab illo maledicto eripere ex hoc quod iustificare non poterat. Ad quod ostendendum utitur quodam syllogismo in secunda figura, et est talis: iustitia est ex fide, sed lex ex fide non est; ergo lex iustificare non potest. Circa hoc ergo primo ponit conclusionem, cum dicit **quoniam autem in lege nemo iustificatur**;

secundo autem maiorem, cum dicit **quia iustus ex fide vivit**;

tertio minorem, cum dicit **lex autem non est ex fide**.

141. Dicit ergo: dico quod per legem maledictio inducta est, nec tamen ab illa maledictione lex eripit, quia manifestum est quod **nemo in lege iustificatur apud Deum**, id est per opera legis.

Circa quod intelligendum, quod illi qui negaverunt Vetus Testamentum, ex hoc verbo occasionem sumpserunt. Et ideo dicendum est quod nemo iustificatur in lege, id est per legem. Nam per eam cognitio quidem peccati habebatur, ut dicitur Rom. V, sed non habebatur per eam iustificatio. Rom. III, 20: *ex operibus legis nullus iustificabitur.*

Sed contra Iac. II, 21 dicitur: *nonne Abraham ex operibus iustificatus est?*

Respondeo. Dicendum est, quod iustificare potest accipi dupliciter: vel quantum ad executionem iustitiae et manifestationem, et hoc modo iustificatur homo, id est, iustus ostenditur, ex operibus operatis. Vel quantum ad habitum iustitiae infusum, et hoc modo non iustificatur quis ex operibus, cum habitus iustitiae qua

them in their works: *a good understanding to all that do it* (Ps 111:10).

Yet the holy patriarchs, although they were of the works of the law, were nevertheless saved by faith in one to come, by trusting in His grace and by fulfilling the law at least spiritually. *For Moses*, says a Gloss, *did indeed command many things which no one could fulfill, in order to tame the pride of the Jews who said: there are many willing and able, but no one to command.*

139. But a difficulty arises about saying **cursed is everyone**. For it is said: *bless, and curse not* (Rom 12:14).

I answer that to curse is nothing else but to say evil. I can therefore say that good is evil and evil good, and again, that good is good and evil evil. The first is what the Apostle forbids when he says, *curse not*, i.e., do not say that good is evil and evil good. But the second is lawful. Hence when we denounce sin, we do indeed curse, not by way of calling good evil but by saying that evil is evil. Therefore it is lawful to curse a sinner, i.e., to say that he is addicted to evil or is evil.

140. Then when he says, **but that in the law**, he shows the inability of the law to snatch us from that curse, for it could not make one just. To show this he makes use of a syllogism in the second figure. Justice is by faith, but the law is not by faith. Therefore the law cannot justify. With respect to this, therefore: first, he states the conclusion when he says, **but that in the law no man is justified**;

second, the major premise, when he says **because the just man lives by faith**;

third, the minor, when he says **but the law is not of faith**.

141. Therefore he says: I say that by the law a curse was introduced, and yet the law cannot extricate one from that curse, because it is obvious that **in the law no man is justified with God**, i.e., through the works of the law.

On this point it should be noted that those who rejected the Old Testament took occasion to do so from this word. Hence it must be said that no one is justified in the law, i.e., through the law. For through it came the knowledge of sin (Rom 3:20); but justification did not come through it: *by the works of the law no flesh shall be justified* (Rom 3:20).

But against this, it is said: *was not Abraham our father justified by works?* (Jas 2:21).

I answer that 'to be justified' can be taken in two senses: either as referring to the execution and manifestation of justice, and in this way a man is justified, i.e., proved just, by the works performed; or as referring to the infused habit of justice, and in this way one is not justified by works, since the habit of justice by which a man is justified before God

homo iustificatur apud Deum, non sit acquisitus, sed per gratiam fidei infusus. Et ideo signanter Apostolus dicit **apud Deum**, quia iustitia quae est apud Deum, in interiori corde est: iustitia autem quae est ex operibus, id est, quae manifestat iustum, est apud homines. Et hoc modo Apostolus accepit **apud Deum**. Rom. II, 13: *non enim auditores, sed factores*, et cetera. Rom. IV, 2: *si ex operibus Abraham iustificatus est, habet gloriam, sed non apud Deum*, et cetera.

Sic ergo patet conclusio rationis, scilicet quod lex iustificare non potest.

142. Consequenter cum dicit **quia iustus**, etc., ponit maiorem, quae est ex auctoritate Scripturae, Hab. II, 4 et introducitur etiam Rom. I, 17 et ad Hebr. X, 38.

Circa quod notandum est, quod in homine est duplex vita, scilicet vita naturae et vita iustitiae. Vita quidem naturae est per animam; unde anima a corpore recedente, corpus remanet mortuum. Vita vero iustitiae est per Deum habitantem in nobis per fidem. Et ideo primum quo Deus est in anima hominis, est fides. Hebr. XI, 6: *accedentem ad Deum oportet credere*. Eph. III, 17: *habitare Christum per fidem*, et cetera.

Et sic dicimus, quod in anima prima indicia vitae apparent in operibus animae vegetabilis: quia anima vegetabilis est, quae primo advenit animali generato, ut Philosophus dicit. Ita quia primum principium quo Deus est in nobis, est fides, ideo fides dicitur principium vivendi. Et hoc est quod hic dicitur **iustus meus ex fide vivit**. Et intelligendum est de fide per dilectionem operante.

143. Minor autem ponitur ibi **lex autem non est**, et cetera.

Et primo ponitur ipsa minor;

secundo probatur, ibi **sed qui fecerit**, et cetera.

144. Dicit ergo **lex non est ex fide**. Sed contra, lex mandat credere quod sit unus Deus, et hoc pertinet ad fidem; ergo lex habebat fidem. Quod autem sit unus Deus, mandatur Deut. VI, *audi, Israel, Dominus Deus tuus*, et cetera.

Respondeo. Dicendum est, quod hic loquitur de observationibus mandatorum legis, secundum quod lex consistit in mandatis et praeceptis caeremonialibus, et dicit quod talis lex non est ex fide. *Fides enim*, ut dicitur Hebr. XI, 1, *est substantia sperandarum rerum, argumentum non apparentium*. Et ideo proprie implet mandatum de fide qui non sperat ex hoc aliqua praesentia et visibilia consequi, sed bona invisibilia et aeterna. Lex ergo quia promittebat terrena et praesentia, ut dicitur Is. I, 19: *si volueritis et audieritis me, bona terrae comedetis*, ideo non est ex fide, sed ex cupiditate potius, vel ex timore,

is not acquired but infused by the grace of faith. Therefore the Apostle says significantly, **with God**, because the justice which is before God is interior in the heart, whereas the justice which is by works, i.e., which manifests that one is just, is before men. And it is in this sense that the Apostle says, **with God**: *for not the hearers of the law, but the doers are just before God* (Rom 2:13); *for if Abraham were justified by works, he has glory, but not before God* (Rom 4:2).

Thus, therefore, the conclusion of his reasoning is obvious, namely, that the law can not justify.

142. Then when he says, **because the just man lives by faith**, he presents the major premise, which is based on Scriptural authority, i.e., Habakkuk (Hab 2:4), and restated in Romans (Rom 1:17) and Hebrews (Heb 10:38).

Concerning this point it should be noted that in man there is a twofold life; namely, the life of nature and the life of justice. Now the life of nature is from the soul; hence when the soul is separated from the body, the body continues but is dead. But the life of justice is through God dwelling in us by faith. Therefore the first way in which God is in the soul of man is by faith: *he who comes to God must believe* (Heb 11:6); *that Christ may dwell by faith in your hearts* (Eph 3:17).

Accordingly, we say that in the soul the first signs of life appear in the works of the vegetative soul, because the vegetative soul is the first to be present in a generated animal, as the Philosopher says. Similarly, because the first principle whereby God exists in us is faith, faith is called the principle of living. And this is what he means when he says, **the just man lives by faith**. Furthermore, this is to be understood of faith acting through love.

143. The minor premise is set down at, **but the law is not of faith**.

First, the minor is set down;

second, it is proved, at **but he who does those things**.

144. He says therefore that **the law is not of faith**. But this seems to conflict with the truth that the law commands one to believe that there is one God, which pertains to faith. Therefore the law had faith. And that there is one God is stated in Deuteronomy: *hear, O Israel, the Lord our God is one Lord* (Deut 6:4).

I answer that he is speaking here about keeping the commandments of the law insofar as the law consists of ceremonial precepts and moral precepts. This is the law that is not of faith. For *faith*, as is said, *is the substance of things to be hoped for, the evidence of things that do not appear* (Heb 11:1). Therefore, strictly speaking, he fulfills the command of faith who does not hope to obtain from it anything present and visible, but things invisible and eternal. Therefore, because the law promised earthly and present things, as it is said: *if you be willing and will hearken to me, you shall eat the good things of the land* (Isa 1:19), it is not of faith but

rather of cupidity or fear, especially in regard to those who kept the law in a carnal manner. Nevertheless, some did live spiritually in the law; but this was not because of the law but because of faith in a mediator.

145. And that the law is not of faith he proves when he says, ***but he who does those things***, i.e., the works of the law, ***shall live in them***, namely, in the present life, i.e., will be immune from temporal death and will be preserved in the present life.

Or again: I say that the ***law is not of faith***, and this is obvious, because ***he who does those things, shall live in them***. As if to say: the precepts of the law are not concerned with what is to be done, even though it proclaims something that must be believed. Therefore its power is not from faith but from works. He proves this on the ground that when the Lord willed to confirm it he did not say, *he that believes*, but ***he who does those things, shall live in them***. But the new law is from faith: *he that believes and is baptized shall be saved* (Mark 16:16).

Nevertheless, the law is something fashioned and produced by faith. That is why the old law is compared to the new as the works of nature to the works of the intellect. For certain works of the intellect appear in the works of nature, not as though natural things understand, but because they are moved and ordained to reach their end by an intellect. In like manner, in the old law are contained certain things that are of faith: not that the Jews held them precisely as being of faith, but that they held them only as protestations and figures of the faith of Christ, in virtue of whose faith the just were saved.

Lecture 5

3:13Christus nos redemit de maledicto legis, factus pro nobis maledictum: quia scriptum est: *maledictus omnis qui pendet in ligno*: [n. 146]

3:14ut in gentibus benedictio Abrahae fieret in Christo Jesu, ut pollicitationem Spiritus accipiamus per fidem. [n. 151]

3:13Χριστὸς ἡμᾶς ἐξηγόρασεν ἐκ τῆς κατάρας τοῦ νόμου γενόμενος ὑπὲρ ἡμῶν κατάρα, ὅτι γέγραπται, Ἐπικατάρατος πᾶς ὁ κρεμάμενος ἐπὶ ξύλου,

3:14ἵνα εἰς τὰ ἔθνη ἡ εὐλογία τοῦ Ἀβραὰμ γένηται ἐν Χριστῷ Ἰησοῦ, ἵνα τὴν ἐπαγγελίαν τοῦ πνεύματος λάβωμεν διὰ τῆς πίστεως.

3:13**Christ has redeemed us from the curse of the law, being made a curse for us** (for it is written: *cursed is everyone who hangs on a tree*). [n. 146]

3:14**That the blessing of Abraham might come on the gentiles through Christ Jesus: that we may receive the promise of the Spirit by faith.** [n. 151]

146. Posito damno a lege illato, et defectu legis ab illo eripere non valentis, hic consequenter ostendit virtutem Christi ab ipso damno liberantis. Et

primo ostendit quomodo per Christum ab ipso damno liberamur;

secundo quomodo etiam super hoc auxilium a Christo acquirimus, ibi *ut in gentibus*, et cetera.

Circa primum tria facit.

Primo enim ponit liberationis auctoritatem;

secundo liberationis modum, ibi *factus pro nobis*, etc.;

tertio testimonium propheticum, ibi *quia scriptum est*, et cetera.

147. Dicit ergo primo: quicumque servabant opera legis erant sub maledicto sicut dictum est, nec per legem liberari poterant. Ideo necesse fuit aliquem habere, qui nos liberaret, et iste fuit Christus. Et ideo dicit **Christus redemit nos de maledicto legis**, et cetera. Rom. VIII, 3: *quod impossibile erat legi*, etc., *Deus mittens Filium suum*, scilicet Christum, et cetera. **Redemit**, inquam, **nos**, scilicet Iudaeos, pretioso sanguine suo, Apoc. V, 9: *redemisti nos in sanguine*, et cetera. Is. XLIII, 1: *noli timere, quia redemi te*, et cetera. **De maledicto legis**, id est, de culpa et poena. Infra IV, v. 5: *ut eos qui sub lege erant redimeret*; Os. XIII, 14: *de morte redimam eos*.

148. Modum liberationis ponit cum dicit **factus pro nobis maledictum**. Ubi notandum quod maledictum est quod dicitur malum. Et secundum duplex malum potest dici duplex maledictum, scilicet maledictum culpae et maledictum poenae. Et utroque modo potest hoc legi dupliciter **factus est pro nobis maledictum**.

Et primo quidem de malo culpae. Nam Christus redemit nos de malo culpae. Unde sicut redemit nos de morte mortuus, ita redimit nos de maledicto culpae factus maledictum, scilicet culpae; non quidem quod in eo peccatum esset aliquod, *qui peccatum non fecit, nec dolus*, etc., ut dicitur I Petr. II, v. 22, sed secundum opinionem hominum, et praecipue Iudaeorum qui reputabant eum peccatorem. Io. XVIII, 30: *si non esset hic*

146. Having explained the curse brought on by the law, as well as the law's incapacity to deliver from sin, he now shows forth Christ's power to set one free from this curse.

First, he shows how through Christ we are set free of that curse;

second, how in addition we receive help from Christ, at **that the blessing of Abraham**.

As to the first, he does three things.

First, he presents the author of the liberation;

second, the manner of liberation, at **being made a curse for us**;

third, the testimony of the prophets, at **for it is written**.

147. Therefore, he says first: all who observed the works of the law were under a curse, as has been said, and they could not be delivered by the law. Hence it was necessary to have someone who should set us free, and that someone was Christ. Hence he says, **Christ has redeemed us from the curse of the law**: for what the law could not do . . . *God, sending his own Son* (Rom 8:3), i.e., Christ. He **has redeemed**, I say, **us**, namely, the Jews, with his own precious blood: *you have redeemed us in your blood* (Rev 5:9); *fear not, for I have redeemed you* (Isa 43:1), **from the curse of the law**, i.e., from guilt and penalty: *that he might redeem those who were under the law* (Gal 4:5); *I will redeem them from death* (Hos 13:14).

148. Then when he says, **being made a curse for us**, he sets forth the manner of the deliverance. Here it should be noted that a curse is that which is said as an evil. Now it is according to two kinds of evil that there can be two kinds of curse, namely, the curse of guilt and the curse of punishment. And with respect to each this passage can be read, namely, **he was made a curse for us**.

First of all with respect to the evil of guilt, for Christ redeemed us from the evil of guilt. Hence, just as in dying he redeemed us from death, so he redeemed us from the evil of guilt by being made a curse, i.e., of guilt; not that there was really any sin in him, for *he did not sin, neither was guile found in his mouth* (1 Pet 2:22), but only according to the opinion of men and particularly the Jews who regarded him as a sinner: *if he were not a malefactor, we*

malefactor, non tibi tradidissemus eum. Et ideo de hoc dicitur II Cor. V, 21: *eum qui non noverat peccatum, fecit pro nobis peccatum.*

Dicit autem **maledictum**, non *maledictus*, ut ostendat quod Iudaei eum sceleratissimum reputabant. Unde dicitur Io. IX, 16: *non est hic homo a Deo*, etc.; et Io. X, 33: *de bono opere non lapidamus te, sed de peccato et de blasphemia.*

Et ideo dicit **factus est pro nobis maledictum**, in abstracto; quasi dicat: factus est ipsa **maledictio**.

149. Secundo exponitur de malo poenae. Nam Christus liberavit nos a poena, sustinendo poenam et mortem nostram: quae quidem in nos provenit ex ipsa maledictione peccati. In quantum ergo hanc maledictionem peccati suscepit, pro nobis moriendo, dicitur esse factus pro nobis maledictum. Et est simile ei quod dicitur Rom. VIII, 3: *misit Deus Filium suum in similitudinem carnis peccati*, id est, mortalis. *Eum qui non noverat peccatum*, scilicet Christum, qui peccatum non fecit, Deus scilicet Pater, *pro nobis fecit peccatum*, II Cor. V, 21, id est fecit pati peccati poenam, quando scilicet oblatus est propter peccata nostra.

150. Consequenter ponit Scripturae testimonium cum dicit **quia scriptum est: maledictus omnis**, et cetera. Et hoc Deut. XXVII.

Ubi sciendum, secundum Glossam, quod in Deuteronomio, unde accipitur hoc verbum, tam in nostris, quam in Hebraeis codicibus habetur: *maledictus a Deo omnis*, etc., quod quidem, scilicet *a Deo*, in antiquis Hebraeorum voluminibus non habetur, unde creditur quod a Iudaeis post passionem domini appositum sit ad infamiam Christi.

Potest autem exponi auctoritas de malo poenae et de malo culpae. De malo quidem culpae sic **maledictus omnis qui pendet in ligno**, non propter hoc quod pendet in ligno, sed pro culpa pro qua pendet. Et hoc modo Christus aestimatus maledictus in cruce pendens, propter hoc quod maxime tali poena punitus fuit. Et secundum hoc continuatur ad praecedentia. Dominus enim praecepit in Deuteronomio, ut qui suspensus fuerit, in vespera deponatur; et ratio huius est, quia haec poena erat caeteris abiectior et ignominiosior. Dicit ergo: vere factus est pro nobis maledictum, quia ipsa mors crucis, quam sustinuit, sufficit ad maledictionem, hoc modo exponendo de malo culpae, sed solum aestimatione Iudaeorum, **quia scriptum est maledictus omnis**, et cetera.

De malo vero poenae sic exponitur **maledictus omnis qui**, etc., quia ipsa poena est maledictio, scilicet quod sic mortuus est. Et est hoc modo exponendo vere

would not have delivered him up to you (John 18:30). Hence it is said of him, *him who knew no sin he has made sin for us* (2 Cor 5:21).

But he says, *a curse*, and not *accursed*, to show that the Jews regarded him as the worst type of criminal. Hence it is said, *this man is not of God who does not keep the sabbath* (John 9:16) and *not for a good work do we stone you, but for sin and for blasphemy* (John 10:33).

Therefore he says, **being made for us a curse** in the abstract. As though to say: he was made **curse** itself.

149. Second, it is explained with respect to the evil of punishment. For Christ freed us from punishment by enduring our punishment and our death which came upon us from the very curse of sin. Therefore, inasmuch as he endured this curse of sin by dying for us, he is said to have been made a curse for us. This is similar to what is said in Romans: *God sent his own Son in the likeness of sinful flesh and of sin* (Rom 8:3), i.e., of mortal sin. *Him who knew no sin*, namely, Christ, who committed no sin, God (namely, the Father) *has made sin for us* (2 Cor 5:21), i.e., made him suffer the punishment of sin, namely, when he was offered for our sins.

150. Then he gives the testimony of Scripture when he says, **for it is written: 'cursed is everyone who hangs on a tree'** (Deut 21:23).

Here it should be noted, according to a Gloss, that in Deuteronomy, from which this passage is taken, our version as well as the Hebrew version has: *cursed by God is everyone who hangs on a tree*. However, the phrase *by God* is not found in the ancient Hebrew volumes. Hence it is believed to have been added by the Jews after the passion of Christ in order to defame him.

But it is possible to expound this authority both with respect to the evil of punishment and the evil of guilt. Of the evil of punishment thus: **cursed is everyone who hangs on a tree**, not precisely because he hangs on a tree, but because of the guilt for which he hangs. And in this way Christ was thought to be cursed, when he hung on the cross, because he was being punished with an extraordinary punishment. And according to this explanation, there is a continuity with the preceding. For the Lord commanded in Deuteronomy that anyone who had hung on a tree should be taken down in the evening; the reason being that this punishment was more disgraceful and ignominious than any other. He is saying, therefore: truly was he made a curse for us, because the death of the cross which he endured is tantamount to a curse—thus explaining the evil of guilt, although it was only in the minds of the Jews—because *it is written: 'cursed is everyone who hangs on a tree'*.

But with respect to the evil of punishment, **cursed is everyone who hangs on a tree** is explained thus: the punishment itself is a curse, namely, that he should die in this way. Explained in this way, he was truly cursed by God, because

maledictus a Deo, quia Deus ordinavit quod hanc poenam sustineret, ut nos liberaret.

151. Consequenter cum dicit *ut in gentibus benedictio*, etc., ponit spem quam per Christum, super hoc quod per eum liberamur de maledicto, acquirimus, ut dicitur Rom. V, 16: *non sicut delictum, ita et donum*; immo multo maius, scilicet quia liberat a peccato, et confert gratiam.

Primo ergo ponit fructum, et quibus datur, dicens *ut in gentibus benedictio Abrahae*, etc., quasi dicat: factus est pro nobis maledictum, non solum ut maledictionem removeret, sed ut in gentibus, quae non sub maledictione legis erant, fieret benedictio Abrahae promissa Gen. XXII, 18: *in semine tuo benedicentur omnes gentes*, et cetera. Et haec quidem benedictio facta est nobis, id est, impleta est, per Christum, qui est de semine Abrahae, cui dictae sunt promissiones *et semini suo, qui est Christus*, ut dicitur infra.

Quae quidem benedictio et fructus est *ut pollicitationem Spiritus accipiamus*, id est, promissiones quas Spiritus Sanctus facit in nobis, scilicet de beatitudine aeterna, qui quasi arra et pignus nobis traditus ipsam nobis promittit, ut habetur Eph. I, 14 et II Cor. c. VI. Et quidem in pignore datur ad certitudinem. Nam pignus est quaedam certa promissio de re accipienda. Rom. V: *non enim accepistis spiritum servitutis*, etc., et infra: *si filii, et haeredes*.

Vel *pollicitationem Spiritus accipiamus*, id est, Spiritum Sanctum, quasi dicat: accipiamus pollicitationem de Spiritu Sancto factam semini Abrahae, Ioel II, 28: *effundam de Spiritu meo*, etc.; quia per Spiritum Sanctum coniungimur Christo, et efficimur semen Abrahae, et digni benedictione.

152. Secundo ostendit per quid proveniat nobis iste fructus, dicens *per fidem*, per quam quidem et haereditatem aeternam acquirimus. Ad Hebr. IX: *accedentem ad Deum oportet credere quia est, et inquirentibus se remunerator sit*. Per fidem etiam acquirimus Spiritum Sanctum, quia, ut dicitur Act. V, 32, *Dominus dat Spiritum Sanctum obedientibus sibi*, scilicet per fidem.

God decreed that he endure this punishment in order to set us free.

151. Then when he says, *that the blessing of Abraham might come on the gentiles through Christ Jesus*, he touches on the hope which we acquire through Christ in addition to being freed from the curse: *not as the offense, so also the gift* (Rom 5:16), but much greater, namely, because he both frees us from sin and confers grace.

First, therefore, he mentions the fruit and those to whom it is given, saying, *that the blessing of Abraham might come on the gentiles through Christ Jesus*. As if to say: he was made a curse for us not only to remove a curse but also to enable the gentiles, who were not under the curse of the law, to receive the blessing promised to Abraham: *in your seed shall all the nations of the earth be blessed* (Gen 22:18). And this blessing was made to us, i.e., fulfilled, through Christ, who is of the seed of Abraham to whom the promises were made 'and to your seed', which is Christ (Gal 3:16).

Now this blessing, this fruit, is *that we may receive the promise of the Spirit*, i.e., the promises which the Holy Spirit, given to us as a pledge and a deposit, works in us concerning eternal happiness which he promises to us (Eph 1:14; 2 Cor 6). Furthermore, in the pledge is contained a guarantee, for a pledge is an assured promise concerning something to be received: *for you have not received the spirit of bondage again in fear, but you have received the Spirit of adoption of sons* (Rom 8:15), and, *and if sons, heirs also* (Rom 8:17).

Or: *that we may receive the promise of the Spirit*, i.e., the Holy Spirit. As if to say: that we may receive the promise made to the seed of Abraham concerning the Holy Spirit: *upon my servants I will pour forth my Spirit* (Joel 2:29). For it is through the Spirit that we are joined to Christ and become children of Abraham, worthy of the blessing.

152. Second, he shows how this fruit comes to us, saying, *by faith*, through which also we obtain an eternal inheritance: *he that comes to God must believe that he is, and is a rewarder to them that seek him* (Heb 11:6). Through faith, too, we receive the Holy Spirit, because as is said in Acts: *the Lord gives the Holy Spirit to those who obey him* (Acts 5:32), namely, through faith.

Lecture 6

³:¹⁵Fratres (secundum hominem dico) tamen hominis confirmatum testamentum nemo spernit, aut superordinat. [n. 153]

³:¹⁶Abrahae dictae sunt promissiones, et semini ejus. Non dicit: *et seminibus*, quasi in multis: sed quasi in uno: *et semini tuo*, qui est Christus. [n. 156]

³:¹⁷Hoc autem dico, testamentum confirmatum a Deo: quae post quadringentos et triginta annos facta est lex, non irritum facit ad evacuandam promissionem. [n. 159]

³:¹⁸Nam si ex lege haereditas, jam non ex promissione. Abrahae autem per repromissionem donavit Deus. [n. 161]

³:¹⁵Ἀδελφοί, κατὰ ἄνθρωπον λέγω· ὅμως ἀνθρώπου κεκυρωμένην διαθήκην οὐδεὶς ἀθετεῖ ἢ ἐπιδιατάσσεται.

³:¹⁶τῷ δὲ Ἀβραὰμ ἐρρέθησαν αἱ ἐπαγγελίαι καὶ τῷ σπέρματι αὐτοῦ. οὐ λέγει, Καὶ τοῖς σπέρμασιν, ὡς ἐπὶ πολλῶν, ἀλλ' ὡς ἐφ' ἑνός, Καὶ τῷ σπέρματί σου, ὅς ἐστιν Χριστός.

³:¹⁷τοῦτο δὲ λέγω· διαθήκην προκεκυρωμένην ὑπὸ τοῦ θεοῦ ὁ μετὰ τετρακόσια καὶ τριάκοντα ἔτη γεγονὼς νόμος οὐκ ἀκυροῖ, εἰς τὸ καταργῆσαι τὴν ἐπαγγελίαν.

³:¹⁸εἰ γὰρ ἐκ νόμου ἡ κληρονομία, οὐκέτι ἐξ ἐπαγγελίας· τῷ δὲ Ἀβραὰμ δι' ἐπαγγελίας κεχάρισται ὁ θεός.

³:¹⁵Brethren (I speak after the manner of man), yet a man's testament, if it be confirmed, no man despises nor adds to it. [n. 153]

³:¹⁶To Abraham were the promises made, and to his seed. He does not say: *and to his seeds* as of many. But as of one: *and to your seed*, which is Christ. [n. 156]

³:¹⁷Now this I say: that the testament which was confirmed by God, the law which was made after four hundred and thirty years does not disannul, to make the promise of no effect. [n. 159]

³:¹⁸For if the inheritance is of the law, it is no more of promise. But God gave it to Abraham by promise. [n. 161]

---

153. Postquam Apostolus probavit per auctoritates, quod lex non iustificat, nec ad iustificationem, quae est per fidem, est necessaria, hic consequenter ostendit idem per rationes humanas. Et

circa hoc quatuor facit.

Primo humanam consuetudinem ponit;

secundo assumit promissionem divinam, ibi *Abrahae dictae sunt promissiones*, etc.;

tertio infert conclusionem, ibi *hoc autem dico*, etc.;

quarto ostendit conclusionem sequi ex praemissis, ibi *nam si ex lege*, et cetera.

154. Dicit ergo: aperte quidem prius locutus sum secundum auctoritatem Scripturae non allatae voluntate humana, sed Spiritu Sancto, ut dicitur II Petr. I, 21; sed nunc *secundum hominem dico*, et secundum ea quae humana ratio et consuetudo habet.

Ex quo quidem habemus argumentum, quod ad conferendum de his quae sunt fidei, possumus uti quacumque veritate cuiuscumque scientiae. Deut. XXI, 11: *si videris in numero captivorum mulierem pulchram, et adamaveris eam, voluerisque habere in uxorem, introduces eam in domum tuam*, id est, si sapientia et scientia saecularis placuerit tibi, introduces eam intra terminos tuos, *quae radet caesariem*, etc., id est, resecabit omnes sensus erroneos.

Et inde est quod Apostolus in multis locis in epistolis suis utitur auctoritatibus gentilium, sicut illud I Cor. XV, 33: *corrumpunt bonos mores*, etc., et illud Tit. I, 11: *Cretenses malae bestiae*, et cetera.

153. Having proved by authority that the law does not justify and is not necessary for justification, which is through faith, the Apostle then proves the same point with human reasons.

Concerning this he does four things.

First, he mentions a human custom;

second, he touches on a divine promise, at *to Abraham were the promises made*;

third, he draws his conclusion, at *now this I say*;

fourth, he shows that the conclusion follows from the premises, at *for if the inheritance is of the law*.

154. He says therefore: it is clear that up to now I have been speaking according to the authority of Scripture, which came not by the will of man, but by the Holy Spirit (2 Pet 1:21). But now *I speak after the manner of man* and after the manners which human reason and human custom follow.

Here, indeed, we have an argument to show that in discussions bearing on faith, we may use any truth of any science: *if you see in the number of the captives a beautiful woman and love her and will have her to wife, you shall bring her into your house*, i.e., if you are pleased with worldly wisdom and science, bring it within your boundaries, *and she shall shave her hair, and pare her nails* (Deut 21:11), i.e., you shall cut away all erroneous opinions.

This is why in many places in his epistles the Apostle uses the authority of the gentiles; for example: *evil communications corrupt good manners* (1 Cor 15:33), and *the Cretans are always liars, evil beasts, slothful bellies* (Titus 1:12).

155. Vel quamvis huiusmodi rationes vanae sint et infirmae, quia, ut dicitur in Ps. XCIII, 11: *Dominus scit cogitationes hominum, quoniam vanae sunt*; **tamen hominis confirmatum testamentum nemo spernit aut superordinat**, quia nihil humanum tantam firmitatem habet sicut ultima voluntas hominis; sperneret autem illud aliquis, si diceret quod testamentum hominis confirmatum morte testatoris et testibus non valeret. Si ergo testamentum huiusmodi nemo spernit, dicens non esse servandum, aut spernit, aliquid mutando; multo magis testamentum Dei nullus spernere debet aut superordinare, infringendo illud, vel addendo vel diminuendo. Apoc. ult.: *si quis apposuerit ad haec, apponet Deus super illum plagas scriptas in isto libro, et si quis diminuerit de verbis prophetiae huius, auferet Deus partem eius*, et cetera. Deut. IV, 2: *non addetis ad verbum, quod vobis loquor, neque auferetis ex eo*, et cetera.

156. Consequenter cum dicit **Abrahae dictae sunt promissiones**, etc., assumit promissionem divinam Abrahae factam, quae est quasi quoddam testamentum Dei. Et

primo exponit hanc promissionem seu testamentum;
secundo vero aperit veritatem testamenti, ibi **non dicit: et seminibus**, et cetera.

157. Dicit ergo primo **Abrahae dictae sunt promissiones**, quasi dicat: sicut testamentum hominis est firmum, ita promissiones divinae firmae sunt. Sed numquid Deus aliquas promissiones fecit ante legem? Utique, quia **Abrahae**, qui fuit ante legem, scilicet quod non falleret Deus, **dictae**, id est, factae **sunt promissiones, et semini eius** a Deo. Sed Abrahae factae sunt, ut cui erant implendae, semini vero, ut per quod implerentur.

Dicit autem **promissiones** pluraliter, quia promissio de benedicendo semine multa continebat. Vel quia frequenter idem, id est, aeterna beatitudo sibi promissa est, sicut Gen. c. XII, 3, *in te benedicentur universae cognationes terrae*; item XV, 5, *suscipe caelum, et numera stellas*, etc.; item eodem: *semini tuo dabo terram hanc*, etc.; item XXII, 18: *benedicam tibi et multiplicabo semen tuum sicut stellas caeli*.

Istae ergo promissiones sunt quasi testamentum Dei, quia est quaedam ordinatio de haereditate danda Abrahae et semini suo.

158. Veritatem autem testamenti aperit, cum dicit **non dicit: et seminibus**, et cetera. Quam quidem aperit eodem spiritu quo testamentum conditum est. Et hoc patet ex verbis testamenti. **Non**, inquit, **dicit et seminibus, quasi in multis**, id est, sicut faceret, si de multis illud valeret, **sed quasi in uno, quod est Christus**, quia ipse solus est per quem et in quo omnes poterunt benedici. Nam ipse solus et singularis est, qui non subiacet

155. Or: although such reasons be fruitless and weak, because, as it is said: *the Lord knows the thoughts of men, that they are vain* (Ps 93:11), **yet a man's testament, if it be confirmed, no one despises nor adds to it**, because nothing human has as much power to bind as a man's last will. But someone would be scorning it if he were to say that a man's will, confirmed by his death and by witnesses, had no validity. Therefore, if no one scorns a testament of this kind by saying that it should not be heeded or by modifying it, much less may anyone scorn the testament of God or modify it and weaken it by adding or removing anything: *if any man shall add to these things, God shall add unto him the plagues written in this book: and if any man shall take away from the words of the book of this prophecy, God shall take away his part out of the book of life* (Rev 22:18); *you shall not add to the word that I speak to you, neither shall you take away from it* (Deut 4:2).

156. Then when he says, **to Abraham were the promises made**, he takes up the promise God made to Abraham, which is, as it were, the testament of God.

First, he explains this promise or testament;
second, he discloses the truth contained therein, at **he does not say: 'and to his seeds'**.

157. He says therefore: **to Abraham were the promises made**. As if to say: as the testament of a man is valid, so the divine promises are valid. But did God make any promises before the law? He did; because **to Abraham** who lived before the time of the law **the promises were made, and to his seed**, by God. However, they were made to Abraham as the one for whom they would be fulfilled, and to his seed as the one through whom they would be fulfilled.

And he says, **promises**, using the plural, because the promise that his seed would be blessed contained a number of things: or because the same thing, namely, eternal happiness, was promised to him on a number of occasions. For example, *in you shall all the kindred of the earth be blessed* (Gen 12:3); *look up to heaven and number the stars if you can. And he said to him: so shall your seed be* (Gen 15:5). Again: *to your seed will I give this land* (Gen 15:18); *I will bless you and I will multiply your seed as the stars of heaven* (Gen 22:17).

These promises then, are God's testament, as it were, i.e., a decree concerning the inheritance to be given to Abraham and his seed.

158. The meaning of this testament he explains when he says, **he does not say: 'and to his seeds', as of many; but as of one: 'and to your seed'**. He explains this according to the very spirit in which the testament was made. And this is obvious from the words of the testament: **he does not say: 'and to his seeds', as of many**, i.e., as he would do, if it were valid for many: **but as of one: 'and to your seed', which is Christ**, because he is the only one through whom

maledictioni culpae, etsi maledictio pro nobis dignatus sit fieri. Unde dicitur in Ps. CXL, 10: *singulariter sum ego*, et cetera. Item: *non est qui faciat bonum*, et cetera. Eccle. VII, 29: *virum de mille unum reperi*, scilicet Christum, qui esset sine omni peccato, *mulierem autem ex omnibus non inveni*, quae omnino a peccato immunis esset, ad minus originali, vel veniali.

159. Conclusionem autem infert consequenter cum dicit **hoc autem dico: testamentum**, etc., ubi videamus per ordinem quid sit quod dicit.

Dicit ergo, quod hoc promisit Deus Abrahae, sed hoc est **testamentum**, scilicet ista promissio de haereditate adipiscenda. Ier. XXXI, 31: *feriam domui Israel et domui Iuda foedus novum*, et cetera. **Confirmatum**, quod ideo ponit, ut concordet cum praemissis. Nam supra dixerat **testamentum hominis confirmatum**, et cetera. **A Deo**, scilicet qui promisit. Et confirmatum dico iureiurando. Gen. XXII, 16: *per memetipsum iuravi*, etc., Hebr. VI, 18: *ut per duas res immobiles quibus impossibile est mentiri Deum*, et cetera. **Hoc**, inquam, **testamentum** lex **non facit irritum, quae** quidem **lex facta est**, et data a Deo per Moysen. Io. I, 17: *lex per Moysen data est*, etc., **post quadringentos et triginta**, et cetera. Et quasi exponens quod dixerat, subiungit **non irritum facit ad evacuandam promissionem**. Sic enim irritum fieret praedictum testamentum, si promissio facta Abrahae evacuaretur, id est, in vacuum facta esset, quasi non sufficeret semen Abrahae repromissum ad gentium benedictionem. Per Christum autem non sunt evacuatae promissiones patribus factae, sed confirmatae. Rom. XV, 8: *dico Iesum Christum ministrum fuisse circumcisionis, ad confirmandas promissiones patrum*. Et II Cor. c. I, 20: *quotquot enim promissiones Dei sunt, in illo est*, et cetera.

Hoc autem quod dicitur **post quadringentos et triginta annos**, concordat ei quod habetur Ex. XII, 40: *habitatio filiorum Israel, qua manserunt in Aegypto, fuit quadringentorum triginta annorum*. Et Act. VII, 6: *locutus est dominus*, scilicet Abrahae, *quia erit semen eius accola in terra aliena, et servituti eos subiicient annis quadringentis triginta*.

160. Sed contra est quod dicitur Gen. c. XV, 13: *scito praenoscens, quod peregrinum futurum sit semen tuum, et servituti eos subiicient, et affligent eos annis quadringentis*.

Respondeo. Dicendum quod si fiat computatio annorum a prima promissione facta Abrahae, quae legitur Gen. XII, usque ad exitum filiorum Israel de Aegypto, quando data est lex, sic sunt anni quadringenti triginta, sicut hic scribitur, et Ex. XII, et Act. c. VII. Si autem incipiat computatio a nativitate Isaac de qua legitur Gen.

and in whom all could be blessed. For he alone and exclusively is the one who does not lie under the curse of guilt, in spite of the fact that he deigned to be made a curse for us. Hence it is said, *I am alone until I pass* (Ps 141:10); and again *there is none that does good, no, not one* (Ps 13:3); *one man among a thousand I have found* (namely, Christ, who had been without any sin), *a woman among them all I have not found* (Eccl 7:29), who would be entirely immune from all sin, at least original or venial.

159. Then when he says, **now this I say: that the testament**, he draws his conclusion. Here let us see, in order, what it is that he says.

He says therefore that this is what God promised to Abraham. But this is a **testament**, i.e., a promise that he would obtain an inheritance: *I will make a new covenant with the house of Israel and with the house of Judah* (Jer 31:31). He says, **confirmed**, in keeping with what he said before. For he said above, *a man's testament, if it be confirmed, no man despises nor adds to it*. **By God**, i.e., by the one who promised. **The testament was confirmed**, namely, with an oath: *by my own self have I sworn* (Gen 22:16); *that by two immutable things in which it is impossible for God to lie, we may have the strongest comfort* (Heb 6:18). **This testament**, I say, the law **does not disannul**: the law, namely, **which was made** and given by God through Moses: *for the law was given through Moses* (John 1:17) **after four hundred thirty years**. Then, as if to explain what he had said, he adds, **does not disannul, to make the promise of no effect**. For the aforesaid testament would have been disannulled if the promise made to Abraham were set aside, i.e., made fruitless, as though the seed promised to Abraham were not enough to bless the gentiles. But as a matter of fact, the promises made to the patriarchs were not set aside by Christ but confirmed: *for I say that Christ Jesus was minister of the circumcision to confirm the promises made unto the fathers* (Rom 15:8); *for all the promises of God are in him* (2 Cor 1:20).

After four hundred thirty years: this concords with Exodus: *the abode of the children of Israel that they made in Egypt was four hundred thirty years* (Exod 12:40), and with Acts: *and God said to him*, i.e., to Abraham, *that his seed should sojourn in a strange country and that they shall bring them under bondage four hundred thirty years* (Acts 7:6).

160. But against this, it is said: *know before that your seed shall be a stranger in a land not their own, and they shall bring them under bondage and afflict them four hundred years* (Gen 15:13).

I answer that if you count the years between the first promise made to Abraham (Gen 12), and the exodus of the children of Israel from Egypt, when the law was given, there will be four hundred thirty years, as is written here and in Exodus (Exod 12) and Acts (Acts 7). But if you begin to count from the birth of Isaac, concerning which

XXI, sic sunt tantum quadringenti et quinque anni. Nam viginti quinque anni fuerunt a promissione facta Abrahae usque ad nativitatem Isaac. Abraham enim erat septuaginta quinque annorum quando exivit de terra sua, et facta est ei prima promissio, ut habetur Gen. XII. Centenarius autem fuit, quando natus est Isaac, ut habetur ibidem cap. XXI. Quod autem a nativitate Isaac usque ad exitum filiorum Israel de Aegypto fuerint quadringenti quinque anni, probatur per hoc, quod Isaac fuit sexaginta annorum quando genuit Iacob, ut habetur Gen. XXV; Iacob autem erat centum triginta annorum quando intravit Aegyptum, ut habetur Gen. XXVII. Et sic a nativitate Isaac usque ad introitum Iacob in Aegyptum fuerunt centum nonaginta anni. Ioseph autem fuit triginta annorum, quando stetit coram Pharaone, ut habetur Gen. XLI. Et postea transierunt septem anni fertilitatis et duo sterilitatis, usque ad ingressum Iacob in Aegyptum, ut habetur XLV. Vixit autem Ioseph centum et decem annis, ut habetur Gen. ult. A quibus si subtrahantur triginta novem anni, remanent septuaginta et unus annus. Fuerunt ergo a nativitate Isaac usque ad mortem Ioseph ducenti et sexaginta unus annus. Fuerunt autem in Aegypto filii Israel post mortem Ioseph centum quadraginta quatuor annis, ut Rabanus dicit in Glossa. Fuerunt ergo a nativitate Isaac usque ad exitum filiorum Israel de Aegypto et legem datam quadringenti quinque anni; Scriptura autem non curavit de minutis.

Vel potest dici, quod quinto anno Isaac expulsus fuit Ismael, et remansit solus Isaac haeres Abrahae, a quo tempore fuerunt quadringenti anni.

161. Deinde, cum dicit **nam si ex lege**, etc., ostendit quomodo sequatur ex praemissis, quod lex evacuaret promissiones, si lex necessaria esset ad iustificationem sive benedictionem gentium. Dicit ergo: vere promissio evacuaretur si lex necessaria esset. **Nam si haereditas**, scilicet benedictionis Abrahae, esset **ex lege, iam non** esset **ex repromissione**, id est, ex semine repromisso Abrahae. Si enim semen promissum esset sufficiens ad haereditatem benedictionis consequendam, non fieret iustificatio per legem.

Destruit autem consequens, cum dicit **Abrahae autem donavit Deus**, etc., id est, promisit se daturum, quod ita certum erat ac si statim daret, **per repromissionem**, id est per semen repromissum. Non ergo est ex lege **haereditas**, id est benedictio, de qua dicitur I Petr. III, 9: *in hoc vocati estis, ut benedictionem haereditate possideatis*.

Genesis (Gen 21) speaks, there are only four hundred five years. For twenty-five years elapsed between the promise made to Abraham and the birth of Isaac: for Abraham was seventy-five years old when he left his own country and the first promise was made to him, as is recorded in Genesis (Gen 12); and he was one hundred years old when Isaac was born, as is recorded in the same book (Gen 21). That there were four hundred five years between the birth of Isaac and the exodus of the children of Israel from Egypt is proved by the fact that Isaac was sixty years old when he begot Jacob, as is had in Genesis (Gen 25). Jacob, on the other hand, was one hundred thirty years old when he entered Egypt, as is recorded in Genesis (Gen 47). Therefore from the birth of Isaac to Jacob's entry into Egypt were one hundred ninety years. Now Joseph was thirty years old when he stood before Pharaoh, as is recorded in Genesis (Gen 41). After that there were seven years of plenty and two of want; and it was after that that Jacob came to Egypt, as is recorded in Genesis (Gen 45). But Joseph lived one hundred ten years, as is mentioned in the final chapter of Genesis. If thirty-nine years be subtracted from this there remain seventy-one years. Consequently from the birth of Isaac to Joseph's death there were two hundred sixty-one years. Furthermore, the children of Israel remained in Egypt for one hundred forty-four more years after Joseph's death, as Rabanus says in a Gloss on the Acts (Acts 7). Therefore from the birth of Isaac to the exodus from Egypt and the giving of the law four hundred five years elapsed. However, the Scripture in Genesis (Gen 17) was not concerned with minutiae.

Or it can be said that during Isaac's fifth year Ishmael was cast forth, leaving Isaac the sole heir of Abraham. Reckoning from this date, we have our four hundred years.

161. Then when he says, *for, if the inheritance is of the law, it is no more of promise*, he shows how from the foregoing it follows that the law would nullify the promises, if the law were necessary for justification or for the blessing to come to the gentiles. He says therefore: the promise would indeed be disannulled, if the law were necessary; for *if the inheritance*, namely, of Abraham's blessing, *is of the law, it is no more of promise*, i.e., of the seed promised to Abraham. For if the seed promised to Abraham was enough to obtain the inheritance of the blessing, there would not be justification through the law.

He rejects the consequent, when he says, *but God gave it to Abraham*, i.e., he promised that he would give it; but the promise was as sure as if it had been fulfilled then and there, *by promise*, i.e., through the seed promised. Therefore the *inheritance*, i.e., the blessing, about which it is said: *for unto this you are called, that you may inherit a blessing* (1 Pet 3:9), is not of the law.

Lecture 7

3:19Quid igitur lex? Propter transgressiones posita est donec veniret semen, cui promiserat, ordinata per angelos in manu mediatoris. [n. 162]

3:19Τί οὖν ὁ νόμος; τῶν παραβάσεων χάριν προσετέθη, ἄχρις οὗ ἔλθῃ τὸ σπέρμα ᾧ ἐπήγγελται, διαταγεὶς δι' ἀγγέλων ἐν χειρὶ μεσίτου.

3:19Why then was the law? It was set because of transgressions, until the seed should come to whom he made the promise, being ordained by angels in the hand of a mediator. [n. 162]

3:20Mediator autem unius non est: Deus autem unus est. [n. 169]

3:20ὁ δὲ μεσίτης ἑνὸς οὐκ ἔστιν, ὁ δὲ θεὸς εἷς ἐστιν.

3:20Now a mediator is not of one: but God is one. [n. 169]

162. Postquam ostendit Apostolus et auctoritate Scripturae et consuetudine humana, quod lex iustificare non potuit, hic movet duas dubitationes et solvit. Secunda dubitatio incipit ibi **lex ergo adversus promissa Dei**, et cetera.

Circa primum tria facit.

Primo movet dubitationem;

secundo solvit, ibi **propter transgressiones**, etc.;

tertio quoddam in solutione positum manifestat, ibi **mediator autem**, et cetera.

163. Potest autem esse dubium ex praemissis tale: si lex iustificare non poterat, an esset omnino inutilis. Et hanc dubitationem movet, dicens **quid igitur lex**, etc., sit, id est, ad quid lex utilis fuit? Et hanc punctuationem magis approbat Augustinus ut habetur in Glossa, quam aliam quae sibi primitus melior videbatur, ut distinguatur: **quid igitur?** Et postea dicatur: **lex propter transgressiones**, et cetera.

Similis dubitatio proponitur Rom. III, 1 ubi sic dicitur: *quid igitur amplius Iudaeo*, et cetera.

164. Deinde cum dicit **propter transgressiones**, solvit dubitationem motam, ubi quatuor facit.

Primo proponit legis utilitatem;

secundo legis fructum, ibi **donec veniret semen**, etc.;

tertio legis ministros, ibi **ordinata per angelos**;

quarto legis Dominium, ibi **in manu mediatoris**.

165. Circa primum notandum est, quod lex vetus data est propter quatuor, secundum quatuor ex peccato consecuta, quae enumerat Beda, scilicet propter malitiam, infirmitatem, concupiscentiam et ignorantiam.

Est ergo lex primo data ad reprimendam malitiam, dum scilicet prohibendo peccatum et puniendo, retrahebantur homines a peccato, et hoc tangit dicens **propter transgressiones posita est** lex, id est, ad transgressiones cohibendas: et de hoc habetur I Tim. I, 9: *iusto lex non est posita, sed iniustis*. Cuius ratio potest sumi a Philosopho in IV *Ethicorum*. Homines enim bene dispositi ex seipsis moventur ad bene agendum, et sufficit eis paterna

162. After showing by the authority of Scripture and by a human custom that the law was unable to make one just, the Apostle now raises two questions and solves them. The second question begins at **was the law then against the promises of God** (Gal 3:21).

With respect to the first, he does three things.

First, he raises the question;

second, he solves it, at **it was set because of transgressions**;

third, he elucidates something he presupposed in the course of his solution, at **now a mediator**.

163. The question which might arise from the foregoing is this: if the law was unable to justify, was the law without purpose? This question he raises when he says, **why then was the law?** i.e., what purpose did it serve? This is the punctuation which, as a Gloss says, Augustine favors, although earlier he approved the reading, **what then?** followed by, **the law was set up because of transgressions**.

In Romans, a similar question is raised: *what advantage then does the Jew have, or what is the profit of circumcision?* (Rom 3:1).

164. Then when he says, **it was set because of transgressions**, he solves the question. Here he does four things.

First, he sets down the purpose of the law;

second, the fruit of the law, at **until the seed should come**;

third, the ministers of the law, at **being ordained by angels**;

fourth, the Lord of the law, at **in the hand of a mediator**.

165. With respect to the first, it should be noted that the old law was given for a fourfold purpose, corresponding to the four consequences of sin enumerated by Bede, namely, because of wickedness, weakness, passion, and ignorance.

Hence the law was given first of all to suppress wickedness, since by forbidding sin and by punishing, it restrained men from sin. This he touches on when he says, **the law was set because of transgressions**, i.e., to prevent them. On this point it is said: *the law is not made for the just man but for the unjust* (1 Tim 1:9). The reason for this can be taken from *Ethics* IV of the Philosopher. For men who are well disposed, are inclined to act well of themselves, so that

monita, unde non indigent lege: sed, sicut Rom. II, 14 dicitur, *ipsi sibi sunt lex, habentes opus legis scriptum in cordibus suis.* Sed homines male dispositi indigent retrahi a peccatis per poenas. Et ideo quantum ad istos fuit necessaria legis positio, quae habet coarctativam virtutem.

Secundo, lex data est ad infirmitatem manifestandam. Homines enim de duobus praesumebant. Primo quidem de scientia, secundo de potentia. Et ideo Deus reliquit homines absque doctrina legis, tempore legis naturae, in quo dum in errores inciderunt, convicta est eorum superbia de defectu scientiae, sed adhuc restabat praesumptio de potentia. Dicebant enim *non deest qui impleat, sed deest qui iubeat*, ut dicitur in Glossa super illud Ex. XXIV: *quicquid praeceperit Dominus, faciemus, et erimus obedientes.* Et ideo data est lex, quae cognitionem peccati faceret, *per legem enim cognitio peccati,* Rom. III, 20. Quae tamen auxilium gratiae non dabat ad vitandum peccata, ut sic homo sub lege constitutus et vires suas experiretur, et infirmitatem suam recognosceret, inveniens se sine gratia peccatum vitare non posse, et sic avidius quaereret gratiam. Et haec etiam causa potest ex his verbis accipi, ut dicatur, quod lex posita est propter transgressiones adimplendas, quasi illo modo loquendo quo Apostolus dicit Rom. c. V, 20: *lex subintravit ut abundaret delictum*; quod non est intelligendum causaliter, sed consecutive: quia lege subintrante, abundavit delictum, et transgressiones sunt multiplicatae, dum concupiscentia nondum per gratiam sanata, in id quod prohibebatur, magis exarsit, et factum est peccatum gravius, addita praevaricatione legis scriptae. Et hoc Deus permittebat, ut homines imperfectionem suam cognoscentes, quaererent mediatoris gratiam. Unde signanter dicit **posita est**, quasi debito ordine collocata inter legem naturae et legem gratiae.

Tertio, data est lex ad domandam concupiscentiam populi lascivientis, ut diversis caeremoniis fatigati neque ad idololatriam, neque ad lascivias declinarent. Unde dicit Petrus Act. XV, 10: *hoc est onus, quod neque nos,* et cetera.

Quarto, ad instruendum ignorantiam data est lex in figuram futurae gratiae, secundum illud Hebr. X, 1: *umbram habens lex*, et cetera.

166. Deinde cum dicit **donec veniret semen**, etc., id est Christus, de quo promiserat Deus, per eum benedicendas omnes gentes. Matth. XI, 13: *lex et prophetae usque ad Ioannem*, et cetera. Gen. XII: *in semine tuo*, et cetera.

167. Ministri autem legis ponuntur, cum dicit **ordinata**, id est, ordinanter data, **per angelos**, id est, per nuntios Dei, scilicet Moysen et Aaron. Mal. II, 7: *legem*

fatherly admonitions are enough for them: hence they do not need a law; indeed, as it is said, *they are a law to themselves who show the work of the law written in their hearts* (Rom 2:14). But men who are ill disposed need to be kept from sin by penalties. Hence with respect to such men it was necessary to set down a law which has power to constrain.

Second, the law was set down in order to disclose human weakness. For men gloried in two things: first, in their knowledge; and second, in their power. Hence God left men without the instruction of the law during the period of the law of nature, during which time, as they fell into errors, their pride was convinced of its lack of knowledge, even though they still presumed on their powers. For they said, *many are willing and able, but there is no one to lead,* as a Gloss says on this passage: *all things that the Lord has spoken we will do. We will be obedient* (Exod 24:8). And therefore the law was given which would cause a knowledge of sin, *for by the law is the knowledge of sin* (Rom 3:20). But it did not give the help of grace to avoid sin, so that man, bound by the law, might test his strength and recognize his infirmity. Finding that without grace he was unable to avoid sin, he would more ardently yearn for grace. And this cause can also be derived from these words, if they are taken to mean that the law was set for the sake of filling up transgressions, in the sense in which the Apostle speaks when he says: *now the law entered in that sin might abound* (Rom 5:20). This is to be taken not in a causal but in a sequential sense; for after the law entered in, sin abounded and transgressions multiplied, because concupiscence, not yet healed by grace, lusted after that which was forbidden, with the result that sin became more grievous, being now a violation of a written law. But God permitted this in order that men, recognizing their own imperfection, might seek the grace of a mediator. Hence he says significantly, ***it was set***, i.e., interposed, as it were, between the law of nature and the law of grace.

Third, the law was given in order to tame the concupiscence of a wanton people, so that, worn out by various ceremonies, they would not fall into idolatry or lewdness. Hence Peter says: *this is a yoke which neither our fathers nor we have been able to bear* (Acts 15: 10).

Fourth, the law was given as a figure of future grace in order to instruct the ignorant: *for the law, having a shadow of the good things to come* (Heb 10:1).

166. Then he sets forth the fruit of the law when he says, **until the seed should come**, i.e., Christ, of whom God had promised that through him all nations would be blessed: *for all the prophets and the law prophesied until John* (Matt 11:13); *in your seed shall all the nations of the earth be blessed* (Gen 22:18).

167. The ministers of the law are mentioned when he says, **ordained**, i.e., given in good order, **by angels**, i.e., the messengers of God, namely, Moses and Aaron: *they shall*

requirent ex ore eius, et cetera. *angelus enim Domini*, et cetera. Vel **per angelos**, id est, ministerio angelorum. Act. VII, 35: *accepistis legem in dispositionem angelorum*, et cetera. Et est data per angelos, quia lex non debebat dari per Filium, qui maior est. Hebr. II, 2: *si enim, qui per angelos factus est sermo*, et cetera.

Dicit autem **ordinata**, quia ordinabiliter data est, scilicet inter tempus legis naturalis, qua homines convicti sunt, quod se iuvare non poterant, et tempus gratiae. Nam antequam gratiam acciperent, convincendi erant de lege.

168. Dominus autem legis dicitur Christus. Et ideo dicit **in manu mediatoris**, id est, in potestate Christi. Deut. XXXIII, 2: *in dextera eius ignea lex*. I Tim. II, 5: *mediator Dei et hominum*, et cetera.

Iste mediator significatus est per Moysen, in cuius manu est lex data. Deut. V, 5: *ego sequester et medius fui inter Deum et vos*, et cetera.

169. Deinde, cum dicit **mediator autem**, etc., exponit quod dixit **in manu mediatoris**, quod potest tripliciter exponi.

Uno modo, quia mediator non est unius tantum, sed duorum. Unde cum iste sit mediator Dei et hominis, oportet quod sit Deus et homo. Si enim esset purus homo, vel Deus tantum, non esset verus mediator. Si ergo est verus Deus, cum nullus est mediator sui ipsius, posset videri alicui, quod praeter ipsum sunt alii dii quorum est mediator; et hoc removet, dicens quod **mediator** iste et si **non est unius** tantum, non propter hoc sunt alii dii, sed **Deus unus est**, quia licet ipse alius sit in persona a Deo Patre, non est tamen aliud in natura. Deut. VI, 4: *audi, Israel, Dominus Deus tuus*, et cetera. Eph. IV, 6: *unus Deus*, et cetera.

Secundo modo, quia posset credi, quod iste esset mediator Iudaeorum tantum, ideo dicit: dico quod Christus est **mediator**, sed **non unius**, scilicet Iudaeorum, sed **unus est** omnium, id est, sufficiens ad omnes reconciliandos Deo, quia ipse Deus est. Rom. III, 30: *unus Deus qui iustificavit circumcisionem ex fide, et praeputium per fidem*, et cetera. II Cor. V, v. 19: *Deus erat in Christo mundum reconcilians sibi*, et cetera.

Tertio modo, quia non est mediator unius populi tantum, scilicet Iudaeorum, sed etiam gentilium. Eph. II, 14: *ipse est pax nostra, qui fecit utraque unum*. Et hoc ex parte gentium auferendo idololatriam, et ex parte Iudaeorum observantiam legis.

Specialiter autem mediator est Filius, non Pater, non Spiritus Sanctus, nihilominus tamen unus est Deus.

seek the law at his mouth: because he is the angel of the Lord of hosts (Mal 2:7). Or: **by angels**, i.e., by the ministry of angels: *you have received the law by the disposition of angels* (Acts 7:53). And it was given by angels, because it was not fitting that it be given by the Son, who is greater: *for if the word spoken by angels became steadfast* (Heb 2:2).

Furthermore, he says **ordained**, because it was given in proper sequence, namely, between the time of the law of nature, during which men were convinced they could not help themselves, and the time of grace. For before they should receive grace, they had to be convicted by the law.

168. The Lord of the law is Christ; hence he says, **in the hand of a mediator**, i.e., in the power of Christ: *in his right hand a fiery law* (Deut 33:2); *there is one mediator of God and men, the man Christ Jesus* (1 Tim 2:5).

This mediator was represented by Moses in whose hand the law was given: *I was the mediator, and stood between the Lord and you at that time* (Deut 5:5).

169. Then when he says, **now a mediator is not of one**, he explains what he meant when he said, **in the hand of a mediator**. This can be explained in three ways.

In one way, that a mediator is not of one alone but of two. Hence, since he is the mediator of God and men, it was fitting that he be God and man. For were he purely man or solely God, he would not be a true mediator. Therefore, if he is true God, then since no one is his own mediator, someone might suppose that there are, besides him, other gods of whom he was the mediator. But this he forestalls when he says that although this **mediator is not of one** only, there are not on that account other gods, **but God is one**, because, although he is distinct in person from God the Father, he is not distinct in nature: *hear, O Israel: the Lord our God is one Lord* (Deut 6:4); *one Lord, one faith, one baptism* (Eph 4:6).

In a second way, because someone might believe that he was the mediator of the Jews alone, he says: I say that Christ is **mediator**; but **not of one**, i.e., of the Jews, but **one** of all, i.e., capable of reconciling everyone to God, because he is God: *for it is one God who justifies circumcision by faith and uncircumcision through faith* (Rom 3:30); *for God indeed was in Christ reconciling the world to himself* (2 Cor 5:19).

In a third way, namely, that he is not a mediator of only one people, namely, the Jews, but of the gentiles as well: *for he is our peace, who has made both one* (Eph 2:14); on the part of the gentiles by taking away idolatry, and on the part of the Jews by delivering them from the observances of the law.

Specifically it is not the Father, not the Holy Spirit, but the Son who is mediator; nevertheless, God is one.

Lecture 8

3:21 Lex ergo adversus promissa Dei? Absit. Si enim data esset lex, quae posset vivificare, vere ex lege esset justitia. [n. 170]

3:22 Sed conclusit Scriptura omnia sub peccato, ut promissio ex fide Jesu Christi daretur credentibus. [n. 173]

3:23 Prius autem quam veniret fides, sub lege custodiebamur conclusi in eam fidem quae revelanda erat. [n. 175]

3:24 Itaque lex paedagogus noster fuit in Christo, ut ex fide justificemur. [n. 177]

3:25 At ubi venit fides, jam non sumus sub paedagogo. [n. 179]

3:21 Ὁ οὖν νόμος κατὰ τῶν ἐπαγγελιῶν [τοῦ θεοῦ]; μὴ γένοιτο: εἰ γὰρ ἐδόθη νόμος ὁ δυνάμενος ζῳοποιῆσαι, ὄντως ἐκ νόμου ἂν ἦν ἡ δικαιοσύνη.

3:22 ἀλλὰ συνέκλεισεν ἡ γραφὴ τὰ πάντα ὑπὸ ἁμαρτίαν ἵνα ἡ ἐπαγγελία ἐκ πίστεως Ἰησοῦ Χριστοῦ δοθῇ τοῖς πιστεύουσιν.

3:23 Πρὸ τοῦ δὲ ἐλθεῖν τὴν πίστιν ὑπὸ νόμον ἐφρουρούμεθα συγκλειόμενοι εἰς τὴν μέλλουσαν πίστιν ἀποκαλυφθῆναι.

3:24 ὥστε ὁ νόμος παιδαγωγὸς ἡμῶν γέγονεν εἰς Χριστόν, ἵνα ἐκ πίστεως δικαιωθῶμεν:

3:25 ἐλθούσης δὲ τῆς πίστεως οὐκέτι ὑπὸ παιδαγωγόν ἐσμεν.

3:21 Was the law then against the promises of God: God forbid! For if there had been a law given which could give life, verily justice should have been by the law. [n. 170]

3:22 But the Scripture has concluded all under sin, that the promise, by the faith of Jesus Christ, might be given to those who believe. [n. 173]

3:23 But before the faith came, we were kept shut up under the law, unto that faith which was to be revealed. [n. 175]

3:24 Wherefore the law was our pedagogue in Christ: that we might be justified by faith. [n. 177]

3:25 But after the faith has come, we are no longer under a pedagogue. [n. 179]

---

170. Hic movet Apostolus aliam dubitationem, utrum scilicet lex noceat gratiae. Et primo movet dubitationem, dicens **lex ergo**, etc., quasi dicat: si lex posita est propter transgressiones, numquid lex facit adversus promissa Dei, scilicet ut id quod Deus promisit se facturum per semen repromissum, per alium faciat? **Absit**. Quasi dicat: non. Nam, supra eodem: **lex non irritum facit testamentum ad evacuandas promissiones**, et cetera. Rom. VII, 12: *lex sancta, et mandatum sanctum*.

171. Secundo cum dicit *si enim lex esset data*, etc., solvit dubitationem. Et

primo ostendit, quod lex non est contra promissa Dei;

secundo quod est in obsequium promissorum, ibi *sed conclusit*, et cetera.

172. Dicit ergo, quod licet lex sit posita propter transgressiones, non tamen contrariatur promissioni Dei, quia transgressiones ipsas removere non potest. Si enim eas removeret, tunc manifeste esset contra promissa Dei, quia iustitia esset per alium modum, quam Deus promisit, quia esset per legem et non per fidem, cum tamen dicatur, Hab. II, v. 4: *iustus meus ex fide vivit*. Rom. III, 22: *iustitia Dei est per fidem Iesu Christi*.

Et ideo dicit, quod *si lex esset data* talis, *quae posset vivificare*, id est, tantae virtutis esset, quod posset vitam gratiae, et aeternam beatitudinem conferre, tunc *vere* et non apparenter *iustitia esset ex lege*, si lex faceret quod fides facere dicitur, et sic frustra esset fides. Sed lex

170. Here, the Apostle raises the other question, namely, whether the law is injurious to grace. First, he raises the question, saying, *was the law then against the promises of God?* As if to say: if the law was set because of transgressions, does the law go counter to the promises of God, namely, so that what God promised he would do through the promised seed, he would do through another? *God forbid!* As if to say: no. For earlier he had said: *the law does not disannul, to make the promise of no effect* (Gal 3:17); *the law, indeed is holy and the commandment holy* (Rom 7:12).

171. Second, when he says, *for if there had been a law given*, he answers the question.

First, he shows that the law is not contrary to the promises of God;

second, that the law is in keeping with the promises, at *but the Scripture has concluded*.

172. He says, therefore, that although the law was set because of transgressions, nevertheless, it is not contrary to the promise of God in being unable to remove those transgressions. For if it were to remove them, then it would obviously be against the promises of God, because justice would be obtained by means other than God promised, since it would be through the law and not through faith; whereas it is said: *the just shall live in his faith* (Hab 2:4); *the justice of God is by faith of Jesus Christ* (Rom 3:22).

Hence he says that *if there had been a law given which could give life*, i.e., of such power as to confer grace and eternal happiness, then *verily* and not seemingly, *justice should have been by the law*, if the law were to effect what faith is said to effect. Thus faith would serve no end. But

81

non iustificat, quia *littera*, scilicet legis, *occidit*, ut dicitur II Cor. III, 6 et Rom. c. VIII, 2: *lex enim Spiritus vitae in Christo Iesu*, et cetera.

173. Deinde cum dicit **sed Scriptura conclusit**, etc., ostendit quod lex non solum non contrariatur gratiae, sed est ei etiam in obsequium. Et

primo ostendit quod lex obsequitur promissis Dei;

secundo quomodo hoc obsequium manifestatum est in Iudaeis, ibi **prius autem quam veniret fides**, etc.;

tertio quomodo gentiles etiam sine lege consecuti sunt promissa Dei, ibi **omnes enim filii Dei estis**, et cetera.

174. Circa primum sciendum est, quod lex obsequitur promissis Dei in generali quantum ad duo. Primo quia manifestat peccata. Rom. III, 20: *per legem cognitio peccati*. Deinde quia manifestat infirmitatem humanam, in quantum homo non potest vitare peccatum, nisi per gratiam, quae per legem non dabatur. Et sicut ista duo, scilicet cognitio morbi et impotentia infirmi, multum inducunt ad quaerendum medicum, ita cognitio peccati et propriae impotentiae inducunt ad quaerendum Christum. Sic ergo lex obsecuta est gratiae, inquantum praebuit cognitionem peccati et experientiam propriae impotentiae.

Et ideo dicit **Scriptura**, id est lex scripta, **conclusit**, id est tenuit inclusos Iudaeos, **sub peccato**, id est, ostendit eis peccata, quae faciebant. Rom. VII, 7: *concupiscentiam nesciebam*, et cetera. Item **conclusit**, quia veniente lege sumpserunt occasionem peccati. Rom. c. XI, 32: *conclusit Deus omnia in incredulitate*, et cetera. Et hoc ideo, ut homo quaereret gratiam. Et ideo dicit **ut promissio**, id est, gratia repromissa, **daretur** non solum Iudaeis, sed omnibus **credentibus**, quia illa gratia poterat liberare a peccatis, et haec gratia est **ex fide Iesu Christi**.

175. Deinde cum dicit **prius autem quam veniret**, etc., ponit experimentum huius obsequii manifestatum in Iudaeis. Et

primo ponit obsequium Iudaeorum;

secundo concludit quoddam corollarium, ibi **itaque lex paedagogus**, et cetera.

176. Dicit ergo: si Scriptura, id est, lex scripta, detinuit omnia sub peccato, quas utilitates habebant Iudaei ex lege antequam veniret fides ex gratia? Respondet et dicit: nos Iudaei, ante adventum fidei, **custodiebamur sub lege**, inquantum faciebat nos vitare idololatriam et multa alia mala; **custodiebamur**, inquam, non sicut liberi, sed quasi servi sub timore, et hoc **sub lege**, id est, sub onere legis et dominio. Rom. VII, 1: *lex in homine dominatur quanto tempore vivit*, et cetera. Et **custodiebamur conclusi**, id est, servati ne deflueremus a vita, sed praepararemur **in eam**, id est, tam bonam **fidem, quae**

the law does not give life, because *the letter* of the law *kills* (2 Cor 3:6); *for the law of the Spirit of life, in Christ Jesus, has delivered me from the law of sin and of death* (Rom 8:2).

173. Then when he says, **but the Scripture has concluded all under sin**, he shows that the law is not only not opposed to grace but serves it.

First, he shows that the law serves God's promises;

second, how this service was made manifest in the case of the Jews, at **but before the faith came**;

third, how the gentiles even without the law obtained the promises of God, at **for you are all the children of God** (Gal 3:26).

174. With respect to the first it should be noted that in general the law serves the promises of God in two ways. First, because it exposes sin: *for by the law is the knowledge of sin* (Rom 3:20). Second, because it reveals human infirmity, in the sense that man cannot avoid sin without grace which was not given by the law. And just as these two things, namely, the knowledge of a disease and the infirmity of the patient are a great inducement to seek medical treatment, so the knowledge of sin and of one's impotency lead us to seek Christ. Thus, therefore, is the law the servant of grace, inasmuch as it affords a knowledge of sin and actual experience of one's impotency.

Hence he says, **the Scripture**, i.e., the written law, **has concluded**, i.e., held the Jews enclosed, **under sin**, i.e., showed them the sins they committed: *for I had not known concupiscence, if the law did not say: you shall not covet* (Rom 7:7). Again, **has concluded**, because with the coming of the law they took occasion to sin: *for God has concluded all in unbelief, that he may have mercy on all* (Rom 11:32). And all this in order that they would search for grace. Hence he says, **that the promise**, i.e., the promised grace, **might be given** not only to the Jews, but to all **those who believe**, because that grace was able to free from sin; and this grace is **by the faith of Jesus Christ**.

175. Then when he says, **but, before the faith came, we were kept under the law shut up**, he gives experimental evidence of this service, as manifested in the case of the Jews.

First, he states how the Jews were benefited;

second, he concludes a corollary, at **wherefore the law was our pedagogue**.

176. He says therefore: if Scripture, i.e., the written law, kept all things shut up under sin, what benefits did the Jews derive from the law before faith came by grace? He answers and says: we Jews, before the coming of faith, **were kept shut up under the law**, inasmuch as it made us avoid idolatry and many other evils; we were kept shut up, I say, not as free men, but as servants under fear; and this **under the law**, i.e., under the burden and domination of the law: *the law has dominion over a man as long as it lives* (Rom 7:1). And **we were kept shut up**, i.e., protected, in order that we not be cut off from life, but be made ready **unto that faith**

revelanda erat. Is. LVI, 1: *iuxta est salus mea, ut veniat, et iustitia mea ut reveletur*.

Et dicit *revelanda*, quia cum fides excedat omne humanum ingenium, non potest per proprium sensum haberi, sed ex revelatione et dono Dei. Is. XL, 5: *revelabitur gloria Domini*, et cetera. Vel *in eam fidem, quae revelanda erat* tempore gratiae, in antiquis temporibus multis signis latens. Unde et tempore Christi velum Templi scissum est, Matth. XXVII, 51.

177. Consequenter cum dicit *lex paedagogus*, etc., concludit quoddam corollarium. Et

primo ostendit legis officium;

secundo officii testationem, ibi *at ubi venit plenitudo temporis*, et cetera.

178. Officium autem legis fuit officium paedagogi, et ideo dicit *lex paedagogus noster*, et cetera.

Quamdiu enim haeres non potest consequi beneficium haereditatis, vel propter defectum aetatis seu alicuius debitae perfectionis, conservatur, et custoditur ab aliquo instructore, qui quidem instructor paedagogus dicitur, a paedos, quod est puer, et goge, quod est ductio. Per legem enim Iudaei tamquam imbecilles pueri, per timorem poenae retrahebantur a malo, et promovebantur amore et promissione temporariorum ad bonum. Iudaeis autem promissa erat benedictio futuri seminis de haereditate obtinenda, sed nondum advenerat tempus ipsius haereditatis consequendae. Et ideo necessarium erat, quod conservarentur usque ad tempus futuri seminis et cohiberentur ab illicitis, quod factum est per legem.

Et ideo dicit *itaque*, etc., quasi dicat: ex quo sub lege custodiebamur, *lex fuit noster paedagogus*, id est, dirigens et conservans *in Christo*, id est in via Christi. Et hoc ideo, *ut ex fide* Christi *iustificaremur*. Os. XI, 1: *puer Israel, et dilexi eum*. Ier. c. XXXI, 18: *castigasti me, domine, et eruditus sum*, et cetera. Rom. III, 28: *arbitramur enim hominem iustificari per fidem*, et cetera.

179. Et quamvis lex paedagogus noster esset, non tamen ad perfectam haereditatem ducebat, quia, ut dicitur Hebr. VII, *neminem ad perfectum adduxit lex*, et cetera. Sed hoc officium cessavit postquam venit fides. Et hoc est quod dicit *at ubi venit fides*, scilicet Christi, *iam non sumus sub paedagogo*, id est sub coactione, quae non est necessaria liberis. I Cor. XV: *cum essem parvulus*, et cetera. *Cum autem factus sum vir*, et cetera. II Cor. V, 17: *si qua ergo in Christo nova creatura, vetera transierunt*, et cetera.

which was to be revealed: *my salvation is near to come and my justice to be revealed* (Isa 56:1).

And he says, *to be revealed*, because, since faith surpasses all human ingenuity, it cannot be acquired by one's own skill, but by revelation and by the gift of God: *the glory of the Lord shall be revealed, and all flesh together shall see that the mouth of the Lord has spoken* (Isa 40:5). Or, *unto that faith*, which was to be revealed in the time of grace, but which in olden times was hidden under many signs. Hence in the time of Christ the veil of the Temple was rent (Matt 27:51).

177. Then when he says, *the law was our pedagogue in Christ*, he draws a corollary:

first, he manifests the law's functions;

second, when its function ceased, at *but after the faith is come*.

178. The function of the law was that of a pedagogue; hence he says, *the law was our pedagogue in Christ*.

For as long as the heir cannot obtain the benefits of his inheritance, either because be is too young or because of some other shortcoming, he is sustained, and guarded by a tutor called a pedagogue, from *paedos*, which means 'boy,' and *goge*, which means 'a guiding.' For under the law the just were restrained from evil, as helpless boys are, through fear of punishment; and they were led to progress in goodness by the love and promise of temporal goods. Further, the Jews were promised that through a seed that was to come the blessing of an inheritance would be obtained, but the time for obtaining that inheritance had not yet come. Consequently, it was necessary that until the seed should come, they be kept safe and not do unlawful things. And this was effected by the law.

And therefore he says, *wherefore the law was our pedagogue*. As if to say: by being kept shut up under the law, *the law was our pedagogue*, i.e., it guided and preserved us, *in Christ*, i.e., in the way of Christ. And this was done in order *that we might be justified by the faith* of Christ: *Israel was a child and I loved him* (Hos 11:1); *you have chastised me and I was instructed* (Jer 31:18); *for we account a man to be justified by faith without the works of the law* (Rom 3:28).

179. And although the law was our pedagogue, it did not bring us the full inheritance, because it is said: *the law brought nothing to perfection* (Heb 7:19). But the law's function ended after faith came. Hence he says, *but, after the faith has come*, namely, of Christ, *we are no longer under a pedagogue*, i.e., under constraint, which is not necessary for those who are free: *when I was a child, I spoke as a child, I understood as a child, I thought as a child, but when I became a man I put away the things of a child* (1 Cor 13:11); *if then any be in Christ a new creature, the old things are passed away* (2 Cor 5:17).

Lecture 9

3:26 Omnes enim filii Dei estis per fidem, quae est in Christo Jesu. [n. 180]

3:27 Quicumque enim in Christo baptizati estis, Christum induistis. [n. 182]

3:28 Non est Judaeus, neque Graecus: non est servus, neque liber: non est masculus, neque femina. Omnes enim vos unum estis in Christo Jesu. [n. 185]

3:29 Si autem vos Christi, ergo semen Abrahae estis, secundum promissionem haeredes. [n. 190]

3:26 Πάντες γὰρ υἱοὶ θεοῦ ἐστε διὰ τῆς πίστεως ἐν Χριστῷ Ἰησοῦ.

3:27 ὅσοι γὰρ εἰς Χριστὸν ἐβαπτίσθητε, Χριστὸν ἐνεδύσασθε·

3:28 οὐκ ἔνι Ἰουδαῖος οὐδὲ Ἕλλην, οὐκ ἔνι δοῦλος οὐδὲ ἐλεύθερος, οὐκ ἔνι ἄρσεν καὶ θῆλυ· πάντες γὰρ ὑμεῖς εἷς ἐστε ἐν Χριστῷ Ἰησοῦ.

3:29 εἰ δὲ ὑμεῖς Χριστοῦ, ἄρα τοῦ Ἀβραὰμ σπέρμα ἐστέ, κατ' ἐπαγγελίαν κληρονόμοι.

3:26 For you are all the children of God, by faith in Christ Jesus. [n. 180]

3:27 For as many of you as have been baptized in Christ have put on Christ. [n. 182]

3:28 There is neither Jew nor Greek: there is neither bond nor free: there is neither male nor female. For you are all one in Christ Jesus. [n. 185]

3:29 And if you are Christ's, then are you the seed of Abraham, heirs according to the promise. [n. 190]

---

180. Hic ostendit Apostolus quod ad fructum gratiae gentiles sine obsequio legis pervenerunt, ad quem tamen Iudaei perducti sunt per legis custodiam et obsequium. Et

circa hoc tria facit.

Primo proponit intentum;

secundo manifestat propositum, ibi *quicumque enim in Christo*, etc.;

tertio ex hoc argumentatur, ibi *si autem vos Christi; ergo*, et cetera.

181. Dicit ergo: vere non sumus sub lege, id est, sub paedagogo et coactione, quia sumus filii Dei. Similiter et vos neque sub lege, neque sub paedagogo estis, quia scilicet ad gratiam pervenistis. Ideo *omnes estis filii Dei per fidem*, non per legem. Rom. VIII, v. 15: *non enim accepistis spiritum servitutis*, scilicet timoris, qui dabatur in lege veteri, *sed accepistis Spiritum filiorum*, scilicet caritatis et amoris, qui datur in nova lege per fidem. Io. I, 12: *dedit eis potestatem filios Dei fieri*, et cetera.

Si ergo filii Dei estis per fidem, quare vultis esse servi per legis observantias? Nam sola fides homines facit filios Dei adoptivos. Nullus siquidem est filius adoptivus, nisi uniatur et adhaereat filio naturali. Rom. VIII, v. 29: *quos praescivit conformes fieri imaginis Filii eius*, et cetera. Fides enim facit nos in Christo Iesu filios. Eph. III, 17: *habitare Christum per fidem in cordibus vestris*. Et hoc *in Christo Iesu*, id est filii Dei estis per Iesum Christum.

182. Consequenter cum dicit *quicumque enim in Christo*, etc., manifestat propositum. Et

circa hoc tria facit.

180. Here the Apostle shows that the gentiles obtained the fruit of grace without serving the law, whereas the Jews obtained it by keeping and serving the law.

Concerning this he does three things.

First, he states his proposition;

second, he elucidates it, at *for as many of you*;

third, from this he proceeds to his argument, at *and if you are Christ's*.

181. He says therefore: verily, we are not under the law, i.e., under a pedagogue, or under restraint, because we are the sons of God. In like manner, you, too, are neither under the law nor under a pedagogue; for you have attained to grace. Hence *you are all the children of God by faith* and not through the law: *for you have not received the spirit of bondage* (i.e., of fear which was given in the old law), but *you have received the Spirit of adoption of sons*, namely, of charity and love which is given in the new law through faith (Rom 8:15); *he gave them power to be made the sons of God, to them that believe in his name* (John 1:12).

If, then, you are the sons of God by faith, why do you wish to become slaves by the observances of the law? For faith alone makes man the adopted son of God. Indeed, no one is an adopted son unless he is united to and cleaves to the natural son: *for whom he foreknew, he also predestined to be made conformable to the image of his Son; that he might be the firstborn among many brethren* (Rom 8:29). For faith makes us sons in Jesus Christ: *that Christ may dwell by faith in your hearts* (Eph 3:17). And this *in Christ Jesus*, i.e., you are sons of God through Jesus Christ.

182. Then when he says, *for as many of you as have been baptized in Christ have put on Christ*, he expounds his proposition.

Concerning this he does three things.

Primo proponit propositi manifestationem;

secundo manifestationis expositionem, ibi *non est Iudaeus*, etc.;

tertio assignat manifestationis rationem, ibi *omnes enim vos unum estis*, et cetera.

183. Manifestat autem circa primum quomodo sumus in Christo Iesu filii Dei. Et hoc est quod dicit *quicumque enim in Christo Iesu*, et cetera. Quod potest quadrupliciter exponi. Uno modo, ut dicatur: *quicumque in Christo Iesu baptizati estis*, id est, institutione Christi ad baptismum instructi estis. Mc. c. ult.: *euntes in mundum universum, praedicate Evangelium omni creaturae*, et cetera. *Qui crediderit et baptizatus fuerit*, et cetera.

Alio modo: *quicumque in Christo Iesu baptizati estis*, scilicet per similitudinem, et per configurationem mortis Christi. Rom. VI, v. 3: *quicumque baptizati sumus in Christo Iesu, in morte ipsius baptizati sumus.*

Vel *in Christo Iesu*, id est, in fide Iesu Christi. Nam baptismus non fit nisi in fide, sine qua effectum baptismi nullum consequimur. Mc. ult.: *qui crediderit et baptizatus fuerit, salvus erit*, et cetera.

Vel *in Christo Iesu*, id est, in virtute et operatione eius. Io. I, 33: *super quem videris Spiritum descendentem, hic est qui baptizat.*

Quicumque ergo istis quatuor modis *baptizati estis, Christum induistis*.

184. Ubi sciendum est, quod qui induitur aliqua veste, protegitur ac contegitur ea, et apparet sub colore vestis, colore proprio occultato. Eodem modo et qui induit Christum, protegitur et contegitur a Christo Iesu contra impugnationes et aestus, et in eo nihil aliud apparet nisi quae Christi sunt. Rom. XIII, 14: *induite Dominum Iesum Christum*. Et sicut lignum accensum induitur igne, et participat eius virtutem, ita et qui Christi virtutes accipit, induitur Christo. Lc. ult.: *sedete in civitate donec induamini virtute*, etc., quod in illis locum habet qui interius Christi virtute informantur. Eph. IV, 24: *induite novum hominem, qui secundum*, et cetera.

Et nota, quod Christum aliqui induunt exterius per bonam conversationem, et interius per spiritus renovationem; et secundum utrumque per sanctitatis configurationem, ut tangitur in Glossa.

185. Expositionem autem manifestationis ponit, cum dicit *non est Iudaeus*, etc., quasi dicat: vere dixi, quod *quicumque in Christo Iesu*, et cetera. Quia nihil potest esse in hominibus, quod faciat exceptionem a sacramento fidei Christi et baptismi. Et ponit tres differentias

First, he proposes to explain the proposition;

second, the elucidation of the explanation, at *there is neither Jew*;

third, he assigns the reason behind the explanation, at *for you are all one in Christ Jesus.*

183. With respect to the first, he shows how we are sons of God in Christ Jesus. And he says: *for as many of you as have been baptized in Christ have put on Christ*. Now this can be explained in four ways. In one way, so that *as many of you as have been baptized in Christ* means that it was by Christ's appointment that you have been instructed for baptism: *go into the whole world and preach the Gospel to every creature. He that believes and is baptized shall be saved* (Mark 16:16).

In another way, *as many of you as have been baptized in Christ have put on Christ*, i.e., through a likeness and a configuration of the death of Christ: *we who are baptized in Christ Jesus are baptized in his death* (Rom 6:3).

Or: *in Christ Jesus*, i.e., in the faith of Christ. For baptism comes about only through faith, without which we derive no effect from baptism: *he who believes and is baptized shall be saved; but he who believes not shall be condemned* (Mark 16:16).

Or: *in Christ Jesus*, i.e., through his power and operation: *he upon whom you shall see the Spirit descending, he it is that baptizes* (John 1:33).

Therefore, *as many of you as have been baptized* in any of those four ways *have put on Christ*.

184. Here it should be noted that when someone puts on clothing he is protected and covered by it and his appearance is that of the color of the clothing instead of his own. In the same way, everyone who puts on Christ is protected and covered by Christ Jesus against attack and against the heat; furthermore in such a one nothing appears except what pertains to Christ: *put on the Lord Jesus Christ* (Rom 13:14). Again, just as burning wood takes on fire and shares in fire's activity, so he who receives the virtues of Christ has put on Christ: *stay in the city until you are endued with power from on high* (Luke 24:49). This applies to those who are inwardly clothed with the virtue of Christ: *put on the new man, who according to God is created in justice and holiness of truth* (Eph 4:24).

And note that some put on Christ outwardly by good works and inwardly by a renewal of the spirit; and with respect to both they are configured to his holiness, as is mentioned in a Gloss.

185. He elucidates this teaching when he says, *there is neither Jew nor Greek*. As if to say: truly have I said, that *as many of you as have been baptized in Christ Jesus have put on Christ*, because there is nothing in man that would exclude anyone from the sacrament of the faith of Christ

hominum, ostendens quod per eas nullus excipitur a fide Christi.

186. Prima differentia est quantum ad ritum, cum dicit **non est Iudaeus, neque Graecus**, quasi dicat: ex quo in Christo Iesu baptizatus est, non est differentia, quod propter hoc sit indignior in fide, ex quocumque ritu ad eam venerit, sive ex ritu Iudaico sive Graeco. Rom. III, 29 s.: *an Iudaeorum Deus tantum? Nonne et gentium? Immo et gentium, quoniam quidem unus est Deus, qui iustificavit circumcisionem ex fide, et praeputium per fidem*. Et Rom. X, 12: *non est distinctio Iudaei et Graeci*, et cetera.

Sed contra est quod dicitur Rom. III, 1: *quid ergo amplius est Iudaeo? Multum quidem per omnem modum*.

Respondeo. Dicendum est, quod Iudaei et Graeci possunt considerari dupliciter: uno modo secundum statum in quo erant ante fidem; et sic amplius fuit Iudaeo propter beneficium legis. Alio modo quantum ad statum gratiae, et sic non est amplius Iudaeo; et de hoc intelligitur hic.

187. Secunda differentia est quantum ad statum et conditionem, cum dicit **non est servus, neque liber**, id est, neque servitus, neque libertas, neque nobilitas, neque ignobilitas differentiam facit ad recipiendum effectum baptismi. Iob III, 19: *parvus et magnus ibi sunt, et servus liber a domino suo*. Rom. II, 11: *non est personarum acceptio apud Deum*.

188. Tertia differentia est quantum ad naturam, cum dicit **non est masculus, neque foemina**, quia sexus nullam differentiam facit quantum ad participandum baptismi effectum. Gal. III, 28: **non est masculus, aut foemina**, et cetera.

189. Expositionis vero rationem ponit, cum dicit **omnes enim vos unum estis in Christo Iesu**, quasi dicat: vere nihil horum est per quod differentia fiat in Christo, quia vos omnes, scilicet fideles, unum estis in Christo Iesu, qui in baptismo omnes estis effecti membra Christi, et unum corpus, etsi inter vos sitis diversi. Rom. XII, 5: *omnes unum corpus sumus in Christo*, et cetera. Eph. IV, v. 4: *unum corpus, unus Spiritus*, et cetera. Ubi autem est unitas, differentia non habet locum. Pro hac unitate orat Christus, Io. XVII, 21: *volo, Pater, ut sint unum*, et cetera.

190. Consequenter cum dicit *si autem vos estis*, etc., arguit ad principale propositum hoc modo: dixi quod **Abrahae dictae sunt promissiones et semini eius**, sed vos **estis Abrahae**, ergo ad vos pertinet promissio Abrahae de haereditate consequenda.

and of baptism. And he mentions three differences among men to show that no one is excluded from faith in Christ by any of them.

186. The first difference concerns one's rite. Hence he says: **there is neither Jew nor Greek**. As if to say: since you have been baptized in Christ, the rite from which you came to Christ, whether it was the Jewish or the Greek, is no ground for saying that anyone occupies a less honorable place in the faith: *is he the God of the Jews only? Is he not also of the gentiles? Yes, of the gentiles also. For there is one God that justifies circumcision by faith and uncircumcision through faith* (Rom 3:29). Again: *there is no distinction of the Jew and Greek; for the same is Lord over all* (Rom 10:12).

But this seems to militate against what is said in Romans: *what advantage then does the Jew have? Much every way* (Rom 3:1).

I answer that Jews and Greeks can be considered in two ways. First, according to the state in which they were before faith. In this way, the Jew was greater because of the benefits he derived from the law. In another way, according to the state of grace; and in this way, the Jew is not greater. And this is the sense in which it is taken here.

187. The second difference is with respect to estate, when he says: **there is neither bond nor free**, i.e., neither slavery nor freedom, neither high estate nor low makes a difference so far as receiving the effect of baptism is concerned: *the small and great are there, and the servant is free from his master* (Job 3:19); *there is no respect of persons with God* (Rom 2:11).

188. The third difference concerns the condition of the nature: **there is neither male nor female**, for sex makes no difference as far as sharing in the effect of baptism is concerned. *There is neither male nor female*.

189. The underlying reason for this explanation is set forth when he says, **for you are all one in Christ Jesus**. As if to say: truly, none of these things makes a difference in Christ, because all of you, i.e., believers, are one in Christ Jesus, because through baptism you have all been made members of Christ and you form one body, even though you are distinct individuals: *so we, being many, are one body in Christ, and everyone members one of another* (Rom 12:5); *one body, one Spirit, as you are called in one hope of your calling* (Eph 4:4). Now where there is unity, difference has no place. Indeed it was for this unity that Christ prayed: *that they all may be one, as you, Father, in me, and I in you* (John 17:21).

190. Then when he says, **if you are Christ's, then are you the seed of Abraham, heirs according to the promise**, he argues to his main proposition in the following manner: I have said that **the promises were made to Abraham and to his seed** (Gal 3:16); but you are **of Abraham**; therefore, to you pertains the promise made to Abraham about obtaining the inheritance.

Minorem sic probat: vos estis filii Dei adoptivi, quia estis uniti per fidem Christo, qui est Filius Dei naturalis; sed Christus est filius Abrahae, ut supra eodem: ***quasi in uno, et semini tuo, qui est Christus***; ergo ***si vos estis Christi***, id est, in Christo, ***estis semen Abrahae***, id est, filii, cum Christus filius eius sit. Et si filii, estis et ***haeredes***, id est, ad vos pertinet haereditas ***secundum promissionem*** Abrahae factam. Rom. IX, 8: *non qui filii sunt carnis, hi filii Dei, sed qui sunt filii promissionis, aestimantur in semine.*

Then he proves the minor premise: you are the adopted sons of God, because by faith you are united to Christ, who is the natural Son of God. But Christ is a son of Abraham, as was said above, ***as of one: 'and to your seed', which is Christ***. Therefore, if you are of Christ, i.e., in Christ, ***you are the seed of Abraham***, i.e., sons, because Christ is his son. And if you are the sons, you are ***heirs***, i.e., the inheritance belongs to you ***according to the promise*** made to Abraham: *they that are the children of the flesh are not the children of God; but they that are the children of the promise are accounted for the seed* (Rom 9:8).

Chapter 4

Lecture 1

⁴:¹Dico autem: quanto tempore haeres parvulus est, nihil differt a servo, cum sit dominus omnium: [n. 191]

⁴:²sed sub tutoribus et actoribus est usque ad praefinitum tempus a patre:

⁴:³ita et nos cum essemus parvuli, sub elementis mundi eramus servientes. [n. 197]

⁴:¹Λέγω δέ, ἐφ' ὅσον χρόνον ὁ κληρονόμος νήπιός ἐστιν, οὐδὲν διαφέρει δούλου κύριος πάντων ὤν,

⁴:²ἀλλὰ ὑπὸ ἐπιτρόπους ἐστὶν καὶ οἰκονόμους ἄχρι τῆς προθεσμίας τοῦ πατρός.

⁴:³οὕτως καὶ ἡμεῖς, ὅτε ἦμεν νήπιοι, ὑπὸ τὰ στοιχεῖα τοῦ κόσμου ἤμεθα δεδουλωμένοι·

⁴:¹As long as the heir is a child, he is no different than a servant, though he be lord of all: [n. 191]

⁴:²But is under tutors and governors until the time appointed by the father.

⁴:³So we also, when we were children, were serving under the elements of the world. [n. 197]

---

191. Postquam ostendit Apostolus legis defectum, hic consequenter ostendit gratiae dignitatem. Et

primo per exemplum humanum;

secundo per exemplum Scripturae, ibi **dicite mihi qui sub lege vultis esse**, et cetera.

Circa primum duo facit.

Primo ostendit dignitatem gratiae supra primitivum statum veteris legis, per similitudinem a lege humana sumptam;

secundo ostendit, quod ipsi facti sunt participes huius dignitatis per fidem, ibi **quoniam autem estis filii Dei**, etc.;

tertio arguit ipsos, eo quod hanc dignitatem contemnebant, ibi **sed tunc quidem ignorantes Deum**, et cetera.

Circa primum duo facit.

Primo ponit similitudinem;

secundo adaptat eam ad propositum, ibi **ita et nos cum essemus**, et cetera.

192. Notandum est quod in proposita similitudine quatuor tangit Apostolus.

Primo quidem dignitatem, quia non est servus, sed haeres. Unde dicit **quanto tempore haeres**, etc., quod aptatur et refertur ad populum Iudaeorum, qui fuit haeres promissionis Abrahae, Ps. CXXXIV, 4: *elegit nos in haereditatem sibi* et ad Christum, qui est haeres omnium, Hebr. I, 2: *quem constituit haeredem universorum*.

193. Secundo eius parvitatem. Unde dicit **parvulus est**, quia et Iudaei parvuli erant secundum statum legis. Amos VII, 5: *quis suscitabit Iacob, quia parvulus est?* Similiter et Christus parvulus factus est per Incarnationem. Is. IX, 6: *parvulus natus est nobis*, et cetera.

Sed nota quod Apostolus aliquando assimilat parvulo statum legis, sicut hic, aliquando statum praesentis

191. After pointing out the shortcoming of the law, the Apostle then shows here the dignity of grace.

First, with a human example;

second, with an example from Scripture, at **tell me, you who desire to be under the law** (Gal 4:21).

Regarding the first he does three things:

first, he shows the pre-eminence of grace over the primitive state of the old law by a simile taken from human law;

second, he shows that they have been made partakers of this pre-eminence through faith, at **and because you are sons of God** (Gal 4:6);

third, he censures them for disdaining this preeminence, at **but then indeed, not knowing God** (Gal 4:8).

As to the first, he does two things:

first, he lays down the simile;

second, he adapts it to his proposition, at **so we also, when we were children**.

192. It should be noted that the Apostle touches upon four things in the simile he proposes.

First of all, eminence, because he speaks not of a servant but of an heir. Hence he says, **as long as the heir is a child**. This is applied and referred both to the Jewish people—who were the heirs of the promise to Abraham: *for the Lord has chosen Jacob unto himself; Israel for his own possession* (Ps 134:4)—and to Christ, who is the heir of all things: *whom he has appointed heir of all things* (Heb 1:2).

193. Second, smallness; hence he says, **is a child**, because the Jews were children according to the state of the law: *who shall raise up Jacob, for he is a little one?* (Amos 7:5). Similarly, Christ, too, was become a child through the Incarnation: *for a child is born to us and a son is given to us* (Isa 9:6).

But note that the Apostle sometimes compares the state of the law to a child, as he does here, and sometimes the state

vitae. I Cor. XIII, v. 11: *cum essem parvulus*, et cetera. Cuius ratio est, quia status veteris legis est sicut parvulus, propter imperfectionem cognitionis, in ipsa comparatione ad statum gratiae et veritatis, quae per Christum facta est. Sic et status praesentis vitae, in qua videmus per speculum in aenigmate, est sicut parvulus, comparatus statui futurae vitae, in qua est perfecta Dei cognitio, quia videtur sicuti est.

194. Tertio eius subiectionem, cum dicit **nihil differt a servo, cum sit dominus omnium, sed sub tutoribus**, et cetera. Proprium enim servi est, quod sit subiectus alicui domino. Puer autem, quamdiu parvulus est, quia non habet cognitionem perfectam et usum liberae voluntatis propter defectum aetatis, committitur custodiae aliorum, qui et bona sua defendant: et hi dicuntur tutores; et negotia agant: et hi actores nominantur. Et ideo licet **sit dominus omnium** rerum suarum, tamen in quantum subiicitur aliis, **nihil differt a servo**, quia nec voluntatem liberam habet, imo cogitur: et haec adaptantur ad populum Iudaicum Is. XLIV, 1: *et nunc servus meus Iacob*, et cetera.

195. Sed notandum est, quod in populo Iudaico aliqui erant simpliciter servi, illi scilicet qui propter timorem poenae et cupiditatem temporalium, quae lex promittebat, legem servabant. Aliqui vero erant, qui non erant servi simpliciter, sed, quasi servi existentes, erant vere filii et haeredes: qui licet attenderent exterius ad temporalia et vitarent poenas, nihilominus tamen in eis finem non ponebant sed accipiebant ea, ut figuram spiritualium bonorum. Unde licet viderentur nihil exterius differre a servis, inquantum caeremonias et alia legis mandata servabant, tamen erant domini, quia non ea intentione eis utebantur, ut servi, quia illis utebantur amore spiritualium bonorum, quae praefigurabant: servi vero principaliter timore poenae et cupiditate terrenae commoditatis.

Christus erat etiam quasi servus, quia, licet sit Dominus omnium, secundum illud Ps. CIX, v. 1: *dixit Dominus Domino meo*, etc., tamen nihil videbatur differre a servo in exterioribus, inquantum homo. Phil. II, 7: *exinanivit semetipsum, formam servi accipiens, et habitu inventus ut homo*. Sub tutoribus autem et actoribus erat, quia sub lege factus erat, ut dicitur infra eodem, **factum sub lege**, et hominibus subditus, ut dicitur Lc. II, 51: *erat subditus illis*.

196. Quarto ponit temporis congruitatem, cum dicit **usque ad praefinitum tempus a patre**, quia sicut haeres secundum determinationem patris praefinito tempore sub tutoribus est, ita et lex determinatum tempus habuit a Deo, quamdiu deberet durare, et quamdiu haeres,

of the present life: *when I was a child, I spoke as a child, I understood as a child, I thought as a child* (1 Cor 13:11). The reason for this is that the state of the old law, because of the imperfection of knowledge, is as a child, compared to the state of grace and truth which came through Christ. In like manner, the state of the present life, in which we see through a mirror in a dark manner, is as a child, compared to the state of the future life, in which there is perfect knowledge of God, because he is seen as he is.

194. Third, subjection, when he says, **he is no different than a servant, though he be lord of all: but is under tutors and governors**. For a servant is one who is subject to a lord. But a boy, as long as he is a child, because he does not have fullness of knowledge and use of free will through lack of years, is committed to the care of others who defend his possessions—and these are called tutors—and who handle his affairs—and these are called governors. Therefore, **though he be lord of all** his things, yet, in so far as he is subject to others, **he is no different than a servant**, because he does not have free will but is in fact constrained. And this is applied to the Jewish people: *and now hear, O Jacob, my servant* (Isa 44:1).

195. Here it should be noted that among the Jewish people some were servants in the strict sense; those, namely, who observed the law through fear of punishment and through a desire for the temporal things which the law promised. But there were others who were not servants in the strict sense, but living as servants, were really sons and heirs. These, although outwardly attending to temporal things and avoiding punishments, did not place their end in them but took them as a figure of spiritual goods. Hence, even though on the surface they seemed to differ nothing from servants, inasmuch as they observed the ceremonies and other commandments of the law, they were, nevertheless, lords, because they did not use them with the same frame of mind as servants; for they used them for love of the spiritual goods they prefigured, whereas servants used them chiefly through fear of punishment and with a desire for earthly convenience.

Christ, too was like a servant, because although he is the Lord of all things according to a psalm: *the Lord said to my Lord* (Ps 109:1), nevertheless outwardly, as man, he seemed no different than a servant: *he emptied himself, taking the form of a servant, being made in the likeness of men, and in habit found as a man* (Phil 2:7). Furthermore, he was under tutors and governors, because he was made under the law, as is said below: **made under the law** (Gal 4:4); he was also subject to men, as is said in Luke: *he was subject to them* (Luke 2:51).

196. Fourth, he touches on the correspondence of time, when he says, **until the time appointed by the father**, because just as the heir is under tutors for a definite period of time fixed by the father, so the law had a time fixed by God determining how long it was to endure and how long the

scilicet populus Iudaeorum, esset sub ea. Similiter et praefinitum tempus fuit a Patre, quo Christus non erat facturus miracula et ostensurus Dominium potestatis divinae. Io. II, 4: *nondum venit hora mea*.

197. Hanc similitudinem adaptat, cum dicit consequenter *ita et nos*, et cetera. Et

primo adaptat eam quantum ad Iudaeos;
secundo quantum ad Christum, ibi *at ubi venit plenitudo temporis*.

198. Dicit ergo: dico quod *quanto tempore haeres parvulus*, etc., et *ita nos*, Iudaei, *cum essemus parvuli*, in statu legis veteris, *sub elementis mundi eramus servientes*, id est sub lege, quae temporalia promittebat Is. I, 19: *si volueritis et audieritis me, bona terrae comedetis* et comminabatur poenas temporales.

Vel lex vetus dicitur *elementum*, quia sicut pueris, qui sunt instituendi ad scientiam, primo proponuntur elementa illius scientiae, per quae manuducuntur ad illam scientiam: ita lex vetus proposita est Iudaeis, per quam manuducerentur ad fidem et iustitiam. Supra III, 24: *lex paedagogus noster fuit in Christo*.

Vel, *sub elementis*, id est corporalibus rerum ritibus quos servabant, sicut lunares dies, neomenias et sabbatum. Nec tamen instandum est quod propter hoc non differrent a paganis, qui elementis serviebant huius mundi, cum eis non servirent Iudaei, seu cultum impenderent; sed sub eis Deo serviebant, et eum colebant, gentiles vero elementis servientes, eis divinum cultum impendebant. Rom. I, 25: *servierunt creaturae potius quam Creatori*, et cetera.

Fuit autem necessarium, quod Iudaei sub elementis huius mundi deservirent Deo, quia iste ordo est congruus naturae humanae, ut a sensibilibus ad intellectualia perducantur.

heir, i.e., the Jewish people, where to be under it. Similarly, there was a time fixed by the Father during which Christ was not to perform miracles or show the lordship of his divine power: *my hour is not yet come* (John 2:4).

197. He applies this simile when he says, *so we also, when we were children, were serving under the elements of the world*.

First, he applies it as regarding the Jews;
second, as regarding Christ, at *but when the fullness of the time was come* (Gal 4:4).

198. He says therefore: *I say that as long as the heir is a child he is no different than a servant; so, we Jews also, when we were children* in the state of the old law, *were serving under the elements of the world*, i.e., under the law which promised temporal things—*if you be willing, and will hearken to me, you shall eat the good things of the land* (Isa 1:19)—and threatened temporal punishments.

Or the old law is called *element*, because just as boys who are to be trained in a science are first taught the elements of that science and through them are brought to the fullness of science, so to the Jews was proposed the old law through which they would be brought to faith and justice: *the law was our pedagogue in Christ* (Gal 3:24).

Or, *under the elements*, i.e., the corporeo-religious usages which they observed, such as days of the moon, new moons and the sabbath. But one should not object that on this account they differed nothing from the pagans who served the elements of this world, for the Jews did not serve them or pay them worship; but under them they served and worshipped God, whereas the pagans in serving the elements rendered them divine worship: *they worshipped and served the creature rather than the Creator* (Rom 1:25).

Furthermore, it was necessary that the Jews serve God under the elements of this world, because such an order is in harmony with human nature which is led from sensible to intelligible things.

Lecture 2

4:4 At ubi venit plenitudo temporis, misit Deus Filium suum factum ex muliere, factum sub lege, [n. 199]

4:5ut eos, qui sub lege erant, redimeret, ut adoptionem filiorum reciperemus. [n. 209]

4:4ὅτε δὲ ἦλθεν τὸ πλήρωμα τοῦ χρόνου, ἐξαπέστειλεν ὁ θεὸς τὸν υἱὸν αὐτοῦ, γενόμενον ἐκ γυναικός, γενόμενον ὑπὸ νόμον,

4:5ἵνα τοὺς ὑπὸ νόμον ἐξαγοράσῃ, ἵνα τὴν υἱοθεσίαν ἀπολάβωμεν.

4:4 But when the fullness of the time was come, God sent his Son, made of a woman, made under the law: [n. 199]

4:5 That he might redeem those who were under the law: that we might receive the adoption of sons. [n. 209]

---

199. Hic adaptat Apostolus similitudinem propositam ad Christum. Et

primo ponitur adaptatio;

secundo finis rei, in qua similitudo adaptatur, ibi *ut eos qui sub lege erant*, et cetera.

200. Sciendum est autem quod supra, in similitudine proposita, quatuor ostendit per ordinem, sicut dictum est. Hic autem illa quatuor adaptans ad Christum, incipit ab ultimo, scilicet a determinatione temporis, cuius ratio est, quia idem tempus fuit in quo Christus fuit humiliatus et in quo fideles fuerunt exaltati.

Et ideo dicit *at ubi venit plenitudo temporis*, id est postquam tempus, quod fuerat praefinitum a Deo Patre de mittendo Filio suo, erat completum; et hoc modo accipitur Lc. II, 6: *impleti sunt dies*, et cetera.

Dicitur autem plenum tempus illud propter plenitudinem gratiarum, quae in eo dantur, secundum Ps. LXIV, 10: *flumen Dei repletum est aquis*, et cetera. Item propter impletionem figurarum veteris legis. Matth. V, 17: *non veni solvere legem*, et cetera. Item, propter impletionem promissorum. Dan. IX, 27: *confirmabit autem pactum multis hebdomada una*.

Hoc autem quod dicit *at ubi venit plenitudo temporis*, etc., similiter et in aliis Scripturae locis, ubi tempus circa Christum impleri dicitur, non est referendum ad fatalem necessitatem, sed ad divinam ordinationem, de qua dicitur in Ps. CXVIII, 91: *ordinatione tua perseverat dies*, et cetera.

201. Assignatur autem duplex ratio, quare illud tempus praeordinatum est ad adventum Christi. Una sumitur ex magnitudine. Quia enim magnus est qui venturus erat, oportebat et multis indiciis et multis praeparationibus homines ad adventum eius disponi. Hebr. I, 1: *multifarie multisque modis*, et cetera.

Alia ex conditione venientis. Quia enim medicus erat venturus, oportebat quod ante adventum suum convincerentur homines de morbo, et quantum ad defectum

199. Here the Apostle applies to Christ the simile he has proposed.

First, he makes the application;

second, he discloses the purpose of the reality that corresponds to the simile, at *that he might redeem those who were under the law*.

200. It should be noted that above, in the simile he proposed, there were four items pointed out in order, as has been said. But now, in applying them to Christ, he begins with the last, namely, the fixing of a time. The reason for this is that the time in which Christ was humiliated and in which the faithful were exalted turns out to be the same.

Hence he says: *but, when the fullness of the time was come*, i.e., after the time fixed by God the Father for sending his Son had been accomplished. This is how it is taken in Luke: *her days were accomplished, that she should be delivered* (Luke 2:6).

This time is called 'full' because of the fullness of the graces that are given in it, according to a psalm: *the river of God is filled with water; you have prepared their food: for so is its preparation* (Ps 65:9). Also because of the fulfillment of the figures of the old law: *I have not come to destroy but to fulfill* (Matt 5:17). And because of the fulfillment of the promises: *and he shall confirm the covenant with many, in one week* (Dan 9:27).

However, the fact that he likewise says, *but, when the fullness of time was come*, in other places of Scripture where the time respecting Christ is said to be accomplished, should not be explained in terms of a necessity imposed by fate, but in terms of a divine ordinance, concerning which a psalm states: *by your ordinance the day goes on; for all things serve you* (Ps 119:91).

201. Two reasons are given why that time was preordained for the coming of Christ. One is taken from his greatness: for since he that was to come was great, it was fitting that men be made ready for his coming by many indications and many preparations. *God, who, at sundry times and in diverse manners, spoke in times past to the fathers by the prophets, last of all in these days has spoken to us by his Son* (Heb 1:1).

The other is taken from the role of the one coming: for since a physician was to come, it was fitting that before his coming, men should be keenly aware of their infirmity,

scientiae in lege naturae et quantum ad defectum virtutis in lege scripta. Et ideo oportuit utrumque, scilicet et legem naturae et legem Scripturae, adventum Christi praecedere.

202. Secundo adaptat quantum ad haereditariam dignitatem, cum dicit *misit Deus Filium suum*, scilicet proprium et naturalem. Et si Filius, ergo et haeres. Dicit autem *Filium suum*, id est proprium, naturalem et unigenitum, non adoptivum. Io. III, v. 16: *sic Deus dilexit mundum, ut*, et cetera. *Misit*, inquam, eum non a se separatum, quia missus est per hoc, quod assumpsit humanam naturam, et tamen erat in sinu Patris, Io. I, 18: *unigenitus, qui est in sinu Patris* aeternaliter. Io. III, 13: *nemo ascendit in caelum, nisi qui descendit de caelo, Filius hominis qui est in caelo*, qui, licet descenderit per assumptionem carnis, tamen est in caelo.

Item *misit* eum, non ut esset ubi prius non erat; quia, licet in propria venerit per praesentiam carnis, in mundo tamen erat per praesentiam Deitatis, ut dicitur in Evangelio Io. I, 14. Similiter non misit eum quasi ministrum, quia sua missio fuit assumptio carnis, non depositio maiestatis.

Misit ergo *Deus Filium suum* ad sanandum, inquam, deviationem concupiscibilis, et ad illuminandum ignorantiam rationalis creaturae. Ps. CVI, 20: *misit Verbum suum*, et cetera. Misit etiam ad liberandum a potestate daemonis contra infirmitatem irascibilis. Is. XIX, v. 20: *mittet eis Salvatorem, qui liberet eos*. Item ad remedium ab obligatione aeternae mortis. Os. III, 14: *de manu mortis liberabo eos, de morte redimam eos*. Item ad salvandum ab eorum peccatis. Io. III, 17: *non misit Deus Filium suum in mundum, ut iudicet mundum, sed ut salvetur mundus per ipsum*, et cetera.

203. Tertio adaptat similitudinem quantum ad parvitatem, cum dicit *factum ex muliere*. Is. IX, 6: *parvulus natus est nobis*, et cetera. Phil. II, 7: *exinanivit semetipsum*, et cetera.

Parvum se fecit non dimittendo magnitudinem, sed assumendo parvitatem.

204. In hoc autem quod dicit *factum ex muliere*, cavendi sunt duo errores, scilicet Photini, qui dixit Christum purum hominem esse et ex Virgine principium essendi sumpsisse; et ideo ita dicit ipsum factum ex muliere, quasi totaliter initium ex ea sumpserit.

Sed hoc est falsum, quia est contra illud quod dicitur Rom. I, 3: *qui factus est ei ex semine David secundum carnem*; non dicit secundum personam, quae est ab aeterno, scilicet ipsa hypostasis Filii Dei. Unde sicut cum scutum fit album de novo, non oportet dicere, quod ipsa substantia scuti de novo fiat sed quod ei de novo albedo accesserit, ita ex hoc quod Filius Dei de novo carnem

both as to their lack of knowledge during the law of nature and as to their lack of virtue during the written law. Therefore it was fitting that both, namely, the law of nature and the written law, precede the coming of Christ.

202. Second, he applies it as to his dignity as heir, when he says, **God sent his Son**, namely, his own natural Son; and if Son, then an heir also. He says, **his Son**, i.e., his own, natural, only begotten but not adopted, Son: *God so loved the world as to give his only begotten Son* (John 3:16). He **sent** him, I say, without his being separated from him, for he was sent by assuming human nature, and yet he was in the bosom of the Father: *the only begotten Son, who is in the bosom of the Father eternally* (John 1:18); *And no man has ascended into heaven, but he that descended from heaven, the Son of man, who is in heaven* (John 3:13), who, although he descended by assuming flesh is, nevertheless, in heaven.

Again, **he sent** him, not to be where before he was not; because, although he came unto his own by his presence in the flesh, yet by the presence of his Godhead, he was in the world, as is said in John (John 1:14). Furthermore, he did not send him as a minister, because his mission was the assuming of flesh, not the putting off of majesty.

God, therefore, **sent his Son**, I say, to heal the errantry of the concupiscible part and to illumine the ignorance of the rational part: *he sent his Word and healed them: and delivered them from their destructions* (Ps 106:20). He sent him also to deliver them from the power of the devil against the infirmity of the irascible part: *he shall send them a Savior and defender to deliver them* (Isa 19:20). Also as a deliverer from the chains of eternal death: *I will deliver them out of the hand of death. I will redeem them from death* (Hos 13:14). Also to save them from their sins: *for God sent his Son into the world not to judge the world but that the world may be saved by him* (John 3:17).

203. Third, he applies the simile as to smallness, when he says, **made of a woman**: *for a child is born to us* (Isa 9:6); *he emptied himself taking the form of a servant* (Phil 2:7).

He made himself small not by putting off greatness, but by taking on smallness.

204. In interpreting the passage, **made of woman**, two errors must be avoided; namely, that of Photinus, who said that Christ was solely man and received the beginning of his existence from the Virgin; in other words, that Christ was made of a woman as though deriving his beginning entirely from her.

But this is false, because it contradicts what is said in Romans: *who was made to him of the seed of David, according to the flesh* (Rom 1:3); he does not say according to his person, which exists from eternity, namely, the hypostasis of the Son of God. Hence, just as when a shield newly comes to be white, it is not proper to say that the very substance of the shield newly came to be, but that the

whiteness newly accrued to it; so from the fact that the Son of God newly assumed flesh, it is not proper to say that the person of Christ newly came to be, but that a human nature newly accrued to that person, as when certain things affect a body without that body itself being changed. For certain items affect a thing and change it, such as forms and absolute qualities; but certain other items affect it without changing it. Of this sort is the assuming of flesh precisely as bespeaking a relationship. Hence the person of the Word is in no way changed by it.

That is why in divine matters we employ in a temporal sense terms that signify a relationship; thus, we say in a psalm: *Lord, you have been our refuge* (Ps 89:1); or we say that God became man. But we do not thus use forms and absolute qualities, so as to say: God was made good or wise and so on.

205. Second, one must avoid the error of Ebion, who said that Christ was born of the seed of Joseph, and who was led to this by the saying, **born of a woman**. For according to him the word 'woman' always implies defloration.

But this is erroneous, for in Sacred Scripture 'woman' also denotes the natural sex, according to Genesis: *Adam said: the woman whom you gave to me to be my companion gave to me of the tree* (Gen 3:12). Here he calls her a woman while she was still a virgin.

206. Furthermore, by saying **made of a woman** two errors are destroyed, namely, that of Nestorius saying that Christ did not take his body of the Virgin but of the heavens and that he passed through the Blessed Virgin as through a corridor or channel.

But this is false, for if it were true, he would not, as the Apostle says, have been made of a woman. By the preposition **of** the material cause is denoted.

207. Likewise, the error of Nestorius saying that the Blessed Virgin is not the mother of the Son of God but of the son of a man. But this is shown to be false by the words of the Apostle here, that **God sent his Son made of a woman**. Now one who is made of a woman is her son. Therefore, if the Son of God was made of a woman, namely, of the Blessed Virgin, it is obvious that the Blessed Virgin is the Mother of the Son of God.

Moreover, although he might have said *born* of a woman, he distinctly says **made**, and not *born*. Indeed, for something to be born it must not only be produced of a principle conjoined to it but be made from a principle separate from it. Thus a wooden chest is made by an artisan, but fruit is born from a tree. Now the principle of human generation is twofold, namely, material—and as to this, Christ proceeded from a conjoined principle, because he took the matter of his body from the Virgin; and it is according to this that he is said to be born of her: *of whom was born Jesus who is called Christ* (Matt 1:16). The other is the active principle, which in the case of Christ, so far as he had a principle, i.e., as to the forming of the body, was not conjoined but

formavit illud. Et quantum ad hoc non dicitur natus ex muliere sed factus quasi ex principio exteriori. Ex quo patet, quod hoc quod dixit *ex muliere*, non dicit corruptionem, quia dixisset *natum* et non **factum**.

208. Quarto adaptat similitudinem quantum ad subiectionem, cum dicit **factum sub lege**.

Sed contra est, quod dicitur infra V, 18: *si Spiritu ducimini, non estis sub lege*. Si ergo Christus non solum est spiritualis, sed etiam dator Spiritus, inconvenienter videtur dici quod sit factus sub lege.

Respondeo. Dicendum est quod esse sub lege dicitur dupliciter. Uno modo, ut ly sub, denotet solam observantiam legis, et sic Christus fuit factus sub lege, quia circumcisus fuit et in Templo praesentatus. Matth. V, v. 17: *non veni legem solvere*, et cetera. Alio modo, ut ly sub, denotet oppressionem. Et hoc modo ille dicitur esse sub lege, qui timore legis opprimitur et hoc modo nec Christus, nec viri spiritales dicuntur esse sub lege.

209. Consequenter cum dicit **ut eos qui sub lege**, etc., ponit fructum rei in qua similitudo adaptatur, scilicet quod ideo voluit isto tempore fieri subiectus, ut haeredes fierent magni et liberi.

Et haec duo ponit, et, primo, fructum liberationis contra subiectionem. Et ideo dicit **ut eos qui sub lege erant**, id est sub maledicto et onere legis, liberaret. Supra III, v. 13: **Christus nos redemit de maledicto legis**, et cetera.

Secundo fructum exaltationis, inquantum adoptamur in filios Dei per hoc quod accipimus Spiritum Christi et conformamur ei. Rom. VIII, 9: *si quis Spiritum Christi non habet*, et cetera.

Et haec adoptio specialiter competit Christo, quia non possumus fieri filii adoptivi, nisi conformemur Filio naturali. Rom. VIII, v. 29: *quos praescivit conformes fieri imaginis Filii eius*, et cetera. Et quantum ad hoc dicit **ut adoptionem filiorum reciperemus**, id est ut per Filium Dei naturalem efficeremur filii adoptivi secundum gratiam per Christum.

separate, because the power of the Holy Spirit formed it. And with respect to this he is not said to have been born of a woman, but made, as it were, from an extrinsic principle. From this it is obvious that the saying, *of a woman*, does not denote a defloration; otherwise he would have said born and not **made**.

208. Fourth, he applies the simile as to its aspect of subjection when he says, **made under the law**.

But here a difficulty comes to mind from what is said below, namely: *if you are led by the Spirit, you are not under the law* (Gal 5:18). Hence if Christ is not only spiritual but the giver of the Spirit, it seems unbecoming to say that he was made under the law.

I answer that 'to be under the law' can be taken in two ways: in one way so that 'under' denotes the mere observance of the law, and in this sense Christ was made under the law, because he was circumcised and presented in the Temple: *I am not come to destroy but to fulfill* (Matt 5:17). In another way so that 'under' denotes oppression. And in this way one is said to be under the law if he is oppressed by fear of the law. But neither Christ nor spiritual men are said to be under the law in this way.

209. Then when he says, **that he might redeem those who were under the law**, he sets down the fruit of the reality in which the simile is applied, namely, that the reason why he willed they be subject during that time was that they might become heirs, great and free.

And he mentions both of these things. First, the fruit of freedom as against subjection; hence he says, **that he might redeem those who were under the law**, i.e., under the curse and burden of the law; **Christ has redeemed us from the curse of the law, being made a curse for us** (Gal 3:13).

Second, the fruit of being made great, inasmuch as we are adopted as sons of God by receiving the Spirit of Christ and being conformed to him: *now if any man have not the Spirit of Christ, he is none of his* (Rom 8:9).

This adoption belongs in a special way to Christ, because we cannot become adopted sons unless we are conformed to the natural Son: *for whom he foreknew, he also predestined to be made conformable to the image of his Son* (Rom 8:29). With this in mind, he says, **that we might receive the adoption of sons**, i.e., that through the natural Son of God we might be made adopted sons according to grace through Christ.

Lecture 3

⁴:⁶Quoniam autem estis filii, misit Deus Spiritum Filii sui in corda vestra, clamantem: Abba, Pater. [n. 210]

⁴:⁷Itaque jam non est servus, sed filius: quod si filius, et haeres per Deum. [n. 216]

⁴:⁶Ὅτι δέ ἐστε υἱοί, ἐξαπέστειλεν ὁ θεὸς τὸ πνεῦμα τοῦ υἱοῦ αὐτοῦ εἰς τὰς καρδίας ἡμῶν, κρᾶζον, Αββα ὁ πατήρ.

⁴:⁷ὥστε οὐκέτι εἶ δοῦλος ἀλλὰ υἱός· εἰ δὲ υἱός, καὶ κληρονόμος διὰ θεοῦ.

⁴:⁶And because you are sons, God has sent the Spirit of his Son into your hearts, crying: Abba, Father. [n. 210]

⁴:⁷Therefore, now he is not a servant, but a son. And if a son, an heir also through God. [n. 216]

---

210. Supra Apostolus ostendit beneficium Iudaeis exhibitum, hic ostendit hoc beneficium etiam ad gentiles pertinere. Et

primo proponit ipsum beneficium;

secundo modum adipiscendi, ibi ***misit Deus Spiritum***, etc.;

tertio manifestat eius fructum, ibi ***itaque iam non est***, et cetera.

211. Dicit ergo, quod beneficium adoptionis filiorum Dei non solum pertinet ad eos qui sub lege erant sed etiam ad gentiles. Et ideo dicit: ***quoniam estis filii Dei***, etc., id est quod sitis filii Dei, ista de causa factum est, quia non solum Iudaei, sed etiam omnes alii, qui in Filium Dei credunt, adoptantur in filios, et cetera. Io. I, 12: *dedit eis potestatem filios Dei fieri*, et cetera.

212. Modus autem adipiscendi illud donum est per missionem Spiritus Filii Dei in corda vestra. Augustinus autem dicit, quod Christus in carne existens praedicavit Iudaeis principaliter, gentibus autem perfunctorie. Rom. XV, 8: *dico Christum Iesum ministrum fuisse circumcisionis*, et cetera. Et ideo quidquid pertinet ad statum Iudaeorum, convenienter attribuitur Christo.

Et quia possent dicere isti, Galatas non esse adoptatos in filios Dei, cum Christus ex eis carnem non sumpserit, nec eis praedicaverit, unde non videbantur in aliquo Christo coniungi, ideo Apostolus modum huius adoptionis demonstrans, dicit quod et si non fuerunt coniuncti Christo secundum carnem, scilicet quantum ad gentem, neque secundum praedicationem, tamen fuerunt coniuncti per Spiritum, et ex hoc adoptati sunt in filios Dei. Unde conversio gentilium specialiter attribuitur Spiritui Sancto. Et ideo Petrus, quando fuit reprehensus a Iudaeis, quod ivisset praedicare gentibus, excusavit se per Spiritum Sanctum, dicens, Act. XI, 12, non posse resistere Spiritui Sancto, cuius instinctu hoc fecerat. Et ideo, quia ***misit Deus***, Pater, ***Spiritum Filii sui in corda*** nostra, Iudaeorum scilicet et gentium, coniungimur Christo, et per hoc adoptamur in filios Dei.

213. Sed sciendum est, quod si alicubi in Scriptura invenitur Spiritus Sanctus mitti a Patre, Io. XIV, 26, *Paracletus autem Spiritus Sanctus, quem mittet Pater*, etc.,

210. Above, the Apostle revealed the gift bestowed on the Jews; here he shows that this gift pertains also to the gentiles.

First, he mentions the gift;

second, the means of obtaining it, at ***God has sent the Spirit***;

third, he discloses the fruit of this gift, at ***therefore, now he is not a servant***.

211. He says therefore that the gift of adoption of sons pertains not only to those who were under the law but to the gentiles as well. Hence he says: ***because you are sons of God***, i.e., you are the sons of God, because not only the Jews but all others who believe in the Son of God are adopted as sons: *he gave them power to be made sons of God, to them that believe in his name* (John 1:12).

212. The manner in which that gift is obtained is by the sending of the Spirit of the Son of God into your hearts. Augustine says, however, that Christ, existing in the flesh, preached in a principal manner to the Jews, but to the gentiles as a matter of course: *for I say that Christ Jesus was minister of the circumcision for the truth of God to confirm the promises made unto the fathers* (Rom 15:8). Accordingly, whatever pertains to the condition of the Jews is fittingly adapted to Christ.

And because they might have said that the Galatians had not been adopted as sons of God, since Christ did not assume flesh from them or preach to them, for that reason the Apostle, elucidating the manner of this adoption, says that although they were not related to Christ according to the flesh, i.e., according to race, or by reason of preaching, yet they were united to him through the Spirit and thereby adopted and made sons of God. Hence the conversion of the gentiles is in a special way attributed to the Holy Spirit. Consequently, Peter, when he was blamed by the Jews for going to preach to the gentiles, excused himself through the Holy Spirit, saying that he could not resist the Holy Spirit by whose inspiration he had done this (Acts 11). And so, because ***God*** the Father ***sent the Spirit of his Son into*** our ***hearts***, i.e., the hearts of the Jews and gentiles, we are united to Christ and by that fact are adopted as sons of God.

213. But it should be noted that if in certain passages of Scripture the Holy Spirit is said to be sent by the Father— *but the Paraclete, the Holy Spirit, whom the Father will send*

aliquando vero a Filio, Io. XV, 26, *cum venerit Paracletus, quem ego mittam vobis*, etc., nihilominus tamen Spiritus Sanctus communis est Patri et Filio, et ab utroque procedit et ab utroque datur. Et ideo est, quod ubicumque invenitur quod Pater mittat Spiritum Sanctum, fit mentio de Filio, sicut in praemissa auctoritate dicitur **quem mittet Pater in nomine meo**. Et, similiter, ubi dicitur mitti a Filio, fit mentio de Patre; unde dicit *quem mittam vobis a Patre*. Et etiam hic cum dicit **misit Deus**, Pater, **Spiritum** Sanctum, statim fit mentio de Filio, cum dicit **Filii sui**.

Nec refert si alicubi dicatur Spiritus Sanctus solum a Patre procedere, quia, ex quo Filius mittit eum, manifestum est quod ab ipso procedit. Unde Spiritus Sanctus dicitur Spiritus Filii, sicut mittentis, et sicut a quo procedit, et sicut a quo habet Spiritus Sanctus quidquid habet, sicut et a Patre. Io. c. XVI, 14: *ille me clarificabit, quia de meo accipiet*, et cetera.

214. Dicit autem **in corda**, quia duplex est generatio. Una carnalis, quae fit per semen carnale missum in locum generationis: quod quidem semen, licet sit quantitate parvum, tamen virtute continet totum.

Alia est spiritualis, quae fit per semen spirituale transmissum in locum spiritualis generationis; qui quidem locus est mens seu cor hominis, quia in filios Dei generamur per mentis renovationem. Semen autem spirituale est gratia Spiritus Sancti. I Io. ult.: *qui natus est ex Deo, non peccat: quoniam generatio Dei conservat eum*, et cetera. Et hoc semen est virtute continens totam perfectionem beatitudinis. Unde dicitur pignus et arra beatitudinis Ephes. I, 14; Ez. XXXVI, 26: *dabo spiritum novum*, et cetera.

215. Clamantem, id est clamare facientem, **Abba, Pater**, non magnitudine vocis, sed magnitudine et fervore affectus. Tunc enim clamamus **Abba, Pater**, quando per affectum accendimur calore Spiritus Sancti ad desiderium Dei. Rom. VIII, 15: *non accepistis spiritum servitutis*, et cetera.

Abba, Pater, et cetera. Idem autem est in significatione, *abba*, quod est Hebraeum, et *pater*, quod est Latinum, et *patir*, quod est Graecum. Et utrumque ponit ut ostendat quod gratia Spiritus Sancti communiter se habet quantum ad utrumque populum, quantum est ex se.

216. Consequenter cum dicit **itaque iam non est servus**, etc., ponit fructum huius beneficii.

Et primo quantum ad remotionem omnis mali, a quo liberamur per adoptionem Spiritus Sancti et haec est liberatio a servitute. Et quantum ad hoc dicit **itaque**, scilicet quia Spiritus clamat in nobis, **Pater, iam**, a tempore gratiae, **non est** aliquis nostrum, qui in Christum credimus, **servus**, in timore scilicet serviens. Io. XV, 15: *iam*

in my name (John 14:26)—and in others to be sent by the Son—*but when the Paraclete comes, whom I will send you from the Father* (John 15:26)—the Holy Spirit is nonetheless common to Father and Son and proceeds from both and is sent by both. Accordingly, wherever it is said that the Father sends the Holy Spirit, mention is made of the Son, as in the aforesaid passage: **whom the Father will send in my name**; and where he is said to be sent by the Son, mention is made of the Father; hence he says, *whom I will send to you from the Father* (John 15:26). Even here, when he says, **God** the Father **has sent the** Holy **Spirit**, mention is made at once of the Son, for he adds, **of his Son**.

Nor does it matter that at times the Holy Spirit is only said to proceed from the Father, for the fact that the Son sends him shows that he proceeds from him. Accordingly, the Holy Spirit is called the Spirit of the Son as of the one sending and as of the one from whom he proceeds, as well as of the one from whom the Holy Spirit has whatever he has, just as of the Father: *he shall glorify me, because he shall receive of mine* (John 16:14).

214. But he says, **into your hearts**, because there is a twofold generation: one is carnal and comes about through fleshly seed sent to the place of generation. This seed, small as it is, contains in effect the whole.

The other is spiritual, which comes about by spiritual seed transmitted to the place of spiritual generation, i.e., man's mind or heart, because they are born sons of God through a renewal of the mind. Furthermore, the spiritual seed is the grace of the Holy Spirit: *whoever is born of God does not sin: but the generation of God preserves him and the wicked one does not touch him* (1 John 5:18). This seed contains, in effect, the whole perfection of beatitude; hence it is called the pledge and deposit of beatitude (Eph 1:14); *I will put a new spirit within you* (Ezek 36:26).

215. Crying, i.e., making us cry, **Abba, Father**, not with a loudness of voice but with a great fervor of love. For we cry, **Abba, Father**, when our affections are kindled by the warmth of the Holy Spirit to desire God: *you have not received the spirit of bondage again in fear; but you have received the Spirit of adoption of sons, whereby we cry: Abba, Father* (Rom 8:15).

Abba in Hebrew and *pater* in Greek and 'father' in English all have the same meaning. And he makes mention of both to show that the grace of the Holy Spirit, as such, is related in a common way to both.

216. Then when he says, **therefore, now he is not a servant, but a son**, he mentions the fruit of this gift.

First, as to removing all evil, from which we are freed through adoption by the Holy Spirit. This is freedom from bondage. With respect to this he says: **therefore**, i.e., because the Spirit cries **Father** in us, **now**, from the time of grace, **he**, i.e., each one of us who believes in Christ, **is not a servant**, i.e., serving in fear—I will not now call you

non dicam vos servos, sed amicos, et cetera. Rom. VIII, 15: *non accepistis spiritum servitutis*, et cetera. **Sed** est *filius*. Rom. VIII, 16: *ipse Spiritus testimonium reddit spiritui nostro, quod sumus filii Dei*.

Licet enim conditione servi simus, quia dicitur Lc. XVII, 10: *cum feceritis omnia quae praecepta sunt vobis, dicite: servi inutiles sumus*, tamen non sumus servi malevoli, ex timore scilicet servientes, quia tali servo debentur tortura et compedes; sed sumus servi boni et fideles, et amore servientes, et ideo libertatem per Filium consequimur. Io. VIII, v. 36: *si Filius vos liberaverit, vere liberi eritis*.

217. Secundo, ponit fructum quantum ad consecutionem omnis boni, et quantum ad hoc dicit **quod si filius, et haeres per Deum**, Rom. VIII, 17: *si filii et haeredes, haeredes quidem Dei*, et cetera. Haec autem haereditas est plenitudo omnis boni, cum nihil aliud sit quam ipse Deus, secundum illud Ps. XV, 5: *Dominus pars haereditatis meae*, et cetera. Gen. c. XV, 1: *dixit ad Abraham: ego ero merces tua magna nimis*, et cetera.

Dicit autem **per Deum**, quia sicut Iudaei haereditatem adepti sunt per Dei repromissionem et iustitiam, ita et gentiles per Deum, id est per Dei misericordiam. Rom. XV, 9: *gentes autem super misericordia honorare Deum*, et cetera.

Vel **per Deum**, id est per Dei operationem. Is. XXVI, 12: *omnia opera nostra operatus es in nobis, Domine*.

servants but friends (John 15:15); *you have not received the spirit of bondage again in fear: but you have received the Spirit of adoption of sons* (Rom 8:15)—**but a son**: for the *Spirit himself gives testimony to our spirit that we are the sons of God* (Rom 8:16).

For although we be in the condition of servants, because it is said in Luke: *when you shall have done all these things that are commanded you, say: we are unprofitable servants* (Luke 17:10), we are not ill-disposed servants, i.e., serving in fear—for such a servant is deserving of torture and chains—but we are good and faithful servants, serving out of love. For that reason we obtain freedom through the Son: *if, therefore, the Son shall make you free, you shall be free indeed* (John 8:36).

217. Second, he mentions the fruit as to its effect of attaining every good. With regard to this he says: **and, if a son, an heir also through God**: *and if sons, heirs also: heirs indeed of God and joint heirs with Christ* (Rom 8:17). Now this inheritance is the fullness of all good, for it is nothing other than God himself, according to a psalm: *the Lord is the portion of my inheritance* (Ps 16:5). He said to Abraham: *I am your reward, exceedingly great* (Gen 15:1).

He says, **through God**, because as the Jews obtained the inheritance through the promise and justice of God, so the gentiles too received it through God, i.e., through the mercy of God: *but the gentiles are to glorify God for his mercy* (Rom 15:9).

Or, **through God**, i.e., through the working of God: *you have wrought all our works for us, O Lord* (Isa 26:12).

Lecture 4

⁴:⁸Sed tunc quidem ignorantes Deum, iis, qui natura non sunt dii, serviebatis. [n. 218]

⁴:⁹Nunc autem cum cognoveritis Deum, immo cogniti sitis a Deo: quomodo convertimini iterum ad infirma et egena elementa, quibus denuo servire vultis? [n. 220]

⁴:¹⁰Dies observatis, et menses, et tempora, et annos. [n. 225]

⁴:¹¹Timeo vos, ne forte sine causa laboraverim in vobis. [n. 226]

⁴:⁸Ἀλλὰ τότε μὲν οὐκ εἰδότες θεὸν ἐδουλεύσατε τοῖς φύσει μὴ οὖσιν θεοῖς·

⁴:⁹νῦν δὲ γνόντες θεόν, μᾶλλον δὲ γνωσθέντες ὑπὸ θεοῦ, πῶς ἐπιστρέφετε πάλιν ἐπὶ τὰ ἀσθενῆ καὶ πτωχὰ στοιχεῖα, οἷς πάλιν ἄνωθεν δουλεύειν θέλετε;

⁴:¹⁰ἡμέρας παρατηρεῖσθε καὶ μῆνας καὶ καιροὺς καὶ ἐνιαυτούς.

⁴:¹¹φοβοῦμαι ὑμᾶς μή πως εἰκῇ κεκοπίακα εἰς ὑμᾶς.

⁴:⁸But then indeed, not knowing God, you served those who, by nature, are not gods. [n. 218]

⁴:⁹But now, after you have known God, or rather are known by God: how do you turn again to the weak and needy elements which you desire to serve again? [n. 220]

⁴:¹⁰You observe days and months and times and years. [n. 225]

⁴:¹¹I am afraid of you, lest perhaps I have labored in vain among you. [n. 226]

---

218. Posita dignitate beneficii gratiae, et ostensa per exemplum humanum, hic Apostolus arguit Galatas, qui hanc gratiam contemnebant, utpote ingrati tanto beneficio. Et

primo arguit eos de ingratitudine;

secundo excusat se, quod hoc non facit ex odio et livore, ibi *fratres, obsecro vos, non me laesistis*, et cetera.

Circa primum tria facit.

Primo commemorat statum pristinum;

secundo extollit et commendat beneficium susceptum, ibi *nunc autem cum cognoveritis*, etc.;

tertio exaggerat peccatum commissum, ibi *quomodo convertimini*, et cetera.

219. Dicit ergo *sed tunc*, etc., quasi dicat: nunc estis filii et haeredes per Deum, *sed tunc quidem*, cum gentes essetis. Eph. V, v. 8: *eratis aliquando tenebrae*, etc., *ignorantes Deum*, per infidelitatem, *serviebatis*, cultu latriae, *his qui non sunt natura dii*, sed opinione hominum. I Cor. XII, 2: *cum gentes essetis, ad simulacra muta prout ducebamini euntes*, et cetera. Rom. I, 25: *servierunt creaturae potius quam Creatori*, et cetera.

Hoc autem quod dicit *qui natura non sunt dii*, est ad confutationem Arianorum dicentium Christum Dei Filium non esse Deum per naturam. Quod si verum esset, non esset ei exhibendus cultus latriae, et quicumque exhiberet ei esset idololatra.

Sed potest obiici, quia nos adoramus carnem et humanitatem Christi, ergo sumus idololatrae. Sed dicendum est, quod licet adoremus carnem, seu humanitatem Christi, adoramus tamen eam, ut unitam personae divini Verbi, quod quidem verbum est suppositum divinum. Unde cum adoratio debeatur supposito divinae naturae, quidquid in Christo adoratur, absque errore fit.

218. Having disclosed the pre-eminence of the gift of grace and explained it with a human example, the Apostle here censures the Galatians, who scorned this grace, for being ungrateful for so great a gift.

First, he censures them for ingratitude;

second, he excuses himself, explaining that he does not do this out of hatred or spite, at *brethren, I beseech you* (Gal 4:12).

As to the first he does three things:

first, he calls to mind their earlier state;

second, he extols and commends the gift they have received, at *but now, after that you have known God*;

third, he amplifies the sin committed: *how do you turn again to the weak and needy elements?*

219. He says therefore: *but then indeed, not knowing God, you served those who, by nature, are not gods*. As if to say: you are now sons and heirs through God; *but then indeed*, when you were heathens—*you were heretofore darkness, but now light in the Lord* (Eph 5:8)—*not knowing God*, through lack of faith, *you served* with the worship of *latria*, *those who, by nature, are not gods*, but by the opinion of men: *you know that when you were heathens, you went to dumb idols, according as you were led* (1 Cor 12:2); *they served the creature rather than the Creator* (Rom 1:25).

His statement, *who, by nature, are not gods*, serves to refute the Arians who said that Christ, the Son of God, is not God by nature. For if this were true, it would not be right to render him *latria*, and whoever rendered it would be an idolater.

But someone might object that we adore the flesh and humanity of Christ; consequently, we are idolaters. I answer that even though we adore the flesh or humanity of Christ, we adore it as united to the person of the divine Word, who is a divine hypostasis. Hence, since adoration is due to a person of the divine nature, whatever is adored in Christ is done without error.

220. Consequenter cum dicit *nunc autem cum cognoveritis*, etc., commemorat acceptum beneficium, quasi dicat: si ignorantes eratis et peccabatis, tolerari poterat, nam, caeteris paribus, gravius est peccatum in Christiano, quam in gentili. Sed *nunc cum cognoveritis Deum*, id est sitis conducti ad Dei cognitionem, gravius peccatis quam olim, serviendo et ponendo spem in his in quibus non debetis. Ier. XXXI, 34: *omnes cognoscent me*, et cetera.

Sed hoc quod dicit *imo cogniti sitis a Deo*, videtur contrarietatem habere, cum Deus ab aeterno omnia cognoverit. Eccli. XXIII, 29: *Domino enim Deo antequam crearentur omnia sunt agnita*, et cetera.

Sed dicendum hoc causaliter esse dictum, ut sit sensus *imo cogniti sitis a Deo*, id est Deus fecit quod vos cognosceretis eum. Sic enim Deus dicitur cognoscere, inquantum est causa cognitionis nostrae. Et ideo, quia supra dixit: *cum cognoveritis Deum*, quae fuit vera locutio, statim corrigit et explicat eam praefiguratam innuendo quod non possumus Deum cognoscere ex nobis, nisi per ipsum. Io. I, 18: *Deum nemo vidit unquam, sed unigenitus, qui est in sinu Patris*, et cetera.

221. Consequenter exprobrat peccatum commissum, dicens *quomodo convertimini*, et cetera. Et

primo exaggerat eorum peccatum;
secundo ostendit imminens periculum, ibi *timeo vos ne forte*, etc.;
tertio reducit eos ad salutis statum, ibi *estote sicut ego*, et cetera.
Circa primum duo facit.
Primo proponit peccatum commissum;
secundo de peccato commisso eos convincit, ibi *dies observatis*, et cetera.

222. Sciendum est autem, quod haec littera dupliciter legitur. Uno modo, quia isti Galatae a fide convertebantur ad idololatriam, et ideo dicit *quomodo convertimini* a fide *iterum*, id est denuo, II Petr. II, 21: *melius erat eis non cognoscere viam iustitiae, quam post*, et cetera. Is. XLII, 17: *conversi sunt retrorsum*, etc. *ad elementa*, scilicet mundi, quae sunt *infirma*, per se subsistere non valentia, quia in nihilum deciderent, nisi ea manus cuncta regentis teneret, secundum illud Hebr. I, 3: *portans omnia verbo virtutis suae*, etc. *et egena*, quia egent Deo et seipsis ad invicem, ad complementum universi, *quibus*, scilicet elementis, *denuo*, id est iterum, *servire vultis*, servitute scilicet latriae. Probatio huius manifeste apparet, quia *observatis dies*, scilicet faustos et infaustos, *et menses, et tempora, et annos*, id est constellationes et cursum corporum caelestium, quae omnia ortum

220. Then when he says, *but now, after you have known God, or rather are known by God*, he reminds them of the gift received. As if to say: if you had been ignorant and sinned, it could have been tolerated; for other things being equal, sin in a Christian is more grievous than in a pagan. *But now, after you have known God*, i.e., were brought to a knowledge of God, you sin more gravely than of old by serving and setting your hope on things you ought not: *all shall know me, from the least of them even to the greatest* (Jer 31:34).

But the statement, *or rather are known by God*, seems to cause a difficulty, for God has known all things from eternity: *all things were known to the Lord God before they were created* (Sir 23:29).

I answer that this is said causally, so that the sense is: you *are known by God*, i.e., God has caused you to know him. In this way, God is said to know inasmuch as he is the cause of our knowledge. Hence, because he had previously said, *after you have known God*, which was a true statement, he immediately amends and explains it with a figure of speech by intimating that we cannot know God of ourselves save by him: *no man has seen God at any time: the only begotten Son, who is in the bosom of the Father, he has declared him* (John 1:18).

221. Then he upbraids them for the sin committed, saying: *how do you turn again to the weak and needy elements?*

First, he amplifies their sin;
second, he shows their imminent danger, at *I am afraid of you*;
third, he draws them back to a state of safety, at *be you as I* (Gal 4:12).
As to the first, he does two things:
first, he mentions the sin committed;
second, he convinces them of it, at *you observe days*.

222. It should be pointed out that this passage is interpreted in two ways: in one way, that those Galatians had turned from the faith to idolatry. For this reason he says, *how do you turn* from the faith *again*, i.e., a second time. *For it had been better for them not to have known the way of justice than, after they have known it, to turn back from that holy commandment which was delivered to them* (2 Pet 2:21); *they are turned back* (Isa 42:17). *To the elements*, namely, of the world, which are *weak*, unable by themselves to subsist, because they would lapse into nothingness unless upheld by the hand which rules all things—*upholding all things by the word of his power* (Heb 1:3)—*and needy*, because they need God and one another to fill out the universe, *which*, namely, the elements, *you desire to serve* with the service of *latria again*, i.e., for a second time. And the proof of this is obvious, because *you observe days*, auspicious and inauspicious, *and months and times and years*, i.e., the

habent ab idololatria. Contra quod dicit Ier. X, 2: *a signis caeli nolite metuere, quae gentes*, et cetera.

Et quod observationes huiusmodi malae sint et contra cultum Christianae religionis, patet: quia distinctio dierum, mensium, annorum, et temporum attenditur secundum cursum solis et lunae. Et ideo tales temporum distinctiones observantes, venerantur corpora caelestia, et disponunt actus suos secundum iudicium astrorum, quae nullam directam impressionem habent in voluntate hominis, et in his quae dependent a libero arbitrio. Et ex hoc imminet grave periculum. Unde dicit **timeo ne forte sine causa**, id est inutiliter **laboraverim in vobis**. Et ideo cavendum est fidelibus talia observare; sed nulla debet esse eis suspicio harum rerum, quia prospere potest cedere quidquid sub Dei devotione simpliciter agitur.

Sed numquid licet in aliquo cursum stellarum servare?

Dicendum est, quod corpora caelestia quorumdam quidem effectuum causa sunt, scilicet corporalium: et in istis licet ipsorum cursum attendere; quorumdam autem non sunt causa, scilicet eorum quae dependent a libero arbitrio, seu a fortuna, vel infortunio: et in istis servare cursum astrorum pertinet ad idololatriam.

223. Sed licet haec lectura sustineri possit, non tamen est secundum intentionem Apostoli. Cum enim ipse in tota praecedenti serie huius epistolae, et in sequenti, arguat Galatas de hoc quod a fide transtulerunt se ad observantiam legis, ideo magis ad propositum exponitur de hoc, quod ad legales observantias convertuntur.

Unde dicit: **cum cognoveritis Deum** per fidem, **quomodo convertimini** a fide **ad elementa**, id est ad litteralem legis observantiam? Quae dicitur elementa, quia lex fuit prima institutio divini cultus; **elementa**, dico, **infirma**, quia non perficit iustificando Hebr. c. VII, 19: *neminem ad perfectum adduxit lex*; **egena**, quia non confert virtutes et gratiam, adiuvando per se.

224. Sed quid est quod dicit **convertimini**? Et videtur hoc inconvenienter dictum. Similiter et hoc, quod dicit **denuo**. Nam isti nec Iudaei fuerant, nec alias legalia servaverant.

Ad quod dicendum est, quod cultus Iudaeorum medius est inter cultum Christianorum et gentilium. Nam gentiles colebant elementa ipsa tamquam viva quaedam; Iudaei vero elementis quidem non serviebant, sed Deo sub ipsis elementis, inquantum observationibus corporalium elementorum Deo cultum exhibebant. Supra eodem: **sub elementis huius mundi eramus servientes**.

constellations and the course of the heavenly bodies, all of which observances spring from idolatry, against which Jeremiah says: *be not afraid of the signs of heaven which the heathens fear* (Jer 10:2).

That observances of this sort are evil and contrary to the worship of the Christian religion is plain, because the distinction of days, months, times and years is based on the course of the sun and moon. Therefore, those who observe such distinctions of times are venerating heavenly bodies and arranging their activities according to the evidence of the stars, which have no direct influence on the human will or on things that depend on free will. By this practice they are put in grave danger. Hence he says: **I am afraid lest perhaps I labored in vain**, i.e., fruitlessly, **among you**. Therefore the faithful must avoid observing such things. Indeed, no suggestion of these things should be found among them, for whatever is done simply out of devotion to God can turn out prosperously.

But is it never lawful to look for the influence of the stars on certain things?

I answer that heavenly bodies are the cause of certain effects, namely, bodily. In such things it is lawful to consider their influence. But they are not the cause of certain other things, i.e., of things that depend on free will or on good and bad fortune. Hence, in such cases, to look for the influence of the stars pertains to idolatry.

223. But although this interpretation might be upheld, it does not accord with the Apostle's intention. For since in the entire section preceding this passage, as well as in all that follows it, he is censuring the Galatians for removing themselves from the faith and turning to the observances of the law, it is more in keeping with his intention to expound it as referring to their turning to the legal observances.

Hence he says: **after you have known God** through faith, **how do you turn** from the faith **to the elements**, i.e., to the literal observance of the law? It is called an element, because the law was the prime institution of divine worship. **To elements**, I say, that are **weak**, because they do not bring to perfection by justifying: *for the law brought nothing to perfection* (Heb 7:19), and **needy**, because they do not confer virtues and grace or offer any help of themselves.

224. But what does he mean by **do you turn**? For to say this, as well as to say, **again**, seems inappropriate, for they neither were Jews nor had they formerly observed the law.

I answer that the Jewish worship is midway between the worship of the Christians and that of the gentiles: for the gentiles worshipped the elements as though they were living things; the Jews, on the other hand, did not serve the elements but served God under the elements, inasmuch as they rendered worship to God by the observances of bodily elements: **we were serving under the elements of the world** (Gal 4:3).

But Christians serve God under Christ, i.e., in the faith of Christ. Now when a person reaches a terminus after passing through the middle, if he then decides to return to the middle, it seems to be the same as returning to the very beginning. Therefore, because they had already reached the terminus, namely, faith in Christ, and then returned to the middle, i.e., to the Jewish worship, then because of a resemblance of middle to beginning, the Apostle says that they are turned to the elements and are serving them again.

225. That this is so, he proves when he says: *you observe days* of the Jewish rite, namely, sabbaths and the tenth day of the month and such things, which are mentioned in a Gloss, *and months*, i.e., new moons, as the first and seventh month, as is had in Leviticus 25, *and times*, namely, of the exodus from Egypt, and the practice of going to Jerusalem three times a year, *and years* of jubilee and the seventh year of remission.

226. From this arises a danger, because faith in Christ profits nothing from it. Hence he says: *I am afraid of you, lest perhaps I have labored in vain among you*; and further on: *if you be circumcised, Christ shall profit you nothing* (Gal 5:2).

227. Then when he says, *be as I am, because I also am as you*, he guides them back to the state of salvation. As if to say: *I am afraid of you, lest I have labored in vain among you*. But lest this be so, *be as I am*.

In a Gloss this is taken in three ways. In the first way thus: *be as I am*, namely, abandon the law as I have abandoned it. In a second way thus: *be as I am*, namely, correcting the old error, as I have corrected mine. And this you can do, *because I also am as you*, and yet I have been corrected of my error. In the third way thus: *be as I am*, i.e., live without the law, *because I*, who had the law and was born in the law, *also am now as you* formerly were, namely, without the law.

Christiani vero serviunt Deo sub Christo, id est in fide Christi. Quando autem aliquis pervenit ad terminum, transacto medio, si iterum redire velit ad medium, idem videtur ac si velit redire ad principium. Et ideo Apostolus, quia isti iam pervenerant ad terminum, scilicet ad fidem Christi, et tunc redierunt ad medium, scilicet ad cultum Iudaeorum, inde est, quod propter quamdam conformitatem medii ad principium, dicit eos converti ad elementa, et denuo eis servire.

225. Et quod ita sit probat, cum dicit *dies observatis*, Iudaico ritu, scilicet sabbata, et decimum primi mensis, et huiusmodi, quae dicuntur in Glossa; *menses*, id est Neomenias, ut primum et septimum mensem, ut habetur Lev. XXIII, 5 ss.; *tempora*, scilicet egressionis de Aegypto, et quod Ierosolymam tribus vicibus veniebant per singulos annos. Item *annos* iubilaei, et septimum annum remissionis.

226. Et ex hoc sequitur periculum, quia ex hoc nihil prodest fides Christi. Unde dicit *timeo vos ne forte sine causa*, id est inutiliter, *in vobis laboraverim*. Infra V, 2: *si circumcidimini, Christus vobis nihil proderit*.

227. Consequenter cum dicit *estote sicut ego*, reducit eos ad statum salutis; quasi dicat: ita *timeo vos, ne forte sine causa laboraverim in vobis*, sed ne ita sit, *estote sicut ego*.

Hoc in Glossa tripliciter legitur. Primo modo sic *estote sicut ego*, scilicet legem deserentes, sicut ego dimisi. Secundo modo sic *estote sicut ego*, errorem scilicet pristinum corrigentes, sicut ego errorem meum correxi. Et hoc potestis, *quia ego*, supple sum, *sicut vos*, et tamen de errore meo correctus sum. Tertio modo sic: *estote sicut ego*, scilicet sine lege viventes, *quia ego*, supple: qui legem habui, et in lege natus sum, modo sum *sicut vos*, supple fuistis, scilicet sine lege.

Lecture 5

⁴:¹²Estote sicut ego, quia et ego sicut vos: fratres, obsecro vos. Nihil me laesistis. [n. 228]

⁴:¹³Scitis autem quia per infirmitatem carnis evangelizavi vobis jampridem: [n. 230]

⁴:¹⁴et tentationem vestram in carne mea non sprevistis, [n. 232] neque respuistis: sed sicut angelum Dei excepistis me, sicut Christum Jesum. [n. 233]

⁴:¹⁵Ubi est ergo beatitudo vestra? testimonium enim perhibeo vobis, quia, si fieri posset, oculos vestros eruissetis, et dedissetis mihi. [n. 234]

⁴:¹⁶Ergo inimicus vobis factus sum, verum dicens vobis? [n. 235]

⁴:¹⁷Aemulantur vos non bene: sed excludere vos volunt, ut illos aemulemini. [n. 238]

⁴:¹⁸Bonum autem aemulamini in bono semper: et non tantum cum praesens sum apud vos. [n. 240]

⁴:¹²Γίνεσθε ὡς ἐγώ, ὅτι κἀγὼ ὡς ὑμεῖς, ἀδελφοί, δέομαι ὑμῶν. οὐδέν με ἠδικήσατε·

⁴:¹³οἴδατε δὲ ὅτι δι' ἀσθένειαν τῆς σαρκὸς εὐηγγελισάμην ὑμῖν τὸ πρότερον,

⁴:¹⁴καὶ τὸν πειρασμὸν ὑμῶν ἐν τῇ σαρκί μου οὐκ ἐξουθενήσατε οὐδὲ ἐξεπτύσατε, ἀλλὰ ὡς ἄγγελον θεοῦ ἐδέξασθέ με, ὡς Χριστὸν Ἰησοῦν.

⁴:¹⁵ποῦ οὖν ὁ μακαρισμὸς ὑμῶν; μαρτυρῶ γὰρ ὑμῖν ὅτι εἰ δυνατὸν τοὺς ὀφθαλμοὺς ὑμῶν ἐξορύξαντες ἐδώκατέ μοι.

⁴:¹⁶ὥστε ἐχθρὸς ὑμῶν γέγονα ἀληθεύων ὑμῖν;

⁴:¹⁷ζηλοῦσιν ὑμᾶς οὐ καλῶς, ἀλλὰ ἐκκλεῖσαι ὑμᾶς θέλουσιν, ἵνα αὐτοὺς ζηλοῦτε.

⁴:¹⁸καλὸν δὲ ζηλοῦσθαι ἐν καλῷ πάντοτε, καὶ μὴ μόνον ἐν τῷ παρεῖναί με πρὸς ὑμᾶς,

⁴:¹²Be as I am, because I also am as you: brethren, I beseech you. You have not injured me at all. [n. 228]

⁴:¹³And you know how, through infirmity of the flesh, I preached the Gospel to you heretofore: [n. 230]

⁴:¹⁴And your temptation in my flesh you did not despise, [n. 232] nor reject: but received me as an angel of God, even as Christ Jesus. [n. 233]

⁴:¹⁵Where then is your blessedness? For I bear you witness that, if it could be done, you would have plucked out your own eyes and would have given them to me. [n. 234]

⁴:¹⁶Am I then become your enemy, because I tell you the truth? [n. 235]

⁴:¹⁷They are not zealous in your regard in a good way: but they would exclude you, that you might be zealous for them. [n. 238]

⁴:¹⁸But be zealous for that which is good in a good thing always: and not only when I am present with you. [n. 240]

---

228. Postquam reprehendit Apostolus Galatas, hic ostendit se hoc non ex odio fecisse. Et

primo ostendit se non habere veram causam odii ad eos ullam;

secundo quod nec habet causam aestimatam, ibi *ergo inimicus factus sum vobis*, etc.;

tertio assignat causam praemissae reprehensionis, ibi *filioli mei*, et cetera.

Circa primum duo facit.

Primo ostendit, quod non habet causam odii ad eos;

secundo quod magis habet causam amoris, ibi *scitis autem quod per infirmitatem*, et cetera.

229. Circa primum notandum est, quod consuetudo est boni pastoris in correctione subditorum asperis dulcia miscere, ne scilicet ex nimia severitate frangantur. Lc. X, 34 legitur de Samaritano, quod in curatione sauciati infudit vinum et oleum. E contra, de malis pastoribus dicitur Ez. XXXIV, 4: *cum austeritate imperabatis eis.*

Et ideo Apostolus sicut bonus praelatus ostendit, quod non ex odio increpat eos, blande loquendo eis quantum ad tria. Primo quantum ad caritatis nomen. Unde dicit *fratres*, Ps. CXXXII, 1: *ecce quam bonum*

228. After censuring the Galatians, the Apostle here shows that he did not do so out of hatred. And

first, he shows that he has no true cause of hatred toward them;

second, that he has no supposed cause, at *am I then become your enemy*;

third, he tells precisely why he rebuked them, at *my little children* (Gal 4:19).

As to the first, he does two things:

first, he shows that he has no reason for hating them;

second, that contrariwise he has reason for loving them, at *and you know how, through infirmity of the flesh*.

229. With respect to the first it should be noted that it is customary for a good pastor in correcting his subjects to mingle gentleness with severity, lest they be discouraged by too great severity. For it is written in Luke 10 that the Samaritan in caring for the wounded man poured in oil and wine. On the other hand, it is written of evil pastors in Ezekiel: *you ruled over them with vigor* (Ezek 34:4).

Therefore, as a good prelate, the Apostle shows that he does not rebuke them in a spirit of hatred, for his words are gentle in three respects. First, as to the charitable name he uses, for he says, *brethren*: *behold how good and*

et quam iucundum habitare fratres in unum. Secundo quantum ad modestiae verbum. Unde dicit **obsecro vos**, Prov. XVIII, 23: *cum obsecrationibus loquitur pauper.* Tertio quantum ad excusationem. Unde dicit **nihil me laesistis**, et ego non sum talis, quod habeam odio illos, qui me non offendunt.

230. Secundo ostendit se ad eos habere causam amoris, cum dicit **scitis autem, quod per infirmitatem**, et cetera. Ubi tria ponit ex quibus homines se diligere consueverunt. Primum est mutuum societatis auxilium, et ex hoc etiam amor in hominibus confirmatur, secundum illud Lc. XXII, v. 28: *vos estis, qui permansistis mecum*, et cetera. Et quantum ad hoc dicit **scitis autem**, etc., ubi

primo commemorat tribulationem quam passus est apud eos;

secundo ostendit quomodo ei astiterunt **et tentationem vestram**, et cetera.

231. Dicit ergo quantum ad primum: dico quod **nihil me laesistis**, imo servivistis mihi. **Scitis enim**, id est recordari poteritis, quod **evangelizavi vobis iampridem**, id est transacto tempore, **per infirmitatem carnis**, id est cum infirmitate et afflictione carnis meae, vel cum multis tribulationibus quas patiebar a Iudaeis (qui sunt de carne mea) me persequentibus. I Cor. II, 3: *cum timore et tremore multo fui apud vos.* II Cor. XII, 9: *virtus in infirmitate perficitur.*

232. Et licet haec infirmitas fuerit causa spernendi me, et tentationis vestrae, secundum illud Zach. XIII, 7: *percute pastorem, et dispergentur oves*, etc., vos tamen **tentationem vestram**, quae erat **in carne mea**, id est tribulationem meam, quae erat vobis causa tentationis, **non sprevistis**. Eccli. XI, 2: *non spernas hominem in visu suo.* Quia, ut dicit Dominus Lc. X, 2: *qui vos spernit, me spernit*, et cetera. **Neque respuistis** doctrinam meam et me, quin velletis esse socii tribulationum. Is. XXXIII, 1: *vae qui spernis, nonne et ipse sperneris*, et cetera.

233. Secundum autem, quod confirmat inter homines dilectionem, est mutuus amor et mutua dilectio ad invicem, secundum illud Prov. VIII, 17: *ego diligentes me diligo*, et cetera. Et quantum ad hoc dicit **sed sicut angelum Dei excepistis me**, id est ita honorifice sicut nuntium verba Dei nuntiantem. I Thess. II, v. 13: *cum accepissetis a nobis verbum auditus Dei*, et cetera. Et inde est, quod praedicatores dicuntur angeli. Mal. II, 7: *legem requirent ex ore eius*, et cetera.

Et non solum sicut angelum recepistis, sed **sicut Iesum Christum**, id est ac si Christus ipse venisset, qui

how pleasant it is for brethren to dwell together in unity (Ps 133:1). Second, as to his suppliant language, when he says: **I beseech you**: *the poor will speak with supplications* (Prov 18:28). Third, as to freeing them of blame; hence he says, **you have not injured me at all**, and I am not the type of person who hates those who do not offend me.

230. Second, he shows that he has reason to love them, when he says: **you know how, through infirmity of the flesh, I preached the Gospel to you heretofore**. Here he touches on three things that usually cause men to love one another. The first is the mutual help of fellowship, and this is also the cause of love being consolidated among men, according to Luke: *and you are they who have continued with me in my temptations* (Luke 22:28). Touching upon this he says: **and you know how, through infirmity of the flesh, I preached the Gospel to you heretofore**. Herein he does two things:

first, he recalls the tribulation he suffered among them;

second, he shows how they stood by him **and your temptation**.

231. He says, therefore, with respect to the first: I say that **you have not injured me at all**; rather you have come to my aid. For **you know**, i.e., are able to recall, **how I preached the Gospel to you heretofore**, i.e., in times past, **through infirmity of the flesh**, i.e., with infirmity and affliction in my flesh, or with the many tribulations I suffered from the Jews who are of my flesh and persecuted me: *and I was with you in weakness and in fear and in much tribulation* (1 Cor 2:3); *power is made perfect in infirmity* (2 Cor 12:9).

232. And although this infirmity might have been reason for scorning me and a cause of temptation for you, according to Zacharias: *strike the shepherd and the sheep will be scattered* (Zech 13:7): nevertheless, **your temptation**, which was **in my flesh**, i.e., my tribulation, which was a source of temptation for you, **you did not despise**: *do not despise a man for his look* (Sir 11:2) because as the Lord says in Luke: *he that despises you, despises me* (Luke 10:16). **Nor** did you **reject** me and my teaching, but you were willing to share my tribulations: *woe to you that despise; shall you not also be despised?* (Isa 33:1).

233. The second thing that strengthens love among men is mutual love and affection toward one another: *I love them that love me* (Prov 8:17). As to this he says: **but you received me as an angel of God**, i.e., with the honor accorded to a messenger announcing God's words: *when you received of us the word of the hearing of God, you received it not as the word of men but (as it is indeed) the word of God* (1 Thess 2:13). For this reason preachers are called angels: *they shall seek the law at the priest's mouth, because he is the angel of the Lord of hosts* (Mal 2:7).

And not only as an angel did you receive me, but **even as Christ Jesus**, i.e., as though Christ himself had come,

who, indeed, had come to them in him and spoke in him: *do you seek a proof of Christ that speaks in me?* (2 Cor 13:3). *He that receives you receives me* (Matt 10:40).

But he then rebukes them for their change of heart; hence he says, **where then is your blessedness?** As if to say: did not men think you blessed for honoring me and accepting my preaching? *Where is your fear, your fortitude, your patience and the perfection of your ways?* (Job 4:6)

234. The third thing that strengthens love is doing good to one another. As to this he says: **for I bear you witness that, if it could be done**, i.e., had been just to do so (for that can be done which it is just to do) or had been to the advantage of the Church, **you would have plucked out your own eyes and would have given them to me**. As if to say: you loved me so much that you would have given me not only your external goods but your very eyes.

235. Then when he says: **am I then become your enemy, because I tell you the truth?**, he states the cause of a supposed hatred.

First, the cause on the part of the Apostle;

second, on the part of the false brethren, at **they are not zealous in your regard in a good way**.

236. He says therefore: if you have done me so much good, are you to believe that **I am become your enemy because I tell you the truth?**

The word *enemy* used here can be interpreted in two ways: in one way as meaning that he hates them; in this case the interpretation is **have I become your enemy**, i.e., do I hate you? Hence what follows, namely, **because I tell you the truth**, can be taken as an indication of hatred, even though telling the truth at the proper time and place is a sign of love.

In another way, the word *enemy* can be taken in a passive sense, i.e., so that he is hated by them; then **have I become your enemy**, i.e., do you hate me? and this **because I tell you the truth**, so that telling the truth is set down as the cause of hatred. For men who tell the truth are hated by evil men, since the truth engenders hatred: *they have hated him that rebukes in the gate: and I have abhorred him that speaks perfectly* (Amos 5:10).

237. But on the other hand, it is said in Proverbs: *he who rebukes a man shall afterward find favor with him more than he who by a flattering tongue deceives him* (Prov 28:23).

I answer that the solution to this can be gathered from what is said in Proverbs: *rebuke not a scorner, lest he hate you. Rebuke a wise man and he will love you* (Prov 9:9). For if the one corrected loves the corrector, it is a sign of virtue; conversely, it is a sign of malice if he should hate him. For since a man naturally hates what is contrary to what he loves, then if you hate one who corrects you for evil, it is obvious that you love the evil; but if you love him, you

ostendis te odire peccata. Quia enim homines a principio cum corripiuntur, per amorem ad peccata afficiuntur: inde est, quod in principio peccator corripientem odit, sed postquam iam correctus est et affectum peccati deposuit, corripientem diligit. Et ideo signanter in proposita auctoritate dicitur, quod *postea inveniet gratiam apud eum.*

238. Consequenter cum dicit **aemulantur vos**, etc., ponit aliam causam aestimatam, ex parte scilicet pseudo. Et

primo ponit eam;

secundo excludit eam, ibi **bonum autem aemulamini**, et cetera.

239. Quantum autem ad primum, sciendum est quod, sicut dictum est supra, quidam pseudo ex Iudaeis conversi, circumeuntes ecclesias gentium, praedicabant servari legalia. Et quia Paulus contrarium dicebat, ideo isti detrahebant ei. Et hoc magis faciebant ut excluderent Paulum, quam pro salute eorum.

Et ideo dicit **aemulantur vos**, id est non patiuntur in vobis (quos diligunt potius amore concupiscentiae, quam amicitiae) consortium nostrum. Aemulatio enim est zelus ex amore quocumque proveniens, non patiens consortium in amato. Sed quia amor eorum ad istos non erat bonus, tum quia non amabant eos propter utilitatem ipsorum, sed propter commodum proprium: et hoc patet quia volebant excludere Apostolum ab eis, utpote propriae utilitati contrarium, tum quia hoc cedebat in damnum Galatarum, quia quaerebant in eis lucrum, per quod ipsi damnificabantur, ideo dicit **aemulantur vos**, sed **non bene**, quia non amant bonum vestrum. Et hoc apparet, quia **volunt vos excludere, ut aemulemini illos**, id est, ut nullum recipiatis nisi eos. Prov. III, 31: *ne aemuleris hominem iniustum*, et cetera. Et Prov. XXXI: *non aemuletur cor tuum peccatores.*

240. Hoc autem excludit consequenter cum dicit **bonum autem aemulamini**, etc., quasi dicat: non debetis eos aemulari in doctrina eorum, sed aemulamini bonum doctorem, me scilicet et huiusmodi. I Petr. III, v. 13: *quis est, qui vobis noceat, si boni aemulatores fueritis?*

Sed quia aliquis potest esse bonus doctor, in quo potest esse aliquid mali, ideo addit: **aemulamini bonum** doctorem, sed dico tamen, **in bono**, id est in eo quod bonum est. I Cor. XIV, 1: *sectamini caritatem, aemulamini spiritualia.* Licet autem Apostolus de se loquatur, secundum Glossam, cum dicit **aemulamini bonum**, addit tamen **in bono**, quia, sicut ipse dicit I Cor. IV, 4: *nihil mihi conscius sum, sed non in hoc iustificatus sum.*

indicate that you hate sin. For at first, when men are corrected, they are attached to their sins—that is why a sinner's first reaction is to hate the one correcting him; but after the correction, he puts aside his attachment to sin and loves the one correcting him. And therefore the passage from Proverbs expressly says that later he will find favor with him.

238. Then when he says, **they are not zealous in your regard in a good way**, he states another supposed cause, namely, on the part of the false brethren.

First, he states it;

second, he refutes it, at **but be zealous for that which is good**.

239. As to the first it should be noted that, as has been said above, certain false brethren, converted from Judaism, went about the churches of the gentiles, preaching the observance of the law. Because Paul opposed them, they slandered him. They did this not so much with an eye to their salvation as to get rid of Paul.

Hence the Apostle says, **they are not zealous in your regard in a good way**, i.e., they do not allow you (whom they love with a love not of friendship but of self-interest) to associate with us. For jealous rivalry is zeal that arises from any love whatsoever and does not brook what is loved to be shared. But because their love for them was not good: first of all, because they did not love them so as to advantage them but for their own gain—and this is obvious from the fact that they wanted to keep the Apostle away from them as one opposed to their own advantage—and second, because this was a source of harm to the Galatians—for they sought from them an advantage by which the latter would suffer harm; for these reasons he says, **they are zealous in your regard** but **not in a good way**, because they are not interested in your welfare. And this is obvious, because **they would exclude you, that you might be zealous for them**, i.e., that you might admit none but them: *do not envy the unjust man and do not follow his ways* (Prov 3:31); *do not let your heart envy sinners* (Prov 23:17).

240. But he rejects this when he says, **but be zealous for that which is good in a good thing always**. As if to say: you ought not to be zealous for them in their teaching; but be zealous for a good teacher, i.e., for me and those like me: *and who is he that can hurt you if you be zealous of the good?* (1 Pet 3:13).

But because there can be evil in a good teacher, he adds, **be zealous of the good** teacher, yet say **in a good thing**, i.e., in that which is good: *follow after charity and be zealous for spiritual goods* (1 Cor 14:1). Now, although the Apostle speaks of himself, according to a Gloss, when he says, **be zealous of the good**, yet he adds **in a good thing**, because as he says: *I am not conscious of anything, yet I am not hereby justified* (1 Cor 4:4).

Sed quia aliqui aemulantur doctorem bonum in sua praesentia solum, ideo addit **semper, et non tantum cum praesens sum apud vos**; quia aemulatio in bonum est signum quod ex amore et timore Dei, qui omnia videt, procedat, si etiam in absentia doctoris perseverat. Col. III, 22: *servi, obedite per omnia dominis vestris*, et cetera.

But because some are zealous for a good teacher in his presence alone, he adds: **always, and not only when I am present with you**; because zeal for the good, if it continues even when the teacher is absent, is an indication that it proceeds from love and fear of God who sees all: *servants, obey in all things your masters according to the flesh, not serving to the eye, as pleasing men, but in simplicity of heart, fearing God* (Col 3:22).

Lecture 6

4:19 Filioli mei, quos iterum parturio, donec formetur Christus in vobis: [n. 241]

4:20vellem autem esse apud vos modo, et mutare vocem meam: quoniam confundor in vobis. [n. 245]

4:19τέκνα μου, οὓς πάλιν ὠδίνω μέχρις οὗ μορφωθῇ Χριστὸς ἐν ὑμῖν·

4:20ἤθελον δὲ παρεῖναι πρὸς ὑμᾶς ἄρτι, καὶ ἀλλάξαι τὴν φωνήν μου, ὅτι ἀποροῦμαι ἐν ὑμῖν.

4:19 My little children, of whom I am in labor again, until Christ be formed in you. [n. 241]

4:20 And I would willingly be present with you now and change my voice: because I am ashamed for you. [n. 245]

---

241. Supra Apostolus removit falsam causam correctionis Galatarum, hic consequenter Apostolus dictae correctionis assignat causam veram, quae est dolor de eorum imperfectione. Et ideo

primo dolorem cordis ex quo loquebatur, exprimit;

secundo ponit desiderium de manifestatione huius doloris, ibi *vellem autem*, etc.;

tertio ponit causam doloris, ibi *quoniam confundor*, et cetera.

242. Dolor autem iste ex caritate procedebat, quia dolebat de peccatis eorum. Ps. CXVIII, 158: *vidi praevaricantes, et tabescebam*, et cetera. Et ideo verbum caritatis proponit dicens *filioli mei*.

Signanter autem non eos filios vocat, sed *filiolos*, ut designet eorum imperfectionem, qua diminuti sunt. I Cor. III, 1: *tamquam parvulis in Christo*, et cetera.

243. Sed notandum est, quod puer dum est in parturitione, dicitur filiolus. Et isti tales erant, quia indigebant iterata parturitione, cum tamen parentes carnales semel tantum parturiant filios. Et ideo dicit eis *quos iterum parturio*.

Nam semel eos parturierat in prima conversione, sed quia iam aversi erant ab eo, qui eos vocavit in aliud evangelium, indigebant quod iterato parturiret eos. Ideo dicit *parturio*, id est cum labore et dolore ad lucem fidei reduco. In quo apparet dolor Apostoli. Unde conversio hominis, partus dicitur. Iob XXXIX, 3: *incurvantur ad foetum et pariunt*. Apoc. XII, 2: *clamabat parturiens, et cruciabatur ut pariat*. Et inde est quod Apostolus ex dolore dure eos corrigit, sicut mulier ex dolore partus dure clamat. Is. XLII, v. 14: *quasi parturiens loquar*, et cetera.

244. Et ratio iteratae parturitionis est, quia non estis perfecte formati. Unde dicit *donec Christus formetur in vobis*, id est recipiatis similitudinem eius, quam vestro vitio perdidistis. Et non dicit, *formemini in Christo* sed *formetur Christus in vobis*, ut hoc terribilius insonet auribus eorum.

241. Above, the Apostle dismissed the false cause of his correcting the Galatians; here he discloses the true cause, which is sorrow for their imperfection.

First, he expresses the heartfelt sorrow of which he spoke;

second, he states a desire to manifest this sorrow, at *and I would willingly*;

third, he gives the cause of the sorrow, at *because I am ashamed for you*.

242. This sorrow proceeded from charity, because he grieved for their sins: *I beheld the transgressors and I pined away; because they did not keep your word* (Ps 118:158). And so he addresses them in words of charity, saying, *my little children*.

He purposely does not call them sons, but *little children*, to indicate the imperfection whereby they had become small: *as unto little ones in Christ, I gave you milk to drink, not meat* (1 Cor 3:1).

243. It should be noted that during birth, a child is called a little one. And this is what they were, because they needed to be born again, even though parents according to the flesh bring forth their child only once. Accordingly he says to them, *of whom I am in labor again*.

For he was in labor of them during their first conversion; but since they had now turned from the one who called them, to another gospel, they needed to be brought forth anew. Hence he says, *I am in labor*, i.e., with labor and pain I bring them forth into the light of faith. In these words the Apostle manifests his grief. Hence a man's conversion is called a birth: *they bow themselves to bring forth young* (Job 39:3); *and being with child she cried, travailing in birth and was in pain to be delivered* (Rev 12:2). Therefore it is because of his pain that he rebukes them so sharply, as a woman cries aloud because of the pains of childbirth: *I will speak now as a woman in labor* (Isa 42:14).

244. The reason for the iterated travail is that you are not perfectly formed. Hence he says: *until Christ be formed in you*, i.e., until you receive his likeness, which you have lost through your sin. He does not say, *that you may be formed in Christ*, but *until Christ be formed in you*, to make it resound more terrifyingly on their ears.

Nam Christus per fidem formatam formatur in corde. Eph. III, 17: *habitare Christum per fidem*, et cetera. Sed quando quis non habet fidem formatam, iam in eo moritur Christus. II Petr. I, 19: *donec dies illucescat*, et cetera. Et sic secundum hominis profectum in fide, Christus in homine proficit, et, e converso, secundum defectum deficit. Quando ergo fides in homine efficitur informis per peccatum, Christus non est in eo formatus.

Et ideo, quia in istis non erat fides formata, indigebant iterum parturiri, donec Christus in eis formaretur per fidem formatam, scilicet quae per dilectionem operatur.

Vel **donec Christus formetur in vobis**, id est, formosus aliis per vos appareat.

245. Posset autem aliquis dicere: *absens tu dicis talia, sed si esses apud nos, haec non diceres*, secundum illud II Cor. X, v. 10: *praesentia quidem corporis infirma, et sermo contemptibilis*, et cetera. Et ideo ponit desiderium manifestandi dolorem suum asperius, dicens **vellem autem esse apud vos modo et mutare vocem meam**, quasi dicat: modo blandis verbis utor, vocans vos fratres et filios in absentia; sed si essem praesens, asperius corriperem. Nam si quae per litteras scribo, nunc praesens et ore proferrem, durior esset correctio, utpote quia magis possem vocem obiurgantis exprimere, et irascentis resonare clamorem et dolorem pectoris, magis quam per litteras explicare, et magis cor vestrum viva vox ad confusionem de errore vestro et mea turbatione moveret.

246. Et causa huius doloris est, **quia confundor in vobis**, id est, erubesco apud alios pro vobis. Nam, sicut Eccli. XXII, 3 dicitur *confusio est patris de filio indisciplinato*.

Nam, cum filius sit res patris, et discipulus, inquantum huiusmodi, res magistri, magister gaudet de bono quod videt in eo relucere, quasi de bono proprio, et gloriatur, et, e converso, de malo dolet et confunditur. Unde quia isti mutati erant de bono in malum, Apostolus confundebatur inde.

For Christ is formed in the heart by formed faith: *that Christ might dwell in your hearts by faith* (Eph 3:17). But when one does not have formed faith, Christ has already died in him: *until the day dawn and the day star arise in your hearts* (2 Pet 1:19). Thus Christ grows in a man according to his progress in the faith; conversely, as it diminishes, he recedes. Therefore, when the faith of a man is rendered unformed by sin, Christ is not formed in him.

And so, because there was not a formed faith in them, they needed to be brought forth from the womb again until Christ be formed in them through faith, i.e., formed faith, which works through love.

Or, **until Christ be formed in you**, i.e., until Christ appear through you as finely formed to others.

245. Here someone might say: *away from us you say these things, but if you were with us, you would not say them*, according to 2 Corinthians: *his bodily presence is weak and his speech contemptible* (2 Cor 10:10). Therefore, he expresses a desire to manifest his grief more vividly, saying, **I would willingly be present with you now and change my voice**. As if to say: I use gentle language now, calling you friends and sons, in my absence; but if I were present among you, I would correct you more sharply. For if I were present and speaking the things I am now writing in a letter, the correction would be more severe; because I would then be able to express the scolding tones of my rebuke and the cries of my anger and the pain in my heart, much better than I can convey them by letter. And a living voice would more effectively stir your hearts to shame for your error and my anxiety.

246. And the cause of this sorrow is that **I am ashamed for you**, i.e., I blush for you in the presence of others; for as it is said in Sirach: *a son ill taught is the confusion of the father* (Sir 22:3).

For since a son is a thing of the father, and a disciple as such is a thing of his master, a master rejoices in the good he sees reflected in him and glories in it as though it were his own. Conversely, he is pained at evil and is ashamed. Hence because they had been turned from good to evil, for that reason the Apostle is ashamed.

Lecture 7

4:21 Dicite mihi qui sub lege vultis esse: legem non legistis? [n. 247]

4:22 Scriptum est enim: quoniam Abraham duos filios habuit: unum de ancilla, et unum de libera. [n. 249]

4:23 Sed qui de ancilla, secundum carnem natus est: qui autem de libera, per repromissionem:

4:21 Λέγετέ μοι, οἱ ὑπὸ νόμον θέλοντες εἶναι, τὸν νόμον οὐκ ἀκούετε;

4:22 γέγραπται γὰρ ὅτι Ἀβραὰμ δύο υἱοὺς ἔσχεν, ἕνα ἐκ τῆς παιδίσκης καὶ ἕνα ἐκ τῆς ἐλευθέρας.

4:23 ἀλλ' ὁ μὲν ἐκ τῆς παιδίσκης κατὰ σάρκα γεγέννηται, ὁ δὲ ἐκ τῆς ἐλευθέρας δι' ἐπαγγελίας.

4:21 Tell me, you who desire to be under the law, have you not read the law? [n. 247]

4:22 For it is written that Abraham had two sons: the one by a bondwoman and the other by a free woman. [n. 249]

4:23 But he who was of the bondwoman was born according to the flesh: but he who was of the free woman was by promise.

247. Supra Apostolus probavit dignitatem gratiae per consuetudinem humanam hic autem probat eam auctoritate Scripturae. Et

primo proponit factum;

secundo exponit mysterium, ibi *quae sunt per allegoriam dicta*, etc.;

tertio concludit propositum, ibi *itaque, fratres mei, non sumus*, et cetera.

Circa primum duo facit.

Primo excitat ad attentionem;

secundo proponit suam intentionem, ibi *scriptum est enim*, et cetera.

248. Dicit ergo *dicite mihi*, etc., quasi dicat: si vos estis sapientes, attendite ad ea quae obiicio, et si non potestis contradicere, cedatis. Iob VI, 29: *respondete, obsecro, absque contentione*, et cetera. Facio vobis autem hanc obiectionem: aut legistis legem, aut non legistis. Sed si legistis, scire debetis ea quae in ea scripta sunt: sed ipsa probat se dimittendam; si autem non legistis, non debetis recipere quod nescitis. Prov. IV, 25: *palpebrae tuae praecedant gressus tuos*.

Dicit autem *sub lege*, id est sub onere legis. Nam subire aliquod leve non est vis, sed subire grave onus, sicut est onus legis, magnae stultitiae signum esse videtur. Act. XV, v. 10: *hoc est onus, quod neque patres nostri, neque nos portare potuimus*, etc., quod est intelligendum de illis, qui volunt carnaliter esse sub lege.

249. Consequenter cum dicit *scriptum est enim*, etc., proponit suam intentionem, dicens: ideo quaero an legistis legem, quia in ipsa continentur quaedam, quae manifeste dicunt legem non esse tenendam. Et specialiter Apostolus facit mentionem de duobus filiis Abrahae. Et primo ponit unum in quo conveniunt; secundo duo in quibus differunt.

Conveniunt quidem in uno patre. Unde dicit *scriptum est, quoniam Abraham duos filios habuit*. Habuit

247. Above, the Apostle showed the pre-eminence of grace by a human example; here he proves it on the authority of Scripture.

First, he proposes a fact;

second, he expounds its mystery, at *which things are said by an allegory* (Gal 4:24);

third, he concludes his proposition, at *so then, brethren* (Gal 4:31).

As to the first, he does two things:

first, he elicits their attention;

second, he sets forth his intention, at *for it is written*.

248. He says therefore: *tell me, you who desire to be under the law, have you not read the law?* As if to say: if you are wise, consider my objections; if you cannot answer them, yield: *answer, I beseech you, without contention: and speaking that which is just, answer me* (Job 6:29). Now I raise this objection to you. You have either read the law or not. If you have read it, you ought to know the things written in it. But those things prove that it should be abandoned. If you have not read it, you ought not accept what you do not know: *let your eyelids go before your steps* (Prov 4:25).

He says *under the law*, i.e., under the burden of the law. For to shoulder something light is not a feat; but to assume a heavy burden, such as the burden of the law, seems to be a mark of exceeding stupidity: *this is a yoke which neither our fathers nor we have been able to bear* (Acts 15:10); which is to be understood of those who wish to live according to the flesh under the law.

249. Then when he says, *it is written that Abraham had two sons*, he sets forth his intention, saying: the reason I ask whether you have read the law is that it contains certain things which clearly indicate that the law must not be retained. And the Apostle mentions specifically the two sons of Abraham. First, he states one point in which they are alike. Second, two points in which they differ.

They are alike in having the same father. Hence he says, *it is written that Abraham had two sons*. In fact he had

more than two, because after Sarah's death, he fathered other sons of Cetura, as is stated in Genesis 25. But the Apostle does not mention them because they have no role in this allegory. Now two peoples, the Jews and the gentiles, can be signified by those two, i.e., the son of the bondwoman and the son of the free woman—and by the other sons of Cetura, schismatics and heretics.

These two peoples are alike in having one father, for the Jews are the children of Abraham according to the flesh, but the gentiles, by imitating him in faith. Or, they are the sons of Abraham, i.e., of God, who is the Father of all: *have we not all one Father?* (Mal 2:10); *is he the God of the Jews only?* (Rom 3:29).

250. But they differ in two respects: namely, in the condition of their mother, because one is of a bondwoman (Gen 21:10). Yet Abraham did not sin by lying with her, because he approached her in conjugal affection and under God's ordinance; the other, namely, Isaac, whom Sarah, his wife, begot unto him, was born of a free woman: *I will return and come to you at this time, life accompanying, and Sarah your wife shall have a son* (Gen 18:10).

Also, they differ as to the manner of procreation, because **he who was of the bondwoman**, i.e., Ishmael, **was born according to the flesh: but he who was of the free woman**, i.e., Isaac, **was by promise**.

251. Here a twofold misinterpretation must be avoided. The first is lest we understand **born according to the flesh** as though **flesh** refers here to an act of sin, as it does in Romans: *if you live according to the flesh, you shall die* (Rom 8:13), and 2 Corinthians: *for although we walk in the flesh, we do not war according to the flesh* (2 Cor 10:3)—as though Abraham sinned in begetting Ishmael.

The other is lest we suppose, when it is said, **by promise**, that Isaac was not born according to the flesh, i.e., through a carnal union, but by the Holy Spirit. Therefore, it must be said that Ishmael was born according to the flesh, i.e., according to the nature of the flesh. For it is natural among men that from a fertile young woman, such as Hagar was, and from a man advanced in years, a son be born. But that Isaac be born according to promise is beyond the nature of the flesh: for the nature of the flesh cannot achieve that a son be born of an old man and a barren old woman, as Sarah was.

In Ishmael are signified the Jewish people, who were born according to the flesh; in Isaac are signified the gentiles, who were born according to the promise, in which Abraham was promised that he would be the father of many nations: *in your seed shall all the nations of the earth be blessed* (Gen 22:18).

252. Then he discloses the mystery when he says, **which things are said by an allegory** (Gal 4:24).

First, he tells what sort of mystery it is;

secundo exemplificat, ibi *haec enim duo sunt Testamenta*, et cetera.

253. Dicit ergo: haec quae sunt scripta de duobus filiis, etc., *sunt per allegoriam dicta*, id est per alium intellectum. Allegoria enim est tropus seu modus loquendi, quo aliquid dicitur et aliud intelligitur. Unde allegoria dicitur ab allos, quod est alienum, et goge, ductio, quasi in alienum intellectum ducens.

Sed attendendum est, quod allegoria sumitur aliquando pro quolibet mystico intellectu, aliquando pro uno tantum ex quatuor qui sunt historicus, allegoricus, mysticus et anagogicus, qui sunt quatuor sensus Sacrae Scripturae, et tamen differunt quantum ad significationem.

254. Est enim duplex significatio. Una est per voces; alia est per res quas voces significant. Et hoc specialiter est in sacra Scriptura et non in aliis; cum enim eius auctor sit Deus, in cuius potestate est, quod non solum voces ad designandum accommodet (quod etiam homo facere potest), sed etiam res ipsas. Et ideo in aliis scientiis ab hominibus traditis, quae non possunt accommodari ad significandum nisi tantum verba, voces solum significant. Sed hoc est proprium in ista scientia, ut voces et ipsae res significatae per eas aliquid significent, et ideo haec scientia potest habere plures sensus. Nam illa significatio qua voces significant aliquid, pertinet ad sensum litteralem seu historicum; illa vero significatio qua res significatae per voces iterum res alias significant, pertinet ad sensum mysticum.

Per litteralem autem sensum potest aliquid significari dupliciter, scilicet secundum proprietatem locutionis, sicut cum dico *homo ridet*; vel secundum similitudinem seu metaphoram, sicut cum dico *pratum ridet*. Et utroque modo utimur in Sacra Scriptura, sicut cum dicimus, quantum ad primum, quod Iesus ascendit, et cum dicimus quod sedet a dextris Dei, quantum ad secundum. Et ideo sub sensu litterali includitur parabolicus seu metaphoricus.

Mysticus autem sensus seu spiritualis dividitur in tres. Primo namque, sicut dicit Apostolus, lex vetus est figura novae legis. Et ideo secundum quod ea quae sunt veteris legis, significant ea quae sunt novae, est sensus allegoricus.

Item, secundum Dionysium in libro *de Caelesti hierarchia*, nova lex est figura futurae gloriae. Et ideo secundum quod ea quae sunt in nova lege et in Christo, significant ea quae sunt in patria, est sensus anagogicus.

Item, in nova lege ea quae in Capite sunt gesta, sunt exempla eorum quae nos facere debemus, quia *quaecumque scripta sunt, ad nostram doctrinam scripta sunt*; et ideo secundum quod ea quae in nova lege facta sunt

second, he explains it, at *for these are the two Testaments* (Gal 4:24).

253. He says therefore: these things which are written about the two sons *are said by an allegory*, i.e., the understanding of one thing under the image of another. For an allegory is a figure of speech or a manner of narrating, in which one thing is said and something else is understood. Hence 'allegory' is derived from *alos* (alien) and *goge* (a leading), leading, as it were, to a different understanding.

Here it should be noted that allegory is sometimes taken for any mystical meaning: sometimes for only one of the four, which are the historical, allegorical, mystical and anagogical, which are the four senses of Sacred Scripture, all of which differ in signification.

254. For signification is twofold: one is through words; the other through the things signified by the words. And this is peculiar to Sacred Scripture and no writings, since is author is God in whose power it lies not only to employ words to signify (which man can also do), but things as well. Consequently, in the other sciences handed down by men, in which only words can be employed to signify, the words alone signify. But it is peculiar to Scripture that words and the very things signified by them signify something. Consequently this science can have many senses. For that signification by which the words signify something pertains to the literal or historical sense. But the signification whereby the things signified by the words further signify other things pertains to the mystical sense.

There are two ways in which something can be signified by the literal sense: either according to the usual construction, as when I say, *the man smiles*; or according to a likeness or metaphor, as when I say, *the meadow smiles*. Both of these are used in Sacred Scripture; as when we say, according to the first, that Jesus ascended, and when we say according to the second, that he sits at the right hand of God. Therefore, under the literal sense is included the parabolic or metaphorical.

However, the mystical or spiritual sense is divided into three types. First, as when the Apostle says that the old law is the figure of the new law. Hence, insofar as the things of the old law signify things of the new law, it is the allegorical sense.

Then, according to Dionysius in the book *On the Heavenly Hierarchy*, the new law is a figure of future glory; accordingly, insofar as things in the new law and in Christ signify things which are in heaven, it is the anagogical sense.

Furthermore, in the new law the things performed by the Head are examples of things we ought to do—because *whatever things were written, were written for our learning* (Rom 15:3) —accordingly, insofar as the things which in the new law were done in Christ and done in things that

in Christo et in his quae Christum significant, sunt signa eorum quae nos facere debemus: est sensus moralis.

Et omnium horum patet exemplum. Per hoc enim quod dico *fiat lux*, ad litteram, de luce corporali, pertinet ad sensum litteralem. Si intelligatur *fiat lux* id est *nascatur Christus in Ecclesia*, pertinet ad sensum allegoricum. Si vero dicatur *fiat lux* id est ut *per Christum introducamur ad gloriam*, pertinet ad sensum anagogicum. Si autem dicatur *fiat lux* id est *per Christum illuminemur in intellectu et inflammemur in affectu*, pertinet ad sensum moralem.

signify Christ are signs of things we ought to do, it is the moral sense.

Examples will clarify each of these. For when I say, *let there be light*, referring literally to corporeal light, it is the literal sense. But if it be taken to mean *let Christ be born in the Church*, it pertains to the allegorical sense. But if one says, *let there be light*, i.e., *let us be conducted to glory through Christ*, it pertains to the anagogical sense. Finally, if it is said *let there be light*, i.e., *let us be illumined in mind and inflamed in heart through Christ*, it pertains to the moral sense.

Lecture 8

⁴:²⁴quae sunt per allegoriam dicta. Haec enim sunt duo Testamenta. Unum quidem in Monte Sina, in servitutem generans, quae est Agar: [n. 255]

⁴:²⁵Sina enim mons est in Arabia, qui conjunctus est ei quae nunc est Jerusalem, et servit cum filiis suis. [n. 261]

⁴:²⁶Illa autem, quae sursum est Jerusalem, libera est, quae est mater nostra. [n. 263]

⁴:²⁷Scriptum est enim: *laetare, sterilis, quae non paris; erumpe et clama, quae non parturis: quia multi filii desertae, magis quam ejus quae habet virum.* [n. 265]

⁴:²⁴ἅτινά ἐστιν ἀλληγορούμενα: αὗται γάρ εἰσιν δύο διαθῆκαι, μία μὲν ἀπὸ ὄρους Σινᾶ, εἰς δουλείαν γεννῶσα, ἥτις ἐστὶν Ἁγάρ.

⁴:²⁵τὸ δὲ Ἁγὰρ Σινᾶ ὄρος ἐστὶν ἐν τῇ Ἀραβίᾳ, συστοιχεῖ δὲ τῇ νῦν Ἰερουσαλήμ, δουλεύει γὰρ μετὰ τῶν τέκνων αὐτῆς.

⁴:²⁶ἡ δὲ ἄνω Ἰερουσαλὴμ ἐλευθέρα ἐστίν, ἥτις ἐστὶν μήτηρ ἡμῶν:

⁴:²⁷γέγραπται γάρ, Εὐφράνθητι, στεῖρα ἡ οὐ τίκτουσα: ῥῆξον καὶ βόησον, ἡ οὐκ ὠδίνουσα: ὅτι πολλὰ τὰ τέκνα τῆς ἐρήμου μᾶλλον ἢ τῆς ἐχούσης τὸν ἄνδρα.

⁴:²⁴Which things are said by an allegory. For these are the two Testaments. The one from Mount Sinai, engendering unto bondage, which is Hagar. [n. 255]

⁴:²⁵For Sinai is a mountain in Arabia, which has affinity to that which is now Jerusalem, and is in bondage with her children. [n. 261]

⁴:²⁶But that Jerusalem which is above is free, which is our mother. [n. 263]

⁴:²⁷For it is written: *rejoice, you barren, who do not bear: break forth and cry, you who do not travail: for many are the children of the desolate, more than of her who has a husband.* [n. 265]

---

255. Superius posuit Apostolus intellectum mysticum, hic aperit mysterium. Et

primo quantum ad matres;

secundo quantum ad filios, ibi **nos autem fratres**, et cetera.

Per duas autem matres intelligit duo Testamenta. Et ideo

primo ponit significatum;

secundo exponit, ibi **unum quidem in Monte**, et cetera.

256. Dicit ergo hae, scilicet duae uxores, ancilla et libera, **sunt duo Testamenta**, Vetus et Novum. Ier. XXXI, 31: *feriam domui Israel foedus novum*, ecce Novum Testamentum, *non secundum pactum*, etc., ecce Testamentum Vetus. Libera enim significat Testamentum Novum, ancilla vero Vetus.

Ad sciendum autem quid sit testamentum, attendi debet, quod testamentum idem est quod pactum seu foedus eorum quae testibus confirmantur. Unde in Scriptura multoties loco testamenti ponitur foedus vel pactum. Ubicumque autem intervenit foedus, vel pactum, fit aliqua promissio. Et ideo secundum diversitatem promissionum, est diversitas testamentorum. Duo autem sunt nobis promissa, scilicet temporalia in veteri lege et aeterna in nova. Matth. V, 12: *gaudete et exultate*, et cetera. Hae ergo duae promissiones sunt duo Testamenta.

257. Unde Apostolus consequenter cum dicit: **unum quidem**, etc., exponit ipsa. Et

primo quantum ad Vetus;

255. Above, the Apostle spoke of the mystical sense; here he discloses the mystery:

first, as to the mothers;

second, as to the sons, at **now we, brethren** (Gal 4:28).

By the two mothers he understands the two Testaments. Therefore,

first, he states the thing signified;

Second, he explains it: **the one from Mount Sinai**.

256. He says therefore, **these**, i.e., the two wives, the bondwoman and the free woman, **are the two Testaments**, the Old and the New: *I will make with the house of Israel a new covenant* (behold, the New Testament), *not according to the covenant which I made with their fathers* (behold, the Old Testament) (Jer 31:31). For the free woman signifies the New Testament and the bondwoman the Old.

To understand what a testament is, we should consider that a testament is a pact or agreement dealing with matters which are confirmed by witnesses. Hence in Scripture in many places in lieu of testament is put pact or agreement. Now, whenever a pact or agreement is struck, a promise is made. Therefore, according to the diversity of promises there is a diversity of testaments. But two things have been promised to us: temporal things in the old law, and eternal things in the new: *rejoice and be glad because your reward is great in heaven* (Matt 5:12). Hence these two promises are the two Testaments.

257. Hence the Apostle, when he says, **the one from Mount Sinai, engendering unto bondage**, explains them.

First, as to the Old;

secundo quantum ad Novum, ibi **illa autem quae sursum**, et cetera.

258. Ad evidentiam autem litterae sciendum est, circa primum, quod quilibet civis alicuius civitatis dicitur esse filius illius, et ipsa civitas est sicut mater eius. Lc. c. XXIII, 28: *filiae Ierusalem, nolite flere*, et cetera. Thren. ult.: *filii Sion inclyti*, et cetera. Per hoc igitur quod aliqui fiunt alicuius civitatis cives, efficiuntur filii eius.

Duplex autem est civitas Dei, una terrena, scilicet Ierusalem terrestris; alia spiritualis, scilicet Ierusalem caelestis. Per Vetus autem Testamentum homines efficiebantur cives civitatis terrestris, per Novum autem, caelestis.

Et ideo circa hoc duo facit.

Primo ponit mysterium expositum;

secundo expositionis mysticae rationem assignat, ibi *Sina enim*, et cetera.

259. Dicit ergo primo: dico quod significat duo Testamenta, scilicet Vetus et Novum. Et quantum ad hoc dicit: primum **quidem in Monte Sina**, et cetera.

Ubi, primo, ponitur locus in quo datum fuit, quia ad litteram **in Monte Sina**, ut dicitur Ex. XX, cuius, secundum Glossam, mystica ratio est, quia Sina interpretatur mandatum. Unde et ab Apostolo vetus lex vocatur lex Mandatorum, Eph. II, 15; mons autem significat superbiam, Ier. XIII, 16: *antequam offendant pedes vestri ad montes caliginosos*, et cetera. Unde per montem istum in quo data est lex, significatur superbia Iudaeorum duplex: una qua superbiebant contra Deum, Deut. XXXI, 27: *ego scio contentionem tuam*, etc.; alia qua superbicbant contra alias nationes abutentes eo, quod dicitur in Ps. CXLVII, 20: *non fecit taliter omni nationi*, et cetera.

260. Secundo vero proponit ad quid sit datum, quia non ad faciendum liberos, sed filios matris ancillae, **generans in servitutem, quae est Agar**, id est significatur per Agar, quae quidem in servitutem generat, scilicet Vetus Testamentum. Et hoc tripliciter, scilicet quantum ad affectum, quantum ad intellectum et fructum.

Quantum ad intellectum quidem secundum cognitionem, quia in homine est duplex cognitio: una libera, quando scilicet rerum veritatem secundum seipsam cognoscit; alia vero ancilla, id est subiecta velaminibus figurarum. Et talis fuit cognitio Veteris Testamenti.

Quantum ad affectum vero, quia nova lex generat affectum amoris, qui pertinet ad libertatem, nam qui amat, ex se movetur. Vetus autem generat affectum timoris, in quo est servitus; qui enim timet, non ex se, sed ex alio

second, as to the New, at **but that Jerusalem which is above is free**.

258. To understand this text, it must be noted with respect to the first that a citizen of a city is called its son, and the city itself his mother: *daughters of Jerusalem, weep not for me* (Luke 23:28); *the noble sons of Zion* (Lam 4:2). Therefore, by the fact that certain ones become citizens of a city, they are made its sons.

Now there is a twofold city of God: the one of earth, called the earthly Jerusalem, and the other of heaven, called the heavenly Jerusalem. Furthermore, men were made citizens of the earthly city through the Old Testament, but of the heavenly through the New.

Therefore, as to this he does two things:

first, he expounds the mystery;

second, he accounts for the mystical explanation, at **for Sinai**.

259. Therefore, he says first: I say that it signifies the two Testaments, namely, the Old and the New. And with respect to this he says: **the one from Mount Sina, engendering unto bondage**.

Wherein is mentioned first of all the place in which it was given, namely, **from Mount Sinai**, as is recorded in Exodus 20. According to a Gloss the mystical rendition of this is that Sinai is interpreted 'commandment'. Hence in Ephesians 2 the old law is called by the Apostle the law of the Commandments. Now a mountain signifies pride: *before your feet stumble upon the dark mountains* (Jer 13:16). Hence by this mountain on which the law was given a twofold pride of the Jews is signified: one by which they were arrogant against God. *I know your obstinacy and your most stiff neck* (Deut 31:27); the other by which they boasted at the expense of other nations, thus perverting what is said in a psalm: *he has not done in like manner to every nation; and his judgments he has not made manifest to them* (Ps 147:20).

260. Second, he explains the end for which it was given, namely, not to make them free, but to make them children of a bondwoman, **engendering unto bondage, which is Hagar**, i.e., which is signified by Hagar, who engenders unto bondage, namely, the Old Testament. And this it does with respect to three things; namely, feeling, understanding and fruit.

As to understanding, indeed, according to knowledge: because in man is a twofold knowledge. One is free, when he knows the truth of things according to themselves; the other is servile, i.e., veiled under figures, as was the knowledge of the Old Testament.

As to feeling, the new law engenders the feeling of love, which pertains to freedom: for one who loves is moved by his own initiative. The Old, on the other hand, engenders the feeling of fear in which is servitude; for one who fears is moved not by his own initiative but by that of another: *you*

movetur. Rom. VIII, 15: *non accepistis spiritum servitutis iterum in timore*, et cetera.

Sed quantum ad fructum, quia lex nova generat filios quibus debetur haereditas; sed illis, quos vetus generat, debentur munuscula, sicut servis. Io. VIII, 35: *servus non manet in domo in aeternum, filius manet in domo in aeternum*.

261. Rationem mysterii assignat, cum dicit **Sina enim mons est in Arabia**, et cetera. Ubi primo oritur dubitatio, quia cum Sina distet a Ierusalem per viginti fere dietas, videtur falsum quod Sina iunctus sit Ierusalem, ut hic Apostolus dicit.

Sed ad hoc mystice respondetur in Glossa sic, ut Sina sit in Arabia. Arabia enim humilitas vel afflictio interpretatur, in qua datum est Vetus Testamentum, quia homines quasi servi et alieni sub ea affligebantur carnalibus observantiis. Act. XV, v. 10: *hoc est onus, quod neque patres nostri, neque nos*, et cetera. Qui, mons, *coniunctus est*, non per spatii continuitatem sed per similitudinem, **ei quae nunc est Ierusalem**, id est, Iudaico populo; quia sicut ipsi terrena diligunt, et pro temporalibus serviunt sub peccato, ita et mons ille in servitutem generabat.

262. Sed haec non videtur intentio Apostoli. Nam ipse vult, quod Vetus Testamentum, quod in Monte Sina datum est, ex ipso loco servitutis in servitutem generet; quia illud dabatur in Sina, non tamen ibi remanentibus filiis Israel, sed proficiscentibus ad terram promissionis. Ierusalem enim etiam generat filios servitutis, et ideo quantum ad hoc coniungitur Mons Sina cum illa. Et hoc est quod dicit **qui coniunctus est ei**, scilicet per continuationem itineris euntium in Ierusalem, **quae nunc est Ierusalem, et servit cum filiis suis**, servitute scilicet legalium observantiarum (a qua redemit nos Christus) et servitute diversorum peccatorum Io. VIII, 34: *qui facit peccatum, servus est peccati* et (ad litteram) a servitute Romanorum, qui eis dominabantur.

263. Deinde cum dicit **illa autem quae sursum est Ierusalem**, etc., hic consequenter aperit mysterium de libera. Et

primo exponit mysterium;

secundo inducit prophetiam, ibi **scriptum est enim**, et cetera.

264. Primum quidem potest dupliciter intelligi, secundum quod hanc matrem possumus intelligere, vel illam per quam generamur, quae est Ecclesia militans; vel illam matrem in cuius filios generamur, quae est Ecclesia triumphans. I Petr. I, 3: *regeneravit nos in spem vivam*, et

have not received the spirit of bondage again in fear; but you have received the Spirit of adoption of sons (Rom 8:15).

But as to the fruit, the new law begets sons to whom is owed the inheritance, whereas to those whom the old law engenders are owed small presents as to servants: *the servant does not abide in the house forever; but the son abides forever* (John 8:35).

261. Then he gives the explanation of the mystery when he says: **Sinai is a mountain in Arabia, which has affinity to that Jerusalem which now is, and is in bondage with her children**. But here a difficulty arises: for since Sinai is almost twenty days journey from Jerusalem, it seems false that Sinai has affinity to, i.e., borders on, Jerusalem, as the Apostle says here.

To this a Gloss responds in a mystical manner that Sinai is in Arabia, which stands for the abjection or affliction under which the Old Testament was given, because the men under it were oppressed by carnal observances after the manner of slaves and foreigners: *this is a yoke which neither we nor our fathers were able to bear* (Acts 15:10). This mountain neighbors on Jerusalem not by a spatial continuity but by a likeness **to that which is now Jerusalem**, i.e., to the Jewish people, because just as they love earthly things and for the sake of temporal things are under the bondage of sin, so that mountain engendered unto bondage.

262. But this does not seem to be the Apostle's intention. For he wants to bring out that, from the very place of bondage, the Old Testament, which was given on Mount Sinai, engenders unto bondage, because it was given on Sinai not as a place where the children of Israel were to remain, but as a stage in their journey to the promised land. For Jerusalem, too, engenders sons unto bondage. Hence it is with respect to this that Mount Sinai is continuous with her. And this is what he says: **which has affinity to that** (i.e., by being part of the continuous route followed by those going to Jerusalem) **which is now Jerusalem, and is in bondage with her children**, i.e., the bondage of legal observances (from which Christ redeemed us) and of various sins—*he who commits sins is the servant of sin* (John 8:34)—and, literally, from bondage under the Romans who were their masters.

263. Then when he says, **but that Jerusalem which is above is free**, he discloses the mystery of the free woman.

First, he discloses the mystery;

second, he refers to a prophecy, at **for it is written**.

264. The first can be understood in two ways, accordingly as we understand this mother to be the one by whom we are engendered, which is the Church Militant, or the mother whose sons we become, which is the Church Triumphant: *he has regenerated us unto a lively hope by the*

cetera. Sic ergo generamur in praesenti Ecclesia Militante, ut perveniamus ad Triumphantem.

Hoc ergo modo illud exponentes, a quatuor describitur mater nostra, scilicet a sublimitate, cum dicit *sursum*, secundo a nomine, cum dicit *Ierusalem*, tertio a libertate, cum dicit *libera est*, quarto a foecunditate, cum dicit *mater nostra*.

Est ergo sublimis per apertam Dei visionem, et per perfectam Dei fruitionem, et hoc quantum ad Ecclesiam Triumphantem. Is. LX, v. 5: *videbis, et afflues*, et cetera. Col. III, 2: *quae sursum sunt sapite*, et cetera. Item sublimis per fidem et spem, quantum ad Ecclesiam Militantem. Phil. III, 20: *nostra conversatio in caelis*, et cetera. Cant. III, 6 et VIII, 5: *quae est ista quae ascendit*, et cetera.

Sed est etiam pacifica, quia *Ierusalem*, id est, visio pacis. Quod quidem competit Ecclesiae Triumphanti, ut habenti pacem perfectam. Ps. CXLVII, 14: *qui posuit fines tuos pacem*, et cetera. Is. XXXII, 18: *sedebit populus meus in pulchritudine pacis*. Item competit Ecclesiae Militanti, quae in Christo pacem habens quiescit. Io. XVI, 33: *in me pacem habebitis*.

Est etiam *libera*, Rom. VIII, 21: *ipsa creatura liberabitur*, et cetera. Et hoc quantum ad Triumphantem, et etiam quantum ad Militantem, ut Apoc. XXI, 2: *vidi civitatem sanctam Ierusalem*, et cetera.

Sed foecunda est, quia *mater nostra*. Militans quidem ut generans, Triumphans ut in cuius filios generamur. Ps. LXXXVI, 5: *numquid Sion dicet homo*, et cetera. Is. LX, 4: *filii tui de longe venient*, et cetera.

265. *Scriptum est enim*, scilicet Is. LIV, v. 1, secundum enim Septuaginta. Hic ponitur prophetia, per quam

primo probatur libertas matris praedictae;

secundo eius foecunditas, ibi *quia multi filii*, et cetera.

266. Sciendum est autem, circa primum, quod in muliere foecunda, primo quidem est tristitia in pariendo, secundo subsequitur gaudium in suscepta prole, secundum illud Io. XVI, 21: *mulier cum parit*, et cetera. Sed mulier sterilis nec patitur in partu, nec gaudet in prole. Differunt autem parere et parturire, quia parturire dicit conatum ad partum; parere vero dicit eductionem foetus iam facti. In parturitione ergo dolorem experitur foecunda, et in partu gaudium. Sterilis autem dolore parturitionis et gaudio partus privatur.

resurrection of Jesus Christ from the dead (1 Pet 1:3). Hence we are so generated in the present Church Militant as to arrive at the Triumphant.

Therefore in explaining it thus, our mother is described by four things: by her sublimity, when he says, *above*; second, by name, when he says, *Jerusalem*; third by her freedom, when he says, *is free*, fourth, by her fecundity when he says, *our mother*.

She is sublime on account of the face-to-face vision of God and the perfect enjoyment of God; and this, as to the Church Triumphant: *then shall you see, and abound, and your heart shall wonder and be enlarged* (Isa 60:5); *mind the things that are above* (Col 3:2). Again she is sublime through faith and hope as to the Church Militant: *our conversation is in heaven* (Phil 3:20); *who is this that comes up from the desert, flowing with delights?* (Song 8:5).

Further, she is a peacemaker, because she is *Jerusalem*, i.e., a vision of peace. This belongs to the Church Triumphant as having perfect peace: *who has placed peace in your borders* (Ps 147:14); *my people shall sit in the beauty of peace* (Isa 32:18). Likewise it pertains to the Church Militant which possesses the peace of resting in Christ: *in me you shall have peace* (John 16:33).

Furthermore, she is *free*: *because the creature also shall itself be delivered from the servitude of corruption* (Rom 8:21). And this is both as to the Church Triumphant and the Church Militant according to Revelation: *I saw the holy city, the new Jerusalem, coming down out of heaven from God* (Rev 21:2).

Finally, she is fruitful, because she is *our mother*: Militant as engendering; Triumphant as the one whose sons we become: *shall Zion say: this man and that man is born of her?* (Ps 87:5) *Your sons shall come from afar, and your daughters shall rise up at your side* (Isa 60:4).

265. *For it is written*, namely in Isaiah, according to the Septuagint (Isa 54:1). Here is mentioned the prophecy through which is proved,

first of all, that the mother referred to is free, and

second, that she is fruitful, at *for many are the children*.

266. With respect to the first, it should be noted that in a fertile woman there is first sorrow in giving birth, but this is followed by joy in beholding the child: *a woman when she is in labor has sorrow, because her hour is come; but when she has brought forth the child, she remembers no more her anguish for joy that a man is born into the world* (John 16:21). But a barren woman neither suffers the pangs of birth nor has joy in a child. Again there is a difference between bearing and travailing. For the latter refers to the effort to bear, whereas the former refers to the releasing of the fetus now formed. Therefore the fertile woman experiences pain in travail but joy in bearing; the sterile woman, on the other hand, experiences neither the pain of travail nor the joy of bearing.

Sed haec duo propheta indicit sterili, dicens *laetare, sterilis*, etc., ubi loquitur de Ierusalem, quam dicit liberam, significatam per Saram sterilem. Nam Ecclesia sterilis erat, scilicet Ecclesia Militans gentium ante conversionem, quae non offerebat filium Deo, sed diabolo. Unde ad Babylonem dicitur Is. XLVII, v. 9: *sterilitas et viduitas venerunt tibi*, et cetera. Et Ecclesia Triumphans ante passionem Christi sterilis erat, quia non generabantur aliqui in filios eius per introitum gloriae nisi in spe. Posita enim erat romphaea ante ianuam paradisi, ut nullus intrare posset. Huic ergo sterili dicitur *laetare, quae non paris*, etc., quasi dicat: steriles, ut dictum est, non dolent de partu, sed de eo quod non pariunt. I Reg. I, 10: *cum esset Anna amaro animo*, et cetera. Sed tu laetaberis in multitudine filiorum. Is. LX, 5: *tunc dilatabitur et mirabitur cor tuum*, scilicet laetitiam mentis extra ostendens.

Duo enim sunt in partu, scilicet dolor ex eruptione reticulorum, quibus continetur foetus in matrice, et clamor ex ipso dolore. Et ideo dicit tu *quae non parturis*, scilicet Ecclesia Militans, quae non conaris ad partum per desiderium, et Triumphans, quae non parturis dolendo, vel quia nondum venit tempus recipiendi filios: *erumpe*, id est laetitiam quam interius habes manifesta exterius, *et clama* voce laudis. Is. LVIII, 1: *clama, ne cesses*, et cetera.

Et haec duo ad libertatem pertinent, scilicet clamare et erumpere: sic ergo apparet libertas matris.

267. Sequitur foecunditas *quia multi filii*, et cetera.

Sed cum supra dictum sit Ecclesiam liberam significari per Saram, videtur esse dubium an Sara fuerit deserta.

Ad quod sciendum est, quod deserta fuit ab Abraham, ut hic dicitur, non per divortium, sed quantum ad opus carnale. Nam Abraham vacabat quidem operi carnali, non propter concupiscentiam, sed propter prolem suscipiendam. Cum ergo innotuit ei Saram sterilem esse, deseruit eam, non frangens coniugalem thorum, sed quia non utebatur ea ab illo praecise tempore quo Sara introduxit ei ancillam.

Per quod datur intelligi, quod Ecclesia gentium deserta erat a Christo, quia nondum venerat Christus, et quod Ecclesia Triumphans deserta erat ab hominibus, quibus ad eam nondum patebat accessus. Huius ergo *desertae*, scilicet Ecclesiae gentium, sunt *multi filii*, id est plures, *magis quam eius*, scilicet synagogae, *quae*

But these are the two things which the prophet announces to the barren woman: *rejoice, you barren, who do not bear: break forth and cry, you who do not travail*. Herein he speaks of Jerusalem, which he calls free and which is signified by the barren Sarah. For the Church was barren, namely, the Church Militant, of the gentiles before their conversion when they offered their sons not to God but to the devil. Hence it is said to Babylon: *barrenness and widowhood will come upon you, because of the multitude of your sorceries* (Isa 47:9). The Church Triumphant, too, was barren before the passion of Christ, because to her were born no sons who entered into glory, save in hope. For a mighty engine of war blocked the entrance to paradise, so that no one might enter. To this barren one he says: *rejoice you who do not bear*. As if to say: the barren, as has been said, are sorrowful, not because they bear, but because they do not bear: *as Hannah had her heart full of grief, she prayed to the Lord, shedding many tears* (1 Sam 1:10). But you shall rejoice in the great number of your children: *then shall your heart wonder and be enlarged* (Isa 60:5), i.e., you will show the joy in your soul outwardly.

For there are two things in childbirth: the pain from the rupturing of the membrane enclosing the child in the womb, and the crying from pain. Hence he says, *you who do not travail*, i.e., the Church Militant, that makes no effort to bear through desire, and the Church Triumphant, that does not cry for travail; or because the time for having sons has not yet come, *break forth*, i.e., show outwardly the joy you have within and cry with sounds of praise: *cry, cease not, lift up your voice like a trumpet* (Isa 58:1).

These two things, namely, to cry and to break forth, pertain to freedom. Thus the freedom of the mother is made manifest.

267. He follows with the fruitfulness: *for many are the children of the desolate, more than of her who has a husband*.

But since it was said above that the free Church is signified by Sarah, there seems to be some doubt whether Sarah was desolate.

I answer that she was made desolate by Abraham, as it is said here, not by a divorce but with respect to the work of the flesh. For Abraham resorted to the work of the flesh not for the pleasure but to obtain a child. Therefore when he learned that Sarah was barren, he abandoned her; not by forsaking the marriage bed, but by not resorting to her from precisely the time that Sarah introduced the bondwoman to him.

By this we are given to understand that the Church of the gentiles was left desolate by Christ, because Christ had not yet come; and that the Church Triumphant was desolate of men, for whom no means of entry was open. Of this *desolate* woman, i.e., the Church of the gentiles, there are *many children*, i.e., *more than of her*, namely, the synagogue, *who*

habet virum, scilicet Moysen. I Reg. II, 5: *sterilis peperit plurimos, et quae multos filios habebat*, et cetera. Et hoc veniente sponso, scilicet Christo, a quo deserta erat, non dilectione, sed partu postposito.

has a husband, namely, Moses: *the barren has borne many: and she that had many children is weakened* (1 Sam 2:5). And this is due to the coming of the spouse, namely, Christ, by whom she had been left desolate not by want of love, but because the bearing of children had been delayed.

Lecture 9

⁴:²⁸Nos autem, fratres, secundum Isaac promissionis filii sumus. [n. 268]

⁴:²⁹Sed quomodo tunc is, qui secundum carnem natus fuerat, persequebatur eum qui secundum spiritum: ita et nunc. [n. 270]

⁴:³⁰Sed quid dicit Scriptura? *Ejice ancillam, et filium ejus: non enim haeres erit filius ancillae cum filio liberae.* [n. 274]

⁴:³¹Itaque, fratres, non sumus ancillae filii, sed liberae:

⁴:²⁸ὑμεῖς δέ, ἀδελφοί, κατὰ Ἰσαὰκ ἐπαγγελίας τέκνα ἐστέ.

⁴:²⁹ἀλλ' ὥσπερ τότε ὁ κατὰ σάρκα γεννηθεὶς ἐδίωκεν τὸν κατὰ πνεῦμα, οὕτως καὶ νῦν.

⁴:³⁰ἀλλὰ τί λέγει ἡ γραφή; Ἔκβαλε τὴν παιδίσκην καὶ τὸν υἱὸν αὐτῆς, οὐ γὰρ μὴ κληρονομήσει ὁ υἱὸς τῆς παιδίσκης μετὰ τοῦ υἱοῦ τῆς ἐλευθέρας.

⁴:³¹διό, ἀδελφοί, οὐκ ἐσμὲν παιδίσκης τέκνα ἀλλὰ τῆς ἐλευθέρας.

⁴:²⁸Now we, brethren are, as Isaac was, the children of promise. [n. 268]

⁴:²⁹But as then he who was born according to the flesh persecuted him who was according to the spirit, so also it is now. [n. 270]

⁴:³⁰But what does the Scripture say? *Cast out the bondwoman and her son: for the son of the bondwoman shall not be heir with the son* of the free woman. [n. 274]

⁴:³¹So then, brethren, we are not the children of the bondwoman but of the free woman:

---

268. Exposito mysterio quantum ad matres, hic exponit illud quantum ad filios. Et

primo ponit filiorum distinctionem;

secundo principalem conclusionem, ibi *itaque, fratres mei*, et cetera.

Distinctionem autem filiorum ponit quantum ad tria.

Primo quantum ad modum originis;

secundo quantum ad affectum dilectionis, ibi *sed quomodo tunc*, etc.;

tertio quantum ad ius haereditatis, ibi *sed quid dicit Scriptura*, et cetera.

269. Modus autem originis quo aliqui nascuntur filii Abrahae est duplex: quidam origine carnali, sicut Ismael de ancilla; quidam autem non carnali origine, sicut Isaac de libera: non quod naturali opere natus non fuerit, sed quia sicut dictum est supra naturalem virtutem carnis fuit ut de vetula sterili filius nasceretur.

Per hos autem filios intelligitur duplex populus. Nam per Ismaelem intelligitur populus Iudaeorum, qui carnali propagatione est ab Abraham derivatus. Per Isaac autem, populus gentium, qui per imitationem fidei ab Abraham descendit. Et ideo dicit *nos autem, fratres*, scilicet fideles, tam Iudaei, quam gentiles, *secundum Isaac*, id est, in similitudine Isaac, *promissionis filii sumus* facti Abrahae. Rom. IX, 8: *qui sunt filii promissionis aestimantur in semine.*

Sed nota, quod filii carnis Abrahae ad litteram sunt Iudaei, mystice autem, qui propter carnalia et temporalia bona ad fidem veniunt.

268. Having disclosed the mystery as to the mothers, he now discloses it as to the sons.

First, he differentiates between the sons;

second, he sets down the main conclusion, at *so then, brethren*.

He distinguishes the sons on three counts:

first, as to the manner of origin;

second, as to the feeling of love, at *but as then he who was born*;

third, as to their right to the inheritance, at *but what does the Scripture say*.

269. The manner of origin, according to which the sons of Abraham are born, is twofold: one is by origin according to the flesh, as Ishmael, of the bondwoman; the other not according to the flesh, as Isaac, of the free woman—not because he was not born in the way of nature, but because, as has been said, it was beyond the natural power of the flesh for a son to be born of a barren old woman.

Two peoples are understood by these two sons: by Ishmael is understood the Jewish people, who derived from Abraham by carnal propagation; but by Isaac, the people of the gentiles, who descended from Abraham by imitation of his faith. Hence he says: *now we, brethren*, i.e., the faithful, both Jew and gentile, *as Isaac was*, i.e., in the line of Isaac, *are the children of the promise* that was made to Abraham: *they that are the children of the promise are accounted for the seed* (Gen 21; Rom 9:8).

But note that the children of Abraham according to the flesh are, literally, the Jewish people; but, mystically, they are the ones who come to the faith for the sake of carnal and temporal goods.

270. Secundum affectum autem distinguuntur, quia *qui natus erat secundum carnem, persequebatur illum qui natus erat secundum spiritum*.

271. Sed hic est quaestio. Primo quia non legitur, quod Ismael persecutionem aliquam fecerit contra Isaac, sed quod tantum luserit cum eo. Gen. XXI, 9: *cum vidisset Sara filium ancillae Agar ludentem*, et cetera.

Responsio. Dicendum est, quod Apostolus illum ludum dicit persecutionem, quia ludus magni ad parvum est quaedam illusio, cum maior cum parvo ludens intendit eum decipere.

Vel etiam, ut dicunt quidam, Ismael cogebat Isaac adorare imagines luteas quas faciebat. Per hoc autem docebat eum averti a cultu unius Dei, quod est magna persecutio, cum maius malum sit inferre mortem spiritualem, quam corporalem. Quod tamen ideo in Genesi appellatur ludus, quia sub specie ludi hoc faciebat.

272. Est etiam quaestio quomodo filii secundum carnem persecuti fuerint et persequantur filios secundum spiritum.

Sed ad hoc est responsio, quia a principio primitivae Ecclesiae Iudaei persecuti sunt Christianos, ut patet in Actibus Apostolorum, et facerent etiam nunc si possent. Nunc etiam carnales persequuntur in Ecclesia spirituales viros, etiam corporaliter, illi scilicet qui quaerunt gloriam et temporalia lucra in Ecclesia. Unde dicitur in Glossa: *omnes qui in Ecclesia terrenam facultatem quaerunt a Domino, ad hunc Ismaelem pertinent. Ipsi sunt qui contradicunt spiritualibus proficientibus, et detrahunt illis, et habent labia iniqua et linguas dolosas et subdolosas*.

Spiritualiter autem persequuntur spirituales filios, superbi et hypocritae. Nam aliquando aliqui manifeste carnales et mali culpam suam recognoscentes, bonis se humiliant, fatui vero bonitatem, quam ipsi non habent, persequuntur in aliis.

273. Est etiam quaestio, quia haeretici quos nos persequimur, dicunt se natos secundum spiritum, nos vero secundum carnem.

Sed dicendum est, quod duplex est persecutio. Una bona, qua aliquis persequitur alium, ut reducat eum ad bonum, et hanc viri iusti faciunt malis et spirituales carnalibus, vel ut eos corrigant si converti volunt, vel si obstinati sunt in malo, destruant, ne gregem Domini inficiant. Alia persecutio est mala, qua quis persequitur alium, ut pervertat ad malum, et hanc qui secundum carnem nati sunt, faciunt his, qui nati sunt secundum spiritum.

274. Quantum vero ad ius haereditatis, distinguuntur per auctoritatem Scripturae, Gen. XXI, 10: *eiice ancillam*

270. Second, they are distinguished according to affection, because *he who was born according to the flesh persecuted him who was according to the spirit*.

271. But this raises a difficulty. First, because it is not recorded that Ishmael persecuted Isaac, but only that they played together: *when Sarah had seen the son of Hagar, the Egyptian, playing with Isaac her son, she said to Abraham: cast out this bondwoman and her son* (Gen 21:9).

I answer that the Apostle calls this playing a persecution, because there is deception when an older person plays with a younger one; since the older person, in playing with the younger, intends to deceive him.

Or, as some say, Ishmael compelled Isaac to adore the clay images he fashioned. By this he was teaching him to be turned from the worship of the one God; and this was a considerable persecution, since it is a greater evil to cause spiritual death than bodily death. Furthermore, in Genesis this is called a game because he did this under the guise of a game.

272. There is another difficulty, namely, how the children according to the flesh persecuted and do persecute the children according to the spirit?

The answer is that from the beginning of the early Church the Jews persecuted Christians, as is obvious in the Acts of the Apostles, and they would do the same even now, if they were able. Now, however, those who are carnal persecute spiritual men in the Church even as to the body; those, namely, who seek glory and temporal gain in the Church. Hence a Gloss says that *all who seek from the Lord earthly aggrandizement in the Church pertain to this Ishmael. They are the ones who oppose those who are making spiritual progress and slander them. They have iniquity in their mouth, and craft and deceit on their tongues*.

But the ones who spiritually persecute the spiritual sons are the haughty and the hypocrites. For sometimes they who are plainly carnal and evil recognize their guilt and humble themselves before the good; but the foolish persecute in others the goodness they themselves lack.

273. A further question arises from the fact that heretics whom we persecute say that they are the ones born according to the spirit and we according to the flesh.

I answer that there are two kinds of persecution: the good one is that in which a person persecutes another to lead him back to good. And this is what just men do to evil men, and spiritual men to carnal men; either to correct them, if they want to be converted, or, if they are obstinate, to destroy them, lest they contaminate the flock of the Lord. The other type of persecution is evil, namely, when a person persecutes another in order to pervert him; and this is what those who are born according to the flesh do to those who are born according to the spirit.

274. Finally, as to their right to the inheritance, they are distinguished by the authority of Scripture: *cast out the*

et filium eius. In quo datur intelligi, quod Iudaei et persecutores fidei Christianae, et etiam carnales et mali Christiani eiicientur a regno caelesti. Matth. VIII, 11: *multi venient ab oriente*, et cetera. Apoc. XXII, 15: *foris canes et venefici*, et cetera. Ancilla etiam, id est malitia, et ipsum peccatum eiicietur. Eccli. XIV, 20: *omne opus corruptibile in fine deficiet*.

275. Et ratio horum subditur, quia **non erit haeres filius ancillae cum filio liberae**. In mundo enim isto boni sunt malis permixti, et mali bonis. Cant. II, 2: *sicut lilium inter spinas*, et cetera. Sed in aeterna patria non erunt nisi boni. Iudic. XI, 2 dicitur ad Iephte: *haeres in domo patris nostri esse non poteris, quia de adultera natus es*. Quam quidem libertatem habemus a Christo. Unde dicit *qua libertate*, et cetera. Io. VIII, 36: *si filius vos liberaverit, vere liberi eritis*.

bondwoman and her son (Gen 21:10). By this we are given to understand that the Jews and persecutors of the Christian religion, as well as carnal and evil Christians, will be cast out from the kingdom of heaven: *many shall come from the east and the west and shall sit down with Abraham and Isaac and Jacob in the kingdom of heaven* (Matt 8:11); *without are dogs and sorcerers* (Rev 22:15). Furthermore, the bondwoman, i.e., vice and sin itself, will be cast out: *every work that is corruptible shall fail in the end* (Sir 14:20).

275. The reason for all this is added, **for the son of the bondwoman shall not be heir with the son of the free woman**. For in this world the good are mingled with the wicked and the wicked with the good: *as the lily among thorns, so is my love among the daughters* (Song 2:2). But in the eternal fatherland there will be only the good. In Judges it is said to Jephtah: *you cannot inherit in the house of our father, because you are born of a harlot* (Judg 11:2). This freedom we obtain from Christ; hence he says, by the freedom wherewith Christ has made us free: *if therefore the son shall make you free, you shall be free indeed* (John 8:36).

Chapter 5

Lecture 1

⁵:¹qua libertate Christus nos liberavit. State, et nolite iterum jugo servitutis contineri. [n. 276]

⁵:²Ecce ego Paulus dico vobis: quoniam si circumcidamini, Christus vobis nihil proderit. [n. 279]

⁵:³Testificor autem rursus omni homini circumcidenti se, quoniam debitor est universae legis faciendae. [n. 281]

⁵:⁴Evacuati estis a Christo, qui in lege justificamini: a gratia excidistis. [n. 283]

⁵:¹τῇ ἐλευθερίᾳ ἡμᾶς Χριστὸς ἠλευθέρωσεν: στήκετε οὖν καὶ μὴ πάλιν ζυγῷ δουλείας ἐνέχεσθε.

⁵:²Ἴδε ἐγὼ Παῦλος λέγω ὑμῖν ὅτι ἐὰν περιτέμνησθε Χριστὸς ὑμᾶς οὐδὲν ὠφελήσει.

⁵:³μαρτύρομαι δὲ πάλιν παντὶ ἀνθρώπῳ περιτεμνομένῳ ὅτι ὀφειλέτης ἐστὶν ὅλον τὸν νόμον ποιῆσαι.

⁵:⁴κατηργήθητε ἀπὸ Χριστοῦ οἵτινες ἐν νόμῳ δικαιοῦσθε, τῆς χάριτος ἐξεπέσατε.

⁵:¹By the freedom with which Christ has made us free. Stand fast and do not be held again under the yoke of bondage. [n. 276]

⁵:²Behold, I, Paul, tell you that if you be circumcised, Christ shall profit you nothing. [n. 279]

⁵:³And I testify again to every man circumcising himself, that he is a debtor to do the whole law. [n. 281]

⁵:⁴You are made void of Christ, you who are justified in the law are fallen from grace. [n. 283]

---

276. Supra ostendit Apostolus, quod per legem non est iustitia hic vero reducit eos ab errore ad statum rectitudinis. Et

primo quantum ad divina;

secundo quantum ad humana, VI cap., ibi *et si praeoccupatus fuerit homo*, et cetera.

Circa primum duo facit.

Primo proponit admonitionem;

secundo eius rationem assignat, ibi *ecce ego Paulus*, et cetera.

277. Et in admonitione etiam duo ponit. Quorum unum est inductivum ad bonum; secundum est prohibitivum a malo.

Inducit quidem ad bonum, cum dicit *state ergo*, quasi dicat: ex quo per Christum liberati estis a servitute legis, state firma fide, et fixo pede permanentes in libertate. Sic ergo cum dicit *state*, inducit ad rectitudinem. Qui enim stat, rectus est. I Cor. X, 12: *qui se existimat stare*, et cetera. Inducit etiam ad firmitatem. I Cor. XV, 58: *stabiles estote et immobiles*, et cetera. Eph. ult.: *state succincti lumbos vestros*, et cetera.

Prohibet vero et retrahit a malo, cum subdit *et nolite iterum iugo servitutis contineri*, id est non subiiciamini legi, quae in servitutem generat. De quo iugo dicitur Act. XV, 10: *hoc est onus quod neque patres nostri,*

276. Above, the Apostle showed that justice is not through the law; here he leads them back from error to a state of rectitude.

First, with respect to divine matters;

second, with respect to human affairs, at **brethren, even if a man be overtaken in some fault** (Gal 6:1).

As to the first, he does two things:

first, he admonishes them;

second, he gives the reason underlying his admonition, at **behold, I, Paul**.

277. In the admonition itself he includes two things: one is an inducement to good; the other is a caution against evil.

He induces to good when he says, **stand fast**. As if to say: since you have been set free from the bondage of the law through Christ, stand fast and, with your faith firm and feet planted, persevere in freedom. And so when he says, **stand fast**, he exhorts them to rectitude. For he that stands is erect: *he that thinks himself to stand, let him take heed, lest he fall* (1 Cor 10:12). Likewise he exhorts them to be firm: *therefore, be steadfast and unmoveable* (1 Cor 15:58); *stand, therefore, having your loins girt about with truth* (Eph 6:14).

But he cautions and draws them from evil, when he adds: **and do not be held again under the yoke of bondage**, i.e., do not subject yourself to the law which engenders unto bondage. Of this yoke, it is written: *this is a yoke*

neque nos, etc., a quo tantum per Christum liberati estis. Is. IX, 4: *virgam humeri eius*, et cetera.

278. Ideo autem addit *iterum*, non quia prius sub lege fuerint, sed quia, ut Hieronymus dicit, post Evangelium servare legalia adeo peccatum est, ut sit sicut servire idololatriae. Unde quia isti idololatrae fuerant, si subiiciant se iugo circumcisionis et aliarum legalium observationum, quasi ad eadem revertuntur, quibus antea in idololatria servierant.

Secundum Augustinum vero, ut supra dictum est, circa legalium observantias triplex tempus distinguitur, scilicet tempus ante passionem, ante gratiam divulgatam, et post gratiam divulgatam. Post ergo gratiam divulgatam servare legalia est peccatum mortale, etiam ipsis Iudaeis. Sed in tempore medio, scilicet ante gratiam divulgatam, poterant quidem absque peccato etiam illi, qui ex Iudaeis conversi fuerant, legalia servare, dum tamen in eis spem non ponerent; conversis vero ex gentibus non licebat ea servare. Quia ergo Galatae ex Iudaeis non erant, et tamen legalia servare volebant et ponebant in eis spem, ideo revertebantur in iugum servitutis. Nam huiusmodi observatio erat eis sicut idololatria, inquantum non recte sentiebant de Christo, credentes ab ipso sine legalibus salutem consequi non posse.

279. Deinde cum dicit *ecce ego*, etc., exponit praedicta duo. Et
primo secundum,
secundo primum, ibi *nos autem spiritus*, et cetera.
Circa primum duo facit.
Primo ostendit quid sit iugum servitutis, quod non debent subire;
secundo probat, ibi *evacuati estis*, et cetera.
Circa primum duo facit.
Primo ostendit iugum illud esse valde nocivum;
secundo valde onerosum, ibi *testificor autem*, et cetera.

280. Nocivum est quidem iugum legis, quia aufert Dominicae passionis effectum. Et ideo dicit: *nolite contineri iugo servitutis*, quia *ecce ego Paulus*, qui, supple: voce auctoritatis, *dico*, et bene, *si circumcidimini, Christus vobis nihil proderit*, id est, fides Christi.

Sed contra, Act. XVI, 3 dicitur quod Paulus circumcidit Timotheum, ergo fecit quod Christus ei nihil prodesset, ergo decepit eum.

which neither we nor our fathers have been able to bear (Acts 15:10), a yoke from which we have been loosed by Christ alone: *for the yoke of their burden, and the rod of their shoulder, and the scepter of their oppressor, you have overcome* (Isa 9:4).

278. The reason for adding, *again*, is not that they had been under the law before, but that, as Jerome says, to observe the legal ceremonies after the Gospel is so great a sin as to border on idolatry. Hence, because they had been idolaters, if they were to submit themselves to the yoke of circumcision and the other legal observances, they would be, as it were, returning to the very things wherein they had formerly practiced idolatry.

However, according to Augustine in *Epistle 19*, three periods of time are distinguished with respect to the observance of the legal ceremonies: namely, the time before the passion, the time before the spreading of grace, and the time after the spreading of grace. To observe the legal ceremonies after grace has been preached is a mortal sin for the Jews. But during the interim, i.e., before the preaching of grace, they could be observed without sin even by those who had been converted from Judaism, provided they set no hope in them. However, those converted from paganism could not observe them without sin. Therefore, because the Galatians had not come from Judaism but wanted, nevertheless, to observe the legal ceremonies and put their hope in them, they were in effect returning to the yoke of bondage. For in their case, observances of this sort were akin to idolatry, inasmuch as they entertained a false notion concerning Christ, believing that salvation cannot be obtained by him without the observances of the law.

279. Then when he says, *behold, I, Paul, tell you*, he explains these two parts of his admonition:
first, the second part;
second, the first part, at *for we in spirit* (Gal 5:5).
As to the first, he does two things:
first, he shows what the yoke of bondage is to which they should not submit;
second, he proves it, at *you are made void of Christ*.
Regarding the first, he does two things:
first, he shows that this yoke is a source of great harm;
second, that it is terribly burdensome, at *and I testify again*.

280. The yoke of the law is harmful because it nullifies the effect of the Lord's passion. Hence he says, *do not be held again under the yoke of bondage*, because *behold, I, Paul*, who am speaking with the voice of authority, *tell you*, and well, *that if you be circumcised, Christ shall profit you nothing*, i.e., faith in Christ.

But against this is something recorded in Acts, namely, that Paul circumcised Timothy (Acts 16:3). Hence in effect he brought it about that Christ profited him nothing; furthermore, he was deceiving him.

Respondeo. Dicendum est, secundum Hieronymum, quod Paulus non circumcidit Timotheum quasi legem servare intenderit, sed simulavit se circumcidere, faciendo opus circumcisionis. Nam, secundum ipsum, apostoli simulatorie servabant legalia ad vitandum scandalum fidelium ex Iudaeis. Faciebant autem actus legalium, non tamen cum intentione servandi legalia, et sic non exibant a fide. Unde non decepit Timotheum.

Secundum vero Augustinum dicendum est quod apostoli secundum veritatem servabant legalia, et cum intentione ea servandi, quia, secundum apostolorum sententiam, licebat fidelibus ex Iudaeis illo tempore, scilicet ante gratiam divulgatam, ipsa servare. Et ideo quia Timotheus fuit ex matre Iudaea, circumcidit eum Apostolus cum intentione servandi legalia. Quia vero Galatae ponebant spem in legalibus post gratiam divulgatam, quasi sine eis gratia non sufficeret ad salutem, et ideo ea servare volebant, ideo dicit eis Apostolus *si circumcidimini*, et cetera. Sequebatur enim ex hoc, quod non reputarent Christum, in cuius signum data fuit circumcisio. Gen. XVII, 11: *ut sit in signum foederis inter me et vos*, et cetera. Qui ergo circumcidebantur, credebant adhuc signum durare, et tunc signatum nondum venisse, et sic excidebant a Christo.

Sic ergo patet onus legis esse nocivum.

281. Est etiam valde onerosum, quia obligat ad impossibile, et hoc est quod dicit **testificor autem**, etc., quasi dicat: dico quod *si circumcidimini, Christus vobis nihil proderit*. Sed adhuc, **testificor enim omni homini**, scilicet Iudaeo et gentili, et cetera.

Nam quicumque profitetur in aliqua religione, facit se debitorem omnium quae ad observantiam illius religionis pertinent. Et sicut dicit Augustinus: *numquam fuit aliqua religio sine aliquo visibili signo, ad quod obligarentur qui in ipsa religione vivunt; sicut in religione Christiana signum visibile est baptisma, ad quod omnes Christiani tenentur quoad cultum. Obligantur etiam ad omnia quae ad cultum Christianae religionis pertinent.* Signum autem legis Mosaicae fuit circumcisio. Quicumque ergo circumcidebat se, obligabatur ad omnia legalia servanda ac implenda, et hoc est quod dicit **quoniam debitor est universae legis faciendae**, Iac. II, v. 10: *qui offendit in uno, factus est omnium reus*. Quam tamen nullus servare poterat, secundum illud Act. XV, 10: *hoc est onus, quod neque patres nostri, neque nos portare potuimus*, et cetera.

282. Sed dato quod aliquis circumcideretur, ergo secundum praedicta obligat se ad servandum legalia, sed

I answer that, according to Jerome, Paul did not circumcise Timothy as though intending to observe the law, but he feigned circumcision in working circumcision on him. For, according to him, the apostles feigned observing the works of the law to avoid scandalizing the converts from Judaism. In other words, they performed the actions of the law without the intention of observing them, and so they did not depart from the faith. Hence he did not deceive Timothy.

However, according to Augustine, the answer is that the apostles did in very truth observe the works of the law and had the intention of observing them; because, according to the teaching of the apostles, it was lawful at that time, i.e., before grace had become widespread, for converts from Judaism to observe them. Therefore, because Timothy was born of a Jewish mother, the Apostle circumcised him with the intention of observing the law. But because the Galatians were putting their hope in the legal observances after the spreading of grace, as though without them grace was not sufficient to save them, and they observed them in that frame of mind, for that reason the Apostle declared to them that *if you be circumcised, Christ shall profit you nothing*. For it followed from this that they did not correctly estimate Christ, to signify whom circumcision was given: *that it may be a sign of the covenant between me and you* (Gen 17:11). Therefore, those who submitted to circumcision believed that the sign was still in vogue and that the one signified had not yet come. Thus they were fallen away from Christ.

In this way, then, it is plain that the yoke of the law is harmful.

281. Furthermore, it is a heavy burden, because it obliges to the impossible. And this is what he states: **I testify again to every man circumcising himself, that he is a debtor to do the whole law**. As if to say: I say that *if you be circumcised, Christ shall profit you nothing*. But in addition to this, **I testify to every man**, both Jew and gentile, **circumcising himself, that he is a debtor to do the whole law**.

For one who professes a religion makes himself a debtor to all that pertains to the observances of that religion. And, as Augustine says: *there has never been a religion without some visible sign to which those who live in that religion are obligated; as in the Christian religion the visible sign is baptism, which all Christians are held to undergo. Furthermore, they are obligated to everything that pertains to the Christian religion*. Now the sign of the Mosaic law was circumcision. Therefore, whoever circumcised himself was put under obligation to observe and fulfill all the matters of the law. And that is what he says: **he is a debtor to do the whole law**: *whosoever offends in one point, is become guilty of all* (Jas 2:10). No one, however, was able to keep the law, according to Acts: *this is a yoke which neither our fathers nor we have been able to bear* (Acts 15:10).

282. But suppose someone is circumcised; then according to the aforesaid he is obligated to observe all the matters

hoc est peccatum mortale, ergo tenetur peccare mortaliter, et sic videtur esse perplexus.

Respondeo. Dicendum est quod eadem conscientia durante, tenetur servare legalia, puta si aliquis haberet conscientiam, quod, nisi circumcideretur, peccaret mortaliter, et circumcisus, ipsa conscientia durante, peccaret mortaliter, si non observaret legalia: cuius ratio est, quia habere conscientiam de re aliqua facienda, nihil aliud est quam aestimare quod faciat contra Deum, nisi illud faciat. Facere autem contra Deum est peccatum. Sic ergo dico, quod nisi faceret hoc ad quod inducit conscientia, peccaret mortaliter, non quidem ex genere operis, sed ex intentione operantis. Et similiter si facit, peccat; quia huiusmodi ignorantia non excusat, cum sit ignorantia iuris. Nec tamen est perplexus simpliciter, sed secundum quid, quia potest deponere erroneam conscientiam. Et hoc modo hic Apostolus testificatur omni circumcidenti se, quod tenetur ad servandum legem.

283. Consequenter cum dicit *evacuati estis*, etc., probat quae dicit, scilicet quod non debent accipere legis observantiam ratione damni iam praesentis, quod est duplex. Unum est amissio Christi; secundum est amissio gratiae Christi. Primum est causa secundi, ibi *qui in lege*, et cetera.

Dicit ergo *evacuati*, etc.; quasi dicat: vere Christus vobis nihil proderit, quia evacuati estis a Christo, id est, habitatione Christi.

Secundum damnum est amissio gratiae. Ideo dicit *a gratia excidistis*, qui scilicet prius eratis pleni gratia Christi, quia de plenitudine eius accepimus omnes. Io. I, 16: *de plenitudine* Christi *nos omnes accepimus*, et cetera. Et Eccli. XXI, 17: *cor fatui quasi vas confractum, et omnem sapientiam non tenebit*. Vos, dico, *qui in lege iustificamini*, id est creditis iustificari, *a gratia*, scilicet habenda futurae beatitudinis, vel etiam a iam habita, *excidistis*. Apoc. II, 5: *memor esto unde excideris, et age poenitentiam*.

of the law. But this is to sin mortally. Therefore, he is obligated to sin mortally and thus he sins in either case.

I answer that on the assumption that the same conviction prevails, he is obliged to observe the matters of the law: for example, if one is convinced that he would sin mortally unless he were circumcised, then, having become circumcised, if the same conviction remains, he would sin mortally were he not to observe the matters of the law. The reason for this is that the conviction that something must be done is nothing else but a judgment that it would be against God's will not to do it. If this is the case, I say that unless he did what his convictions dictate, he would sin mortally, not by reason of the work done but by reason of his conscience. Likewise, if he does it, he sins, because ignorance of this kind does not excuse him, since he is ignorant of a precept. Nevertheless, he is not absolutely perplexed, but only in a qualified sense, because it is within his power to correct his erroneous conscience. And this is the way the Apostle is here testifying to everyone who circumcises himself that he is obliged to observe the ceremonies of the law.

283. Then when he says, *you are made void of Christ*, he proves what he said, namely, that they must not embrace the observances of the law, because it involves a double injury: first, the loss of Christ; second, the loss of grace. Moreover, the first is the cause of the second, because *you who are justified in the law are fallen from grace*.

He says therefore, *you are made void of Christ*. As if to say: verily Christ will profit you nothing, because *you are made void of Christ*, i.e., of living in Christ.

The second injury is the loss of grace. Hence he says: *you are fallen from grace*, i.e., you who were full of the grace of Christ, *because of his fullness we have all received* (John 1:16); *the heart of a fool is like a broken vessel and no wisdom at all shall it hold* (Sir 22:17). *You*, I say, *who are justified in the law*, i.e., who believe that you are justified, *are fallen*—*be mindful, therefore, from whence you are fallen and do penance* (Rev 2:5)—*from grace*, namely, from possessing future happiness or even from the grace you once had.

Lecture 2

⁵:⁵Nos enim spiritu ex fide, spem justitiae exspectamus. [n. 284]

⁵:⁶Nam in Christo Jesu neque circumcisio aliquid valet, neque praeputium: sed fides, quae per caritatem operatur. [n. 286]

⁵:⁷Currebatis bene: quis vos impedivit veritati non obedire? [n. 288]

⁵:⁸persuasio haec non est ex eo, qui vocat vos. [n. 290]

⁵:⁹Modicum fermentum totam massam corrumpit.

⁵:¹⁰Ego confido in vobis in Domino, quod nihil aliud sapietis: qui autem conturbat vos, portabit judicium, quicumque est ille. [n. 292]

⁵:¹¹Ego autem, fratres, si circumcisionem adhuc praedico: quid adhuc persecutionem patior? ergo evacuatum est scandalum crucis. [n. 294]

⁵:¹²Utinam et abscindantur qui vos conturbant. [n. 297]

⁵:⁵ἡμεῖς γὰρ πνεύματι ἐκ πίστεως ἐλπίδα δικαιοσύνης ἀπεκδεχόμεθα.

⁵:⁶ἐν γὰρ Χριστῷ Ἰησοῦ οὔτε περιτομή τι ἰσχύει οὔτε ἀκροβυστία, ἀλλὰ πίστις δι' ἀγάπης ἐνεργουμένη.

⁵:⁷Ἐτρέχετε καλῶς· τίς ὑμᾶς ἐνέκοψεν [τῇ] ἀληθείᾳ μὴ πείθεσθαι;

⁵:⁸ἡ πεισμονὴ οὐκ ἐκ τοῦ καλοῦντος ὑμᾶς.

⁵:⁹μικρὰ ζύμη ὅλον τὸ φύραμα ζυμοῖ.

⁵:¹⁰ἐγὼ πέποιθα εἰς ὑμᾶς ἐν κυρίῳ ὅτι οὐδὲν ἄλλο φρονήσετε· ὁ δὲ ταράσσων ὑμᾶς βαστάσει τὸ κρίμα, ὅστις ἐὰν ᾖ.

⁵:¹¹ἐγὼ δέ, ἀδελφοί, εἰ περιτομὴν ἔτι κηρύσσω, τί ἔτι διώκομαι; ἄρα κατήργηται τὸ σκάνδαλον τοῦ σταυροῦ.

⁵:¹²ὄφελον καὶ ἀποκόψονται οἱ ἀναστατοῦντες ὑμᾶς.

⁵:⁵For we in spirit, by faith, wait for the hope of justice. [n. 284]

⁵:⁶For in Christ Jesus neither circumcision nor uncircumcision avails anything: but faith that works by charity. [n. 286]

⁵:⁷You did run well. What has hindered you, that you should not obey the truth? [n. 288]

⁵:⁸This persuasion is not from him who calls you. [n. 290]

⁵:⁹A little leaven corrupts the whole lump.

⁵:¹⁰I have confidence in you in the Lord, that you will not be of another mind: but he who troubles you shall bear the judgment, whoever he is. [n. 292]

⁵:¹¹And I, brethren, if I yet preach circumcision, why do I yet suffer persecution? Then is the scandal of the cross made void. [n. 294]

⁵:¹²Would that even those who trouble you were cut off. [n. 297]

---

284. Explicavit Apostolus secundum documentum, scilicet quod non esset subeundum iugum servitutis legis, hic autem redit ad primum, ostendens quod stare debent. Et

primo proponit standi exemplum;

secundo removet stationis impedimentum, ibi *currebatis*, etc.;

tertio assignat standi causam, ibi *vos autem in libertatem*, et cetera.

Circa primum duo facit.

Primo proponit standi exemplum;

secundo causam eius assignat, ibi *nam in Christo Iesu*, et cetera.

285. Dicit ergo: qui in lege volunt iustificari, Christus eis nihil prodest, quia excidunt a gratia. Sed *nos*, scilicet apostoli, stamus per spem, quia scilicet *expectamus spem iustitiae*, id est iustitiam et spem, scilicet aeternam beatitudinem. I Petr. I, 3: *regeneravit nos in spem vivam*, et cetera. Vel, *spem iustitiae*, id est Christum, per quem est nobis spes iustitiae, quia per eum iustificamur. Phil. III, 20: *Salvatorem expectamus*, et cetera. I Cor. I, 30: *qui factus est nobis sapientia, et iustitia, et sanctificatio, et redemptio*, et cetera. Vel *spem iustitiae*, id est spem quae est de iustitia, ut iustificentur non per legem, sed per fidem. Rom. III, 28: *arbitramur hominem*

284. Having explained the second point, namely, that they must not submit to the yoke of serving the law, the Apostle here returns to the first and shows that they must stand fast.

First, he gives an example of standing fast;

second, he removes an obstacle to standing fast, at *you did run well*;

third, he tells them the cause for standing fast, at *for you, brethren, have been called unto liberty* (Gal 5:3).

As to the first, he does two things:

first, he proposes an example of standing fast;

second, he assigns its cause, at *for in Christ Jesus*.

285. He says therefore: those who want to be justified in the law, Christ profits them nothing, because they are fallen from grace. But *we*, namely, the apostles, stand through hope, because we *wait for the hope of justice*, i.e., for justice and hope, namely, eternal happiness: *he has regenerated us unto a lively hope by the resurrection of Jesus Christ from the dead* (1 Pet 1:3). Or, *the hope of justice*, i.e., Christ, by whom we have a hope for justice, because we are justified by him: *we look for the Savior, our Lord Jesus Christ* (Phil 3:20); *who of God is made unto us wisdom and justice and sanctification and redemption* (1 Cor 1:30). Or, *the hope of justice*, i.e., the hope which is concerned with justice; that we be

iustificari per fidem sine operibus legis. Vel **spem iustitiae**, id est rem speratam, in quam tendit iustitia, scilicet vitam aeternam. II Tim. ult.: *in reliquo reposita est mihi corona iustitiae*, et cetera.

Et hoc **ex fide**, quia *iustitia Dei* est *per fidem Iesu Christi*, ut dicitur Rom. III, 22. Quae quidem fides non est ab homine, sed a Spiritu Sancto qui eam inspirat. Rom. VIII, v. 15: *accepistis Spiritum filiorum, in quo clamamus: Abba, Pater*, et cetera.

Sicut ergo fides est ex Spiritu, ita ex fide est spes, ex spe iustitia, per quam pervenimus ad vitam aeternam.

286. Haec autem spes non venit ex circumcisione, neque ex gentilitate, quia nihil faciunt ad hoc. Et ideo dicit **nam in Christo Iesu**, id est in his qui sunt in fide Christi, **neque circumcisio, neque praeputium**, etc., id est indifferentia sunt. **Sed fides**, non informis, sed ea **quae per dilectionem operatur**, Iac. II, 26: *fides sine operibus mortua est*, et cetera. Nam fides est cognitio Verbi Dei, Eph. III, 17: *habitare Christum per fidem*, et cetera. Et hoc Verbum nec perfecte habetur, nec perfecte cognoscitur, nisi etiam habeatur amor quem sperat.

287. Hic sunt duo dubia circa Glossam. Primum est, quod dicit praeputium et circumcisionem esse indifferentia, cum supra dixerit *si circumcidimini, Christus vobis nihil proderit*.

Sed dicendum est, quod ex genere operis sunt indifferentia, scilicet illis, qui non ponunt spem in eis; sed ex intentione operantis non sunt indifferentia. Nam ponentibus in eis spem, mortifera sunt.

Secundum dubium est de hoc, quod dicit quod illi qui non credunt, peiores sunt quam daemones, cum daemones credant et contremiscant.

Respondeo. Dicendum est, quod peiores quidem sunt ex specie operis, sed non quantum ad affectum. Nam daemonibus displicet hoc, quod credunt; nec etiam est tanta nequitia voluntatis in homine qui non credit, quanta in daemone qui odit quod credit.

288. Consequenter cum dicit **currebatis bene**, etc., agitur de impedimento stationis. Et
primo ponit impedimentum;
secundo docet eius remotionem, ibi **nemini consenseritis**, et cetera.

289. Impedimentum stationis eorum magnum erat et nocivum; nam tanto aliquid est magis nocivum, quanto maius bonum privat. Quando ergo aliquis multis bonis spiritualibus privatur, signum est habuisse magnum impedimentum. Et ideo, ut ostendat eos apostolus

justified not by the law but by faith: *we account a man to be justified by faith without the works of the law* (Rom 3:28). Or, **the hope of justice**, i.e., the things we hope for, and unto which justice tends, namely, eternal life: *as to the rest, there is laid up for me a crown of justice which the Lord, the just judge, will render to me in that day* (2 Tim 4:8).

And this **by faith**, because *the justice of God is by the faith of Jesus Christ* (Rom 3:22). Which faith is not of man but of the Holy Spirit who inspires it. *You have received the Spirit of adoption of sons, whereby we cry: Abba, Father* (Rom 8:15).

Therefore, as faith is from the Spirit, so from faith is hope, and from hope the justice through which we reach eternal life.

286. However, this hope does not come from circumcision or from paganism, because these contribute nothing to it. Hence he says, **for in Christ Jesus**, i.e., in those who live in the faith of Christ, **neither circumcision nor uncircumcision avails anything**, i.e., they make no difference; **but faith**, not unformed, but the kind **that works by charity**: *faith without works is dead* (Jas 2:26). For faith is a knowledge of the Word of God—*that Christ may dwell by faith in your hearts* (Eph 3:17)—which Word is not perfectly possessed or perfectly known unless the love which it hopes for is possessed.

287. Here a Gloss raises two problems. The first is that he says circumcision and uncircumcision to be indifferent, whereas above he had said, **if you be circumcised, Christ will profit you nothing**.

I answer that it is from the general nature of the work that they are indifferent, namely, to those who do not put any trust in them; however, they are not indifferent if you consider the intention of the one acting. For they are deadly to those who put their trust in them.

The second problem concerns his saying that those who do not believe are worse than demons, for the demons believe and tremble.

I answer that if you consider the nature of the work, they are worse; but not if you consider the will. For the demons are displeased by the fact of their believing; furthermore, there is not as much malice in the will of a man who does not believe as there is in the demon who hates what he believes.

288. Then when he says, **you did run well**, he deals with the obstacle to standing fast.
First, he mentions the obstacle;
second, he teaches its removal.

289. The obstacle to their standing fast was great and harmful, for the harmfulness of anything is reckoned according to the greater good it hinders. Therefore, when someone is kept from many spiritual goods, it is an indication that he is faced with a great obstacle. Accordingly,

magnum impedimentum habuisse, commemorat eis bona spiritualia, quae amiserunt, cum dicit ***currebatis bene***, etc., scilicet per opera fidei formatae per caritatem, quae instigat ad currendum. Ps. CXVIII, v. 32: *viam mandatorum tuorum cucurri, cum dilatasti cor meum.*

Et hoc quidem fuit olim in vobis, sed dum sic currebatis, estis impediti, et ideo subdit: ***quis vos fascinavit?*** De quo dictum est supra cap. III, 1; et ideo supersedeo ad praesens.

Quis ergo ***vos fascinavit***, id est ***impedivit veritati***, scilicet Evangelicae, ***non obedire?*** Et hoc congrue dicit; nam obedire est voluntatis applicandae ad consensum praecipientis. Et ideo fides est voluntatis et intellectus scientia. Oportet ergo voluntati fidei obedire; hoc autem est volendo credere, quod gratia fidei Christi sufficiat ad salutem sine legalibus observantiis.

290. Excludit autem impedimentum, cum dicit ***nemini***, etc., et hoc ex triplici parte.

Primo ex parte eorum;

secundo ex parte Dei, ibi ***ego confido***, etc.;

tertio ex parte Apostoli, ibi ***ego autem, fratres***, et cetera.

291. Ex parte eorum, cum dicit ***nemini***, et cetera. Ubi primo ostendit quid requiratur ex parte eorum, ut vitent hoc nocumentum, scilicet quod nemini pseudo deinceps consentiant. I Thess. V, 5: *non simus noctis neque tenebrarum*, et cetera. Eph. V, 11: *nolite communicare operibus infructuosis tenebrarum*, etc., et II Tim. II, 17: *et sermo eorum ut cancer serpit*, et cetera. Ex quo datur intelligi, quod nondum erant corrupti, sed sollicitabantur de hoc.

Secundo assignat rationem huius cum dicit ***persuasio enim***, et cetera. Et haec est duplex. Prima, quia homo cum dat se alicui, nihil debet facere nisi quod utile duxerit sibi. Sed vos traditi estis Christo, ergo non debetis audire, vel consentire, nisi his quae sunt ab ipso; ergo ***haec persuasio***, qua vos volunt mittere sub iugo legis, quia ***non est ex eo***, scilicet ex Deo, qui vos vocavit ad vitam, sed ex diabolo, inquantum scilicet deficiens est, et ideo non consenseritis eis. Vel ***non ex eo***, id est contra ipsum. Secunda ratio est, quia posset dici quod non est magnum si paucis consentiatur, cum ex hoc non sit periculum, et ideo dicit quod non est eis consentiendum, nec eorum insidiae sunt contemnendae, sed debent principiis obstare, quia ***modicum fermentum***, etc., id est illi pauci qui vobis persuadent. Vel ***haec persuasio***, parva in principio, ***totam massam corrumpit***, id est congregationem fidelium. Lev. II, 11: *nec quidquam fermenti ac mellis adolebitur in sacrificio Domini.*

in order to show them that they have a great obstacle, he reminds them of the spiritual goods they have lost, when he says: ***you did run well***, namely, by means of the works of faith formed by charity, which incites one to run: *I have run the way of your commandments, when you enlarged my heart* (Ps 119:32).

And this did indeed apply to you formerly; but while you were thus running, you came upon an obstacle. Therefore he says: ***who has bewitched you?*** (Gal 3:1) This has been discussed already in chapter three; hence we pass over it now.

Therefore, ***who has bewitched you***, i.e., ***hindered you, that you should not obey the truth***, namely, of the Gospel? This is appropriately said: for obedience is the application of the will to the edict of the one who commands. That is why faith is a science of the will and of the understanding. It is suitable, therefore, for the will to obey the faith. But this is done by willing to believe that the grace of Christ is sufficient for salvation without the legal observances.

290. Then when he says, ***consent to no one***, he removes the obstacle.

First, on their part;

second, on God's part, at ***I have confidence***;

third, on the Apostle's part, at ***and I, brethren***.

291. On their part when he says, ***consent to no one***. Herein he shows what is required on their part to overcome this obstacle, namely, that henceforth they not give their consent to any deceiver: *we are not of the night nor of the darkness; therefore, let us not sleep* (1 Thess 5:5); *have no fellowship with the unfruitful works of darkness but rather reprove them* (Eph 5:11); *and their speech spreads like a canker* (2 Tim 2:17). From this it can be gathered that they were not yet corrupted, but he was concerned.

Second, he gives an explanation of this, when he says, ***this persuasion is not from him who calls you***, and it is twofold. First, because a man, when he gives himself to someone, ought to do nothing save what is of advantage to the latter. But you have been given to Christ. Therefore, you should not heed or consent to anyone but those who come from him. Hence because ***this persuasion***, by which they wish to set you under the yoke of the law, ***is not from him***, i.e., from God, ***who calls you*** to life, but from the devil, for it is degrading, you should not consent to them. Or, ***not from him***, i.e., against him. The second explanation is that they might suppose that consenting to a few is not a great matter, since it constitutes no danger. But he says that they must not consent to them at all, nor underestimate their artifices; rather they must oppose them at the start, because ***a little leaven corrupts the whole lump***, i.e., those few who are persuading you. Or, ***this persuasion*** small in the beginning ***corrupts the whole lump***, i.e., the congregation of the faithful: *neither shall any leaven or honey be burnt in the sacrifice to the Lord* (Lev 2:11).

292. Then when he says, *I have confidence in you in the Lord, that you will not be of another mind*, he removes the obstacle on the part of God who offers his help to this end. And he mentions a twofold help: one as to the deceivers; the other as to the trouble makers.

He says therefore, *I have confidence in you in the Lord, that you will not be of another mind*. As if to say: I have told you not to obey the deceivers and *I have confidence in you*: I rejoice that in all things I have confidence in you (2 Cor 7:16); *but, dearly beloved, we trust better things of you, and nearer to salvation* (Heb 6:9). *I have confidence*, I say, in this, namely, *that you will not be of another mind* than what I have taught you—*but though we, or an angel from heaven, preach a gospel to you besides that which we have preached to you, let him be anathema* (Gal 1:8); *fulfill my joy, that you be of one mind* (Phil 2:2)—and this with God's help. Hence he says, *in the Lord* God working: *and such confidence we have through Christ towards God* (2 Cor 3:4), because the Lord will give you a mind according with the standard of the Catholic Faith: *it is good to have confidence in the Lord rather than to have confidence in a man* (Ps 117:8).

As to the trouble makers, he says, *he who troubles you shall bear the judgment, whoever he is*, i.e., he that perverts you from right order so as to be turned from spiritual to corporeal things, whereas it should be the contrary: *yet that was not first which was spiritual, but that which is natural; afterwards that which is spiritual* (1 Cor 15:46). And since order is thus perverted, as it was said above: *are you so foolish that, whereas you began by the Spirit, now you would be made perfect by the flesh?* (Gal 3:3), therefore, *he shall bear the judgment*, i.e., he will undergo damnation. For as one who urges another to good is rewarded—*they that instruct many to justice shall shine as stars for all eternity* (Dan 12:3)—so one who urges another to evil is condemned: *because you have troubled us, may the Lord trouble you this day* (Jos 7:25); *cursed be he that makes the blind to wander out of his way* (Deut 27:18). And this, *whoever he is*, i.e., whatever his dignity, he will not be spared.

293. But Porphyry and Julian censure Paul for presumption, and assert that in saying this he defames Peter (since he wrote above that he withstood him to his face) so that the meaning would be: *whoever he is*, i.e., even if it is Peter, he would be punished.

But as Augustine says, one should not believe that Paul was calling down a curse on the Prince of the Church—for it is written in Exodus: *you shall not curse the prince of your people* (Exod 22:28)—or that Peter committed an offense worthy of damnation. Therefore the Apostle is speaking of someone else who, coming from Judea, claimed to be a disciple of the important apostles and with that authority he and other false teachers were subverting the Galatians, *because of false brethren brought in unawares* (Gal 2:4).

294. Consequenter cum dicit *ego autem, fratres*, etc., removet impedimentum ex parte sua. Et

primo ponit sui excusationem;

secundo eorum, qui eum infamabant, obiurgationem, ibi *utinam abscindantur*, et cetera.

Excludit autem falsum quod ei imponebatur. Et

primo aliquid pertinens ad ipsum tantum;

secundo aliquid pertinens ad omnes, ibi *ergo evacuatum est*, et cetera.

295. Sciendum est circa primum, quod pseudo Galatis excusantibus se de eo quod non servabant legalia, quia ita edocti erant ab Apostolo, et dicebant quod Apostolus deceperat eos, et quod in servitutem eorum haec persuaserat eis: et confirmabant, dicentes Paulum praedicasse in Iudaea, et docuisse legalia debere servari.

Et ideo excusat se de hoc Apostolus, dicens *ego autem, fratres, si circumcisionem adhuc praedico*, sicut imponunt mihi pseudo, *quid adhuc persecutionem patior?* Scilicet a Iudaeis. I Cor. IV, 12: *persecutionem patimur*, et cetera. Nam Iudaei specialiter propter hoc persequebantur Paulum, quod praedicabat legalia non debere servari. Act. XXI, 21, dicit Iacobus Paulo: *audierunt de te quia discessionem doceas a Moyse eorum, qui per gentes sunt Iudaeorum, dicens eos non debere circumcidere filios*, et cetera. Patet ergo quod non est verum quod mihi imponunt, alioquin persecutiones adhuc non paterer.

296. Falsum est etiam id quod mihi imponunt per id quod communiter est apud alios, quia si circumcisionem praedico, *evacuatum est scandalum crucis*. Nam non solum ego, sed etiam omnes apostoli *praedicamus Christum crucifixum, Iudaeis quidem scandalum*, etc., ut dicitur I Cor. I, 23. Et de hoc maxime scandalizantur, quia praedicamus, quod per crucem Christi legalia evacuantur. Si ergo praedico circumcisionem, *evacuatum est scandalum*, id est non erit scandalum apud Iudaeos ultra de cruce. Nam patienter sustinerent, immo libenter vellent, quod praedicaremus crucem et legalia simul debere servari.

Vel, secundum Augustinum, *evacuatum est scandalum crucis*, id est evacuata est crux quae est scandalum, quasi dicat: crux perdidit effectum suum et virtutem. Supra II, v. 21: *si enim ex lege esset iustitia, ergo Christus gratis mortuus est*.

Dicit autem Apostolus specialiter *evacuatum est*, etc., ut det intelligere, quod propter hoc Iudaei occiderunt Christum, quia legalia non servabat et ea non esse servanda docebat. Io. IX, 16: *non est hic homo a Deo, quia sabbatum non custodit*.

297. Consequenter obiurgat pseudo, qui eum infamaverant, dicens *utinam abscindantur*, etc., quasi dicat:

294. Then when he says, *and I, brethren*, he removes the obstacle on his part.

First, he presents his defense;

second, he rebukes his slanderers, at *would that even those who trouble you*.

He refutes the false charge against him:

first, a charge that pertains to himself alone;

second, one that pertains to all, at *then is the scandal of the cross*.

295. With respect to the first, it should be noted that the false brethren, when the Galatians excused themselves from observing the legal ceremonies because they had been so taught by the Apostle, declared that the Apostle misled them and that he persuaded them to this in order to lord it over them. As confirmation of this they alleged that when he preached in Judea, Paul taught that the legal ceremonies should be observed.

But the Apostle clears himself of this, when he says, *and I, brethren, if I yet preach circumcision, why do I yet suffer persecution* from the Jews? *We are persecuted and we suffer it* (1 Cor 4:12). For the Jews persecuted Paul precisely because he taught that the legal ceremonies should not be observed. Indeed, in Acts, James says to Paul: *they have heard of you that you teach those Jews who are among the gentiles to depart from Moses; saying that they ought not to circumcise their children nor walk according to custom* (Acts 21:21). It is plain, therefore, that their charge is not true; otherwise, he would not have suffered their persecutions.

296. False, too, is that which they impute to me because of something generally held by others; because if I preach circumcision, *then is the scandal of the cross made void*. For not only I but all the apostles *preach Christ crucified, to the Jews indeed a stumbling-block and unto the gentiles, foolishness* (1 Cor 1:23). And the main reason why they are scandalized is because we preach that through the cross of Christ the legal ceremonies are made void. Therefore, if I preach circumcision, *the scandal of the cross is made void*, i.e., there will no longer be a stumbling-block for the Jews from the cross. For they would endure it patiently; indeed, they would welcome it, if along with the cross we preached the obligation to observe the legal ceremonies.

Or, according to Augustine on this passage: *the scandal of the cross is made void*, i.e., the cross is made void; which is a scandal. As if to say: the cross has lost its effect and its power: *if justice be by the law, then Christ died in vain* (Gal 2:21).

Now the Apostle specifically says, *the scandal of the cross is made void*, to denote that the reason the Jews killed Christ was because he did not observe the legal ceremonies and taught that they were not to be observed: *this man is not of God who does not keep the sabbath* (John 9:16).

297. Then he rebukes the false brethren who had slandered him, saying, *would that even those who trouble you*

ipsi conturbant vos in hoc quod volunt vos circumcidi: sed utinam non solum circumcidantur, sed totaliter castrentur.

Sed contra Rom. XII, 14: *benedicite, et nolite maledicere*, et cetera.

Ad hoc est duplex responsio. Prima est, quod non maledixit Apostolus eis, sed potius benedixit, quia optavit eis ut spiritualiter castrentur, ut servarent spiritualem castitatem, cassando caeremonialia, secundum illud Matth. XIX, 12: *sunt quidam eunuchi, qui se castraverunt propter regnum caelorum*.

Secundo quod optat eis sterilitatem prolis quam habent eunuchi, ut scilicet non generent. Unde ait **utinam et abscindantur**, etc., id est vim generandi perdant in vobis, et aliis. Et hoc merito, quia generant filios in errorem, et redigunt eos in servitutem legis. Os. c. IX, 14: *dabo eis vulvam sine liberis, ut ubera arentia*.

were cut off. As if to say: they trouble you on one matter, namely, they want you to be circumcised; but I wish that they be not only circumcised but wholly emasculated.

But this is contrary to Romans: *bless, and curse not* (Rom 12:14).

To this there are two responses: first, that the Apostle was not calling down an evil on them but rather a blessing; because he was wishing them to be emasculated spiritually, i.e., abolish the legal ceremonies, that they might preserve spiritual chastity: *there are eunuchs who have made themselves such for the kingdom of heaven* (Matt 19:12).

The second is that he is wishing them the impotence that eunuchs have, so that they might not procreate. Hence he says: **would that even those who trouble you were cut off**, i.e., that they lose the power of engendering among you and others. And this deservedly, because they engender sons unto error and subject them to the bondage of the law: *give them a womb without children, and dry breasts* (Hos 9:14).

Lecture 3

⁵:¹³Vos enim in libertatem vocati estis, fratres: tantum ne libertatem in occasionem detis carnis, sed per caritatem Spiritus servite invicem. [n. 298]

⁵:¹⁴Omnis enim lex in uno sermone impletur: diliges proximum tuum sicut teipsum. [n. 303]

⁵:¹⁵Quod si invicem mordetis, et comeditis: videte ne ab invicem consumamini. [n. 306]

⁵:¹³Ὑμεῖς γὰρ ἐπ' ἐλευθερίᾳ ἐκλήθητε, ἀδελφοί· μόνον μὴ τὴν ἐλευθερίαν εἰς ἀφορμὴν τῇ σαρκί, ἀλλὰ διὰ τῆς ἀγάπης δουλεύετε ἀλλήλοις.

⁵:¹⁴ὁ γὰρ πᾶς νόμος ἐν ἑνὶ λόγῳ πεπλήρωται, ἐν τῷ Ἀγαπήσεις τὸν πλησίον σου ὡς σεαυτόν.

⁵:¹⁵εἰ δὲ ἀλλήλους δάκνετε καὶ κατεσθίετε, βλέπετε μὴ ὑπ' ἀλλήλων ἀναλωθῆτε.

⁵:¹³For you, brethren, have been called unto liberty. Only do not make liberty an occasion to the flesh: but by charity of the Spirit serve one another. [n. 298]

⁵:¹⁴For all the law is fulfilled in one word: you shall love your neighbor as yourself. [n. 303]

⁵:¹⁵But if you bite and devour one another: take heed that you be not consumed one of another. [n. 306]

---

298. Proposito exemplo standi et remoto eius impedimento, hic innuit modum ipsius. Et

primo ponit modum standi;
secundo exponit, ibi *omnis enim lex*, et cetera.
Circa primum tria facit.
Primo ponit conditionem status;
secundo removet abusum standi;
tertio innuit standi modum.

299. Conditio quidem standi est libertas. Omnis enim status conditio pertinet ad servitutem vel ad libertatem; sed status fidei Christi, ad quem inducit Apostolus, ad libertatem pertinet et est ipsa libertas. Et ideo dicit *vos enim*, etc., quasi dicat: recte conturbant vos, quia abducunt a meliore in peius, quia *vos vocati estis*, scilicet a Deo, *in libertatem* gratiae. Rom. VIII, 15: *non accepistis spiritum servitutis iterum in timore, sed accepistis Spiritum adoptionis filiorum*, et cetera. Supra IV, 31: *non sumus ancillae filii, sed liberae*, et cetera. Vos, inquam, qui liberi estis per Christum, volunt ducere in servitutem.

300. Abusus autem status est si in deterius prolabatur, et libertas spiritus pervertatur in servitutem carnis. Galatae autem iam liberi erant a lege, sed ne credant eis licere peccata committere, quae lex prohibebat, ideo Apostolus subdit abusum libertatis, dicens *tantum ne*, etc., quasi dicat: liberi estis, ita tamen, quod non abutamini libertate vestra, impune vobis peccandum esse arbitrantes. I Cor. VIII, 9: *videte ne forte haec licentia vestra offendiculum fiat infirmis*.

301. Modus autem standi est per caritatem, unde dicit *sed per caritatem Spiritus*, et cetera.

Status autem totus est in caritate, sine qua homo nihil est, I Cor. XIII, 1 s. Et secundum diversos gradus caritatis distinguuntur diversi status. Sic ergo status gratiae est

298. Having proposed an example of standing fast, and having eliminated an obstacle thereto, he now establishes its mode.

First, he establishes the mode of standing;
second, he gives an explanation, at *for all the law*.
As to the first he does three things:
first, he sets down the condition of a state;
second, he describes its abuse;
third, he asserts its mode.

299. The condition of standing fast is liberty. For the condition of any given state pertains either to liberty or to bondage; but the state of faith in Christ, to which the Apostle urges them, pertains to liberty and is liberty itself. Hence he says: *for you, brethren, have been called unto liberty*. As if to say: they are indeed troubling you; for they are drawing you from what is better to what is worse, because *you have been called* by God *unto* the *liberty* of grace: *you have not received the spirit of bondage again in fear, but you have received the Spirit of adoption of sons* (Rom 8:15); *we are not the children of the bondwoman but of the free woman* (Gal 4:31). You, I say, who are free in Christ, they want to lead into bondage.

300. But a state is being misused if it declines, and if liberty of the spirit is perverted into slavery of the flesh. Now the Galatians were free of the law; but lest they suppose this to be a license to commit sins forbidden by the law, the Apostle touches on abuse of liberty, saying, *only do not make liberty an occasion to the flesh*. As if to say: you are free, but not so as to misuse your liberty by supposing that you may sin with impunity: *but take heed, lest perhaps this your liberty become a stumbling-block to the weak* (1 Cor 8:9).

301. Now the mode of standing fast is through charity; hence he says: *but by charity of the Spirit serve one another*.

In fact the whole state consists in charity, without which a man is nothing (1 Cor 13:1ff.). Moreover, it is according to the various degrees of charity that various states

non per affectum carnis, ***sed per caritatem Spiritus***, id est quae procedit a Spiritu Sancto, per quem debemus invicem esse subiecti et servire. Infra VI, 2: ***alter alterius onera portate***, et cetera. Rom. XII, 10: *honore invicem praevenientes*, et cetera.

302. Sed cum superius dicat quod sint vocati in libertatem, quid est quod modo dicit ***servite invicem***?

Ad quod dicendum est, quod hoc exigit caritas, ut invicem serviamus, et tamen libera est. Sciendum est tamen, quod, sicut Philosophus dicit, liber est qui est causa sui, servus autem est causa alterius, vel ut moventis, vel ut finis: quia servus nec a se movetur ad opus, sed a domino, et propter utilitatem domini sui. Caritas ergo quantum ad causam moventem libertatem habet, quia a se operatur. II Cor. V, 14: *caritas Christi urget nos*, spontanee, scilicet ad operandum. Servus autem est, cum postpositis propriis utilitatibus, accommodat se utilitatibus proximorum.

303. Consequenter cum dicit ***omnis lex***, etc., exponit quae dicit, et

primo de dilectione,

secundo de libertate non danda in occasionem carnis, ibi ***Spiritu ambulate***, et cetera.

Circa primum monet ad caritatem sectandam:

primo propter utilitatem quam consequimur in impletione;

secundo propter damnum caritatis neglectae quod incurrimus, ibi ***quod si invicem***, et cetera.

304. Utilitas autem, quam consequimur ex impletione caritatis, maxima est, quia in ea implemus totam legem. Et ideo dicit ***omnis enim***, etc., quasi dicat: ideo caritas est habenda, quia omnis lex in uno sermone impletur, scilicet in uno praecepto caritatis. Rom. XIII, 8: *qui diligit proximum, legem implevit*. Et in eodem capite dicitur: *plenitudo legis est dilectio*. Et ideo dicit I Tim. I, 5: *finis praecepti est caritas*.

Sed contra, quia dicitur Matth. XII: *in his duobus mandatis*, scilicet de dilectione Dei et proximi, *tota lex pendet et prophetae*; non ergo in uno praecepto tantum impletur.

Respondeo. Dicendum est quod in dilectione Dei includitur dilectio proximi. I Io. IV, v. 21: *hoc mandatum habemus a Deo, ut qui diligit Deum, diligat et fratrem suum*. Et e converso proximum diligimus propter Deum: impletur ergo tota lex in uno praecepto caritatis.

Praecepta enim legis reducuntur ad illud praeceptum. Nam omnia praecepta vel sunt moralia, vel sunt caeremonialia, vel iudicialia. Moralia quidem sunt praecepta Decalogi, quorum tria pertinent ad dilectionem Dei, alia septem ad dilectionem proximi. Iudicialia autem sunt ut quicumque furatur aliquid reddat quadruplum, et his

are distinguished. Consequently, the state of grace does not exist in virtue of a desire of the flesh but ***by charity of the Spirit***, i.e., a charity which proceeds from the Holy Spirit, through whom we should be subject to and serve one another: ***bear one another's burdens*** (Gal 6:2); *with honor preventing one another* (Rom 12:10).

302. But since he said earlier that they have been called unto liberty, why does he now say, ***serve one another***?

I answer that charity requires that we serve one another; nevertheless, it is free. Here one might interject that, as the Philosopher says, he is free who is for his own sake; whereas he is a slave who is for the sake of another as of a mover or an end. For a slave is moved to his work not by himself but by a master and for the benefit of his master. Charity, therefore, has liberty as to its moving cause, because it works of itself: *the charity of Christ presses us* spontaneously, to work (2 Cor 5:14). But it is a servant when, putting one's own interests aside, it devotes itself to things beneficial to the neighbor.

303. Then when he says, ***for all the law is fulfilled in one word***, he explains what he says:

first, about charity;

second, about not making liberty an occasion to the flesh, at ***walk in the Spirit*** (Gal 5:16).

As to the first, he admonishes them to follow charity:

first, because of the benefit we obtain in fulfilling charity;

second, because of the injury incurred by neglecting charity, at ***but if you bite***.

304. Now the benefit we obtain in fulfilling charity is of the highest order, because in it we fulfill the whole law; hence he says, ***for all the law in fulfilled in one word***. As if to say: charity must be maintained, because the whole law is fulfilled in one word, namely, in the one precept of charity: *he that loves his neighbor has fulfilled the law* (Rom 13:8) and *love is the fulfillment of the law* (Rom 13:10). Wherefore he says in 1 Timothy: *the end of the commandment is charity* (1 Tim 1:5).

However, it is said in Matthew: *on these two commandments*, namely, of the love of God and of neighbor, *depends the whole law and the prophets* (Matt 22:40). Therefore, it is not fulfilled in the one precept alone.

I answer that in the love of God is included love of neighbor: *this commandment we have from God, that he, who loves God, love also his brother* (1 John 4:21). Conversely, we love our neighbor for the love of God. Consequently, the whole law is fulfilled in the one precept of charity.

For the precepts of the law are reduced to that one precept. Indeed, precepts are either moral or ceremonial or judicial. The moral are the precepts of the Decalogue: three concern the love of God, and the other seven the love of neighbor. The judicial are, for example, that whosoever steals anything shall restore fourfold, and others like this;

similia, quae similiter ad dilectionem proximi pertinent. Caeremonialia vero sunt sacrificia et huiusmodi quae reducuntur ad dilectionem Dei.

Et sic patet, quod omnia in uno praecepto caritatis implentur *diliges proximum tuum sicut teipsum*: et est scriptum Lev. XIX, 18.

305. Dicit autem *sicut teipsum*, non *quantum teipsum*, quia homo secundum ordinem caritatis magis debet se diligere, quam alium.

Exponitur autem tripliciter: uno modo ut referatur ad veritatem dilectionis. Amare enim est velle bonum alicui. Et ideo dicimur amare aliquem cui volumus bonum, et etiam bonum illud amamus, quod ei volumus; sed diversimode, quia cum volo bonum mihi, me diligo simpliciter propter me, bonum autem illud quod mihi volo, diligo non propter se, sed propter me. Tunc ergo diligo proximum sicut meipsum, id est eodem modo quo meipsum, quando volo ei bonum propter se, non quia est mihi utilis, vel delectabilis.

Secundo modo, ut referatur ad iustitiam dilectionis. Unaquaeque enim res est inclinata velle sibi illud, quod potissimum est in ea; potissimum autem in homine est intellectus, et ratio; ille ergo diligit se, qui vult sibi bonum intellectus et rationis. Tunc ergo diligis proximum sicut teipsum, quando vis ei bonum intellectus et rationis.

Tertio modo, ut referatur ad ordinem, scilicet ut sicut te diligis propter Deum, ita et proximum propter ipsum diligas, scilicet ut ad Deum perveniat.

306. Consequenter cum dicit *quod si invicem*, etc., inducit ad caritatem sectandam ex damno quod incurrimus si eam negligamus. Ubi loquitur Galatis adhuc quasi spiritualibus, abstinens a commemoratione maiorum vitiorum et, eorum quae minora videntur mentionem facit, scilicet de vitiis linguae.

Et ideo dicit *quod si invicem*, etc., quasi dicat: in dilectione omnis lex impletur, *quod si vos invicem mordetis*, id est in parte famam, proximo detrahendo, aufertis: qui enim mordet, non totum accipit, sed partem. *Et comeditis*, id est totam famam aufertis et totaliter detrahendo confunditis. Nam qui comedit, totum absorbet. Iac. IV, 11: *nolite detrahere alterutrum, fratres mei*, et cetera.

Si ita, inquam, caritatem negligitis, *videte* damnum quod imminet vobis, scilicet quod *ab invicem consumamini*. Phil. III, 2: *videte canes, videte malos operarios*, et cetera. Is. c. XLIX, 4: *et vane fortitudinem meam consumpsi*, et cetera. Nam sicut Augustinus dicit: *vitio contentionis et invidiae, perniciosa iurgia inter homines nutriuntur, quibus consumitur societas et vita.*

and they pertain absolutely to the love of neighbor. The ceremonial concern sacrifices and related matters which are reduced to love of God.

And so it is plain that all are fulfilled in the one precept of charity, *you shall love your neighbor as yourself*, which is also written in Leviticus (Lev 19:18).

305. He says, *as yourself*, not *as much as yourself*, because according to the order of charity a man should love himself more than his neighbor.

Now this is explained in three ways: first, as referring to the genuineness of the love. For to love is to will good to someone: hence we are said to love both the one to whom we will a good and the very good which we will to someone; but not in the same way. For when I will a good to myself, I love myself absolutely for myself, but the good which I will to myself, I do not love for itself but for myself. Accordingly, I love my neighbor as myself in the same way that I love myself, when I will him a good for his sake, and not because it is useful or pleasant for me.

In a second way, as referring to the justice of love. For each thing is inclined to want for itself that which is most eminent in it; but in man, understanding and reason are the most eminent. He, therefore, loves himself who wants for himself the good of understanding and reason. Accordingly, you then love your neighbor as yourself, when you will him the good of understanding and reason.

In a third way, as referring to order, i.e., that just as you love yourself for the sake of God, so you love your neighbor for the sake of God, namely, that he may attain to God.

306. Then when he says, *but if you bite and devour one another*, he urges them to follow charity, because of the harm we incur if we neglect it. Here he continues to speak to the Galatians as to spiritual men, not bringing up their greater vices but mentioning ones that seem to be minor, such as sins of the tongue.

Hence he says: *if you bite and devour one another, take heed that you be not consumed one of another*. As if to say: all the law is fulfilled in love; *but if you bite one another*, i.e., partially destroy the good name of your neighbor by slander (for one who bites takes not the whole but a part) *and devour*, i.e., destroy his good name entirely, and completely shame him by slander (for he that devours, consumes all): *detract not one another, my brethren; he that detracts his brother detracts the law* (Jas 4:11).

If you neglect charity in that way, I say, *take heed* for the calamity that threatens you, namely, *that you be not consumed one of another*: *beware of dogs, beware of evil workers, beware of the concision* (Phil 3:2); *I have spent my strength without cause and in vain* (Isa 49:4). For as Augustine says, *by the vice of contention and envy, pernicious rivalries are bred among men, and both life and society are thereby brought to ruin.*

Lecture 4

5:16 Dico autem: Spiritu ambulate, et desideria carnis non perficietis. [n. 307]

5:17 Caro enim concupiscit adversus spiritum, spiritus autem adversus carnem: haec enim sibi invicem adversantur, ut non quaecumque vultis, illa faciatis. [n. 310]

5:16Λέγω δέ, πνεύματι περιπατεῖτε καὶ ἐπιθυμίαν σαρκὸς οὐ μὴ τελέσητε.

5:17ἡ γὰρ σὰρξ ἐπιθυμεῖ κατὰ τοῦ πνεύματος, τὸ δὲ πνεῦμα κατὰ τῆς σαρκός: ταῦτα γὰρ ἀλλήλοις ἀντίκειται, ἵνα μὴ ἃ ἐὰν θέλητε ταῦτα ποιῆτε.

5:16I say then: walk in the Spirit: and you shall not fulfill the lusts of the flesh. [n. 307]

5:17 For the flesh lusts against the spirit, and the spirit against the flesh: for these are contrary to one another, so that you do not do the things that you would. [n. 310]

---

307. Postquam Apostolus manifestavit in quo consistit status spiritualis, quia scilicet in caritate, consequenter hic agit de causa status, scilicet de Spiritu Sancto, quem dicit esse sequendum. Ubi ponit triplex beneficium Spiritus Sancti. Quorum primum est liberatio a servitute carnis; secundum est liberatio a servitute legis; et tertium est collatio vitae seu securitas a damnatione mortis.

Secundum, ibi *quod si ducimini*, et cetera. Tertium, ibi *si Spiritu vivimus*, et cetera.

Circa primum duo facit.

Primo ponit primum beneficium Spiritus;

secundo beneficii necessitatem ostendit, ibi *caro enim*, et cetera.

308. Dicit ergo: dico quod debetis *per caritatem Spiritus* invicem servire, quia nihil prodest sine caritate. Sed hoc *dico in Christo*, id est per fidem Christi, *spiritu ambulate*, id est mente et ratione. Quandoque enim mens nostra spiritus dicitur, secundum illud Ephes. IV, 23: *renovamini spiritu mentis vestrae*; et I Cor. IV: *psallam spiritu, psallam et mente*. Vel *Spiritu ambulate*, id est Spiritu Sancto proficite bene operando. Nam Spiritus Sanctus movet et instigat corda ad bene operandum. Rom. c. VIII, 14: *qui Spiritu Dei aguntur*, et cetera.

Ambulandum est ergo *spiritu*, id est mente, ut ipsa ratio sive mens legi Dei concordet, ut dicitur Rom. VII, 16. Nam spiritus humanus per se vanus est, et nisi regatur aliunde, fluctuat hac atque illac, ut dicitur Eccli. c. XXXIV, 6, *et sicut parturientis cor tuum phantasias patitur nisi ab Altissimo fuerit emissa visitatio*, et cetera. Unde de quibusdam dicitur Ephes. IV, 17: *ambulant in vanitate sensus sui*, et cetera. Non ergo perfecte stare potest ratio humana, nisi secundum quod est recta a Spiritu divino.

Et ideo dicit Apostolus *Spiritu ambulate*, id est per Spiritum Sanctum regentem et ducentem, quem sequi debemus sicut demonstrantem viam. Nam cognitio supernaturalis finis non est nobis nisi a Spiritu Sancto. I Cor. II, 9: *oculus non vidit, nec auris audivit, nec*

307. After indicating what the spiritual state consists in, namely, in charity, the Apostle then deals with the cause of the state, namely, of the Holy Spirit whom he says they must follow. And he mentions three benefits obtained from the Holy Spirit. First, freedom from the bondage of the flesh; second, freedom from the bondage of the law; third, the conferring of life, or security from the damnation of death;

second, at **but if you are led by the Spirit** (Gal 5:18); third, at **if we live in the Spirit** (Gal 5:25).

As to the first, he does two things:

first, he sets down the first benefit of the Spirit;

second, he shows the need for this benefit, at **for the flesh**.

308. He says therefore: I say that you are obliged **by charity of Spirit** (Gal 5:13) to serve one another, because nothing profits without charity. But this **I say in Christ**, i.e., by the faith of Christ, **walk in the spirit**, i.e., in the mind and reason. For sometimes our mind is called a spirit, according to Ephesians: *be renewed in the spirit of your mind* (Eph 4:23), and *I will sing with the spirit, I will sing also with the understanding* (1 Cor 14:15). Or, **walk in the Spirit**, i.e., make progress in the Holy Spirit, by acting well. For the Holy Spirit moves and incites hearts to do well: *whosoever are led by the Spirit of God, they are the sons of God* (Rom 8:14).

One should walk, therefore, **by the spirit**, i.e., the mind, so that one's reason or mind is in accord with the law of God, as it is said in Romans (Rom 7:16). For the human spirit is fickle, and unless it is governed from elsewhere, it turns now in one direction and now in another, as is said in Sirach: *the heart fancies as that of a woman in travail. Unless it be a vision sent forth from the Most High, do not set your heart upon them* (Sir 34:6). Hence Ephesians says of certain ones: *they walk in the vanity of their mind* (Eph 4:17). Therefore the human reason cannot stand perfectly except to the extent that it is governed by the divine Spirit.

Accordingly the Apostle says, **walk in the Spirit**, i.e., under the rule and guidance of the Holy Spirit, whom we should follow as one pointing out the way. For knowledge of the supernatural end is in us only from the Holy Spirit: *eye has not seen nor ear heard, neither has it entered into the*

in cor hominis ascendit, etc., et sequitur: *nobis autem revelavit Deus per Spiritum suum*. Item sicut inclinantem. Nam Spiritus Sanctus instigat, et inclinat affectum ad bene volendum. Rom. VIII, 14: *qui Spiritu Dei aguntur*, et cetera. Ps. CXLII, 10: *Spiritus tuus bonus deducet me in terram rectam.*

309. Ideo autem Spiritu ambulandum est quia liberat a corruptione carnis. Unde sequitur *et desideria carnis non perficietis*, id est delectationes carnis, quas caro suggerit. Hoc desiderabat Apostolus, dicens Rom. c. VII, 24: *infelix ego homo, quis me liberabit de corpore mortis huius? Gratia Dei*, et cetera. Et postea concludit in octavo capite: *nihil ergo damnationis est his, qui sunt in Christo Iesu, qui non secundum carnem ambulant.* Huius rationem, ibidem, subiungit dicens: *quia lex Spiritus vitae in Christo Iesu liberavit me a lege*, et cetera.

Et hoc est speciale desiderium sanctorum, ut non perficiant desideria ad quae caro instigat, ita tamen, quod in hoc non includantur desideria quae sunt ad necessitatem carnis, sed quae sunt ad superfluitatem.

310. Consequenter cum dicit *caro enim concupiscit*, etc., ponit necessitatem huius beneficii, quae est ex impugnatione carnis et spiritus. Et

primo ponit ipsam impugnationem;

secundo manifestat eam per evidens signum, ibi *haec enim invicem adversantur*, et cetera.

311. Dicit ergo: necessarium est quod per spiritum carnis desideria superetis. Nam *caro concupiscit adversus spiritum*.

Sed hic videtur esse dubium, quia cum concupiscere sit actus animae tantum, non videtur quod competat carni.

Ad hoc dicendum est, secundum Augustinum, quod caro dicitur concupiscere inquantum anima secundum ipsam carnem concupiscit, sicut oculus dicitur videre, cum potius anima per oculum videat. Sic ergo anima per carnem concupiscit, quando ea, quae delectabilia sunt secundum carnem, appetit. Per se vero anima concupiscit, quando delectatur in his quae sunt secundum spiritum, sicut sunt opera virtutum et contemplatio divinorum et meditatio sapientiae. Sap. VI, 21: *concupiscentia itaque sapientiae deducet ad regnum perpetuum*, et cetera.

312. Sed, si caro concupiscit per spiritum, quomodo concupiscit adversus eum? In hoc, scilicet quod concupiscentia carnis impedit concupiscentiam spiritus. Cum enim delectabilia carnis sint bona quae sunt infra nos, delectabilia vero spiritus bona quae sunt supra nos, contingit quod cum anima circa inferiora, quae sunt carnis, occupatur, retrahitur a superioribus, quae sunt spiritus.

heart of man what things God has prepared for them that love him, and immediately is added, *but to us God has revealed them by his Spirit* (1 Cor 2:9). Also as one who inclines us. For the Holy Spirit stirs up and turns the affections to right willing: *whosoever are led by the Spirit of God, they are the sons of God* (Rom 8:14); *your good Spirit shall lead me into the right land* (Ps 142:10).

309. Now one ought to walk in the Spirit, because it frees him from the defilement of the flesh. Hence he follows with: *and you shall not fulfill the lusts of the flesh*, i.e., the pleasures which the flesh suggests. This the Apostle yearned for, saying: *unhappy man that I am, who shall deliver me from the body of this death?* (Rom 7:24). Later he concludes: *there is now therefore no condemnation to them that are in Christ Jesus, who walk not according to the flesh* (Rom 8:1). And at once he gives the reason for this: *for the law of the Spirit of life in Christ Jesus has delivered me from the law of sin and of death* (Rom 8:2).

And this is the special desire of the saints, that they not fulfill the desires to which the flesh stirs them, but always understanding that in this are not included desires which pertain to the necessities of the flesh, but those that pertain to superfluities.

310. Then when he says, *for the flesh lusts against the spirit*, he tells why this benefit is needed, namely, because of the struggle between flesh and spirit.

First, he asserts that there is a struggle;

second, he elucidates this by an obvious sign, at *for these are contrary to one another*.

311. He says therefore: it is necessary that by the spirit you overcome the desires of the flesh, *for the flesh lusts against the spirit*.

But one might have a doubt here, because, since lusting is an act of the soul alone, it does not seem to come from the flesh.

I answer that, according to Augustine, the flesh is said to lust inasmuch as the soul lusts by means of the flesh, just as the eye is said to see, when as a matter of fact, it is the soul that sees by means of the eye. Consequently, the soul lusts by means of the flesh, when it seeks, according to the flesh, things which are pleasurable. But the soul lusts by means of itself, when it takes pleasure in things that are according to the spirit, as virtuous works, contemplation of divine things, and meditation of wisdom: *the desire of wisdom leads to the everlasting kingdom* (Wis 6:21).

312. But if the flesh lusts by means of the spirit, how does it lust against it? It does so in the sense that the lusting of the flesh hinders the desires of the spirit. For since the pleasures of the flesh concern goods which are beneath us, whereas the pleasures of the spirit concern goods which are above us, it comes to pass that when the soul is occupied with the lower things of the flesh, it is withdrawn from the higher things of the spirit.

313. Sed videtur etiam dubium de hoc quod dicit, scilicet quod **spiritus concupiscit adversus carnem**. Si enim accipiamus hic spiritum pro Spiritu Sancto, concupiscentia autem Spiritus Sancti sit contra mala, consequens videtur quod caro, adversus quam concupiscit Spiritus, sit mala, et sic sequitur error Manichaei.

Respondeo. Dicendum est quod spiritus non concupiscit adversus naturam carnis, sed adversus eius desideria, quae scilicet sunt ad superfluitatem. Unde et supra dictum est: **desideria carnis**, scilicet superflua, **non perficietis**. In necessariis enim spiritus non contradicit carni, quia, ut dicitur Ephes. c. V, 29, *nemo carnem suam odio habuit*.

314. Consequenter cum dicit **haec enim**, etc., ponit signum compugnationis, quasi dicat: experimento patet, quod contra se invicem pugnant et **adversantur**, intantum **ut non quaecumque vultis**, bona scilicet vel mala, **illa faciatis**, id est, facere permittamini. Rom. VII, 19: *non quod volo bonum, hoc ago, sed quod*, et cetera.

Non tamen tollitur libertas arbitrii. Cum enim liberum arbitrium sit ex hoc quod habet electionem, in illis est libertas arbitrii, quae electioni subsunt. Non autem omnia quae in nobis sunt simpliciter subsunt nostrae electioni, sed secundum quid. In speciali enim possum vitare hunc, vel illum motum concupiscentiae seu irae, sed in generali omnes motus irae vel concupiscentiae vitare non possumus, et hoc propter corruptionem fomitis ex primo peccato introductam.

315. Sed notandum est quod quatuor sunt genera hominum circa concupiscentias, quorum nullus facit quaecumque vult.

Nam intemperati, qui ex proposito sequuntur carnales passiones, secundum illud Prov. c. II, 14: *laetantur cum malefecerint*, faciunt quidem quod volunt, inquantum ipsas passiones sequuntur, sed inquantum ipsa eorum ratio remurmurat, et ei displicet, faciunt quae non volunt.

Incontinentes autem qui habent propositum abstinendi, et tamen a passionibus vincuntur, faciunt quidem quod non volunt, inquantum ipsas passiones contra eorum propositum sequuntur, et sic intemperati faciunt plus de eo quod volunt.

Continentes autem, qui vellent omnino non concupiscere, faciunt quod volunt dum non concupiscunt, sed quia omnino non concupiscere non possunt, faciunt quod nolunt.

Temperati vero, quod volunt quidem faciunt, inquantum in carne domata non concupiscunt, sed quia non ex toto domari potest, quin in aliquo repugnet spiritui, sicut nec malitia intantum crescere potest quin ratio

313. But his further statement that **the spirit lusts against the flesh** may cause a problem. For if we take *spirit* for the Holy Spirit, and the desire of the Holy Spirit is against evil things, it seems to follow that the flesh against which the Spirit lusts is evil—which is the Manichean error.

I answer that the spirit does not lust against the nature of the flesh, but against its desires, namely, those that concern superfluities; hence he said above, **you shall not fulfill the lusts of the flesh**, i.e., superfluous things. For in things necessary the spirit does not contradict the flesh, as we are told in Ephesians: *no man hates his own flesh* (Eph 5:29).

314. Then when he says, **for these are contrary to one another**, he gives evidence of the struggle. As if to say: it is obvious from experience that they fight and struggle against one another, insofar as **you do not do**, i.e., are not suffered to do, **the things**, good or evil, **that you would**: *the good which I will I do not: but the evil which I will not, that I do* (Rom 7:19).

However, free will is not taken away. For since free will consists in having choice, there is freedom of the will with respect to things subject to choice. But not all that lies in us is fully subject to our choice, but only in a qualified sense. In specific cases we are able to avoid this or that movement of lust or anger, but we cannot avoid all movements of anger or lust in general—and this by reason of the *fomes* introduced by the first sin.

315. Here it should be noted that with respect to lusts there are four categories of men who do not that which they would.

For intemperate men, who of set intention follow the passions of the flesh—according to Proverbs: *they are glad when they have done evil* (Prov 2:14)—do, indeed, what they will, inasmuch as they follow their passions; but inasmuch as their reason complains and is displeased, they are doing what they would not.

But incontinent persons, who resolve to abstain but are, nevertheless, conquered by their passions, do what they would not, inasmuch as they follow such passions contrary to what they resolved. As between these two types, the intemperate do more of the things that they would.

Those, however, who are continent, i.e., who would prefer not to lust at all, do what they intend, as long as they are not subject to lust; but because they cannot completely repress lust, they do what they would not.

Finally, those who are temperate do what they would, inasmuch as there is no lust in the tamed flesh; but because it cannot be totally tamed so as never to rise up against the spirit—just as neither can malice so abound that reason

remurmuret, ideo, cum aliquando concupiscunt, faciunt quod nolunt, plus tamen de eo, quod volunt.

would never complain—therefore, in those instances in which they do lust, they are doing what they would not; but for the most part they do what they would.

Lecture 5

⁵:¹⁸Quod si Spiritu ducimini, non estis sub lege. [n. 316]

⁵:¹⁹Manifesta sunt autem opera carnis, quae sunt fornicatio, immunditia, impudicitia, luxuria, [n. 319]

⁵:²⁰idolorum servitus, veneficia, inimicitiae, contentiones, aemulationes, irae, rixae, dissensiones, sectae, [n. 324]

⁵:²¹invidiae, homicidia, ebrietates, comessationes, et his similia, quae praedico vobis, sicut praedixi: quoniam qui talia agunt, regnum Dei non consequentur.

⁵:¹⁸εἰ δὲ πνεύματι ἄγεσθε, οὐκ ἐστὲ ὑπὸ νόμον.

⁵:¹⁹φανερὰ δέ ἐστιν τὰ ἔργα τῆς σαρκός, ἅτινά ἐστιν πορνεία, ἀκαθαρσία, ἀσέλγεια,

⁵:²⁰εἰδωλολατρία, φαρμακεία, ἔχθραι, ἔρις, ζῆλος, θυμοί, ἐριθεῖαι, διχοστασίαι, αἱρέσεις,

⁵:²¹φθόνοι, μέθαι, κῶμοι, καὶ τὰ ὅμοια τούτοις, ἃ προλέγω ὑμῖν καθὼς προεῖπον ὅτι οἱ τὰ τοιαῦτα πράσσοντες βασιλείαν θεοῦ οὐ κληρονομήσουσιν.

⁵:¹⁸But if you are led by the Spirit, you are not under the law. [n. 316]

⁵:¹⁹Now the works of the flesh are manifest, which are fornication, uncleanness, immodesty, luxury, [n. 319]

⁵:²⁰Idolatry, witchcrafts, enmities, contentions, emulations, wraths, quarrels, dissensions, sects, [n. 324]

⁵:²¹Envies, murders, drunkenness, revellings, and such like. Of which I foretell to you, as I have foretold to you, that they who do such things shall not obtain the kingdom of God.

316. Postquam ostendit Apostolus, quod per Spiritum liberamur a desideriis carnis, hic consequenter ostendit, quod per ipsum liberamur a servitute legis. Et

primo proponit beneficium Spiritus;

secundo manifestat per effectum, ibi ***manifesta sunt opera carnis***, et cetera.

317. Dicit ergo: dico quod si Spiritu ambuletis, non solum desideria carnis non perficietis, sed quod plus est, ***si Spiritu ducimini*** (quod fit quando facitis quod Spiritus suggerit, ut director et gubernator, non autem id ad quod sensus et affectus proprius instigat), ***non estis sub lege***. Ps. CXLII, 10: *Spiritus tuus bonus deducet me in terram rectam*, non quidem ut coactor, sed ut gubernator.

318. Ex his autem verbis vult Hieronymus, quod post adventum Christi nullus habens Spiritum Sanctum tenetur servare legem.

Sed sciendum est, quod hoc quod dicit ***si Spiritu ducimini***, iam ***non estis sub lege***, potest referri ad praecepta legis, vel caeremonialia, vel moralia.

Si quidem referatur ad caeremonialia, sciendum est, quod aliud est servare legem, aliud esse sub lege. Servare legem est facere opera legis, non habendo spem in eis; sed esse sub lege est ponere spem in operibus legis. In primitiva autem Ecclesia erant aliqui iusti servantes legem, sed non sub lege, inquantum servabant opera legis sed non erant sub lege, quasi in eis spem ponentes. Sic etiam Christus sub lege fuit. Supra IV, 4: ***factum sub lege***, et cetera. Et sic excluditur opinio Hieronymi.

Si autem referatur ad moralia, sic esse sub lege potest intelligi dupliciter, vel quantum ad obligationem: et sic omnes fideles sunt sub lege, quia omnibus data est. Unde dicitur Matth. V, 17: *non veni solvere legem*, et cetera. Vel

316. After showing that through the Spirit we are freed from the desires of the flesh, the Apostle here shows that through him we are released from the bondage of the law.

First, he mentions a benefit of the Spirit;

second, he manifests it by certain effects, at ***now the works of the flesh are manifest***.

317. He says therefore: I say that if you walk in the Spirit, not only will you not carry out the desires of the flesh, but, what is more, ***if you are led by the Spirit*** (which happens when you do what the Spirit suggests, as director and guide, and not what your sense desires urge), you are not ***under the law***: *your good Spirit shall lead me into the right land*, not by compelling, but by guiding (Ps 143:10).

318. Jerome infers from these words that after the coming of Christ no one having the Holy Spirit is obliged to observe the law.

But it should be recognized that the saying, ***if you are led by the Spirit, you are not under the law***, can be referred either to the ceremonial or to the moral precepts of the law.

If it is referred to the ceremonial precepts, then it is one thing to observe the law and another to be under the law. For to observe the law is to carry out the works of the law without putting any hope in them; but to be under the law is to put one's hope in the works of the law. Now in the early Church there were some just men who observed the law without being under the law, inasmuch as they observed the works of the law; but they were not under the law in the sense of putting their hope in them. In this way even Christ was under the law: ***made under the law*** (Gal 4:4). Thus Jerome's opinion is excluded.

But if it is referred to the moral precepts, then to be under the law can be taken in two ways: either as to its obliging force, and then all the faithful are under the law, because it was given to all—hence it is said: *I have not come to destroy*

quantum ad coactionem: et sic iusti non sunt sub lege, quia motus et instinctus Spiritus Sancti, qui est in eis, est proprius eorum instinctus; nam caritas inclinat ad illud idem quod lex praecipit. Quia ergo iusti habent legem interiorem, sponte faciunt quod lex mandat, ab ipsa non coacti. Qui vero voluntatem male faciendi habent, comprimuntur tamen pudore vel timore legis, isti coguntur. Et sic iusti sunt sub lege obligante tantum, non cogente, sub qua sunt solum iniusti. II Cor. III, 17: *ubi Spiritus Domini, ibi libertas*. I Tim. I, 9: *iusto non est lex posita*, scilicet cogens.

319. Consequenter cum dicit **manifesta sunt autem opera**, etc., probat quae dixit per effectum. Et

primo ponit opera carnis, quae contrariantur Spiritui Sancto;

secundo ostendit quomodo opera Spiritus non prohibentur a lege, ibi **adversus huiusmodi**, et cetera.

Circa primum duo facit.

Primo ponit opera carnis, quae prohibentur a lege;

secundo ponit opera Spiritus, quae ab ea non prohibentur, ibi **fructus autem**, et cetera.

Circa primum duo facit.

Primo proponit opera carnis;

secundo subdit nocumentum, quod ex his sequitur, ibi **quae praedico**, et cetera.

320. Dubitatur autem circa primum. Primo quidem de hoc quod Apostolus hic quaedam ponit, quae non pertinent ad carnem, quae tamen dicit esse opera carnis, sicut **idolorum servitus**, **sectae**, **aemulationes**, et huiusmodi.

Respondeo. Dicendum est, secundum Augustinum Lib. XIV de Civ. Dei, c. II, quod secundum carnem vivit quicumque vivit secundum seipsum. Unde caro hic accipitur pro toto homine. Quidquid ergo provenit ex inordinato amore sui, dicitur opus carnis.

Vel dicendum est, quod aliquod peccatum potest dici carnale dupliciter, scilicet quantum ad consummationem: et sic dicuntur carnalia illa tantum quae consummantur in delectatione carnis, scilicet luxuria et gula; et quantum ad radicem: et sic omnia peccata dicuntur carnalia, inquantum ex corruptione carnis anima aggravatur, ut dicitur Sap. IX, 15; ex quo intellectus debilitatus facilius decipi potest, et impeditur a sua perfecta operatione. Unde et ex hoc sequuntur vitia, scilicet haereses, sectae, et alia huiusmodi. Et hoc modo dicitur quod fomes est principium omnium peccatorum.

321. Secundo dubitatur, quia cum Apostolus dicat **qui talia agunt, regnum Dei** non **consequentur**, et nullus excludatur a regno Dei, nisi pro peccato mortali, sequitur ergo quod omnia quae enumerat sint peccata

the law but to fulfill it (Matt 5:17)—or as to its compelling forces, and then the just are not under the law, because the movements and breathings of the Holy Spirit in them are their inspiration; for charity inclines to the very things that the law prescribes. Therefore, because the just have an inward law, they willingly do what the law commands and are not constrained by it. But those who would do evil but are held back by a sense of shame or by fear of the law are compelled. Accordingly, the just are under the law as obliging but not as compelling, in which sense the unjust alone are under it: *where the Spirit of the Lord is, there is liberty* (2 Cor 3:17); *the law*, as compelling, *is not made for the just man* (1 Tim 1:9).

319. Then when he says, **the works of the flesh are manifest**, he proves what he has said through certain effects.

First, he mentions the works of the flesh which are opposed to the Holy Spirit;

second, he shows how the works of the Spirit are not forbidden by the law, at **against such there is no law** (Gal 5:23).

As to the first, he does two things:

first, he mentions the works of the flesh that are forbidden by the law;

second, the works of the Spirit which are not forbidden by it, at **but the fruit of the Spirit** (Gal 5:22).

As to the first, he does two things:

first, he enumerates the works of the flesh;

second, he mentions the harm that follows from them, at **of which I foretell to you**.

320. With respect to the first, two doubts arise. First, as to the Apostle's mentioning things that do not pertain to the flesh, but which he says are works of the flesh, such as **idolatry**, **sects**, **emulations**, and the like.

I answer that, according to Augustine in *The City of God* XIV, he lives according to the flesh who lives according to himself. Hence flesh is taken here as referring to the whole man. Accordingly, whatever springs from disordered self-love is called a work of the flesh.

Or, one should say that a sin can be called 'of the flesh' in two ways: namely, with respect to fulfillment, and in this sense only those are sins of the flesh that are fulfilled in the pleasure of the flesh, namely, lust and gluttony; or with respect to their root, and in this sense all sins are called sins of the flesh, inasmuch as the soul is so weighed down by the weakness of the flesh that the enfeebled intellect can be easily misled and hindered from operating perfectly (Wis 9:15). As a consequence, certain vices follow therefrom, namely, heresies, sects and the like. In this way it is said that the *fomes* is the source of all sins.

321. The second doubt is that, since the Apostle says that **they who do such things shall not obtain the kingdom of God**, whereas no one is excluded from the kingdom of God except for mortal sin, it follows that all the sins enumerated

mortalia. Cuius contrarium videtur, quia inter ista enumerat multa quae non sunt peccata mortalia, sicut est **contentio**, **aemulatio**, et huiusmodi.

Respondeo. Dicendum est quod omnia haec enumerata sunt aliquo modo mortalia; sed quaedam quidem secundum genus suum, sicut **homicidium**, **fornicatio**, **idolorum servitus** et huiusmodi; quaedam vero secundum suam consummationem, sicut **ira** cuius consummatio est in nocumentum proximi. Unde si accedit consensus de ipso nocumento, est peccatum mortale. Et similiter comestio ordinatur ad delectationem cibi, sed si in huiusmodi delectationibus ponat quis finem suum, peccat mortaliter: et ideo non dicit *comestiones*, sed ***comessationes***; et similiter intelligendum est de aliis similibus.

322. Tertio dubitatur de ordine et numeratione eorum.

Circa quod dicendum est quod cum Apostolus in diversis locis, diversa vitia et diversimode enumerat, non intendit enumerare omnia vitia ordinate et secundum artem, sed illa tantum in quibus abundant et in quibus excedunt illi ad quos scribit. Et ideo in eis non est quaerenda sufficientia, sed causa diversitatis.

323. His ergo habitis sciendum est, quod Apostolus enumerat quaedam vitia carnis, quae contingunt circa ea quae non sunt necessaria vitae; quaedam vero circa ea quae sunt necessaria vitae.

Circa primum ponit quaedam vitia quae sunt hominis ad seipsum, quaedam contra Deum quaedam contra proximum.

Contra seipsum sunt quatuor, quae ideo primo ponit quia manifeste ex carne procedunt, quorum duo pertinent ad actum carnalem luxuriae, scilicet ***fornicatio***, quae est quando scilicet accedit solutus ad solutam, vel quantum ad naturalem usum luxuriae. Aliud est ***immunditia*** quantum ad usum contra naturam. Eph. V, 5: *omnis fornicator aut immundus, et cetera.* II Cor. XII, 21: *qui non egerunt poenitentiam super immunditia et fornicatione et impudicitia, et cetera.*

Alia duo ordinantur ad ipsos actus. Unum scilicet exterius, sicut tactus, aspectus, oscula, et huiusmodi; et quantum ad hoc dicit: ***impudicitia***, Eph. IV, 19: *qui desperantes, semetipsos tradiderunt impudicitiae, et cetera.* Aliud interius, scilicet in cogitationibus immundis; et quantum ad hoc dicit ***luxuria***, I Tim. V, v. 11: *cum enim luxuriatae fuerint in Christo nubere volunt, et cetera.*

324. Contra Deum ponit duo, quorum unum est per quod impeditur ab hostibus Dei cultus divinus; et quantum ad hoc dicit ***idolorum servitus***, I Cor. X, 7: *neque*

are mortal sins. But the contrary seems to be the case, because in this list he enumerates many that are not mortal sins, such as **contention**, **emulation**, and the like.

I answer that all the sins listed here are mortal one way or another: some are so according to their genus, as **murder, fornication, idolatry**, and the like; but others are mortal with respect to fulfillment, as **anger**, whose fulfillment consists in harm to neighbor. Hence if one consents to that harm, there is mortal sin. In like manner, eating is directed to the pleasure of food, but if one places his end in such pleasures, he sins mortally; accordingly, he does not say *eating* but ***revellings***. And the same must be said of the others that are like this.

322. Third, there is a doubt about the order followed in this list.

However, it should be recognized that when the Apostle varies his enumeration of various vices in various texts, it is not his intention to enumerate all the vices in perfect order and according to the rules of the art, but only those in which the persons to whom he is writing abound and in which they are excessive. Therefore in these lists one should look not for completeness but for the cause of the variation.

323. Having settled these doubts, we should next observe that the Apostle lists certain vices of the flesh that concern things not necessary to life and others that concern things necessary to life.

As to the first, he mentions certain vices that a man commits against himself; then those that are against God; finally, those that are against the neighbor.

Against the self there are four. These he mentions first, because they obviously spring from the flesh. Two of these pertain to the carnal act of lust, namely, ***fornication***, when an unmarried man becomes one with an unmarried woman with respect to the natural use of lust. The other is ***uncleanness*** as to a use which is contrary to nature—*no fornicator or unclean . . . has inheritance in the kingdom of Christ and of God* (Eph 5:5); *they have not done penance for the uncleanness and fornication and lasciviousness that they have committed* (2 Cor 12:21).

The other two are ordained to the aforesaid acts: one is performed outwardly, as touches, looks, kisses and the like; as to these he says, ***immodesty***: *who despairing, have given themselves up to immodesty unto the working of all uncleanness* (Eph 4:19). The other inwardly, namely, unclean thoughts; as to this he says, ***luxury***: *when they have grown wanton in Christ, they will marry* (1 Tim 5.11).

324. Against God he lists two: one of these is that whereby divine worship is hindered by the enemies of God; as to this he says, ***idolatry***: *neither become idolaters as some*

idololatrae efficiamini, et cetera. Sap. XIV, 27: *infandorum enim idolorum cultura omnis mali causa est et initium et finis.*

Aliud est per quod initur pactum cum daemonibus; et quantum ad hoc dicit **veneficia**, quae fiunt per magicas artes, et dicuntur veneficia a veneno, quia fiunt in nocumentum hominum. I Cor. X, 20: *nolo vos fieri socios daemoniorum.* Apoc. ult.: *foris canes, et venefici*, et cetera.

325. Contra proximum autem ponit novem, quorum primum est **inimicitia**, ultimum vero **homicidium**, quia ab hoc devenitur ad illud.

Primum ergo est inimicitia in corde, quae est odium erga proximum. Matth. X, 36: *inimici hominis domestici eius.* Et ideo dicit **inimicitiae**. Ex hac autem oritur dissensio in verbis. Et ideo dicit **contentiones**, quae est impugnatio veritatis cum confidentia clamoris. Prov. XX, 3: *honor est homini qui se separat a contentionibus.* Secundum est aemulatio, quae consistit in hoc, quod ad idem obtinendum cum alio contendit. Unde dicit **aemulationes**, quae ex contentione oriuntur. Tertium est cum unus impeditur per alium ad rem eamdem tendentem, et ex hoc irascitur contra eum, et ideo dicit **irae**, Iac. I, 20: *ira enim viri*, et cetera. Eph. IV, 26: *sol non occidat super iracundiam vestram.* Quartum cum ex ira animi pervenitur ad percussiones; et quantum ad hoc dicit **rixae**. Prov. IV: *odium suscitat rixas.* Quintum ex his, scilicet **dissensiones**, et si quidem in rebus humanis sint, dicuntur dissensiones, quando scilicet partialitates fiunt in Ecclesia. Rom. XVI, 17: *observetis eos qui dissensiones et offendicula praeter doctrinam quam vos didicistis, faciunt, et declinate ab illis.* Si in rebus divinis, sic dicuntur **sectae**, id est, haereses. II Petr. II, 1: *introducent sectas perditionis*, et cetera. Et, ibidem: *sectas non metuunt introducere blasphemantes.* Ex his autem sequitur **invidia**, quando illi quos aemulantur, prosperantur. Iob V, 2: *parvulum occidit invidia*, et cetera. Ex his autem sequuntur **homicidia** cordis et operis. I Io. IV: *qui odit fratrem suum, homicida est.*

326. Quantum vero ad vitia quae pertinent ad ordinationem circa vitae necessaria, ponit duo, unum quantum ad potum; unde dicit **ebrietates**, scilicet assiduae, Lc. XXI, 34: *attendite ne graventur corda vestra crapula et ebrietate*, et cetera. Aliud vero quantum ad cibum, et quantum ad hoc dicit **comessationes**, Rom. XIII, 13: *non in comessationibus et ebrietatibus.*

of them (1 Cor 10:7); *for the worship of abominable idols is the cause and beginning and end of all evil* (Wis 14:27).

The other is that in which a pact is struck with demons; as to this he says, **witchcrafts**, which are performed through magical arts, and are called in Latin *veneficia*, from venom, because they result in great harm to man: *I do not want you to be made partakers with devils* (1 Cor 10:20); *without are dogs and sorcerers* (Rev 22:15).

325. Against one's neighbor he enumerates nine, the first of which is **enmity** and the last **murder**, because from the former, one comes to the latter.

The first, therefore, is animosity in the heart, which is hatred toward one's neighbor: *and a man's enemies shall be of his own household* (Matt 10:36); hence he says **enmities**: from which arise verbal disputes. And so he says, **contentions**, which are attacks on the truth with the confidence of shouting: *it is an honor for a man to separate himself from quarrels* (Prov 20:3). The second is emulation, which consists in contending with another to obtain a same thing; hence he says, **emulations**, which arise from contention. The third arises when one is hindered by someone else who is tending to a same thing, so that on this account anger arises against him. Hence he says, **wraths**: *the anger of men does not work the justice of God* (Jas 1:20); *do not let the sun go down on your anger* (Eph 4:26). The fourth is when anger of spirit leads to blows; and with respect to this he says, **quarrels**: *hatred stirs up strifes* (Prov 10:12). The fifth, namely, **dissensions**, arise from quarrels: if they concern human matters they are called dissensions: for example, when factions arise in the Church—*mark them who make dissensions and offences contrary to the doctrine which you have learned, and avoid them* (Rom 16:17) —if they concern divine matters, they are called **sects**, i.e., heresies: *they shall bring in sects of perdition, and deny the Lord who bought them*, and *they do not fear to bring in sects, blaspheming* (2 Pet 2:1, 10). From these **envy** follows, when those with whom they vie are prosperous: *envy slays the little one* (Job 5:2). And from these follow **murders** in heart and deed: *whoever hates his brother is a murderer* (1 John 3:15).

326. Finally, of vices that pertain to the ordering of the necessaries of life, he mentions two: one concerns drink; hence he says, **drunkenness**, i.e., continual: *take heed lest perhaps your hearts be overcharged with surfeiting and drunkenness and the cares of this life* (Luke 21:34). The other concerns food, touching which he says, **revellings**: *not in rioting and drunkenness* (Rom 13:13).

Lecture 6

5:22 Fructus autem Spiritus est caritas, gaudium, pax, patientia, benignitas, bonitas, longanimitas, [n. 327]

5:22Ὁ δὲ καρπὸς τοῦ πνεύματός ἐστιν ἀγάπη, χαρά, εἰρήνη, μακροθυμία, χρηστότης, ἀγαθωσύνη, πίστις,

5:22 But the fruit of the Spirit is charity, joy, peace, patience, benignity, goodness, longanimity, [n. 327]

---

327. Positis operibus carnis, hic consequenter Apostolus manifestat opera Spiritus. Et

primo manifestat ea;

secundo ostendit quomodo lex se habet ad opera Spiritus et ad opera carnis, ibi *adversus huiusmodi*, et cetera.

328. Circa primum enumerat bona spiritualia quae nominat *fructus*.

Ex quo incidit quaestio, quia illud dicitur fructus, quo fruimur, sed actibus nostris non debemus frui, sed Deo solo; ergo huiusmodi actus quos enumerat hic Apostolus non debent dici *fructus*.

Item, Glossa dicit quod huiusmodi opera Spiritus sunt propter se appetenda; quod autem propter se appetitur non refertur ad aliud, ergo virtutes et earum opera non sunt referenda ad beatitudinem.

Respondeo. Dicendum est quod *fructus* dicitur dupliciter, scilicet ut acquisitus, puta ex labore vel studio, Sap. III, 15: *bonorum laborum gloriosus est fructus*, et ut productus, sicut fructus producitur ex arbore. Matth. c. VII, 18: *non potest arbor bona fructus malos facere*. Opera autem Spiritus dicuntur fructus non ut adepti sive acquisiti, sed ut producti; fructus autem qui est adeptus, habet rationem ultimi finis, non autem fructus productus. Nihilominus tamen fructus sic acceptus duo importat, scilicet quod sit ultimum producentis, sicut ultimum quod producitur ab arbore est fructus eius, et quod sit suave sive delectabile. Cant. II, 3: *fructus eius dulcis gutturi meo*. Sic ergo opera virtutum et Spiritus sunt quid ultimum in nobis. Nam Spiritus Sanctus est in nobis per gratiam, per quam acquirimus habitum virtutum, et ex hoc potentes sumus operari secundum virtutem.

Sunt etiam delectabilia, et sunt etiam fructuosa. Rom. VI, 22: *habetis fructum vestrum in sanctificationem*, id est in operibus sanctificatis, et ideo dicuntur *fructus*.

Dicuntur etiam flores respectu futurae beatitudinis, quia sicut ex floribus accipitur spes fructus, ita ex operibus virtutum habetur spes vitae aeternae et beatitudinis. Et sicut in flore est quaedam inchoatio fructus, ita in operibus virtutum est quaedam inchoatio beatitudinis, quae tunc erit quando cognitio et caritas perficientur.

Et per hoc patet responsio ad illud quod secundo obiicitur. Nam aliquid potest dici propter se appetendum

327. Having listed the works of the flesh, the Apostle then manifests the works of the Spirit.

First, he manifests them;

second, he shows how the law is related to the works of the Spirit and to the works of the flesh, at *against such* (Gal 5:23).

328. As to the first, he enumerates the spiritual goods which he calls *fruits*.

But here a question arises, because fruit is something we enjoy; but we should enjoy not our acts, but God alone. Therefore, acts of this kind, which the Apostle lists here, ought not be called *fruits*.

Furthermore, a Gloss says that these works of the Spirit are to be sought for themselves; but that which is sought for itself is not referred to something else. Therefore virtues and their works are not to be referred to happiness.

I answer that *fruit* is said in two ways: namely, as something acquired, for example, from labor or study—*the fruit of good labors is glorious* (Wis 3:15)—and as something produced, as fruit is produced from a tree: *a good tree cannot bear evil fruit* (Matt 7:18). Now the works of the Spirit are called fruits, not as something earned or acquired, but as produced. Furthermore, fruit which is acquired has the character of an ultimate end; not, however, fruit which is produced. Nevertheless, fruit so understood implies two things: namely, that it is the last thing of the producer, as the last thing produced by a tree is its fruit, and that it is sweet or delightful: *his fruit was sweet to my palate* (Song 2:3). So, then, the works of the virtues and of the Spirit are something last in us. For the Holy Spirit is in us through grace, through which we acquire the habit of the virtues; these in turn make us capable of working according to virtue.

Furthermore, they are delightful and even fruitful: *you have your fruit unto sanctification* (Rom 6:22), i.e., in holy works. And that is why they are called *fruits*.

But they are also called flowers, namely, in relation to future happiness; because just as from flowers hope of fruit is taken, so from works of the virtues is obtained hope of eternal life and happiness. And as in the flower there is a beginning of the fruit, so in the works of the virtues is a beginning of happiness, which will exist when knowledge and charity are made perfect.

From this the answer to the second objection is plain. For something can be said to be worthy of being sought for

itself in two ways, according as 'for' designates formal cause or final cause. Works of the virtues are to be sought for themselves formally but not finally, because they are a delight in themselves. For a sweet medicine is formally sought for itself, because it has something within itself that makes it pleasant, namely, sweetness, which however is sought for an end, namely, for the sake of health. But a bitter medicine is not sought formally for itself, because it does not please by reason of its form; yet it is sought for something else finally, namely, for health, which is its end.

This explains why the Apostle calls the effects of the flesh **works**, but the fruits of the Spirit he calls **fruits**.

For it has been pointed out that a fruit is something last and sweet, produced from a thing. On the other hand, that which is produced from something but not according to nature, does not have the character of fruit but is, as it were, an alien growth. Now the works of the flesh and sins are alien to the nature of those things which God has planted in our nature. For God planted in human nature certain seeds, namely, a natural desire of good and knowledge, and he added gifts of grace: and therefore, because the works of the virtues are produced naturally from these, they are called **fruits**, but the works of the flesh are not. And for this reason, the Apostle says: *what fruit, therefore, had you then in those things of which you are now ashamed?* (Rom 6:21)

It is plain, therefore, from what has been said, that the works of the virtues are called **fruits of the Spirit**, both because they have a sweetness and delight in themselves and because they are the last and congruous products of the gifts.

329. The difference from one another of the gifts, beatitudes, virtues and fruits is taken in the following way.

In a virtue can be considered the habit and the act. Now the habit of a virtue qualifies a person to act well. If it enables him to act well in a human mode, it is called a virtue. But if it qualifies one for acting well, above the human mode, it is called a gift. Hence the Philosopher, above the common virtues, puts certain heroic virtues: thus, to know the invisible things of God darkly is in keeping with the human mode, and such knowledge pertains to the virtue of faith; but to know the same things more penetratingly and above the human mode pertains to the gift of understanding.

But as to the act of a virtue, it is either perfective, and in this way is a beatitude; or it is a source of delight, and in this way it is a fruit. Of these fruits it is said in Revelation: *on both sides of the river was the tree of life, bearing twelve fruits* (Rev 22:2).

330. He says, therefore, **the fruit of the Spirit**, which arises in the soul from the sowing of spiritual grace, is **charity, joy, peace, patience, longanimity**, which indeed are thus distinguished because fruits perfect one either inwardly or outwardly.

Primo ergo ponit illos qui perficiunt interius; secundo illos qui perficiunt exterius, ibi **bonitas**, et cetera.

Interius autem homo perficitur et dirigitur et circa bona et circa mala. II Cor. VI, 7: *per arma iustitiae a dextris et a sinistris*.

Circa bona autem perficiunt, primo quidem in corde per amorem. Nam sicut inter motus naturales primus est inclinatio appetitus naturae ad finem suum, ita primus motuum interiorum est inclinatio ad bonum, qui dicitur amor, et ideo primus fructus est **caritas**, Rom. V, 5: *caritas Dei diffusa est in cordibus nostris*, et cetera. Et ex caritate perficiuntur aliae, et ideo dicit Apostolus, Col. III, v. 14: *super omnia caritatem habentes*, et cetera. Ultimus autem finis, quo homo perficitur interius, est **gaudium**, quod procedit ex praesentia rei amatae. Qui autem habet caritatem, iam habet quod amat. I Io. IV, 16: *qui manet in caritate, in Deo manet, et Deus in eo*. Et ex hoc consurgit gaudium. Phil. IV, 4: *gaudete in Domino semper*, et cetera.

Gaudium autem istud debet esse perfectum. Et ad hoc duo requiruntur. Primo ut res amata sufficiens sit amanti propter suam perfectionem. Et quantum ad hoc dicit **pax**. Tunc enim amans pacem habet, quando rem amatam sufficienter possidet. Cant. ult.: *ex quo facta sum coram eo quasi pacem reperiens*, et cetera. Secundo vero ut adsit perfecta fruitio rei amatae, quod similiter per pacem habetur, quia, quidquid superveniat, si perfecte aliquis fruatur re amata, puta Deo, non potest impediri ab eius fruitione. Ps. CXVIII, 165: *pax multa diligentibus legem tuam, et non est illis scandalum*. Sic ergo gaudium dicit caritatis fruitionem, sed pax caritatis perfectionem. Et per haec homo interius perficitur quantum ad bona.

331. Circa mala etiam perficit Spiritus Sanctus et ordinat, et primo contra malum quod perturbat pacem, quae perturbatur per adversa. Sed ad hoc perficit Spiritus Sanctus per patientiam, quae facit adversa patienter tolerare, et ideo dicit **patientia**. Lc. XXI, 19: *in patientia vestra possidebitis animas vestras*. Iac. I, 4: *patientia opus perfectum habet*. Secundo, contra malum impediens gaudium est dilatio rei amatae, ad quod Spiritus opponit longanimitatem, quae expectatione non frangitur. Et quantum ad hoc dicit **longanimitas**. Habacuc II, 3: *si moram fecerit, expecta eum, quia*, et cetera. II Cor. VI, 6: *in longanimitate*, et cetera. Et ideo dicit Dominus Matth. c. X, 22: *qui perseveraverit usque in finem*, et cetera.

332. Consequenter cum dicit **bonitas**, etc., ponit fructus Spiritus, qui perficiunt quantum ad exteriora.

First, he mentions those that perfect inwardly; second, those that perfect outwardly.

Now a man is perfected and directed inwardly both as to good things and as to evil: *by the armor of justice on the right hand and on the left* (2 Cor 6:7).

With respect to good things a person is perfected, first of all, in his heart through love. For just as in natural movements there is first an inclination of a nature's appetite to its end, so the first of the inward movements is the inclination to good, i.e., love; accordingly, the first fruit is **charity**: *the charity of God is poured forth in our hearts by the Holy Spirit who is given to us* (Rom 5:5). And through charity the others are perfected; wherefore, the Apostle says in Colossians: *but above all these things have charity, which is the bond of perfection* (Col 3:14). But the ultimate end that perfects man inwardly is **joy**, which proceeds from the presence of the thing loved. And he that has charity already has what he loves: *he that abides in charity abides in God and God in him* (1 John 4:16). And from this springs joy: *rejoice in the Lord always; again I say, rejoice* (Phil 4:4).

But this joy should be perfect, and for this two things are required: first, that the object loved be enough to perfect the lover. And as to this he says, **peace**. For it is then that the lover has peace, when he adequately possesses the object loved: *I am become in his presence as one finding peace* (Song 8:10). Second, that there be perfect enjoyment of the thing loved, which is likewise obtained by peace, because whatever else happens, if someone perfectly enjoys the object loved, say God, he cannot be hindered from enjoying it: *much peace have they that love your law and to them there is no stumbling-block* (Ps 119:165). In this way, therefore, joy connotes the fruition of charity, but peace the perfection of charity. And by these is man inwardly made perfect as to good things.

331. Also with respect to evils, the Holy Spirit perfects and adjusts a person: first, against the evil that disturbs peace, which is disturbed by adverse objects. Touching this the Holy Spirit perfects one by patience, which makes for patient endurance of adversities; hence he says, **patience**: *in your patience you shall possess your souls* (Luke 21:19); *and patience has a perfect work* (Jas 1:4). Second, against the evil which hinders joy, namely, the deferment of the object loved, the Spirit opposes long-suffering, which is not broken by delay. As to this he says, **longanimity**: *if it make any delay, wait for it; for it shall surely come, and it shall not be slack* (Hab 2:3): *in long-suffering* (2 Cor 6:6). Hence the Lord says: *he that shall persevere unto the end, he shall be saved* (Matt 10:22).

332. Then when he says, **goodness, benignity**, he mentions the fruits of the Spirit that perfect a man with respect to external things.

Hominis autem exteriora sunt vel id quod est iuxta ipsum, vel id quod est supra ipsum, vel id quod est infra ipsum. Iuxta ipsum est proximus, supra ipsum Deus, infra ipsum natura sensitiva et corpus.

Sic ergo quantum ad proximum perficit primo quidem in corde per rectam et bonam voluntatem. Et quantum ad hoc dicit **bonitas**, id est rectitudo et dulcedo animi.

Si enim homo omnes alias potentias bonas habeat, non potest dici bonus homo nisi habeat bonam voluntatem, secundum quam omnibus aliis bene utitur. Cuius ratio est, quia bonum dicit aliquod perfectum. Est autem duplex perfectio. Prima, scilicet quae est ipsum esse rei; secunda vero est eius operatio: et haec est maior quam prima. Illud ergo dicitur simpliciter perfectum quod pertingit ad perfectam sui operationem, quae est secunda eius perfectio. Cum ergo homo per voluntatem exeat in actum cuiuslibet potentiae, voluntas recta facit bonum usum omnium potentiarum, et, per consequens, ipsum hominem bonum. Et de hoc fructu dicitur Eph. V, 9: *fructus enim lucis est in omni bonitate*, et cetera.

Secundo vero in opere, ut scilicet sua communicet proximo, et quantum ad hoc dicit **benignitas**, id est, largitas rerum. II Cor. IX, v. 7: *hilarem enim datorem*, et cetera. Benignitas enim dicitur quasi bona igneitas, quae facit hominem fluere ad subveniendum necessitatibus aliorum. Sap. I, 6: *benignus est enim Spiritus sapientiae*, et cetera. Col. III, 12: *induite vos ergo sicut electi Dei, sancti et dilecti, viscera misericordiae, benignitatem*, et cetera. Item perficiunt etiam quantum ad mala ab aliis illata, ut mansuete ferat ac sustineat proximi molestias; et quantum ad hoc dicit **mansuetudo**, Matth. XI, 29: *discite a me, quia*, et cetera. Prov. III, 34: *mansuetis dabit gratiam*.

333. Ad id vero quod est supra nos, scilicet Deus, ordinat Spiritus per fidem, unde dicit ***fides***, quae est cognitio quaedam invisibilium cum certitudine. Gen. XV, 6: *credidit Abraham Deo, et reputatum est ei ad iustitiam*. Hebr. XI, 6: *accedentem ad Deum oportet credere*, cetera. Et ideo Eccli. I, v. 34: *beneplacitum est Deo fides, et mansuetudo*, et cetera.

334. Ad id quod est infra nos, scilicet corpus, dirigit Spiritus, et primo quantum ad actus exteriores corporis, quod fit per modestiam, quae ipsis actibus seu dictis modum imponit; et quantum ad hoc dicit **modestia**, Phil. IV, 5: *modestia vestra*, et cetera.

Secundo vero quantum ad appetitum sensitivum interiorem, et quantum ad hoc dicit **continentia**, quae etiam a licitis abstinet, et **castitas**, quae licitis recte utitur, secundum Glossam.

Vel aliter, continentia dicitur ex eo quod licet homo impugnetur a pravis concupiscentiis, tamen per rationis vigorem se tenet, ne abducatur; et ideo continentiae

Now external to man are things next to him, above him and beneath him. Next to him is the neighbor; above him is God; beneath him is his sensitive nature and body.

In regard to his neighbor he perfects men, first of all, from the heart with a right and good will. Concerning this he says, **goodness**, i.e., rectitude and gentleness of spirit.

For if a man has all his other powers good, he cannot be said to be good unless he has a good will, according to which he uses all the others well. The reason for this is that the good denotes something perfect. But perfection is twofold: the first concerns the being of a thing; the second, its operation; and the latter is greater than the former. For that is called perfect in the absolute sense which has attained its perfect operation, which is its second perfection. Therefore, since it is by his will that man exercises the act of any power, right will makes for the good use of all the powers, and, consequently, makes the man himself good. Of this fruit it is said in Ephesians: *the fruit of the light is in all goodness and justice and truth* (Eph 5:9).

Second, he perfects a man in his deeds, so that he will share with his neighbor. Concerning this he says, **benignity**, i.e., giving: *the Lord loves a cheerful giver* (2 Cor 9:7). For benignity is said to be, as it were, a good fire, which makes a man melt to relieve the needs of others: *for the Spirit of wisdom is benevolent* (Wis 1:6); *put on, therefore, as the elect of God, holy and beloved, the bowels of mercy, benignity* (Col 3:12). Again, they perfect one with respect to evils inflicted by others, so that one meekly bears and endures harassment from another. Touching this he says, **mildness** (Gal 5:23): *learn of me, because I am meek and humble of heart* (Matt 2:29); *to the meek he will give grace* (Prov 3:34).

333. With respect to what is above us, namely, God, the Spirit establishes right order through faith; hence he says, ***faith***, which is a knowledge of invisible things with certainty: *Abraham believed God and it was reputed to him unto justice* (Gen 15:6); *he that comes to God must believe that he is* (Heb 11:6). On this account it is said in Sirach: *that which is agreeable to the Lord is faith and meekness* (Sir 1:34).

334. Touching what is beneath us, namely, the body, the Spirit directs us first as to the outward acts of the body by modesty, which moderates its deeds or utterances—concerning this he says, **modesty** (Gal 5:23): *let your modesty be known to all men* (Phil 4:5).

Second, as to the interior appetite, and concerning this he says **continency**, which abstains even from things that are lawful; and **chastity**, which correctly uses what is lawful, as a Gloss says.

Or, another way: continence refers to the fact that although a man be assailed by base desires, yet by the vigor of his reason he holds fast lest he be carried away. According

nomen sumptum est ab eo quod aliquis in impugnatione tenet se. Castitas vero dicitur ex eo quod quis nec impugnatur, nec abducitur, et dicitur a castigando. Nam illum dicimus bene castigatum, qui in omnibus ordinate se habet.

335. Circa hoc duo dubitantur. Primo quia cum fructus Spiritus adversentur operibus carnis, videtur quod Apostolus debuerit ponere tot fructus spiritus, quot posuit opera carnis, quod non fecit.

Ad quod dicendum est quod ideo non fecit, quia plura sunt vitia quam virtutes.

Secundo dubitatur, quia fructus Spiritus hic positi non respondent operibus carnis.

Ad hoc dicendum est quod Apostolus non intendit hic tradere artem virtutum et vitiorum, et ideo non ponit unum contra aliud, sed aliqua enumerat de istis et aliqua de illis, secundum quod expediens videtur praesenti intentioni.

Nihilominus tamen si diligenter consideretur, alijqualiter sibi contra respondent. Nam *fornicationi*, quae est amor illicitus, contra respondet *caritas*; *immunditiae* vero, *impudicitiae* et *luxuriae*, quae sunt carnales illecebrae, et ex fornicatione proveniunt, contra ponitur *gaudium*, quod est spiritualis delectatio consequens ex caritate, ut dictum est. Ei vero quod est *idolorum servitus*, contra ponitur *pax*. Ei vero quod dicit *veneficia*, etc., usque ad *dissensiones*: *patientia, longanimitas* et *bonitas*. Ei vero quod dicitur *sectae*, contra ponitur *fides*. Ei vero quod dicitur *invidiae*, *benignitas*. Ei autem quod dicitur *homicidia*, *mansuetudo*. Ei quod dicitur *ebrietas, comessationes*, et his similia, contra ponitur *modestia, continentia* et *castitas*.

to this the word 'continence' is taken from a person's holding fast under attack. But chastity is taken from the fact that one is neither attacked nor carried away, and is derived from 'chastening.' For we call him well-chastened who is rightly tempered in all things.

335. Concerning the aforesaid, two problems arise. The first is that since the fruits of the Spirit are opposed to the works of the flesh, it seems that the Apostle should have mentioned as many fruits of the spirit as he mentioned works of the flesh—which he did not do.

I answer that he did not do so, because there are more vices than virtues.

The second problem is that the fruits of the Spirit mentioned do not correspond to the works of the flesh.

I answer that since it is not the Apostle's intention here to teach the art of the virtues and vices, he does not set one against the other; but he mentions as many of the one and as many of the other as are suited to his present objective.

Yet a more diligent consideration discloses that they are in some fashion set in opposition. For in opposition to *fornication*, which is illicit love, is set *charity*; in opposition to *uncleanness*, *immodesty*, and *luxury*, which are allurements of the flesh that arise from fornication, is set *joy*, which is the spiritual delight produced by charity, as has been said. In opposition to what are called *witchcrafts, enmities, contentions, dissensions*, are set *patience, longanimity*, and *goodness*. To what are called *sects, faith* is set in opposition. To what is called *murder, benignity*. To what are called *drunkenness, revellings*, and the like, are opposed *modesty, continency* and *chastity*.

Lecture 7

5:23mansuetudo, fides, modestia, continentia, castitas. Adversus huiusmodi non est lex. [n. 336]

5:24Qui autem sunt Christi, carnem suam crucifixerunt cum vitiis et concupiscentiis. [n. 338]

5:25Si Spiritu vivimus, Spiritu et ambulemus. [n. 339]

5:26Non efficiamur inanis gloriae cupidi, invicem provocantes, invicem invidentes. [n. 341]

5:23πραΰτης, ἐγκράτεια· κατὰ τῶν τοιούτων οὐκ ἔστιν νόμος.

5:24οἱ δὲ τοῦ Χριστοῦ [Ἰησοῦ] τὴν σάρκα ἐσταύρωσαν σὺν τοῖς παθήμασιν καὶ ταῖς ἐπιθυμίαις.

5:25εἰ ζῶμεν πνεύματι, πνεύματι καὶ στοιχῶμεν.

5:26μὴ γινώμεθα κενόδοξοι, ἀλλήλους προκαλούμενοι, ἀλλήλοις φθονοῦντες.

5:23Mildness, faith, modesty, continency, chastity. Against such there is no law. [n. 336]

5:24And they who are Christ's have crucified their flesh, with the vices and concupiscences. [n. 338]

5:25If we live in the Spirit, let us also walk in the Spirit. [n. 339]

5:26Let us not be made desirous of vainglory, provoking one another, envying one another. [n. 341]

---

336. Enumeratis operibus carnis, et Spiritus, hic consequenter ex utrisque concludit, quod qui Spiritum sequuntur, non sunt sub lege. Et utitur tali probatione: ille est sub lege qui est obnoxius legi, id est qui facit contraria legi; sed illi qui aguntur Spiritu, non faciunt opera contraria legi, ergo non sunt sub lege.

Primo ergo ostendit propositum ex parte operum Spiritus;

secundo ex parte operum carnis, ibi *qui autem sunt*, et cetera.

337. Dicit ergo: dico quod qui aguntur Spiritu, non faciunt opera contraria legi, quia aut faciunt opera Spiritus, et *adversus huiusmodi non est lex*, id est contra opera Spiritus, sed Spiritus docet ea. Nam sicut lex exterius docet opera virtutum, ita et Spiritus interius movet ad illa. Rom. VII, 22: *condelector enim legi Dei secundum interiorem hominem*, et cetera.

Aut faciunt opera carnis, et haec in his qui Spiritu Dei aguntur, non sunt contraria legi.

338. Unde dicit *qui autem sunt Christi*, id est qui Spiritum Dei habent. Rom. VIII, v. 9: *qui Spiritum Dei non habet, hic non est eius*. Illi ergo Spiritu Dei aguntur, qui sunt Christi. Isti, inquam, *carnem suam crucifixerunt*, et cetera. Non autem dicit: vitia et concupiscentias vitant, quia bonus medicus tunc bene curat, quando adhibet remedia contra causam morbi. Caro autem est radix vitiorum. Si ergo volumus vitare vitia, oportet domare carnem. I Cor. IX, 27: *castigo corpus meum*, et cetera.

Quia vero caro domatur per vigilias, ieiunia et labores—Eccli. XXXIII, 28: *servo malevolo tortura et compedes*, etc.—ad haec autem opera moventur ex devotione quam habent ad Christum crucifixum, ideo signanter dicit *crucifixerunt*, id est Christo crucifixo se conformaverunt, affligendo carnem suam, et cetera. Rom. VI, 6:

336. Having enumerated the works of the flesh and of the Spirit, the Apostle then concludes from both, that those who follow the Spirit are not under the law. The proof he uses is this: he is under the law who is liable to the law, i.e., who does things contrary to the law. But those who are led by the Spirit do not the works contrary to the law. Therefore, they are not under the law.

First, therefore, he proves the proposition on the part of the works of the Spirit;

second, on the part of the works of the flesh, at *and they who are Christ's*.

337. He says, therefore: I say that those who are led by the Spirit do not the works that are contrary to the law, because they either do the works of the Spirit, and *against such there is no law*, i.e., against the works of the Spirit, but the Spirit teaches such works. For as the law outwardly teaches works of virtue, so the Spirit inwardly moves one to them: *for I am delighted with the law of God according to the inward man* (Rom 7:22).

Or they do the works of the flesh; and in those who are led by the Spirit, such works are not contrary to the law.

338. Hence he says, *they that are Christ's*, i.e., who have the Spirit of God; for *if any man have not the Spirit of Christ, he is none of his* (Rom 8:9). Accordingly, those are led by the Spirit of God who are Christ's. *They*, I say, *have crucified their flesh, with the vices and concupiscences*. He does not say that they shun vices and concupiscences, because a good physician cures well when he applies remedies against the cause of the disease. But the flesh is the root of vices. Therefore, if we would shun vices, the flesh must be tamed: *I chastise my body and bring it under subjection* (1 Cor 9:27).

But because the flesh is tamed by vigils, fasts and labors—*torture and fetters are for a malicious slave; send him to work that he be not idle* (Sir 33:28)—and one is led to such works out of devotion to Christ crucified, therefore he specifically says, *they have crucified*, i.e., conformed themselves to Christ crucified by afflicting their flesh: *our*

vetus homo noster simul crucifixus est, et cetera. Supra II: *ut Deo vivam, Christo confixus sum cruci*, et cetera.

Quia vero non crucifigunt carnem destruendo naturam, quia *nemo carnem suam odio habuit*, ut dicitur Eph. V, 29, sed quantum ad ea quae contrariantur legi, ideo dicit **cum vitiis**, id est cum peccatis, **et concupiscentiis**, id est passionibus, quibus anima inclinatur ad peccandum. Non enim bene crucifigit carnem qui etiam passionibus locum non aufert, aliter cum ratio non semper invigilet ad peccata vitandum, ut oportet, posset quandoque cadere. Eccli. XVIII, 30: *post concupiscentias tuas non eas*, et cetera. Rom. XIII, 14: *carnis curam ne feceritis in desideriis*, et cetera.

339. Consequenter cum dicit *si Spiritu vivimus*, etc., ponit tertium beneficium Spiritus Sancti, quod confert vitam. Et

primo ponit beneficium Spiritus Dei;

secundo excludit vitia spiritus mundi, ibi **non efficiamur**, et cetera.

340. Dicit ergo, connumerans se eis quibus scribit: dico quod debemus ambulare per Spiritum, quia et per ipsum vivimus, et non per carnem. Rom. VIII, 12: *debitores sumus non carni*, et cetera. *Si* ergo *Spiritu vivimus*, debemus in omnibus ab ipso agi.

Sicut enim in vita corporali corpus non movetur nisi per animam per quam vivit, ita in vita spirituali omnis motus noster debet esse a Spiritu Sancto. Io. VI, 64: *Spiritus est qui vivificat*. Act. XVII, 28: *in ipso vivimus, movemur, et sumus*.

341. Et ne ea quae dicta sunt de Spiritu intelligantur de spiritu mundi, de quo dicitur I Cor. II, 12: *nos autem non spiritum huius mundi accepimus*, ideo hoc consequenter removet Apostolus, dicens **non efficiamur**, etc., ubi tria excludit propria spiritus mundi, scilicet inanem gloriam, iracundiam, et invidiam, quibus tribus convenienter aptari potest nomen spiritus.

Significat enim spiritus quamdam inflationem. Unde secundum hoc illi dicuntur vani spiritus, qui sunt inflati per inanem gloriam. Is. XXV, 4: *spiritus robustorum quasi turbo impellens parietem*, et cetera. Et quantum ad hoc dicit **non efficiamur inanis gloriae cupidi**, id est, gloriae saecularis. Cum enim vanum sit quod nec solide firmatur, nec veritate fulcitur, nec utilitate amatur, ideo gloria huius mundi vana est, quia caduca, et non solida, Is. XL, v. 6: *omnis caro foenum*, etc., et quia falsa, I Mac. II, 62: *gloria hominis peccatoris, stercus et vermis*, et cetera. Sed vera gloria est in propriis bonis hominis, quae sunt bona spiritualia, et hanc habent sancti. II Cor. I, 12: *gloria nostra haec est, testimonium conscientiae nostrae*, et cetera. Et quia inutilis et infructuosa: nam quantumcumque gloriam habeat quis ex testimonio

old man is crucified with him that the body of sin may be destroyed (Rom 6:6); *that I may live to God: with Christ I am nailed to the cross* (Gal 2:19).

But because they do not crucify the flesh by destroying nature, for *no one hates his own flesh* (Eph 5:29), but with respect to matters that are contrary to the law, for that reason he says, **with the vices**, i.e., with the sins, **and concupiscences**, i.e., passions, whereby the soul is inclined to sin. For he does not crucify his flesh well who leaves room for passions; otherwise, since reason is not always alert to avoid sin, as it ought, he might fall at some time: *do not go after your lusts, but turn away from your own will* (Sir 18:30); *do not make provision for the flesh in its concupiscence* (Rom 13:14).

339. Then when he says, *if we live in the Spirit, let us also walk in the Spirit*, he mentions the third benefit of the Holy Spirit, namely, the conferring of life.

First, he mentions this benefit of the Spirit of God;

second, he rejects the vices of the spirit of the world, at **let us not be made desirous**.

340. Therefore, including himself with those to whom he writes, he says: I say that we ought to walk by the Spirit, because we live by him and not by the flesh: *we are debtors not to the flesh to live according to the flesh* (Rom 8:12). Therefore, *if we live in the Spirit*, we ought in all things to be led by him.

For as in bodily life the body is not moved save by the soul, by which it has life, so in the spiritual life all of our movements should be through the Holy Spirit: *it is the Spirit that gives life* (John 6:64); *in him we live and move and are* (Acts 17:28).

341. But lest the things said of the Spirit be understood of the spirit of the world—concerning which it is said in 1 Corinthians: *we have received not the spirit of this world* (1 Cor 2:12)—the Apostle forestalls this when he says, **let us not be made desirous of vainglory, provoking one another, envying one another**. Here he excludes things proper to the spirit of the world, namely, vainglory, anger and envy, all three of which are aptly described by the word 'spirit.'

For 'spirit' denotes a swelling. According to this, then, those are called vain spirits who are swollen with vainglory: *the blast of the mighty is like a whirlwind beating against a wall* (Isa 25:4). Concerning this he says, **let us not be made desirous of vainglory**, i.e., of worldly glory. For since that is vain which is not solidly established nor supported by truth nor loved for any usefulness, then the glory of this world is vain, because it is frail and not solid: *all flesh is grass* (Isa 40:6). Furthermore, it is false—*the glory of a sinful man is dung and worms* (1 Mac 2:62)—whereas true glory concerns goods appropriate to man, i.e., the goods of the Spirit, such as holy men have: *our glory is this, the testimony of our conscience* (2 Cor 1:12). Furthermore, this glory is useless and fruitless: for however great the glory one acquires from the testimony of men, he cannot on that

saecularium, non potest propter hoc consequi finem suum, quem consequitur testimonio Dei. I Cor. I, 31: *qui gloriatur, in Domino glorietur*.

Non autem dicit: *non habeatis inanem gloriam* sed ***non efficiamini cupidi***, quia gloria sequitur aliquando fugientes eam, et si eam oportet recipi, non tamen ametur.

Item significat quamdam impetuositatem. Prov. XXVII, 4: *impetum concitati spiritus ferre quis poterit?* Et significat iracundiam. Et quantum ad hoc dicit ***invicem provocantes***, scilicet ad contentionem, vel litem, vel alia illicita. Rom. XIII, 13: *non in contentione et aemulatione*, et cetera.

Item est spiritus tristitiae, de quo dicitur Prov. XVII, 22: *spiritus exsiccat ossa*. Et quantum ad hoc dicit ***invicem invidentes***. Prov. XIV, 30: *putredo ossium, invidia*, et cetera. Cuius ratio est, quia ipsa sola crescit ex bono.

account achieve his end, which is achieved by the testimony of God: *he that glories, let him glory in the Lord* (1 Cor 1:31).

He does not say, *do not have vainglory*, but ***be not made desirous of vainglory***, because glory sometimes follows those who seek to avoid it, and if they are obliged to receive it, they should not love it.

Furthermore, spirit connotes vehemence: *who can bear the violence of one provoked?* (Prov 27:4). It also connotes wrath. And as to this he says, ***provoking one another***, namely, to quarrels and fights or other unlawful things: *not in contention and envy* (Rom 13:13).

Furthermore, it is a spirit of sadness, of which it is said in Proverbs: *a sorrowful spirit dries up the bones* (Prov 17:22). And concerning this he says, ***envying one another***: *envy is the rottenness of the bones*, because it alone feeds on the good (Prov 14:30).

Chapter 6

Lecture 1

⁶:¹Fratres, etsi praeoccupatus fuerit homo in aliquo delicto, vos, qui spirituales estis, hujusmodi instruite in spiritu lenitatis, considerans teipsum, ne et tu tenteris. [n. 342]

⁶:²Alter alterius onera portate, et sic adimplebitis legem Christi. [n. 346]

⁶:³Nam si quis existimat se aliquid esse, cum nihil sit, ipse se seducit. [n. 349]

⁶:⁴Opus autem suum probet unusquisque, et sic in semetipso tantum gloriam habebit, et non in altero. [n. 351]

⁶:⁵Unusquisque enim onus suum portabit. [n. 352]

⁶:¹Ἀδελφοί, ἐὰν καὶ προλημφθῇ ἄνθρωπος ἔν τινι παραπτώματι, ὑμεῖς οἱ πνευματικοὶ καταρτίζετε τὸν τοιοῦτον ἐν πνεύματι πραΰτητος, σκοπῶν σεαυτόν, μὴ καὶ σὺ πειρασθῇς.

⁶:²Ἀλλήλων τὰ βάρη βαστάζετε, καὶ οὕτως ἀναπληρώσετε τὸν νόμον τοῦ Χριστοῦ.

⁶:³εἰ γὰρ δοκεῖ τις εἶναί τι μηδὲν ὤν, φρεναπατᾷ ἑαυτόν·

⁶:⁴τὸ δὲ ἔργον ἑαυτοῦ δοκιμαζέτω ἕκαστος, καὶ τότε εἰς ἑαυτὸν μόνον τὸ καύχημα ἕξει καὶ οὐκ εἰς τὸν ἕτερον·

⁶:⁵ἕκαστος γὰρ τὸ ἴδιον φορτίον βαστάσει.

⁶:¹Brethren, even if a man be overtaken in some fault, you, who are spiritual, instruct such a one in the spirit of meekness, considering yourself, lest you also be tempted. [n. 342]

⁶:²Bear one another's burdens: and so you shall fulfill the law of Christ. [n. 346]

⁶:³For if any man think himself to be something, whereas he is nothing, he deceives himself. [n. 349]

⁶:⁴But let everyone prove his own work: and so he shall have glory in himself only and not in another. [n. 351]

⁶:⁵For everyone shall bear his own burden. [n. 352]

---

342. Postquam Apostolus reduxit Galatas ad statum veritatis quantum ad res divinas, hic consequenter reducit eos quantum ad res humanas, instruens eos qualiter se habeant ad homines. Et

primo qualiter se habeant ad rectos;

secundo, quomodo ad perversos, ibi *videte qualibus litteris*, et cetera.

Circa primum tria facit.

Primo docet qualiter superiores se habeant ad inferiores;

secundo qualiter aequales ad coaequales, ibi *alter alterius*, etc.;

tertio qualiter inferiores ad superiores, ibi *communicet autem is*, et cetera.

Circa primum duo facit.

Primo ponit admonitionem;

secundo assignat admonitionis rationem, ibi *considerans teipsum*, et cetera.

343. Quia ergo de peccatis multa dixerat, ne aliquis a peccato immunis in peccatores desaeviret, ideo admonitionem de mansuetudine et misericordia eis proponit, dicens *fratres, etsi praeoccupatus fuerit homo*, et cetera. Ubi tria ponit quae faciunt admonitionem. Primum est surreptio. Nam quando aliqui ex malitia peccant, minus digni sunt venia. Iob XXXIV, 27: *qui quasi de industria recesserunt*, et cetera. Sed quando aliquis

342. After leading the Galatians back to the state of truth as to divine things, the Apostle then leads them back as to things human, instructing them how to behave toward men.

First, how to act toward the upright;

second, toward those who are wicked, at *see what a letter I have written* (Gal 6:11).

With respect to the first, he does three things:

first, he teaches how superiors should act toward inferiors;

second, how equals toward equals, at *bear one another's burdens*;

third, how inferiors toward superiors, at *and let him who is instructed* (Gal 6:6).

Regarding the first he does two things:

first, he sets forth the admonition;

second, he assigns the reason for the admonition: *considering yourself, lest you also be tempted*.

343. Therefore, because he had said so much about sin, then, lest anyone free of sin be severe toward sinners, he gives them an admonition about meekness and mercy, saying: *brethren, even if a man be overtaken in some fault, you, who are spiritual, instruct such a one in the spirit of meekness*. Herein he lays down the three elements which form the admonition. The first consists in being come upon unawares. For when some sin out of malice, they are

praeoccupatur tentationibus et inducitur ad peccandum, facilius debet ei venia concedi, et ideo dicit **etsi praeoccupatus fuerit**, etc., id est imprudenter et ex surreptione lapsus, ut nequeat vitare.

Secundum est peccatorum paucitas. Nam aliqui ex consuetudine peccant. Os. IV, 2: *maledictum, et mendacium, et homicidium, et furtum, et adulterium inundaverunt, et sanguis sanguinem tetigit*, et cetera. Et contra tales severius est agendum. Et hoc excluditur, cum dicit **in aliquo**, quasi non usu quotidiano peccans.

Tertium est peccatorum qualitas. Nam quaedam peccata consistunt in transgressione, quaedam vero in omissione. Graviora autem sunt prima secundis: quia illa opponuntur praeceptis negativis, quae obligant semper et ad semper, haec vero opponuntur praeceptis affirmativis quae cum non obligent ad semper, non potest sciri determinate quando obligant. Unde dicitur in Ps. XVIII, 13: *delicta quis intelligit?* et cetera. Et quantum ad hoc dicit **delicto**. Vel, secundum Glossam, delictum est peccatum ex ignorantia.

344. His ergo praemissis, ad misericordiam eos qui corrigunt monet, et hi sunt spirituales, ad quos pertinet correctio. Unde dicit **vos qui spirituales estis, huiusmodi instruite**. I Cor. II, 15: *spiritualis iudicat omnia, et ipse a nemine iudicatur*, et cetera. Et huius ratio est, quia rectum iudicium habet de omnibus, quia circa unumquodque recte dispositus est, sicut qui sanum gustum habet, recte iudicat de sapore; solus autem spiritualis bene dispositus est circa agenda; et ideo ipse solus de eis bene iudicat.

Sed quia nomen spiritus rigorem quemdam et impulsum designat, secundum illud Is. XXV, v. 4: *spiritus robustorum quasi turbo impellens parietem*, etc., non tamen est credendum quod viri spirituales sint nimis rigidi in corrigendo. Nam hoc spiritus huius mundi facit, sed Spiritus Sanctus suavitatem quamdam et dulcorem efficit in homine. Sap. XII, v. 1: *o quam bonus et suavis est Spiritus tuus, Domine*, et cetera. Et ideo dicit **in spiritu lenitatis**. Ps. CXL, 5: *corripiet me iustus in misericordia*, et cetera. Contra quod dicitur de quibusdam Ez. XXXIV, 4: *cum austeritate imperabatis eis*, et cetera.

Dicit autem **instruite**, et non *corrigite*, quia loquitur de praeoccupatis delinquentibus, qui indigent instructione; vel quia omnis peccans est ignorans. Prov. XIV, 22: *errant qui operantur malum*.

345. Rationem autem admonitionis subdit, dicens **considerans teipsum**, etc., quasi dicat: ita fiat, ut dixi,

less worthy of forgiveness: *who as it were on purpose have revolted from him and would not understand all his ways* (Job 34:27). But when one is overtaken by temptation and lured into sin, pardon should be granted him more readily. That is why he says, **even if a man be overtaken in some fault**, i.e., fall through want of circumspection and because of trickery, so that he could not escape, **instruct such a one in the spirit of meekness**.

The second is infrequency of sin. For some sin as a matter of custom: *cursing and lying and killing and theft and adultery have overflowed and blood has touched blood* (Hos 4:2). Against such sinners more severe measures should be taken. And this is excluded when he says, **in some**, implying that he is speaking of those who do not sin as a daily practice.

The third is the quality of the sin. For some sins consist in commission and some in omission. And the first is more grave than the second, because the former are opposed to negative precepts which bind always and at every moment; whereas with the latter, being opposed to affirmative precepts, since they do not bind one at every moment, it cannot be known definitely when they do bind. Hence it is said in a psalm: *who can understand faults?* (Ps 19:12). And touching this he says, **in some fault**. Or, according to a Gloss, a fault is a sin committed through ignorance.

344. Having stated these things, he recommends that mercy be shown by those who correct others. These are spiritual men whose office is to correct. Hence he says, **you who are spiritual, instruct such a one in the spirit of meekness**: *the spiritual man judges all things, and he himself is judged of no man* (1 Cor 2:15). The reason for this is that he has a correct judgment of all things, being rightly disposed to each thing, as a person with a healthy taste is the best judge of flavor. Now the spiritual man alone is rightly disposed concerning moral actions. Therefore he alone judges well of them.

But although the name 'spirit' suggests unyielding energy, according to the saying of Isaiah: *for the spirit of the mighty is like a whirlwind beating against a wall* (Isa 25:4), it should not be supposed that spiritual men are over-strict in correcting. For the spirit of this world does that, but the Holy Spirit produces a certain gentleness and sweetness in a man: *O, how good and sweet is your Spirit, O Lord, in all things* (Wis 12:1). Hence he says, **in the spirit of meekness**: *the just man shall correct me in mercy and shall reprove me* (Ps 141:5). Contrariwise, it is said of some in Ezekiel: *you ruled over them with vigor and with a high hand* (Ezek 34:4).

Furthermore, he says, **instruct**, and not *correct*, because he is speaking of those who fall by being overtaken, and these need instruction; or because every sinner falls through some lack of knowledge: *they err that work evil* (Prov 14:22).

345. He adds a reason for the admonition, saying, **considering yourself, lest you also be tempted**. As if to say: you

should do as I say, because you, too, are weak. For as long as we are in this mortal life, we are prone to sin. But nothing so breaks a man from severity in correcting as fear of his own fall: *judge of the disposition of your neighbor by yourself* (Sir 31:18).

346. But how they ought to act towards equals he shows when he says, **bear one another's burdens**.

First, he sets down the admonition;

second, he assigns a reason for it, at **and so you shall fulfill the law**;

third, he removes an obstacle to the admonition, at **for if any man think himself**.

347. Here he admonishes them to support one another, saying, **bear one another's burdens**. And this is to be done in three ways. In one way by patiently enduring the bodily or spiritual defects of another: *we that are stronger ought to bear the infirmities of the weak* (Rom 15:1). In a second way by coming to one another's aid in their needs: *communicating to the necessities of the saints* (Rom 12:13). In a third way by making satisfaction through prayers and works for the punishment one has incurred: *a brother that is helped by his brother is like a strong city* (Prov 18:19).

348. Now the reason for this admonition is the fulfillment of the law of Christ. But this is charity: *the fulfillment of the law is love* (Rom 13:10). Hence he says: **and you shall fulfill the law of Christ**, i.e., charity.

There are three reasons why charity is specifically linked with the law of Christ. First, because by it the new law is distinguished from the old; for the former is a law of fear, but the latter of love. Hence Augustine says: *fear and love is the slight difference between the old law and the new*. Second, because Christ expressly promulgated his law in terms of charity: *by this shall all men know that you are my disciples, if you have love one for another* (John 13:35); again: *a new commandment I give unto you: that you love one another, as I have loved you*. Third, because Christ fulfilled it and left us an example how to fulfill it; for he bore our sins out of charity: *surely he has borne our infirmities* (Isa 53:4); *who himself bore our sins in his body upon the tree, that we, being dead to sins, should live to justice* (1 Pet 2:24); *he himself shall carry them that are with young* (Isa 40:11).

Thus, then, ought we to carry one another's burdens out of charity, that so we may fulfill the law of Christ.

349. The obstacle to fulfilling the above admonition is pride. And to exclude this he says, **for if any man think himself to be something, whereas he is nothing, he deceives himself**.

First, he censures such pride;

second, he points out how to avoid it, at **but let everyone prove his own work**;

third, he gives a reason for avoiding it, at **for everyone shall bear**.

350. Dicit ergo: *facite ut dixi*. Sed contingit aliquem onus alterius non portare, quia praefert se aliis. Unde dicebat ille Lc. c. XVIII, 11: *non sum sicut caeteri hominum*, et cetera. Et ideo dicit **nam si quis existimat se aliquid esse**, id est in mente sua superbe iudicat se magnum esse in comparatione peccantis, **cum nihil sit**, ex se, quia quidquid sumus hoc est ex gratia Dei, secundum illud Apostoli I Cor. XV, 10: *gratia Dei sum id quod sum*. Qui, inquam, tale aliquid facit, **ipse se seducit**, id est a veritate se dividit. Is. XL, 17: *omnes gentes quasi non sint*, et cetera. Lc. XVII, 10: *cum feceritis omnia quae praecepta sunt vobis, dicite: servi inutiles sumus*, et cetera.

351. Remedium autem vitandi, est propriorum defectuum consideratio. Nam ex hoc quod aliquis alienos et non suos defectus considerat, videtur sibi aliquid esse in comparatione ad alios, in quibus defectus intuetur, et suos non considerans, superbit. Et ideo dicit **opus autem**, scilicet interius et exterius, **suum**, id est proprium, **probet**, id est diligenter examinet, **unusquisque**. I Cor. XI, v. 28: *probet seipsum homo*, et cetera. **Et sic in seipso**, id est in propria conscientia, **gloriam habebit**, id est gloriabitur et gaudebit. II Cor. I, 12: *gloria nostra haec est, testimonium conscientiae nostrae*. **Et non in altero**, id est non in laude alterius.

Vel sic: **in semetipso**, id est per ea quae sui ipsius sunt, **gloriam habebit**, id est gloriabitur in consideratione sui, **et non in altero**, id est non consideratione alterius. II Cor. XII, 9: *libenter gloriabor in infirmitatibus meis*, et cetera.

Vel **in semetipso**, id est in Deo qui in eo habitat, gloriabitur, id est eius erit gloria, **et non in altero** quam in Deo. II Cor. X, 17: *qui gloriatur, in Domino glorietur*.

352. Ratio vitandi superbiam est praemium vel poena unicuique pro merito vel demerito reddenda. Unde dicit **unusquisque enim onus suum portabit**. Quod videtur contrarium ei quod dixerat **alter alterius onera portate**.

Sed sciendum est quod ibi loquitur de onere sustinendae infirmitatis, quod debemus mutuo portare; hic loquitur de onere reddendae rationis, quod quilibet pro se portabit, sive sit onus praemii, sive poenae. Nam onus aliquando quidem pondus poenae, aliquando praemii significat. II Cor. IV, 17: *aeternum gloriae pondus operatur*, et cetera. Is. III, 10-11. *dicite iusto, quoniam bene, quoniam fructum adinventionum suarum comedet, vae impio in malum*, et cetera.

Si autem dicantur aliqui rationem reddere pro aliis, puta praelati pro subditis, secundum illud Ez. III, 18:

350. He says therefore: *do as I say*. But it sometimes happens that one does not carry another's burdens, because he prefers himself to others. Hence such a one said in Luke: *I am not as the rest of men, extortioners, unjust, adulterers* (Luke 18:11). Therefore he says, **for if any man think himself to be something**, i.e., through pride, judge in his own mind that he is greater in comparison to a sinner, **whereas he is nothing of himself**, because whatever we are is from the grace of God, according to the saying of the Apostle: *but by the grace of God I am what I am* (1 Cor 15:10), anyone, I say, who acts thus **deceives himself**, i.e., cuts himself off from the truth: *all nations are before him as if they had no being at all* (Isa 40:17); *when you have done all these things that are commanded you, say: we are unprofitable servants: we have done what we ought to do* (Luke 17:10).

351. Now the way to avoid such a failing is to consider one's own defects, for it is because one considers the defects of others and not his own that he seems to himself to be something in comparison to others in whom he observes defects; and not considering his own, he has a feeling of pride. Hence he says, **but let everyone prove**, i.e., diligently examine, **his own work**, both inward and outward: *let a man prove himself* (1 Cor 11:28), **and so in himself**, i.e., in his own conscience, **he shall have glory**, i.e., shall glory and rejoice—*for our glory is this, the testimony of our conscience* (2 Cor 1:12)—**and not in another**, i.e., not in being praised by someone else.

Or thus: **in himself**, i.e., in things that are his own, **he shall have glory**, i.e., he will glory by considering himself; **and not in another**, i.e., not by considering others: *gladly, therefore, will I glory in my infirmities, that the power of Christ may dwell in me* (2 Cor 12:9).

Or, **in himself**, i.e., in God who dwells in him, **he shall have glory**, i.e., the glory will be his; **and not in another** save in God: *he that glories, let him glory in the Lord* (2 Cor 10:17).

352. The reason for avoiding pride is the reward or punishment that will be rendered to each one according to his merits or demerits. Hence he says, **for everyone shall bear his own burden**. But this seems contrary to what he had said earlier, namely, **bear one another's burdens**.

But it should be known that he was speaking there of the burden of supporting weakness, a burden which we ought to carry one for another; but now he is speaking of the burden of rendering an account. This, everyone will carry for himself, whether it be a burden of reward or of punishment. For 'burden' signifies the weight sometimes of punishment, sometimes of reward: *working for us an eternal weight of glory* (2 Cor 4:17); *say to the just man that it is well, for he shall eat the fruit of his doings. Woe to the wicked unto evil: for the reward of his hands shall be given him* (Isa 3:10).

But if some are said to render an account for others, as prelates for subjects, according to Ezekiel: *I will require his*

sanguinem eius de manu tua requiram, etc., et Hebr. ult.: *obedite praepositis vestris, ipsi enim pervigilant quasi rationem reddituri pro animabus vestris*, non est contrarium dicto Apostoli: quia non puniuntur pro peccatis subditorum, sed pro propriis, quae in custodia subditorum commiserunt.

Est ergo vitanda superbia et peccatum, quia unusquisque onus suum, id est mensuram gratiae suae offert Deo in die iudicii, tamquam manipulos bonorum operum. Ps. CXXV, 6: *venientes autem venient cum exultatione*. Et hoc quantum ad bonos. Vel **onus suum portabit**, id est poenam pro proprio peccato.

blood at your hand (Ezek 3:20); and Hebrews: *obey your prelates . . . for they watch, being ones who will render an account of your souls* (Heb 13:17), this is not contrary to the words of the Apostle, because they are not punished for the sins of their subjects but for their own, which they committed in ruling them.

Therefore pride and sin are to be avoided, because everyone will present to God on the day of judgment his own burden, i.e., the measure of his own grace as sheaves of good works: *but coming they shall come with joyfulness, carrying their sheaves* (Ps 126:6), and this refers to those who are good. Or: **shall bear his own burden**, i.e., each the punishment for his own sin.

Lecture 2

6:6 Communicet autem is qui catechizatur verbo, ei qui se catechizat, in omnibus bonis. [n. 353]

6:7 Nolite errare: Deus non irridetur. Quae enim seminaverit homo, haec et metet. [n. 355]

6:8 Quoniam qui seminat in carne sua, de carne et metet corruptionem: qui autem seminat in Spiritu, de Spiritu metet vitam aeternam. [n. 357]

6:9 Bonum autem facientes, non deficiamus: tempore enim suo metemus non deficientes. [n. 361]

6:10 Ergo dum tempus habemus, operemur bonum ad omnes, maxime autem ad domesticos fidei. [n. 362]

6:6Κοινωνείτω δὲ ὁ κατηχούμενος τὸν λόγον τῷ κατηχοῦντι ἐν πᾶσιν ἀγαθοῖς.

6:7Μὴ πλανᾶσθε, θεὸς οὐ μυκτηρίζεται· ὃ γὰρ ἐὰν σπείρῃ ἄνθρωπος, τοῦτο καὶ θερίσει·

6:8ὅτι ὁ σπείρων εἰς τὴν σάρκα ἑαυτοῦ ἐκ τῆς σαρκὸς θερίσει φθοράν, ὁ δὲ σπείρων εἰς τὸ πνεῦμα ἐκ τοῦ πνεύματος θερίσει ζωὴν αἰώνιον.

6:9τὸ δὲ καλὸν ποιοῦντες μὴ ἐγκακῶμεν, καιρῷ γὰρ ἰδίῳ θερίσομεν μὴ ἐκλυόμενοι.

6:10ἄρα οὖν ὡς καιρὸν ἔχομεν, ἐργαζώμεθα τὸ ἀγαθὸν πρὸς πάντας, μάλιστα δὲ πρὸς τοὺς οἰκείους τῆς πίστεως.

6:6 And let him who is instructed in the word communicate to him who instructs him, in all good things. [n. 353]

6:7 Do not be deceived: God is not mocked. For what things a man shall sow, those also shall he reap. [n. 355]

6:8 For he who sows in his flesh, of the flesh also shall reap corruption. But he who sows in the Spirit, of the Spirit shall reap life everlasting. [n. 357]

6:9 And in doing good, let us not fail. For in due time we shall reap, not failing. [n. 361]

6:10 Therefore, while we have time, let us work good to all men, but especially to those who are of the household of the faith. [n. 362]

---

353. Postquam Apostolus ostendit qualiter superiores se habeant ad inferiores, et aequales aequalibus, hic consequenter ostendit qualiter inferiores se habeant ad superiores, dicens inferiores debere superioribus ministrare et obsequi. Et

circa hoc tria facit.

Primo monet ut ministrent prompte;

secundo ut ministrent perseveranter, ibi ***bonum autem facientes, non deficiamus***, etc.;

tertio, ut ministrent communiter, ibi ***ergo dum tempus habemus***, et cetera.

Circa primum duo facit.

Primo ponit monitionem ministerii;

secundo excusationem excludit, ibi ***nolite errare***, et cetera.

354. Dicit ergo: dictum est supra, quomodo superiores se debeant habere ad inferiores, scilicet leniter corripiendo et instruendo, nunc autem restat videre qualiter inferior superiori obsequatur, et ideo dicit ***communicet autem is, qui catechizatur***, id est docetur verbo Dei, ***ei qui se catechizat***, id est qui eum docet; communicet, inquam, ***in omnibus bonis***.

Sed notandum est quod discipulus potest dupliciter communicare se docenti. Primo ut accipiat bona doctoris, et sic dicitur ***communicet is qui catechizatur***, id est commune sibi faciat quod est docentis, eum imitando. I Cor. XI, 1: *imitatores mei estote*, et cetera. Sed quia contingit doctores aliquando minus bona facere, ideo

353. After showing how those who are greater should act toward those below them, and how equals should act toward equals, the Apostle then shows here how those who are lesser should serve and revere those who are over them.

About this he does three things:

first, he advises that they serve readily;

second, that they serve perseveringly, at ***and in doing good, let us not fail***;

third, that they serve all, ***therefore, while we have time***.

Regarding the first he does two things:

first, he lays down the admonition to serve;

second, he forestalls an excuse, at ***be not deceived***.

354. He says therefore: we have indicated above how those who are greater should act toward those who are below them, namely, by correcting them in a gentle manner and by instructing. Now, however, there remains to see how the lesser should accommodate themselves to those who are higher. Therefore he says, ***let him who is instructed in the word***, i.e., taught the word of God, ***communicate to him who instructs him***, i.e., who teaches him; let him, I say, communicate to him ***in all good things***.

But it should be noted that a disciple can communicate in two ways with his teacher. First, so as to receive good things from the teacher; and so it is said, ***let him who is instructed in the word communicate***, i.e., make common to himself what belonged to the teacher, by imitating him: *be imitators of me, as I also am of Christ* (1 Cor 11:1). But

non sunt in hoc imitandi, et ideo subdit *in omnibus bonis*. Matth. c. XXIII, 3: *quaecumque dixerint vobis, servate et facite: secundum opera eorum nolite facere*.

Secundo ut communicet bona sua docenti. Hoc enim a Domino praecipitur I Cor. IX, v. 14, ubi dicitur: *qui Evangelio serviunt, de Evangelio vivant*. Unde Matth. X, 10: *dignus est operarius cibo suo*. Et Lc. X, 7: *dignus est operarius mercede sua*. Et Apostolus dicit I Cor. IX, 11: *si vobis spiritualia seminamus*, et cetera. Et ideo hic dicit *communicet autem is*, etc., id est doctus doctori *in omnibus bonis* quae habet; nam etiam temporalia bona quaedam dicuntur. Is. I, 19: *si volueritis et audieritis me, bona terrae comedetis*. Matth. c. VII, 11: *si vos cum sitis mali, nostis bona dare*, et cetera.

Dicit autem, *in omnibus*, quia non solum communicare debet indigenti, sed et sententiam et consilium, potentiam et quidquid habet, generaliter debet proximo communicare. I Petr. IV, 10: *unusquisque sicut accepit gratiam, in alterutrum illam administrantes*, et cetera. De ista communicatione dicitur Rom. XII, v. 13: *necessitatibus sanctorum communicantes*; Eccli. XIV, 15: *in divisione sortis da et accipe*.

355. Consequenter cum dicit *nolite errare*, etc., excusationem excludit, et

primo excludit eam;

secundo rationem exclusionis assignat, ibi *quae enim seminaverit homo*, et cetera.

356. Dicit ergo *nolite errare, Deus non irridetur*. Quod quidem dupliciter intelligi potest secundum duas praemissas expositiones.

Secundum primam quidem sic: tu dicis quod debemus imitari doctores etiam in bonis, sed non possum eos imitari nisi in his quae faciunt: nihil autem video in ipsis nisi malum; ergo debeo eos imitari in malo. Sed hoc excludit, dicens *nolite errare, Deus non irridetur*. Error est hoc dicere. Nam mala praelatorum non excusant nos. Non enim sunt subditis in exemplum, nisi in his quibus imitantur Christum, qui est pastor absque peccato; unde et signanter dicit Io. c. X, 11: *ego sum Pastor Bonus*, et cetera. Et Apostolus I Cor. IV, 16 et XI, 1 dicit: *imitatores mei estote, sicut et ego Christi*; quasi dicat: in his me imitamini, in quibus ego imitor Christum. Etsi per mala praelatorum excusatis vos apud homines, tamen *Deus non irridetur*, id est, non potest falli. Iob XIII, 9: *aut decipietur ut homo fraudulentiis vestris?* Unde dicitur Prov. III, 34: *delusores ipse deludet*.

because teachers might at times not do what is good, they are not to be imitated in this Hence he adds, *in all good things*: *whatsoever they shall say to you, observe and do: but according to their works, do not do* (Matt 23:3).

Second, that he communicate his own goods to the teacher. For this is commanded by the Lord: *they who preach the Gospel should live by the Gospel* (1 Cor 9:14); *the workman is worthy of his meat* (Matt 10:10); *the laborer is worthy of his hire* (Luke 10:7); and the Apostle says, *if we have sown unto you spiritual things, is it a great matter if we reap your carnal things?* (1 Cor 9:11). And therefore he says here, *let him who is instructed in the word communicate to him who instructs*, i.e., the one taught should communicate to the teacher, *in all good things* that he has; for even temporal things are called goods: *if you be willing and will hearken to me, you shall eat the good things of the land* (Isa 1:19); *if you then, being evil, know how to give good gifts to your children: how much more will your Father who is in heaven give good things to them that ask him?* (Matt 7:11).

But he says, *in all good things*, because one should not communicate solely to those who are in dire need; but whatever one has he ought universally to communicate to his neighbor, including knowledge and advice and influence: *as every man has received grace, administering the same one to another* (1 Pet 4:10). Of this sharing it is said in Romans: *communicating to the necessities of the saints* (Rom 12:13); *in dividing by lot, give and take* (Sir 14:15).

355. Then when he says, *do not be deceived: God is not mocked*, he forestalls an excuse.

First, he forestalls it;

second, he gives a reason for this, at *for what things a man shall sow*.

356. He says, therefore: *do not be deceived: God is not mocked*. his can be taken in two ways, according to the two explanations given above.

According to the first, this way: you say that we ought to imitate our teachers even in good things, but I cannot imitate them save in the things they do; and the only thing I observe in them is evil. Therefore, I ought to imitate them in evil. But he dismisses this, when he says, *do not be deceived: God is not mocked*. As if to say: it is erroneous to say this, for the evils of the prelates do not excuse us, because they are an example to their subjects only in those matters in which they imitate Christ, who is the shepherd without sin. Hence he expressly says in John: *I am the Good Shepherd* (John 10:11); and the Apostle says in 1 Corinthians: *be imitators of me, as I also am of Christ* (1 Cor 4:16; 11:1). As if to say: imitate me in those things in which I imitate Christ. And although you excuse yourself before men because of the evil acts of prelates, yet *God is not mocked*, i.e., cannot be deceived: *shall he be deceived as a man, with your deceitful dealings?* (Job 13:9) Hence it is said in Proverbs: *he shall scorn the scorners* (Prov 3:34).

Secundum autem secundam expositionem sic introducitur. Possent autem dicere: pauperes sumus, nihil habemus quod communicare possimus. Sed hoc excludit, dicens **nolite errare**, id est nemo excusatum vane se existimet paupertatem praetendendo, **Deus non irridetur**, id est non potest falli, scit enim corda nostra et non ignorat facultates. Excusatio verisimilis hominem potest fallere et placare, Deum non potest fallere.

357. Rationem autem huius assignat, dicens **quae enim seminaverit homo**, et cetera. Et

primo in generali,

secundo in speciali, ibi **quoniam qui seminat**, et cetera.

358. Dicit ergo, secundum primam expositionem: vere erratis, hoc credentes, quia Deus reddet singulis pro meritis propriis. Nam **quae seminaverit homo, haec et metet**, id est secundum opera sua bona vel mala, parva vel magna, praemiabitur vel punietur.

Secundum autem secundam expositionem: **quae seminaverit homo**, id est secundum beneficia sua parva vel magna, et quantum ad qualitatem operum, et quantum ad quantitatem beneficiorum praemiabitur. II Cor. IX, 6: *qui parce seminat, parce et metet*, et cetera.

359. Rationem autem specialiter assignat, dicens **quoniam qui seminat in carne sua**, et cetera. Quae quidem ratio habet duas partes secundum duas seminationes carnis et Spiritus. Primo ergo agit de seminatione carnis.

Ubi dicendum est, quid sit seminare in carne; secundo quid est de carne metere corruptionem.

Seminare quidem in carne, est operari pro corpore vel pro carne; sicut si dicam: ego multum expendi in isto homine, id est, multa feci pro eo. Ille ergo in carne seminat, qui ea quae facit, etiam si quae bona videantur, facit in fomentum et utilitatem carnis.

De carne autem metere corruptionem, dicit et infert, quia semen fructificat ut plurimum secundum conditionem terrae. Unde videmus quod in aliquibus terris semen frumenti degenerat in siliginem, vel in aliquod aliud. Conditio autem carnis est, ut sit corruptibilis, et ideo **qui in carne seminat**, id est studium suum ponit et opera, oportet quod ipsa opera corrumpantur et pereant. Eccli. XIV, 20: *omne opus corruptibile, in fine perdetur*. Rom. VIII, 13: *si secundum carnem vixeritis, moriemini*.

360. Secundo agit de seminatione spiritus, dicens: **qui autem seminat in spiritu**, id est ordinat studium suum ad servitutem Spiritus, ex fide et caritate serviendo iustitiae, **metet** quidem **de spiritu** secundum conditionem eius. Conditio autem spiritus est quod sit

But according to the second explanation it is understood in the following manner. They could say: we are poor and have nothing to communicate. But he rejects this, saying, **do not be deceived**, i.e., think not to excuse yourself in vain, by pretending poverty; **God is not mocked**, i.e., cannot be deceived, for he knows our hearts and is not unaware of our possessions. A likely excuse may deceive a man and satisfy him; but it cannot deceive God.

357. He assigns the reason for this, saying, **for what things a man shall sow, those also shall he reap**.

First, in a general way;

second, in a specific way, at **for he who sows**.

358. He says therefore with respect to the first explanation: surely you err in believing this, because God will render to each one according to his own merits: **for what things a man shall sow, those also shall he reap**, i.e., he will be rewarded or punished according to his works, be they good or evil, great or small.

But according to the second explanation: **what things a man shall sow, those also shall he reap**; i.e., he will be rewarded according to his good deeds, great or small, both as to the quality of the works and the quantity of the good deeds: *he that sows sparingly, shall also reap sparingly; and he who sows in blessings, shall also reap blessings* (2 Cor 9:6).

359. Then he assigns a specific reason, saying, **for he who sows in his flesh, of the flesh also shall reap corruption**. Now this reason has two parts, according to the two sowings: namely, in the flesh and in the Spirit. First therefore, he treats of the sowing in the flesh,

where we must first of all see what it is to sow in the flesh; second, what it is to reap corruption of the flesh.

To sow in the flesh is to work for the body and for the flesh. As though I were to say: I have spent much on that man, i.e., I have done many things for him. Hence he sows in the flesh who in all that he does, even in things that seem good, does them to favor and benefit the flesh.

But with respect to reaping corruption of the flesh, he says and infers, that because seed fructifies for the most part according to the condition of the land, we see that on some lands wheat seeds degenerate into siligo or something else. Now the condition of the flesh is that it is corruptible; hence **he who sows in his flesh**, i.e., directs his works and interest to the flesh, must expect that those works corrupt and perish: *every work that is corruptible shall fail in the end* (Sir 14:20); *for if you live according to the flesh, you shall die* (Rom 8:13).

360. Second, he treats of the sowing in the spirit, saying, **but he who sows in the spirit**, i.e., directs his interest to the service of the Spirit by serving justice through faith and charity, **shall reap of the spirit** according to its condition. Now the condition of the spirit is that it is the principle of

life: *it is the spirit that gives life* (John 6:64), and not just any life, but eternal life; since the spirit is immortal. Hence, *of the spirit he shall reap life everlasting: to him that sows justice there is a faithful reward* (Prov 11:18), because it never withers.

But note that when he treats of the sowing in the flesh, he says, *in his flesh*, because the flesh is ours, as part of our nature; but when he speaks of the seed of the spirit, he does not say *his own*, because the spirit in us is not from ourselves but from God.

361. Then when he says, **and in doing good, let us not fail**, he counsels perseverance in ministering, because we should do good not only for a time but always. This can be referred to those already mentioned, namely, to superiors, to equals, and to those who are lower. As if to say: whatever our station, whether prelates towards subjects, or equals toward equals, or subjects toward prelates, **in doing good, let us not fail**, i.e., in doing good works; because in reaping we shall not fail: *whatsoever your hand is able to do, do it earnestly* (Sir 9:10); *be steadfast and unmovable* (1 Cor 15:58).

And it is important that we do not fail; because we hope for an eternal and unfailing reward. Hence he adds: **for in due time we shall reap, not failing**. Therefore Augustine says: *if a man puts no limit on his works, God will put none on his reward*.

But note that he says, **in due time**: because a farmer does not immediately reap the fruit of what he sows, but at the suitable time: *behold the husbandman waits for the precious fruit of the earth; patiently bearing till he receive the early and latter rain* (Jas 5:7). Of this harvest it is said: *who sows in blessings shall also reap of the blessings, eternal life* (2 Cor 9:6).

362. Then when he says, **while we have time, let us work good to all men**, he advises everyone to minister, saying: since we shall reap, not failing, then **while we have time**, i.e., in this life, which is the time for sowing: *I must work the works of him that sent me, while it is day: the night comes, when no man can work* (John 9:4); *whatsoever your hand is able to do, do it earnestly; for neither work nor reason nor wisdom nor knowledge shall be in hell whither you are hastening* (Sir 9:10).

As long, I say, as we have time, **let us work good**, and this **to all men** who are bound to us through a divine likeness, inasmuch as all of us have been made to the image of God.

363. But this seems to be contrary to Sirach: *give to the good and do not receive the sinner* (Sir 12:5). Therefore we are not obliged to do good to everyone.

I answer that in the sinner are two things: namely, his nature and his guilt. Now the nature in everyone, including an enemy, must be loved and upheld: *love your enemies*

diligite inimicos vestros, et cetera. Culpa vero in eo est expellenda. Sic ergo dictum est: *da iusto, et non recipias peccatorem*, ut scilicet peccatori non ideo benefacias, quia peccator est, sed quia homo. Unde Augustinus: *non sis ad iudicandum remissus, nec ad subveniendum inhumanus*. Persequamur ergo in malis propriam iniquitatem, misereamur in eisdem communem conditionem.

364. Sed quia non possumus omnibus benefacere, ordinem benefaciendi subdit **maxime autem ad domesticos fidei**, qui scilicet non solum natura nobis sunt similes, sed etiam sunt uniti fide et gratia. Eph. II, 19: *non estis hospites et advenae, sed estis cives sanctorum, et domestici Dei*, et cetera. Ergo omnibus impendenda est misericordia, sed praeponendi sunt iusti, qui sunt ex fide: quia I Tim. V, 8 dicitur: *qui suorum et maxime domesticorum curam non habet, fidem negavit, et est infideli deterior*.

Sed dubitatur hic, utrum liceat plus unum diligere, quam alium.

Ad quod sciendum, quod amor potest dici maior vel minor dupliciter. Uno modo ex obiecto; alio modo ex intensione actus. Amare enim aliquem, est velle ei bonum. Potest ergo aliquis alium magis alio diligere, aut quia vult ei maius bonum, quod est obiectum dilectionis, aut quia magis vult ei bonum, id est ex intensiori dilectione.

Quantum ergo ad primum, omnes aequaliter debemus diligere, quia omnibus debemus velle bonum vitae aeternae. Sed quantum ad secundum, non oportet quod omnes aequaliter diligamus: quia cum intensio actus sequatur principium actionis, dilectionis autem principium sit unio et similitudo, illos intensius et magis debemus diligere, qui sunt nobis magis similes et uniti.

(Matt 5:44). But the guilt in them is to be shunned. Therefore, when it is said, *give to the just and do not receive the sinner*, the meaning is that you ought not to do good to the sinner precisely as he is a sinner, but because he is a human being. Hence Augustine says: *do not be remiss in judging, or inhuman in helping*. Therefore, in evil men let us attack their sin, but show mercy to our common condition.

364. But because we cannot do good to everyone, he presents the order in which it is to be done, when he adds: **but especially to those who are of the household of the faith**, who, namely, are not only akin to us in nature but united by faith and grace: *you are no more strangers and foreigners: but you are fellow citizens of the saints and the domestics of God* (Eph 2:19). Therefore mercy must be extended to everyone but preferably to the just who share in the faith, because it is said: *but if any man does not have care of his own and especially those of his house, he has denied the faith and is worse than an infidel* (1 Tim 5:8).

But here it might be asked whether it is lawful to love one more than another.

To answer this, it should be noted that love can be called greater or less in two ways. In one way, from the standpoint of the object; in another, from the intensity of the act. For to love someone is to will good to him. Accordingly, one can love one person more than another, either because he wills him a greater good, which is the object of love, or because he more intensely wills him a good, i.e., with a more intense love.

Therefore, with respect to the first, we ought to love everyone equally, because we ought to wish the good of eternal life to everyone; but with respect to the second, it is not necessary that we love all equally, because since the intensity of an act results from the principle of the action, and the principle of the action is union and similarity, we ought to love in a higher degree and more intensely those who are more like us and more closely united to us.

Lecture 3

6:11Videte qualibus litteris scripsi vobis mea manu. [n. 365]

6:12Quicumque enim volunt placere in carne, hi cogunt vos circumcidi, tantum ut crucis Christi persecutionem non patiantur. [n. 367]

6:13Neque enim qui circumciduntur, legem custodiunt: sed volunt vos circumcidi, ut in carne vestra glorientur. [n. 369]

6:11Ἴδετε πηλίκοις ὑμῖν γράμμασιν ἔγραψα τῇ ἐμῇ χειρί.

6:12ὅσοι θέλουσιν εὐπροσωπῆσαι ἐν σαρκί, οὗτοι ἀναγκάζουσιν ὑμᾶς περιτέμνεσθαι, μόνον ἵνα τῷ σταυρῷ τοῦ Χριστοῦ μὴ διώκωνται·

6:13οὐδὲ γὰρ οἱ περιτεμνόμενοι αὐτοὶ νόμον φυλάσσουσιν, ἀλλὰ θέλουσιν ὑμᾶς περιτέμνεσθαι ἵνα ἐν τῇ ὑμετέρᾳ σαρκὶ καυχήσωνται.

6:11See what a letter I have written to you with my own hand. [n. 365]

6:12For those who desire to please in the flesh constrain you to be circumcised, only that they may not suffer the persecution of the cross of Christ. [n. 367]

6:13For neither they themselves who are circumcised keep the law: but they will have you be circumcised, that they may glory in your flesh. [n. 369]

---

365. Postquam Apostolus monuit Galatas qualiter se habeant ad homines rectos et iustos, hic docet quomodo se habeant ad haereticos et perversos. Et

primo insinuat modum scribendi monitionem;

secundo ipsam monitionem subiungit, ibi *quicumque enim*, et cetera.

366. Circa primum sciendum quod consuetudo erat apud haereticos depravandi et falsificandi Scripturas canonicas, nec non et permiscendi aliqua eorum quae haeresim sapiant; propter hoc consuetudo fuit ab Apostolo servata, quod quando aliqua contra eos scribebat, in fine litterae aliqua scriberet, ut depravari non posset, et ita innotesceret eis de eius conscientia processisse, sicut I Cor. c. ult. dicit: *salutatio mea manu Pauli*. Totam enim epistolam per alium, eo dictante, scribi faciebat, et postea in fine aliquid propria manu addebat. Et secundum hunc modum ea quae sequuntur, ab isto loco scripsit Paulus manu propria. Unde dicit *videte qualibus litteris scripsi vobis manu propria*, ut scilicet praedicta firmius teneatis, ut scientes a me hanc epistolam missam magis obediatis.

Sic ergo praelati debent propria manu scribere, ut quod docent verbo et scripto, ostendant exemplo. Ideo dicitur Is. XLIX, 16: *in manibus*, id est in operibus meis, *descripsi te*, et cetera. Ex. XXXII, 15 dicitur de Moyse, quod descendit portans duas tabulas lapideas scriptas digito Dei.

367. Monitionem autem subiungit, dicens *quicumque enim placere volunt*, et cetera. Et

primo aperit seducentium intentionem;

secundo ostendit suam intentionem eis esse contrariam, ibi *mihi autem absit gloriari*, etc.;

365. After admonishing the Galatians how to behave towards men who are upright and just, the Apostle here teaches them how to act toward heretics and the perverse.

First, he insinuates the way he is writing the admonition;

second, he sets forth the admonition, at *for those who*.

366. As to the first, it should be noted that heretics were wont to distort and falsify the canonical Scriptures and append things that savored of heresy. Because of this, whenever the Apostle wrote anything against them, he followed the practice of writing something at the end of the epistle, so that it could not be distorted. In this way it could be known that it came from him with full knowledge of its contents. Thus in 1 Corinthians he says: *the salutation of me, Paul, with my own hand* (1 Cor 16:21). For he allowed the entire epistle to be written by someone else at his dictation; then, at the end, he added something in his own hand. According to this procedure, then, whatever followed from that place on, Paul wrote in his own hand. Hence he says; *see what a letter I have written to you with my own hand*; to the end, namely, that you might firmly hold to the foregoing, and that knowing this epistle is sent by me, you might obey better.

In this way, then, prelates ought to write in their own hand, so that what they teach by word and script, they may show by example. Hence it is said in Isaiah: *I have graven you in my hands*, i.e., works (Isa 49:16); and it is said of Moses that he descended carrying two stone tablets written by the finger of God (Exod 32:15).

367. He then follows with the admonition, saying, *for those who desire to please in the flesh constrain you to be circumcised*.

First, he exposes the intention of the seducers;

second, he shows that his intention is contrary to theirs, at *but God forbid that I should glory* (Gal 6:14);

third, he adds his warning to those who are subject to him, at **and whoever shall follow this rule** (Gal 6:16).

Regarding the first, he does two things:

first, he discloses the evil intention of the seducers;

second, he proves what he says, at **for neither they themselves**.

368. Concerning the first, he lays down one fact and two intentions that are mutually related. The fact concerns those who urged circumcision, from which they intended two things, one for the sake of the other; namely, that they might thereby please the Jews for having introduced the observances of the law in the Church of the gentiles. And this is what he says: *those who desire to please*, namely, the unbelieving Jews, **they constrain you to be circumcised** not by absolute force, but, as it were, by placing a condition, saying: *unless you are circumcised after the manner of Moses, you cannot be saved* (Acts 15:1).

They further intended to derive some security from this. For the Jews persecuted the disciples of Christ, because of the preaching of the cross: *but we preach Christ crucified, unto the Jews, indeed, a stumbling-block, and unto the gentiles, foolishness* (1 Cor 1:23). And this because through the preaching of the cross the works of the law were made void. For if the apostles had preached, along with the cross of Christ, that the legal ceremonies were to be observed, the Jews would not have persecuted the apostles. Hence he said: *and I, brethren, if I yet preach circumcision, why do I yet suffer persecution?* (Gal 5:11). Therefore, in order to escape persecution from the Jews, some urged circumcision. So he says: and they do this for the **only** reason **that they may not suffer the persecution of the cross of Christ**, a persecution which is inflicted because of the cross of Christ.

Or they did this to escape the persecution not only of the Jews but of the gentile unbelievers. For the Roman emperors, Gaius Caesar and Octavius Augustus, promulgated laws that wherever there were Jews, they might observe their own rite and ceremonies. Consequently, anyone who believed in Christ and was not circumcised was subject to persecution from the gentiles and Jews. Therefore, in order that they might not be troubled because of their faith in Christ and that they might live in peace, they constrained them to be circumcised, as is mentioned in a Gloss.

369. But because the false brethren might say that they urged circumcision not for that reason, but solely because of their zeal for the law, then excluding this, he proves his proposition thus, when he says: *for neither they themselves who are circumcised keep the law*.

For it is obvious that if through zeal for the law they urged certain ones to observe the law, they should also command the law to be fulfilled in other matters. But neither those who are circumcised nor the false brethren keep the law in other matters, namely, in moral matters, which are more important in the law, and in other observances:

legis circumcisionem inducunt. Rom. II, 25: *circumcisio quidem prodest, si legem observes*. **Sed** ideo **volunt vos circumcidi, ut in carne vestra**, id est in carnali vestra circumcisione, **glorientur**, apud Iudaeos, eo quod tam multos proselytos faciant. Matth. c. XXIII, 15: *vae vobis, scribae et Pharisaei, qui circuitis mare et aridam, ut faciatis unum proselytum*, et cetera.

none of you keeps the law (John 7:19). Therefore it was not from zeal for the law that they urged circumcision: *circumcision profits, indeed, if you keep law* (Rom 2:25). **But** the reason why **they will have you be circumcised** is **that in your flesh**, i.e., in your fleshly circumcision, **they may glory** among the Jews for making so many proselytes: *woe to you, scribes and Pharisees, hypocrites; because you go round about the sea and the land to make one proselyte; and when he is made, you make him the child of hell twofold more than yourselves* (Matt 23:15).

Lecture 4

⁶:¹⁴Mihi autem absit gloriari, nisi in cruce Domini nostri Jesu Christi: per quem mihi mundus crucifixus est, et ego mundo. [n. 370]

⁶:¹⁴ἐμοὶ δὲ μὴ γένοιτο καυχᾶσθαι εἰ μὴ ἐν τῷ σταυρῷ τοῦ κυρίου ἡμῶν Ἰησοῦ Χριστοῦ, δι' οὗ ἐμοὶ κόσμος ἐσταύρωται κἀγὼ κόσμῳ.

⁶:¹⁴But God forbid that I should glory, save in the cross of our Lord Jesus Christ, by whom the world is crucified to me, and I to the world. [n. 370]

⁶:¹⁵In Christo enim Jesu neque circumcisio aliquid valet, neque praeputium, sed nova creatura. [n. 374]

⁶:¹⁵οὔτε γὰρ περιτομή τί ἐστιν οὔτε ἀκροβυστία, ἀλλὰ καινὴ κτίσις.

⁶:¹⁵For in Christ Jesus neither circumcision nor uncircumcision avails anything, but a new creature. [n. 374]

370. Postquam Apostolus exposuit pravam seducentium intentionem, hic insinuat suam. Et

primo ponit suam intentionem;

secundo ostendit intentionis huius signum, ibi *per quem mihi mundus*, etc.;

tertio rationem intentionis assignat, ibi *in Christo Iesu*, et cetera.

371. Dicit ergo: intentio seducentium apparet, quia illi gloriantur in carne, sed ego aliam gloriam quaero, scilicet in cruce. Et hoc est quod dicit *mihi absit gloriari*, et cetera. Vide quod ubi mundi philosophus erubuit, ibi Apostolus thesaurum reperit. Quod illi visum est stultitia, Apostolo factum est sapientia et gloria, ut dicit Augustinus. Unusquisque enim in ea re gloriatur, per quam reputatur magnus. Sic qui reputat se magnum in divitiis, gloriatur in eis, et sic de aliis. Qui enim in nullo alio se magnum reputat, nisi in Christo, gloriatur in solo Christo. Talis autem erat Apostolus. Unde dicebat supra II, v. 20: *vivo ego, iam non ego, vivit vero in me Christus*.

Et ideo non gloriatur nisi in Christo, praecipue autem in cruce Christi, et hoc quia in ipsa inveniuntur omnia, de quibus homines gloriari solent. Nam gloriantur aliqui de magnorum (puta regum aut principum) amicitia: et hoc maxime Apostolus invenit in cruce, quia ibi ostenditur evidens signum divinae amicitiae, Rom. V, 8: *commendat autem suam caritatem Deus in nobis*, et cetera. Nihil enim sic caritatem suam ad nos ostendit, sicut mors Christi. Unde Gregorius: *o inaestimabilis dilectio caritatis. Ut servum redimeres, Filium tradidisti*.

Item gloriantur aliqui de scientia. Et hanc Apostolus excellentiorem invenit in cruce. I Cor. II, 2: *non enim aestimavi me aliquid scire inter vos, nisi Iesum Christum*, et cetera. Nam in cruce est perfectio totius legis, et tota ars bene vivendi.

Item gloriantur aliqui de potentia. Et hanc Apostolus maximam habuit per crucem. I Cor. c. I, 18: *verbum*

370. After unmasking the sinister intention of the seducers, the Apostle here insinuates his own intention.

First, he states his intention;

second, he gives a sign of this intention, at *by whom the world is crucified to me*;

third, the reason for this intention, at *for in Christ Jesus*.

371. He says therefore: the intention of the seducers is obvious, for they glory in the flesh; but I seek my glory elsewhere, namely, in the cross. And this is what he says: *but God forbid that I should glory, save in the cross of our Lord Jesus Christ*. Notice that where the worldly philosopher felt shame, there the Apostle found his treasure: what the former regarded as foolish became for the Apostle wisdom and glory, as Augustine says. For each person glories in that through which he is considered great. Thus a person who regards himself as great in his riches, glories in them; and so on for other things. For one who regards himself to be great in nothing but Christ glories in Christ alone. But the Apostle was such a one; hence he says: *I do not live now: but Christ lives in me* (Gal 2:20).

Accordingly he glories in nothing but Christ and particularly in the cross of Christ; and this because in it are found all the things about which men usually glory. For some glory in the friendship of the great, such as of kings and princes; and this friendship the Apostle found most of all in the cross, because there an obvious sign of divine friendship is shown: *but God commends his charity towards us; because when as yet we were sinners according to the time, Christ died for us* (Rom 5:8). For nothing shows his mercy to us as much as the death of Christ. Hence Gregory: *O inestimable love of charity! To redeem the servant, he delivered his Son*.

Again, some glory in knowledge; and of this the Apostle found a more excellent one in the cross: *for I did not judge myself to know anything among you but Jesus Christ and him crucified* (1 Cor 2:2). For in the cross is the perfection of all law and the whole art of living well.

Again, some glory in power; and of this the Apostle found the highest form through the cross: *the word of*

Again, some glory in newly-found freedom; and this the Apostle obtained through the cross: *our old man is crucified with him that the body of sin may be destroyed, to the end that we may serve sin no longer* (Rom 6:6).

Again, some glory in being accepted into some famous fellowship; but by the cross of Christ, we are accepted into the heavenly ranks: *making peace through the blood of his cross, both as to the things that are on earth and the things that are in heaven* (Col 1:20).

Again, some glory in the triumphal banners of conquest; but the cross is the triumphal ensign of Christ's conquest over the demons: *and despoiling the principalities and powers, he has exposed them confidently in open show, triumphing over them in himself* (Col 2:15); *blessed is the wood by which justice comes* (Wis 14:7).

372. The sign of his own intention he shows, saying **by whom the world is crucified to me, and I to the world**. But since this which he says, **but God forbid that I should glory, save in the cross of our Lord Jesus Christ**, is an exceptive proposition which includes one affirmative and one negative statement, he is really giving two signs that prove both statements.

First, he proves the negative one, namely, that he does not glory save in the cross. He does this when he says, **by whom the world is crucified to me, and I to the world**. For that in which a person glories is not dead in his heart, but rather that which he scorns: *I am forgotten as one dead, from the heart* (Ps 31:12).

But it is plain that the world and all things in it were dead in the heart of Paul: *I count all things as dung, that I may gain Christ* (Phil 3:8). Therefore he does not glory in the world or in the things that are in the world. And this is what he says: verily, **I glory in nothing save in the cross of Christ, by whom**, namely, Christ crucified, **the world is crucified to me**, i.e., is dead in my heart, so that I covet nothing in it.

373. Second, he proves the affirmative, namely, that he glories in the cross of Christ, saying that he is crucified to the world.

For a person who glories in something treasures it and desires to make it known; but the Apostle treasures nothing or desires to make nothing known except what pertains to the cross of Christ; therefore, he glories in it alone. And this is what he says: **and I to the world**, namely, I am crucified. As if to say: I carry the marks of the cross and I am considered as dead. Therefore, as the world abhors the cross of Christ, so it abhors me: *for you are dead and your life is hid with Christ in God* (Col 3:3).

374. The reason why he glories in nothing else is given when he says, **for in Christ Jesus neither circumcision nor uncircumcision avails anything, but a new creature**.

In illo siquidem maxime gloriatur, quod valet et adiuvat ad coniungendum Christo, hoc enim Apostolus desiderat, scilicet cum Christo esse. Et quia non valet ad hoc ritus Iudaicus, nec gentilium observantia, sed crux Christi solum, ideo solum in ea gloriatur. Et hoc est quod dicit **in Christo neque circumcisio aliquid valet**, id est ritus Iudaicus, **neque praeputium**, id est gentilitatis observantia, id est ad iustificandum et iungendum Christo, sed ad hoc valet **nova creatura**. Quod quidem patet ex his quae dicta sunt supra v. 6 (quasi eisdem verbis): **in Christo enim Iesu neque circumcisio aliquid valet, neque praeputium, sed fides quae per dilectionem operatur**. Fides ergo caritate formata est nova creatura. Creati namque et producti sumus in esse naturae per Adam; sed illa quidem creatura vetusta iam erat, et inveterata, et ideo Dominus producens nos, et constituens in esse gratiae, fecit quamdam novam creaturam. Iac. I, 18: *ut simus initium aliquod creaturae eius*.

Et dicitur **nova**, quia per eam renovamur in vitam novam; et per Spiritum Sanctum, Ps. CIII, 30: *emitte Spiritum tuum, et creabuntur, et renovabis faciem terrae*. Et per crucem Christi, II Cor. V, 17: *si qua est in Christo nova creatura*, et cetera.

Sic ergo per novam creaturam, scilicet per fidem Christi et caritatem Dei, quae diffusa est in cordibus nostris, renovamur, et Christo coniungimur.

Indeed, he glories mainly in that which avails and helps in joining him to Christ; for it is this the Apostle desires, namely, to be with Christ. And because the Jewish rite and the observances of the gentiles are of no avail in this regard, but only the cross of Christ, therefore he glories in it alone. And this is what he says: **for in Christ Jesus neither circumcision**, i.e., the Jewish rite, **nor uncircumcision**, i.e., gentile observances, **avails anything**, i.e., to justify us and join us to Christ, **but a new creature** avails for us. This, indeed, is obvious from what was said above, in almost the same words: **for in Christ Jesus neither circumcision nor uncircumcision avails anything: but faith that works by charity** (Gal 5:6). Therefore, faith informed by charity is the new creature. For we have been created and made to exist in our nature through Adam, but that creature is already old. Therefore, the Lord in producing us and establishing us in the existence of grace has made a new creature: *that we might be some beginning of his creature* (Jas 1:18).

And it is called **new**, because by it we are reborn into a new life by the Holy Spirit—*you shall send forth your Spirit and they shall be created: and you shall renew the face of the earth* (Ps 104:30)—and by the cross of Christ: *if then any be in Christ a new creature, the old things are passed away; behold all things are made new* (2 Cor 5:17).

In this way, then, by a new creature, i.e., by the faith of Christ and the charity of God which has been poured out in our hearts, we are made new and are joined to Christ.

Lecture 5

⁶:¹⁶Et quicumque hanc regulam secuti fuerint, pax super illos, et misericordia, et super Israël Dei. [n. 375]

⁶:¹⁷De cetero, nemo mihi molestus sit: ego enim stigmata Domini Jesu in corpore meo porto. [n. 377]

⁶:¹⁸Gratia Domini nostri Jesu Christi cum spiritu vestro, fratres. Amen. [n. 380]

⁶:¹⁶καὶ ὅσοι τῷ κανόνι τούτῳ στοιχήσουσιν, εἰρήνη ἐπ' αὐτοὺς καὶ ἔλεος, καὶ ἐπὶ τὸν Ἰσραὴλ τοῦ θεοῦ.

⁶:¹⁷Τοῦ λοιποῦ κόπους μοι μηδεὶς παρεχέτω, ἐγὼ γὰρ τὰ στίγματα τοῦ Ἰησοῦ ἐν τῷ σώματί μου βαστάζω.

⁶:¹⁸Ἡ χάρις τοῦ κυρίου ἡμῶν Ἰησοῦ Χριστοῦ μετὰ τοῦ πνεύματος ὑμῶν, ἀδελφοί· ἀμήν.

⁶:¹⁶And whoever shall follow this rule, peace on them and mercy: and upon the Israel of God. [n. 375]

⁶:¹⁷Henceforth let no man be troublesome to me: for I bear the marks of the Lord Jesus in my body. [n. 377]

⁶:¹⁸The grace of our Lord Jesus Christ be with your spirit, brethren. Amen. [n. 380]

375. Aperta intentione seducentium, et insinuata sua, hic consequenter Apostolus monet eos, et

primo ad sui imitationem;

secundo ut desistant ab eius molestatione, ibi *de caetero nemo*, etc.;

tertio implorat eis gratiae auxilium ad praedictorum impletionem.

376. Dicit ergo primo: intentio mea est, ut nonnisi in cruce Christi glorier, quod et vos debetis facere, quia ***quicumque hanc regulam***, quam ego scilicet teneo, ***secuti fuerint***, scilicet hanc rectitudinem gloriandi. II Cor. X, 13: *non in immensum gloriamur, sed secundum mensuram regulae, et cetera*. ***Pax super illos***, scilicet gloriantes quia nonnisi in Christo gloriantur. ***Pax***, inquam, qua quietentur et perficiantur in bono. Pax enim est tranquillitas mentis. Cant. VIII, 10: *ex quo facta sum coram illo quasi pacem reperiens*. Col. III, 15: *pax Christi exultet in cordibus vestris, in qua, et cetera*. ***Et misericordia***, per quam liberentur a peccatis. Thren. III, 22: *misericordiae Domini, quia non sumus consumpti*. Sap. IV, 15: *gratia Dei et misericordia in sanctos eius, et respectus in electos illius*, qui scilicet sunt Israel. Rom. II, 28: *non enim qui in manifesto Iudaeus est*. Ille ergo est ***Israel Dei***, qui est spiritualiter Israel coram Deo. Io. I, 47: *ecce vere Israelita, in quo dolus non est*. Rom. c. IX, 6: *non enim omnes qui sunt ex Israel, hi sunt Israelitae, et cetera. Sed qui filii sunt promissionis existimantur in semine*. Unde et ipsi gentiles facti sunt Israel Dei per mentis rectitudinem. Israel rectissimus interpretatur. Gen. XXXII: *Israel erit nomen tuum, et cetera*.

377. Consequenter cum dicit ***de caetero nemo***, etc., monet, ut desistant a sui molestatione. Et

primo ponit admonitionem;

secundo rationem eius assignat, ibi: ***ego enim stigmata***.

375. Having disclosed the intention of the seducers and intimated his own, the Apostle counsels them:

first, to imitate him;

second, to desist from being troublesome to him, at ***henceforth***;

third, he begs grace for them to carry out the aforesaid.

376. First, therefore, he says: my intention is to glory only in the cross of Christ. And you, too, should do this, because ***whoever shall follow this rule*** which I follow, namely, this proper way of glorying—*but we will not glory beyond our measure and according to the measure of the rule which God has measured to us* (2 Cor 10:13)—***peace on them***, namely, on those who glory, because they glory in Christ alone: ***peace***, I say, by which they are set at rest and made perfect in good. (For peace is tranquility of mind: *since I am become in his presence as one finding peace* (Song 8:10); and in Colossians: *and let the peace of Christ rejoice in your hearts, wherein also you are called in one body* (Col 3:15). ***And mercy***, by which we are set free of our sins: *the mercies of the Lord that we are not consumed* (Lam 3:22); *the grace of God and his mercy is with his saints, and he has respect to his chosen*, namely, who are his Israel (Wis 4:15); *for he is not a Jew who is so outwardly* (Rom 2:28). He, therefore, is ***the Israel of God*** who is spiritually an Israel before God: *behold an Israelite indeed, in whom there is no guile* (John 1:47); *for all are not Israelites that are of Israel: neither are all they that are the seed of Abraham, children; but in Isaac shall your seed be called; that is to say, not they that are the children of the flesh are the children of God but they that are the children of the promise, are accounted for the seed* (Rom 9:6). Hence even the gentiles have become the Israel of God by uprightness of mind; for Israel means 'most upright': *Israel will be your name* (Gen 32:28).

377. Then when he says, ***henceforth let no man be troublesome to me***, he admonishes them to bother him no more.

First, he gives the admonition;

second, he gives a reason for it, at ***for I bear the marks***.

378. He says therefore: **henceforth let no man be troublesome to** me. This can be explained in two ways. In one way, **henceforth** can be taken as one word so that the sense is: **henceforth**, i.e., from now on. In another way it might be taken as two words, so that the sense is: let no man be troublesome to me about anything else. As if to say: I glory in the cross alone; with respect to anything else, *let no man be troublesome to me*, because I care about nothing else. But the first is better.

His saying, *let no man be troublesome to me*, can be referred to the false brethren, who were troubling the Apostle by raising difficulties and murmuring about the legal observances: *but as for me, when they were troublesome, I was clothed with haircloth* (Ps 35:13). Or it can be referred to hearers who do not grasp his meaning. As if to say: *let no one be troublesome to me*, i.e., let no one who hears me show himself to be such as to make it necessary for me to labor with him again, namely, by understanding in a way other than I have taught.

379. The reason for this admonition he assigns when he says, *for I bear the marks of the Lord Jesus in my body*.

For stigmata are, strictly speaking, certain marks branded on one with a hot iron; as when a slave is marked on the face by his master, so that no one else will claim him, but will quietly let him remain with the master whose marks he bears. And this is the way the Apostle says he bears *the marks of the Lord*, branded, as it were, as a slave of Christ; and this, because he bore the marks of Christ's passion, suffering many tribulations in his body for him, according to the saying of 1 Peter: *Christ suffered for us, leaving you an example, that you should follow his steps* (1 Pet 2:21); *always bearing about in our body the mortification of Jesus, that the life also of Jesus may be made manifest in our mortal flesh* (2 Cor 4:10).

According to this there are two ways of connecting this with the preceding. In one way, as has been said: *let no man be troublesome to me: for I bear the marks of our Lord Jesus in my body*; consequently, no one has any right over me except Christ. In another way: *let no man be troublesome to me*, because I have many other conflicts and marks that trouble me in the persecutions I suffer; and it is cruel to add affliction to one already afflicted. Hence the complaint of Job: *he has torn me with wound upon wound* (Job 16:15). Nevertheless, the first is better.

380. Then he implores the help of God's grace, saying: *the grace of our Lord Jesus Christ*, by which you may carry out the foregoing, *be with your spirit*, i.e., with your understanding, so that you may understand the truth.

Or, *with your spirit*, with which you should observe the law, rather than in a carnal manner: *for you have not received the spirit of bondage again in fear; but you have received the Spirit of adoption of sons* (Rom 8:15).

Commentary on the Letter of Saint Paul to the Ephesians

Introduction

St. Thomas Aquinas combined attention to the literal sense of Holy Scripture with a profound theological understanding of the salvific mysteries revealed in the Old and New Testaments. In his Prologue to the Pauline corpus that precedes his commentary on St. Paul's letter to the Romans, Aquinas sees the importance for St. Paul of the grace who is Christ Jesus as true God and true man. The letter to the Romans deals with Christ's grace in itself, while 1 Corinthians is concerned with the sacraments of grace, and 2 Corinthians with the dignity of the ministers of the sacraments. Galatians shows how the sacraments of the New Law fulfill and surpass those of the Old Law. Then Paul continues by revealing how the grace of Christ effects the unity of His Body, the Church. Ephesians reveals the unity of the Church as the whole Christ, head and members. Aquinas's lectures on Romans and Ephesians, along with those on the Gospel of John, are prestine examples of his profound theological understanding of the mystery revealed in the life, death, and resurrection of Our Lord Jesus Christ for the whole of creation and human history.

In developing the main theme of his lectures on Ephesians, the unity of the faithful in Christ, Aquinas continually pointed out the central position of Christ in salvation history. The whole of Chapter One pivots around the blessings which men have received in Christ. Through him we are chosen, predestined, and adopted as God's children, worthy to partake of eternal beatitude and bodily resurrection (Lect. 1). The Father loves us because he sees his own Son in us; only Christ can justify and save us (Lect. 2). The life giving mystery revealed through the Apostles is the advent of God in Christ and the recapitulation of everything in Him (Lect. 3). The acceptance of this mystery in faith is dependent on Christ (Lect. 5). As Christ is the model and form of our justice, so his exultation sets the pattern for mankind's resurrection (Lect. 7). In this exultation Christ exercises a supreme fullness of power over the entire universe (Lect. 8).

This sets the stage for Chapter Two in which St. Thomas comments on the effects of Christ's power. The slavery to sin in which Jew and pagan were plunged (Lect. 1) was destroyed by God's unique mercy, justifying us in Christ (Lect. 2). Only Christ can accomplish this salvation (Lect. 3). The alienation between Jew and pagan (Lect. 4) was completely overcome by the unification of mankind effected in Christ as truly God and truly man (Lect. 5). Now all the races of men have access by Christ, in the Spirit, to the Father (ibid.). A new community of men is formed whose foundation is Christ (Lect. 6).

In the lectures on Chapter Three the special role of the Apostles in disseminating knowledge of this mystery is discussed. The blessings outlined in Chapters One and Two are reiterated in the context of this apostolic mission. Christ is Lord of history (Lect. 3), and the essence of our faith consists in affirming his true divinity and true humanity (Lect. 5). The moral exhortations and precepts of Chapters Four to Six are to assist the Ephesians in preserving the ecclesial unity Christ has established and strengthened by his gifts. St. Thomas certainly cannot be accused of failing to impress on his students the profoundly Christological nature of mankind's return to God.

The lectures on Ephesians exhibit all the characteristics of Thomas' exegesis. The Prologue considers the four causes of the letter while allegorizing on a verse from Psalm 74. Parallel passages from other parts of Scripture are generously sprinkled throughout the commentary. Since it is a transcription or *reportatio* by Reginald, these quotations are often jotted down without any introductory phrase linking them to the previous thought. Yet the connection is not difficult to perceive in the majority of cases since they substantiate or illustrate what preceded.

Aquinas's typically thirteenth century interest in the theological import of the biblical text is evident on every page. Though few in number, similarities to the twelfth century biblical moral school of exegesis can also be detected. Thus, in Lecture 4 of Chapter One he describes how civil elections were performed at his time. A contemporary maxim is quoted in Lecture 6 of Chapter Five when Thomas assures his students that the caution St. Paul was recommending had nothing in common with that advised in the saying "si non caste, tamen

caute." An echo of Stephen Langton's concern for reform can be heard in his categorical statement that bishops, the successors of the Apostles, are to leave temporal administration to deacons since their spiritual duties are a full time job (Ch. 4, Lect. 4).

Dialectical procedures are well represented. Objections and answers regarding the Apostle's thought are frequent, and in Chapter Five we are told how Paul demonstrated one of his minor (Lect. 3) and major premises (Lect. 5). The general lines of St. Thomas' divisions of the letter to the Ephesians are excellent. The excellent study of Aquinas's exegesis in Christopher Baglow's Modus et Forma: A New Approach to the Exegesis of St. Thomas Aquinas (Rome: Analecta Biblica, 2002) establishes how the detailed divisions of the texts in Aquinas's lectures on the Scriptural texts was to show the unity of the entire book or letter. The following is an outline of the main sections and their more prominent subdivisions as given by St. Thomas.

Outline

	Chapter and Verse	Lecture
THE GREETING	1:1-2	1

THE NARRATIVE: meant to fortify the Ephesians in the good of ecclesial unity

Chapter One: By reason of Christ and his blessings

a. The blessings offered to all men	1:3-7	1-2
b. The unique gifts given the Apostles	1:8-12	3-4
c. The blessings bestowed on the Ephesians	1:13-14	5
1. Paul's affection for them has grown	1:15-16a	6
2. He prays that they be blessed evermore	1:16b-19a	6
d. Christ, the form and exemplar of all blessings:		
1. Especially in his Resurrection and Exultation	1:19b-21	7
2. So that he orders the universe & the Church	1:22-23	8

Chapter Two: By reason of the Ephesians' own past experience

a. Their sinful state & unmerited justification and salvation in Christ	2:1-10	1-3
b. Their Gentile condition and Christ's goodness	2:11-13	4
1. In making them, with the Jews, one New Man	2:14-18	5
2. Now both share in God's blessings	2:19-22	6

Chapter Three: By reason of Paul's solicitude for them and the special graces he has received

a. The dignity of his mission because of		
1. His knowledge of divine mysteries	3:3-6	1
2. His part in carrying these mysteries into effect and their outcome	3:7-12	2-3
b. Paul's trials and his prayer that they remain strong in faith and love	3:13-17	4
c. If they do, a knowledge of divine mysteries will be granted to them also	3:18-20	5
d. A Thanksgiving to God for giving us Christ and the Church	3:21	5

Chapter Four: AN EXHORTATION: urging them on to higher goods, especially unity

I. An admonition to preserve ecclesial unity
    a. The admonition itself   4:1-4   1
    b. The form of this ecclesial unity:
        1. That which is common to every member   4:5-6   2
        2. What is particular to each individual:
            a) The source of these different gifts   4:7-11   3-4
            b) The fruit of this diversity, Christ's body   4:12-16   4-5

II. How they are to remain in Christian unity
    a. General norms for everyone:
        1. Christ's teaching is contrary to pagan sins   4:17-21   6-7
        2. The conditions for knowing Christ's doctrine   4:22-24   7
    b. General precepts applicable to everyone:
        1. Avoid spiritual sins and follow Christ's example   4:25-5:2   4:8-5:1

Chapter Five:
        2. Avoid carnal sins; Paul speaks of punishment and warns against these sins   5:3-14   2-5
        3. Exhortation to newness of life and thanksgiving   5:15-21   6-7

    c. Particular precepts for different groups
        1. For husbands and wives, the mystery of Christ and the Church   5:22-23   8-10

Chapter Six:
        2. For children and parents   6:1-4   1
        3. For slaves and their masters   6:5-9   2

THE CONCLUSION: indicating by whose power these precepts will be fulfilled

I. Trust in God, he will provide spiritual armor for the struggles Christians must undergo   6:10-17   3-4

II. A final prayer, farewells and doxology   6:18-24   5

No critical edition of St. Thomas Aquinas' scriptural commentaries has yet been undertaken. The present translation is based on the Parma edition of his complete works. I have also consulted the Piana edition as used by Raphael Cai, O.P., for the Marietti edition. Quotations from the Bible and the text of St. Paul's letter to the Ephesians are taken from the Douay Rheims translation of the Vulgate, except when textual variations or clarity called for a direct translation from Aquinas' version.

Throughout the work my objective has been to produce an accurate and readable translation. I wish to thank the Aquinas Institute for the Study of Sacred Doctrine for making this translation available again. It was originally published by Magi Books, Inc. with a longer introduction and extensive endnotes.

Reverend Matthew L. Lamb
Ave Maria University
Feast of St. Benedict 2012

Commentary on the Letter of Saint Paul to the Ephesians

Prologue

Psalm 75:3

Liquefacta est terra et omnes qui habitant in ea: ego confirmavi columnas ejus.	ἐτάκη ἡ γῆ καὶ πάντες οἱ κατοικοῦντες ἐν αὐτῇ, ἐγὼ ἐστερέωσα τοὺς στύλους αὐτῆς. διάψαλμα.	The earth is melted, and all that dwell therein: I have strengthened its pillars.

1. Sicut dicit sapiens: *non minor est virtus quam quaerere parta tueri*, ideo non immerito commendatur Apostolus, quia etsi Ephesios in fide non fundavit, tamen fundatos in fide confirmavit, ut ipse loquens de ecclesia Ephesiorum, vere possit dicere: **ego confirmavi columnas eius**; ego videlicet, Israelita natione, Christianus religione, apostolus dignitate.

Israelita dico natione; *nam et ego Israelita sum, ex semine Abrahae de tribu Beniamin* II Cor. XI, 22. Item Christianus religione. Gal. II, 19 s.: *ego enim per legem mortuus sum legi, ut Deo vivam: Christo confixus sum cruci: vivo ergo iam non ego, vivit vero in me Christus: quod autem nunc vivo in carne, in fide vivo filii Dei.* Item apostolus dignitate. I Cor. XV, 9: *ego sum minimus apostolorum.* De his tribus II Cor. XI, 22: *Israelitae sunt, et ego; semen Abrahae sunt, et ego; ministri Christi sunt, et ego; ut minus sapiens dico, plus ego.*

Talis debet esse praedicator sapientiae salutaris, scilicet Israelita quo ad contemplationem Dei, Christianus quo ad religionem fidei, apostolus quo ad auctoritatem officii.

Ego, ergo, Iudaeus per originem, quaerens Deum per fidem, apostolus Dei per imitationem, **confirmavi**, et cetera. Confirmavi ne a fide vacillarent, sicut artifex confirmat aedificium, ne cadat. Unde dictum est Petro Lc. XXII, v. 32: *et tu aliquando conversus confirma fratres tuos*, quod fecit Paulus. Unde ei competit illud Iob IV, 4: *vacillantes confirmaverunt sermones tui.* Confirmavit item ne pseudo timerent, sicut episcopus confirmat puerum ad robur contra pusillanimitatem, unde dictum est de David in Ps. LXXXVIII, 21: *inveni David servum meum, oleo sancto meo unxi eum; manus enim mea auxiliabitur ei, et brachium meum confortabit eum,*

1. Wisely has it been remarked that: *no less energy is spent in retaining possessions than in acquiring them.* Although St. Paul did not initiate the Ephesians into the faith, the Apostle is justly praised for having strengthened them in it. Of the church at Ephesus he rightfully can claim: *I have strengthened its pillars*—I who am an Israelite in nationality, a Christian in religion, an apostle in dignity.

A Jew by birth, for *I am an Israelite sprung from Abraham's seed in the tribe of Benjamin* (2 Cor 11:22). A Christian in religion, *for I, through the law, am dead to the law, that I may live to God; with Christ I am nailed to the cross. And I live, now not I; but Christ lives in me. And the life that I live now in the flesh, I live in the faith of the Son of God* (Gal 2:19–20). An apostle in dignity since *I am the least of the apostles* (1 Cor 15:9). Concerning these three it is written: *they are Israelites: so am I. They are the seed of Abraham: so am I. They are the ministers of Christ, so am I. I speak as one less wise: I am more* (2 Cor 11:22–23).

Everyone who proclaims saving wisdom, like Paul, must be an Israelite in his contemplation of God, a Christian in his religious faith, an apostle in his function's authority.

I, therefore, am a Jew by birth, seeking God through faith, and am an apostle of God through imitation. *I have strengthened* them lest they falter in their faith, as the workman will buttress a building against a fall. *And when you have turned back, strengthen your brothers* (Luke 22:32), was spoken to Peter and accomplished by Paul. And it may be applied to him that *your words have upheld the stumbler* (Job 4:4). The bishop confirms a boy to fortify him against becoming spiritless; similarly, Paul has strengthened the Ephesians not to fear unreasonably. In this connection, it is written of David: *I have found David my servant: with my holy oil I have anointed him. For my hand shall help him:*

nihil proficiet inimicus in eo, et cetera. Ps. XXXII, 6: *verbo Domini*, per Paulum scripto, *caeli*, id est Ephesii, *firmati sunt*, etc., scilicet ne praemium gloriae amitterent, sicut praelatus vel princeps confirmat donum, ne postea auferatur. Ps. XL, 13: *me autem propter innocentiam suscepisti, et confirmasti me in conspectu tuo in aeternum*. Has confirmationes petebat Ps. LXVII, 29 dicens: *confirma hoc, Deus, quod operatus es in nobis*, et cetera. Has promittebat Apostolus II Thess. ult.: *fidelis autem Deus qui confirmabit vos, et custodiet a malo*.

Ego, ergo, ***confirmavi columnas eius***, scilicet fideles ecclesiae Ephesiorum.

Fideles enim ecclesiae dicuntur columnae, quia debent esse recti, erecti, et fortes. Recti per fidem, erecti per spem, fortes per caritatem.

Recti dico per fidem, fides enim ostendit rectam viam veniendi ad patriam, unde significatur per columnam nubis, de qua Ex. c. XIII, 21: *Dominus autem praecedebat eos, ad ostendendam viam per diem in columna nubis*. Fides enim ad modum nubis habet obscuritatem, quia cum aenigmate; dissolutionem, quia evacuatur; humiditatem, quia excitat ad devotionem.

Erecti per spem, spes enim dirigit ad superna, unde significatur per columnam fumi, de qua dicitur Iud. XX, 40: *viderunt quasi columnam fumi de civitate ascendentem*. Spes enim ad modum fumi ex igne, id est ex caritate, provenit, in altum ascendit, in fine deficit, id est in gloria.

Fortes per caritatem, *fortis enim est ut mors dilectio*, ut dicitur Cant. VIII, 6; unde significatur per columnam ignis qui omnia consumit, de quo Sap. XVIII, 3: *ignis ardentem columnam ducem habuerunt ignotae viae*. Sicut enim ignis illuminat diaphana, examinat metalla, exterminat cremabilia, sic caritas illuminat opera, examinat intentionem, et omnia vitia exterminat.

Iam apparet quae sit causa huius epistolae efficiens, quia Paulus, quod notatur ibi *ego*. Finalis, quia confirmatio, quod notatur ibi ***confirmavi***. Materialis, quia Ephesii, quod notatur ibi ***columnas eius***. Formalis patet in divisione epistolae, et modo agendi.

2. Huic epistolae praemittit glossator prologum sive argumentum, ubi principaliter duo facit: primo describit eos, secundo, rationem et modum scribendi subdit, ibi *hos collaudat Apostolus*, et cetera. Ephesinos vero quibus scribit, describit a tribus. Primo, a regione, quia *Ephesii sunt Asiani* ab Asia Minore; secundo, a religione, quia *hi acceperunt verbum veritatis* Christianae; tertio a stabilitate, quia *perstiterunt in fide*. Primum respicit patriam; secundum, gratiam; tertium, perseverantiam.

and my arm shall strengthen him (Ps 89:21–22). *By the word of the Lord*, written through Paul, *the heavens*, applying to the Ephesians, *were established* (Ps 33:6) lest they lose their prize of glory, just as a prelate or prince ratifies a gift to protect it against theft. *Because of my perfection you have supported me, and set me before you forever* (Ps 41:13). This strengthening power is asked for where it is written: *send, my God, your strength; strengthen, God, what you have built for us* (Ps 68:29). The Apostle promised these divine aids: *but the Lord is faithful, who will strengthen and keep you from evil* (2 Thess 3:3).

I have strengthened its pillars, namely, the faithful of the church at Ephesus.

They are referred to as pillars since they must be straightforward, upright, and strong—straightforward through faith, upright through hope, and strong because of charity.

I say straightforward through faith because faith reveals the straight and true way to arrive at the fatherland; it is symbolized by the pillar of cloud: *and the Lord went before them to show the way by day in a pillar of a cloud* (Exod 13:21). Faith, similar to clouds, is opaque with its mysteries, dissolves when it gives way to vision, and moistens by arousing devotion.

The faithful are upright through hope, for hope points heavenwards; it is symbolized by the column of smoke: *the signal rose from the city as a pillar of smoke* (Judg 20:40). Hope, like smoke from fire, springs from charity, ascends upward, and finally vanishes in glory.

The faithful must be strong through charity, *for love is strong as death* (Song 8:6); hence, it is symbolized by a pillar of fire capable of consuming everything: *therefore, they received a burning pillar of fire for a guide on the unknown journey* (Wis 18:3). As fire makes the surroundings visible, puts metals to the test, and destroys what can burn, so charity enlightens human actions, examines one's motives, and exterminates all vices.

The efficient cause of this letter is, of course, St. Paul; this cause was ascribed to the *I* of the psalm (Ps 75:3). The final cause is to fortify, designated by the *have strengthened*. The material cause is the Ephesians, as noted under *its pillars*. The formal cause will be understood in the structural divisions of the letter and its method of presentation.

2. A glossator prefaces this letter with a prologue or summary expressing two main ideas: first, he describes the recipients; second, he gives the reason and circumstances of writing, at *the Apostle praises them*. The Ephesians, to whom he wrote, are described in three ways: first, by their locality, *the Ephesians are Asians*, coming from Asia Minor; second, by their religion, *they have accepted the word* of Christian *truth*; third is their constancy, *they have remained steadfast in the faith*. The first has reference to their home country, the second to grace, and the third to perseverance.

Hos collaudat Apostolus, et cetera. Hic subdit etiam rationem et modum scribendi, ubi implicat quatuor. Primo, Scripturae rationem; secundo actorem, qui est *Apostolus scribens*; tertio, locum a quo scribit, quia *a Roma de carcere*; quarto, nuntium per quem scribit, quia *per Tychicum diaconum*; littera satis patet.

At *the Apostle praises them* he adds the reason and circumstance for writing, which involves four things: first, the reason for Scripture; second, the author, who is *the Apostle*; third, the place from which he writes, which is *from a prison in Rome*; fourth, the messenger through whom he writes, who is *Tychicus, a deacon*.

Chapter 1

Lecture 1

1:1 Paulus apostolus Jesu Christi per voluntatem Dei, omnibus sanctis qui sunt Ephesi, et fidelibus in Christo Jesu. [n. 4]

1:2 Gratia vobis, et pax a Deo Patre nostro, et Domino Jesu Christo.

1:3 Benedictus Deus et Pater Domini nostri Jesu Christi, qui benedixit nos in omni benedictione spirituali in caelestibus in Christo, [n. 5]

1:4 sicut elegit nos in ipso ante mundi constitutionem, ut essemus sancti et immaculati in conspectu ejus in caritate. [n. 8]

1:5 Qui praedestinavit nos in adoptionem filiorum per Jesum Christum in ipsum: secundum propositum voluntatis suae, [n. 9]

1:1 Παῦλος ἀπόστολος Χριστοῦ Ἰησοῦ διὰ θελήματος θεοῦ τοῖς ἁγίοις τοῖς οὖσιν [ἐν Ἐφέσῳ] καὶ πιστοῖς ἐν Χριστῷ Ἰησοῦ·

1:2 χάρις ὑμῖν καὶ εἰρήνη ἀπὸ θεοῦ πατρὸς ἡμῶν καὶ κυρίου Ἰησοῦ Χριστοῦ.

1:3 Εὐλογητὸς ὁ θεὸς καὶ πατὴρ τοῦ κυρίου ἡμῶν Ἰησοῦ Χριστοῦ, ὁ εὐλογήσας ἡμᾶς ἐν πάσῃ εὐλογίᾳ πνευματικῇ ἐν τοῖς ἐπουρανίοις ἐν Χριστῷ,

1:4 καθὼς ἐξελέξατο ἡμᾶς ἐν αὐτῷ πρὸ καταβολῆς κόσμου, εἶναι ἡμᾶς ἁγίους καὶ ἀμώμους κατενώπιον αὐτοῦ ἐν ἀγάπῃ,

1:5 προορίσας ἡμᾶς εἰς υἱοθεσίαν διὰ Ἰησοῦ Χριστοῦ εἰς αὐτόν, κατὰ τὴν εὐδοκίαν τοῦ θελήματος αὐτοῦ,

1:1 Paul, an apostle of Jesus Christ, by the will of God, to all the saints who are at Ephesus and to the faithful in Christ Jesus. [n. 4]

1:2 Grace be to you and peace, from God the Father and from the Lord Jesus Christ.

1:3 Blessed be the God and Father of our Lord Jesus Christ, who has blessed us with every spiritual blessing in heavenly places, in Christ: [n. 5]

1:4 Even as he chose us in him before the foundation of the world, that we should be holy and unspotted in his sight in charity. [n. 8]

1:5 He destined us unto the adoption of children through Jesus Christ unto himself: according to the purpose of his will: [n. 9]

---

3. Hanc epistolam scribit Apostolus ad Ephesios. Ephesii sunt Asiani ab Asia Minore, quae est pars Graeciae. Hi non fuerunt per Apostolum Paulum in fide fundati, sed confirmati. Iam enim antequam veniret ad eos, erant conversi, ut haberi potest Act. XIX, v. 1: *factum est cum Apollo esset Corinthi*, et cetera. Post conversionem vero suam et Apostoli confirmationem, in fide perstiterunt, nec pseudo receperunt. Non ergo reprehensione, sed consolatione digni erant. Ideo Paulus eis non increpatoriam, sed consolatoriam scribit epistolam. Scribit autem eis ab urbe Roma per Tychicum diaconum.

Intentio vero eius est, eos in bonis habitis confirmare, et ad altiora provocare.

Modus autem agendi patet in divisione epistolae.

Primo ergo ponit salutationem, in qua suum affectum ad eos demonstrat;

secundo narrationem, in qua eos in bonis habitis confirmat, ibi **benedictus Deus**, etc., usque ad IV cap.;

tertio, exhortationem, in qua eos ad ulteriora bona provocat, a cap. IV usque ad locum illum cap. VI ***de caetero, fratres, confortamini in Domino***, etc.;

3. The Apostle writes this letter to the Ephesians who were Asians, coming from Asia Minor which is part of Greece. They were not initiated into the faith by the Apostle Paul but he did strengthen them in it. Even before he had met them, they had been converted, as can be gathered: *it happened that, while Apollo was at Corinth, Paul passed through the upper country and came to Ephesus, where he found certain disciples* (Acts 19:1). Once they were converted and fortified by the Apostle, they were steadfast in the faith, not succumbing to false doctrine. Thus, they were entitled to encouragement rather than reprimand; and Paul's letter has a tone of reassurance and not of rebuke. He wrote them from the city of Rome through the deacon, Tychicus.

The Apostle's intention is to strengthen them in good habits, and spur them on to greater perfection.

The method of presentation can be seen in the division of the letter:

first, the greeting, in which he shows his affection for them;

second, the narrative, in which he strengthens them in good habits, from ***blessed be God*** until chapter four;

third, the exhortation, in which he urges them on to greater perfection, from chapter four until chapter six at ***be strong in the Lord***;

quarto epistolae conclusionem, in qua eos ad certamen spirituale confortat a loco isto *de caetero*, usque in finem.

4. In salutatione primo ponitur persona salutans; secundo, personae salutatae, ibi *sanctis omnibus*, etc.; tertio forma salutationis, ibi *gratia vobis*, et cetera.

In prima, primo nominat personam, ibi *Paulus*; secundo personae auctoritatem, ibi *apostolus Christi*; tertio auctoritatis datorem, ibi *per voluntatem Dei*.

Dicit ergo: *Paulus apostolus*. Paulus nomen est humilitatis, apostolus vero nomen dignitatis, quia *qui se humiliat, exaltabitur*, Lc. XIV, 11 et XVIII, 14. *Apostolus*, inquam, *Iesu*, non Satanae, sicut pseudo. V. 11: *non est ergo magnum si ministri eius*, scilicet Satanae, *transfigurentur velut ministri iustitiae*, et cetera. Apostolus, inquam, et hoc non meis meritis, sed *per voluntatem Dei*. Econtra est in multis. Os. VIII, 4: *ipsi regnaverunt, et non ex me*, et cetera. *Sanctis omnibus*, scilicet *qui sunt Ephesi, et fidelibus*, supple scribit. Vel ego Paulus scribo sanctis exercitio virtutum quo ad mores; fidelibus, rectitudine cognitionis quo ad fidem. Vel sanctis, id est maioribus et perfectis; fidelibus, id est minoribus et imperfectis. *Et fidelibus*, inquam, *in Christo*, non in factis suis.

Gratia vobis et pax, et cetera. Hic subditur salutationis forma, in qua implicantur tria, donum quodlibet gratificantia: doni sufficientia, ibi *gratia vobis et pax*, datoris potentia, ibi *a Deo patre*, mediatoris excellentia, ibi *et Domino Iesu Christo*. Tunc enim gratum est donum quando sufficiens est quod datur; quando a potente datur, ut quando a rege, vel principe datur; quando per solemnem nuntium datur, ut per filium.

Dicit ergo: *gratia*, scilicet iustificationis a culpa, *et pax*, id est tranquillitas mentis, vel reconciliatio ad Deum, quoad liberationem a debita poena pro offensa. *Vobis*, supple sit, ex hoc, scilicet *a Deo Patre nostro*, a quo bona cuncta procedunt. Iac. I, 17: *omne datum optimum*, et cetera. *Et Domino Iesu Christo*, sine quo nulla bona dantur. Ideo fere omnes orationes finiuntur: *per Dominum nostrum Iesum Christum*.

Spiritum Sanctum non nominat, quia cum sit nexus Patris et Filii, intelligitur in extremis, vel intelligitur in donis sibi appropriatis, quae sunt gratia et pax.

5. Deinde cum dicit *benedictus Deus*, etc., hic, gratias agendo, eos in bono confirmat, et hoc tribus modis.

Primo, ratione sumpta ex parte Christi, a quo multa bona adepti sunt, capite isto;

fourth, the conclusion of the letter, in which he fortifies them for the spiritual combat, from *be strong* until the end.

4. In the salutation, the person greeting comes first, second those greeted, at *to all the saints*, and third the formula of greeting, at *grace be to you*.

In reference to the first, he gives the name of the person, *Paul*; second, that person's authority as an *apostle of Christ*; lastly, the giver of this authority, *by the will of God*.

He says *Paul* which is a name of humility, whereas the title of apostle is one of dignity; the reason is that *he that humbles himself shall be exalted* (Luke 14:11; 18:14). *An apostle*, I mean, *of Jesus* and not one of the pseudo-apostles who are of Satan: *it is no great thing if his*— that is, Satan's—*ministers be transformed as the ministers of justice* (2 Cor 11:15). I am an apostle, he says, not by my own merits but *by the will of God*. In many instances it is just the opposite—*they have reigned, but not by me* (Hos 8:4). He writes *to all the saints who are at Ephesus and to the faithful*. Either this could mean, I, Paul, write about morals to those who are holy through the exercise of virtues; and about faith to those who believe with true knowledge. Or, it may mean, to the saints who are the elders and perfect, and to the faithful who are less experienced and imperfect. They are said to believe *in Christ Jesus* and not in their own deeds.

At *grace be to you and peace*, he adds the formula of greeting which indicates three qualities which make any gift pleasing: the sufficiency of the gift, in *grace be to you and peace*; the power of the giver, *from God our Father*; and the excellence of the mediator, *and from the Lord Jesus Christ*. For a gift is pleasing when what is given is sufficient and is offered by someone in power, as a king or prince, and is presented by a solemn messenger, for example, by his son.

He mentions *grace* meaning justification from sin, *and peace* which is calmness of mind, or reconciliation to God, in regard to the freedom from punishment due to sin. May this be *to you*, *from God our Father* from whom every good comes: *every good giving and every perfect gift is from above, coming down from the Father of lights* (Jas 1:17). *And the Lord Jesus Christ* without whom no blessings are given. That is why nearly all prayers are concluded: *through our Lord Jesus Christ*.

The Holy Spirit is not mentioned in the greeting formula since he is the bond uniting Father and Son and is understood when they are mentioned; or he is understood in the gifts appropriated to him, grace and peace.

5. Then when he says *blessed be God*, in giving thanks he strengthens them in good, and he does this in three ways: first, by giving as a reason Christ, from whom they have received so many gifts, in chapter one;

secundo, ratione sumpta ex parte ipsorum, qui de praeterito statu malo, ad bonum praesens translati sunt, cap. II, ibi *et vos cum essetis mortui*, etc.;

tertio, ratione sumpta ex parte Apostoli, cuius ministerio et diligentia in bono statu positi, confirmati sunt, cap. III, ibi *huius rei gratia*, et cetera.

Iterum prima in tres dividitur, quia

primo gratias agendo, tangit beneficia generaliter;

secundo, beneficia exhibita ipsis apostolis specialiter, ibi *quae superabundavit in nobis*, etc.;

tertio, beneficia exhibita ipsis Ephesiis specialiter, ibi *in quo et vos cum audivissetis*, et cetera.

Beneficia vero exhibita generaliter humano generi tangit sex.

Primum benedictionis, in certitudine futurae beatitudinis, ibi *benedictus*, et cetera.

Secundum electionis, in praeordinata separatione a massa perditionis, ibi *sicut elegit nos in ipso*, et cetera.

Tertium praedestinationis, in praeordinata associatione cum bonis, scilicet cum filiis adoptionis, ibi *qui praedestinavit nos*, et cetera.

Quartum gratificationis, in collatione gratiae, ibi *in quo gratificavit nos*, et cetera.

Quintum redemptionis, in liberatione a poena, id est, a Diaboli servitute, ibi *in quo habemus redemptionem*, et cetera.

Sextum remissionis in deletione culpae, ibi *remissionem peccatorum*, et cetera.

Circa beneficium benedictionis, tangit duo. Primo, praeconium, quod debet impendi, ibi *benedictus Deus*, etc.; secundo, beneficium, propter quod debet impendi, ibi *qui benedixit nos*, et cetera.

6. Dicit ergo *benedictus*, scilicet a me, a vobis, et ab aliis, scilicet corde, et ore, et opere, id est laudatus, *Deus et Pater*, id est ille, qui est Deus per essentiam divinitatis, et Pater propter proprietatem generationis. Incidit autem copulatio, non ratione suppositionis, quia idem est suppositum, sed ratione significationis essentialiter et relative. *Pater*, inquam, *Domini nostri Iesu Christi*, id est Filii, qui est Dominus noster secundum divinitatem, Iesus Christus secundum humanitatem.

7. *Qui*, scilicet Deus, *benedixit nos* in spe in praesenti, sed in futuro benedicet in re. Ponit autem praeteritum pro futuro propter certitudinem. Benedixit, inquam, nos, licet nostris meritis maledictos, *in omni benedictione spirituali*, scilicet quantum ad animam, et quantum ad corpus. Tunc enim erit corpus spirituale. I Cor. XV, 44: *seminatur corpus animale, resurget corpus spirituale*. Benedictione, inquam, habita, *in caelestibus*, id est in caelo; et hoc, *in Christo*, id est per Christum, vel in Christo

second, by reason of they themselves who have been transformed from a former evil condition to their present good one, at *when you were dead* (Eph 2:1);

third, because of the Apostle himself, whose ministry and solicitude has confirmed them in their good state, at *for this cause* (Eph 3:1).

The first is divided into three sections:

first, in giving thanks he touches on blessings in a general way;

second, the blessings given the apostles in particular, at *which has superabounded in us* (Eph 1:8);

third, the blessings especially granted to the Ephesians themselves, at *in him you also, who have heard* (Eph 1:13).

He treats of six blessings offered generally to the human race:

first, that of praising God in the certainty of future beatitude, at *blessed*;

second, that of being chosen in the foreordained separation from those headed toward destruction, at *even as he chose us*;

third, that of predestination in the foreordained community of the good, namely, of the adopted sons, at *he destined us*;

fourth, that of becoming pleasing to God through the gift of grace, at *in which he has graced us* (Eph 1:6);

fifth, that of being redeemed, liberated from the punishment of diabolical slavery, at *in whim we have redemption* (Eph 1:7);

sixth, that of being pardoned by having sin blotted out, at *the forgiveness of sins* (Eph 1:7).

Regarding the benefit of praise two aspects are touched on: first, the praise itself which should be rendered, at *blessed be God*; second, the blessing on account of which it should be rendered, at *who has blessed us*.

6. He says that God should be *blessed* or praised by you, me and others with our hearts, tongues and actions. He who is *God* by the divine essence *and Father* because of his property of generating. The copula *and* is not placed between God and Father to designate two separate persons, for there is only one Father, but to denote what he is by his essence and what he is in relation to the Son. *Father*, I say, *of our Lord Jesus Christ*, that is, of the Son who is our Lord because of his divinity, and Jesus Christ according to his humanity.

7. God *who has blessed us* with hope in the present while in the future he will bless us with the reality. He puts the verb in the past tense, instead of the future, on account of his certainty. Even though by our own merits we were cursed, he blessed us *with every spiritual blessing* both for soul and for body. For then the body will be spiritual: *it is sown a natural body: it shall rise a spiritual body* (1 Cor 15:44). This will occur by a blessing enjoyed *in heavenly places*, that is, in heaven, and *in Christ* since it

operante. Ipse enim est qui *reformabit corpus humilitatis nostrae*, etc., Phil. III, 21.

Valde appetenda est benedictio haec. Et ratione efficientis, quia **Deus** est benedictio haec; et ratione materiae, quia **nos benedixit**; et ratione formae, quia **in omni benedictione spirituali** benedicit; et ratione finis, quia **in caelestibus** benedicit. Ps. CXXVII, 4: *ecce benedicetur homo, qui timet Dominum.*

8. Deinde cum dicit **sicut elegit nos**, etc., tangitur beneficium electionis, ubi commendatur electio ista, quia libera, ibi **sicut elegit nos in ipso**, quia aeterna, ibi **ante mundi constitutionem**, quia fructuosa, ibi **ut essemus**, etc., quia gratuita, ibi **in caritate**.

Dicit ergo: ita benedicet nos, non nostris meritis, sed ex gratia Christi, **sicut elegit nos**, et gratis, a massa perditionis separando, praeordinavit nos **in ipso**, id est per Christum. Io. XV, 16: *non vos me elegistis, sed ego elegi vos*, et cetera. Et hoc **ante mundi constitutionem**, id est ab aeterno, antequam fieremus. Rom. IX, 11: *cum nondum nati fuissent*, et cetera. **Elegit**, inquam, non quia sancti essemus, quia nec eramus, sed ad hoc elegit nos **ut essemus sancti**, virtutibus, **et immaculati**, a vitiis. Utrumque enim facit electio secundum duas partes iustitiae. Ps. XXXIII, v. 15: *declina a malo, et fac bonum.*

Sancti, inquam, **in conspectu eius**, id est interius in corde, ubi ipse solus conspicit. I Reg. XVI, 7: *Deus autem intuetur cor*. Vel **in conspectu eius**, id est ut eum inspiciamus, quia visio est tota merces, secundum Augustinum. Et hoc fecit, non nostris meritis, sed in caritate sua, vel nostra, qua nos formaliter sanctificat.

9. Deinde cum dicit **qui praedestinavit**, etc., subdit tertium beneficium, scilicet praedestinationis, in praeordinata associatione cum bonis. Ubi circa praedestinationem implicat sex. Primo actum aeternum, ibi **praedestinavit**, secundo, temporale obiectum, ibi **nos**, tertio, praesens commodum, ibi **in adoptionem**, etc., quarto, fructum futurum, ibi **in idipsum**, quinto, modum gratuitum, ibi **secundum propositum**, sexto, effectum debitum, ibi **in laudem gloriae**, et cetera.

Dicit ergo **qui**, scilicet Deus, **praedestinavit nos**, id est sola gratia praeelegit, **in adoptionem filiorum**, id est ut associaremur cum aliis filiis adoptionis in bonis, quae habituri sunt; ideo dicit **in adoptionem filiorum**. Rom. VIII, 15: *non enim accepistis spiritum servitutis iterum in timore, sed accepistis Spiritum adoptionis filiorum*; et infra: *adoptionem filiorum expectantes.*

will be through Christ or by Christ's action, for he himself *will transform our lowly body* (Phil 3:21).

This blessing is greatly to be desired. And this by reason of its efficient cause since **God** is the one who blesses; and by reason of its material cause since **he has blessed us**; and because of the formal cause since he blessed us **with every spiritual blessing**; and on account of the end, because he blessed us **in heavenly places**. *Behold, thus shall the man be blessed that fears the Lord* (Ps 128:4).

8. Next, at **he chose us**, he treats of the blessing of election; he sets forth the advantages of this election because: it is free, **as he chose us in him**; it is eternal, **before the foundation of the world**; it is fruitful, **that we should be holy**; and it is gratuitous, **in charity**.

Therefore he states: he will bless us in the same way—not through our merits but from the grace of Christ—**as he chose us** and, separating us from those headed to destruction, freely foreordained us **in him**, that is, through Christ. *You have not chosen me; but I have chosen you* (John 15:16). This happened **before the foundation of the world**, from eternity, before we came into being. *For when the children were not yet born, nor had done any good or evil, that the purpose of God according to election, might stand* (Rom 9:11). **He chose us**, I say, not because we were holy—we had not yet come into existence—but that **we should be holy** in virtues **and unspotted** by vices. For election performs this twofold action of justice: *turn away from evil and do good* (Ps 33:15).

Saints, I assert, **in his sight**; interiorly in the heart where he alone can see: *the Lord sees the heart* (1 Sam 16:7). Or, **in his sight** may mean that we may gaze on him since the beatific vision, according to Augustine, is the whole of our reward. He will accomplish this, not by our merits, but in his charity; or, by our charity with which he formally sanctifies us.

9. Then, at **he destined us**, he adds the third blessing, that of predestination in the foreordained community of those who are good. Six characteristics of predestination are sketched here. First, it is an eternal act, **he destined**; second, it has a temporal object, **us**; third, it offers a present privilege, **the adoption of children through Jesus Christ**; fourth, the result is future, **unto himself**; fifth, its manner of being realized is gratuitous, **according to the purpose of his will**; sixth, it has a fitting effect, **unto the praise of the glory of his grace** (Eph 1:6).

Hence he affirms that God, who **destined us**, has forechosen us by grace alone **unto the adoption of children** that we might share with the other adopted children the goods yet to come—thus he says **unto the adoption of children**. *For you have not received the spirit of bondage again in fear; but you have received the Spirit of adoption of sons*, and further on, *waiting for the adoption of the sons of God, the redemption of our body* (Rom 8:15, 23).

It must be through contact with fire that something starts to burn since nothing obtains a share in some reality except through whatever is that reality by its very nature. Hence the adoption of sons has to occur through the natural Son.

For this reason the Apostle adds **through Jesus Christ**, which is the third characteristic touched on in this blessing, namely, the mediator who draws all to himself. *God sent his Son, made of a woman, made under the law, that he might redeem them who were under the law, that we might receive the adoption of sons* (Gal 4:4–5). This is accomplished **unto himself**, that is, inasmuch as we are conformed to him and become servants in the Spirit. *See what love the Father has bestowed upon us, that we should be called the sons of God; and so we are . . . we know that when he shall appear we shall be like him* (1 John 3:1–2).

10. Here it should be noted that the likeness of the predestined to the Son of God is twofold. One is imperfect, which is through grace. It is called imperfect, first, because it only concerns the reformation of the soul. **Be renewed in the spirit of your mind, and put on the new man, who according to God is created in justice and holiness of truth** (Eph 4:23–24). Second, even with the soul it retains some imperfection, *for we know in part* (1 Cor 13:9).

However, the second likeness, which will be in glory, will be perfect; both as regards the body—*he will transform our lowly body to be like his glorious body.* (Phil 3:21)—and in regard to the soul, because *when the perfect comes, the imperfect shall pass away* (1 Cor 13:10).

What the Apostle says, therefore, about his predestinating us unto the adoption of children can refer to the imperfect assimilation to the Son of God possessed in this life through grace. But it is more probable that it refers to the perfect assimilation to the Son of God which will exist in the fatherland. In reference to this adoption it is written: *even we ourselves groan within ourselves, waiting for the adoption of the sons of God* (Rom 8:23).

11. Divine predestination is neither necessitated on God's part nor due to those who are predestined; it is rather **according to the purpose of his will**. This is the fourth characteristic which recommends the blessing to us, for it springs from pure love. Predestination, according to reason, presupposes election, and election love.

A twofold cause of this immense blessing is designated here. One is the efficient cause— which is the simple will of God—**according to the purpose of his will**. *Therefore, he has mercy on whomever he wills; and whomever he wills he hardens* (Rom 9:18). *Of his own will he has given us birth by the word of truth* (Jas 1:18). **Unto the praise of the glory of his grace** (Eph 1:6) specifies the final cause which is that we may praise and know the goodness of God. Once again this eminent blessing is recommended inasmuch as the

Causa enim divinae praedestinationis est voluntas mera Dei, finis vero cognitio eius bonitatis.

12. Unde notandum est, quod Dei voluntas nullo modo habet causam, sed est prima causa omnium. Nihilominus tamen potest ei aliqua ratio assignari dupliciter, scilicet vel ex parte volentis, et sic quaedam ratio divinae voluntatis est eius bonitas, quae est obiectum voluntatis divinae, et movet eam. Unde ratio omnium eorum quae Deus vult, est divina bonitas. Prov. XVI, 4: *universa propter semetipsum operatus est Deus*. Ex parte autem voliti, ratio divinae voluntatis potest esse aliquod esse creatum, sicut dum vult coronare Petrum, quia legitime certavit; sed hoc non est causa volendi sed est causa quod ita fiat.

Sciendum tamen est, quod effectus sunt ratio voluntatis divinae ex parte voliti, ita scilicet quod effectus prior sit ratio ulterioris; sed tamen cum venitur ad primum effectum, non potest ultra assignari aliqua ratio illius effectus, nisi voluntas divina; puta, Deus vult hominem habere manum, ut serviat rationi, et hominem habere rationem, quia voluit eum esse hominem, et hominem esse voluit propter perfectionem universi. Et quia hic est primus effectus in creatura, non potest assignari aliqua ratio universi ex parte creaturae, sed ex parte creatoris, quae est divina voluntas. Ergo secundum hunc modum, nec praedestinationis potest ex parte creaturae ratio aliqua assignari, sed solum ex parte Dei.

Nam, effectus praedestinationis sunt duo, scilicet gratia et gloria. Effectuum autem qui ad gloriam ordinantur, potest quidem ex parte voliti assignari ratio, scilicet gratia; puta, Petrum coronavit quia legitime certavit, et hoc quia fuit firmatus in gratia; sed gratiae, quae est primus effectus, non potest aliqua ratio assignari ex parte hominis, quod sit ratio praedestinationis; quia hoc esset ponere, quod principium boni operis sit in homine ex seipso et non per gratiam, quod est haeresis Pelagiana, quae dicit principium boni operis esse ex parte nostra.

Sic ergo patet, quod ratio praedestinationis est simplex Dei voluntas; propter quod dicit Apostolus **secundum propositum voluntatis suae**.

13. Qualiter autem intelligatur, quod Deus omnia facit et vult propter suam bonitatem, sciendum est, quod aliqua operari propter finem, potest intelligi dupliciter. Vel propter finem adipiscendum, sicut infirmus accipit medicinam propter sanitatem; vel propter amorem finis diffundendi, sicut medicus operatur propter sanitatem alteri communicandam. Deus autem nullo exteriori a se bono indiget, secundum illud Ps. XV, 2: *bonorum meorum non eges*. Et ideo cum dicitur, quod Deus vult et facit

homage it results in is in accord with itself. For the cause of divine predestination is simply the will of God, while the end is a knowledge of his goodness.

12. Whence it should be realized that God's will in no way has a cause but is the first cause of everything else. Nevertheless, a certain motive can be assigned to it in two ways. On the part of the one willing, the motive for the divine will is his own goodness which is the object of the divine will, moving it to act. Hence, the reason for everything that God wills is his own goodness: *Yahweh has made everything for his own purpose* (Prov 16:4). On the side of what is willed, however, some created existent can be a motive for the divine will; for example, when he wills to crown Peter because he has fought well (2 Tim 4:7–8). But this latter is not the cause of God's willing; rather it is a cause of it happening the way it did.

Nonetheless, it should be acknowledged how, in the realm of what is willed, effects are a motive for the divine will in such a way that a prior effect is the reason for a later one. But when the primary effect is arrived at, no further reason can be given for that effect except the divine will. For instance, God wills that men should have hands that they might be of service to his mind; and that man possess a mind since he wills him to be a man; and he wills man to exist for the sake of the perfection of the universe. Now since this is what is primarily effected in creation, no further reason for the universe can be assigned on the part of creatures themselves, but only on the part of the Creator, which is the divine will. In this perspective, neither can predestination find any reason on the part of the creature but only on the part of God.

For there are two effects of predestination, grace and glory. Within the realm of what is willed by God, grace can be identified as a reason for the effects which are oriented towards glory. For example, God crowned Peter because he fought well, and he did this because he was strengthened in grace. But no reason for the grace, as a primary effect, can be found on the part of man himself which would also be the reason for predestination. This would be to assert that the source of good works was in man by himself and not by grace. Such was the heretical teaching of the Pelagians who held that the source of good works exists within ourselves.

Thus it is evident that the reason for predestination is the will of God alone, on account of which the Apostle says *according to the purpose of his will*.

13. To understand how God creates everything and wills it because of his own goodness, it should be realized that someone can work for an end in two ways: either in order to attain an end, as the sick take medicine to regain their health; or out of a love of spreading the end, as a doctor will work to communicate health to others. But God needs absolutely nothing external to himself. *You have no need of my goods* (Ps 16:2). Therefore, when it is said that God wills and performs everything on account of his own goodness,

omnia propter bonitatem suam, non intelligitur quod faciat aliquid propter bonitatem sibi communicandam, sed propter bonitatem in alios diffundendam.

Communicatur autem divina bonitas creaturae rationali proprie, ut ipsa rationalis creatura eam cognoscat. Et sic omnia quae Deus in creaturis rationalibus facit, creat ad laudem et gloriam suam, secundum illud Is. c. XLIII, 7: *omnem, qui invocat nomen meum, in gloriam meam creavi eum*, ut scilicet cognoscat bonitatem, et cognoscendo laudet eam. Et ideo subdit Apostolus **in laudem gloriae gratiae suae**, id est ut cognoscat quantum Deus sit laudandus et glorificandus.

Non dicit autem *in laudem iustitiae*; nam iustitia ibi locum habet ubi invenitur debitum, vel etiam redditur; quod autem praedestinatur ad vitam aeternam, non est debitum, ut dictum est, sed gratia pure gratis data.

Nec solum dicit **gloriae**, sed addit **gratiae**, quasi gloriosae gratiae, quae est gratia, in qua ostenditur magnitudo gratiae, quae consistit etiam in magnitudine gloriae, et modo dandi, quia nullis meritis praecedentibus, sed adhuc immeritis existentibus eam dat. Unde Rom. V, 8 s., *commendat autem Deus suam caritatem in nobis, quoniam si cum adhuc peccatores essemus, secundum tempus Christus pro nobis mortuus est*, etc., et parum post, *cum inimici essemus, reconciliati sumus Deo*.

Patet ergo quod praedestinationis divinae nulla alia causa est, nec esse potest, quam simplex Dei voluntas. Unde patet etiam, quod divinae voluntatis praedestinantis non est alia ratio, quam divina bonitas filiis communicanda.

this should not be understood as though he acted in order to confer goodness on himself but rather to communicate goodness to others.

This divine goodness is properly communicated to rational creatures in order that the rational creature himself might know it. Thus, everything that God performs in reference to rational creatures is for his own praise and glory: *everyone who calls upon my name, whom I have created for my glory, whom I have formed and made* (Isa 43:7) so that he may know what goodness is, and in this knowledge praise it. The Apostle thus adds **unto the praise of the glory of his grace**, that man might realize how much God must be praised and glorified.

Nor does he say *unto the praise of justice*. For justice enters into the picture only where a debt is present or is to be returned. But for man to be predestined to eternal life is not due to him—as was said, it is a grace given in perfect freedom.

Nor does he simply say *of the glory*, but annexes **of his grace** as though it were of a glorious grace. And grace is just this; the greatness of grace is revealed in that it consists in the greatness of glory, and it is revealed also in the way it is bestowed; for he gives it without any preceding merits when men are unworthy of it. *God proves his love for us in that while we were yet sinners Christ died for us*; and a little further on, *when we were enemies, we were reconciled to God by the death of his Son* (Rom 5:8; 10).

By now it must be clear how divine predestination neither has nor can have any cause but the will of God alone. This, in turn, reveals how the only motive for God's predestinating will is to communicate the divine goodness to others.

Lecture 2

1:6in laudem gloriae gratiae suae, in qua gratificavit nos in dilecto Filio suo. [n. 15]

1:7In quo habemus redemptionem per sanguinem ejus, remissionem peccatorum secundum divitias gratiae ejus, [n. 17]

1:6εἰς ἔπαινον δόξης τῆς χάριτος αὐτοῦ ἧς ἐχαρίτωσεν ἡμᾶς ἐν τῷ ἠγαπημένῳ,

1:7ἐν ᾧ ἔχομεν τὴν ἀπολύτρωσιν διὰ τοῦ αἵματος αὐτοῦ, τὴν ἄφεσιν τῶν παραπτωμάτων, κατὰ τὸ πλοῦτος τῆς χάριτος αὐτοῦ,

1:6Unto the praise of the glory of his grace, in which he has graced us, in his beloved Son. [n. 15]

1:7In whom we have redemption through his blood, the remission of sins, according to the riches of his grace, [n. 17]

---

14. Hic ponit Apostolus quartum beneficium, scilicet gratificationis in collatione gratiae. Circa quod duo facit.

Primo tangit huius beneficii collationem;

secundo ostendit conferendi modum et conditionem, ibi *in quo habemus redemptionem*, et cetera.

15. Dicit ergo primo: ego dico, quod praedestinati sumus in adoptionem filiorum, in laudem gloriae gratiae suae, et dico gratiam, *in qua gratificavit nos*, et cetera.

Circa quod sciendum est quod idem est aliquid esse gratum alicui et esse dilectum ei. Ille enim est mihi gratus quem diligo. Cum ergo Deus dilexerit nos ab aeterno, nam elegit nos ante mundi constitutionem in caritate, sicut dictum est, quomodo ergo in tempore gratificavit?

Et dicendum est quod illos quos ab aeterno in seipso dilexit, in tempore prout sunt in naturis propriis gratificat, et illud quidem quod ab aeterno est, factum non est; quod vero in tempore est, fieri dicitur. Unde hic Apostolus dicit *gratificavit*, id est gratos fecit, quod simus digni dilectione sua. I Io. III, v. 1: *videte qualem caritatem dedit nobis Deus Pater, ut filii Dei nominemur, et simus*.

Consuevit autem distingui duplex gratia, scilicet gratis data, quae sine meritis datur, Rom. XI, 6: *si autem gratia, iam non ex operibus, alioquin gratia, iam non est gratia*, et gratia gratum faciens, quae nos facit Deo gratos et acceptos, de qua dicitur hic.

16. Notandum est autem, quod aliqui diliguntur propter alium, et aliqui propter seipsos. Cum enim aliquem multum diligo, diligo illum, et quidquid ad illum pertinet; nos autem a Deo diligimur, sed non propter nos ipsos, sed in eo, qui per seipsum dilectus est Patri. Et ideo Apostolus addit *in dilecto Filio*, pro quo, scilicet, nos diligit, inquantum sumus ei similes. Dilectio enim fundatur super similitudine. Unde dicitur Eccli. c. XIII, 19: *omne animal diligit sibi simile*. Filius autem est per naturam suam similis Patri, et ideo principaliter et per se dilectus est, et ideo naturaliter et excellentissimo modo est Patri dilectus. Nos autem sumus filii per adoptionem, inquantum scilicet sumus conformes Filio eius, et ideo quamdam participationem divini

14. Now the Apostle writes of the fourth blessing, that of becoming pleasing to God through the gift of grace. Regarding this he does two things:

first, he touches on the giving of this blessing;

second, he shows the manner and conditions of its bestowal, at *in whom we have redemption*.

15. Hence he first asserts: we are predestined unto the adoption of sons, for the praise of the glory of his grace—that grace, I say, *in which he has graced us in his beloved Son*.

In this respect, it should be noted that to be loved by someone is identical to being pleasing to him. For he whom I love is pleasing to me. Now, since God loved us from eternity—he chose us before the foundation of the world in love, as has been said—how has he made us pleasing to himself in time?

A reply is that those whom he loves eternally in himself, he renders pleasing in time according as they exist in their own natures. The former is from eternity and is not created, the latter happens in time and is said to come into being. Hence the Apostle says that *he has graced us*, that is, made us pleasing that we should be worthy of his love. *See what love the Father has bestowed upon us, that we should be called the sons of God; and so we are* (1 John 3:1).

Two types of grace are customarily distinguished: grace freely given without being merited—*and, if by grace, it is now not by works; otherwise grace is no more grace* (Rom 11:6)—and grace which makes us pleasing and acceptable to God. The latter is the grace dealt with here.

16. Notice how persons can be loved for the sake of others, or for their own sake. For when I love someone very much, I love him and whatever belongs to him. We are loved by God, not for what we are in ourselves, but in him who by himself is beloved of the Father. Thus the Apostle adds *in his beloved Son* on account of whom he loves us and to the degree that we are like him. For love is based on similarity: *every beast loves its like: so also every man his neighbor* (Sir 13:15). By his own nature, the Son is similar to the Father, he is beloved before all else and essentially. Hence he is naturally, and in a most excellent way, loved by the Father. We, on the other hand, are sons through adoption to the degree that we are conformed to his Son; in this way we enjoy a certain participation in the divine

amoris habemus. Io. XIII, v. 35: *Pater diligit Filium, et omnia dedit in manu eius; qui credit in Filium, habet vitam aeternam.* Col. I, 13: *transtulit nos in regnum Filii dilectionis suae.*

17. Deinde cum dicit *in quo habemus redemptionem*, etc., ponit modum ipsius.

Circa hoc autem duo facit. Quia

primo proponit modum ex parte Christi;

secundo ex parte Dei, ibi *secundum divitias gratiae eius*, et cetera.

18. Ex parte Christi ponit duplicem modum, nam Christus per duo nos gratificavit. Sunt enim duo in nobis quae repugnant gratificationi divinae, scilicet peccati macula, et poenae noxa. Et sicut mors repugnat vitae, ita peccatum repugnat iustitiae, ita ut per hoc elongati a Dei similitudine, Deo grati non essemus. Sed per Christum nos gratificavit. Primo quidem ablata poena, et quantum ad hoc dicit, quod in Christo *habemus redemptionem*, scilicet a servitute peccati. I Petr. I, 18: *non corruptibilibus auro vel argento redempti estis de vana vestra conversatione paternae traditionis, sed pretioso sanguine*, et cetera. Apoc. V, 9: *redemisti nos Deo in sanguine tuo.*

Secundo dicimur redempti, quia a servitute, qua propter peccatum detinebamur, nec per nos plene satisfacere poteramus, per Christum liberati sumus, quia moriendo pro nobis satisfecit Deo Patri, et sic abolita est noxa culpae. Unde dicit *in remissionem peccatorum*. Io. I, 29: *ecce Agnus Dei, ecce qui tollit peccata mundi.* Lc. ult. 46: *oportebat Christum pati et resurgere a mortuis die tertia, et praedicari in nomine eius poenitentiam et remissionem peccatorum.*

19. Modus autem ex parte Dei ponitur, cum dicit *secundum divitias*, etc., quasi dicat, quod Deus gratificans nos, non solum culpam remisit nobis, sed Filium suum dedit, qui pro nobis satisfecit. Et hoc fuit ex superabundanti gratia, qua voluit per hoc honorem humanae naturae conservare, dum, quasi per iustitiam, homines a servitute peccati et mortis voluit liberare per mortem Filii sui. Et ideo dicit *secundum divitias gratiae eius*, quasi dicat: hoc quod redempti sumus et gratificati sumus per satisfactionem Filii eius, fuit ex abundanti gratia et misericordia, prout immeritis tribuitur misericordia et miseratio.

20. Haec autem, quae dicta sunt, prosecuti sumus secundum expositionem Glossae, quae quidem expositio videtur extorta, quia idem continetur in uno, quod in alio. Nam idem est dictu *elegit nos* et *praedestinavit nos*.

love. *The Father loves the Son, and has given all things into his hand. He who believes in the Son has life everlasting* (John 3:35–36). *He has transferred us into the kingdom of the Son he loves* (Col 1:13).

17. Next, when he says *in whom we have redemption*, he sets down the way itself that grace is given.

Concerning this he sets down two things:

first, the way it is given on the part of Christ;

second, on the part of God, at *according to the riches of his grace*.

18. On the part of Christ he writes of two ways through which Christ has made us pleasing. For within us there exists two antagonisms to the divine good pleasure, the stains of sin and the hurt of punishment. Justice is as opposed to sin as life is to death, so that through sin, having departed from our likeness to God, we cease being pleasing to God. But through Christ he has made us pleasing. First, indeed, by abolishing the punishment; and in reference to this he says that in Christ *we have redemption* from the slavery of sin. *You know that you were not redeemed with corruptible things, as gold or silver, from the vain manner of life handed down from your fathers: but with the precious blood of Christ, as of a lamb unspotted and undefiled* (1 Pet 1:18–19). *You have redeemed us for God, by your blood* (Rev 5:9).

Second, we are said to be redeemed because through Christ we are freed from a slavery in which we were caught as a result of sin without ourselves being capable of fully making satisfaction. By dying for us, Christ has satisfied the Father and thus the penalty of sin was abolished. Whence he says *unto the remission of sins*. *Behold the Lamb of God, who takes away the sin of the world* (John 1:29). *It is written that Christ should suffer and rise from the dead on the third day, and that penance and remission of sins should be preached in his name* (Luke 24:46–47).

19. The way we are blessed with grace on God's part is set down in *according to the riches of his grace*. As though he said: in making us pleasing to himself, God not only forgave us our sins, but he gave his own Son to make reparation on our behalf. This was from an overflowing graciousness by which he willed to preserve the human race's honor while, as though in justice, willing men to be freed from the slavery of sin and death through the death of his own Son. Thus, in saying *according to the riches of his grace* he seems to state: that we were redeemed and made pleasing through the satisfaction of his Son comes from an overflowing grace and mercy, since mercy and compassion are bestowed on those having no claim to it.

20. In what has been said so far we have followed the interpretation of a Gloss which seems to be a far-fetched exposition since the same idea expressed in one phrase occurs in another. *He chose us* is the same as to say *he destined us*.

Et idem dicitur per hoc, quod dicit *ut essemus sancti et immaculati*, et per hoc quod dicit *in adoptionem filiorum*.

Propter quod sciendum est, quod est consuetudo Apostoli, ut cum loquitur in aliqua difficili materia, quae immediate sequuntur, sunt praemissorum expositio, nec est ibi inculcatio verborum, sed expositio, et hunc modum servat hic Apostolus. Unde, servato eodem verborum pondere, aliter a principio dividamus, et dicamus, quod pars ista, *benedictus Deus*, etc., dividitur primo in tres partes, quia Apostolus primo reddit gratiarum actionem, ibi *benedictus Deus*, etc.; secundo recitat omnium beneficiorum simul largitionem, ibi *qui benedixit nos in omni benedictione spirituali*, etc.; tertio ponit divinorum beneficiorum in speciali apertam expressionem, ibi *sicut elegit*, et cetera. Et haec dividitur in duas partes, quia primo beneficia distincte exprimit; secundo ea exponit, ibi *qui praedestinavit nos*, et cetera.

Explicat autem beneficia: primo quantum ad electionem; secundo quantum ad ea quae sequuntur, ibi *ut essemus sancti*, et cetera.

Exponit autem primo de electione. Est enim duplex electio, scilicet praesentis iustitiae, et praedestinationis aeternae. De prima Io. VI, 71: *nonne duodecim vos elegi, et unus ex vobis diabolus est?* Et de hac Apostolus non intendit hic, quia ista non fuit *ante mundi constitutionem*, et ideo statim manifestat de qua intelligit, quia de secunda, scilicet de aeterna praedestinatione; propter quod dicit *praedestinavit nos*, et cetera. Et quia dicit *in Christo*, scilicet ut Christo essemus similes et conformes, secundum quod adoptamur in filios, ideo subdit *in adoptionem filiorum per Iesum Christum*. Hoc vero, quod dicit *in caritate*, exponit cum dicit *in quo habemus redemptionem per sanguinem eius*, quasi dicat: nos habemus, et cetera. Quod vero dicit *et immaculati*, exponit cum dicit *in remissionem peccatorum*. Hoc vero quod dicit *in conspectu eius*, exponit, dicens *in laudem gloriae gratiae suae*.

And the same idea is expressed in that *we should be holy and unspotted* as in *unto the adoption of children*.

In this regard it should be known that the customary procedure of the Apostle, when speaking of a difficult subject, is to explain what went before by what immediately follows. This is not verbal proliferation but an exposition; and this is the method the Apostle uses here. Retaining the same import of the words, we may divide it differently from the beginning, at *blessed be God* (Eph 1:3), into three sections. First, the Apostle gives thanks in *blessed be God*. Second, he mentions conjointly the bestowal of all blessings in *who has blessed us with every spiritual blessing in heavenly places, in Christ*. Third, he gives a clear expression of the divine blessings in particular, at *as he chose*. This latter is divided into two parts: first, he distinctly formulates the blessings; second, he interprets them, at *he destined us* (Eph 1:5).

He formulates the blessings: first, as regards election; second, as regards its consequences, at *that we should be holy* (Eph 1:4).

First, he treats of election, for there are two types of election, one involving a present justification and another an eternal predestination. Concerning the first it is written: *have not I chosen you twelve? And one of you is a devil?* (John 6:71). But this is not what the Apostle refers to since it did not occur *before the foundation of the world* (Eph 1:4). So he immediately clarifies what he means, that it is the second type, eternal predestination. Thus he says *he destined us* (Eph 1:5). As he said *in Christ* to signify that we are assimilated and conformed to Christ in proportion as we are adopted children, so he adds *unto the adoption of children through Jesus Christ*. What he means by *in charity* he explains when he says *in whom we have redemption through his blood*. As though he affirmed: we have redemption. *Unspotted* is expounded by *unto the remission of sins*; while *in his sight* is explained by *unto the praise of the glory of his grace*.

Lecture 3

1:8quae superabundavit in nobis in omni sapientia et prudentia: [n. 22]	1:8ἧς ἐπερίσσευσεν εἰς ἡμᾶς ἐν πάσῃ σοφίᾳ καὶ φρονήσει	1:8Which has superabounded in us, in all wisdom and prudence, [n. 22]
1:9ut notum faceret nobis sacramentum voluntatis suae, secundum beneplacitum ejus, quod proposuit in eo, [n. 25]	1:9γνωρίσας ἡμῖν τὸ μυστήριον τοῦ θελήματος αὐτοῦ, κατὰ τὴν εὐδοκίαν αὐτοῦ ἣν προέθετο ἐν αὐτῷ	1:9That he might make known unto us the mystery of his will, according to his purpose, which he has purposed in him, [n. 25]
1:10in dispensatione plenitudinis temporum, instaurare omnia in Christo, quae in caelis et quae in terra sunt, in ipso; [n. 28]	1:10εἰς οἰκονομίαν τοῦ πληρώματος τῶν καιρῶν, ἀνακεφαλαιώσασθαι τὰ πάντα ἐν τῷ Χριστῷ, τὰ ἐπὶ τοῖς οὐρανοῖς καὶ τὰ ἐπὶ τῆς γῆς: ἐν αὐτῷ,	1:10In the dispensation of the fullness of times, to re-establish all things in Christ, that are in heaven and on earth, in him. [n. 28]

21. Positis beneficiis communiter omnibus collatis, hic Apostolus ponit beneficia specialiter apostolis collata. Dividitur autem haec pars in duas, quia

primo proponit beneficia singulariter apostolis collata;

secundo ostendit causam eorum, ibi *in quo et nos sorte vocati*, et cetera.

Circa primum tria facit, quia

primo proponit singularia apostolorum beneficia quantum ad excellentiam sapientiae;

secundo quantum ad specialem revelationem sacramenti absconditi, ibi *ut notum faceret*, etc.;

tertio exponit quid sit illud sacramentum, ibi *secundum beneplacitum*, et cetera.

22. Dicit ergo primo: dico quod secundum divitias gratiae eius omnes fideles communiter, tam vos quam nos, habemus redemptionem et remissionem peccatorum per sanguinem Christi; *quae* quidem gratia *superabundavit in nobis*, id est abundantius fuit, quam in aliis.

23. Ex quo apparet temeritas illorum (ut non dicam error), qui aliquos sanctos praesumunt comparare apostolis in gratia et gloria. Manifeste enim patet ex verbis istis, quod apostoli habent gratiam maiorem quam aliqui alii sancti, post Christum et Virginem Matrem.

Si vero dicatur alios sanctos tantum mereri posse quantum et apostoli meruerunt et per consequens tantam gratiam habere, dicendum est quod bene argueretur si gratia pro meritis daretur; quod si ita esset, *iam non esset gratia*, ut dicitur Rom. XI, 6.

Et ideo sicut Deus praeordinavit aliquos sanctos ad maiorem dignitatem, ita et abundantiorem gratiam eis infudit, sicut Christo homini, quem ad unitatem personae assumpsit, contulit gratiam singularem. Et gloriosam Virginem Mariam, quam in matrem elegit et quantum ad animam et quantum ad corpus gratia implevit; et sic apostolos, sicut ad singularem dignitatem vocavit, ita et singularis gratiae privilegio dotavit; propter quod

21. Having set down the blessings generally given to all, the Apostle now turns to those favors especially granted to the apostles. This section is divided into two parts:

first, he proposes the special blessings given the apostles;

second, he indicates their cause, at *in whom we are also called by lot* (Eph 1:11).

In reference to the first he does three things:

first, he sets down the particular blessings of the apostles as regards the excellence of their wisdom;

second, as regards a unique revelation of the hidden mystery, at *that he might make known*;

third, he suggests what this mystery is, at *according to his purpose*.

22. He first states: according to the riches of his grace all the faithful together, both you and we, possess redemption and the remission of sins through the blood of Christ. This grace *has superabounded in us* who have it more fully than others.

23. Whence the rashness—not to say error—of those who dare equate the grace and glory of some saints with that of the apostles. For this passage openly asserts that the apostles are more fully graced than the other saints, except for Christ and his Virgin Mother.

However, should it be claimed that other saints were able to merit as much as the apostles merited, and consequently would have as much grace, it must be said that this would be a good argument if grace was given according to merits—but if that were the case, *grace is no more grace* (Rom 11:6).

Greater dignity was preordained by God to some saints, and hence he infused grace more abundantly into them. For example, he imparted a unique grace to Christ as man when he assumed the humanity into the unity of his person. He endowed with special graces in both her body and soul, the glorious Virgin Mary whom he chose to be his mother. Similarly, those God called to a unique dignity, the apostles, were gifted with a corresponding favor of grace. Thus the Apostle states: *ourselves also, who have the first*

dicit apostolus Rom. VIII, 23: *nos ipsi primitias Spiritus habentes*. Glossa: *tempore prius, et caeteris abundantius*.

Temerarium est ergo aliquem sanctum apostolis comparare.

24. Superabundavit ergo gratia Dei in apostolis ***in omni sapientia***. Nam apostoli praepositi sunt Ecclesiae sicut pastores. Ier. c. III, 15: *dabo vobis pastores secundum cor meum, et pascent vos scientia et doctrina*.

Duo autem spectant ad pastores, scilicet ut sint sublimes in cognitione divinorum, et industrii in actione religionis. Nam subditi instruendi sunt in fide, et ad hoc necessaria est sapientia, quae est cognitio divinorum, et quantum ad hoc dicit ***in omni sapientia***. Lc. XXI, 15: *ego dabo vobis os et sapientiam, cui non poterunt resistere nec contradicere omnes adversarii vestri*.

Item, gubernandi sunt subditi in exterioribus, et ad hoc necessaria est prudentia; dirigit enim in temporalibus, et quantum ad hoc dicit ***prudentia***. Matth. X, 16: *estote ergo prudentes*, et cetera.

Sic ergo apparet beneficium apostolorum quantum ad excellentiam sapientiae.

25. Sequitur eorum beneficium quantum ad excellentiam revelationis, ibi ***ut notum faceret sacramentum***, etc., quasi dicat: sapientia nostra non est ut sciamus naturas rerum et siderum cursus et huiusmodi, sed in solo Christo. I Cor. II, 2: *non enim iudicavi me scire aliquid inter vos, nisi Christum Iesum*, et cetera. Unde hic dicit ***ut notum faceret sacramentum***, id est sacrum secretum, scilicet mysterium Incarnationis, quod fuit ab initio absconditum.

Causam autem huius sacramenti absconditi subdit, dicens ***voluntatis***. Nam effectus futuri non cognoscuntur, nisi cognitis causis, sicut eclipsim futuram non cognoscimus, nisi cognoscendo causam eius. Cum ergo causa mysterii Incarnationis sit voluntas Dei: quia propter nimiam caritatem quam Deus habuit ad homines, voluit incarnari, Io. III, v. 16: *sic enim Deus dilexit mundum, ut Filium suum unigenitum daret*, voluntas autem Dei occultissima est, I Cor. II, 11: *quae Dei sunt, nemo novit, nisi Spiritus Dei*, causa ergo Incarnationis occulta fuit, nisi quibus Deus revelavit per Spiritum Sanctum, sicut Apostolus dicit I Cor. II, 10.

Dicit ergo ***ut notum faceret sacramentum***, id est sacrum secretum, quod ideo est secretum, quia ***voluntatis suae***. Matth. XI, 25: *confiteor tibi, Domine, Pater caeli et terrae, quia abscondisti haec a sapientibus et prudentibus, et revelasti ea parvulis*. Item Col. c. I, 26: *mysterium, quod absconditum fuit a saeculis et generationibus; nunc*

fruits of the Spirit (Rom 8:23). And a Gloss comments: *their share is first in time and more copious than others*.

What rashness, therefore, to put some later saint on the same level with the apostles.

24. God's grace has superabounded in the apostles, ***in all wisdom***. For the apostles are set over the Church to be her pastors: *and I will give you pastors according to my own heart: and they shall feed you with knowledge and doctrine* (Jer 3:15).

Two qualities should characterize pastors: a profound knowledge of divine truths and an assiduous fulfillment of religious actions. They must teach those trusted to them the true faith; this requires that wisdom which consists in a knowledge of the divine, concerning which he remarks ***in all wisdom***. *For I will give you a mouth and wisdom, which all your adversaries shall not be able to resist and gainsay* (Luke 21:15).

They also need ***prudence*** to guide their subjects in external and temporal affairs: *be therefore prudent as serpents and simple as doves* (Matt 10:16).

Thus the special blessing of wisdom given to the apostles is clearly expressed.

25. The reception of an uncommon revelation is their next blessing, ***that he might make known unto us the mystery***. As if he had said: our wisdom does not consist in discovering the natures of material realities, nor the course of the stars, or such like; rather, it concerns Christ alone. *I decided not to know any thing among you, but Jesus Christ, and him crucified* (1 Cor 2:2). Hence he says ***that he might make known the mystery***, that is, the sacred secret, hidden from the beginning, the mystery of the Incarnation.

He adds the cause of this hidden mystery when he says ***his will***. Future events are known only if their causes are; for example, we can determine a future eclipse only by knowing what causes an eclipse. Now the mystery of the Incarnation has God's will as its cause since he willed to become incarnate on account of his intense love for men: *for God so loved the world, as to give his only begotten Son* (John 3:16). Yet God's will is more hidden than anything else: *no one knows what pertains to God, but the Spirit of God* (1 Cor 2:11). So, the cause of the Incarnation was concealed from everyone except those to whom God revealed it through the Holy Spirit, as the Apostle mentions: *God has revealed to us through the Spirit. For the Spirit searches everything, even the depths of God* (1 Cor 2:10).

Hence he affirms ***that he might make known the mystery*** which is a sacred secret—a secret because it is ***of his will***. *I thank you, Father, Lord of heaven and earth, for hiding these things from the wise and clever and revealing them to little children* (Matt 11:25). *The mystery, hidden from ages and generations, and now made manifest to his saints, to*

autem manifestatum est sanctis eius, quibus voluit Deus notas facere divitias gloriae sacramenti huius.

26. Quid autem sit hoc sacramentum, exponit dicens *secundum beneplacitum*, et cetera.

Quae quidem sententia intricata est, et debet sic construi: *ut notum faceret*, etc., quod quidem sacramentum est *instaurare omnia in Christo*, id est per Christum. Omnia dico, *quae in caelis et in terra sunt*. Instaurare, inquam, in eo, scilicet Christo, cum *dispensatione plenitudinis temporum*, et hoc *secundum beneplacitum eius*. Ubi tria tangit, scilicet sacramenti causam, temporis congruitatem, et sacramenti utilitatem.

27. Causam quodam modo tangit, cum dicit *secundum beneplacitum*. Licet autem quidquid Deo placet, bonum sit, hoc tamen beneplacitum Dei anthonomastice bonum dicitur, quia per ipsum ad perfectam fruitionem bonitatis perducimur. Ps. CXLVI, 11: *beneplacitum est domino super timentes eum*, et cetera. Rom. XII, 2: *ut probetis quae sit voluntas Dei bona, et beneplacens, et perfecta*.

28. Congruitas temporis fuit *in dispensatione plenitudinis*, de qua dicitur Gal. c. IV, 4: *at ubi venit plenitudo temporis, misit Deus Filium suum factum ex muliere*.

Unde Apostolus hic excludit quaestionem frivolam, quam gentiles quaerere consueverunt. Ut enim dicitur Iob XXIV, 1, *ab Omnipotente non sunt abscondita tempora*, unde sicut omnia ordinat et dispensat, ita et tempora, dispensando et accommodando ea effectibus quos producit secundum congruentiam eorum. Sicut autem aliis effectibus ab eo productis tempora ordinata sunt, ita et certum tempus praeordinavit ab aeterno mysterio Incarnationis. Quod quidem tempus, secundum Glossam, existens fuit postquam homo convictus fuit de sua insipientia ante legem scriptam, dum scilicet creaturas colebat ut Creatorem, ut dicitur Rom. I, 22: *dicentes se esse sapientes, stulti facti sunt*; et de impotentia per legem scriptam, quam implere non poterat. Ut sic homines adventum Christi, de sua sapientia et virtute non praesumentes, non contemnerent, sed, quasi infirmi et quodammodo ignari, Christum avidius affectarent.

29. Et effectus huius sacramenti est *instaurare omnia*. Nam inquantum facta sunt propter hominem, omnia instaurari dicuntur. Amos IX, 11: *suscitabo tabernaculum David quod cecidit, et reaedificabo aperturas murorum eius, et ea quae corruerant, instaurabo*.

Omnia, inquam, *quae in caelis*, id est angelos: non quod pro angelis mortuus sit Christus, sed quia redimendo hominem, reintegratur ruina angelorum. Ps. CIX, 6: *implevit ruinas*, et cetera. Ubi cavendus est

whom God would make known the riches of the glory of this mystery (Col 1:26–27).

26. He then explains something about this mystery, at *according to his purpose*.

His thought is involved and should be construed as: *that he might make known unto us the mystery of his will*, which mystery is *to re-establish all things in Christ*, that is, through Christ. All, namely, that are *in heaven and on earth*. This re-establishment in Christ must be *in the dispensation of the fullness of times* which, in turn, is *according to his purpose*. Thus, three aspects of the mystery are touched on: the mystery's cause, the fittingness of the time of its appearance, and its purpose.

27. *According to his purpose* briefly sums up the cause. Although whatever pleases God is good, God's pleasure in making known this mystery is autonomastically said to be good because through it we are led to perfectly enjoy goodness. *Yahweh is pleased with those who fear him, who rely on his strength* (Ps 147:11); *that you may prove what is the good and the acceptable and the perfect will of God* (Rom 12:2).

28. The suitable time was *in that dispensation of the fullness of times*. *But when the fullness of the time came, God sent his Son, made of a woman, made under the law, that he might redeem them who were under the law, that we might receive the adoption of sons* (Gal 4:4–5).

The pointless problem pagans used to raise is thus brushed aside by the Apostle. *Times are not hidden from the Almighty* (Job 24:1). He orders and arranges everything, including time; for he manages and accommodates the passage of time to those events which he wills to exist at the right moment. Just as other events effected by him had their specified time, likewise he eternally preordained a time for the mystery of the Incarnation. This time, a Gloss points out, occurred after man was convinced of his own stupidity before the written law, when he worshiped creatures instead of the Creator—for, *professing themselves to be wise, they became fools* (Rom 1:22)—and of his own absolute inability to live up to the prescriptions of the written law. Thus men, no longer trusting in their own wisdom and power, would not consider Christ's advent as unimportant. Weak, and to a certain extent ignorant, they would eagerly desire the Christ.

29. The mystery's purpose is to *re-establish all things*. Inasmuch as everything was made for mankind, everything is said to be re-established: *in that day I will raise up the booth of David that had fallen; I will close up its breaches and rebuild it as long ago* (Amos 9:11).

Everything that is in heaven, namely, the angels. Christ did not die for the angels, but in redeeming mankind *he shall fill the ruins* (Ps 110:6) left by the sin of the angels. Beware of the error Origen fell into, as if the damned angels

error Origenis, ne per hoc credamus angelos damnatos redimendos esse per Christum, ut ipse finxit.

Et quae in terris, inquantum caelestia terrenis pacificat. Col. I, 20: *pacificans per sanguinem crucis eius, sive quae in terris, sive quae in caelis sunt*; quod est intelligendum quantum ad sufficientiam, etsi omnia non restaurentur quantum ad efficaciam.

were to be redeemed through Christ; this was only a figment of his imagination.

And what is on earth insofar as he reconciles heavenly and earthly realities: *making peace through the blood of his cross, both as to the things that are on earth and the things that are in heaven* (Col 1:20). This must be understood in reference to the sufficiency of the redemption, even though, with respect to its efficacy, everything will not be re-established.

Lecture 4

1:11in quo etiam et nos sorte vocati sumus praedestinati secundum propositum ejus qui operatur omnia secundum consilium voluntatis suae: [n. 31]

1:12ut simus in laudem gloriae ejus nos, qui ante speravimus in Christo; [n. 35]

1:11ἐν ᾧ καὶ ἐκληρώθημεν προορισθέντες κατὰ πρόθεσιν τοῦ τὰ πάντα ἐνεργοῦντος κατὰ τὴν βουλὴν τοῦ θελήματος αὐτοῦ,

1:12εἰς τὸ εἶναι ἡμᾶς εἰς ἔπαινον δόξης αὐτοῦ τοὺς προηλπικότας ἐν τῷ Χριστῷ:

1:11 In whom we also are called by lot, being predestined according to the purpose of him who works all things according to the counsel of his will. [n. 31]

1:12 That we may be for the praise of his glory: we who before hoped in Christ: [n. 35]

---

30. Supra posuit Apostolus abundantiam gratiae, quam ipse et alii apostoli a Christo receperunt. Ne autem crederet aliquis eos propriis meritis eam recepisse, ideo consequenter ostendit, quod gratis eam receperunt, vocati a Deo non propriis meritis.

Dividitur autem pars ista in tres: quia

primo proponit gratuitam vocationem;

secundo voluntariam Dei praedestinationem, ibi *praedestinati secundum propositum eius*, etc.;

tertio utriusque finem, ibi *ut simus in laudem gloriae eius*, et cetera.

31. Dicit ergo: dixi quod huiusmodi gratia superabundavit in nobis, et quod in Christo omnia restaurata sunt. *In quo etiam*, id est per quem Christum, *nos sorte sumus vocati*, id est non nostris meritis, sed divina electione. Col. I, 12: *gratias agentes Deo et Patri, qui dignos nos fecit in partem sortis sanctorum, in lumine*, et cetera. Ps. XXX, 16: *in manibus tuis sortes meae*.

32. Ad huius autem intellectum sciendum est quod multa fiunt inter homines, quae fortuita videntur et contingentia; quae tamen sunt secundum divinam providentiam ordinata. Sors nihil aliud est, quam exquisitio providentiae divinae de aliquo contingenti et humano. Unde Augustinus super illud Ps. XXX, 16: *in manibus tuis sortes meae*, dicit quod sors non est aliquod malum, sed in rebus dubiis divinam exquirens voluntatem.

Est autem in sortibus triplex peccatum vitandum. Primo quidem superstitionis; nam omnis vana et illicita religio superstitio est. Tunc ergo in sortibus incurritur peccatum illicitae superstitionis, quando in eis initur aliquod pactum cum daemonibus. Unde dicitur Ez. XXI, 21: *stetit rex Babylonis in bivio in capite duarum viarum divinationem quaerens, commiscens sagittas. Interrogavit idola, exta consuluit.* Commiscere enim sagittas, ad sortilegium pertinet et interrogare idola ad superstitionem. Et ibi sortilegium damnatur inter peccata ad superstitionem pertinentia.

Secundo vitandum est peccatum tentationis Dei; nam quamdiu per se homo aliquid potest facere et scire quid debeat facere, si tunc a Deo sorte, vel aliquo alio loco tali exploret quid facere debeat, Deum tentat. Quando autem necessitas imminet, neque ipse per

30. Previously the Apostle wrote of how he and the other apostles received an abundance of grace from Christ. Lest anyone imagine they had it coming to them the Apostle quickly affirms that they were called by God gratuitously, not for their personal merits.

This section is divided into three parts:

first, the gratuity of the call;

second, God's freedom in predestination, at *according to the purpose*;

third, what is the end of both the vocation and the predestination, at *for the praise of his glory*.

31. I have indicated, he says, that grace has superabounded in us and that everything has been re-established in Christ. The same Christ *in whom we also are called by lot*, not by our own merits but by a divine choice: *giving thanks to God the Father, who has made us worthy to be partakers of the lot of the saints in light* (Col 1:12) because *my lots are in your hands* (Ps 31:16).

32. To understand this it should be realized that many human events which seem to occur by fate and chance, in reality are arranged according to divine providence. Casting lots is no more than a search for divine guidance in contingent and human affairs. Augustine, commenting on: *my lots are in your hands* (Ps 31:15), teaches that casting lots is not an evil, but a means of discovering God's will in a doubtful issue.

Nonetheless, three sins must be avoided. The first is superstition; for any religion which is shallow and immoral is superstition. The forbidden sin of superstition would be incurred when the casting of lots is performed in league with the devil. *The king of Babylon stood in the highway, at the head of two ways, seeking divination, shuffling arrows: he consulted the idols and looked at the liver* (Ezek 21:26). The shuffling of the arrows is related to sortilege, and the questioning of idols belongs to superstition. Sortilege, moreover, is condemned there among sins pertaining to superstition.

Second, the sin of tempting God must be shunned. As long as a man can discover and accomplish by himself what he ought to do, he tempts God if he resorts to lots, or any other such method, to ascertain what he should do. Only when unavoidably threatened by situations where one is

seipsum iuvari potest, tunc licite a Deo inquirit quid faciere debeat. II Par. XX, 12: *cum ignoremus quid agere debeamus, hoc solum habemus residui, ut oculos nostros dirigamus ad te.*

Tertio vitandum est peccatum vanitatis, quod fit si de inutilibus et impertinentibus ad nos inquiramus, ut puta de futuris contingentibus. Unde dicitur Act. I, 7: *non est vestrum nosse tempora, vel momenta, quae Pater posuit in sua potestate.*

33. Potest ergo secundum hoc triplex sors accipi, scilicet quaedam divisoria, quaedam consultoria et quaedam divinatoria.

Divisoria est cum aliqui dividentes haereditatem et concordare non valentes, mittunt sortes, puta annulum, vel chartam, vel aliquid tale ostendendo, dicentes: ille cuicumque evenerit, habebit partem istam in haereditate. Et huiusmodi sortes possunt mitti licite. Prov. XVIII, 18: *contradictiones comprimit sors: et inter potentes quoque diiudicat*, id est inter volentes dividere.

Consultoria autem fit, quando quis dubitans quid facere debeat, consulit Deum, mittens sortes. Ionae I, 7 dicitur, quod quando supervenit tempestas illa in mari, consuluerunt Deum, sortem mittentes, ut scirent cuius peccato tempestas illa venisset. Et hic modus licitus est, maxime in necessitatibus et in electionibus potestatum saecularium. Unde faciunt rotulos de cera, in quorum quibusdam ponunt aliquas chartas, et in quibusdam non, quos bussulos vocant, ut illi quibus veniunt bussuli cum chartis, habeant voces in electione. Sed hoc, ante adventum Spiritus Sancti, Apostoli fecerunt etiam in electione spirituali, Act. I, 26, quando sors cecidit super Mathiam; sed hoc post adventum Spiritus Sancti amplius non licet in praedictis electionibus, quia hoc faciendo iniuriaretur Spiritui Sancto. Credendum est enim, quod Spiritus Sanctus providet Ecclesiae suae de bonis pastoribus. Unde post adventum Spiritus Sancti quando apostoli elegerunt septem diaconos, non miserunt sortes; et ideo in nulla electione ecclesiastica hoc modo licet.

Divinatoria autem sors est inquisitio de futuris soli divinae cognitioni reservatis. Et haec semper habet vanitatem admixtam, nec potest sine vitio curiositatis fieri.

Quia ergo sors nihil aliud est quam inquisitio rerum quae ex divina voluntate fiunt, gratia autem eius ex sola divina voluntate dependet, inde est, quod gratia divinae electionis dicitur sors, quia Deus per modum sortis secundum occultam providentiam, non ex alicuius meritis, per gratiam internam vocat.

34. Deinde cum dicit **praedestinati**, etc., ponit voluntariam Dei praedestinationem, de qua dicitur Rom. VIII, 30: *quos praedestinavit, hos et vocavit.* Cuius quidem praedestinationis ratio non sunt merita nostra,

powerless by himself can a man licitly resort to questioning God with lots concerning what he must do. *But as we know not what to do, we can only turn our eyes to you* (2 Chr 20:12).

Vanity is the third sin. It is committed if we inquire into futile matters not pertaining to us; for example, contingent events in the future. *It is not for you to know the times or moments, which the Father has put in his own power* (Acts 1:7).

33. Relative to this purpose for which they are cast, there are three types of lots: some are divisory, others are consultatory, while still others are divinatory.

Divisory lots are those which people cast when they are dividing an inheritance and cannot agree. Using a certain slip of paper or the like they declare: whoever it will fall to shall have this part of the inheritance. Such lots can be cast lawfully: *the lot puts an end to disputes, and decides between powerful contenders* (Prov 18:18) when they wish to divide in this way.

Consultatory lots are used when someone doubts what he should do and consults God by casting lots. Jonah recounts how, when the great storm came upon them at sea, they cast lots to seek information from God that they might know for whose sin the tempest had occurred (Jonah 1:7). This method is licit, especially in necessities and in the elections of secular rulers. Hence, men will make small wax balls called 'bussuli,' of which some contain slips of paper and others none. Whoever draws a 'bussulus' with the paper inside has a voice in the election. This was done also, previous to the Holy Spirit's coming, in spiritual elections, evidenced in the choice of Mathias by lot (Acts 1:26). Now that the Holy Spirit has come, however, it is no longer lawful in these elections since making use of them would be an insult to the Holy Spirit. It must be believed, after all, that the Holy Spirit will provide his Church with good pastors. After the Holy Spirit's advent, therefore, when the apostles chose the seven deacons (Acts 6), they did not cast lots. Thus, this method is not lawful in any ecclesiastical election.

Divinatory lots augur future events reserved to the divine knowledge alone. They always are colored by vainglory, nor can they be resorted to without a sinful curiosity.

Lots, therefore, are nothing other than a questioning concerning realities whose occurrence depends on the divine will. Since grace depends on the divine will alone, the grace of divine election is termed a lot. For God, as though by lot, according to his hidden providence, calls men through an inner grace and not on account of anyone's merits.

34. Next, when he says **predestined according to his purpose**, he writes of the free predestination of God concerning which it is written: *and those he predestined he has also called* (Rom 8:30). The reason for this predestination

sed mera Dei voluntas, propter quod subdit **secundum propositum eius**. Rom. c. VIII, 28: *scimus quoniam diligentibus Deum omnia cooperantur in bonum, his qui secundum propositum vocati sunt sancti*.

Quod autem secundum propositum praedestinaverit, probat, quia non solum hoc, sed etiam omnia alia, quae Deus facit, **operatur secundum consilium voluntatis suae**. Ps. CXXXIV, 6: *omnia quaecumque voluit dominus fecit*. Is. XLVI, 10: *consilium meum stabit, et omnis voluntas mea fiet*.

Non autem dicit *secundum voluntatem*, ne credas quod sit irrationabilis, sed **secundum consilium voluntatis suae**, id est secundum voluntatem suam quae est ex ratione, non secundum quod ratio importat discursum, sed secundum quod designat certam et deliberatam voluntatem.

35. Ultimo autem tangit finem utriusque, scilicet praedestinationis et vocationis, scilicet laudem Dei. Unde dicit **ut simus in laudem gloriae eius nos, qui ante speravimus in Christo**, et per nos, qui credimus in Christo, laudetur gloria Dei. Is. LV, 12: *montes et colles cantabunt coram Deo laudem*. Laus autem gloriae Dei, ut dicit Ambrosius, est cum multi acquiruntur ad fidem, sicut gloria medici est cum multos acquirit et curat. Eccli. II, 9: *qui timetis Dominum, sperate in illum, et in oblectatione veniet vobis misericordia*.

is not our merits but the will of God alone, on account of which he adds **according to the purpose of him**. *And we know that to those who love God, all things work together unto good; to those who are called saints according to his purpose* (Rom 8:28).

He approves of what he has predestined according to his purpose since not only this, but also everything else that God does he **works according to the counsel of his will**. *Whatever he wills Yahweh does, in heaven and on earth, in the seas and in all the depths* (Ps 135:6). *My counsel shall stand, and what I like I shall do* (Isa 46:10).

He did not say *according to his will* lest you would believe it was irrational, but **according to the counsel of his will**. This means, according to his will which arises from reason; not that reason here implies any transition in his thoughts, but it rather indicates a certain and deliberate will.

35. Finally, he briefly mentions the end of one's predestination and vocation, namely, the praise of God. Thus he states **that we may be for the praise of his glory, we who before hoped in Christ**. Through us, who believe in Christ, the glory of God is extolled. *The mountains and hills shall sing praise before you* (Isa 55:12). The praise of God's glory, as Ambrose remarks, occurs when many persons are won over to the faith, as a doctor's glory is in a large clientele and their cure. *You who fear the Lord, hope for good things, for everlasting joy and mercy* (Sir 2:9).

Lecture 5

1:13in quo et vos, cum audissetis verbum veritatis, Evangelium salutis vestrae, in quo et credentes signati estis Spiritu promissionis Sancto, [n. 37]

1:14qui est pignus haereditatis nostrae, in redemptionem acquisitionis, in laudem gloriae ipsius. [n. 43]

1:13ἐν ᾧ καὶ ὑμεῖς ἀκούσαντες τὸν λόγον τῆς ἀληθείας, τὸ εὐαγγέλιον τῆς σωτηρίας ὑμῶν, ἐν ᾧ καὶ πιστεύσαντες ἐσφραγίσθητε τῷ πνεύματι τῆς ἐπαγγελίας τῷ ἁγίῳ,

1:14ὅ ἐστιν ἀρραβὼν τῆς κληρονομίας ἡμῶν, εἰς ἀπολύτρωσιν τῆς περιποιήσεως, εἰς ἔπαινον τῆς δόξης αὐτοῦ.

1:13 In whom you also, after you had heard the word of truth (the Gospel of your salvation), in whom also believing, you were signed with the Holy Spirit of promise. [n. 37]

1:14 Who is the pledge of our inheritance, unto the redemption of acquisition, unto the praise of his glory. [n. 43]

36. Postquam enarravit Apostolus beneficia collata communiter omnibus fidelibus, exhibita specialiter apostolis, hic consequenter enumerat beneficia ipsis Ephesiis collata.

Dividitur autem pars ista in duas, quia

primo proponit beneficia eis exhibita;

secundo insinuat affectum suum ex ipsis beneficiis excitatum, ibi *propterea et ego audiens*, et cetera.

Prima iterum in tres dividitur, secundum tria beneficia eis exhibita; quia

primo proponit beneficium praedicationis;

secundo beneficium conversionis ad fidem, ibi *in quo et credentes signati estis*;

tertio beneficium iustificationis, ibi *signati estis*, et cetera.

37. Dicit ergo quantum ad primum *in quo*, scilicet Christo, *et vos cum audivissetis*, id est cuius beneficio et virtute audivistis, *verbum veritatis*, id est verbum praedicationis, in quantum ipse Christus ad vos praedicatores misit. Rom. X, 14: *quomodo audient sine praedicante? Quomodo vero praedicabunt, nisi mittantur?* Item infra eodem: *ergo fides ex auditu, auditus autem per verbum Dei.* Eius ergo beneficio audiunt, qui praedicatores eis mittit. Lc. XI, 28: *beati qui audiunt verbum Dei, et custodiunt illud.*

38. Hoc verbum praedicationis tripliciter commendat Apostolus. Primo a veritate cum dicit *verbum veritatis* quippe quia accipit originem a Christo, de quo dicitur Io. c. XVII, 17: *sermo tuus veritas est*; Iac. I, v. 18: *voluntarie genuit nos verbo veritatis suae.*

Secundo quia est annuntiatio bona. Unde dicit *Evangelium*, quod quidem annuntiat summum bonum et vitam aeternam, et anthonomastice verbum fidei, Evangelium dicitur, quasi Annuntiatio summi boni. Is. LII, 7: *quam pulchri pedes annuntiantis et praedicantis pacem, annuntiantis bonum, praedicantis salutem,* eodem 41, *super montem excelsum ascende tu qui evangelizas Sion.* Et hoc est quantum ad futura bona.

36. Once the Apostle has enumerated the blessings offered generally to all the faithful, then those especially given the apostles, he begins to recount those granted to the Ephesians themselves.

This section is divided into two parts:

first, he sets down the favors shown them;

second, he describes his feelings aroused by the favors, at *wherefore, I also* (Eph 1:15).

The first is divided into three parts according to the three blessings granted to them:

first, the blessing of preaching;

second, the blessing of conversion to the faith, at *in whom also believing*;

third, the blessing of justification, at *were signed*.

37. In reference to the first point he says: Christ *in whom you also, after you had heard*, that is, by whose favor and power you have heard the proclamation of the *word of truth* since Christ himself has sent those who preach it to you. *How shall they believe him of whom they have not heard? And how shall they hear, without a preacher? And how shall they preach unless they be sent? . . . faith, then, comes by hearing; and hearing by the word of Christ* (Rom 10:14–15, 17). They hear through the blessing of him who sends them the preachers: *blessed are they who hear the word of God and keep it* (Luke 11:28).

38. The Apostle mentions the threefold recommendation of this preached word. It is, first of all, true; *a word of truth*. Indeed, it could be nothing else since its source is Christ, concerning whom it is written: *your word is truth* (John 17:7); *for of his own will he has begotten us by the word of truth* (Jas 1:18).

Second, it is a proclamation of good news. Hence he says *the Gospel*: it announces the highest good and eternal life. 'Word of faith' is antonomastically applicable to the Gospel as the communication of the highest good. *How beautiful upon the mountains are the feet of him who brings good news and preaches salvation . . . go up on a high mountain, lady-messenger of Zion* (Isa 52:7; 40:9). This refers to future goods.

Tertio describitur et commendatur quantum ad bona praesentia, quia salvat. Unde dicit *salutis vestrae*, id est quod creditum dat salutem. Rom. I, 16: *non enim erubesco Evangelium: virtus enim Dei est in salutem omni credenti*. I Cor. XV, 1: *notum autem vobis facio, fratres, Evangelium, quod praedicavi vobis, quod et accepistis, in quo et statis, per quod et salvamini*.

39. Quantum autem ad beneficium conversionis ad fidem, dicit *in quo*, scilicet Christo, id est, in cuius operatione vos *credentes, signati estis*. Quod quidem beneficium ideo apponitur fidei, quia fides necessaria est audientibus. Frustra enim quis audiret verbum veritatis, si non crederet, et ipsum credere est per Christum. Infra II, 8: *gratia enim estis salvati per fidem. Et hoc non ex vobis, donum enim Dei est*.

40. Quantum vero ad beneficium iustificationis dicit *signati estis*, et hoc *per Spiritum Sanctum*, qui datus est vobis, de quo dicit tria, scilicet quod est signum, et quod est Spiritus promissionis, et quod est pignus haereditatis.

41. Signum quidem est inquantum per eum infunditur caritas in cordibus nostris, qua distinguimur ab his qui non sunt filii Dei. Et quantum ad hoc dicit *signati estis*, scilicet divisi a grege diaboli. Infra cap. IV, v. 30: *nolite contristare Spiritum Sanctum Dei, in quo signati estis*, et cetera. Sicut enim homines gregibus suis apponunt signa, ut ab aliis distinguantur, ita Dominus gregem suum, id est populum suum, spirituali signo voluit signari.

Dominus autem populum peculiarem habuit, in Veteri quidem Testamento Iudaeos. Ez. XXXIV, 31: *vos autem greges mei, greges pascuae meae homines estis*. Unde Ps. XCIV, v. 7: *nos autem populus eius, et oves pascuae eius*. Sed quia hic grex in pascuis corporalibus pascebatur, scilicet in doctrina corporali et in bonis temporalibus, Is. I, 19: *si volueritis et audieritis me, bona terrae comedetis*, ideo eum Dominus corporali signo, scilicet circumcisionis, ab aliis separavit et distinxit. Gen. XVII, 13: *eritque pactum meum in carne vestra*. Prius autem dicitur: *circumcidetis carnem praeputii vestri, ut sit signum foederis inter me et vos*.

In Novo autem Testamento gregem habuit populum Christianum. I Petr. II, 25: *conversi estis nunc ad pastorem et episcopum animarum vestrarum*. Io. X, 27: *oves meae vocem meam audient*, et cetera. Sed grex iste pascitur in pascuis doctrinae spiritualis et spiritualibus bonis, ideo eum signo spirituali ab aliis Dominus distinxit. Hoc autem est Spiritus Sanctus, per quem illi qui Christi sunt, distinguuntur ab aliis qui non sunt eius. Quia autem Spiritus Sanctus amor est, ergo tunc Spiritus Sanctus datur alicui, quando efficitur amator Dei et proximi. Rom. V, 5: *caritas Dei diffusa est in cordibus nostris per Spiritum Sanctum*, et cetera.

The present goods are what describe and recommend the preached word in the third place, for it saves. Thus he says *of your salvation*; if believed in, it gives salvation. *I am not ashamed of the Gospel. For it is the power of God unto salvation to all who believe* (Rom 1:16). *Now I make known unto you, brothers, the Gospel which I preached to you, which also you have received and wherein you stand, by which also you are saved* (1 Cor 15:1).

39. Regarding the blessing of conversion to the faith, he states *in whom*, namely, Christ, by whose action you *also believing, were signed*. This blessing is applied to faith since faith is necessary for those who listen. In vain would anyone listen to the word of truth if he did not believe, and the believing itself is through Christ. *By grace you are saved through faith, and that not of yourselves, for it is the gift of God* (Eph 2:8).

40. Concerning the blessing of justification he mentions that *you were signed with the Holy Spirit* who was given to you. Concerning this Spirit three things are said: he is a sign, the Spirit of the promise, and the pledge of our inheritance.

41. He is a sign inasmuch as through him charity is infused into our hearts, thereby distinguishing us from those who are not the children of God. Relating to this be says *you were signed*, set apart from Satan's fold. *Do not grieve the Holy Spirit of God; whereby you are sealed unto the day of redemption* (Eph 4:30). Just as men brand a mark on their own herds to differentiate them from others, so the Lord willed to seal his own flock, his people, with a spiritual sign.

The Lord had the Jews as his own people in the Old Testament. *And you, my flocks, the flocks of my pastures are men* (Ezek 34:31). *And we are the people of his pasture and the sheep of his hand* (Ps 95:7). This flock was fed on the earthly pastures of material teachings and temporal goods: *if you be willing and obedient, you shall eat the good things of the land* (Isa 1:19). The Lord, therefore, differentiated and set them apart from others by means of the bodily sign of circumcision. *And my covenant shall be in your flesh* (Gen 17:13); before this it says, *you shall circumcise the flesh of your foreskin, that it may be for a sign of the covenant between me and you* (Gen 17:11).

In the New Testament the flock he had is the Christian people: *you have returned to the shepherd and guardian of your souls* (1 Pet 2:25). *My sheep hear my voice; and I know them; and they follow me* (John 10:27). This flock is fed on the pastures of spiritual doctrine and spiritual favors; hence the Lord differentiated it from others by a spiritual sign. This is the Holy Spirit through whom those who are of Christ are distinguished from the others who do not belong to him. But since the Holy Spirit is love, he is given to someone when that person is made a lover of God and neighbor. *God's love has been poured into our hearts through the Holy Spirit which has been given to us* (Rom 5:5).

Signum ergo distinctionis est caritas, quae est a Spiritu Sancto. Io. XIII, 35: *in hoc cognoscent omnes, quia mei discipuli estis, si dilectionem habueritis ad invicem*. Spiritus ergo Sanctus est quo signamur.

42. Spiritus vero promissionis dicitur triplici ratione. Primo quia promissus est fidelibus. Ez. XXXVI, 26: *spiritum novum ponam in medio vestri*. Et Ez. XXXVII, 6: *dabo vobis spiritum novum*. Secundo quia datur cum quadam promissione; ex hoc enim ipso quod datur nobis, efficimur filii Dei. Nam per Spiritum Sanctum efficimur unum cum Christo, Rom. VIII, 9: *si quis autem Spiritum Dei non habet, hic non est eius*, et per consequens efficimur filii Dei adoptivi, ex quo habemus promissionem haereditatis aeternae, quia *si filii, et haeredes* Rom. VIII, 17.

43. Tertio dicitur **pignus**, inquantum facit certitudinem de promissa haereditate. Nam Spiritus Sanctus inquantum adoptat in filios Dei, est Spiritus promissionis, et ipsemet est signum promissionis adipiscendae.

Sed, ut dicitur in Glossa, alia littera habet **qui est arra haereditatis**, et forte melius, quia pignus est aliud a re pro qua datur, et redditur postquam ille, qui pignus recipit, rem sibi debitam recipit. Arra autem non est aliud a re pro qua datur, nec redditur; quia datur de ipso pretio, quod non est auferendum, sed complendum. Deus autem dedit nobis caritatem tamquam pignus, per Spiritum Sanctum, qui est Spiritus veritatis et dilectionis. Et ideo huiusmodi non est aliud, quam quaedam particularis et imperfecta participatio divinae caritatis et dilectionis, quae quidem non est auferenda, sed perficienda, ideo magis proprie dicitur arra quam pignus.

Tamen potest nihilominus et pignus dici. Nam per Spiritum Sanctum Deus nobis diversa dona largitur, quorum quaedam manent in patria, ut caritas, quae *nunquam excidit*, I Cor. XIII, 8; quaedam vero propter sui imperfectionem non manent, sicut fides et spes, quae *evacuabuntur* ut ibidem dicitur. Sic ergo Spiritus Sanctus dicitur arra per respectum ad ea quae manent, pignus vero per respectum ad ea quae evacuabuntur.

44. Ad quid autem signati sumus, subdit, dicens **in redemptionem**. Nam si aliquis de novo aliqua animalia acquireret et adderet gregi suo, imponeret eis signa acquisitionis illius. Christus autem acquisivit populum ex gentibus. Io. X, 16: *alias oves habeo, quae non sunt ex hoc ovili, et illas oportet me adducere*, et cetera. Et ideo impressit eis signum acquisitionis. I Petr. II, 9: *gens sancta, populus acquisitionis*. Act. XX, 28: *quam acquisivit sanguine suo*.

Sed quia Christus acquisivit populum istum, non sic quod nunquam fuerit suus, sed quia aliquando fuerat suus, sed opprimebatur a servitute diaboli, in quam

Therefore, the distinctive sign is charity which comes from the Holy Spirit: *by this shall all men know that you are my disciples, if you have love one for another* (John 13:35). The Holy Spirit is he by whom we are signed.

42. The Spirit is described as a promise for three reasons. First, he is promised to those who believe: *I will put a new spirit within you . . . and I will give you a new spirit* (Ezek 36:26; 37:6). Second, he is given with a certain promise, because by the very fact that he is given to us we become the children of God. For through the Holy Spirit we are made one with Christ: *anyone who does not have the Spirit of God, does not belong to him* (Rom 8:9). As a result we are made adopted children of God, and thus we have the promise of an eternal inheritance since *if sons, heirs also* (Rom 8:17).

43. Third, he is termed a **pledge** inasmuch as he makes us certain of the promised inheritance. Adopting us into the children of God, the Holy Spirit is the Spirit of promise who also is the seal of the promise yet to be attained.

However, as is mentioned in a Gloss, a variant reading has **who is the earnest of our inheritance**, and perhaps this is a better rendering. For a pledge differs from the object in place of which it is given, and it must be returned once he who has received the pledge obtains the object due him. An earnest, however, does not differ from the object in place of which it is given, nor is it returned since it is a partial payment of the price itself, which is not to be withdrawn but completed. God communicates charity to us as a pledge, through the Holy Spirit who is the Spirit of truth and love. Hence, this is nothing else than an individual and imperfect participation in the divine charity and love; it must not be withdrawn but brought to perfection. More fittingly, therefore, it is referred to as an earnest rather than as a pledge.

Nevertheless, it can also be called a pledge. For through the Holy Spirit God grants us a variety of gifts. Some of these will remain in the fatherland, as charity which *never comes to an end* (1 Cor 13:8); while others will not last on account of their imperfection, such as faith and hope *which shall be done away* with (1 Cor 13:10). Hence, the Holy Spirit is called an earnest in reference to what will remain, and a pledge with respect to what will be done away with.

44. He adds the purpose for which we are signed as **unto the redemption**. For when a man buys new animals and adds them to his flock, he puts a mark on them to the effect that he has purchased them. Now Christ has purchased a people from the gentiles. *Other sheep I have that are not of this fold; them also I must bring. And they shall hear my voice; and there shall be one fold and one shepherd* (John 10:16). And on them he imprints a sign of purchase: *a holy nation, a purchased people* (1 Pet 2:9) which he *has purchased with his own blood* (Acts 20:28).

Christ acquired this people, not because they never were his, but because they previously belonged to him and yet, by sinning, had sold themselves into a diabolical slavery

peccando se redegit, ideo non dicit simpliciter acquisivit, sed addit *in redemptionem*, quasi dicat: non simpliciter de novo acquisiti, sed quasi a servitute diaboli per sanguinem eius redempti. I Petr. I, 18: *non corruptibilibus auro et argento redempti estis*, et cetera. Acquisivit ergo Christus nos redimendo, non quod accrescat inde aliquid Deo; quia bonorum nostrorum non indiget. Iob XXXV, 7: *si iuste egeris, quid donabis ei? Aut quid de manu tua recipiet?*

Ad quid autem acquisiverit nos Christus, subdit *in laudem gloriae ipsius*, id est ut ipse Deus laudetur. Is. XLIII, 7: *qui invocat nomen meum, in gloriam meam creavi eum*.

which oppressed them. So it does not simply state that he acquired them but adds **unto redemption**, as though to say: you are not strictly a new acquisition; you are re-purchased from the slavery of the devil through his blood. *You were not redeemed with corruptible things as gold or silver, from the vain manner of life handed down from your fathers, but with the precious blood of Christ* (1 Pet 1:18–19). Christ purchased us, therefore, through a redemption; not that this added anything to God since he needs none of our goods. *If you are righteous, what do you give him, or what does he receive of your hand?* (Job 35:7).

The purpose for which Christ acquired us is **unto the praise of his glory**, that God himself be praised since *everyone who calls upon my name, I have created him for my glory* (Isa 43:7).

Lecture 6

1:15Propterea et ego audiens fidem vestram, quae est in Domino Jesu, et dilectionem in omnes sanctos, [n. 46]

1:16non cesso gratias agens pro vobis, [n. 47] memoriam vestri faciens in orationibus meis: [n. 48]

1:17ut Deus Domini nostri Jesu Christi, Pater gloriae, det vobis Spiritum sapientiae et revelationis [n. 49] in agnitione ejus, [n. 52]

1:18illuminatos oculos cordis vestri, ut sciatis quae sit spes vocationis ejus, [n. 52] et quae divitiae gloriae haereditatis ejus in sanctis, [n. 54]

1:15Διὰ τοῦτο κἀγώ, ἀκούσας τὴν καθ' ὑμᾶς πίστιν ἐν τῷ κυρίῳ Ἰησοῦ καὶ τὴν ἀγάπην τὴν εἰς πάντας τοὺς ἁγίους,

1:16οὐ παύομαι εὐχαριστῶν ὑπὲρ ὑμῶν μνείαν ποιούμενος ἐπὶ τῶν προσευχῶν μου,

1:17ἵνα ὁ θεὸς τοῦ κυρίου ἡμῶν Ἰησοῦ Χριστοῦ, ὁ πατὴρ τῆς δόξης, δώῃ ὑμῖν πνεῦμα σοφίας καὶ ἀποκαλύψεως ἐν ἐπιγνώσει αὐτοῦ,

1:18πεφωτισμένους τοὺς ὀφθαλμοὺς τῆς καρδίας [ὑμῶν] εἰς τὸ εἰδέναι ὑμᾶς τίς ἐστιν ἡ ἐλπὶς τῆς κλήσεως αὐτοῦ, τίς ὁ πλοῦτος τῆς δόξης τῆς κληρονομίας αὐτοῦ ἐν τοῖς ἁγίοις,

1:15Wherefore, I also, hearing of your faith that is in the Lord Jesus and of your love towards all the saints, [n. 46]

1:16I do not cease to give thanks for you, [n. 47] remembering you in my prayers, [n. 48]

1:17That the God of our Lord Jesus Christ, the Father of glory, may give unto you the Spirit of wisdom and of revelation, [n. 49] in the knowledge of him: [n. 52]

1:18The eyes of your heart enlightened that you may know what the hope is of his calling [n. 52] and what are the riches of the glory of his inheritance in the saints. [n. 54]

---

45. Postquam enumeravit Apostolus beneficia Ephesiis collata per Christum, hic ostendit quomodo affectus suus crevit ad eos.

Dividitur autem haec pars in tres partes, quia

primo praemittitur bonorum, quae audivit de eis, commemoratio;

secundo de perceptis beneficiis gratiarum debita actio, ibi *non cesso gratias agens*, etc.;

tertio subditur pro futuris beneficiis eius oratio, ibi *memoriam vestri faciens*, et cetera.

46. Bona autem quae de eis audivit, sunt duo, unum quo ordinantur ad Deum, et hoc est fides, et quantum ad hoc dicit *propterea et ego audiens fidem vestram, quae est in Christo Iesu*, quae quidem facit habitare Deum in homine. Infra III, 17: *habitare Christum per fidem in cordibus vestris*. Item, corda purificat. Act. XV, 9: *fide purificans corda eorum*. Item, sine lege iustificat. Rom. III, 28: *arbitramur iustificari hominem per fidem sine operibus legis*.

Secundum quo ordinantur ad proximum, et hoc est dilectio, et quantum ad hoc dicit *et dilectionem*, id est opera caritatis, quae quidem dilectio est spirituale signum, quod homo sit discipulus Christi. Io. XIII, 35: *in hoc cognoscent omnes, quia mei estis discipuli, si dilectionem*, et cetera. Et ibidem XIII, 34: *mandatum novum do vobis, ut diligatis invicem*, et cetera.

Dilectionem, dico, *in omnes sanctos*. Nam omnes quos ex caritate diligimus, debemus eos diligere vel ideo quia sancti sunt, vel ut sancti sint. Gal. VI, 10: *dum*

45. After enumerating the blessings conferred on the Ephesians through Christ, the Apostle now reveals how his affection for them has grown.

This section is divided into three parts:

first, he begins by relating the good reports he has heard concerning them;

second, he gives the thanks due for the blessings they have received, at *I do not cease to give thanks*;

third, he adds a prayer for future blessings, at *remembering you*.

46. There were two good things which he heard about them. One was their faith by which they were properly orientated toward God; regarding this he remarked: *wherefore, I also, hearing of your faith that is in the Lord Jesus*. Indeed, faith makes God dwell in man: *that Christ may dwell by faith in your hearts* (Eph 3:17). Again, it purifies hearts: *purifying their hearts by faith* (Acts 15:9). Moreover, it justifies without recourse to the law: *for we account a man to be justified by faith, without the works of the law* (Rom 3:28).

The second good is love by which they are properly orientated toward their neighbor; in reference to this he says *and of your love* consisting in works of charity. This love is a spiritual sign that a man is a disciple of Christ: *a new commandment I give you: that you love one another, as I have loved you, so also you must love one another. By this shall all men know that you are my disciples, if you have love one for another* (John 13:34–35).

This *love*, I say, *is towards all the saints*. For everyone whom we love with charity, we ought to love either because they are holy or in order that they become holy. While we

tempus habemus, operemur bonum ad omnes, maxime autem ad domesticos fidei, et cetera.

47. Deinde cum dicit **non cesso**, etc., agit Apostolus gratias de bonis et beneficiis huiusmodi auditis, dicens **non cesso gratias agens**, et cetera.

Contra, quia non semper poterat continue pro eis gratias agere.

Respondeo. Apostolus dicit **non cesso**, id est horis debitis; vel **non cesso** quia affectus gratias agendi pro vobis sine cessatione habitualiter est in me. Col. I, 9: *non cessamus pro vobis orantes, et postulantes*, et cetera. Rom. I, 9–10: *sine intermissione memoriam vestri facio semper in orationibus meis*.

48. Consequenter orat Apostolus pro beneficiis eis in futurum concedendis, et quantum ad hoc dicit **memoriam vestri**, et cetera. Et haec dividitur in tres, quia

primo proponit quaedam quae eis petit;
secundo exponit ea, ibi **in agnitionem eius**, etc.;
tertio ostendit exemplar et formam illorum, ibi **secundum operationem potentiae**, et cetera.

49. Dicit ergo quantum ad primum: non solum gratias ago quantum ad beneficia praeterita, quae recepistis, et quantum ad bona audita de vobis, sed etiam oro ut omnino in futurum accrescant. **Memoriam vestri faciens in orationibus meis**, pro his scilicet, **ut Deus Domini nostri Iesu Christi, Pater gloriae**, et cetera.

Ubi sciendum quod Dominus noster Iesus Christus et Deus et homo est. Et inquantum homo est, Deum habet, cum sit compositus ex anima et corpore, quorum utrique, cum sint creaturae, competit Deum habere; secundum autem quod Deus est, Patrem habet. Io. XX, 17: *ascendo ad Patrem meum et Patrem vestrum; Deum meum et Deum vestrum*. Similiter etiam secundum quod est Deus, est gloria Patris. Hebr. I, 3: *qui cum sit splendor gloriae*, et cetera. Est etiam gloria nostra, quia ipse est vita aeterna. I Io. c. ult., 20: *simus in vero Filio eius, hic est verus Deus, et vita aeterna*.

Sic ergo dicit **ut Deus Domini nostri Iesu Christi**, secundum quod est homo, et **Pater** eiusdem, secundum quod est Deus; **Pater**, inquam, **gloriae**, scilicet Christi, qui est gloria eius, Prov. X, 1: *gloria patris filius sapiens*, etc., et gloriae nostrae, inquantum dat omnibus gloriam.

50. Deinde cum dicit **det vobis**, etc., ponit ea quae petit, quae sunt duo.

Ubi sciendum est, quod quaedam sunt dona communia omnibus sanctis, scilicet illa quae sunt necessaria ad salutem, ut fides, spes, caritas, et haec habebant, ut iam patet. Alia autem sunt dona specialia, et quantum ad hoc pro eis orat; primo quidem pro dono sapientiae, et quantum ad hoc dicit **ut det vobis Spiritum sapientiae**, quem nullus potest dare, nisi Deus. Sap. IX, 17: *sensum*

have time, let us work good to all men, but especially to those who are of the household of the faith (Gal 6:10).

47. Next, at **I do not cease**, the Apostle gives thanks for these goods and blessings he has heard about, saying **I do not cease to give thanks for you**.

On the contrary, however, he could not have continually offered thanks for them.

I reply. In saying **I do not cease**, the Apostle means at the required times; or, **I do not cease** because my attitude of thanksgiving for you is without intermission habitually in me. *We do not cease to pray for you, and to beg that you may be filled with the knowledge of his will, in all wisdom and spiritual understanding* (Col 1:9). *I remember you constantly, always in my prayers making request* (Rom 1:9–10).

48. Consequently, the Apostle prays for the blessings that must be given them in the future, and concerning this he says **remembering you in my prayers**. This has three divisions:

first, he sets down certain ones that he asks for them;
second, he explains these, at **in the knowledge**;
third, he discloses the exemplar and form of these blessings, at **according to the operation of the might** (Eph 1:19).

49. In regard to the first he says: not only do I give thanks for past benefits which you have received and for the good reports concerning you, but I also pray that, by all means, these increase in the future, **remembering you in my prayers** in behalf of these to **the God of our Lord Jesus Christ, the Father of glory**.

It must be acknowledged, at this point, that our Lord Jesus Christ is both God and man. Insofar as he is man, he is related to God, since he is composed of body and soul, both of which, being creatures, are necessarily related to God. But according as he is God, he is related to the Father. *I ascend to my Father and to your Father, to my God and to your God* (John 20:17). Likewise, as God he is the glory of the Father: *who, being the brightness of his glory, and the figure of his substance* (Heb 1:3). He is also our glory because he himself is life eternal: *we are in his true Son, Jesus Christ. This is the true God and eternal life* (1 John 5:20).

Therefore, he states **the God of our Lord Jesus Christ** in relation to him as man, and **his Father** in reference to him as God. I say the **Father of glory**, that is, of Christ who is his glory. *A wise son is the glory of his father* (Prov 10:1); and of our glory, inasmuch as he communicates glory to all.

50. Then he writes down the two things he asks for: **the Spirit of wisdom and of revelation**.

It must be realized here that certain gifts are common to all the saints and are necessary for salvation, such as faith, hope and charity. These they already possessed, as is evident. Then there are other special gifts; he prays that they receive these. First is the gift of wisdom when he says **the Spirit of wisdom** whom no one can bestow except God:

autem tuum quis sciet, nisi tu dederis sapientiam, et miseris Spiritum Sanctum tuum de altissimis?

Secundo orat pro dono intellectus, et hoc consistit in revelatione spiritualium secretorum, propter quod dicit **et revelationis**, quae etiam a solo Deo est. Dan. II, 28: *est Deus in caelis revelans mysteria.*

51. Exponit autem quae sint ista quae petit, et
primo quod pertinet ad donum sapientiae;
secundo quod pertinet ad donum intellectus, ibi **ut sciatis, quae sit spes**, et cetera.

52. Ad donum autem sapientiae pertinet cognitio divinorum. Unde petere donum sapientiae est petere quod habeant cognitionem Dei, et hoc petit ibi **in agnitionem Dei**, etc., quasi dicat: hoc peto ut per Spiritum sapientiae habeatis **illuminatos oculos cordis vestri in agnitionem**, scilicet clariorem, **eius**, scilicet Dei. Ps. XII, 4: *illumina oculos meos*, et cetera.

Hoc est contra eos, qui habent oculos illuminatos tantum ad temporalia cognoscenda, cum magis tamen sit necessarium et etiam gloriosum cognoscere Deum. Ier. III, 23 s.: *non glorietur sapiens in sapientia sua, et non glorietur dives in divitiis suis; sed in hoc glorietur, qui glorietur, scire et nosse me.*

53. Ad donum autem intellectus tria pertinentia ponit: unum quantum ad statum praesentem, et duo quantum ad futurum.

Ad statum vero praesentem pertinet spes, quae est necessaria ad salutem. Rom. VIII, v. 24: *spe enim salvi facti sumus*, et cetera. Et quantum ad hoc dicit **ut sciatis quae**, id est quanta, **sit spes vocationis eius**, id est virtus spei, et de quanta re sit. Quae quidem et maxima est, quia de maximis. I Petr. I, v. 3: *regeneravit nos in spem vivam per resurrectionem Iesu Christi ex mortuis*, et cetera. Et fortissima virtutum. Hebr. VI, 18: *fortissimum solatium habeamus, qui confugimus ad tenendam propositam spem; quam sicut anchoram habemus animae*, et cetera.

54. Sed quia ea quae speramus, sunt de futura vita, ideo alia duo pertinent ad vitam futuram; unum quidem pertinet ad omnes iustos communiter, quod est praemium essentiale, et quantum ad hoc, dicit **et quae divitiae gloriae**, et cetera. Ubi ponit quatuor ad illa dona pertinentia. Primum est, quod sunt copiosissima, et quantum ad hoc, dicit **divitiae**. Prov. I, 33: *abundantia perfruetur, terrore malorum sublato.* Ps. CXI, 3: *gloria et divitiae in domo eius*, et cetera. Prov. c. VIII, 18: *mecum sunt divitiae et gloria*, et cetera.

who ever knew your counsel, unless you had given wisdom, and sent your Holy Spirit from above? (Wis 9:17)

The second gift prayed for is that of understanding which consists in the revelation of spiritual mysteries that God alone can give, on account of which he says **and of revelation**: *there is a God in heaven who reveals mysteries* (Dan 2:28).

51. Next, he explains what he asks for:
first, what pertains to the gift of wisdom;
second, what pertains to the gift of understanding, at **that you may know what the hope is**.

52. To the gift of wisdom belongs the knowledge of divine realities. Hence, to ask for the gift of wisdom is to ask that they enjoy a knowledge of God. He begs for this in saying **in the knowledge of him**, as if to say: I ask that, through the Spirit of wisdom, you may have **the eyes of your heart enlightened in** a clearer **knowledge** of God. *Look at me, answer me, Yahweh my God! Enlighten my eyes; turn away the sleep of death* (Ps 13:3).

This is the opposite of those whose eyes are enlightened only with respect to temporal reality when it is more necessary and more glorious to know God. *Let not the wise man glory in his wisdom . . . and let not the rich man glory in his riches: but let anyone who boasts glory in this, that he understands and knows me* (Jer 9:23–24).

53. Three aspects pertain to the gift of understanding, one of which has reference to the present life, and two to the future.

Hope, which is necessary for salvation, belongs to the present condition: *for we are saved by hope* (Rom 8:24). Concerning this he says **that you may know what**, that is, how great **the hope is of his calling**, meaning the virtue of hope and what an immense reality it is concerned with. This hope is of the utmost importance because it concerns the greatest realities: *he has given us a new birth to a living hope, by the resurrection of Jesus Christ from the dead* (1 Pet 1:3). It is also the strongest of the virtues: *that we who have fled for refuge may have strong encouragement to hold fast to the hope set before us. This we have as a sure and firm anchor of the soul, which enters behind the veil* (Heb 6:18–19).

54. Yet, since what we hope for concerns the future life, the other two aspects of the gift of understanding pertain to the future. One, the essential reward, is common to all the just; regarding which he says **what are the riches of the glory of his inheritance in the saints**. Here he writes down four characteristics of those gifts. First, they are most abundant, which he implies in **riches**. *He who obeys me will enjoy abundance, and be at ease without fear of evil* (Prov 1:33); *glory and wealth shall be in his house* (Ps 112:3); *riches and honor are with me, enduring wealth and prosperity* (Prov 8:18).

Secundo quod sunt clarissima, et quantum ad hoc dicit **gloriae**. Rom. II, 10: *gloria autem, et honor, et pax omni operanti bonum*, et cetera.

Tertio quod sunt stabilissima, et quantum ad hoc dicit **haereditatis**. Ea enim quae haereditaria sunt, stabiliter possidentur. Eccli. XXXI, 11: *stabilita sunt bona illius in domino*. Ps. XV, 5: *dominus pars haereditatis meae et calicis*, et cetera.

Quarto, quod erunt intima, et quantum ad hoc dicit **in sanctis**. Rom. VIII, 18: *non sunt condignae passiones huius temporis*, et cetera. II Cor. IV, 17: *supra modum in sublimitate gloriae pondus operatur in nobis*.

55. Aliud quod ponit pertinens ad futuram gloriam, est quod specialiter pertinet ad apostolos, unde dicit **et quae sit** (supple sciatis) **supereminens magnitudo virtutis eius in nos**, scilicet apostolos. Quasi dicat: licet omnibus sanctis abundanter divitias gloriae tribuat, supereminentius tamen tribuet apostolis. Magnitudo enim virtutis ostenditur in effectu. Unde quanto magis effectus virtutis divinae in aliquo invenitur, tanto ibi virtus divina maior ostenditur, licet in seipsa sit una et indivisa. Et ideo, quia maior effectus virtutis divinae est in apostolis, ideo magnitudo virtutis erit in eis.

Et quod maior sit in eis effectus ostendit, dicens **qui credimus**, id est qui sumus primitiae credentium. II Cor. IV, 13 s.: *nos credimus, propter quod et loquimur, scientes quod ille, qui suscitavit Iesum, et nos cum Iesu suscitabit*. Propter quod dicebat II Tim. c. I, 12: *scio cui credidi*, et cetera.

Ideo illi inter vos per quos alii instructi sunt et vocati ad fidem, sicut doctores, praeeminentius praemiabuntur; quia, ut dicitur in Glossa *quoddam incrementum gloriae habebunt summi doctores ultra illud quod communiter omnes habebunt* propter quod Dan. XII, 3 docti assimilantur splendori firmamenti, sed doctores assimilantur stellis: *qui autem docti fuerint, fulgebunt quasi splendor firmamenti, et qui ad iustitiam erudiunt multos, quasi stellae in perpetuas aeternitates*.

Second, they have the greatest clarity, regarding which he says **of glory**. *Glory, honor and peace to everyone who does good* (Rom 2:10).

Third, they are the most enduring, in reference to which he states **of his inheritance**, for what is hereditary is possessed permanently. *His goods will be established* (Sir 31:11); *Yahweh, you have portioned my cup of smooth wine; you have cast my lot. The lines have fallen on rich land for me; the Most High has marked out my estate* (Ps 16:5).

Fourth, he indicates that they will be most profound, as **in the saints**. *The sufferings of this time are not worthy to be compared with the glory to come that shall be revealed in us* (Rom 8:18); *for this slight momentary affliction is preparing for us an incomparable eternal weight of glory* (2 Cor 4:17).

55. The other aspect which he sets down is in reference to the future glory and pertains especially to the apostles. Hence he asks **that you may know ... what is the exceeding greatness of his power towards us** (Eph 1:19), the apostles. He seems to say: although he bestows the riches of his glory abundantly on all the saints, he grants them in an exceedingly great measure to the apostles. For the greatness of a power is gauged by what it does. Hence, the more the divine power accomplishes in someone, the more is that divine power revealed there—even though it is one and undivided in itself. Therefore, since a greater effect of the divine power is present in the apostles, the greatness of this power will reside in them.

He shows what this greater effect present in them is by saying **we who believe** (Eph 1:19), we who are the first-fruits among those who believe. *We also believe. For which cause we speak also, knowing that he who raised up Jesus will raise us up also with Jesus* (2 Cor 4:13). *I know whom I have believed and I am certain that he is able to keep what I have committed unto him until the last day* (2 Tim 1:12).

Those among you, therefore, through whom others are taught and called to the faith—such as the doctors of the sacred sciences—will be rewarded in a preeminent way. Thus a Gloss states how *the great doctors will enjoy a certain increase in glory above that commonly possessed by all*. For the same reason, the educated are likened to the brightness of the sky, while the doctors are the stars themselves: *those who are wise will shine like the brightness of the sky: and those who turn many to justice, as stars for all eternity* (Dan 12:3).

Lecture 7

1:19et quae sit supereminens magnitudo virtutis ejus in nos, qui credimus secundum operationem potentiae virtutis ejus, [n. 56]

1:20quam operatus est in Christo, suscitans illum a mortuis, [n. 58] et constituens ad dexteram suam in caelestibus: [n. 60]

1:21supra omnem principatum, et potestatem, et virtutem, et dominationem, [n. 62] et omne nomen, quod nominatur non solum in hoc saeculo, sed etiam in futuro. [n. 64]

1:19καὶ τί τὸ ὑπερβάλλον μέγεθος τῆς δυνάμεως αὐτοῦ εἰς ἡμᾶς τοὺς πιστεύοντας κατὰ τὴν ἐνέργειαν τοῦ κράτους τῆς ἰσχύος αὐτοῦ

1:20ἣν ἐνήργησεν ἐν τῷ Χριστῷ ἐγείρας αὐτὸν ἐκ νεκρῶν, καὶ καθίσας ἐν δεξιᾷ αὐτοῦ ἐν τοῖς ἐπουρανίοις

1:21ὑπεράνω πάσης ἀρχῆς καὶ ἐξουσίας καὶ δυνάμεως καὶ κυριότητος καὶ παντὸς ὀνόματος ὀνομαζομένου οὐ μόνον ἐν τῷ αἰῶνι τούτῳ ἀλλὰ καὶ ἐν τῷ μέλλοντι·

1:19And what is the exceeding greatness of his power towards us, who believe according to the operation of the might of his power, [n. 56]

1:20Which he wrought in Christ, raising him up from the dead [n. 58] and setting him on his right hand in the heavenly places. [n. 60]

1:21Above all principality and power and virtue and dominion [n. 62] and every name that is named, not only in this world, but also in that which is to come. [n. 64]

---

56. Enumeratis beneficiis, quae Apostolus conferenda optat Ephesiis in futurum, hic consequenter ponit formam et exemplar illorum beneficiorum. Sicut autem vita Christi est forma et exemplar iustitiae nostrae, ita et gloria et exaltatio Christi est forma et exemplar gloriae et exaltationis nostrae. Ideo hic Apostolus duo facit, quia

primo proponit formam exaltationis beneficiorum et donorum in generali;

secundo manifestat eam in speciali, ibi *suscitans illum a mortuis*, et cetera.

57. Forma autem et exemplar operationis divinae in nos, est operatio divina in Christo. Et quantum ad hoc dicit *secundum operationem*, id est ad similitudinem operationis, *potentiae virtutis eius*, id est virtuosae potentiae Dei, *quam operatus est in Christo*, exaltans caput illud, supple: ita virtuose operabitur in nobis. Phil. III, 20 s.: *salvatorem expectamus Dominum nostrum Iesum Christum, qui reformabit corpus humilitatis nostrae*, et cetera.

Nos autem exaltari ad similitudinem exaltationis Christi frequenter legimus in Scriptura. Rom. VIII, 17: *si compatimur, ut et glorificemur*. Item Apoc. III, 21: *qui vicerit, dabo ei sedere mecum in throno meo, sicut et ego vici et sedi cum Patre meo in throno eius*.

58. Consequenter explicat formam et exemplar in speciali, manifestans ea quae pertinent ad exaltationem Christi, loquendo de Christo inquantum est homo, dicens *suscitans illum*, et cetera.

Circa quod tria beneficia ponit exaltationis Christi.

Primum est transitus de morte ad vitam, et quantum ad hoc dicit *suscitans illum a mortuis*.

Secundum est exaltatio ad gloriam altissimam, et quantum ad hoc dicit *constituens illum ad dexteram suam*.

56. Once he has listed the blessings which he hopes will be granted to the Ephesians in the future, the Apostle discusses the form and exemplar of those benefits. As the life of Christ is the form and exemplar of our justice, so Christ's glory and exultation is the form and exemplar of our glory and exaltation. Here the Apostle makes two points:

first, he proposes in a general manner the form of our exaltation with its blessings and gifts;

second, he discusses it in detail, at *raising him up from the dead*.

57. The divine activity in Christ is the form and exemplar of the divine activity in us. In reference to this he states *according to the operation*, that is, in the likeness of the operation, *of the might of his power*, meaning the powerful might of God, *which he wrought in Christ* exalting him who is the head. Understand that in this way he will mightily act in us. *We await a savior, the Lord Jesus Christ, who will transfigure our wretched body to be like his glorious body by the power which enables him to subject all things to himself* (Phil 3:20–21).

In Scripture we frequently read that we will be exalted in the likeness of Christ's exaltation: *provided we suffer with him, so as also to be glorified with him* (Rom 8:17); *he who conquers I will grant him to sit with me in my throne; as I myself have conquered and sat down with my Father on his throne* (Rev 3:21).

58. As a result, he specifies the form and exemplar in more detail, showing what pertains to the exaltation of Christ while speaking of him inasmuch as he is man, at *raising him*.

He writes of three favors in the exaltation of Christ:

first, the transition from death to life, in regard to which he adds *raising him up from the dead*;

second, the exaltation to the utmost heights of glory, in regard to which he says *setting him on his right hand*;

Tertium est sublimatio ad potentiam maximam, et quantum ad hoc dicit *et omnia subiecit sub pedibus eius*.

59. Dicit ergo quantum ad primum: dico quod hoc erit *secundum operationem* quam operatus est *in Christo*, scilicet Deus Pater eadem virtute, quam habet cum Christo. Unde et ipse Christus seipsum resuscitavit, et Deus Pater eum resuscitavit. Rom. c. VIII, 11: *si Spiritus eius, qui suscitavit Iesum a mortuis habitat in vobis, qui suscitavit Iesum a mortuis, vivificabit et mortalia corpora vestra*.

60. Quantum vero ad secundum dicit *constituens illum*, et cetera. Quae quidem celsitudo gloriae potest tripliciter considerari, scilicet per comparationem ad Deum, per comparationem ad corporales creaturas, et per comparationem ad creaturas spirituales.

Si ergo consideretur per comparationem ad Deum, sic constitutus est ad dexteram suam, quae quidem dextera non est intelligenda pars corporalis, quia, ut dicitur Io. IV, v. 24, *spiritus est Deus*, sed metaphorice dicitur, ut sicut per dexteram intelligitur nobilior et virtuosior pars hominis ita cum dicimus Christum Iesum constitutum ad dexteram Dei, intelligatur secundum humanitatem constitutus in potioribus bonis Patris, et secundum divinitatem intelligatur aequalis Patri. Unde Ps. CIX, 1: *dixit Dominus Domino meo: sede a dextris meis*, et cetera. Item Mc. ult.: *et Dominus quidem Iesus postquam locutus est eis, assumptus est in caelum, et sedet ad dexteram Dei*.

In comparatione vero ad corporales creaturas dicit *in caelestibus*. Nam corpora caelestia tenent supremum locum in comparatione ad alia corpora. Infra, IV, 10: *qui descendit, ipse est et qui ascendit super omnes caelos*.

In comparatione vero ad spirituales creaturas, primo dicit Christum exaltatum super aliquas specialiter; secundo super omnes generaliter, ibi *et super omne nomen*, et cetera.

61. Ad horum autem intelligentiam sciendum est, quod novem sunt ordines angelorum, quorum quatuor Apostolus tangit hic, qui quidem sunt medii. Nam supra eos sunt tres superiores, scilicet throni, cherubim et seraphim. Sub eis autem sunt duo inferiores, scilicet archangeli et angeli. Qui quidem novem ordines distinguuntur in tres hierarchias, id est, sacros principatus, in quarum qualibet assignantur tres ordines.

Sed in assignatione ordinum hierarchiae primae conveniunt omnes doctores in hoc scilicet quod supremus ordo ipsius sit seraphim, secundus cherubim, tertius throni. In assignatione vero ordinum aliarum duarum hierarchiarum, scilicet mediae et infimae, discordant Dionysius et Gregorius. Nam Dionysius in supremo ordine mediae hierarchiae ponit dominationes, in secundo virtutes, in tertio potestates, descendendo. In supremo vero ordine infimae hierarchiae posuit principatus, in

third, an elevation to the greatest of power, in regard to which he says *and he has subjected all things under his feet* (Eph 1:22).

59. Concerning the first he states that it was *according to the operation which* God the Father *wrought in Christ* by the same power which he shares with Christ. Christ both restored himself to life and was restored to life by the Father. *And, if the Spirit of him that raised up Jesus from the dead dwell in you, he that raised up Jesus Christ from the dead shall quicken also your mortal bodies, because of his Spirit that dwells in you* (Rom 8:11).

60. *Setting him on his right hand* refers to the second element in Christ's exaltation. This height of glory can be viewed in three perspectives: in its relation to God, to material creatures, and to spiritual creatures.

Considered in relation to God, he is seated at his right hand; this is not to be thought of as a bodily organ—*God is spirit* (John 4:24)—but as a metaphorical way of speaking. The right hand is taken as a nobler and stronger part of man; so when we say that Christ Jesus is seated at the right hand of God, it should be understood that according to his humanity he partakes of the Father's choicest blessings, and according to his divinity it is understood as equality with the Father. *Yahweh spoke to my Lord: take the throne at my right* (Ps 110:1). *And the Lord Jesus, after he had spoken to them, was taken up into heaven and sat on the right hand of God* (Mark 16:19).

In heavenly places defines the relation of Christ's exaltation to material creatures. For the heavenly bodies occupy the highest place in comparison to the other bodies; yet, *he that descended is the same also who ascended above all the heavens* (Eph 4:10).

In relation to spiritual creatures, he first mentions that Christ is exalted over certain specific ones, and second, over all of them generally, at *above every name*.

61. To understand this, note that there are nine ranks of angels, of which the Apostle here mentions only the four middle ranks. Above these are the three superior ranks of the thrones, cherubim and seraphim. Below them are the two lower ranks of the archangels and the angels. These nine ranks are also differentiated into three hierarchies, or sacred authorities, each of which embraces three ranks.

All the doctors agree in assigning the ranks of the first hierarchy. The highest rank is the seraphim, second are the cherubim, third are the thrones. In assigning the ranks among the middle and lower hierarchies, however, Dionysius and Gregory disagree. Dionysius, in descending order, places the dominions as first in the middle hierarchy, the virtues second, and the powers third. In the first rank of the lower hierarchy he puts the principalities, second are the archangels and third are the angels. This listing of the ranks

secundo archangelos, in tertio angelos. Et haec assignatio ordinum concordat litterae praesenti. Nam Apostolus ascendendo incipit a supremo infimae hierarchiae, qui est septimus.

Gregorius autem aliter ordinat, quia ponit principatus in medio dominationum et potestatum, quod pertinet ad secundum ordinem mediae hierarchiae; virtutes vero ponit in medio potestatum et archangelorum, quod pertinet ad supremum ordinem infimae hierarchiae. Et haec assignatio etiam fulcimentum habet ex verbis Apostoli, Col. III ubi dicit *sive throni, sive dominationes, sive principatus, sive potestates*, ubi illos ordines enumerat descendendo.

Sed, reservata ordinatione Gregorii, usquequo legamus epistolam ad Colossenses, ad praesens viam Dionysii magis competentem praesenti litterae prosequemur.

62. Ad cuius intellectum sciendum est, quod potest considerari tripliciter ordo rerum. Primo quidem secundum quod sunt in prima omnium causa, scilicet in Deo; secundo vero secundum quod sunt in causis universalibus; tertio secundum determinationem ad speciales effectus.

Et quia omnia quae fiunt in creaturis ministrantur per angelos, ideo secundum triplicem acceptionem ordinis rerum distinguuntur tres angelicae hierarchiae, ad quarum unam pertinet accipere rationes rerum in ipso rerum vertice, scilicet Deo; ad aliam vero pertinet accipere rationes rerum in causis universalibus; ad aliam vero in propriis effectibus. Nam quanto mentes angelicae sunt superiores, tanto divinam illuminationem in maiori universalitate recipiunt. Et ideo ad supremam hierarchiam pertinet administratio rerum in comparatione ad Deum. Propter quod ordines hierarchiae istius denominantur per comparationem ad Deum, quia seraphim dicuntur ardentes, et uniti Deo per amorem. cherubim vero quasi lucentes, in quantum supereminenter divina secreta cognoscunt. Throni vero dicuntur sic, in quantum in eis Deus sua iudicia exercet.

Et de istis tribus ordinibus nullam facit hic Apostolus mentionem.

Ad mediam hierarchiam pertinet rerum administratio per comparationem ad causas universales. Unde denominantur ordines hierarchiae illius nominibus ad potestatem pertinentibus, cum causae universales sint virtute et potestate in inferioribus et particularibus. Ad potestates autem, quae habent universale regimen, tria pertinent. Primo quod sint aliqui per imperium dirigentes; secundo quod sint aliqui qui impedimenta executionis repellant; tertio quod sint aliqui qui ordinent qualiter alii imperium exequantur. Horum autem primum pertinet ad **dominationes**, quae, ut dicit Dionysius, sunt

is in accord with the present text where the Apostle begins, in an ascending order, from the first rank of the lower hierarchy, the seventh down from the seraphim.

Gregory, on the other hand, arranges them differently. He places the principalities between the dominions and the powers, which is the second rank of the middle hierarchy; while he puts the virtues between the powers and the archangels, which is the first rank of the lower hierarchy. This arrangement is supported by the Apostle's words: *for in him were all things created in heaven and on earth, visible and invisible, whether thrones, or dominions, or principalities, or powers* (Col 1:16), where he enumerates those ranks in a descending order.

Reserving Gregory's classification until we lecture on the letter to the Colossians, for the present we will follow Dionysius's approach since it accords with the text at hand.

62. To understand this, it should be realized that the structure of reality can be considered in three ways: first, according as it is present in the first cause of everything, namely in God; second, according as it is in the universal causes; third, according to the arrangement of individual causes.

Since everything that happens among creatures occurs with the assistance of the angels, the three angelic hierarchies are distinguished according to the threefold way of conceiving the structure of reality. To one it belongs to grasp the intelligible patterns of things in the very summit of reality, God; it pertains to another to grasp the intelligible patterns of reality in the universal causes; still another understands these patterns in the individual causes. For the higher the angelic minds are, the more do they receive divine illumination with greater universality. Therefore, the governance of reality in relation to God pertains to the first hierarchy. On this account, the ranks of that hierarchy are named with reference to God. The seraphim are so called because they are burning with love and through it are united to God. The cherubim are, as it were, radiant inasmuch as they possess a supereminent knowledge of divine mysteries. The thrones are so termed inasmuch as in them God carries out his judgments.

Of these three ranks the Apostle makes no mention here.

To the middle hierarchy belongs the governance of things in relation to the universal causes. Hence the ranks of this hierarchy have names associated with power since the universal causes are present in the lower and individual things by their power and strength. Three tasks pertain to these powers which govern universally. First, some must give direction by their commands; second, others must dispose of any impediments to the fulfillment of those commands; third, some must arrange how others will carry out the commands. Of these, the first belongs to the **dominions** who, as Dionysius remarks, are free from any

liberae ab omni subiectione, nec ad exteriora mittuntur sed eis, qui mittuntur, imperant. Secundum vero pertinet ad **virtutes**, quae praebent facilitatem ad imperium implendum. Tertium vero pertinet ad **potestates** imperium exequentes.

Ad infimam autem hierarchiam pertinet administratio rerum in comparatione ad speciales effectus, unde nominibus ad eos pertinentibus nuncupantur. Unde angeli dicuntur illi, qui exequuntur ea quae pertinent ad salutem singulorum; Archangeli vero qui exequuntur ea quae pertinent ad salutem et utilitatem magnorum. **Principatus** vero dicuntur illi, qui praesunt singulis provinciis.

63. His ergo expositis, Christus super omnes est.

De his vero quatuor Apostolus specialem mentionem facit. Cuius ratio est, quia horum quatuor ordinum nomina a dignitate imponuntur; et quia agit de dignitate Christi, ideo hic specialiter eos nominat, ut ostendat Christum omnem dignitatem creatam excedere.

64. Consequenter cum dicit **et omne nomen quod nominatur**, etc., ostendit Christum exaltatum esse communiter supra omnem creaturam spiritualem.

Dixerat enim supra Christum esse exaltatum super omnes creaturas spirituales, quae a potestate denominantur, sed quia praeter illos angelorum ordines, in Sacra Scriptura quidam alii ordines caelestium spirituum inveniuntur, scilicet seraphim et cherubim et throni, et de istis non fecerat mentionem, ideo ostendit Christum, secundum quod homo, supra omnes huiusmodi ordines esse exaltatum: propter quod subiungit, dicens **et super omne nomen**, etc., id est, non solum principatus sed super omne nominabile.

Sciendum est enim, quod nomen imponitur ad cognoscendum rem, unde significat rei substantiam, cum significatum nominis sit diffinitiva ratio rei. Cum ergo dicit **et omne nomen quod nominatur**, dat intelligere quod exaltatus est supra omnem substantiam, de qua potest haberi notitia et quae possit nomine comprehendi. Quod dico ut excludatur substantia divinitatis, quae incomprehensibilis est. Unde Glossa dicit **supra omne nomen**, id est nominabile.

Et ne intelligatur, quod sit supra nomen Dei, ideo subdit **quod nominatur**. Nam maiestas divina nullo nomine concludi, vel nominari potest.

Addit autem **non solum in hoc saeculo, sed etiam in futuro**, quia multa fiunt in hoc saeculo, quae notitia comprehendimus et nominamus: quaedam tamen sunt in futuro saeculo, quae hic comprehendi non possunt, nec etiam nominari, quia, ut dicitur I Cor. c. XIII, 9: *ex parte cognoscimus, et ex parte prophetamus*. Nominantur tamen haec a beatis, qui sunt in futuro saeculo. Huiusmodi autem sunt de quibus dicit Apostolus II Cor. XII, 4, quod

subordination; nor are they sent out on external missions but they give orders to those who are sent. The second pertains to the **virtues** who facilitate the execution of the commands. The third belongs to the **powers** who carry out the commands.

On the lower hierarchy devolves the guidance of things in relation to individual causes, and they are named from what is consigned to them. Hence, those called angels carry out what pertains to the salvation of individual persons. The salvation and utility of greater personages is entrusted to the archangels. **Principalities** is the name of those who preside over each of the provinces.

63. Christ is above all of these ranks that have been discussed.

The Apostle only makes a special mention of four of them. The reason is that the names of these four ranks are given them for their dignity, and since he is dealing with the dignity of Christ, he names them especially to show that Christ surpasses all created dignity.

64. Consequently, when he says **and above every name that is named**, he teaches that Christ has been exalted above every spiritual creature in general.

He had stated previously that Christ was exalted above all the spiritual creatures whose names were related to power. However, in Sacred Scripture, besides those ranks of angels, other ranks of celestial spirits are mentioned; for instance, the seraphim (Isa 6), cherubim (Ezek 10, 11, and 41), and thrones (Psalms), which he did not speak of. Therefore, he shows that Christ, as man, is exalted above all of these ranks by adding **above every name that is named**, that is, above not only those who exercise authority but also everything capable of being named.

For it should be recognized that a name is given to understand the object referred to; it signifies the object's substance when what the name designates is the precise intelligibility of the object. In asserting **every name that is named** he lets us know that the exaltation is above every substance which can be known and comprehended by a name. I say this to exclude the substance of divinity which is incomprehensible; so a Gloss remarks that **above every name** means everything that can be named.

And lest it be thought that he is above the name of God, he inserts **that is named**. For the divine majesty can be neither contained nor designated by a name.

Not only in this world, but also in that which is to come is added because there are many facts in this life that we grasp through knowledge and which we name, whereas those of the future life cannot be comprehended or named: *we know in part; and we prophesy in part* (1 Cor 13:9). Nevertheless, the blessed in the future life do name these latter; they are those realities of which the Apostle says that *he heard things that cannot be told, which man may not utter*

audivit arcana verba, quae non licet homini loqui. Et tamen super haec omnia exaltatus est Christus. Phil. II, v. 9: *dedit illi nomen, quod est super omne nomen.*

(2 Cor 12:4). Yet Christ is even exalted above these. *He gave him a name which is above all names* (Phil 2:9).

Lecture 8

1:22Et omnia subjecit sub pedibus ejus: et ipsum dedit caput supra omnem Ecclesiam, [n. 66]

1:23quae est corpus ipsius, et plenitudo ejus, qui omnia in omnibus adimpletur. [n. 70]

1:22καὶ πάντα ὑπέταξεν ὑπὸ τοὺς πόδας αὐτοῦ, καὶ αὐτὸν ἔδωκεν κεφαλὴν ὑπὲρ πάντα τῇ ἐκκλησίᾳ,

1:23ἥτις ἐστὶν τὸ σῶμα αὐτοῦ, τὸ πλήρωμα τοῦ τὰ πάντα ἐν πᾶσιν πληρουμένου.

1:22And he has subjected all things under his feet and has made him head over all the Church, [n. 66]

1:23Which is his body and the fullness of him who is filled all in all. [n. 70]

65. Supra egit Apostolus de exaltatione Christi, et quantum ad eius transitum de morte ad vitam in illa particula *suscitans illum*, etc.; et de eius exaltatione ad gloriam altissimam, in illa particula *et constituens ad dexteram*, etc., hic agit de eius exaltatione quantum ad potestatem maximam.

Circa quod duo facit, quia

primo agit de Christi potestate respectu totius creaturae;

secundo de eius potestate respectu Ecclesiae, ibi *et ipsum dedit*, et cetera.

66. Dicit ergo, quod respectu totius creaturae habet universalem potestatem, quia *omnia subiecit*, scilicet Deus Pater, *sub pedibus eius*.

Ubi sciendum est, quod hoc quod dicit *sub pedibus*, potest accipi dupliciter. Uno modo, ut sit locutio figurativa et similitudinaria, ut scilicet per hoc detur intelligi, quod omnis creatura totaliter est subiecta potestati Christi. Illud enim est a nobis omnino subiectum, quod pedibus conculcamus. Et de ista potestate dicitur Matth. ult.: *data est mihi omnis potestas in caelo et in terra*. Hebr. II, 8: *in eo enim, quod ei omnia subiiciuntur, nihil dimisit non subiectum ei*.

Alio modo, ut sit locutio metaphorica. Nam per pedes intelligitur infima pars corporis, per caput vero suprema. Licet autem in Christo divinitas et humanitas non habeant rationem partis, tamen divinitas, quae est supremum in Christo, intelligitur per caput, I Cor. XI, 3: *caput vero Christi Deus*, humanitas vero, quae infima est, intelligitur per pedes, Ps. CXXXI, 7: *adorabimus in loco ubi steterunt pedes eius*. Est ergo sensus, quod omnia creata non solum subiecit Pater Christo inquantum est Deus, cui ab aeterno omnia sunt subiecta, sed etiam humanitati eius.

67. Advertendum est autem hic, quod Christo subiiciuntur aliqua dupliciter, quia quaedam voluntarie, et quaedam involuntarie. Hoc autem Origenes non intelligens, sumpsit ex hoc verbo Apostoli occasionem erroris, dicens, quod omnia quae subiiciuntur Christo participant salutem, quia ipse est vera salus. Et ideo dixit, quod omnes daemones et damnati aliquando salvabuntur, cum subiiciantur sub pedibus Christi. Hoc autem est contra sententiam Domini Matth. XXV, 41: *discedite a me, maledicti, in ignem aeternum, qui paratus est*

65. The Apostle has previously dealt with the exaltation of Christ both from the viewpoint of his passing over from death to life, at *raising him* (Eph 1:20), and from that of his exaltation to the highest glory, at *setting him on his right hand*. Now he treats of the immense power of his exaltation.

Concerning this he does two things:

first, he discusses the power of Christ with respect to the whole of creation;

second, his power in relation to the Church, at *has made him*.

66. He affirms that, with respect to the whole of creation, Christ has universal power since God the Father *has subjected all things under his feet*.

The phrase *under his feet* can be taken in two ways. In one it is a figurative and symbolic way of saying that every creature is totally subject to the power of Christ. What we trample under foot is certainly subjected to us. Regarding this power it is written: *all power is given to me in heaven and in earth* (Matt 28:18). *For in subjecting all things to him, he left nothing not subjected to him* (Heb 2:8).

In another acceptation it is a metaphorical way of speaking. By the feet the lowest part of the body is understood, and by the head the highest. Although the humanity and divinity should not be thought of as parts of Christ, nonetheless the divinity is preeminent in Christ and may be understood as his head—*the head of Christ is God* (1 Cor 11:3). The humanity is lower and may be taken as the feet—*let us worship at his footstool* (Ps 132:7). The meaning of this passage is then that the Father has not only subjected all of creation to Christ as he is God, to whom everything is subject from eternity, but also to his humanity.

67. Notice how something may be subjected to Christ in two ways, some are so voluntarily and others involuntarily. Origen overlooked this distinction so that this saying of the Apostle occasioned an error on his part. He claimed that everything subjected to Christ, who is true salvation, must share in salvation. He concluded that the demons and damned will be saved at some time since they are subjected under Christ's feet. But this is contrary to the Lord's pronouncement: *depart from me, you cursed, into everlasting fire, which was prepared for the devil and his angels*; and he

diabolo et angelis eius; et concludit in fine capituli: *ibunt hi in supplicium aeternum*.

Dicendum est ergo, quod **omnia subiecit sub pedibus eius**, sed quaedam voluntarie tamquam Salvatori, puta iustos, qui in vita praesenti implent voluntatem Dei, et isti subiiciuntur ei ut impleat eorum desiderium et voluntatem, expectantes illud quod dicitur de bonis Prov. X, 24: *desiderium suum iustis dabitur*. Quaedam vero subiiciuntur ei invite tamquam iudici, ut Christus de his suam voluntatem faciat. Et isti sunt mali, de quibus potest intelligi illud Lc. XIX, 27: *verumtamen inimicos meos illos qui noluerunt me regnare super se, adducite huc et interficite coram me*.

68. Deinde cum dicit **et ipsum dedit caput**, etc., agit de potestate Christi respectu Ecclesiae.

Circa quod tria facit; quia
primo ponit habitudinem Christi ad Ecclesiam;
secundo habitudinem Ecclesiae ad Christum;
tertio exponit illam habitudinem.

69. Quantum ad primum dicit **et ipsum dedit**, Deus Pater, **caput super omnem Ecclesiam**, scilicet tam Militantem, quae est hominum in praesenti viventium, quam Triumphantem, quae est ex hominibus et angelis in patria.

Christus enim secundum quasdam communes rationes caput est etiam angelorum, Col. c. II, 10: *qui est caput omnis principatus et potestatis*; sed secundum speciales rationes est Christus caput hominum spiritualiter.

Nam caput triplicem habitudinem habet ad membra. Primo quidem quo ad praeeminentiam in situ; secundo, quo ad diffusionem virtutum, quia ab eo omnes sensus derivantur in membra; item, quo ad conformitatem in natura. Sic ergo quantum ad praeeminentiam et quantum ad diffusionem Christus est caput angelorum. Nam Christus praeest angelis, etiam secundum humanitatem. Hebr. I, v. 4: *tanto melior angelis effectus, quanto prae illis differentius nomen haereditavit*. Item Christus, etiam secundum quod homo, angelos illuminat et in eis influit, ut Dionysius probat ex verbis Is. LXIII, 1 scilicet: *quis est iste, qui venit de Edom*, etc., dicens haec verba esse supremorum angelorum. Quod autem sequitur: *ego qui loquor iustitiam*, dicit esse verba Christi eis immediate respondentis. Ex quo datur intelligi quod non solum inferiores, sed etiam superiores angelos Christus illuminat.

Quantum autem ad naturae conformitatem, Christus non est caput angelorum, quia *non angelos apprehendit, sed semen Abrahae, ut dicitur* Hebr. II, 16 sed est caput hominum tantum. Cant. IV, 9: *vulnerasti cor meum, soror mea*, scilicet per naturam, *et sponsa* per gratiam.

70. Quantum ad habitudinem Ecclesiae ad Christum, dicit **quae est corpus eius**, scilicet inquantum est

concludes at the end of the chapter, *and these shall go into everlasting punishment* (Matt 25:41, 46).

It must be held, therefore, that **he has subjected all things under his feet**, some as willingly, as to their Savior, such as the just who fulfill God's will in the present life, and are subjected to him that they may satisfy their desire and will, awaiting for what is said of the good: *to the just their desire shall be given* (Prov 10:24). Others, however, are subjected to him unwillingly, as to their judge, that Christ may accomplish his own will in their regard. These are the wicked of whom it may be understood to be written: *but as for those my enemies, who would not have me reign over them, bring them here and kill them before me* (Luke 19:27).

68. Next, at **has made him head**, he deals with Christ's power with respect to the Church.

In reference to this he makes three points:
first, he sets down the relation of Christ to the Church.
second, he lays out the relation of the Church to Christ;
third, he explains this relationship.

69. Concerning the first, at **and made him head**, he says God the Father **made him head over all the Church**, both of the Church Militant, composed of men living in the present, and of the Church Triumphant, made up of the men and angels in the fatherland.

On account of certain general reasons, Christ is even the head of the angels—*who is the head of all principality and power* (Col 2:10)—whereas Christ is spiritually the head of mankind for special reasons.

For the head has a threefold relationship with the other members. First, it has a preeminent position; second, its powers are diffused since all the senses in the members are derived from it; third, it is of the same nature as the other members. Thus, Christ is head of the angels in regard to preeminence and the diffusion of his power. Even in his humanity Christ surpasses the angels: *being made so much better than the angels as he has inherited a more excellent name than they* (Heb 1:4). Moreover, even as man, Christ enlightens and influences them; Dionysius proves this from what is written: *who is this that comes from Edom, with dyed garments from Bosra?* (Isa 63:1), claiming that these words are those of the highest angels. The response which follows: *it is I, announcing justice mighty to save*, he says are the words of Christ who immediately answers them. From this it should be understood that Christ not only illumines the lower but also the higher angels.

With respect to a conformity of nature, Christ is not the head of the angels, *for surely he did not take angels to himself, but he took the line of Abraham* (Heb 2:16); but in this respect he is the head of men only. *You have wounded my heart, my sister*, through nature, *and my spouse*, through grace (Song 4:9).

70. He speaks of the relation of the Church to Christ at **which is his body**, inasmuch as she is subject to him,

ei subiecta, et recipit ab eo influentiam, et habet naturam conformem cum Christo. I Cor. XII, 12: *sicut enim corpus unum est et habet multa membra, omnia autem membra corporis cum sint multa, unum tamen corpus sunt, ita et Christus; etenim in uno Spiritu omnes nos in unum corpus baptizati sumus.*

71. Exponit autem quod dixit, **quae est corpus ipsius**, subdens **et plenitudo eius**, et cetera.

Quaerenti enim cur in corpore naturali sint tot membra, scilicet manus, pedes, os et huiusmodi, respondetur hoc esse ideo ut deserviant diversis operibus animae, quorum ipsa potest esse causa, principium, et quae sunt virtute in ipsa. Nam corpus est factum propter animam, et non e converso. Unde secundum hoc corpus naturale est quaedam plenitudo animae. Nisi enim essent membra cum corpore completa, non posset anima suas operationes plene exercere.

Similiter itaque est hoc de Christo et de Ecclesia. Et quia Ecclesia est instituta propter Christum, dicitur quod Ecclesia est **plenitudo eius**, scilicet Christi, id est, ut omnia, quae virtute sunt in Christo, quasi quodam modo in membris ipsius Ecclesiae impleantur, dum scilicet omnes sensus spirituales, et dona, et quidquid potest esse in Ecclesia, quae omnia superabundanter sunt in Christo, ab ipso deriventur in membra Ecclesiae et perficiantur in eis. Unde subdit **qui omnia in omnibus adimpletur**, scilicet dum hunc quidem, qui est membrum Ecclesiae, facit sapientem secundum perfectam sapientiam, quae est in ipso: illum vero iustum secundum perfectam iustitiam, et sic de aliis.

receives his influence, and shares the same nature with Christ. *Just as the body is one and has many members, and all the members of the body, though many, are one body, so it is with Christ. For in one Spirit were we all baptized into one body* (1 Cor 12:12–13).

71. He explains **which is his body** by adding **the fullness of him**.

To one asking why there are so many members in a natural body—hands, feet, mouth, and the like it could be replied that they are to serve the soul's variety of activities. The soul itself is the cause and principle of these members, and what they are, the soul is virtually. For the body is made for the soul, and not the other way around. From this perspective, the natural body is a certain fullness of the soul; unless the members exist with an integral body, the soul cannot exercise fully its activities.

This is similar in the relation of Christ and the Church. Since the Church was instituted on account of Christ, the Church is called the **fullness** of Christ. Everything which is virtually in Christ is, as it were, filled out in some way in the members of the Church. For all spiritual understanding, gifts, and whatever can be present in the Church—all of which Christ possesses superabundantly—flow from him into the members of the Church, and they are perfected in them. So he adds **who is filled all in all** since Christ makes this member of the Church wise with the perfect wisdom present in himself, and he makes another just with his perfect justice, and so on with the others.

Chapter 2

Lecture 1

2:1Et vos, cum essetis mortui delictis et peccatis vestris, [n. 73]

2:2in quibus aliquando ambulastis secundum saeculum mundi hujus, secundum principem potestatis aëris hujus, spiritus, qui nunc operatur in filios diffidentiae, [n. 74]

2:3in quibus et nos omnes aliquando conversati sumus in desideriis carnis nostrae, facientes voluntatem carnis et cogitationum, et eramus natura filii irae, sicut et ceteri: [n. 80]

2:1Καὶ ὑμᾶς ὄντας νεκροὺς τοῖς παραπτώμασιν καὶ ταῖς ἁμαρτίαις ὑμῶν,

2:2ἐν αἷς ποτε περιεπατήσατε κατὰ τὸν αἰῶνα τοῦ κόσμου τούτου, κατὰ τὸν ἄρχοντα τῆς ἐξουσίας τοῦ ἀέρος, τοῦ πνεύματος τοῦ νῦν ἐνεργοῦντος ἐν τοῖς υἱοῖς τῆς ἀπειθείας·

2:3ἐν οἷς καὶ ἡμεῖς πάντες ἀνεστράφημέν ποτε ἐν ταῖς ἐπιθυμίαις τῆς σαρκὸς ἡμῶν, ποιοῦντες τὰ θελήματα τῆς σαρκὸς καὶ τῶν διανοιῶν, καὶ ἤμεθα τέκνα φύσει ὀργῆς ὡς καὶ οἱ λοιποί·

2:1And you, when you were dead in your offences and sins, [n. 73]

2:2Wherein in time past you walked according to the course of this world, according to the prince of the power of this air, of the spirit that now works on the children of unbelief: [n. 74]

2:3In which also we all conversed in time past, in the desires of our flesh, fulfilling the will of the flesh and of our thoughts, and were by nature children of wrath, even as the rest: [n. 80]

---

72. Supra enumeravit Apostolus beneficia humano generi per Christum communiter exhibita, hic Apostolus commemorat eadem per comparationem ad eorum statum praeteritum. Status autem eorum praeteritus dupliciter considerari potest. Primo quidem quantum ad statum culpae; secundo quantum ad statum gentilitatis eorum. Apostolus ergo duo facit, quia

primo commemorat beneficia quantum ad primum statum eis exhibita;

secundo commemorat ea per comparationem ad statum secundum, ibi *propter quod memores estote*, et cetera.

Prima iterum in duas, quia

primo recitat Apostolus statum culpae ipsorum;

secundo beneficium gratiae iustificationis, ibi *Deus autem, qui dives est*, et cetera.

Prima iterum in duas, quia

primo commemorat statum culpae quantum ad gentiles;

secundo quantum ad Iudaeos, ibi *in quibus et nos*, et cetera.

Prima iterum in duas, quia

primo praemittit beneficii generalitatem;

secundo subdit huius necessitatem, ibi *cum essemus mortui*, et cetera.

73. Dicit ergo: dico quod Deus magnifice operatur in fidelibus *secundum operationem potentiae virtutis eius, quam operatus est in Christo*, et hoc quia suscitavit illum a mortuis; secundum hanc ergo operationem ad huius operationis exemplum convivificavit nos, vita scilicet gratiae de morte peccati. Os. VI, 3: *vivificabit*

72. Above, the Apostle enumerated the blessings bestowed on the human race in general through Christ. Here the Apostle sets them in relief by comparing them to mankind's former condition. Their past state can be considered in two ways: first as a state of sin, and second as a state of paganism. Therefore, the Apostle does two things:

first, he recounts the blessings shown them in regard to their first state;

second, he recalls those related to their second state, at *for which cause be mindful* (Eph 2:11).

The first part has two sections:

first, the Apostle describes their state of sin;

second, he describes the blessing of the grace of justification, at *but God who is rich* (Eph 2:4).

Again, the first part has two divisions:

first, he calls to mind the state of sin with reference to the pagans;

second, then with reference to the Jews, at *in which also we all*.

Once more the first has two parts:

first, he sets down the generality of the blessing;

second, he adds its necessity, at *when you were dead*.

73. God, he says, is wondrously active in the faithful, *according to the operation of the might of his power, which he wrought in Christ*, (Eph 1:19) in raising him from the dead. Hence, according to this activity, and after the example of this operation, he has restored us to the life of grace from the death of sin. *He will revive us after two days: on*

nos post duos dies, in die tertia suscitabit nos, et cetera. Col. III, v. 1: *si consurrexistis cum Christo, quae sursum sunt quaerite*, et cetera.

74. Necessitatem vero huius beneficii ostendit, cum dicit **cum essetis mortui**, et cetera. Ubi optime describit eorum culpam.

Primo quantum ad multitudinem, **quia cum essetis mortui**, scilicet morte spirituali, quae pessima est. Ps. XXXIII, 22: *mors peccatorum pessima*. Peccatum enim mors dicitur, quia per ipsum homo a domino, qui est vita, separatur. Io. XIV, 6: *ego sum via, veritas, et vita*.

Mortui, inquam, **in delictis et peccatis vestris**, ecce multitudo. In delictis quidem quantum ad omissa, Ps. XVIII, 13: *delicta quis intelligit*, etc., et peccatis quantum ad commissa. **In quibus aliquando ambulastis**, quod ideo dicit, ut multitudinem peccatorum exaggeret. Nam aliqui si ad horam mortui sunt in peccatis et in delictis, cessant tamen aliquando, et peccare desistunt; sed isti, de malo in peius procedentes et ambulantes, proficiebant.

Simile habetur Phil. III, 18: *multi enim ambulant, quos saepe dicebam vobis, nunc autem et flens dico*, et cetera. Ier. II, 5: *ambulaverunt post vanitatem suam, et vani facti sunt*.

75. Secundo describit eorum culpam quantum ad causam quae ponitur duplex.

Una ex parte huius mundi, quia alliciebantur a rebus mundi. Et quantum ad hoc dicit **secundum saeculum mundi huius**, id est secundum saecularem vitam rerum mundanarum, quae vos alliciunt. I Io. II, 15: *si quis diligit mundum, non est caritas Patris in eo*. Propter quod praemittit: *nolite diligere mundum*.

76. Alia causa est ex parte daemonum, quibus serviebant, de quibus dicitur Sap. XIV, v. 27: *infandorum idolorum cultura, omnis mali causa est et initium*. Et quantum ad hoc dicit **et secundum principem potestatis**. Quam quidem causam describit tripliciter.

Primo quidem quantum ad potestatem, dicens **secundum principem potestatis**, id est, potestatem exercentem, non quod habeat eam naturaliter, cum nec dominus, nec creator sit ex natura, sed inquantum dominatur hominibus qui se ei peccando subiiciunt. Io. XII, v. 31: *nunc princeps huius mundi eiicietur foras*. Et XIV, 30: *venit princeps huius mundi, et in me non habet quidquam*.

77. Secundo quantum ad habitationem, quia **aeris huius**, id est qui habet potestatem in hoc aere caliginoso.

Ubi sciendum est quod de istis daemonibus duplex est opinio apud doctores. Quidam enim dixerunt daemones qui ceciderunt, non fuisse de supremis ordinibus, sed de inferioribus, qui praesunt corporibus inferioribus.

the third day he will raise us up and we shall live in his sight (Hos 6:3). *If you have been raised with Christ, seek the things that are above, where Christ is sitting at the right hand of God* (Col 3:1).

74. He demonstrates the need for such a blessing when he states **when you were dead** where he describes so well their sin.

First of all, he depicts the multitude of their sins at **and you, when you were dead** with the worst type of death, spiritual death. *The death of the wicked is very worst* (Ps 34:22). Sin is termed a death because by it man is separated from God who is life: *I am the way, and the truth, and the life* (John 14:6).

Dead I say, **in your offenses and sins**—behold the great number! For offenses are what they omitted—*who can discover errors?* (Ps 19:13)—while sins are what they committed. **Wherein in time past you walked** is added to give an account of the great number of sins. For if some are dead in offenses and sins at one time, they nonetheless cease at another time and leave off sinning; but these keep up their pace in going from bad to worse.

Similarly it is written: *for many, as I have often told you and now tell you with tears, conduct themselves as enemies of the cross of Christ* (Phil 3:18). *They have gone after worthlessness and become worthless* (Jer 2:5).

75. Second, he describes the twofold cause of their sin.

One arises from this world insofar as they are attracted by the things of the world. Concerning this he states **according to the course of this world**; you were allured by mundane matters into a worldly life. *If any man love the world, the charity of the Father is not in him*. Hence the command: *love not the world, nor the things which are in the world* (1 John 2:15).

76. The other cause was the devils whom they served: *the worship of abominable idols is the beginning and cause and end of all evil* (Wis 14:27). In reference to this he says **according to the prince of the power of this air**, and he portrays three aspects of this cause.

First, as regards their strength he says **the prince of the power**. He exerts a power, not by the fact that he has it naturally, since he is neither the lord nor creator by nature, but to the degree that he dominates over men who subject themselves to him by sinning. *Now shall the prince of this world be cast out* (John 12:31); *for the prince of this world is coming; he has no power over me* (John 14:30).

77. Second, concerning their dwelling place he says **of this air**, that is, he has power in this darksome atmosphere.

Here it should be noted that two opinions exist among the doctors. For some held that the demons who had fallen were not from the higher ranks, but from the lower ones in charge of the lower bodies. It is evident that the whole of

Constat autem totam creaturam corporalem administrari a Deo, ministerio angelorum. Et haec est opinio Ioannis Damasceni, scilicet quod primus eorum qui ceciderunt, praeerat ordini terrestrium, quod forte sumptum est ex dicto Platonis, qui ponebat quasdam substantias caelestes seu mundanas. Et secundum hoc exponitur hoc quod dicit *aeris huius*, id est ad hoc creati, ut praesiderent aeri huic.

Alii vero volunt, et melius, quod fuerint de supremis ordinibus, ita quod hoc quod dicit *aeris huius*, sit ad ostendendum ipsum aerem esse habitationem ipsorum in poenam eorum. Unde Iudas in sua canonica dicit: *angelos vero qui non servaverunt suum principatum, sed dereliquerunt suum domicilium, in iudicium Dei magni, vinculis aeternis sub caligine reservavit*.

Ratio autem quare non statim post eorum casum retrusi sunt in Infernum, sed dimittuntur in aere, est, quia Deus noluit quod ipsis peccantibus eorum creatio totaliter frustraretur, et ideo dedit eos hominibus in exercitium quo bonis praepararent coronam, malis autem aeternam mortem. Et quia usque ad diem iudicii est nobis tempus belli et merendi, ideo usque tunc in aere permanebunt; post diem vero iudicii retrudentur in Infernum.

Advertendum etiam quod una littera habet *spiritus*, et sic est genitivi casus, et ponitur singulare pro pluralibus, quasi dicat: *spirituum*. Alia littera habet *spiritum*, et tunc est accusativi casus, ut dicatur: *secundum principem spiritum*, id est, qui princeps est spiritus.

78. Tertio quantum ad operationem, ibi, cum dicit *qui nunc operatur in filios diffidentiae*, id est in illos qui a se repellunt fructum passionis Christi, qui erant filii diffidentiae. Vel quia de aeternis non habent fidem, nec spem salutis per Christum: et in talibus princeps potestatis aeris huius libere *operatur*, ducens eos quo vult: de quibus infra IV, 19, dicitur: *qui desperantes semetipsos tradiderunt impudicitiae, in operationem immunditiae*.

Vel *diffidentiae*, id est de quibus eis est diffidendum, id est qui ex malitia peccant, in quibus princeps huius mundi etiam operatur ad nutum. De his enim qui ex ignorantia et infirmitate peccant, non est diffidendum, nec in eis princeps iste operatur ad nutum.

79. Sed contra. De nemine est desperandum quamdiu vivit.

Respondeo. Dicendum est quod de aliquo potest esse duplex spes. Una ex parte hominis, alia ex parte divinae gratiae. Et sic de aliquo potest desperari ex parte sua, de quo tamen desperandum non est ex parte Dei, sicut desperandum erat de Lazaro iacente in sepulcro, quod resurgeret ex parte sua, de quo tamen desperandum non erat ex parte Dei, a quo resuscitatus est. De illis ergo, qui ex malitia sunt multum in peccatis demersi, si attendatur

material creation is governed by God through the ministry of angels. Thus John Damascene was of the opinion that the first of those who had fallen had been in charge of the terrestrial order. He may have derived this from Plato's talk about certain celestial or worldly substances. In this perspective *of this air* is interpreted that they were created to preside over this atmosphere.

Others preferred, and with better reason, that those angels who sinned were from the highest ranks. *Of this air* then designates that this atmosphere is the place of their punishment. Jude refers to this in his canonical letter: *and the angels who did not keep their own position but left their proper dwelling he has kept in everlasting chains under darkness until the judgment of the great day* (Jude 1:6).

The reason why they were not immediately thrust into hell after their fall, but released in the atmosphere, was because God did not want the creation of those who had sinned to be totally frustrated. Hence, he sent them to try men, by which the good would be prepared for glory and the wicked for eternal death. The time of our warfare and of merit will last until the day of judgment, till then they will remain in the atmosphere; after the day of judgment, however, they will be thrust back into hell.

Observe also how one reading has *of the spirit* which, as a genitive singular, stands for the plural *of the spirits*. Another reading gives *spirit* in the accusative case; as if to say: *according to the prince spirit*, that is, the prince who is a spirit.

78. Third, he describes their activity when he states *that now works on the children of despair*. They are the children of despair who reject the fruit of Christ's passion. Or, those who have no faith in eternal realities nor hope in salvation through Christ. In these the prince of the power of this air freely *works*, leading them wherever he wishes. Later it is said of them: *who despairing, have given themselves up to licentiousness, unto the working of all uncleanness, unto covetousness* (Eph 4:19).

Perhaps, *of despair* means those of whom we should despair because they sin out of malice; the prince of this world doing whatever he pleases in them. For no one should despair of those who sin from ignorance or weakness, nor does that prince do whatever he wants with them.

79. On the contrary, however, one should never despair of anyone else as long as he lives.

I reply. Our hope in someone can be twofold. On the one hand, it can be in the man, and on the other, in divine grace. Thus someone may be despaired of as far as he himself is concerned, but never must confidence in God be lost. For instance, people rightly despaired of Lazarus's power to bring himself back to life once he had been placed in the tomb, but no trust should have been lost in the God who raised him up. Therefore, those who out of malice are

eorum virtus, desperari potest, Ps. LXVIII, 3: *infixus sum in limo profundi, et non est substantia*, non tamen si attendatur virtus divina.

De istis autem filiis diffidentiae dicitur infra V, 6: ***nemo vos seducat inanibus verbis. Propter hoc enim venit ira Dei in filios diffidentiae***.

80. Deinde cum dicit **in quibus et nos omnes**, etc., commemorat Apostolus statum culpae quantum ad Iudaeos, ostendens eos omnes in peccato fuisse, secundum illud Rom. III, 9: *causati sumus Iudaeos et Graecos omnes sub peccato esse*.

Attendenda est tamen differentia circa hoc, quia Apostolus, agens de culpa gentilium, assignavit duas causas culpae fuisse. Unam scilicet ex parte mundi, aliam ex parte daemonum, quos colebant. Quia ergo Iudaei erant similes gentilibus in statu culpae, quantum ad primam causam, non autem quantum ad secundam, ideo Apostolus non facit mentionem de culpa eorum, nisi quantum ad causam quae est ex parte mundi.

Circa quod tria facit.

Primo commemorat eorum culpam quantum ad peccatum cordis;

secundo quantum ad peccatum operis;

tertio quantum ad peccatum originis.

81. Peccatum vero cordis insinuat per desideria carnis, et quantum ad hoc dicit **in quibus**, scilicet peccatis seu delictis, **nos omnes**, scilicet Iudaei, **aliquando conversati sumus**, agentes vitam nostram, **in desideriis carnis nostrae**, id est, carnalibus. Tit. III, 3: *eramus enim aliquando et nos insipientes et increduli, errantes et servientes desideriis et voluptatibus variis*, et cetera. Rom. XIII, 14: *carnis curam ne feceritis in desideriis*.

82. Peccatum vero operis nihil aliud est quam expressio interioris concupiscentiae. Est autem quaedam concupiscentia carnis, sicut sunt concupiscentiae naturales, puta cibi per quam conservatur individuum, et venereorum per quam conservatur species; et quantum ad hoc dicit **facientes voluntatem**, etc., id est, ea in quibus caro delectatur. Rom. VIII, 8: *qui autem in carne sunt, Deo placere non possunt*.

Quaedam vero est concupiscentia cognitionis, eorum scilicet quae non veniunt ex desideriis carnis, sed ex ipso appetitu animae, ut honoris ambitio et propriae excellentiae, et huiusmodi; et quantum ad hoc dicit **et cogitationum**, id est exequentes illas concupiscentias, quae causantur ex instinctu cogitationum nostrarum.

83. Peccatum vero originis insinuat dicens **et eramus natura filii irae**. Quod quidem peccatum ex primo parente non solum in gentiles, sed etiam in Iudaeos transfunditur. Rom. V, 12: *sicut per unum hominem in hunc mundum peccatum intravit, et per peccatum mors; ita et*

sunk in their many sins can be despaired of from the point of view of their own strength: *I have sunk into the abysmal mire, where there is no footing* (Ps 69:3). But no one should despair if it is a question of the divine power.

Concerning these children of despair it mentions further on: ***let no man deceive you with vain words. For because of these things comes the anger of God upon the children of unbelief*** (Eph 5:6).

80. Next, at **in which also we all**, the Apostle recalls the sinful state of the Jews, thereby demonstrating how everyone had sinned, according to what is written: *for we have charged both Jews and Greeks, that they are all under sin* (Rom 3:9).

Nevertheless, a difference should be noted. The Apostle had designated two causes when dealing with the sin of the gentiles, one on the side of the world and the other on that of the demons whom they worshiped. The Jews were like the gentiles in their sinful condition in regard to the first cause, but not the second; hence, the Apostle only mentions their sin as arising from worldly causes.

In reference to this he makes three points:

first, he recounts their guilt regarding sins of the heart;

second, regarding the sins of action;

third, regarding original sin.

81. A sin of the heart is implied in carnal desires. About this he asserts: **in which** sins and offenses **also we all** who are Jews **conversed in time past**, leading our life **in the** carnal **desires of our flesh**. *For we ourselves also were once foolish, disobedient, led astray, slaves to various passions and pleasures, living in malice and envy, hateful, and hating one another* (Titus 3:3). *Put on the Lord Jesus Christ; and make no provision for the desires of the flesh* (Rom 13:14).

82. Sin in action is nothing else than a manifestation of inner concupiscence. A certain concupiscence of the flesh exists, which consists of the natural concupiscences; for example, for food through which the individual maintains his own life, and for sexual relations by which the species is preserved. Regarding these he says **fulfilling the will of the flesh**, doing what the flesh delights in. *And they who are in the flesh cannot please God* (Rom 8:8).

Another concupiscence exists, that of thought. These desires do not spring from the flesh but from the appetitive faculty of the soul, such as the ambition for honors, for one's own excellence and the like. Of these he states **and of our thoughts**, that is, inordinate desires are followed once they are caused by the prompting of our reflections.

83. Original sin is hinted at in **and we were by nature children of wrath**. This sin of the first parent was not only passed on to the gentiles but to the Jews also: *wherefore as by one man sin entered into this world, and by sin death;*

in omnes homines mors pertransivit, in quo omnes peccaverunt.

Et sicut homines per baptismum mundantur a peccato originali solum quantum ad personas proprias, unde generant filios baptizandos, ita circumcisio mundabat ab originali personas solum, sed generabant adhuc circumcidendos. Et hoc est quod dicit **eramus natura**, id est per originem naturae, non quidem naturae ut natura est, quia sic bona est et a Deo, sed naturae ut vitiata est, **filii irae**, id est vindictae, poenae et Gehennae, et hoc **sicut et caeteri**, id est gentiles.

and so death passed upon all men, in whom all have sinned (Rom 5:12).

Baptism cleanses only the individual person who receives it from original sin; his children must also be baptized. Likewise, circumcision cleansed only the individual from original sin; the children they begot still had to be circumcised. Thus he says **we were by nature**, that is, from the earliest beginning of nature—not of nature as nature since this is good and from God, but of nature as vitiated—**children of** an avenging **wrath**, aimed at punishment and hell, **even as the rest**, that is, the gentiles.

Lecture 2

²:⁴Deus autem, qui dives est in misericordia, propter nimiam caritatem suam, qua dilexit nos, [n. 85]

²:⁵et cum essemus mortui peccatis, convivificavit nos in Christo (cujus gratia estis salvati), [n. 88]

²:⁶et conresuscitavit, et consedere fecit in caelestibus in Christo Jesu: [n. 88]

²:⁷ut ostenderet in saeculis supervenientibus abundantes divitias gratiae suae, in bonitate super nos in Christo Jesu. [n. 89]

²:⁴ὁ δὲ Θεὸς πλούσιος ὢν ἐν ἐλέει, διὰ τὴν πολλὴν ἀγάπην αὐτοῦ ἣν ἠγάπησεν ἡμᾶς,

²:⁵καὶ ὄντας ἡμᾶς νεκροὺς τοῖς παραπτώμασιν συνεζωοποίησεν τῷ Χριστῷ χάριτί ἐστε σεσῳσμένοι

²:⁶καὶ συνήγειρεν καὶ συνεκάθισεν ἐν τοῖς ἐπουρανίοις ἐν Χριστῷ Ἰησοῦ,

²:⁷ἵνα ἐνδείξηται ἐν τοῖς αἰῶσιν τοῖς ἐπερχομένοις τὸ ὑπερβάλλον πλοῦτος τῆς χάριτος αὐτοῦ ἐν χρηστότητι ἐφ' ἡμᾶς ἐν Χριστῷ Ἰησοῦ.

²:⁴But God (who is rich in mercy) for his exceeding charity with which he loved us [n. 85]

²:⁵Even when we were dead in sins, has quickened us together in Christ (by whose grace you are saved) [n. 88]

²:⁶And has raised us up together and has made us sit together in the heavenly places, through Christ Jesus. [n. 88]

²:⁷That he might show in the ages to come the abundant riches of his grace, in his bounty towards us in Christ Jesus. [n. 89]

---

84. Postquam exaggeravit Apostolus statum culpae inficientis, hic commendat beneficium gratiae iustificantis.

Circa quam duo facit.

Primo ipsum beneficium ponit;

secundo seipsum exponit, ibi *gratia enim estis*, et cetera.

Beneficium autem illud describit quantum ad tres causas.

Primo quantum ad causam efficientem;

secundo quantum ad causam formalem, seu exemplarem;

tertio quantum ad causam finalem.

85. Efficiens autem causa beneficii divini iustificantis, est caritas Dei. Et quantum ad hoc dicit *Deus autem qui dives est in misericordia, propter nimiam caritatem*.

Dicit autem *propter nimiam caritatem*, quia dilectionis divinae possumus considerare quadruplicem bonitatem et efficientiam. Primo quia nos in esse produxit. Sap. XI, 25: *diligis enim omnia quae sunt, et nihil odisti eorum quae fecisti*, et cetera. Secundo quia ad imaginem suam nos fecit, et capaces beatitudinis suae. Deut. XXXIII, 2–3: *cum eo sanctorum millia, in dextra illius ignea lex, dilexit populos, omnes sancti in manu illius sunt*. Tertio quia homines per peccatum corruptos reparavit. Ier. XXXI, 3: *in caritate perpetua dilexi te, et ideo*, et cetera. Quarto quia pro salute nostra Filium proprium dedit. Io. III, 16: *sic Deus dilexit mundum, ut Filium suum unigenitum daret*. Unde Gregorius: *o inaestimabilis dilectio caritatis. Ut servum redimeres, Filium tradidisti*.

86. Dicit autem *qui dives est in misericordia*, quia cum amor hominis causetur ex bonitate eius qui diligitur, tunc homo ille qui diligit, diligit ex iustitia, inquantum

84. After giving an account of their state of festering sin, the Apostle recounts here the blessing of the grace of justification.

Concerning this he does two things:

first, he sets down the blessing itself;

second, he explains it, at *for by grace* (Eph 2:8).

The blessing is described with reference to its three causes:

first, the efficient cause;

second, the formal or exemplary cause;

third, the final cause.

85. The efficient cause of the divine blessing of justification is God's charity: *but God, who is rich in mercy, for his exceeding charity with which he loved us*.

He states *for his exceeding charity* since we can think of a fourfold goodness and efficacy of the divine love. First, it brought us into existence: *for you love all things that are, and hate none of the things which you have made* (Wis 11:25). Second, he made us according to his own image, capable of enjoying his own beatitude: *he came from Miribath-Kadesh and with him thousands of saints. At his right hand a fire blazed forth. He has loved the people; all the saints are in his hand* (Deut 33:2–3). Third, he renewed men corrupted by sin: *I have loved them with an everlasting love; therefore have I drawn you, taking pity on you* (Jer 31:3). Fourth, for our salvation he gave over his own Son: *for God so loved the world, as to give his only begotten Son* (John 3:16). Hence Gregory exclaims: *O the incalculable love of your charity! To redeem slaves you delivered up your Son*.

86. He then asserts *who is rich in mercy*. When a man's love is caused from the goodness of the one he loves, then that man who loves does so out of justice, inasmuch as it is

iustum est quod talem amet. Quando vero amor causat bonitatem in dilecto, tunc est amor procedens ex misericordia. Amor autem quo Deus amat nos, causat in nobis bonitatem, et ideo misericordia ponitur hic quasi radix amoris divini. Is. LXIII, 7: *largitus est in eis secundum indulgentiam suam, et secundum multitudinem misericordiarum suarum.* Ibidem: *multitudo viscerum tuorum et miserationum tuarum super me.*

87. Dicitur autem Deus **dives in misericordia**, quia habet eam infinitam et indeficientem, quod non habet homo.

In tribus enim homo miseretur cum termino et limitatione. Primo quidem largiendo beneficia temporalia, et haec misericordia est finita, non excedens limites propriae facultatis. Tob. IV, 8: *quomodo potueris, ita esto misericors*; sed Deus *dives est* etiam *in omnes qui invocant illum*, ut dicitur Rom. X, 12.

Secundo est finita misericordia hominis quia non remittit nisi offensam propriam, et in hoc etiam modus esse debet, ut scilicet non sic passim remittat, ut ille cui remittit efficiatur procacior, pronior et facilior ad iterum offendendum. Eccle. VIII, 11: *etenim quia non profertur cito contra malos sententia, absque timore ullo filii hominum perpetrant mala.* Deo autem nihil nocere potest, et ideo potest omnem offensam remittere. Iob c. XXXV, 6: *si peccaveris, quid ei nocebis?* Et parum post: *porro si iuste egeris, quid donabis ei?*

Tertio, homo miseretur poenam remittendo, et in hoc etiam est modus servandus, scilicet ut non facias contra legis superioris iustitiam: Deus autem poenam omnium remittere potest, cum non obstringatur aliqua superioris lege. Iob XXXIV, 13: *quem constituit alium super terram, et quem posuit super orbem quem fabricatus est?*

Sic ergo misericordia Dei est infinita, quia non coarctatur angustiis divitiarum, neque timore nocumenti restringitur, et neque lege superioris.

88. Causa vero exemplaris beneficii est, quia in Christo collata est. Et quantum ad hoc dicit **cum essemus mortui peccatis, convivificavit nos in Christo**, et cetera. Ubi tangit triplex beneficium, id est: iustificationis, resurrectionis a mortuis, et ascensionis in caelum, per quae tria Christo assimilamur.

Dicit ergo quantum ad primum, ut legatur littera suspensive, **Deus autem, qui dives est**, etc., **cum essemus mortui peccatis, convivificavit nos in Christo**, id est simul vivere fecit cum Christo. Os. VI, 3: *vivificabit nos post duos dies*, et cetera. Convivificavit, inquam, hic scilicet per viam iustitiae. Ps. LXV, v. 9: *qui posuit animam meam ad vitam.* Et hoc **in Christo**, id est per gratiam Christi, **cuius**, scilicet Christi, **gratia estis salvati**. Rom. VIII, 24: *spe enim salvi sumus.*

just that he love such a person. When, however, love causes the goodness in the beloved, then it is a love springing from mercy. The love with which God loves us produces goodness in us; hence mercy is presented here as the root of the divine love: *the favors of Yahweh I will recall, the praises of Yahweh for all that Yahweh has done for us . . . which he has given according to his kindness and the multitude of his mercies* (Isa 63:7). And *where is your zealous care and might, your surge of pity and mercy toward me?* (Isa 63:15).

87. God is said to be **rich in mercy** because he possesses an infinite and unfailing mercy, which man does not.

For man has a mercy that is bounded or limited in three ways. First, in bestowing temporal benefits, man's mercy is restricted by the amount of his own possessions. *If you have little, do not be afraid to give from that little* (Tob 4:8); whereas God *enriches all who call upon him* (Rom 10:12).

Second, the mercy of man is limited since he can only pardon offenses against himself. Even with these there ought to be a certain qualification; he should not forgive so indiscriminately that whoever is pardoned becomes more bold, prone and ready to offend again. *For, because sentence is not speedily pronounced against the evil, the hearts of the sons of men are fully set to do evil* (Eccl 8:11). But nothing can harm God and hence he can forgive every offense: *if you sin, what harm do you do to him?* And a little further on, *and if you act rightly, what do you give him?* (Job 35:6–7)

Third, a man shows mercy in remitting punishment; yet here too a qualification must be observed: he must not contravene the justice of a higher law. God, on the other hand, can remit all punishment since he is not bound by any higher law: *who gave him charge over the earth? Or who else set the land in its place?* (Job 34:13).

Thus the mercy of God is infinite because it is not limited by a scarcity of wealth, nor is it restricted through a fear of injury, nor by any higher law.

88. The exemplary cause of the blessing is that it is granted in Christ. In reference to this he states **even when we were dead in sins, he has quickened us together in Christ**. He touches upon a triple blessing: justification, resurrection from the dead, and ascension into heaven—through these three we are assimilated to Christ.

He states that the whole text might be read, concerning the first: **God, who is rich in mercy, for his exceeding charity with which he loved us, even when we were dead in sins, has quickened us together in Christ**, that is, he has made us live together with Christ. *He will revive us after two days: on the third day he will raise us up and we shall live in his sight* (Hos 6:3). He has quickened us, I say, through a life of justice: *who placed us among the living* (Ps 66:9). This occurs in Christ, that is, through the grace of Christ **by whose grace you are saved**. *For we are saved by hope* (Rom 8:24).

Regarding the second, he says *and has raised us up together* with Christ—in reality, in regard to the soul, and in hope, in regard to the body. *He who raised Jesus Christ from the dead will give life to your mortal bodies also through his Spirit which dwells in you* (Rom 8:11).

In respect to the third he asserts *and has made us sit together in the heavenly places in Christ Jesus*, now through hope, and in the future in reality. *Where I am, there also will my servant be. If anyone serves me, my Father will honor him* (John 12:26). *He who conquers I will grant him to sit with me in my throne; as I myself have conquered and sat down with my Father on his throne* (Rev 3:21).

In these the Apostle uses the past tense in place of the future, proclaiming as already accomplished what has yet to be done, on account of the certitude of hope. Thus God has *quickened us* in soul, he *has raised us up* in body, and *has made us sit* with Christ in both body and soul.

89. Consequently, when he says *that he might show*, he discloses the final cause of the blessing which has been given. It can be read in two ways, depending on whether *ages to come* pertains to the present or future life.

If it applies to this life, then age is a certain measure of time and a period of one generation. As though he affirmed: I am saying that we who are the first-fruits of those who sleep (1 Thess 4:12ff), *he has quickened in Christ that he might show in the ages to come*, to those who will exist after us, *the abundant riches of his grace*. And this is not on account of our merits, but in his own *bounty towards us in Christ Jesus*, that is, through Christ Jesus. *Christ Jesus came into the world to save sinners; of these I am the foremost. But I have received mercy for this reason, that in me first Christ Jesus might display his perfect patience, as an example for those who would believe in him for eternal life* (1 Tim 1:15–16).

Therefore, God has communicated copious gifts of grace to the early saints that later generations would more easily be converted to Christ.

90. Or, *age* can be taken in reference to the next life, of which it is written: *for eternity I shall not cease to exist* (Sir 24:14). Although there will then be only one age, since it will be eternity, he nevertheless says *in the ages to come* on account of the numerous saints who will participate in eternity; there are said to be as many ages as there are shared-in eternities. Of these ages it is written: *your kingdom is a kingdom of all ages* (Ps 145:13).

In this sense he affirms: I say that he has vivified us in hope, namely, through Christ or in grace *that he might show in the ages to come*, that is, that he might bring to perfection in the next life, *the abundant riches of his grace*. Such an abundant grace with which, even in this world, he forgives many sins and confers the greatest of gifts, will superabound even more in the next life, since there it will be

indeficienter habetur. Io. X, 10: *ego veni ut vitam*, scilicet gratiae, *habeant* in hoc mundo, *et abundantius habeant*, scilicet gloriae in patria.

Et hoc **in bonitate sua**. Ps. LXXII, 1: *quam bonus Israel Deus*. Thren. III, 25: *bonus est dominus sperantibus in eum, animae quaerenti illum*.

Et hoc **supra nos**, id est supra nostrum desiderium, supra nostrum intellectum, et supra capacitatem nostram. Is. LXIV, 4: *oculus nos vidit, Deus, absque te, quae praeparasti expectantibus te*.

Et hoc **in Christo Iesu**, id est, per Christum Iesum, quia sicut gratia nobis confertur per Christum, ita et gloria consummata. Ps. LXXXIII, 12: *gratiam et gloriam dabit dominus*. Per ipsum enim beatificamur, per quem iustificamur.

91. Dicit autem **ut ostenderet**, quia thesaurus gratiae in nobis est occultus, quia habemus ipsum *in vasis fictilibus*, ut dicitur II Cor. IV, 7; et I Io. III, 1: *videte qualem caritatem dedit nobis Pater: ut filii Dei nominemur et simus*. Et parum post: *nunc filii Dei sumus, et nondum apparuit*, et cetera. Sed ille thesaurus occultus, quia nondum apparuit, in saeculis supervenientibus ostenditur, quia in patria omnia erunt nobis aperta, quae ad manifestam sanctorum gloriam pertinent. Rom. VIII, 18: *non sunt condignae passiones huius temporis ad futuram gloriam, quae revelabitur in nobis*.

enjoyed unfailingly. *I have come that they might have a life*, namely, of grace in this world, *and have it more abundantly* in the fatherland of glory (John 10:10).

This occurs **in his own bounty**. *Israel, how good God is to those who are pure of heart!* (Ps 73:1). *Yahweh is good to those who wait for him, to the soul that seeks him* (Lam 3:25).

This is **towards us**; it is beyond our desire, our understanding, and beyond our capacity: *no eye has seen any God but you acting like this for those who wait for him* (Isa 64:4).

And this is **in Christ Jesus**, that is, through Christ Jesus; for as grace is bestowed on us through Christ, so also is glory communicated, which is grace brought to perfection. *Yahweh God bestows favors and honors* (Ps 84:12). Through the same person we are beatified, through whom we are justified.

91. He says **that he might show** because the treasure of grace is hidden within us; we have it *in earthen vessels* (2 Cor 4:7). *Behold what manner of charity the Father has bestowed upon us, that we should be called and should be the sons of God*, after which comes: *we are now sons of God, and it has not yet been revealed what we shall be. We know that when he shall appear we shall be like to him* (1 John 3:1–2). But that hidden treasure, although it has not yet been revealed, is shown in the ages to come, since in the fatherland everything relating to the transparent glory of the saints will be unveiled before us. *The sufferings of this time are not worthy to be compared with the glory to come that shall be revealed in us* (Rom 8:18).

Lecture 3

^{2:8}Gratia enim estis salvati per fidem, et hoc non ex vobis: Dei enim donum est: [n. 93]

^{2:9}non ex operibus, ut ne quis glorietur. [n. 96]

^{2:10}Ipsius enim sumus factura, creati in Christo Jesu in operibus bonis, quae praeparavit Deus ut in illis ambulemus. [n. 97]

^{2:8}τῇ γὰρ χάριτί ἐστε σεσῳσμένοι διὰ πίστεως· καὶ τοῦτο οὐκ ἐξ ὑμῶν, θεοῦ τὸ δῶρον·

^{2:9}οὐκ ἐξ ἔργων, ἵνα μή τις καυχήσηται.

^{2:10}αὐτοῦ γάρ ἐσμεν ποίημα, κτισθέντες ἐν Χριστῷ Ἰησοῦ ἐπὶ ἔργοις ἀγαθοῖς οἷς προητοίμασεν ὁ θεὸς ἵνα ἐν αὐτοῖς περιπατήσωμεν.

^{2:8}For by grace you are saved through faith: and that not of yourselves, for it is the gift of God. [n. 93]

^{2:9}Not of works, that no man may glory. [n. 96]

^{2:10}For we are his workmanship, created in Christ Jesus in good works, which God has prepared that we should walk in them. [n. 97]

---

92. Supra commemorans Apostolus beneficium Dei quo liberati sumus a peccato, interposuerat quod gratia Christi eramus salvati, nunc autem illud probare intendit.

Circa quod duo facit.

Primo enim proponit intentionem suam;

secundo manifestat propositum, ibi **et hoc non ex vobis**, et cetera.

93. Dicit ergo primo: bene dixi cuius gratia estis salvati; et certe adhuc dico secure, **enim**, pro *quia*, **estis salvati gratia**. I Cor. XV, 10: *gratia Dei sum id quod sum*. Rom. III, 24: *iustificati gratis per gratiam ipsius*.

Idem enim est salvari et iustificari. Salus enim importat liberationem a periculis; unde perfecta salus hominis erit in vita aeterna, quando ab omnibus periculis immunis erit, sicut navis dicitur esse salvata, quando venit ad portum. Is. LX, 18: *occupabit salus muros tuos, et portas tuas laudatio*.

Huius autem salutis spem suscipiunt homines, dum in praesenti iustificantur a peccato, et secundum hoc dicuntur salvati esse, secundum illud Rom. VIII, 24: *spe enim salvati sumus*.

Haec autem salvatio gratiae est **per fidem** Christi. Concurrit enim ad iustificationem impii, simul cum infusione gratiae, motus fidei in Deum in adultis. Lc. VIII, 48: *vade in pace, fides tua te salvum fecit*. Rom. V, 1: *iustificati enim ex fide, pacem habeamus*.

94. Deinde cum dicit **et hoc non ex vobis**, etc., manifestat quod dixerat, et

primo quantum ad fidem quae est fundamentum totius spiritualis aedificii;

secundo quantum ad gratiam, ibi **ipsius enim sumus factura**, et cetera.

95. Circa primum excludit duos errores, quorum primus est: quia dixerat quod per fidem sumus salvati, posset quis credere quod ipsa fides esset a nobis et quod

92. When the Apostle was recounting above the blessing of God by which we have been freed from sin, he inserted that we had been saved by Christ's grace. Now he intends to prove this.

He makes two points concerning it:

first, he sets down his intention;

second, he clarifies the point in question, at **and that not of yourselves**.

93. I rightly declared, he says of the first, by whose grace you were saved; and indeed, I still confidently say **for**, in place of *because*, **by grace you are saved**. *By the grace of God, I am what I am* (1 Cor 15:10), *being justified freely by his grace* (Rom 3:24).

For to be saved is the same as to be justified. Salvation implies a freedom from dangers; hence, man's perfect salvation will be in eternal life when he will be immune from all dangers, as a ship is said to be safe when it has arrived at port. *You shall call your walls 'salvation' and your gates 'praise'* (Isa 60:18).

Men receive the hope of this salvation when they are justified from sin in the present, and are thus referred to as saved: *for we are saved by hope* (Rom 8:24).

But this salvation of grace is **by faith** in Christ. In the justification of an adult who has sinned, the movement of faith towards God coincides with the infusion of grace. *Your faith has saved you. Go in peace* (Luke 8:48). *Being justified, therefore, by faith, we are at peace with God through our Lord Jesus Christ* (Rom 5:1).

94. When he next says **and that not of yourselves**, he clarifies what he had spoken of:

first, regarding faith, which is the foundation of the whole spiritual edifice;

second, regarding grace, at **for we are his workmanship**.

95. He eliminates two errors concerning the first point. The first of these is that, since he had said we are saved by faith, anyone can hold the opinion that faith itself originates

credere in nostro arbitrio constitutum est. Et ideo hoc excludens, dicit **et hoc non ex vobis**.

Non enim sufficit ad credendum liberum arbitrium, eo quod ea quae sunt fidei, sunt supra rationem. Eccli. III, 25: *plurima supra sensum hominis ostensa sunt tibi*. I Cor. c. II, 11: *quae Dei sunt nemo novit, nisi Spiritus Dei*, et cetera. Et ideo quod homo credat, hoc non potest ex se habere, nisi Deus det, secundum illud Sap. IX, 17: *sensum autem tuum quis sciet, nisi ut dederis sapientiam, et miseris Spiritum Sanctum tuum de altissimis?* Propter quod subdit **Dei enim donum est**, scilicet ipsa fides. Phil. I, 29: *vobis autem donatum est pro Christo non solum ut in eum credatis, sed ut etiam pro eo patiamini*, et cetera. I Cor. XII, 9: *alii enim datur fides in eodem Spiritu*.

96. Secundo excludit alium errorem. Posset enim aliquis credere quod fides daretur nobis a Deo merito operum praecedentium, et, ad hoc excludendum, subdit **non ex operibus**, scilicet praecedentibus, hoc donum meruimus aliquando, quod salvati sumus, quoniam hoc ex gratia, ut supra dictum est, secundum illud Rom. XI, 6: *si autem gratia, iam non ex operibus, alioquin gratia iam non est gratia*.

Subdit autem rationem quare Deus salvat homines per fidem, absque meritis praecedentibus, **ut ne quis glorietur** in seipso, sed tota gloria in Deum referatur. Ps. CXIII, 1: *non nobis, domine, non nobis*, et cetera. I Cor. c. I, 29: *ut non glorietur omnis caro in conspectu eius, ex ipso autem vos estis in Christo Iesu*.

97. Deinde cum dicit **ipsius enim factura sumus**, etc., manifestat quod dixerat quantum ad gratiam. Circa quod duo facit.

Primo manifestat gratiae infusionem;

secundo declarat gratiae praedestinationem, ibi **quae praeparavit Deus**, et cetera.

98. Duo autem ad rationem gratiae pertinent, quae etiam iam dicta sunt, quorum primum est ut id quod est per gratiam, non insit homini per seipsum, vel a seipso, sed ex dono Dei. Et quantum ad hoc dicit **ipsius enim factura sumus**, quia scilicet quidquid boni nos habemus, non est ex nobis ipsis, sed ex Deo faciente. Ps. XCIX, 3: *ipse fecit nos, et non ipsi nos*. Deut. XXXII, v. 6: *nonne ipse est Pater tuus, qui possedit, fecit et creavit te?*

Et continuatur immediate cum praecedenti, ut dicatur: **ne quis glorietur**, quia scilicet **ipsius factura sumus**. Vel potest continuari cum eo quod supra dixerat: **gratia enim salvati sumus**.

99. Secundo, pertinet ad rationem gratiae, ut non sit ex operibus praecedentibus, et hoc exprimitur in hoc

within ourselves and that to believe is determined by our own wishes. Therefore to abolish this he states **and that not of yourselves**.

Free will is inadequate for the act of faith since the contents of faith are above human reason. *Matters too great for human understanding have been shown to you* (Sir 3:25). *No one knows what pertains to God except the Spirit of God* (1 Cor 2:11). That a man should believe, therefore, cannot occur from himself unless God gives it, according to what is written: *who could ever have known your will, had you not given wisdom and sent your Holy Spirit from above* (Wis 9:17). For this reason he adds **for it is the gift of God**, namely, faith itself. *For you have been granted, for the sake of Christ, not only to believe in him, but also to suffer for him* (Phil 1:29). *To another, faith is given in the same Spirit* (1 Cor 12:9).

96. The second error he rejects is that anyone can believe that faith is given by God to us on the merit of our preceding actions. To exclude this he adds **not of** preceding **works** that we merited at one time to be saved; for this is the grace, as was mentioned above, and according to what is written: *if by grace, it is not now by works; otherwise grace is no more grace* (Rom 11:6).

He follows with the reason why God saves man by faith without any preceding merits, **that no man may glory** in himself but refer all the glory to God. *Not for our sake, Yahweh, not for our sake, but for the sake of your name display your glory, because of your kindness, because of your faithfulness* (Ps 115:1-2). *That no flesh should glory in his sight. It is due to him that you are in Christ Jesus, who became for us wisdom from God, justice, sanctification and redemption* (1 Cor 1:29-30).

97. Next, at **for we are his workmanship**, he clarifies what he had said regarding grace. Concerning this he does two things:

first, he clarifies the infusion of grace;

second, he declares the predestination of grace, at **which God has prepared**.

98. There are two essential characteristics of grace, which have already been spoken of. The first of these is that what exists through grace is not present in man through himself or by himself, but from the gift of God. In reference to this he states **for we are his workmanship**, because whatever good we possess is not from ourselves but from the action of God. *Know that Yahweh is God: he made us, the Almighty* (Ps 100:3). *Is he not your Father, who created you, made you and fashioned you?* (Deut 32:6).

This is immediately linked with what went before: **that no man may glory, for we are his workmanship**. Or, it can be joined with what was said above: **for by grace you are saved**.

99. The second essential characteristic of grace is that it is not from previous works; this is expressed when he adds

quod subdit ***creati***. Est enim creare, aliquid ex nihilo facere, unde quando aliquis iustificatur sine meritis praecedentibus, dici potest creatus, quasi ex nihilo factus. Haec autem actio, scilicet creatio iustitiae, fit virtute Christi, Spiritum Sanctum dantis. Propter quod subdit ***in Christo Iesu***, id est per Christum Iesum. Gal. ult.: *in Christo enim Iesu neque circumcisio aliquid valet, neque praeputium, sed nova creatura.* Ps. CIII, 30: *emitte Spiritum tuum, et creabuntur.*

Ulterius, non solum datur nobis habitus virtutis et gratiae sed interius per Spiritum renovamur ad bene operandum. Unde subdit ***in operibus bonis***, quia scilicet ipsa bona opera sunt nobis a Deo. Is. XXVI, 12: *omnia enim opera nostra operatus es in nobis.*

100. Et quia *quos praedestinavit hos et vocavit*, scilicet per gratiam, ut dicitur Rom. VIII, 30, ideo subdit de praedestinatione, dicens ***quae***, scilicet bona opera, ***praeparavit Deus***. Nihil enim aliud est praedestinatio, quam praeparatio beneficiorum Dei, inter quae beneficia computantur et ipsa bona opera nostra. Dicitur autem Deus nobis aliqua praeparare, inquantum disposuit se nobis daturum. Ps. LXIV, 10: *parasti cibum illorum, et cetera.*

Sed ne aliquis intelligeret bona opera sic esse nobis praeparata a Deo, ut nihil ad illa per liberum arbitrium cooperaremur, ideo subdit ***ut in illis ambulemus***, quasi dicat: sic nobis ea praeparavit, ut ea nos ipsi nobis per liberum arbitrium impleremus. *Dei enim adiutores sumus*, ut dicitur I Cor. III, 9. Propter quod dicebat de seipso Apostolus I Cor. c. XV, 10: *gratia eius in me vacua non fuit, sed abundantius omnibus laboravi, non ego autem, sed gratia Dei mecum.*

Signanter autem dicit ***ambulemus***, ut designet boni operis profectum, secundum illud Io. XII, 35: *ambulate, dum lucem habetis.* Infra V, 8: ***ut filii lucis ambulate***.

created. To create anything is to produce it from nothing; hence, when anyone is justified without preceding merits, he can be said to have been created as though made from nothing. This creative action of justification occurs through the power of Christ communicating the Holy Spirit. On this account he adds ***in Christ Jesus***, that is, through Christ Jesus. *For in Christ Jesus neither circumcision nor uncircumcision means anything, but a new creation* (Gal 6:15). *Send forth your Spirit, they are created anew* (Ps 104:30).

Moreover, not only are the habits of virtue and grace given to us, but we are inwardly renewed through the Spirit in order to act uprightly. Whence he goes on ***in good works*** since the good works themselves are made possible to us by God. *For you have accomplished all we have done* (Isa 26:12).

100. Since *those he predestined he also called* (Rom 8:30) through grace, therefore he adds something concerning predestination, saying, ***which*** good works ***God has prepared***. For predestination is nothing else than the pre-arrangement of God's blessings, among which blessings our good works themselves are numbered. God is said to prepare something for us insofar as he disposes himself to give it to us. *Provide the land with grain, for you prepared it for this* (Ps 65:9).

Lest anyone imagine that good works are prepared for us by God in such a way that we do not cooperate in their realization through our free will, he annexes ***that we should walk in them***. As though he said: thus has he prepared them for us, that we might perform them for ourselves through our free will. *For we are God's co-workers* (1 Cor 3:9). For this reason the Apostle said of himself: *by the grace of God, I am what I am. And his grace in me has not been in vain; rather I have worked harder than all of them—yet not I, but the grace of God that is with me* (1 Cor 15:10).

He expressly says ***we should walk*** to designate a progress in good works, in line with that saying: *walk while you have the light, so that darkness may not overtake you* (John 12:35); ***walk then as children of the light*** (Eph 5:8).

Lecture 4

²:¹¹Propter quod memores estote quod aliquando vos gentes in carne, qui dicimini praeputium ab ea quae dicitur circumcisio in carne, manu facta: [n. 102]

²:¹²quia eratis illo in tempore sine Christo, alienati a conversatione Israël, et hospites testamentorum, promissionis spem non habentes, et sine Deo in hoc mundo. [n. 105]

²:¹³Nunc autem in Christo Jesu, vos, qui aliquando eratis longe, facti estis prope in sanguine Christi. [n. 108]

²:¹¹Διὸ μνημονεύετε ὅτι ποτὲ ὑμεῖς τὰ ἔθνη ἐν σαρκί, οἱ λεγόμενοι ἀκροβυστία ὑπὸ τῆς λεγομένης περιτομῆς ἐν σαρκὶ χειροποιήτου,

²:¹²ὅτι ἦτε τῷ καιρῷ ἐκείνῳ χωρὶς Χριστοῦ, ἀπηλλοτριωμένοι τῆς πολιτείας τοῦ Ἰσραὴλ καὶ ξένοι τῶν διαθηκῶν τῆς ἐπαγγελίας, ἐλπίδα μὴ ἔχοντες καὶ ἄθεοι ἐν τῷ κόσμῳ.

²:¹³νυνὶ δὲ ἐν Χριστῷ Ἰησοῦ ὑμεῖς οἵ ποτε ὄντες μακρὰν ἐγενήθητε ἐγγὺς ἐν τῷ αἵματι τοῦ Χριστοῦ.

²:¹¹For which cause be mindful that you, being heretofore gentiles in the flesh, who are called uncircumcision by that which is called circumcision in the flesh, made by hands: [n. 102]

²:¹²That you were at that time without Christ, alienated from Israel's way of life, and strangers to the testament, having no hope of the promise and without God in this world. [n. 105]

²:¹³But now in Christ Jesus, you, who at one time were far off, are made near by the blood of Christ. [n. 108]

---

101. Prosecuto beneficio Dei gentilibus exhibito quantum ad liberationem a peccato, hic recitat Apostolus beneficium eis exhibitum a liberatione a statu gentilitatis.

Circa quod duo facit.

Primo commemorat conditionem status praeteriti;

secundo recitat beneficia eis exhibita in statu praesenti, ibi **nunc autem in Christo Iesu**, et cetera.

Circa primum duo facit.

Primo commemorationis status praeteriti ponit exhortationem;

secundo ipsemet status praeteriti declarat conditionem, ibi **quia aliquando**, et cetera.

102. Dicit ergo **propter quod**, ut scilicet advertere possitis, quod omnia sint nobis data ex Dei gratia, **memores estote**. Deut. IX, 7: *memento et ne obliviscaris quomodo ad iracundiam provocaveris dominum Deum tuum*, et cetera. Deut. XVI, 3: *memineris diei egressionis tuae de Aegypto, omnibus diebus vitae tuae*.

103. Secundo cum dicit **quia aliquando** commemorat praeteriti status conditionem et

primo quantum ad mala quae habebant;

secundo quantum ad bona quibus privabantur, ibi **qui eratis illo in tempore**, et cetera.

104. Circa primum ponit tria mala. Primo gentilitatis crimen, quo idolis serviebant, cum dicit **quia aliquando vos gentes eratis**. I Cor. XII, 2: *scitis quoniam cum Gentes essetis, ad simulacra muta prout ducebamini euntes*.

Quidam vero libri habent: **vos qui gentes eratis**, et tunc pendet constructio usque ibi **nunc autem in Christo Iesu**, et cetera.

101. Once he has outlined God's blessing to the gentiles in freeing them from sin, the Apostle recalls the favor shown them in their liberation from the state of paganism.

Concerning this he does two things:

first, he recounts the condition of their former state;

second, he describes the blessings granted them in their present state, at **but now in Christ Jesus**.

He does two things about the first:

first, he prefaces the recollections of their past state with an exhortation;

second, he discusses the condition of the past state itself, at **at one time**.

102. Thus he says **for which cause**, that you might advert to the fact that everything comes to us by God's grace, **be mindful**: remember and do not forget how you provoked Yahweh your God in the dessert (Deut 9:7), *that you may remember the day of your coming out of Egypt, all the days of your life* (Deut 16:3).

103. When he states **that you, being heretofore gentiles** he recounts, in the second place, the condition of their past state:

first, as regards the evils they endured;

second, as regards the goods of which they were deprived, at **you were at that time**.

104. In reference to the first he exposes three evils. First was the crime of paganism, by which they were accustomed to worship idols; this he implies in **that you, being heretofore gentiles**. *You know that when you were heathens, you went to dumb idols according as you were led* (1 Cor 12:2).

Some books have **you who were gentiles** and omit everything until **but now in Christ Jesus**.

Secundo recitat eorum carnalem conversationem, cum dicit *in carne*, id est carnaliter viventes. Rom. VIII, 8: *qui autem in carne sunt, Deo placere non possunt*.

Tertio recitat contemptus eorum vilipensionem, qua a Iudaeis vilipendebantur. Unde dicit **qui dicebamini praeputium**, id est incircumcisio, *ab ea*, scilicet circumcisione, **quae dicitur circumcisio manufacta in carne**, id est a Iudaeis tali circumcisione circumcisis. Et dicit **manufacta** ad differentiam circumcisionis spiritualis, de qua dicitur Col. II, v. 11: *in quo circumcisi estis circumcisione non manufacta in expoliatione corporis carnis, sed in circumcisione Christi consepulti ei in baptismo*. Et sequitur parum post: *vos cum mortui essetis in delictis et praeputio carnis vestrae, convivificavit cum illo, condonans vobis omnia*, et cetera.

105. Deinde cum dicit *qui eratis illo in tempore*, etc., commemorat bona quibus privabantur, et

primo participatione sacramentorum;

secundo Dei cognitione, ibi *et sine Deo in hoc mundo*.

106. Circa primum ponit tria sacramenta, quorum participatione privabantur. Primo Christi dignitatem; unde dicit **qui eratis illo in tempore sine Christo**, id est sine promissione Christi, quae facta est Iudaeis. Ier. XXIII, 5: *suscitabo David germen iustum*, et cetera. Zach. IX, 9: *exulta satis, filia Sion, iubila, filia Ierusalem, ecce Rex tuus venit tibi iustus et salvator*.

Secundo tangit societatem sanctorum, qua privabantur quamdiu in Gentilitate permanebant, cum dicit **alienati a conversatione Israel**, quia scilicet Iudaeis cum gentibus non erat licitum conversari. Deut. VII, 2–3: *non inibis cum eis foedus, non miserebris eorum, neque sociabis cum eis coniugia*, et cetera. Io. IV, v. 9: *non enim coutuntur Iudaei Samaritanis*.

Et quantum ad illos qui in Iudaismo recipiebantur contemptibiliter cum fiebant proselyti. Unde subditur **et hospites testamentorum**, quasi dicat: huiusmodi proselyti, quando convertebantur ad Iudaeos et fiebant proselyti, non sicut cives sed sicut hospites recipiebantur ad percipiendum testamenta Dei.

Dicit autem **testamentorum** in plurali; quia Iudaeis Vetus Testamentum erat exhibitum, et Novum erat promissum; quia, ut dicitur Eccli. XLIV, 25: *testamentum suum confirmavit super caput Iacob*; quod potest intelligi de Veteri Testamento. Promiserat enim Deus dare aliud testamentum. Bar. II, 35: *statuam illis testamentum ulterum sempiternum*. Hoc autem reddidit illis, quorum *adoptio est filiorum* Dei *et gloria et testamentum*, ut dicitur Rom. IX, 4.

Ponit etiam aliud beneficium quo privabantur, scilicet spem futurorum bonorum, cum dicit **promissionis**

Second, he discusses their carnal way of life, saying *in the flesh*, that is, living lustfully. *And they who are in the flesh cannot please God* (Rom 8:8).

Third, he speaks of the repugnance and contempt with which the Jews despised them. Hence he mentions **who are called uncircumcision by that** type of circumcision **which is called circumcision in the flesh** as the circumcised Jews performed this circumcision. He says **made by hands** to distinguish it from the spiritual circumcision spoken of: *in whom you also were circumcised with a circumcision not hand-made, by putting off the body of the flesh, but in the circumcision of Christ, buried with him in baptism . . . and when you were dead in your sins and the uncircumcision of your flesh, he has brought you to life together with him, forgiving you all offenses* (Col 2:11–13).

105. Next, at **you were at that time**, he recounts the good things of which they were deprived:

first, a share in the sacraments;

second, a knowledge of God, at **and without God in this world**.

106. Regarding the first he sets down three sacraments they were deprived of sharing in. They were, first of all, without the dignity of Christ; whence he affirms **that you were at that time without Christ**, without the promise of a Christ as was made to the Jews. *I will raise up for David a just branch; and a king shall reign and shall be wise* (Jer 23:5). *Rejoice greatly, O daughter of Zion, shout for joy, O daughter of Jerusalem: See, your King is coming to you, triumphant and victorious* (Zech 9:9).

They were deprived, in the second place, from the society of the saints as long as they remained in paganism. He says they were **alienated from Israel's way of life**, since the Jews were not permitted to mix with the gentiles. *You shall not make any league with them, nor show them mercy. Neither shall you make marriages with them* (Deut 7:2–3). *Jews do not communicate with Samaritans* (John 4:9).

With respect to those who—not without contempt—were accepted into Judaism when they became proselytes he adds and **strangers to the testaments**. As though he asserted: these converts, when they went over to Judaism and became proselytes, were accepted to partake of God's covenants as strangers rather than as citizens.

He says **testaments** in the plural since the Old Testament was offered the Jews and the New was promised. *The Lord made his covenant rest upon the head of Jacob* (Sir 44:25) can be understood of the Old Testament. God promised to give them another covenant: *and I will make an everlasting covenant with them* (Bar 2:35). This latter was granted to those *to whom belong the adoption as children, the glory and the testament* (Rom 9:4).

He also sets down another blessing of which they were deprived: the hope of future goods, when he says **having**

spem non habentes; quia, ut dicitur Gal. III, 16, *Abrahae dictae sunt promissiones, et semini eius.*

107. Ulterius ponit summam damnificationem qua damnificantur, scilicet ob Dei ignorantiam, ibi *et sine Deo in hoc mundo*, id est sine cognitione Dei. Ps. LXXV, 2: *notus in Iudaea Deus*: non autem gentibus, ut dicitur I Thess. IV, 5: *non in passione desiderii, sicut et gentes, quae ignorant Deum*; quod tamen intelligitur de cognitione quae est per fidem. Nam de cognitione naturali dicitur Rom. I, 21: *qui cum cognovissent Deum, non sicut Deum glorificaverunt*, et cetera.

108. Consequenter cum dicit **nunc autem in Christo**, etc., commemorat beneficia eis exhibita in statu conversionis per Christum.

Circa quod duo facit, quia

primo ostendit quomodo facti sunt participes bonorum quibus ante privabantur;

secundo ostendit quod ad illa bona non sicut hospites, sed sicut cives recipiuntur, ibi **ergo non estis hospites**, et cetera.

Prima iterum in duas, quia

primo commemorat huiusmodi beneficia in generali;

secundo in speciali, ibi **in ipso enim est pax nostra**, et cetera.

109. Dicit ergo primo: dixi quod **in illo tempore eratis sine Christo, alienati a conversatione Israel**, **nunc autem**, id est postquam conversi estis ad Christum, vos qui estis **in Christo**, id est qui ei adhaeretis per fidem et caritatem. I Io. IV, 16: *qui manet in caritate, in Deo manet, et Deus in eo*. Gal. ult.: *in Christo enim Iesu neque circumcisio aliquid valet, neque praeputium, sed nova creatura.*

Vos, inquam, **qui aliquando eratis longe**, id est elongati a Deo, non loco, sed merito, Ps. CXVIII, 155: *longe a peccatoribus salus*, et a conversatione sanctorum et participatione testamentorum, ut dictum est, iam **facti estis prope**, Deo scilicet et sanctis eius, et testamentis. Is. LX, 4: *filii tui de longe venient*, et cetera. Mc. VIII, 3: *quidam enim ex eis*, scilicet gentibus, *de longe venerunt*, scilicet de regione dissimilitudinis et statu gentilitatis. **Vos** autem modo **facti estis prope**, scilicet **in sanguine Christi**, id est per sanguinem eius, quo vos Christus attraxit. Io. XII, 32: *ego si exaltatus fuero a terra, omnia traham ad meipsum*. Et hoc propter nimiam caritatem, quae potissime in morte crucis manifestatur. Ier. XXXI, 3: *in caritate perpetua dilexi te, ideo attraxi te miserans.*

no hope of the promise since *to Abraham were the promises made and to his seed* (Gal 3:16).

107. Finally, he writes of the greatest injury from which they suffered, ignorance of God. **And without God in this world** means without the knowledge of God. *God has shown himself in Judah* (Ps 76:2), but not among the gentiles: *not in the passion of lust, like the gentiles that do not know God* (1 Thess 4:5). This must be understood of the knowledge obtainable through faith, for Romans speaks of their natural knowledge: *although they knew God, they did not glorify him as God or give him thanks* (Rom 1:21).

108. After this, when he says **but now in Christ**, he recalls the blessings offered them through Christ in their condition after conversion.

Concerning this he does two things:

first, he shows how they were made partakers of the goods previously denied them;

second, he shows that their participation in those goods is not that of strangers but of citizens, at **you are no more strangers** (Eph 2:19).

The first part again has two sections:

first, he depicts these blessings in a general way;

second, he in a specific way, at **for he is our peace** (Eph 2:14).

109. With respect to the first: I have mentioned that **you were at that time without Christ, alienated from Israel's way of life**. **But now**, after you have been converted to Christ, you are **in Christ Jesus**, intimately united to him through faith and love. *He who remains in love remains in God, and God in him* (1 John 4:16). *For in Christ Jesus neither circumcision nor uncircumcision means anything, but a new creature* (Gal 6:15).

You, I say, **who at one time were far off**, severed from God, not by space but by what you deserved, because it is said: *keep distant from the wicked your salvation* (Ps 119:155), as well as association with the saints and a share in the covenants, as has already been said. Now you **are made near** to God and to his saints and covenants. *Your sons shall come from afar and your daughters shall be carried in arms* (Isa 60:4). *For some of them*, namely, the gentiles, *have come from far away* (Mark 8:3), from the land of distortion and the state of paganism. Yet now **you are made near by the blood of Christ**, that is, through his blood by which Christ draws you: *and I, if I be lifted up from the earth, will draw all things to myself* (Isa 12:32). This was on account of his vehement love which most forcefully revealed itself in the death of the cross. *I have loved you with an everlasting love. Therefore have I drawn you close, taking pity on you* (Jer 31:3).

Lecture 5

²:¹⁴Ipse enim est pax nostra, qui fecit utraque unum, et medium parietem maceriae solvens, inimicitias in carne sua, [n. 111]

²:¹⁵legem mandatorum decretis evacuans, ut duos condat in semetipso in unum novum hominem, faciens pacem: [n. 115]

²:¹⁶et reconciliet ambos in uno corpore, Deo per crucem, interficiens inimicitias in semetipso. [n. 117]

²:¹⁷Et veniens evangelizavit pacem vobis, qui longe fuistis, et pacem iis, qui prope. [n. 119]

²:¹⁸Quoniam per ipsum habemus accessum ambo in uno Spiritu ad Patrem. [n. 121]

²:¹⁴Αὐτὸς γάρ ἐστιν ἡ εἰρήνη ἡμῶν, ὁ ποιήσας τὰ ἀμφότερα ἓν καὶ τὸ μεσότοιχον τοῦ φραγμοῦ λύσας, τὴν ἔχθραν, ἐν τῇ σαρκὶ αὐτοῦ,

²:¹⁵τὸν νόμον τῶν ἐντολῶν ἐν δόγμασιν καταργήσας, ἵνα τοὺς δύο κτίσῃ ἐν αὐτῷ εἰς ἕνα καινὸν ἄνθρωπον ποιῶν εἰρήνην,

²:¹⁶καὶ ἀποκαταλλάξῃ τοὺς ἀμφοτέρους ἐν ἑνὶ σώματι τῷ θεῷ διὰ τοῦ σταυροῦ, ἀποκτείνας τὴν ἔχθραν ἐν αὐτῷ.

²:¹⁷καὶ ἐλθὼν εὐηγγελίσατο εἰρήνην ὑμῖν τοῖς μακρὰν καὶ εἰρήνην τοῖς ἐγγύς·

²:¹⁸ὅτι δι' αὐτοῦ ἔχομεν τὴν προσαγωγὴν οἱ ἀμφότεροι ἐν ἑνὶ πνεύματι πρὸς τὸν πατέρα.

²:¹⁴For he is our peace, who has made both one, and breaking down the middle barrier of partition, the enmities in his flesh: [n. 111]

²:¹⁵Making void the law of commandments contained in decrees: that he might make the two in himself into one new man, making peace [n. 115]

²:¹⁶And might reconcile us both to God in one body by the cross, killing the enmities in himself. [n. 117]

²:¹⁷And coming, he preached peace to you who were far off: and peace to those who were near. [n. 119]

²:¹⁸For by him we both have access in one Spirit to the Father. [n. 121]

---

110. Commemoratis beneficiis collatis ipsis Ephesiis in generali per Christum, hic ea commemorat in speciali.

Circa quod duo facit.

Primo ostendit qualiter appropinquaverunt populo Iudaico;

secundo qualiter propinquiores facti sunt Deo, ibi ***ut reconciliet ambos***, et cetera.

Prima iterum in tres, quia

primo ostendit causam appropinquationis,

secundo modum,

tertio finem.

Secunda ibi ***et medium parietem***, et cetera.

Tertia ibi ***ut duos***, et cetera.

111. Causa autem appropinquationis est Christus, propter quod dicit ***ipse enim est pax nostra***, et cetera. Et est emphatica locutio ad maiorem rei expressionem, quasi dicat: bene dico quod facti estis prope, sed hoc factum est per Christum, quia ***ipse est pax nostra***, id est causa pacis nostrae. Unde dicebat Io. XIV, 27: *pacem meam do vobis*.

Hic autem modus loquendi fieri consuevit, quando totum quod est in effectu dependet ex causa, sicut cum dicimus de Deo quod ipse est salus nostra, quia quidquid salutis est in nobis causatur a Deo. Quia ergo quidquid pacis est in nobis causatur a Christo, et per consequens quidquid appropinquationis, quia homo quando pacificatus est cum alio, secure potest ambulare seu appropinquare ad ipsum, ideo dicit quod est ***pax nostra***. Nam in eius nativitate angeli annuntiaverunt pacem. Lc. II, 14:

110. Having recounted the blessings imparted to the Ephesians through Christ in a general way, he now recounts them in a specific way.

Concerning this he makes two points:

first, he shows how they have converged with the Jewish people;

second, how they are drawn closer to God, at ***reconcile us both***.

The first has three divisions:

first, he reveals the cause of this convergence;

second, its manner;

third, its purpose.

The second he reveals at ***the middle barrier***;

the third at ***that he might make***.

111. Christ is the cause of this drawing together, for which reason he affirms ***for he is our peace, who has made both one***. This is an emphatic way of speaking to better express the reality, as though he said: rightly do I say that you are drawn near each other, but this occurs through Christ since ***he is himself our peace***, that is, he is the cause of our peace. *My peace I give you* (John 14:27).

It is usual to adopt this way of speaking when the totality of the effect depends on its cause; for instance, we say that God himself is our salvation because whatever salvation is present in us is caused by God. In the same way, whatever peace we possess is caused by Christ and, as a result, whatever convergence men have with one another. For when a man is at peace with another he can securely walk towards or approach him. Hence, ***he is our peace***. Angels announced peace at his birth: *glory to God in the highest;*

gloria in altissimis Deo, et in terra pax, et cetera. Ipso etiam Christo in corpore existente, mundus maximam pacem habuit, qualem ante non habuerat. Ps. LXXI, v. 7: *orietur in diebus eius iustitia*, et cetera. Ipse etiam resurgens pacem annuntiavit. Lc. ult.: *dixit eis: pax vobis*.

Sequitur *qui fecit utraque unum*, quia scilicet Christus utrumque populum, videlicet Iudaeorum colentium Deum verum et gentilium, ab huiusmodi Dei cultura alienatorum, coniunxit in unum. Io. X, 16: *alias oves habeo quae non sunt ex hoc ovili*, etc., usque ibi: *et fiet unum ovile et unus pastor*. Ez. c. XXXVII, 22: *rex unus erit omnibus imperans*, et cetera.

112. Modus autem appropinquationis ostenditur cum subdit *et medium parietem*, et cetera. Hic autem modus est per remotionem eius quod dividebat.

Debemus autem ad intellectum litterae imaginari unum magnum campum, et multos homines ibi congregatos, in quo quidem per medium protendatur et elevetur unus paries dividens eos, ita quod non videatur populus unus, sed duo. Quicumque ergo removeret parietem, coniungeret illorum hominum congregationem in turbam unam, et efficeretur populus unus. Sic intelligendum est quod hic dicitur. Mundus enim iste est sicut ager, Matth. XIII, 38: *ager est mundus*; hic autem ager, scilicet mundus, plenus est hominibus, Gen. I, 28: *crescite, et multiplicamini, et replete terram*. In isto autem agro est paries, quia quidam sunt ex una parte, quidam ex alia; hic autem paries potest dici lex vetus secundum carnales observantias, in qua Iudaei conclusi custodiebantur, ut dicitur Gal. c. III, 23: *sub lege custodiebamur conclusi in eam fidem, quae revelanda erat*. Cant. II, v. 9: *ipse stat post parietem nostrum*; quia videlicet Christus per veterem legem figurabatur. Christus autem hunc parietem removit, et ita cum nullum remaneret interstitium, factus est populus unus Iudaeorum et gentium. Et hoc est quod dicit: dico quod *fecit utraque unum*, hoc modo scilicet *solvens medium parietem*.

113. Parietem dico *maceriae*, non muri. Tunc enim est paries maceriae, quando lapides in eo non conglutinantur cemento, nec ad hoc erigitur, ut duret in perpetuum, sed usque ad tempus praefinitum.

Vetus ergo lex est paries maceriae propter duo. Primo quia non conglutinabatur caritate, quae est quasi cementum conglutinans singulos sibi invicem, et omnes simul Christo. Infra IV, 3: *solliciti servare unitatem Spiritus in vinculo pacis*. Vetus enim lex est lex timoris, inducens homines per poenas et comminationes ad observantias mandatorum. Et si qui, illo tempore legis, eam ex caritate observabant, iam pertinebant ad Novum Testamentum, ut dicit Augustinus, quod est lex amoris.

and on earth peace to those he is pleased with (Luke 2:14). Indeed, while Christ lived in the body the world enjoyed the greatest peace, the like of which it had never before possessed. *May the just man flourish in his days, and peace pour down till the moon be no more* (Ps 72:7). He himself proclaimed peace when he arose from the dead: *he said to them: peace be with you* (Luke 24:36).

It follows that he *has made both one*, joining into unity both the Jews who worshiped the true God and the gentiles who were alienated from God's cult. *And other sheep I have, that are not of this fold; them also I must bring. And they shall hear my voice; and there shall be one fold and one shepherd* (John 10:16). *One king shall be king over them all. And they shall no more be two nations, neither shall they be divided any more into two kingdoms* (Ezek 37:22).

112. The manner of convergence is revealed when he states *and breaking down the middle barrier of partition*. The method, then, consists in removing what is divisive.

To understand the text we should imagine a large field with many men gathered on it. But a high barrier was thrown across the middle of it, segregating the people so that they did not appear as one people but two. Whoever would remove the barrier would unite the crowds of men into one multitude, and one people would be formed. What is said here should be understood in this way. For the world is likened to a field: *the field is the world* (Matt 13:38); this field of the world is crowded with men: *increase and multiply, and fill the earth* (Gen 1:28). A barrier, however, runs down the field, some are on one side and the rest on the other. The old law can be termed such a barrier; its carnal observances kept the Jews confined: *before the faith came, we were under the guardianship of the law, confined in anticipation of the faith which was to be revealed* (Gal 3:23). Christ was symbolized through the old law: *see, he stands behind our wall* (Song 2:9). Christ, however, has put an end to this barrier and, since no division remained, the Jews and the gentiles became one people. This is what he says: I affirm that *he has made both one* by the method of *breaking down the middle barrier*.

113. I say a barrier *of partition* and not a wall. A barrier of partition is one in which the stones are not mortared together with cement; it is not built to last permanently but only for a specified time.

The old law was a barrier of partition for two reasons. First, because it was not mortared together with charity which is, as it were, the cement uniting individuals among themselves and everyone together with Christ. *Careful to keep the unity of the Spirit in the bond of peace* (Eph 4:3). The old law is a law of fear, persuading men to observe its commands by punishments and threats. While that law was in force, those who kept it out of love belonged by anticipation, as Augustine holds, to the New Testament which is the law of love. *For you have not received the spirit of bondage*

Rom. VIII, 15: *non enim accepistis Spiritum servitutis iterum in timore*, et cetera.

Secundo, vetus lex est paries maceriae quia non fuit data ut perpetuo duraret, sed usque ad tempus praefinitum. Gal. IV, 1 ss.: *quanto tempore haeres parvulus est, nihil differt a servo, cum sit dominus omnium, sed sub tutoribus et actoribus est usque ad praefinitum tempus a patre: ita et nos cum essemus*, et cetera.

114. Sed hic incidit quaestio quia dicit **parietem maceriae solvens**, contrarium dicitur Matth. V, 17: *non veni solvere legem, sed adimplere*.

Respondeo. Dicendum est, quod in veteri lege erant praecepta moralia et caeremonialia. Moralia quidem praecepta Christus non solvit, sed adimplevit, superaddendo consilia, et exponendo ea quae scribae et Pharisaei male intelligebant. Unde dicebat Matth. V, 19: *nisi abundaverit iustitia vestra plus quam scribarum*, et cetera. Et iterum: *dictum est antiquis: diliges proximum tuum, et odio habebis inimicum tuum. Ego autem dico vobis: diligite inimicos vestros*, et cetera. Caeremonialia vero praecepta solvit quidem quantum ad eorum substantiam, sed adimplevit quantum ad illud quod figurabant, adhibens figuratum figurae.

Est ergo intelligendum quod hic dicit **solvens**, scilicet quantum ad observantiam legis carnalis. Et solvere hoc, scilicet parietem maceriae, est solvere inimicitias quae erant inter Iudaeos et gentiles: quia isti volebant legem servare, illi vero minime, ex quo oriebatur inter eos ira et invidia.

Sed certe has inimicitias Christus solvit **in carne sua** assumpta. Nam in eius nativitate statim pax hominibus annuntiata est. Lc. II, v. 14. Vel **in carne sua**, scilicet immolata, quia, ut dicitur infra V, 2: **tradidit semetipsum pro nobis oblationem et hostiam Deo**. In quo quidem sacrificio impleta sunt omnia illa sacrificia, et cessaverunt. Hebr. X, 14: *una enim oblatione consummavit in sempiternum sanctificatos*.

115. Quid autem sit iste paries insinuat, dicens quod est **lex mandatorum**, quasi dicat: solvens parietem, hoc est legem mandatorum, et cetera.

Dicitur autem lex vetus **lex mandatorum**, non quia aliae leges mandatis careant; nova enim lex mandata habet. Io. XIII, 34: *mandatum novum do vobis*. Sed propter duo: primo quidem propter magnum numerum mandatorum legalium, intantum quod ab hominibus servari non possunt, secundum illud Act. XV, 10: *hoc est onus*

again in fear but you have received the Spirit of adoption of sons (Rom 8:15).

Second, the old law is a barrier of partition because it was not meant to last permanently but only for a definite time. *As long as the heir is a child, he is no different from a servant, though he is master of all; but he is under tutors and governors until the time appointed by his father. So we also, when we were children, were slaves to the elemental powers of the world* (Gal 4:1–3).

114. A problem arises here since he says **breaking down the middle barrier of partition** because, on the contrary, it is written: *do not think that I have come to destroy the law or the prophets. I have not come to destroy, but to fulfill* (Matt 5:17).

I reply. The old law contained both moral and ceremonial precepts. The moral commandments were not destroyed by Christ but fulfilled in the counsels he added and in his explanations of what the scribes and Pharisees had wrongly interpreted: *unless your justice abounds more than that of the scribes and Pharisees, you shall not enter into the kingdom of heaven* (Matt 5:20). And further on: *you have heard that it has been said: you shall love your neighbor and hate your enemy. But I say to you: love your enemies; do good to those who hate you; and pray for those who persecute and calumniate you* (Matt 5:43–44). He abolished the ceremonial precepts with regard to what they were in themselves, but he fulfilled them with regard to what they prefigured, adding what was symbolized to the symbol.

It should be understood, therefore, that in saying **breaking** he refers to the observance of the carnal law. To break down this barrier of partition is to destroy the hostility between the Jews and gentiles. The former wanted to observe the law and the latter had little inclination to do so, from which anger and jealousy sprung up between them.

But certainly, Christ has abolished this animosity **in his** assumed **flesh**. For at his birth peace was immediately proclaimed to men (Luke 2:14). Or, **in his** immolated **flesh** since he **has delivered himself for us, an oblation and a sacrifice to God** (Eph 5:2). In this sacrifice all the former sacrifices were fulfilled and came to an end. *For by a single offering he has perfected forever those who are sanctified* (Heb 10:14).

115. What that barrier was he implies when he says **the law of commandments**, as though he said: breaking down the barrier which is the law of the commandments.

The old law is termed **the law of commandments**, not because other laws lacked injunctions since the new law has commandments: *a new commandment I give you* (John 13:34). There are two reasons why this title is applied to the old law. One is the great number of legal injunctions it contained, so many that men could not possibly keep them

quod neque nos, neque patres nostri portare potuimus. Iob XI, v. 6: *quod multiplex sit lex eius*, et cetera.

Vel dicitur **mandatorum**, id est, factorum. Rom. III, 27: *ubi est ergo gloriatio tua? Exclusa est. Per quam legem? Factorum? Non, sed per legem fidei.* Unde sicut baptismus Ioannis dicitur baptismus aquae, quia tantum exterius mundabat, interius autem non sanctificabat: ita et lex vetus dicitur lex factorum, quia praecipiebat tantum quid facere deberent, sed non conferebat gratiam, per quam ad legem implendam iuvarentur. Lex vero nova dirigit in agendis, praecipiendo, et iuvat ad implendum, gratiam conferendo.

Evacuans dico, sicut imperfectum evacuatur per perfectum, et umbra per veritatem. I Cor. XIII, 10: *cum autem venerit quod perfectum est, evacuabitur quod ex parte est*, scilicet imperfectio et umbra veteris legis, de qua Hebr. X, 1: *umbram enim habens lex futurorum bonorum*, et cetera.

Et hoc **decretis**, id est, praeceptis Novi Testamenti, per quae excluditur lex. Lev. XXVI, v. 10: *comedetis vetustissima veterum*, id est, praecepta legis naturae simul cum nova lege; et, praeceptis eius susceptis, *vetera proiicietis*, id est caeremonialia praecepta veteris legis quantum ad eorum substantiam, ut dictum est.

116. Finem vero appropinquationis ostendit, dicens **ut duos condat in se**, et cetera. Qui quidem finis est ut dicti duo populi efficiantur unus populus. Quae autem uniuntur, oportet uniri in aliquo uno, et quia lex dividebat, non poterant in lege uniri; Christus autem in lege succedens, et fides eius (sicut veritas figurae) eos in semetipso condidit. Io. XVII, 22: *ut sint unum, sicut et nos unum sumus*. Matth. XVIII, 20: *ubi enim sunt duo vel tres congregati in nomine meo, ibi ego sum in medio eorum*.

Et hoc **in uno novo homine faciens pacem**, id est in semetipso Christo, qui dicitur novus homo propter novum modum suae conceptionis. Ier. XXXI, 22: *creavit Dominus novum super terram, foemina circumdabit virum.* Item propter novitatem gratiae quam contulit. Gal. ult.: *in Christo enim Iesu neque circumcisio aliquid valet, neque praeputium, sed nova creatura.* Infra IV, 23: **renovamini spiritu mentis vestrae, et induite novum hominem, qui**, et cetera. Item propter nova mandata quae attulit. Io. XIII, 34: *mandatum novum do vobis, ut diligatis invicem*, et cetera.

all, according to what is written: *now, therefore, why tempt God to put a yoke upon the necks of the disciples which neither our fathers nor we have been able to bear?* (Acts 15:10); *that he would tell you the secrets of wisdom, and that his law is manifold* (Job 11:6).

Or, it is called **of commandments** meaning *of works*. *Where then is your boasting? It is excluded. By what law? Of works? No, but by the law of faith* (Rom 3:27). Thus the baptism of John was called a baptism of water since it would cleanse only externally and not sanctify interiorly. Likewise, the old law was termed a law of works because it ordained only what must be done, but did not confer the grace through which men would have been assisted in fulfilling the law. The new law, on the other hand, regulates what must be done by giving commands, and it aids in fulfilling them by bestowing grace.

I affirm that Christ was **making void the law of commandments** as the imperfect is made void by the perfect and the shadow by the truth. *When the perfect comes, the imperfect will pass away* (1 Cor 13:10), that is, the imperfection and shadow of the old law: *the law has a shadow of the good things to come, not the very image of the things* (Heb 10:1).

This happened **in decrees**, referring to the precepts of the New Testament through which the law was annulled. *You shall eat the oldest of the old store; and, the new coming on*, that is, the precepts of the natural law together with the new law; and having received these precepts *you shall cast away the old* (Lev 26:10), meaning the ceremonial precepts of the old law as they were in themselves, as was mentioned above.

116. He reveals the purpose of the convergence when he states **that he might make the two in himself**. The end is that the aforementioned two peoples would be formed into one people. Whatever unites must come together in some unity, and since the law divided they could not be united in that law. But Christ took the place of the law, and faith in him, as the truth of those symbols, made them one in himself. *That they may be one as we also are one* (John 17:22); *for, where there are two or three gathered together in my name, there am I in the midst of them* (Matt 18:20).

This is **into one new man, making peace**. That is, into Christ himself who is called a new man on account of the new manner of his conception: *for the Lord has created a new thing upon the earth: a woman shall encompass a man* (Jer 31:22). Another factor is the novelty of the grace he bestows: *for in Christ Jesus neither circumcision nor uncircumcision has any meaning, but a new creature* (Gal 6:15); **and be renewed in the spirit of your mind, and put on the new man who according to God is created** (Eph 4:23). Christ is also a new man on account of the new commands he sets forth: *a new commandment I give you: that you love one another as I have loved you* (John 13:34).

Et licet ista videatur esse intentio Apostoli, tamen in Glossa paries duplicatur: quia ex parte Iudaeorum ponitur lex quasi obstaculum, ex parte vero gentium est idololatria.

117. Consequenter cum dicit **ut reconciliet ambos**, etc., ostendit qualiter Deo appropinquaverunt.

Circa quod duo facit.

Primo manifestat eorum reconciliationem ad Deum;

secundo ponit manifestationem reconciliationis, ibi **et veniens evangelizavit**, et cetera.

118. Sciendum est quod dilectio proximi est via ad pacem Dei; quia ut dicitur I Io. IV, 20: *qui enim non diligit fratrem suum quem videt, Deum quem non videt quomodo potest diligere?* Et Augustinus dicit quod nullus putet habere pacem cum Christo, si discors fuerit cum Christiano. Primo ergo ponit pacem hominum invicem factam per Christum, et exinde pacem hominum ad Deum. Propter quod dicit **ut reconciliet ambos**, iam unitos, **in uno corpore** Ecclesiae, scilicet in Christo. Rom. XII, 5: *multi unum corpus sumus in Christo.* Reconciliet, inquam, **Deo** per fidem et caritatem. II Cor. V, 19: *Deus erat in Christo mundum reconcilians sibi.*

Et hoc fecit **per crucem, interficiens inimicitias in semetipso**, quia Iudaeorum et gentilium, quae erant per legem, inimicitias interfecit, implens figuras Veteris Testamenti; sed inimicitias quae erant inter Deum et homines per peccatum interfecit in semetipso, quando per mortem crucis delevit peccatum. Gal. I, v. 4: *qui dedit semetipsum pro peccatis nostris.* Hebr. IX, 28: *Christus semel oblatus est ad multorum exhaurienda peccata.*

Dicit ergo: **interficiens inimicitias**, id est peccata, **in semetipso**, in immolatione corporis sui. Col. I, 20: *pacificans per sanguinem crucis eius, sive quae in caelis, sive quae in terris sunt.* Rom. V, 10: *cum inimici essemus, reconciliati sumus Deo per mortem Filii eius.* Item Col. I, 19: *in Christo complacuit omnem plenitudinem habitare, et per eum reconciliare omnia in ipso.*

Quia ergo Christus satisfecit sufficienter pro peccatis nostris, consequens fuit ut soluto pretio fieret reconciliatio.

119. Manifestationem vero huius reconciliationis ponit, dicens: **et veniens evangelizavit**, et cetera. Ponit autem

primo pacis seu reconciliationis annuntiationem;

secundo pacis causam et rationem, ibi: **quoniam per ipsum habemus accessum** et cetera.

120. Est ergo manifesta Dei reconciliatio ad hominem per Christum, quia ipse Christus non solum reconciliavit nos Deo, et interfecit inimicitias, sed etiam **veniens**, scilicet in carne, **evangelizavit**, id est annuntiavit, **pacem**. Vel **veniens** post resurrectionem, quando stetit

This appears to correspond to the Apostle's intention, yet in a Gloss the barrier is duplicated. On the side of the Jews the law is said to be the obstacle, while on the gentile's side it is idolatry.

117. When he states **and might reconcile us both**, he discloses how both draw near to God.

Concerning this he does two things:

first, he treats of their reconciliation to God;

second, he writes of the manifestation of this reconciliation, at **and coming, he preached peace**.

118. It should be realized that love of neighbor is the way to peace with God; for, as is mentioned: *he who does not love his brother whom he sees, how can he love God whom he does not see?* (1 John 4:20) Let no one pretend he has peace with Christ, Augustine asserts, if he quarrels with another Christian. Hence, he first mentions the peace among themselves that Christ brought to men and then the peace of men with God. For this reason he says **that he might reconcile us both** the united peoples **in one body** of the Church, namely, in Christ. *We, being many, are one body in Christ* (Rom 12:5). Then he reconciles us **to God** through faith and charity: *for God indeed was in Christ, reconciling the world to himself* (2 Cor 5:19).

He achieved this **by the cross, killing the enmities in himself**. In fulfilling the Old Testament symbols, he killed the hostility that had arisen through the law between the Jews and the gentiles. But the hostility that existed between God and men through sin, he killed in himself when he blotted out sin through the death of the cross. He *who gave himself for our sins* (Gal 1:4); *Christ was offered once to carry away the sins of many* (Heb 9:28).

Therefore, he says **killing the enmities**, that is, sins, **in himself**, meaning in the immolation of his own body, *making peace through the blood of his cross, both as to the things that are on earth and the things that are in heaven* (Col 1:20). *When we were enemies, we were reconciled to God by the death of his Son* (Rom 5:10). *God wanted all fullness to dwell in him, and through him, to reconcile all things unto himself* (Col 1:19–20).

Since Christ satisfied sufficiently for our sins, reconciliation occurred as a consequence of his having paid the price (1 Cor 6:20).

119. The manifestation of the reconciliation is set down in **and coming, he preached**, where he touches on:

first, the proclamation of peace or reconciliation;

second, the cause and reason of this peace, at **for by him we both have access**.

120. The reconciliation of God to man through Christ has been made known because Christ himself not only reconciled us to God and destroyed the hostilities, but also **coming** in the flesh **he preached** and proclaimed **peace**. Or, **coming** after the resurrection when he stood in the midst

in medio discipulorum, et dixit eis: *pax vobis*, Lc. ult., Is. LXI, 1: *ad annuntiandum mansuetis misit me*, et cetera. Et Is. LII, 7: *quam pulchri pedes supra montes annuntiantis et praedicantis pacem, annuntiantis bonum, praedicantis salutem*, et cetera.

Evangelizavit, inquam, non uni populo tantum, sed **vobis** gentibus **qui longe fuistis**, quibus etsi non in persona propria, tamen per apostolos suos annuntiavit pacem. Matth. ult.: *euntes ergo docete omnes Gentes, baptizantes*, et cetera. Is. XXXIII, 13: *audite, qui longe estis, quae fecerim, et cognoscite*, et cetera. Et pacem **his qui prope**, supple annuntiavit Christus in persona propria. Rom. XV, 8: *dico enim Christum Iesum ministrum fuisse circumcisionis propter veritatem Dei, ad confirmandas promissiones patrum*. Is. LIV, 15: *ecce, accola veniet qui non erat mecum, advena quondam tuus adiungetur tibi*.

121. Causam autem pacis et formam ostendit dicens **quoniam per ipsum habemus accessum ambo**, id est, duo populi, **in uno Spiritu**, id est, uniti unione Spiritus Sancti. Infra IV, 3: **solliciti servare unitatem Spiritus**, et cetera. I Cor. XII, 11: *haec autem omnia operatur unus atque idem Spiritus*, et cetera.

Sic autem habemus accessum **ad Patrem** per Christum, quoniam Christus operatur per Spiritum Sanctum. Rom. VIII, 9: *si quis autem Spiritum Christi non habet, hic non est eius*. Et ideo quidquid fit per Spiritum Sanctum, etiam fit per Christum.

Per hoc etiam quod dicit, **ad Patrem**, intelligendum est quod etiam pertinet ad totam Trinitatem, quia propter essentiae unitatem in Patre est Filius et Spiritus Sanctus, et in Spiritu Sancto est Pater et Filius. Ideo cum dicit **ad Patrem**, specialiter ostendit quod quidquid Filius habet, a Patre habet, et ab eo etiam se habere recognoscit.

of the disciples and said: *peace be to you* (Luke 24:36). *He has sent me to bring good news to the afflicted, to heal the brokenhearted* (Isa 61:1). *How beautiful upon the mountains are the feet of the messenger who preaches peace, brings good news and announces salvation* (Isa 52:7).

He preached, I say, not to one people only but **to you** gentiles **that were far off**; although not in his own person, nonetheless he proclaimed peace to you through his apostles. *Go, therefore, and teach all nations* (Matt 28:19). *Hear, you that are far off, what I have done: and you that are near, know my strength* (Isa 33:13). Christ in his own person announced the **peace to those who were near**. For I say that Christ became a servant of the circumcised to show God's truthfulness, to confirm the promises made to the patriarchs (Rom 15:8). *Behold, an inhabitant will come who was not with me; he who was a foreigner to you before will be joined to you* (Isa 54:15).

121. He indicates the cause and form of peace by saying *for by him we both have access*, that is, the two peoples, **in one Spirit**, meaning we are joined by the union of the Holy Spirit. *Careful to keep the unity of the Spirit in the bond of peace* (Eph 4:3). *One and the same Spirit produces all these* (1 Cor 12:11).

The way we enjoy access **to the Father** is through Christ since Christ works through the Holy Spirit. *Now if anyone does not have the Spirit of Christ, he does not belong to him* (Rom 8:9). Hence, whatever happens through the Holy Spirit also occurs through Christ.

When he says **to the Father**, it must be understood as pertaining to the whole Trinity. For, by reason of the unity of the divine essence, the Son and the Holy Spirit are in the Father, and the Father and the Son are in the Holy Spirit. In saying **to the Father** he especially shows that whatever the Son possesses he has from the Father, and that he recognizes he has it from the Father.

Lecture 6

2:19 Ergo jam non estis hospites, et advenae: sed estis cives sanctorum, et domestici Dei, [n. 123]

2:20 superaedificati super fundamentum apostolorum, et prophetarum, ipso summo angulari lapide Christo Jesu: [n. 126]

2:21 in quo omnis aedificatio constructa crescit in templum sanctum in Domino, [n. 131]

2:22 in quo et vos coaedificamini in habitaculum Dei in Spiritu. [n. 132]

2:19 ἄρα οὖν οὐκέτι ἐστὲ ξένοι καὶ πάροικοι, ἀλλὰ ἐστὲ συμπολῖται τῶν ἁγίων καὶ οἰκεῖοι τοῦ θεοῦ,

2:20 ἐποικοδομηθέντες ἐπὶ τῷ θεμελίῳ τῶν ἀποστόλων καὶ προφητῶν, ὄντος ἀκρογωνιαίου αὐτοῦ Χριστοῦ Ἰησοῦ,

2:21 ἐν ᾧ πᾶσα οἰκοδομὴ συναρμολογουμένη αὔξει εἰς ναὸν ἅγιον ἐν κυρίῳ,

2:22 ἐν ᾧ καὶ ὑμεῖς συνοικοδομεῖσθε εἰς κατοικητήριον τοῦ θεοῦ ἐν πνεύματι.

2:19 Now therefore you are no more strangers and foreigners: but you are fellow citizens with the saints and the domestics of God, [n. 123]

2:20 Built upon the foundation of the apostles and prophets, Jesus Christ himself being the chief corner stone: [n. 126]

2:21 In whom all the building, being framed together, grows up into a holy temple in the Lord. [n. 131]

2:22 In whom you also are built together into a habitation of God in the Spirit. [n. 132]

---

122. Ostenso supra quod ad spiritualia beneficia simul admissae sunt gentes cum Iudaeis hic ostendit quod in illis beneficiis gentiles non sunt minoris dignitatis quam sunt ipsi Iudaei, sed aeque plenarie ad Christi beneficia sint admissi.

Circa quod duo facit, quia
primo proponit intentum,
secundo manifestat propositum per exemplum, ibi *superaedificati*, et cetera.

Circa primum duo facit.

Primo excludit id quod erat in statu praeterito a statu praesenti;
secundo concludit id quod competit praesenti statui, ibi *sed estis cives*, et cetera.

123. Quia ergo Apostolus concludendo inducit hoc quod dicit *ergo iam*, etc., considerandum est, quod similitudo sequitur ex praemissis: primo quidem ex hoc quod ambo coniuncti, sunt Deo reconciliati; secundo quod ambo habent accessum in uno Spiritu ad Patrem. Quia ergo simul sunt configurati toti Trinitati: Patri ad quem habent accessum, Filio per quem, Spiritui Sancto in quo uno accedunt, in nullo ergo deficiunt a spiritualium bonorum participatione.

124. Ad intellectum autem litterae sciendum est, quod collegium fidelium quandoque in Scripturis vocatur domus, secundum illud I Tim. III, 15: *ut scias quomodo in domo Dei oporteat te conversari, quae est Dei Ecclesia.* Quandoque autem vocatur civitas, secundum illud Ps. CXXI, 3: *Ierusalem quae aedificatur ut civitas.*

Civitas enim habet collegium politicum: domus autem oeconomicum, inter quae quidem duplex differentia invenitur. Nam qui sunt de collegio domus communicant sibi in actibus privatis; qui vero sunt de collegio civitatis, communicant sibi in actibus publicis. Item, qui

122. Once he has made it clear that the gentiles have been admitted to spiritual blessings together with the Jews, he goes on to teach that in these blessings the gentiles are not of less eminence than the Jews themselves; they enjoy a completely equal access to Christ's blessings.

In reference to this he does two things:
first, he presents what he has in mind;
second, he clarifies this presentation by an example, at *built upon the foundation*.

Regarding the first he makes two points:
first, he excludes what was true of their past state from their present state;
second, he concludes to what is fitting for their present state, a *but you are fellow citizens*.

123. In drawing a conclusion, the Apostle says *now therefore you are no more strangers and foreigners*, and it should be recognized that a similar conclusion follows from the premises. First, indeed, from this, that both Jews and gentiles are united and are reconciled to God. In the second place, they both have access in one Spirit to the Father. Together they are conformed to the whole Trinity; to the Father whom they approach, to the Son through whom, and to the Holy Spirit in whom they have access in unity. Hence, they in no way lack a share in spiritual goods.

124. To understand the text it must be realized that the community of the faithful is sometimes referred to as a house in the Scriptures: *that you may know how to behave yourself in the household of God, which is the Church of the living God* (1 Tim 3:15). At other times it is called a city: *Jerusalem, which is built as a city* (Ps 122:3).

A city possesses a political community whereas a household has a domestic one, and these differ in two respects. For those who belong to the domestic community share with one another private activities; but those belonging to the civil community have in common with one another

sunt in collegio domus, reguntur ab uno qui vocatur paterfamilias; sed qui sunt in collegio civitatis reguntur a rege. Ita enim est paterfamilias in domo, sicut rex in regno.

Sic igitur collegium fidelium aliquid habet de civitate, et aliquid de domo. Sed si consideretur rector collegii, pater est Matth. VI, v. 9: *Pater noster, qui es in caelis*, et cetera. Hier. c. III, 19: *Patrem vocabis me, et post me ingredi non cessabis*; et sic collegium est domus. Si vero ipsos subditos consideres, sic civitas est, quia communicabant sibi in actibus praecipuis, scilicet fidei, spei et caritatis. Et hoc modo si fideles considerentur in se, est collegium civitatis; si vero rector collegii attendatur, est collegium domus.

Et ideo Apostolus duo verba ponit hic, scilicet **hospites et advenae**. Hoc enim sunt hospites ad domum, quod advenae ad civitatem. Hospes enim dicitur quasi extraneus a domo. Eccli. XXIX, 31: *vita nequam, hospitandi de domo in domum*. Advena vero est qui extraneus venit ad civitatem. Ac si dicat Apostolus: olim eratis extranei a collegio fidelium, sicut hospites a domo, et advenae ad civitatem, quemadmodum et proselyti ad legem veterem; sed nunc non est ita, quia **iam non estis hospites**, et cetera. Is. LIV, 15: *ecce accola veniet qui non erat mecum, advena quondam tuus adiungetur tibi*.

125. Consequenter cum dicit **sed estis cives sanctorum**, etc.; concludit quod convenit statui praesenti, dicens **sed estis cives sanctorum**, etc., quasi dicat: quia collegium fidelium dicitur civitas in comparatione ad subditos, et domus in comparatione ad rectorem, collegium, ad quod vocati estis, est civitas sanctorum et domus Dei. Ps. LXXXVI, v. 3: *gloriosa dicta sunt de te, civitas Dei*. Unde Augustinus: *duas civitates faciunt duo amores. Nam amor Dei usque ad contemptum sui*, scilicet hominis amantis, *facit civitatem Ierusalem caelestem, amor vero sui usque ad contemptum Dei, facit civitatem Babylonis*. Quilibet ergo vel est civis sanctorum, si diligit Deum usque ad contemptum sui, Prov. ult.: *omnes domestici eius vestiti sunt duplicibus*, si vero diligit se usque ad contemptum Dei, est civis Babylonis.

126. Consequenter cum dicit **superaedificati**, etc., manifestat propositum.

Consuetum est in Scripturis quod in figura, quae metonymia dicitur, continens ponatur pro contento, sicut quandoque domus pro his qui sunt in domo: secundum hunc ergo modum loquitur Apostolus de his qui sunt

public activities. Second, the head of the family governs the domestic community; while those in the civil community are ruled by a king. Hence, what the king is in the realm, this the father is in the home.

The community of the faithful contains within it something of the city and something of the home. If the ruler of the community is thought of, he is a father: *our Father, who is in heaven* (Matt 6:9); *you will call me Father and will not turn from following me* (Jer 3:19). In this perspective, the community is a home. But if you consider the subjects themselves, it is a city since they have in common with one another the particular acts of faith, hope and charity. In this way, if the faithful are considered in themselves, the community is a civil one; if, however, the ruler is thought of, it is a domestic community.

This is why the Apostle writes the two words here: **strangers and foreigners**. For what the stranger is to the home, that the foreigner is to the city. A stranger is an outsider, as it were, of a family: *it is a miserable life to go from house to house, and where you are a stranger you may not open your mouth* (Sir 29:24). A foreigner is as an alien to the city into which he comes. As though the Apostle said: formerly you were estranged from the community of believers, as strangers to a home and foreigners to a state—and as the proselytes were to the old law—but this is true no longer, for **you are no more strangers and foreigners**. *Behold, an inhabitant will come who was not with me; he who was a foreigner to you will be joined to you* (Isa 54:15).

125. Next, at **but you are fellow citizens**, he draws the conclusion of what their present state is, stating **but you are fellow citizens with the saints and the domestics of God**. As if he had said: since the community of the faithful is termed a city in relation to its subjects, and a home relative to its ruler, the assembly to which you are called is the city of the saints and the house of God. *He who made perfect the glorious dwellings of Jacob speaks in you, city of God* (Ps 87:3). Hence Augustine remarks: *two loves have formed two cities. For the love of God, even to the contempt of self*, namely, of the man loving, *builds the heavenly city of Jerusalem. But the love of self, even to the contempt of God, builds the city of Babylon*. Everyone, then, either is a citizen with the saints if he loves God to the contempt of self: *she shall not fear for her house in the cold of snow, for all her domestics are clothed with double garments* (Prov 31:21); or, if he loves himself even to the contempt of God, he is a citizen of Babylon.

126. Consequently, when he says **built upon the foundation**, he clarifies what has been said.

It is customary in the Scriptures that the figure, called metonymy, is used where the container is substituted for what it contains, as a house sometimes refers to those who are in the house. The Apostle employs this figure of speech

in domo Dei, scilicet de fidelibus, sicut de una domo, et comparat eos aedificio. Et

circa hoc duo facit, quia
primo proponit intentum,
secundo ostendit quod huius aedificii participes facti sunt ipsi Ephesii, ibi *in quo et vos coaedificamini*, et cetera.

Circa primum duo facit.
Primo proponit huius aedificii fundamentum;
secundo ipsius constructionem seu complementum, ibi *in quo omnis aedificatio constructa*, et cetera.

127. Fundamentum autem ponit duplex: unum secundarium, et aliud principale. Secundarium quidem fundamentum sunt apostoli et prophetae. Et quantum ad hoc dicit eos non esse hospites, sed cives, qui iam pertinent ad aedificium spirituale, utpote *superaedificati supra fundamentum apostolorum et prophetarum*, id est, qui sunt apostoli et prophetae, id est, super doctrinam eorum.

Vel aliter: *supra fundamentum apostolorum et prophetarum*, id est, supra Christum qui est fundamentum apostolorum et prophetarum; quasi dicat: in eodem fundamento superaedificati estis in quo apostoli et prophetae sunt aedificati, qui ex Iudaeis fuerunt.

Hae autem expositiones duae tantum quo ad verba differunt; sed prima convenientior est, quia si alia convenientior esset, tunc pro nihilo adiungeret *ipso summo angulari lapide Christo Iesu*, cum ipse Iesus sit summum fundamentum. Secundum ergo primum modum magis consonat, ita tamen quod praecipuus lapis et summum fundamentum sit Christus. Quantum vero ad sententiam nihil differunt, quia idem est dicere Christum esse fundamentum, et doctrinam apostolorum et prophetarum, cum Christum tantum, non seipsos, praedicaverint; unde accipere eorum doctrinam est accipere Christum crucifixum. I Cor. I, 23: *nos autem praedicamus Christum crucifixum* idest I Petr. I, 12: *quibus revelatum est, quia non sibi ipsis*, et cetera. Item I Cor. II, 16: *nos autem sensum Christi habemus*.

128. Notandum est quod apostoli dicuntur fundamenta. Ps. LXXXVI, 1: *fundamenta eius in montibus sanctis*. Is. LIV, 11: *fundabo te in sapphiris*, id est, in caelestibus viris. Expresse autem dicuntur fundamenta Apoc. XXI, 14: *murus civitatis habens fundamenta duodecim, et in ipsis nomina duodecim apostolorum*. Qui intantum dicuntur fundamenta, inquantum eorum doctrina Christum annuntiant. Matth. XVI, 18: *super hanc petram aedificabo Ecclesiam meam*.

Dicit autem *apostolorum et prophetarum*, ut designet, quod utraque doctrina est necessaria ad salutem. Matth. XIII, 52: *scriba doctus in regno caelorum similis*

concerning those who are in the house of God, the faithful; as though they were one house, he compares them to a building.

Regarding this he does two things:
first, he sets down what he intended;
second, he shows that the Ephesians themselves have become parts of this building, at *in whom you also are built*.

Concerning the first he does two things:
first, he describes the foundation of this building;
second, its construction or completeness, at *all the building, being framed together*.

127. He writes of two foundations: one is primary and another secondary. The apostles and prophets are the secondary foundation. In this regard he states that the Ephesians are not strangers but fellow citizens who belong already to the spiritual edifice which is *built upon the foundation of the apostles and prophets*, that is, upon the teaching of the apostles and prophets.

Or, *upon the foundation of the apostles and prophets* means upon Christ who is the foundation of the apostles and prophets. As though he said: you are built upon the same foundation on which the apostles and prophets, who were Jewish, were built.

These two interpretations only differ in words. Yet the first is more appropriate; if the second was the better one there would be no point in adding *Jesus Christ himself being the chief cornerstone* since he would be the principal foundation. Hence this is more in harmony with the first; although Christ would be both the chief stone and the principal foundation. In meaning, however, they are in no way different since it is the same to say that Christ is the foundation, and that the teaching of the apostles and prophets is; after all, they proclaimed Christ alone, and not themselves. To accept their doctrine is to accept Christ crucified: *we preach Christ crucified* (1 Cor 1:23); *it was revealed to them that they were not serving themselves but you, in the things which have been announced to you by those who preached the good news to you* (1 Pet 1:12). *We have the mind of Christ* (1 Cor 2:16).

128. Notice that the apostles are designated as foundations: *O city founded by him on the holy mountains* (Ps 87:1). *I will lay your foundations with sapphires* (Isa 54:11), that is, with saintly men. They are expressly called foundations: *and the wall of the city had twelve foundations, and on them were the twelve names of the twelve apostles of the Lamb* (Rev 21:14). They are referred to as foundations to the degree that their doctrine proclaims Christ. *Upon this rock I will build my Church* (Matt 16:18).

Both *apostles and prophets* are alluded to so that he might indicate that the doctrine of both is necessary for salvation. Therefore, *every scribe instructed in the kingdom of*

est homini patrifamilias, qui profert de thesauro suo nova et vetera. Item ut ostendat concordiam inter utramque, alterius ad alteram, dum idem est utriusque fundamentum. Nam quod prophetae praedixerunt futurum, apostoli praedicaverunt factum. Rom. I, 1 s.: *Paulus servus Iesu Christi, vocatus apostolus, segregatus in Evangelium Dei, quod ante promiserat per prophetas suos.*

129. Principale vero fundamentum tantum est Christus Iesus, et quantum ad hoc dicit **ipso summo**, et cetera. Ubi tria dicit de eo, scilicet quod sit lapis, quod angularis, et quod summus.

Lapis quidem est propter fundamenti firmitatem. Unde dicitur Matth. VII, 25, quod domus quae fundata erat supra petram, firmiter aedificata erat, intantum quod nec pluvia, nec flumina, nec venti potuerunt eam destruere. Non sic autem de domo fundata super arenam. Dan. II, 45: *lapis abscissus de monte sine manibus.*

Angularis autem dicitur propter utriusque coniunctionem; nam ut in angulo duo parietes uniuntur, sic in Christo populus Iudaeorum et gentium uniti sunt. Ps.: *lapidem quem reprobaverunt aedificantes, hic factus est in caput anguli.* Act. IV, 11 s.: *hic est lapis qui reprobatus est a vobis aedificantibus, qui factus est in caput anguli, et non est in aliquo alio salus.* Et hoc idem de se introducit Matth. XXI, 42: *numquid legistis in Scripturis: lapidem quem reprobaverunt aedificantes, hic factus est in caput anguli*, et cetera.

Summus autem dicitur propter dignitatis celsitudinem. Is. XXVIII, 16: *ecce ego mittam in fundamentis Sion lapidem angularem, probatum, pretiosum, in fundamento fundatum.*

130. Sed non est idem de fundamento in aedificio spirituali et in aedificio materiali. Materiale namque aedificium fundamentum habet in terra, et ideo oportet ut principalius fundamentum sit magis infimum. Spirituale vero aedificium fundamentum habet in caelo, et ideo oportet quod fundamentum quanto est principalius, tanto sit sublimius: ut sic imaginemur civitatem quamdam descendentem de caelo, cuius fundamentum in caelo existens, et aedificium demissum ad nos, videatur inferius; secundum illud Apoc. XXI, v. 2: *vidi civitatem sanctam Ierusalem descendentem de caelo*, et cetera.

131. Consequenter cum dicit **in quo omnis aedificatio**, etc., agit de constructione aedificii. In qualibet autem aedificii constructione quatuor requiruntur. Primo aedificii fundatio, secundo constructio, tertio augmentatio, quarto consummatio: quae quidem breviter tangit.

Primum, cum dicit **in quo**, scilicet fundamento, qui Christus est principaliter, et doctrina apostolorum et prophetarum secundario, quia, ut dicitur I Cor. III, 11: *fundamentum aliud nemo potest ponere praeter id*, et cetera.

heaven is like a householder who brings forth out of his treasure new things and old (Matt 13:52). Also, that he might show the harmony between the two, of the one with the other, since there is an identical foundation to both. What the prophets foretold was to come, the apostles proclaimed as accomplished. *Paul, a servant of Jesus Christ, called to be an apostle, set apart for the Gospel of God, which he had promised before by his prophets in the holy Scriptures, concerning his Son* (Rom 1:1–3).

129. Christ Jesus alone is the principal foundation, in reference to this he says **himself being the chief cornerstone**. Here he states three things about him; he is a stone, is placed at the corner, and is the chief one.

He is a stone on account of the strength of the foundation. Whence Matthew speaks of the house founded on a rock and built solidly (Matt 7:25); neither rains, nor floods, nor winds could destroy it. Such was not the case with the house built on sand. *You saw a stone cut out of the mountain without a hand being put to it* (Dan 2:45).

He is called a corner stone on account of the convergence of both Jews and gentiles. As two walls are joined at the corner, so in Christ the Jewish and pagan peoples are united. *The stone which the builders rejected became the cornerstone* (Ps 118:22): *this is the stone rejected by you, the builders, which became the cornerstone. And there salvation in no one else* (Acts 4:11–12). And Christ applies this text to himself: *have you never read in the Scriptures: the stone which the builders rejected has become the cornerstone?* (Matt 21:42)

He is referred to as the chief one by reason of his heavenly dignity: *see, I am laying a stone in Zion, a tested stone, a cornerstone, a precious stone, a foundation stone* (Isa 28:16).

130. The foundation of a spiritual edifice contrasts with that of a material building. For a material building rests on a foundation in the earth, and the more important the foundation is, the deeper must it be. A spiritual structure, on the other hand, has its foundation in heaven; as a result, the more principal the foundation, the higher it necessarily is. Thus we could imagine a city, as it were, coming down from heaven with its foundation in heaven and the building itself appearing to come downward towards us below, according to what is written: *I John, saw the holy city, the new Jerusalem, coming down out of heaven from God* (Rev 21:2).

131. Next, at **in whom all the building**, he treats of the building's construction. In erecting any building four stages are requisite. First is the foundation of the edifice, second is the construction, third its increase, and fourth is the completion. He briefly touches on these.

In saying **in whom** he designates the foundation which principally is Christ and secondarily the doctrine of the apostles and prophets: *for other foundation no man can lay, but that which is laid, which is Christ Jesus* (1 Cor 3:11).

Secundo vero tangit secundum, cum dicit **omnis aedificatio constructa**. Et quidem si intelligatur allegorice, designat ipsam Ecclesiam, quae tunc construitur quando homines ad fidem convertuntur. Si autem moraliter intelligatur, significat animam sanctam, et tunc eiusmodi aedificatio construitur, quando bona opera superaedificantur super Christum. Prov. XIV, 1: *sapiens mulier aedificat domum suam*. I Cor. III, 10: *unusquisque videat quomodo superaedificet*. In hoc ergo fundamento, scilicet Christo, omnis aedificatio spiritualis construitur, Iudaeorum vel gentilium, a Deo per auctoritatem. Ps. CXXVI, 1: *nisi dominus aedificaverit domum*, et cetera. Hebr. III, v. 4: *omnis namque domus fabricatur ab aliquo, qui autem omnia creavit, Deus est*. Sed instrumentaliter construitur aedificium vel ab homine qui seipsum aedificat, vel a praelatis.

Tertium tangit cum dicit **crescit in templum**, etc.; quod quidem fit quando multiplicantur qui salvi fiunt. Act. VI, 7: *verbum Domini crescebat, et multiplicabatur numerus discipulorum in Ierusalem valde*. Crescit etiam quando homo crescit in bonis operibus, et in gratia crescit quantum ad hoc, quod fit templum sanctum. Templum enim a Deo inhabitatur, et ideo oportet quod sit sanctum. Ps. XLV, 5: *sanctificavit tabernaculum suum Altissimus*. Et quia nos debemus inhabitari a Deo, ut Deus in nobis habitet, ad hoc nos parare debemus, ut sancti simus. I Cor. III, 16: *nescitis quia templum Dei estis, et Spiritus Dei habitat in vobis*; Apoc. c. XXI, 3: *ecce tabernaculum Dei cum hominibus, et habitabit cum eis*.

Sed numquid statim a principio, cum caritatem habemus, templum Dei sumus?

Respondeo. Dicendum est quod sic. Et quanto magis proficimus, tanto magis Deus habitat in nobis. Et ideo ad hoc aedificium, quarto, requiritur perfectio et consummatio, quod ostendit, cum dicit **in Domino**.

132. Consequenter cum dicit **in quo et vos**, etc., ostendit quomodo gentiles facti sunt participes huius aedificii, dicens **in quo**, scilicet aedificio, non solum superaedificantur Iudaei, sed etiam vos Ephesii **coaedificamini**, id est ad similitudinem aliorum aedificamini. I Petr. II, 4 s.: *ad quem accedentes lapidem vivum, ab hominibus quidem reprobatum, a Deo autem electum et honorificatum, et ipsi tamquam lapides vivi superaedificamini domus spiritualis*. Et ideo subdit **in habitaculum Dei**, ut scilicet Deus in vobis inhabitet per fidem. Infra III, 17: **habitare Christum per fidem in cordibus vestris**. Hoc autem non potest fieri sine caritate, quia *qui manet in caritate, in Deo manet*, etc., I Io. IV, 16. Caritas autem datur nobis per Spiritum Sanctum. Rom. V, 5: *caritas Dei diffusa est in cordibus nostris per Spiritum Sanctum qui datus est nobis*. Ideo subdit **in Spiritu Sancto**.

He discusses the second briefly in ***all the building being framed together***. Understood allegorically, this signifies the Church herself which is built up when men are converted to the faith. Taken morally it signifies a sanctified soul, and then this building is erected when good works are built upon Christ. *Lady wisdom builds her house* (Prov 14:1); *let each man take care how he builds on it* (1 Cor 3:10). With Christ as foundation, every spiritual edifice—whether of the Jews or of the gentiles—is constructed by God's power. *If Yahweh does not build the palace, in vain do its builders work on it* (Ps 127:1). *Every house is built by someone; but the builder of all things is God* (Heb 3:4). Yet the building is constructed instrumentally either by the man who builds it up himself, or by prelates.

He touches on the third when he states ***grows up into a holy temple***; this happens when the number of those saved increases. *The word of the Lord continued to spread, and the number of the disciples multiplied greatly in Jerusalem* (Acts 6:7). It also grows when a man makes progress in good works, and he grows in grace to the degree that he becomes a holy temple. A temple is the dwelling plate of God and must be holy: *the Most High sanctifies his dwelling* (Ps 46:5). Since we should be inhabited by God, that he might live in us, we ought to prepare ourselves in order to be holy. *Do you not know that you are the temple of God, and that the Spirit of God dwells in you?* (1 Cor 3:16). *See, God's dwelling is with men, and he will dwell with them* (Rev 21:3).

But are we not temples of God from the instant we possess charity?

I reply that it is so. And the more we progress, so much the more will God dwell within us. Hence, the fourth requisite to this building is its perfection and completion, which he states to be ***in the Lord***.

132. Finally, at ***in whom you also***, he indicates how the gentiles have become participants of the building. ***In which*** building not only are the Jews incorporated, but also you Ephesians ***are built together***, that is, you are incorporated like the others. *Come to him, the living stone, rejected indeed by men, but chosen and honored by God. Be yourselves like living stones built into a spiritual house* (1 Pet 2:4–5). Therefore he adds ***into a habitation of God*** that God may dwell in you through faith; ***that Christ may dwell by faith in your hearts*** (Eph 3:17). Yet this cannot happen without charity since *he who remains in love remains in God and God in him* (1 John 4:16). And charity is bestowed on us through the Holy Spirit: *the love of God is poured forth in our hearts by the Holy Spirit who is given to us* (Rom 5:5). Thus he adds ***in the Spirit***.

Chapter 3

Lecture 1

³:¹Hujus rei gratia, ego Paulus vinctus Christi Jesu, pro vobis gentibus, [n. 134]

³:²si tamen audistis dispensationem gratiae Dei, quae data est mihi in vobis: [n. 135]

³:³quoniam secundum revelationem notum mihi factum est sacramentum, sicut supra scripsi in brevi, [n. 136]

³:⁴prout potestis legentes intelligere prudentiam meam in mysterio Christi: [n. 138]

³:⁵quod aliis generationibus non est agnitum filiis hominum, sicuti nunc revelatum est sanctis apostolis ejus et prophetis in Spiritu, [n. 139]

³:⁶gentes esse cohaeredes, et concorporales, et comparticipes promissionis ejus in Christo Jesu per Evangelium: [n. 142]

³:¹Τούτου χάριν ἐγὼ Παῦλος ὁ δέσμιος τοῦ Χριστοῦ [Ἰησοῦ] ὑπὲρ ὑμῶν τῶν ἐθνῶν

³:²εἴ γε ἠκούσατε τὴν οἰκονομίαν τῆς χάριτος τοῦ θεοῦ τῆς δοθείσης μοι εἰς ὑμᾶς,

³:³[ὅτι] κατὰ ἀποκάλυψιν ἐγνωρίσθη μοι τὸ μυστήριον, καθὼς προέγραψα ἐν ὀλίγῳ,

³:⁴πρὸς ὃ δύνασθε ἀναγινώσκοντες νοῆσαι τὴν σύνεσίν μου ἐν τῷ μυστηρίῳ τοῦ Χριστοῦ,

³:⁵ὃ ἑτέραις γενεαῖς οὐκ ἐγνωρίσθη τοῖς υἱοῖς τῶν ἀνθρώπων ὡς νῦν ἀπεκαλύφθη τοῖς ἁγίοις ἀποστόλοις αὐτοῦ καὶ προφήταις ἐν πνεύματι,

³:⁶εἶναι τὰ ἔθνη συγκληρονόμα καὶ σύσσωμα καὶ συμμέτοχα τῆς ἐπαγγελίας ἐν Χριστῷ Ἰησοῦ διὰ τοῦ εὐαγγελίου,

³:¹For this cause, I Paul, the prisoner of Jesus Christ, for you gentiles: [n. 134]

³:²If yet you have heard of the dispensation of the grace of God which is given me towards you: [n. 135]

³:³How that, according to revelation, the mystery has been made known to me, as I have written above in a few words: [n. 136]

³:⁴As reading, you may understand my prudence in the mystery of Christ, [n. 138]

³:⁵Which in other generations was not known to the sons of men, as it is now revealed to his holy apostles and prophets in the Spirit: [n. 139]

³:⁶That the gentiles should be fellow heirs and of the same body: and co-partners of his promise in Christ Jesus, by the Gospel [n. 142]

---

133. Supra commemoravit Apostolus multa Dei beneficia humano generi et ipsis apostolis collata, hic commemorat specialia Dei beneficia sibi tradita.

Primo ergo proponit intentionem suam in generali;
secundo exponit per partes in speciali, ibi **quoniam secundum revelationem**, et cetera.
Circa primum duo facit.
Primo ponit suam conditionem quantum ad patientiam et tribulationes quas pertulit;
secundo quantum ad dona gratiae quae Deus sibi contulit, ibi **si tamen audistis**, et cetera.

134. Dicit ergo: dixi *in quo et vos coaedificamini*, etc., **huius rei gratia**, id est ut aedificemini et convertamini ad Christum, *ego Paulus*, qui tantus sum, quia apostolus Iesu Christi et magister gentium in fide et veritate, nunc **vinctus** Romae. Nam hanc epistolam de urbe scripsit, ubi in vinculis tenebatur. II Tim. II, 9: *laboro usque ad vincula quasi male operans*. Infra IV, 1: **obsecro vos itaque ego Paulus vinctus in Domino**. Ex quo apparet eius tribulatio et passio in squalore carceris.

133. The Apostle has previously recounted the many blessings of God granted to the human race and the apostles themselves here he turns to God's special blessings bestowed on himself.

First he sets forth his thought in a general way.
Second, he explains each part of it in detail, at **how that, according to revelation**.
Concerning the first he does two things:
first, he describes his condition in respect to patience and the sufferings he endures;
second, in reference to the gifts of grace God has given him, at **you have heard**.

134. He remarks: I have said that *you also are built together into a habitation of God* (Eph 2:22); *for this cause*, of your edification and conversion to Christ, *I, Paul*, am *a prisoner* at Rome; my greatness is in being an apostle of Jesus Christ and a teacher of faith and truth to the nations. He wrote this letter from Rome where he was kept under custody. *I labor even into bands, as an evildoer* (2 Tim 2:9); *I therefore, a prisoner in the Lord* (Eph 4:1). Certainly this indicates his suffering and pain amid the prison's squalor.

Sed quia poena non facit martyrem sed causa, ideo addit suarum tribulationum causam. Duplex est autem causa pro qua quis martyrii causam prosequitur. Una si patiatur pro fide Christi, vel pro quacumque alia virtute. I Petr. IV, 15: *nemo vestrum patiatur quasi homicida, aut maledicus, aut alienorum appetitor, si autem ut Christianus, non erubescat*. Et quantum ad hoc dicit **vinctus Christi Iesu**.

Alia, si patiatur pro Ecclesiae utilitate, et quantum ad hoc ait **pro vobis gentibus**, id est tantum intendo conversionem vestram, et verbum salutis vobis praedico, quod traditus sum carceri. II Cor. I, 6: *tribulamur pro vestra exhortatione et salute*. Col. I, 24: *nunc gaudeo in passionibus pro vobis*.

135. Consequenter cum dicit *si tamen audistis*, etc., ponit donum gratiae sibi commissum, quasi dicat: dico quod sum pro vobis gentibus vinctus, **si tamen audistis**, id est intellexistis, **dispensationem gratiae, quae data est mihi pro vobis**.

Quod potest intelligi dupliciter. Uno modo ut dispensatio accipiatur passive, et sit sensus **si tamen audistis dispensationem gratiae**, etc., id est si intellexistis quod mihi hoc donum, scilicet apostolatus in gentibus, est dispensatum. Nam, ut dicitur infra IV, 7: **unicuique data est gratia secundum mensuram donationis Christi**. Et infra: **ipse dedit quosdam quidem apostolos, quosdam autem prophetas**, et cetera. Unde mihi dispensatum est a Domino Christo, id est venit in sortem, gratia Dei haec ut in vobis fructum faciam. Col. I, 23: *factus sum ego minister*, et cetera. Dico **dispensationem Dei quae data est mihi in vobis**, id est eorum dispensatio tradita est mihi.

Alio modo, ut dispensatio accipiatur active, ut sit sensus **si tamen audistis dispensationem**, etc., id est si intellexistis quod mihi datum sit, ut dona gratiae dispensem per communicationem sacramentorum, et hoc **in vobis**. I Cor. IV, 1: *sic nos existimet homo ut ministros Christi*.

136. Consequenter cum dicit **quoniam secundum revelationem**, etc., manifestat conditionem suam per partes et in speciali.

Circa quod duo facit, quia

primo ponit quod pertinet ad dignitatem officii, scilicet dispensationem gratiae;

secundo illud quod pertinet ad experientiam patientiae, scilicet tribulationem, ibi *quapropter peto ne deficiatis*, et cetera.

Prima iterum in duas.

Primo ostendit gratiae dispensationem quantum ad diversorum mysteriorum cognitionem;

Since it is not punishment that makes the martyr, but the cause of the punishment, he inserts the cause of his tribulations. There are two causes in behalf of which someone can pursue martyrdom. One, if he should suffer for faith in Christ, or for any other virtue. *But let none of you suffer as a murderer, or a thief, or a slanderer, or a coveter of other men's things. But, if as a Christian, let him not be ashamed* (1 Pet 4:15–16). With respect to this he affirms that he is **a prisoner of Jesus Christ**.

The other is if one suffers for the utility of the Church, in regard to which he says **for you gentiles**, that is, I long so much for conversion, and thus preach the word of salvation to you, that I have been thrown into prison. *We are in tribulation for your exhortation and salvation* (2 Cor 1:6). *I now rejoice in my sufferings for you* (Col 1:24).

135. Then he makes known the gift of grace given him, as though he said: I assert that I am a prisoner for you gentiles, *if yet you have heard of*, that is, understood **the dispensation of the grace of God which is given me towards you**.

This may be understood in two ways. In one, the dispensation is taken in a passive sense. Here, **if you have heard of the dispensation of the grace** means, if you have understood that this gift of being an apostle among the nations was dispensed to me. For, as is mentioned below: **to everyone of us is given grace, according to the measure of the giving of Christ . . . he gave some apostles, and some prophets** (Eph 4:7, 11). Whence the Lord Christ has given to me, that I should bear fruit among you, and this has fallen to my lot by God's grace. *I am made a minister of the Gospel* (Col 1:23). I say the **dispensation of the grace of God which is given me towards you**, that is, I have been entrusted with dispensing those graces.

In a second way, dispensation is taken actively so that the sense of **if you have heard of the dispensation of the grace** is, if you have understood what has been granted to me: that I might dispense gifts of grace through communicating the sacraments to **you**. *Let a man so account of us as of the ministers of Christ and the dispensers of the mysteries of God* (1 Cor 4:1).

136. Subsequently, when he says **how that, according to revelation**, he makes known the several aspects of his condition in detail.

In reference to which he does two things:

first, he treats of what pertains to the dignity of his office, namely, the dispensation of grace;

second, what pertains to his experience of patience, namely, tribulations, at *wherefore I pray you not to faint* (Eph 3:13).

The first part contains two sections:

first, he discusses the dispensation of grace regarding the knowledge of various mysteries;

secundo quantum ad ipsorum executionem, ibi *cuius factus sum minister*, et cetera.

Prima iterum in duas.

Primo ponit mysteriorum Christi sibi datam cognitionem; secundo exponit quod sit istud mysterium, ibi *esse gentes cohaeredes*, et cetera.

Circa cognitionem suam tria facit. Primo quod sit certa, secundo quod sit plena, tertio quod sit excellens.

137. Certa quidem est, quia non est per humanam industriam, nec per humanam intentionem, quae falli potest, Sap. IX, 14: *cogitationes enim mortalium timidae, et incertae providentiae nostrae*, sed per legem divinam quae certissima est. Et ideo dicit *quoniam secundum revelationem*, et cetera. Gal. I, v. 12: *neque enim ego ab homine accepi illud, neque didici; sed per revelationem Iesu Christi*. II Cor. III, 18: *nos vero revelata facie gloriam Domini speculantes*, et cetera.

138. Item plena est, quia perfecte revelatum est mihi, et committo vestro iudicio, quia ego in verbis paucis hoc expressi, in quibus cognoscere potestis quod perfectam cognitionem habeam de mysteriis fidei. Et quantum ad hoc dicit *sicut scripsi in brevi*, id est in paucis verbis, ita aperte, quod eo modo hoc *potestis legentes intelligere*. Cant. IV, 11: *favus distillans labia tua*, et cetera.

Labium quidem breve quid est. Et sic labia doctoris sunt *favus distillans*, quando brevibus et paucis verbis multa et magna insinuat.

Sed attende, ut dicit Augustinus, quod debet intendere hoc doctor, quod scilicet intelligatur. Et quamdiu ad hoc laborat, verba sua non sunt superflua, sed si postquam intelligitur, eis immoratur, superflua sunt eius verba.

Dicit autem *prudentiam meam*, secundum illud Prov. IX, 10: *scientia sanctorum prudentia*. Quae quidem non est mundana sed divina et caelestis, propter quod dicit *in mysterio Christi*.

139. Est etiam excellens, quia solis apostolis est revelata; unde subdit *quod aliis generationibus non est agnitum*. Licet enim mysteria Christi prophetis et patriarchis fuerint revelata, non tamen ita clare sicut apostolis. Nam prophetis et patriarchis fuerunt revelata in quadam generalitate; sed apostolis manifestata sunt quantum ad singulares et determinatas circumstantias.

140. Hoc autem quod dicit *quod aliis generationibus*, etc., potest dupliciter exponi.

Uno modo ut per generationes tempora generationum accipiantur, iuxta illud Ps. CXLIV, v. 13: *dominatio tua in omni generatione, et generatione*. Et tunc est sensus, *quod aliis generationibus*, id est temporibus, *non est agnitum filiis hominum*, id est rationalibus creaturis, scilicet nec hominibus, nec angelis. Matth. XI, 25:

second, regarding how these mysteries are carried into effect, at *of which I am made a minister* (Eph 3:7).

Once more the first section has two divisions:

first, he sets down the knowledge of the mysteries of Christ that was granted to him; second, he explains what that mystery is, at *that the gentiles should be fellow heirs*.

He makes three points in regard to his knowledge: first, it is certain; second, it is full; third, it is preeminent.

137. Certain it is indeed, for he did not acquire it through human effort or human thought, which can err: *the thoughts of mortal men are timid, and our counsels uncertain* (Wis 9:14). Instead it is through the divine law which is most certain. Hence he says *according to revelation the mystery has been made known to me. For neither did I receive it of man; nor did I learn it but by the revelation of Jesus Christ* (Gal 1:12). *We all, beholding the glory of the Lord with open face, are transformed into the same image* (2 Cor 3:18).

138. Moreover, it is full since it is revealed perfectly to me, and I entrust it to your judgment. I write of it in few words, in which you can recognize that I enjoy a perfect knowledge of the mysteries of faith. And in regard to this he says as *I have written above in a few words* clearly, that *as reading, you may understand*. *Your lips . . . are as a dropping honeycomb* (Song 4:11).

Lips are small, and those of a doctor of the sacred sciences are as *a dropping honeycomb* when he conveys many and profound thoughts in a few short words.

Nevertheless, note that Augustine remarks how a doctor should aim at being understood. As long as he strives for this his words are not superfluous, but if he remains on a point after he is understood he wastes his words.

He adds *my prudence* since *the knowledge of the holy is prudence* (Prov 9:10). This is not worldly but divine and heavenly, for which reason he states *in the mystery of Christ*.

139. It is also preeminent since it was revealed to the apostles alone. Hence he adds *which in other generations was not known*. For although the mysteries of Christ were revealed to the prophets and patriarchs, they were more clearly revealed to the apostles. To the prophets and patriarchs they were revealed in vague generality; but they were shown in their singular and determinate circumstances to the apostles.

140. *Other generations* admits of a twofold explanation.

In one, by generations the times of the generations are understood: *your dominion endures throughout all generations* (Ps 145:13). Then the meaning is *which in other generations*, that is, times, the mystery *was not known to the sons of men*, to no rational creature, neither to men nor to angels. *You have hid these things from the wise and the*

abscondisti haec a sapientibus et prudentibus, et revelasti ea parvulis. **Sicut nunc revelatum est sanctis apostolis eius et prophetis in Spiritu**, ipsis scilicet in eo spiritu Novi Testamenti interpretantibus Scripturas, et explanantibus legem. Lc. c. VIII, 9: *vobis datum est nosse mysterium regni Dei, caeteris autem*, et cetera. Lc. X, 23: *beati oculi qui vident quae vos videtis*, et infra XXIV: *dico autem vobis, quod multi reges et prophetae voluerunt videre quae vos videtis, et non viderunt*, et cetera.

141. Alio modo potest exponi ut per **generationes** accipiantur homines generati, secundum illud Matth. XXIII, 36: *venient haec omnia super generationem istam*, et cetera. Et tunc est sensus **quod aliis generationibus**, id est hominibus in praecedentibus generationibus generatis, **non est cognitum**, etc., sicut prius. Unde Is. LIII, 1: *quis credidit auditui nostro, et brachium Domini cui revelatum est?*

Sed hoc quidem sacramentum fidei revelatum est aliquibus patribus Veteris Testamenti, secundum illud Io. VIII, 56: *Abraham pater vester exultavit ut videret diem meum; vidit, et gavisus est*. Et etiam prophetis, secundum illud Ioel II, 28: *post haec effundam de Spiritu meo super omnem carnem, et prophetabunt filii vestri et filiae vestrae*.

Sed eis quidem revelatum est in quadam generalitate, apostolis vero clare et perfecte. Et hoc propter tria. Primo quia ipsi apostoli habuerunt revelationem immediate a Filio Dei, secundum illud Io. I, 18: *unigenitus Filius qui est in sinu Patris, ipse enarravit*. Prophetae vero et patres Veteris Testamenti, ipsi edocti sunt per angelos, vel per aliquas similitudines. Unde dicitur Is. VI, 6: *volavit ad me unus de seraphim, et in manu eius calculus, quem*, et cetera. Et ideo ipsi apostoli clarius acceperunt. Secundo, quia non in figuris et in aenigmatibus, sicut prophetae, viderunt, sed revelata facie gloriam Domini speculantes. Lc. X, 23: *beati oculi qui vident quae vos videtis*. Tertio, quia apostoli constituti fuerunt executores et dispensatores huius sacramenti, et ideo oportebat quod melius ipsi essent instructi quam alii. Io. IV, 38: *alii laboraverunt, et vos in labores eorum introistis*.

142. Consequenter cum dicit **esse gentes**, etc., manifestat quid sit illud sacramentum.

Circa quod sciendum est quod Iudaei triplicem praerogativam habebant respectu gentilium, scilicet promissionis haereditatis. Rom. c. IV, 13: *non enim per legem promissio Abrahae, aut semini eius, ut haeres esset mundi, sed per iustitiam fidei*. Ps. XV, 5: *Dominus pars haereditatis meae*, et cetera. Item per specialem a gentibus aliis distinctionem et electionem. Deut. VII, 6: *te elegit Dominus Deus tuus, ut sis ei populus peculiaris de cunctis populis qui sunt super terram*. Unde Ps. XCIX, 3: *nos*

prudent, and have revealed them to little ones (Matt 11:25). **As it is now revealed to his holy apostles and prophets in the Spirit**, to them, namely, who interpret the Scriptures and explain the law in the spirit of the New Testament. *To you it is given to know the mystery of the kingdom of God; but to the rest in parables* (Luke 8:10). *And turning to his disciples he said: blessed are the eyes that see the things which you see. For I say to you that many prophets and kings have desired to see the things that you see and have not seen them* (Luke 10:23–24).

141. Another interpretation takes **generations** in the sense of human generations, according to what is written: *all these things shall come upon this generation* (Matt 23:26). Then the meaning is **which in other generations**, that is, to those who were born in the preceding generations it **was not known**, as above. *Who has believed our report? And to whom is the arm of the Lord revealed?* (Isa 53:1)

But certainly this sacrament of faith was revealed to some of the Old Testament fathers, according to what is written: *Abraham, your father, rejoiced that he might see my day; he saw it and was glad* (John 8:56). And also to the prophets, according to another passage: *and it shall come to pass after this, that I will pour out my Spirit upon all flesh: and your sons and your daughters shall prophesy* (Joel 2:28).

It was revealed to them in certain generalities, but to the apostles clearly and completely. Three reasons account for this. First, because the apostles received the revelation immediately from the Son of God: *the only begotten Son who is in the bosom of the Father, he has declared him* (John 1:18). The prophets and fathers of the Old Testament, on the other hand, were taught by angels, or through some similar imagery: *and one of the seraphim flew to me: and in his hand was a live coal which he had taken with the tongs off the altar* (Isa 6:6). Hence, the apostles received it more clearly. Second, they did not see in symbols and riddles as the prophets did, but were given a plain view of the Lord's glory: *blessed are the eyes that see the things which you see* (Luke 10:23). Third, since the apostles were meant to carry into effect and communicate this sacrament, it was necessary for them to be more instructed in it than others. *Others have labored; and you have entered into their labors* (John 4:38).

142. Consequently, when he states **that the gentiles should be fellow heirs**, he makes known what the sacrament is.

In reference to it, it should be recognized that the Jews enjoyed three prerogatives with respect to the gentiles. They had the promised inheritance: *for not through the law was the promise to Abraham or to his seed, that he should be heir of the world; but through the justice of faith* (Rom 4:13); *the Lord is the portion of my inheritance* (Ps 15:5). Another was their special election, by which they were set apart from the gentiles: *the Lord your God has chosen you to be his peculiar people of all peoples that are upon the earth* (Deut 7:6). We

autem populus eius et oves pascuae eius. Cant. VI, 8: *una est columba mea, perfecta mea*, et cetera. Item per Christi promissionem. Gen. XII, 3: *in te benedicentur universae cognationes terrae.*

Haec autem tria gentes non habebant. Supra II, 12: *qui eratis illo tempore sine Christo, alienati a conversatione Israel*. Sed ad haec tria recepti sunt per fidem. Primo quidem, quantum ad participationem haereditatis, et, quantum ad hoc, dicit **cohaeredes**, scilicet ipsis Iudaeis in haereditate caelesti. Matth. VIII, 11: *multi ab oriente et occidente venient, et recumbent cum Abraham, Isaac et Iacob in regno caelorum*, et cetera. Secundo ad speciale collegium fidelium, et, quantum ad hoc, dicit **et concorporales**, id est in unum corpus. Io. X, 16: *alias oves habeo quae non sunt ex hoc ovili*, id est gentes, *et illas oportet me adducere, et vocem meam audient, et fiet unum ovile et unus pastor*. Tertio, ad participationem gratiae repromissae, et quantum ad hoc dicit **et comparticipes**, scilicet promissionum quae factae sunt Abrahae. Rom. XV, 8: *dico autem Christum fuisse ministrum circumcisionis propter veritatem Dei ad confirmandas promissiones patrum, gentes autem super misericordia honorare Deum.*

Et haec omnia consecutae sunt gentes non per Moysem, sed **in Christo**. Io. I, 17: *lex per Moysem data est, gratia et veritas per Iesum Christum facta est*. II Petr. I, 4: *per quem maxima et pretiosa nobis promissa donavit*, et cetera. Item, nec per impletionem legis, quia hoc est iugum quod *neque patres nostri, neque nos portare potuimus*, ut dicitur Act. XV, 10, sed per Evangelium, per quod omnes salvantur. Rom. I, 16: *non enim erubesco Evangelium, virtus enim Dei est in salutem omni credenti*. I Cor. XV, 1: *notum vobis facio Evangelium quod praedicavi vobis, quod et accepistis, in quo et statis, per quod et salvamini.*

are his people and the sheep of his pasture (Ps 100:3); *one is my dove: my perfect one is but one* (Song 6:8). Finally, they had the promise of a Christ: *in you shall all the kindred of the earth be blessed* (Gen 12:3).

These three the gentiles did not enjoy: **you were at that time without Christ, alienated from Israel's way of life** (Eph 2:12). By faith, however, they have received these three. First, they have received them as regards a share in the inheritance; concerning this he says **fellow heirs** with the Jews in the heavenly inheritance. *And I say to you that many shall come from the east and the west, and shall sit down with Abraham and Isaac and Jacob in the kingdom of heaven* (Matt 8:11). Second, as regards the chosen community of believers; thus he states **of the same body**, that is, in one body. *And other sheep I have that are not of this fold*, namely, the gentiles, *them also I must bring. And they shall hear my voice; and there shall be one fold and one shepherd* (John 10:16). Third, as regards a participation in the promised grace; he says they are **co-partners of his promise**, the promises made to Abraham. *For I say that Christ Jesus was minister of the circumcision for the truth of God, to confirm the promises made unto the fathers; but that the gentiles are to glorify God for his mercy* (Rom 15:8–9).

The gentiles have acquired all this, not through Moses, but **in Christ**. *For the law was given by Moses; grace and truth came by Jesus Christ* (John 1:17), *by whom he has given us most great and precious promises* (2 Pet 1:4). Moreover, these did not come through fulfilling the law, whose yoke *neither our fathers nor we have been able to bear* (Acts 15:10), but by the Gospel through which all men are saved. *For I am not ashamed of the Gospel. For it is the power of God unto salvation to every one that believes; to the Jew first and to the Greek* (Rom 1:16). *Now I make known unto you, brethren, the Gospel which I preached to you, which also you have received and wherein you stand, by which also you are saved* (1 Cor 15:1–2).

Lecture 2

3:7cujus factus sum minister secundum donum gratiae Dei, quae data est mihi secundum operationem virtutis ejus. [n. 144]

3:8 Mihi omnium sanctorum minimo data est gratia haec, in gentibus evangelizare investigabiles divitias Christi, [n. 147]

3:9et illuminare omnes, quae sit dispensatio sacramenti absconditi a saeculis in Deo, qui omnia creavit: [n. 150]

3:7οὗ ἐγενήθην διάκονος κατὰ τὴν δωρεὰν τῆς χάριτος τοῦ θεοῦ τῆς δοθείσης μοι κατὰ τὴν ἐνέργειαν τῆς δυνάμεως αὐτοῦ.

3:8ἐμοὶ τῷ ἐλαχιστοτέρῳ πάντων ἁγίων ἐδόθη ἡ χάρις αὕτη, τοῖς ἔθνεσιν εὐαγγελίσασθαι τὸ ἀνεξιχνίαστον πλοῦτος τοῦ Χριστοῦ,

3:9καὶ φωτίσαι [πάντας] τίς ἡ οἰκονομία τοῦ μυστηρίου τοῦ ἀποκεκρυμμένου ἀπὸ τῶν αἰώνων ἐν τῷ θεῷ τῷ τὰ πάντα κτίσαντι,

3:7 Of which I am made a minister, according to the gift of the grace of God, which is given to me according to the operation of his power. [n. 144]

3:8 To me, the least of all the saints, is given this grace, to preach among the gentiles the unsearchable riches of Christ: [n. 147]

3:9 And to enlighten all men, that they may see what is the dispensation of the mystery which has been hidden from eternity in God who created all things: [n. 150]

---

143. Postquam ostendit Apostolus esse sibi gratiam dispensatam quantum ad mysteriorum divinorum cognitionem, hic ostendit hoc idem quantum ad ipsorum mysteriorum executionem. Et

circa hoc duo facit.

Primo commemorat auxilium gratiae praestitum sibi ad exequendum;

secundo, ostendit sibi commissum officium ministerii, ibi *mihi omnium sanctorum minimo*, et cetera.

Prima in duas.

Primo tangit ministeriorum divinorum executionem;

secundo ostendit auxilium sibi datum ad exequendum, ibi *secundum donum gratiae*, et cetera.

144. Executio autem divinorum sibi commissa est per modum ministerii, et quantum ad hoc dicit: dico quod hoc ministerium est mihi commissum, scilicet gentes esse cohaeredes per Evangelium, per quod gentes participes fiunt promissionis Dei in Christo Iesu, *cuius ego* Paulus *factus sum minister*, etc.; quasi dicat: non ego impleo vel exequor ut a me vel ut meum, sed sicut ministerium quod Dei est. Act. IX, 15: *vas electionis est mihi iste*, et cetera. Unde apostolus I Cor. IV, 1: *sic nos existimet homo ut ministros Christi et dispensatores mysteriorum Dei*.

145. Deinde cum dicit *secundum donum gratiae*, etc., tangit auxilium sibi praestitum ad ministeriorum executionem.

Huiusmodi autem auxilium duplex fuit. Unum quidem ipsa facultas exequendi, aliud ipsa operatio, sive actualitas. Facultatem autem dat Deus infundendo virtutem et gratiam, per quas efficitur homo potens et aptus ad operandum; sed ipsam operationem confert inquantum operatur in nobis interius movendo et instigando ad bonum.

143. After the Apostle has discussed the grace given him relative to the knowledge of divine mysteries, he indicates the same with respect to carrying these mysteries themselves into effect.

Concerning this he makes two points:

first, he acknowledges the assistance of grace granted him to put them into practice;

second, he speaks of the ministerial duty confided to him, at *to me, the least of all the saints*.

The first has two divisions:

first, he briefly treats of putting divine mysteries into effect;

second, he shows how help has been given him, at *according to the gift of the grace of God*.

144. The realization of divine realities was committed to him by way of a ministry. He says in relation to this: I assert that this ministry has been entrusted to me, that the gentiles are co-heirs by the Gospel and through it they share as well in God's promise in Christ Jesus, *of which I am made a minister*. As though he stated: I do not fulfill or carry out this mystery as if it came from me or was mine, but as a ministry belonging to God. *For this man is to me a vessel of election, to carry my name before the gentiles* (Act 9:15). *Let a man so account of us as of the ministers of Christ and the dispensers of the mysteries of God* (1 Cor 4:1).

145. When he writes *according to the gift of the grace of God* he touches on the aid granted him to carry out the mysteries.

This type of assistance was twofold. One was the capacity to put them into effect, and another was the actuality or action itself. God bestows the capability by infusing the power and grace through which a man is able and fit for action; while he confers the action itself insofar as he moves us interiorly and spurs us on to good.

Et ideo hoc accipiens Apostolus a Deo, dicit quantum ad primum: dico quod *factus sum minister*, sed certe non meis meritis, nec virtute propria, sed *secundum donum gratiae Dei quae data est mihi*, quia scilicet idoneus efficior ad executionem divinorum mysteriorum, qui fui prius persecutor. I Cor. XV. 10: *plus omnibus laboravi, non ego, sed gratia Dei mecum.*

Quantum ad secundum dicit *secundum operationem*, quam Deus efficit, inquantum *virtus eius* operatur in nobis et velle et perficere pro bona voluntate.

146. Potest autem hoc aliter exponi secundum Glossam, ut quod dictum est modo referatur ad praecedentia, scilicet dicatur quod esse gentes cohaeredes et concorporales, et comparticipes promissionis eius, scilicet Dei Patris, hoc quidem donum dedit Deus gentibus in Christo, id est per Christum, et hoc *secundum operationem virtutis eius*, id est per hoc quod potenter operatus est, suscitando Christum a morte.

147. Consequenter cum dicit *mihi enim sanctorum minimo*, etc., ostendit officium commissum, cuius quidem commissionis gratia commendatur ex tribus.

Primo quidem ex personae suae conditione;

secundo ex commissorum magnitudine, ibi *evangelizare investigabiles*, etc.;

tertio ex fructus utilitate, ibi *ut innotescat*, et cetera.

148. Commendat igitur officium sibi commissum ex personae conditione. Si enim rex aliquis, aliquod quidem magnum officium alicui magno principi et excellenti committeret, non multum ei magnam gratiam faceret, quantum ad hunc magnum, si poneret in magno officio; sed si magnum et arduissimum officium alicui parvo committat, multum eum magnificat, et magnam gratiam facit ei, et tanto magis quanto officii excellentia excedit ipsum. Secundum ergo hunc modum Paulus gratiam sibi commissi officii commendat, dicens *mihi enim omnium sanctorum minimo data est gratia haec.*

Et vocat se *minimum*, non ex potestate sibi commissa, sed ex consideratione status praeteriti. I Cor. XV, 9: *ego sum minimus apostolorum, qui non sum dignus vocari apostolus, quoniam persecutus sum Ecclesiam Dei.* Is. LX, 22: *minimus erit in mille, et parvulus in gentem fortissimam.*

Et hoc *in gentibus*, id est inter gentes, Gal. II, 8-9: *qui enim operatus est Petro in apostolatum circumcisionis, operatus est et mihi inter gentes. Et cum cognovissent gratiam Dei, quae data est mihi inter gentes*, et cetera.

149. Secundo commendatur huiusmodi commissionis gratia ex officii magnitudine, quod est revelare

Receiving both from God, the Apostle acknowledges the first in saying: **I am made a minister**, certainly not on my own merits, nor by my own power, but **according to the gift of the grace of God which is given to me**. For I was made worthy to realize the divine mysteries which previously I had persecuted. *I have labored more abundantly than all they. Yet not I, but the grace of God with me* (1 Cor 15:10).

In reference to the second he states **according to the operation** which God effects inasmuch as **his power** works within us both to will and to act in accord with good will.

146. This can be interpreted in another way according to a Gloss. What is said here refers to what immediately preceded. For it is said that the pagans have become co-heirs, and of the same body, and co-partners of God the Father's promise; and this is a gift God gave the gentiles in Christ. That is, they come through Christ, **according to the operation of his power** in that he has powerfully acted in raising Christ from the dead.

147. Next, at **to me, the least of all the saints**, he speaks of the duty entrusted to him; the grace of such a commission has three qualities to recommend it:

first, the condition of the person to whom it is entrusted;

second, the greatness of what is confided, at **to preach among the gentiles**;

third, the good that results as its fruit, at **that through the manifold wisdom** (Eph 3:10).

148. The office confided to him is recommended from this person's condition. For if some king entrusted an important office to a great and high-ranking prince, he would not be doing him a very great favor since he would be placing an important person in an important position. But if he entrusts a great and exceedingly difficult duty to an insignificant person, he would greatly honor him and do him a considerable favor; the more so in proportion as the eminence of the office exceeds him. In this fashion Paul praises the gratuity of the office confided to himself: **to me, the least of all the saints, is given this grace.**

He calls himself the **least**, not because of the power granted him, but in recognition of his former state: *for I am the least of the apostles, who am not worthy to be called an apostle, because I persecuted the Church of God* (1 Cor 15:9). *The least shall become a thousand, and a little one a most strong nation* (Isa 60:22).

This duty was to be fulfilled **among the gentiles**, that is, throughout the nations. *For he who wrought in Peter to the apostleship of the circumcision wrought in me also among the gentiles. And, when they had known the grace that was given to me, James and Cephas and John, who seemed to be pillars, gave to me and Barnabas the right hands of fellowship; that we should go unto the gentiles, and they unto the circumcision* (Gal 2:8-9).

149. Second, the grace of his mission is commended by reason of the magnitude of his task: to reveal and clarify the

great and hidden secrets of God. Think of the greatness of Christ and of the salvation of the faithful which he accomplished. The entire Gospel concerns these two.

Regarding the first he says **to preach among the gentiles the unsearchable riches of Christ**, as if to assert: this grace is given to me that I might proclaim the good. *Christ sent me not to baptize, but to preach the Gospel* (1 Cor 1:17). *Woe unto me if I do not preach the Gospel* (1 Cor 9:16).

This good is **the unsearchable riches of Christ** which are true wealth. ***God who is rich in mercy . . . has quickened us together in Christ*** (Eph 2:4); *or despise you the riches of his goodness, and patience, and longsuffering?* (Rom 2:4) *The same is Lord over all, rich unto all that call upon him* (Rom 10:12). These riches are unsearchable indeed, he affirms, since they are as great as his mercy, which can be neither understood nor analyzed. *Riches of salvation, wisdom and knowledge: the fear of the Lord is his treasure* (Isa 33:6), referring to Christ since reverence of the Lord found its most plentiful expression in Christ. *And he shall be filled with the Spirit of the fear of the Lord* (Isa 11:3).

In Christ *are hid all the treasures of wisdom and knowledge* (Col 2:3). They are unsearchable because Christ's wisdom and knowledge cannot be perfectly analyzed. *Perhaps you will comprehend the steps of God, and will find out the Almighty perfectly?* (Job 11:7) The implied answer is, no. For creatures, from whom a trace of their creator shines forth, do not provide us with a perfect understanding of him. Struck by the wonder of these riches, the Apostle exclaimed: *O the depth of the riches of the wisdom and of the knowledge of God! How incomprehensible are his judgments, and how unsearchable his ways!* (Rom 11:33). *Who has searched out the wisdom of God that goes before all things?* (Sir 1:3).

150. Concerning the second—to make known the salvation which comes from Christ to those who believe—he says **to enlighten all men**, not only the Jews, but the gentiles as well, through preaching and miracles. *I will enlighten all that hope in the Lord* (Sir 24:45). *This man is to me a vessel of election, to carry my name before the gentiles, and kings, and the children of Israel* (Acts 9:15); *you are the light of the world* (Matt 5:14).

To enlighten, I say, insofar as I can, all who want to believe. For God *will have all men to be saved and to come to the knowledge of the truth* (1 Tim 2:4) in order that they might understand **what is the dispensation of the mystery**. For these mysteries would be of no use if they were not imparted, as if he claimed: I shall enlighten men on how awe-inspiring the mystery of our redemption is, and from what an immense love it was accomplished. **Unsearchable riches** of this sort are imparted to you through Christ.

151. Yet it might be objected: what you speak of is known to all, even if it is great. The Apostle gives a negative reply, saying it **has been hidden from eternity**.

Ubi sciendum est quod omnia quae sunt in effectu, latent virtute in suis causis, sicut in virtute solis continentur omnia quae sunt in generabilibus et corruptibilibus. Sed tamen ibi quaedam sunt abscondita, quaedam manifesta. Nam calor est manifeste in igne; aliquorum vero ratio, quae occulto modo producit, latet in eo. Deus autem est omnium rerum causa efficiens, sed producit quaedam, quorum ratio potest esse manifesta, illa scilicet quae mediantibus causis secundis producit. Aliqua vero sunt in eo abscondita, illa scilicet quae immediate per seipsum producit.

Et quia sacramentum humanae redemptionis per seipsum operatus est Deus, ideo in eo solo hoc sacramentum est absconditum. Et hoc est quod dicit **absconditi a saeculis in Deo**, id est in sola notitia Dei. Investigare autem secreta primae causae maximum est. I Cor. II, 6: *sapientiam loquimur inter perfectos: sapientiam vero non huius saeculi, neque principum huius saeculi, qui destruuntur, sed loquimur Dei sapientiam in mysterio, quae abscondita est, quam praedestinavit Deus ante saecula*. **Qui**, inquam, **omnia creavit**.

Here it should be noted how everything present in an effect is concealed in the power of its causes. For example, in the power of the sun is contained everything that exists among those things which are able to be generated and able to corrupt. Nevertheless, certain effects are hidden there, and others are evident. For instance, heat is evidently in fire while the intelligibility of other effects, which it produces in a more hidden manner, are concealed in it. Now God is the efficient cause of everything; he makes some things whose intelligibility is able to be manifest, namely, those created through the mediation of second causes. Other effects, however, which he immediately produces by himself are hidden in him.

Since God accomplished by himself the mystery of human redemption, this mystery is hidden in him alone. Thus he states that it is **hidden from eternity in God**, known to him only. Yet, to seek out the secrets of the first cause is the greatest wisdom: *we speak wisdom among the perfect; yet not the wisdom of this world, neither of the princes of this world that come to nothing. But we speak the wisdom of God in a mystery, a wisdom which is hidden, which God ordained before the world* (1 Cor 2:6-7). **He**, I say, **who created all things**.

Lecture 3

3:10ut innotescat principatibus et potestatibus in caelestibus per Ecclesiam, multiformis sapientia Dei, [n. 153]

3:11secundum praefinitionem saeculorum, quam fecit in Christo Jesu Domino nostro: [n. 154]

3:12in quo habemus fiduciam, et accessum in confidentia per fidem ejus. [n. 156]

3:10ἵνα γνωρισθῇ νῦν ταῖς ἀρχαῖς καὶ ταῖς ἐξουσίαις ἐν τοῖς ἐπουρανίοις διὰ τῆς ἐκκλησίας ἡ πολυποίκιλος σοφία τοῦ θεοῦ,

3:11κατὰ πρόθεσιν τῶν αἰώνων ἣν ἐποίησεν ἐν τῷ Χριστῷ Ἰησοῦ τῷ κυρίῳ ἡμῶν,

3:12ἐν ᾧ ἔχομεν τὴν παρρησίαν καὶ προσαγωγὴν ἐν πεποιθήσει διὰ τῆς πίστεως αὐτοῦ.

3:10That the manifold wisdom of God may be made known to the principalities and powers in heavenly places through the Church, [n. 153]

3:11According to a pre-determining of the ages which he realized in Christ Jesus our Lord: [n. 154]

3:12In whom we have assurance and access with confidence by the faith of him. [n. 156]

---

152. Posita dignitate officii ex magnitudine commissorum, hic commendat Apostolus officii dignitatem ex utilitate effectus, quae quidem est revelatio magnarum rerum magnis personis. Sunt autem circa hoc tria consideranda.

Primo quidem quibus sit revelatum, et quantum ad hoc dicit **ut innotescat principatibus**, etc.;

secundo per quem reveletur, quia **per Ecclesiam**;

tertio quid reveletur, quia **multiformis sapientia Dei**.

Ad cuius quidem sapientiae descriptionem quatuor tangit Apostolus.

Primo eius multiplicitatem, ibi **multiformis sapientia Dei**;

secundo modum multiplicitatis, ibi **praefinitionem saeculorum**;

tertio multiplicitatis auctoritatem; unde subdit **quam fecit in Christo Iesu Domino nostro**;

quarto auctoritatis effectum, ibi **in quo habemus fiduciam et accessum**.

153. Est ergo **sapientia**, quae revelatur, **multiformis**, et haec quidem multiformitas tangitur Iob XI, 5: *utinam Deus loqueretur tecum et aperiret labia sua tibi, ut ostenderet tibi secreta sapientiae, et quam multiplex sit lex eius*, et cetera. Sap. VII, 22: *est enim in illa*, scilicet sapientia divina, *Spiritus intelligentiae, sanctus, unicus et multiplex*, et cetera. Multiplex scilicet in effectibus; unicus, scilicet in essentia.

154. Modus autem multiplicitatis revelatae scientiae est **secundum praefinitionem saeculorum**, id est distinctionem et determinationem diversorum temporum. Deus enim ordinat alia esse in uno tempore, alia in alio, et secundum hoc huiusmodi sapientia **multiformis** dicitur **secundum praefinitionem saeculorum**, quia diversa tempora diversis ornat effectibus.

155. Auctor autem huius multiplicitatis est Christus; unde dicit **quam fecit** Deus **in Christo Iesu Domino**

152. Once he has set forth the dignity of his office that arises from the magnitude of what it entrusts to him, the Apostle here gives evidence of his office's worth from the utility of its effect. This consists in the revelation of great realities to eminent persons. Three points are to be considered regarding this:

first, to whom the revelation is directed, regarding which he says **be made known to the principalities**;

second, through whom it is made known, namely, **through the Church**;

third, what is revealed, namely, **the manifold wisdom of God**.

The Apostle touches on four points in his description of this wisdom:

first, its many facets, at **the manifold wisdom of God**;

second, the way in which it is so manifold, at **according to a pre-determining of the ages**;

third, the source of this multiplicity, at **which he realized in Christ Jesus our Lord**;

fourth, the effect of its coming from that source, at **in whom we have assurance and access with confidence**.

153. The **wisdom** which is revealed is **manifold**, and this manifoldness is touched upon elsewhere: *and I wish that God would speak with you, and would open his lips to you, that he might show you the secrets of wisdom, and that his law is manifold* (Job 11:5). *For in her*, namely, divine wisdom, *is the Spirit of understanding: holy, one, manifold* (Wis 7:22). Manifold that is, in her effects, yet one in her essence.

154. The way this revealed knowledge is many-sided is **according to a pre-determining of the ages**, meaning the differentiation and limitation of the various times. For God plans something to exist at one time, and others at another time. In this fashion such wisdom is referred to as **manifold according to a pre-determining of the ages** since he provides different times with different events.

155. The source of this multiplicity is Christ; hence he says **which** God **realized in Christ Jesus our Lord**, that is,

nostro, id est per Christum. Ipse enim mutat tempora et statum eorum. Hebr. I, 1: *multifarie multisque modis*, etc., *per quem fecit et saecula*.

Potest autem hoc quod dicit **quam fecit**, etc., referri vel ad aeternam praedestinationem: nam ipsam fecit Pater in Filio suo. Supra I, 4: ***elegit nos in ipso ante mundi constitutionem, ut essemus sancti***. Ipse enim Filius est sapientia Patris, nihil autem diffinit, vel praeordinat aliquid, nisi per sapientiam.

Vel potest referri ad praedestinationis aeternae completionem, quam Deus Pater per Filium consummavit. I Cor. X, 11: *in quos fines saeculorum devenerunt*, supple sumus.

156. Effectus autem auctoris est magnitudo fructus, qui nobis a Christo provenit, quod ponitur, cum dicit **in quo habemus fiduciam**, et cetera.

Circa quod duo facit.

Primo ponit bona quae recipimus;

secundo appropriatum per quod recipimus, ibi **per fidem eius**.

157. Bona autem quae recipimus, sunt duo: unum quod pertinet ad spem obtinendi, et quantum ad hoc dicit **in quo**, scilicet Christo, **habemus fiduciam**, scilicet veniendi ad caelum et aeternam haereditatem. Io. XVI, 33: *confidite, ego vici mundum*. II Cor. III, 4: *fiduciam talem habemus per Christum ad Deum*.

Aliud bonum pertinet ad obtinendi facultatem, et quantum ad hoc dicit **et accessum in confidentia**, scilicet habemus. Hebr. IV, v. 16: *adeamus cum fiducia ad thronum gloriae eius*. Ier. III, 19: *Patrem vocabis me, et post me ingredi non cessabis*. Rom. V, 2: *per quem accessum habemus per fidem in gratia ista, in qua stamus, et gloriamur in spe gloriae filiorum Dei*.

158. Per quid autem haec dentur nobis, subdit, dicens **per fidem eius**, scilicet Christi. Rom. V, 1: *iustificati ex fide pacem habemus ad Deum per Dominum nostrum Iesum Christum*.

Ut ergo breviter comprehendamus, dico quod revelata est sapientia Dei multiformis varietatis, secundum distinctionem et praefinitionem saeculorum, quae dedit nobis fiduciam et accessum ad Patrem per fidem eius.

159. Quibus autem revelata sit ista multiformis sapientia Dei ostendit, et tunc sumitur ista littera superius dimissa, **ut innotescat principatibus et potestatibus**, ex qua apparet magnitudo. Et quia etiam in terris sunt principes et potestates, addit **in caelestibus**, id est in caelo, ubi nos erimus.

Notandum est autem hic, quod principatus et potestates sunt duo ordines, qui ex ipsorum nomine praeeminentiam in operando designant. Potestatis ordo

through Christ. For he himself alters times and their states: *God, who, at sundry times and in diverse manners, spoke in times past to the fathers by the prophets, last of all in these days has spoken to, us by his Son, whom he has appointed heir of all things, by whom also he made the ages* (Heb 1:1–2).

Which he realized in Christ Jesus may refer to eternal predestination since the Father accomplishes this in his Son: **he chose us in him before the foundation of the world, that we should be holy** (Eph 1:4). For the Son himself is the wisdom of the Father, and nothing is determined or foreordained except through wisdom.

Or this may refer to the fulfillment of eternal predestination which God the Father brings to completion through the Son. We are those *upon whom the ends of the ages have come* (1 Cor 10:11).

156. The effect of this source consists in a great fruit which comes to us from Christ. This is expressed at **in whom we have assurance**.

Concerning this he does two things:

first, he puts down the goods we receive;

second, he designates through what we receive them, at **by the faith of him**.

157. There are two goods which we obtain. One pertains to the hope of attaining to our reward; and in reference to this he says **in whom**, namely Christ, **we have assurance** of arriving at heaven and our eternal inheritance. *Have confidence, I have overcome the world* (John 16:33). *Such assurance we have, through Christ, towards God* (2 Cor 3:4).

The second good pertains to the power of attaining to our reward; in respect to which he states that we have **access with confidence**. *Let us go, therefore, with confidence to the throne of his glory* (Heb 4:16). *You shall call me Father and shall not cease to walk after me* (Jer 3:19). *By whom also we have access through faith into this grace wherein we stand, and glory in the hope of the glory of the sons of God* (Rom 5:2).

158. The means by which these are given us is **by the faith of him**, namely, of Christ. *Being justified, therefore, by faith, let us have peace with God, through our Lord Jesus Christ* (Rom 5:1).

That we might summarize briefly, I assert that God's many-faceted wisdom is revealed in the differentiation and pre-determining of the ages, which gives us assurance and access to the Father by faith in him.

159. He discusses those to whom the manifold wisdom of God is revealed in that text previously not mentioned: that it **may be made known to the principalities and powers**, from which its greatness is evident. And, since there are also princes and potentates on earth, he adds **in heavenly places** meaning in heaven, where we shall be.

Note here that principalities and powers are two ranks which, by their very names, designate a preeminence in action. The rank of powers is ordered to check any hindrances

to salvation, while the rank of principalities takes the lead and gives commands that salvation might be carried into effect properly.

The regulative function of the principality rank is evident from what is written: *princes went before joined with singers... the princes of Judah are their leaders* (Ps 67:26–28).

The repressive function of the powers is also clear: *will you then not be afraid of the power? Do what is good; and you shall have praise from the same. For he is God's minister to you, for good. But, if you do what is evil, fear; for he does not bear the sword in vain. For he is God's minister; an avenger to execute wrath upon him that does evil* (Rom 13:3–4).

Hence, those to whom the mystery is made known are eminent: the holy angels by whom the saints are directed and protected.

160. The means through which the manifold wisdom of God is made known to them is designated by his saying **through the Church**. This presents no small problem. For a Gloss has *that is, through the apostles preaching in the Church*. One way this could be understood is that the angels are taught by the apostles, and this seems somewhat rational. For we notice that in heaven the higher angels, who are enlightened immediately by God, illumine and teach the lower angels who are not enlightened immediately by God. Therefore, it does not seem unreasonable that the apostles should teach the angels since they were taught immediately by God according to what is written: *the only begotten Son who is in the bosom of the Father, he has declared him* (John 1:18).

This interpretation would be sufficient were it not for another factor. For there are two natures in Christ, the divine and the human. The apostles were taught immediately by Christ in his human nature; but the angels immediately intuit the divine nature—even the lower angels, otherwise they would not be happy, since the beatitude of a rational creature can consist in the vision of the divine essence alone. It certainly would be unseemly and absurd for us to maintain that the saints in the fatherland could be taught by even the most perfect of those still on their way. Although among men born of women none greater than John the Baptist has arisen, yet *he that is the lesser in the kingdom of heaven is greater than he* (Luke 7:28). To hold that the demons could be instructed by men is, at first glance, credible. But that the blessed could be educated by pilgrims when they immediately behold the Word, the spotless mirror reflecting all being, should not be held and does not appear proper.

Therefore, it must be asserted that the angels are instructed **through the Church**, that is, through the apostolic preaching, as the Gloss maintains, in such a way that they are not taught by the apostles, but in them. Augustine remarks, in his *Super Genesim ad Litteram*, that before God created material beings, he impressed on the angelic minds

creata sint, rationes rerum naturalium indidit mentibus angelorum, quo fit ut angeli dupliciter res naturales cognoscerent, quia cognoverunt eas in Verbo, et haec cognitio dicitur matutina. Item, cognoverunt eas in naturis propriis, et haec dicitur cognitio vespertina.

Ulterius notandum est, quod sunt quaedam rationes mysteriorum gratiae totam creaturam excedentes, et huiusmodi rationes non sunt inditae mentibus angelorum, sed in solo Deo sunt occultae. Et ideo angeli non cognoscunt eas in seipsis, nec etiam in Deo, sed cognoscunt eas secundum quod in effectibus explicantur. Cum igitur rationes pertinentes ad multiformem sapientiam Dei, sint huiusmodi, scilicet in solo Deo absconditae, et postmodum in istis forinsecis effectibus explicatae, manifestum est, quod angeli eas, nec in seipsis, nec in ipso Verbo, nec etiam ab apostolis, nec a viatoribus aliis cognoverunt; sed in ipsis apostolis explicatas, prius in mente divina latentes, cognoverunt. Sicut domus quae est in mente artificis, vel conceptu de domo facienda, nullus scire potest quamdiu latet in mente, nisi solum ille qui solus illabitur animabus, scilicet Deus; sed postquam conceptus est iam in effectu extrinseco explicatus, quia domus iam facta est; sic aliquis de domo iam facta, quae prius latebat in mente artificis, edocetur, non autem edocetur per domum, sed in domo.

161. Unde iam restat ut aliter exponatur hoc quod dicit ***ut innotescat principatibus***, etc., ut illa coniunctio ut accipiatur non causaliter, sed quodammodo consecutive, et legatur sic: ***illuminare quae sit dispensatio sacramenti absconditi a saeculis in Deo, qui omnia creavit***, ita tamen absconditi, ***ut innotescat principatibus***, etc., id est, istud sacramentum ita fuit absconditum in Deo, quod inde innotuit principatibus et potestatibus non ab aeterno, sed a saeculo, quia omnis creatura principium habet; et hoc, non per Ecclesiam terrenam, sed caelestem, quia ibi est vera Ecclesia, quae est mater nostra et ad quam tendimus et a qua nostra Ecclesia Militans est exemplata. Et sic ly ***per***, designat ordinem naturae tantum, ut dicatur ***per Ecclesiam*** caelestem, id est, de uno in aliud, sicut dicitur: illud factum est notum per totum regnum vel civitatem, quia nova currunt ab uno in alium, secundum quod verba currunt; sicut dicitur Act. c. IX, 42 de suscitatione Thabitae beghinae sancti Petri: *notum autem factum est per universam Ioppen, et crediderunt multi*, et cetera.

Magister tamen, aliter recitat lecturam Augustini, hoc modo ***illuminare quae sit dispensatio***, etc., et hoc

the intelligible patterns of natural realities—the 'before' designating the order of nature and not of time, since from the standpoint of time everything was created together. As a result, angels know natural things in two ways. They know them in the Word, and this is termed their morning knowledge; and they know them in their own proper natures, and this is referred to as their evening knowledge.

Further, there exist certain intelligible patterns of the mysteries of grace which transcend the whole of creation. These intelligible patterns are not impressed on the angelic minds but are hidden in God alone. Thus the angels do not grasp them in themselves, nor even in God, but only as they unfold in their effects. Now, the intelligible patterns relative to God's manifold wisdom belong to this category. They are hidden in God and gradually unfold in external effects. Clearly, therefore, the angels will understand them neither in themselves, nor in the Word, nor by the apostles or any other wayfarer. Rather, they know the mysteries previously hidden in the divine mind as they unfold in the apostles themselves. This is like the case of a house, or the concept of a house to be built, in the mind of an architect. As long as it remains in his mind it can be known to no one—except God who alone penetrates into human souls. However, once the concepts are realized externally in the construction, in the house after it is built, anyone can learn from the building what previously was concealed in the architect's mind. Yet, they are not taught by the house but in the house.

161. There is still another interpretation of ***that it may be made known to the principalities and powers*** in which the conjunction is not taken causally, but in a certain way, consecutively. Thus it would read: to make known ***what is the dispensation of the mystery hidden from eternity in God who has created all things***; hidden, nonetheless, in such a way that ***it was made known to principalities and powers***. The mystery was concealed in God in such a manner that he later revealed it to the principalities and powers, not from eternity but from the time they began to exist, for every creature has a beginning. This was not through the earthly Church but through the heavenly one—the true Church who is our mother and to whom we tend, on whom our Church Militant is patterned. Thus the ***through*** signifies only a natural sequence, so that the mysteries are made known ***through the*** heavenly ***Church*** in the sense that it is passed on from one to another, as when it is said: that fact is known throughout a whole realm or city because the news travelled from one person to another in their conversations, as it is written of St. Peter's raising of Tabitha: *and it was made known throughout all Joppe; and many believed in the Lord* (Acts 9:42).

On the other hand, the Teacher comments on the text of Augustine in such a way that ***to enlighten all men, that***

per Ecclesiam, id est, omnes qui sunt in Ecclesia terrena, sed hoc non est secundum intentionem Augustini.

162. Hic posset quaeri, utrum angeli a principio mundi cognoverint mysterium Incarnationis.

Respondet Magister dicens, quod angelis maioribus notum fuit, sed non minoribus. Unde ipsi, scilicet angeli minores, interrogant, Is. LXIII, 1: *quis est iste qui venit de Edom tinctis vestibus de Bosra?*

Sed opinio haec est contra Beatum Dionysium. Dionysius enim duas interrogationes angelorum de Christo factas ex Sacra Scriptura accipit. Unam ex Ps. XXIII, 8: *quis est iste Rex Gloriae?* Item accipit aliam ex Is. LXIII, v. 1: *quis est iste, qui venit de Edom?* et cetera. Prima autem interrogatio, secundum eum, est inferiorum angelorum, secunda supremorum; quod patet, quia primae non Deus respondet, sed alius, unde dicit: *Dominus virtutum ipse est Rex Gloriae*. Secundae vero respondet ipse Deus immediate, unde dicit: *ego qui loquor iustitiam, et propugnator sum ad salvandum*. Vult ergo Dionysius, quod utrique aliquid ignoraverunt et aliquid sciverunt: quia a principio omnes sciverunt mysterium Incarnationis in generali, sed rationes in speciali didicerunt tempore procedente seu processu temporis, secundum quod in effectibus extrinsecis explicabantur.

they may see what is the dispensation of the mystery which has been hidden from eternity in God (Eph 3:9) occurs **through the Church**, that is, to all men who are in the earthly Church. But this is not in accord with Augustine's thought.

162. Here it could be asked whether the angels knew of the mystery of the Incarnation from the beginning of the world.

The Teacher replies that it was known to the higher angels but not the lower ones. So the lower angels ask: *who is this that comes from Edom, with dyed garments from Bosra?* (Isa 63:1).

This opinion contradicts that of Blessed Dionysius who sees in the Holy Scriptures two questions asked by the angels about Christ. The first is: *who is this King of Glory?* (Ps 24:8) and the other is: *who is this that comes from Edom?* (Isa 63:1) According to Dionysius, the first is asked by the lower angels and the second by the higher. He bases this on the fact that God does not reply to the first, but someone else says: *the Lord of hosts, he is the King of Glory* (Ps 23:10). Whereas the second is answered by God immediately: *I, that speak justice and am a defender to save* (Isa 63:1). Hence, Dionysius prefers to say that both were ignorant of some aspects of the mystery and knew others. From the beginning all knew the mystery of the Incarnation in a general fashion, but as time passed or in the temporal process, they learned its detailed intelligible patterns when they were explicated in external events.

Lecture 4

³:¹³Propter quod peto ne deficiatis in tribulationibus meis pro vobis: quae est gloria vestra. [n. 164]

³:¹⁴Hujus rei gratia flecto genua mea ad Patrem Domini nostri Jesu Christi, [n. 165]

³:¹⁵ex quo omnis paternitas in caelis et in terra nominatur, [n. 169]

³:¹⁶ut det vobis secundum divitias gloriae suae, virtute corroborari per Spiritum ejus in interiorem hominem, [n. 170]

³:¹⁷Christum habitare per fidem in cordibus vestris: in caritate radicati, et fundati, [n.172]

³:¹³διὸ αἰτοῦμαι μὴ ἐγκακεῖν ἐν ταῖς θλίψεσίν μου ὑπὲρ ὑμῶν, ἥτις ἐστὶν δόξα ὑμῶν.

³:¹⁴Τούτου χάριν κάμπτω τὰ γόνατά μου πρὸς τὸν πατέρα,

³:¹⁵ἐξ οὗ πᾶσα πατριὰ ἐν οὐρανοῖς καὶ ἐπὶ γῆς ὀνομάζεται,

³:¹⁶ἵνα δῷ ὑμῖν κατὰ τὸ πλοῦτος τῆς δόξης αὐτοῦ δυνάμει κραταιωθῆναι διὰ τοῦ πνεύματος αὐτοῦ εἰς τὸν ἔσω ἄνθρωπον,

³:¹⁷κατοικῆσαι τὸν Χριστὸν διὰ τῆς πίστεως ἐν ταῖς καρδίαις ὑμῶν, ἐν ἀγάπῃ ἐρριζωμένοι καὶ τεθεμελιωμένοι,

³:¹³Wherefore I pray you not to faint at my tribulations for you, which is your glory. [n. 164]

³:¹⁴For this cause I bend my knees to the Father of our Lord Jesus Christ, [n. 165]

³:¹⁵From whom all paternity in heaven and earth is named: [n. 169]

³:¹⁶That he would grant you, according to the riches of his glory, to be strengthened by his Spirit with might unto the inward man: [n. 170]

³:¹⁷That Christ may dwell by faith in your hearts: that, being rooted and founded in charity, [n.172]

---

163. Postquam egit Apostolus de dignitate officii, quod pertinet ad suam conditionem, hic consequenter agit de his quae pertinent ad suam afflictionem, scilicet de passionibus suis.

Circa quod duo facit.

Primo exhortatur eos ne pro suis tribulationibus conturbentur sed habeant patientiam;

secundo, quia ad hoc quod homo non conturbetur necessarium est divinum auxilium, praemittit orationem, ut impleant hoc per divinam gratiam, ibi *huius rei gratia*, et cetera.

164. Dicit ergo primo: ex magnitudine officii mei et firmitate eius, quam habeo per fidem Christi, accidit quod tribulationes patior; nec me conturbant, nec a Christo avellere possunt. Rom. VIII, 35: *quis nos separabit a caritate Christi? Tribulatio?* etc.; quasi dicat: nihil. **Propter quod** induco vos et **peto, ne deficiatis in tribulationibus meis**, ne scilicet occasione tribulationum mearum deficiatis omnino a fide et ab operibus bonis. Hebr. XII, 3: *non fatigemini animis vestris deficientes*.

Dico autem quod vos non debetis deficere, quia sunt **pro vobis**, id est, pro utilitate vestra. II Cor. I, 6: *sive tribulamur pro vestra exhortatione et salute, sive consolamur pro vestra consolatione, sive exhortamur pro vestra exhortatione et salute, quae operatur tolerantiam passionum earumdem, quas et nos patimur, ut spes nostra firma sit pro vobis, scientes quoniam sicut socii passionum estis, sic eritis et consolationum*. Vel dicit **pro vobis**, id est pro

163. After the Apostle has dealt with the dignity of the office belonging to his position, he goes on to speak of his tribulations and sufferings.

In reference to this he does two things:

first, he exhorts them lest they be troubled by his sufferings; they should have patience;

second, since divine assistance is necessary if man is not to become agitated, he prays that they might accomplish this through divine grace, at *for this cause*.

164. About the first he says: due to the importance and security of my office, which I have through faith in Christ, it happens that I suffer tribulations; but they neither daunt me nor can they tear me away from Christ. *Who then shall separate us from the love of Christ? Shall tribulation? Or distress? Or famine? Or nakedness? Or danger? Or persecution? Or the sword?* (Rom 8:35). As though he affirmed that nothing can. **Wherefore I** urge and **pray you not to faint at my tribulations**. My sufferings should not be an occasion for you to fail in faith or in good works at all. *Think diligently upon him that endures such opposition from sinners against himself; that you be not wearied, fainting in your minds* (Heb 12:3).

I declare that you must not be disheartened because they are *for you*, for your own utility. *Whether we be in tribulation, it is for your exhortation and salvation; or whether we be comforted, it is for your consolation; or whether we be exhorted, it is for your exhortation and salvation, which works the enduring of the same sufferings which we also suffer, that our hope for you may be steadfast, knowing that as you are partakers of the sufferings, so shall you be also of the consolation* (2 Cor 1:6–7). Or, he says *for you* meaning, for

vestra probatione. Sap. III, v. 6: *tamquam aurum in fornace probavit electos dominus*, et cetera.

Quae est gloria vestra, etc., scilicet si non deficiatis, sed stetis fortes in tribulationibus. Nam *qui perseveraverit usque in finem*, et cetera.

Alio modo: **quae est gloria vestra**, id est tolerantia passionum nostrarum, est pro vobis ad gloriam, in hoc quod Deus exposuit apostolos suos et prophetas tribulationibus et passionibus propter salutem vestram. Os. c. VI, 5: *propterea dolavi in prophetis, et occidi eos*, et cetera. II Cor. I, 14: *gloria vestra sumus, sicut vos nostra*, et cetera.

165. Consequenter cum dicit **huius rei gratia**, etc., implorat eis auxilium per orationem, ut per exhortationem suam proficiant. Et

primo orationem praemittit;

secundo quasi securus de exauditione, gratias agit, ibi **ei autem qui potens est**, et cetera.

Item, prima in tres, quia

primo proponit orationis obiectum;

secundo orationis intentum, ibi **ut det vobis secundum divitias**, etc.;

tertio orationis fructum, ibi **ut possitis comprehendere**, et cetera.

166. Oratio autem redditur exaudibilis per humilitatem. Ps. ci, 18: *respexit in orationem humilium*, et cetera. Eccli. XXXV, 21: *oratio humiliantis se, nubes penetrabit*, et cetera. Et ideo statim orationem suam ab humilitate incipit, dicens **huius rei gratia**, scilicet ne deficiatis a fide, **flecto genua mea ad Patrem**, etc., quod est signum humilitatis propter duo. Primo quia qui genua flectit, quodam modo parvificat se, et subiicit se ei, cui genua flectit: unde per huiusmodi ostenditur recognitio propriae fragilitatis et parvitatis.

Secundo quia in genu est fortitudo corporis. Quando ergo quis genua flectit, protestatur debilitatem suae virtutis. Et inde est, quod exteriora signa corporalia exhibentur Deo ad conversionem, et exercitium spirituale animae interioris. In oratione Manasses: *flecto genua cordis mei*, et cetera. Is. XLV, 23: *mihi curvabitur omne genu*, et cetera.

167. Deinde describit orationis obiectum, quod est Deus, et describit eum ex duobus: primo ex affinitate, secundo ex auctoritate.

Ex affinitate enim erigimur ad orandum cum fiducia. Et quantum ad hoc dicit **ad Patrem Domini nostri Iesu Christi**, scilicet cuius nos filii sumus. Iac. I, 17: *omne datum optimum*, et cetera. Is. LXIII, 16: *tu enim, Domine, Pater noster*, et cetera.

your testing: *as gold in the furnace he has proved them, and as a victim of a holocaust he has received them* (Wis 3:6).

Which is your glory if you do not fall but remain steadfast in sufferings, for *he that shall persevere unto the end, he shall be saved* (Matt 10:22).

In a different way, **which is your glory** signifies that the endurance of our trials is to your own glory in that God exposes his apostles and prophets to sorrows and pains on account of your salvation. *For this reason have I hewed them in the prophets, I have slain them by the words of my mouth* (Hos 6:5). *We are your glory, as you also are ours, in the day of our Lord Jesus Christ* (2 Cor 1:14).

165. As a consequence he goes on, at **for this cause**, to implore assistance for them through a prayer that they might derive advantage from his exhortation.

First, he sets down the prayer.

Second, confident of its being heard, he adds a thanksgiving, at **now to him who is able** (Eph 3:20).

The first part has three sections:

first, he mentions to whom the prayer is addressed;

second, the intention of the prayer, at **that he would grant you, according to the riches**;

third, the prayer's fruit, at **you may be able to comprehend**.

166. Humility makes a prayer worthy of being heard: *he has had regard to the prayer of the humble: and he has not despised their petition* (Ps 102:17). And, *the prayer of him that humbles himself shall pierce the clouds: and till it come near he will not be comforted* (Sir 35:21). Therefore, he immediately starts his prayer in humility, saying **for this cause** that you fail not in the faith **I bend my knees to the Father**. This is a symbol of humility for two reasons. First, a man belittles himself, in a certain way, when he genuflects, and he subjects himself to the one he genuflects before. In such a way he recognizes his own weakness and insignificance.

Second, physical strength is present in the knees; in bending them a man confesses openly to his lack of strength. Thus external, physical symbols are shown to God for the purpose of renewing and spiritually training the inner soul, as in the prayer of Manasse: *I bend the knee of my heart*; and *for every knee shall be bowed to me: and every tongue shall swear* (Isa 45:24).

167. He describes next the person to whom the prayer is directed, God, whom he portrays in his nearness and in his authority.

For from his close relationship to us we are encouraged to pray with confidence. In this regard he states **to the Father of our Lord Jesus Christ** and whose children we are also. *Every best gift and every perfect gift is from above, coming down from the Father of lights* (Jas 1:17). *You, O Lord, are our Father, our redeemer: from everlasting is your name* (Isa 63:16).

Ex auctoritate autem confirmatur obtinendi quod petimus fiducia, quia ipse est *ex quo omnis paternitas in caelo et in terra nominatur*.

168. Hic posset quaeri utrum in caelo sit paternitas.

Posset dici breviter, quod *in caelo*, id est in Deo vel in divinis, est paternitas, quae est principium omnis paternitatis. Sed de hac non quaeritur ad praesens, quia cuilibet fideli nota est. Sed quaeritur utrum *in caelis*, id est utrum in angelis sit aliqua paternitas.

Ad hoc dico quod paternitas est tantum in viventibus et cognoscentibus. Est autem duplex vita. Una secundum actum, alia secundum potentiam. Vita quidem secundum potentiam, est habere opera vitae in potentia. Unde dormiens quantum ad actus exteriores, dicitur vivere in potentia. Vivere autem secundum actum est, quando exercet quis opera vitae in actu. Sic autem non solum qui dat potentiam vitae, pater est eius cui dat; sed qui dat actum vitae, ille etiam pater dici potest. Quicumque ergo inducit aliquem ad aliquem actum vitae, puta ad bene operandum, intelligendum, volendum, amandum, pater eius dici potest. I Cor. IV, 15: *nam si decem millia paedagogorum habeatis in Christo, sed non multos patres*, et cetera. Cum ergo inter angelos unus alterum illuminet, perficiat et purget, et isti sint actus hierarchici, manifestum est quod unus angelus est pater alterius, sicut magister est pater discipuli.

169. Utrum autem paternitas, quae est in caelis et in terra, derivetur a paternitate, quae est in divinis, dubitatur. Et videtur quod non; quia nomina sic imponimus secundum quod res nominatas cognoscimus; quidquid autem cognoscimus, est per creaturas, ergo nomina imposita a nobis rebus ipsis, plus et prius conveniunt creaturis quam ipsi Deo.

Respondeo et dico quod nomen alicuius rei nominatae a nobis dupliciter potest accipi, quia vel est expressivum, aut significativum conceptus intellectus, quia voces sunt notae, vel signa passionum, vel conceptuum qui sunt in anima, et sic nomen prius est in creaturis, quam in Deo. Aut inquantum est manifestativum quidditatis rei nominatae exterius, et sic est prius in Deo. Unde hoc nomen *paternitas*, secundum quod significat conceptionem intellectus nominantis rem, sic per prius invenitur in creaturis quam in Deo, quia per prius creatura innotescit nobis, quam Deus; secundum autem quod significat ipsam rem nominatam, sic per prius est in Deo quam in nobis, quia certe omnis virtus generativa in nobis est a Deo. Et ideo dicit: *ex quo omnis paternitas in caelo et in terra nominatur*, quasi dicat: paternitas quae est in ipsis creaturis, est quasi nominalis seu vocalis, sed illa paternitas divina, qua Pater dat totam naturam Filio, absque omni imperfectione, est vera paternitas.

We are confirmed in the hope of obtaining what we ask for with confidence by his authority since from him *all paternity in heaven and earth is named*.

168. At this point the question arises if there is any paternity in heaven.

A quick answer would be that *in heaven* means that paternity is present in God and in divinity, and that this is the source of all fatherhood. But this is not questioned here, since it is known to all the faithful. It is asked whether *in heaven*, that is, in the angels, there is any paternity.

To this I reply that paternity exists only among beings who live and who know. But life is twofold: it is either actual or potential. To possess the vital activities in potency is to be potentially alive; for example, a person who is sleeping is said to be potentially alive in regard to external actions. But when someone actually performs the vital activities, he is alive in act. Thus, not only he who transmits the potency to life is the father of him to whom he gives it, but also he who communicates an act of life can be called a father. Therefore, whoever stimulates another to some vital act, whether it be to good activity, to understanding, to willing or loving, can be given the name of father. *For if you have ten thousand instructors in Christ, yet not many fathers* (1 Cor 4:15). Likewise, in the hierarchical acts by which one angel illumines, perfects, and purifies another, it is evident that that angel is the father of the other—just as a teacher is the father of his disciples.

169. Some doubt that the fatherhood in heaven and on earth is derived from the paternity which exists in the divinity. It seems not to be, for we give names in accordance with our knowledge of the reality named. And whatever we do know is through creatures; hence, the names we give to the things themselves are applicable primarily, and to a greater degree, to creatures rather than God.

I reply and state that the name of anything we name can be taken in two ways. In one it is expressive or symbolic of an intellectual concept, since words are the marks or signs of the impressions or concepts that are in the soul. In this perspective a name refers to creatures more primarily than to God. However, inasmuch as it discloses the quiddity of the external object which is named, it refers more primarily to God. Therefore, the word *paternity*, when it signifies a concept formed by our intellect as it is naming a thing, will primarily be applicable to creatures instead of God since creatures are more known to us than God. But when it signifies the reality itself which has been named, then this reality is primarily in God rather than in us. For certainly all the power to procreate present in us is from God. So he says *from whom all paternity in heaven and earth is named* as though to affirm: the fatherhood present in creatures is, as it were, nominal or vocal; but the divine fatherhood, by which the Father communicates his whole nature to the Son without any imperfection, is true paternity.

170. Consequenter cum dicit *ut det vobis*, etc., ostendit orationis intentum. Et primo facit hoc; secundo ostendit per quid posset impetrare suum propositum, ibi *per Spiritum eius*, et cetera.

171. Dicit ergo: dico quod peto ne deficiatis, sed stetis viriliter. Scio tamen quod hoc ex vobis facere non potestis sine dono Dei, ideo peto, *ut det vobis*. Iac. I, 17: *omne datum optimum*, et cetera. Et hoc quidem *secundum divitias gloriae suae*, id est secundum copiam maiestatis eius et magnificentiae. Ps. CXI, 3: *gloria et divitiae in domo eius*. Prov. VIII, 18: *mecum sunt divitiae et gloria*. Divitiae, inquam, quae faciunt *virtute corroborari*. Is. XL, 29: *qui dat lasso virtutem, et his qui non sunt fortitudinem et robur multiplicat*. Et hoc *in interiori homine*, quia nisi in interioribus fortificetur homo, faciliter ab hoste superatur. Is. IX, 7: *confirmet illud et corroboret in iudicio et iustitia, amodo et usque in sempiternum*.

172. Tunc resumatur illa particula interposita, scilicet *per Spiritum*, in qua ostendit per quid obtinere potest quod petit. Ipse enim Spiritus, qui roborat, est Spiritus fortitudinis et est causa non deficiendi in tribulationibus, quem obtinemus per fidem quae est fortissima: quia fides est substantia rerum sperandarum, id est facit in nobis subsistere res sperandas. Unde I Petr. V, 9: *cui resistite fortes in fide*. Et ideo subiungit *habitare Christum per fidem*, et hoc *in cordibus vestris*. I Petr. III, 15: *Dominum autem Christum sanctificate in cordibus vestris*.

Per quod? Dico quod non solum per fidem, quae, ut donum est fortissima, sed etiam per caritatem quae est in sanctis. Et ideo subdit *in caritate radicati et fundati*. I Cor. XIII, 7: *omnia suffert, omnia credit, omnia sperat, omnia sustinet, caritas numquam excidit*. Cant. ult.: *fortis est ut mors dilectio*. Unde sicut arbor sine radice, et domus sine fundamento de facili ruit, ita spirituale aedificium, nisi sit in caritate fundatum et radicatum, durare non potest.

170. Next, at *that he would grant you*, he discloses what he prays for: first, he does this; second, he shows through whom he can ask for what he desires, at *by his Spirit*.

171. Thus he says: I ask that you do not give up, but be steadfast like men. Yet I know that by yourselves you cannot achieve this without God's gift, so I beg *that he would grant* it to *you* since *every best gift and every perfect gift is from above, coming down from the Father of lights* (Jas 1:17). He will do this *according to the riches of his glory*, that is, in accord with his overflowing majesty and grandeur. *Glory and riches are in his house* (Ps 112:3), and *with me are riches and glory* (Prov 8:18). Riches, I say, which will cause you to *be strengthened with might*. *It is he that gives strength to the weary, and increases force and might to them that are not* (Isa 40:29). This is for *the inward man* because a man is overcome easily by his enemy if he is not inwardly fortified. *Establish him and strengthen him with judgment and with justice, from henceforth and forever* (Isa 9:7).

172. Inserted in the above is the phrase *by his Spirit* indicating through whom petitions are granted. The Spirit himself who fortifies is the Spirit of fortitude, and is the source of our not yielding under sufferings. We receive him through a faith which is most strong because it is the substance of the realities we hope for—that is, it makes these desired realities exist within us. *Resist, strong in faith* (1 Pet 5:9). And Paul adds *that Christ may dwell by faith in your hearts*. *Sanctify the Lord Christ in your hearts* (1 Pet 3:15).

With what? I claim that it should not only be through faith, which as a gift is the strongest, but also through the charity that is in the saints. Thus he adds *being rooted and founded in a charity* which *bears all things, believes all things, hopes all things, endures all things. Charity never falls away* (1 Cor 13:7-8), for *love is strong as death* (Song 8:6). A tree without roots, or a house lacking a foundation are destroyed easily. In a similar manner, a spiritual edifice not rooted and founded in charity cannot last.

Lecture 5

3:18ut possitis comprehendere cum omnibus sanctis, quae sit latitudo, et longitudo, et sublimitas, et profundum: [n. 174]

3:19scire etiam supereminentem scientiae caritatem Christi, ut impleamini in omnem plenitudinem Dei. [n. 178]

3:20Ei autem, qui potens est omnia facere superabundanter quam petimus aut intelligimus, secundum virtutem, quae operatur in nobis: [n. 183]

3:21ipsi gloria in Ecclesia, et in Christo Jesu, in omnes generationes saeculi saeculorum. Amen. [n. 186]

3:18ἵνα ἐξισχύσητε καταλαβέσθαι σὺν πᾶσιν τοῖς ἁγίοις τί τὸ πλάτος καὶ μῆκος καὶ ὕψος καὶ βάθος,

3:19γνῶναί τε τὴν ὑπερβάλλουσαν τῆς γνώσεως ἀγάπην τοῦ Χριστοῦ, ἵνα πληρωθῆτε εἰς πᾶν τὸ πλήρωμα τοῦ θεοῦ.

3:20Τῷ δὲ δυναμένῳ ὑπὲρ πάντα ποιῆσαι ὑπερεκπερισσοῦ ὧν αἰτούμεθα ἢ νοοῦμεν κατὰ τὴν δύναμιν τὴν ἐνεργουμένην ἐν ἡμῖν,

3:21αὐτῷ ἡ δόξα ἐν τῇ ἐκκλησίᾳ καὶ ἐν Χριστῷ Ἰησοῦ εἰς πάσας τὰς γενεὰς τοῦ αἰῶνος τῶν αἰώνων: ἀμήν.

3:18You may be able to comprehend, with all the saints, what is the breadth and length and height and depth, [n. 174]

3:19To know also the charity of Christ, which surpasses all knowledge: that you may be filled unto all the fullness of God. [n. 178]

3:20Now to him who is able to do all things more abundantly than we desire or understand, according to the power that works in us: [n. 183]

3:21To him be glory in the Church and in Christ Jesus, unto all generations, world without end. Amen. [n. 186]

---

173. Supra ostendit Apostolus petitionis suae pro Ephesiis, et orationis intentum, scilicet corroborationem spiritus in fide et caritate, hic consequenter ostendit eius quam petiit corroborationis per fidem et caritatem fructum, qui est quaedam cognitio. Ideo

primo proponit ipsam notitiam;

secundo ipsius notitiae et cognitionis efficaciam, ibi *ut impleamini in omnem plenitudinem Dei*.

174. Dicit ergo: ita sitis, charissimi, *in caritate radicati et fundati, ut possitis comprehendere*, et cetera. Quod quidem dupliciter legi potest. Primo modo, ut magis sequamur intentionem Apostoli.

Sciendum est ergo quod tam in futuro quam in praesenti cognitio Dei est nobis necessaria; nam in futuro gaudebimus et de cognitione Dei et de cognitione assumptae humanitatis. Io. XVII, 3: *haec est vita aeterna, ut, cognoscant*, et cetera. Io. X, 9: *ingredietur*, scilicet in contemplatione divinitatis, *et egredietur*, scilicet in contemplatione humanitatis, *et pascua inveniet*. Et quia fides est inchoatio illius futurae cognitionis, quia *est substantia rerum sperandarum*, etc., ut dicitur Hebr. XI, v. 1 quasi iam in nobis res sperandas per modum cuiusdam inchoationis facit subsistere. Inde est quod fides nostra in his duobus consistit, scilicet in divinitate et humanitate Christi. I Cor. II, 2: *non enim iudicavi me scire aliquid inter vos, nisi Iesum Christum*, et cetera.

Secundum hoc ergo

primo praemittit eis cognitionem divinitatis;

secundo cognitionem mysteriorum humanitatis, ibi *scire etiam supereminentem scientiae*, et cetera.

173. Previously the Apostle revealed the object of his petition or prayer in behalf of the Ephesians, a strengthening of spirit in faith and charity. Consequently, he here shows the fruit of this strengthening through faith and charity; it is a certain type of knowledge. He sets forth:

first, the knowledge itself;

second, the effective power of this awareness or knowledge, at *that you may be filled*.

174. He says: you ought to be so *rooted and founded in charity* (Eph 3:17), dearly beloved, that *you may be able to comprehend, with all the saints, what is the breadth and length and height and depth*. This can be read in two ways. In the first way we are more in accord with the Apostle's thought.

The knowledge of God is necessary for us both in the future life and in the present. For in the future we shall rejoice in our knowledge of God and in our perception of the humanity he assumed. *Now this is eternal life: that they may know you, the only true God, and Jesus Christ, whom you have sent* (John 17:3). Men will *go in* by the contemplation of the divinity, and will *go out* by the contemplation of the humanity, *and shall find pastures* (John 10:9). Faith inaugurates that future knowledge; it is *the substance of things hoped for* (Heb 11:1), already making the realities we desire exist within us in an inchoate manner. For this reason our faith consists in the divinity and humanity of Christ. *For I did not judge myself to know anything among you, but Jesus Christ; and him crucified* (1 Cor 2:2).

In accord with this he discusses:

first, the knowledge of divinity;

second, the knowledge of the mysteries of the humanity, at *to know also the charity of Christ*.

175. Cognitionem autem divinitatis manifestat eis sub his verbis *ut possitis*, etc., quasi dicat: corroboramini per fidem et caritatem, quia si sic estis, pervenietis ad vitam aeternam, ubi habebitis Deum praesentem et perfecte eum cognoscetis.

Quod autem Deus manifestetur amanti, patet Io. XIV, 21: *qui diligit me, diligetur a Patre meo, et ego diligam eum, et manifestabo ei meipsum*; quod vero manifestetur credenti, patet, prout dicitur Is. VII, 9, secundum aliam litteram: *nisi credideritis, non intelligetis*. Oportet enim ut secundum fidem et caritatem corroboremini, ut possitis comprehendere.

176. Ubi sciendum est quod *comprehendere* quandoque ponitur pro includere, et tunc oportet quod comprehendens contineat in se totaliter comprehensum. Quandoque autem ponitur pro apprehendere, et tunc dicit remotionem distantiae et insinuat propinquitatem. Primo autem modo a nullo intellectu creato Deus comprehendi potest. Iob XI, 7: *forsitan vestigia Dei comprehendes, et usque ad perfectum Omnipotentem reperies?* Quasi dicat: non, quia sic posset eum perfecte cognoscere quantum cognoscibilis est. Et de hac cognitione non intelligitur quod dicitur *ut possitis comprehendere*, sed secundo modo. Et est una de tribus dotibus, et de hac loquitur Apostolus, cum dicit *ut possitis comprehendere*, id est Deum habere praesentem et praesentialiter cognoscere. Phil. c. III, 12: *sequor autem si quomodo comprehendam, in quo*, et cetera.

Et haec comprehensio est communis omnibus sanctis eius. Ideo subdit *cum omnibus sanctis*. Ps. CXLIX, 9: *gloria haec est omnibus sanctis eius*. Talibus autem dicitur illud I Cor. IX, 24: *sic currite ut comprehendatis*, et cetera.

177. *Quae sit latitudo*, et cetera. Notandum quod verba ista videntur ortum habere ex verbis Iob XI, 7: *forsan*, inquit, *vestigia Dei comprehendes?* Quasi dicat: incomprehensibilis est; huius autem incomprehensibilitatis causam assignat, dicens: *excelsior caelo est, et quid facies? Profundior Inferno est, et unde cognosces? Longior terra mensura eius, et latior mari*. Ex quo videtur quod Iob ostendat eum esse comprehensibilem, attribuens ei quadruplicem differentiam dimensionum. His enim verbis alludens Apostolus dicit *ut possitis comprehendere, quae sit latitudo*, etc.; quasi dicat: habeatis tantam fidem et caritatem, ut possitis tandem comprehendere quod comprehensibile est. Et hoc modo exponit Dionysius.

Non est tamen aliquo modo intelligendum has dimensiones corporaliter esse in Deo, quia *spiritus est Deus*, ut dicitur Io. IV, 24. Sunt tamen in Deo metaphorice. Unde per *latitudinem* designatur dimensio

175. He reveals the knowledge of the divinity to them with the words: *that you may be able to comprehend, with all the saints*. As though he said: be strong in faith and charity for if you are, you will gain life eternal where you will enjoy God's presence and perfectly know him.

It is evident that God reveals himself to one who loves: *he that loves me shall be loved of my Father; and I will love him and will manifest myself to him* (John 14:21). It is also clear that he shows himself to one who believes, as a variant reading puts it: *unless you believe, you will not understand* (Isa 7:9). You must be fortified by faith and charity in order that you might be able to comprehend.

176. It should be noted that sometimes *to comprehend* means 'to enclose,' and then it is necessary that the comprehending totally contains within itself what is comprehended. At other times it means 'to apprehend,' and then it affirms a remoteness or distance and yet implies proximity. No created intellect can comprehend God in the first manner. *Perhaps you will comprehend the steps of God, and will find out the Almighty perfectly?* (Job 11:7) The answer implied is, no. For this would be to know him perfectly insofar as he is knowable. And this type of knowledge is not referred to in *that you may be able to comprehend*, but rather the second kind. This latter is one of the three dowries, and it is of it that the Apostle speaks here when he says *that you may be able to comprehend*, meaning, that you may enjoy the presence of God and know him face to face. *Not as though I had already attained, or were already perfect; but I follow after, if I may by any means comprehend, wherein I am also comprehended by Christ Jesus* (Phil 3:12).

Such comprehension is common to all his saints; so he adds *with all the saints*. *This glory is to all his saints* (Ps 149:9). *So run that you may comprehend* (1 Cor 9:24).

177. Note that the words *what is the breadth and length and height and depth* seem to owe their origin to the passage: *perhaps*, he says, *you will comprehend the steps of God?* (Job 11:7–9), as if he stated that God is incomprehensible. Then he gives the reason for this incomprehensibility by saying: *he is higher than the heaven, and what will you do? He is deeper than hell, and how will you know? The measure of him is longer than the earth, and broader than the sea*. Yet from this it appears that Job, in attributing the four different dimensions to him, shows that he is comprehensible. Alluding to these words the Apostle asserts that *you may be able to comprehend what is the breadth and length and height and depth*, as though he said: may you possess sufficient faith and charity that you might comprehend him to the extent that he is able to be comprehended. Dionysius explains the text in this way.

Under no pretext should these dimensions be conceived as physically applicable to God, since *God is spirit* (John 4:24). They are in God metaphorically. *Breadth* designates the dimension or extension of his power and divine

seu extensio virtutis, et sapientiae divinae super omnia. Eccli. I, 10: *effudit illam*, scilicet sapientiam, *super omnia opera sua*. Per **longitudinem** designatur aeterna eius duratio. Ps. ci, 13: *tu autem, Domine, in aeternum permanes*, et cetera. Ps. XCII, 5: *domum tuam, Domine, decet sanctitudo in longitudinem dierum*. Per **sublimitatem** vel celsitudinem vero, perfectio et nobilitas naturae eius, quae in infinitum excedit creaturam. Ps. CXII, 4: *excelsus super omnes gentes Dominus*. **Et profundum**, id est incomprehensibilitas sapientiae eius. Eccle. VII, 25: *alta profunditas*, scilicet sapientiae divinae, *quis inveniet eam?*

Sic ergo patet quod finis fidei et caritatis nostrae est ut perveniamus ad perfectam fidei cognitionem, qua cognoscamus infinitam suae virtutis extensionem, aeternam et infinitam eius durationem, suae perfectissimae naturae celsitudinem, suae sapientiae profunditatem et incomprehensibilitatem, eo modo sicut est attingendum.

178. Consequenter, quia adhuc alia cognitio est necessaria, scilicet cognitio mysteriorum humanitatis, ideo subdit **scire etiam supereminentem scientiae**, et cetera. Ubi sciendum est quod quidquid est in mysterio redemptionis humanae et Incarnationis Christi, totum est opus caritatis. Nam quod incarnatum est, ex caritate processit. Supra II, 4: **propter nimiam caritatem suam qua dilexit nos**, et cetera. Quia vero mortuus fuit, ex caritate processit Io. XV, 13: *maiorem hac dilectionem nemo habet*, etc.; infra V, 2: **Christus dilexit nos, et tradidit semetipsum pro nobis oblationem et hostiam Deo**. Propter hoc dicit Gregorius: *o inaestimabilis dilectio caritatis. Ut servum redimeres, Filium tradidisti*. Et ideo scire caritatem Christi, est scire omnia mysteria Incarnationis Christi et redemptionis nostrae, quae ex immensa caritate Dei processerunt, quae quidem caritas excedit omnem intellectum creatum et omnium scientiam, cum sit incomprehensibilis cogitatu. Et ideo dicit **supereminentem scientiae**, scilicet naturali et omnem intellectum creatum excedentem, Phil. IV, 7: *et pax Dei, quae exsuperat omnem sensum*; **caritatem Christi**, id est, quam Deus Pater fecit per Christum. II Cor. V, 19: *Deus erat in Christo mundum reconcilians sibi*.

179. Alio modo potest legi, ut referatur ad perfectionem caritatis nostrae, quasi dicat: corroboramini **in caritate radicati et fundati**, et hoc **ut possitis comprehendere**, non solum cognoscere, **cum omnibus sanctis**, quia hoc donum, scilicet caritatis, commune est omnibus, cum nullus possit esse sanctus sine caritate, ut dicitur Ephes. c. III. **Possitis**, inquam, comprehendere **quae sit latitudo**, scilicet caritatis, quae se extendit usque ad inimicos. Ps. CXVIII, 96: *latum mandatum tuum nimis*. Lata est enim caritas ad suam diffusionem. Ps. XVII, 20: *eduxit me in latitudinem Dominus*. **Longitudo** autem eius attenditur quantum ad sui perseverantiam, quia

wisdom over all being. *And he poured her out*, namely wisdom, *upon all his works* (Sir 1:10). By **length** his eternal duration is signified: *but you, O Lord, endures forever* (Ps 102:12), and *holiness becomes your house, O Lord, unto length of days* (Ps 93:5). **Height** or loftiness denotes the perfection and nobility of his nature which infinitely exceeds all creation: *the Lord is high above all nations: and his glory above the heavens* (Ps 113:4). In **depth** the incomprehensibility of his wisdom is intimated: *it is a great depth, this divine wisdom, who shall find it out?* (Eccl 7:25).

Clearly, therefore, the fulfillment of our faith and charity is to arrive at a perfect knowledge of the faith, by it we shall know, to the degree we can attain to it, the infinite extension of his power, the unbounded eternity of his duration, the loftiness of his most perfect nature, and the incomprehensibility and depth of his wisdom.

178. Next, since further knowledge is also necessary—a knowledge of the mysteries of the humanity—he goes on **to know also the charity of Christ**. For whatever occurred in the mystery of human redemption and Christ's Incarnation was the work of love. He became incarnate out of charity: *for his exceeding charity with which he loved us even when we were dead in sins, has quickened us together in Christ* (Eph 2:4–5). That he died also sprang from charity: *greater love than this no man has, that a man lay down his life for his friends* (John 15:13). And **Christ also has loved us and has delivered himself for us, an oblation and a sacrifice to God** (Eph 5:2). On this account St. Gregory exclaimed: *O the incalculable love of your charity! To redeem slaves you delivered up your Son*. It follows that to know Christ's love is to know all the mysteries of Christ's Incarnation and our redemption. These have poured out from the immense charity of God; a charity exceeding every created intelligence and the knowledge of all of them because it cannot be grasped in thought. Thus he says **which surpasses all** natural **knowledge** and every created intellect: *the peace of God, which surpasses all understanding, keep your hearts and minds in Christ Jesus* (Phil 4:7). For **the charity of Christ** is what God the Father has accomplished through Christ: *God indeed was in Christ, reconciling the world to himself* (2 Cor 5:19).

179. The other manner in which this passage can be read is in reference to the perfection of our charity, as though he stated: be strong, **rooted and founded in charity** (Eph 3:17), that **you may be able to comprehend**—and not merely know—**with all the saints**; this gift of charity is common to all, no one can be holy without charity, as the third chapter of Ephesians indicates. **May you, I say, comprehend what is the breadth** of charity, extending, as it does, even to one's enemies: *your commandment is exceeding broad* (Ps 119:96). For charity is broad in its diffusion: *and the Lord brought me forth into a broad place* (Ps 18:19). Its **length** is seen in its durability since, never stopping, it

numquam deficit, sed hic incipit et perficitur in gloria. I Cor. XIII, v. 8: *caritas numquam excidit*. Cant. ult.: *aquae multae non potuerunt extinguere caritatem*. **Sublimitas** autem eius attenditur quantum ad intentionem caelestium, ut scilicet Deus non diligatur propter temporalia, quia huiusmodi caritas esset infirma, sed ut diligatur propter se tantum. Iob XL, v. 5: *in sublime erigere, et esto gloriosus*. **Profundum** vero attenditur quantum ad originem ipsius caritatis. Nam hoc quod Deum diligimus, non est ex nobis, sed a Spiritu Sancto, quia, ut dicitur Rom. V, 5, *caritas Dei diffusa est in cordibus nostris per Spiritum Sanctum*, et cetera. Hoc ergo quod unus habet caritatem longam, latam, sublimem et profundam, et alius non, venit ex profundo divinae praedestinationis. Eccli. I, 2: *profundum abyssi quis dimensus est*.

Ergo, **ut possitis comprehendere**, id est perfecte consequi cum omnibus sanctis, **quae sit latitudo**, ut extendatur caritas vestra usque ad inimicos, quae sit **longitudo**, ut scilicet numquam deficiat, quae sit **sublimitas**, ut scilicet propter seipsum Deus diligatur, et quid sit **profundum**, scilicet praedestinationis, et cetera.

180. Sciendum est autem hic quod Christus, in cuius potestate fuit eligere genus mortis quod vellet, quia ex caritate mortem subiit, elegit mortem crucis, in qua praedictae quatuor dimensiones sunt. Ibi est **latitudo**, scilicet in ligno transverso, cui affixae sunt manus, quia opera nostra debent per caritatem dilatari usque ad inimicos. Ps. XVII, 20: *eduxit me in latitudinem Dominus*. Ibi est **longitudo** in ligno erecto, cui innititur totum corpus, quia caritas debet esse perseverativa, quae sustinet et salvat hominem. Matth. X, 22: *qui autem perseveraverit usque in finem, hic salvus erit*. Ibi est **sublimitas** in ligno superiori, cui caput inhaeret, quia spes nostra debet elevari ad aeterna et divina. I Cor. XI, 3: *caput viri Christus est*. Ibi etiam est **profundum** in ligno quod latet sub terra et sustinet crucem, et tamen non videtur, quia profundum amoris divini sustinet nos, nec tamen videtur; quia ratio praedestinationis ut dictum est excedit intellectum nostrum.

Sic ergo debemus comprehendere virtutem caritatis nostrae et Christi, et adhuc scire caritatem Christi **supereminentem scientiae**, scilicet humanae, quia nullus potest scire quantum Christus dilexit nos, vel scire etiam caritatem scientiae Christi, quae habetur cum scientia Christi. **Caritatem**, dico, **supereminentem**, scilicet alii caritati, quae est sine scientia.

181. Sed numquid est verum quod caritas quae est cum scientia supereminet caritati quae est sine scientia? Et videtur quod non, quia sic malus theologus esset supereminentioris caritatis quam sancta vetula.

Respondeo. Dico quod hoc intelligitur de scientia afficiente: nam ex vi cognitionis inducitur ad magis diligendum, quia, quanto Deus magis cognoscitur, tanto et

begins in this life and is perfected in glory: *charity never falls away* (1 Cor 13:8), and *many waters cannot quench charity* (Song 8:7). Its **height** is perceived in its motivation which is heavenly; God is not loved to obtain temporal advantages—which love would be feeble—but he is loved for his own sake alone. *Set yourself up on high and be glorious* (Job 40:5). **Depth** signifies the source of charity itself. For our love of God does not spring from ourselves, but from the Holy Spirit: *the charity of God is poured forth in our hearts, by the Holy Spirit who is given to us* (Rom 5:5). Hence, for one person to possess a love which is lasting, extensive, sublime and deep, while another person does not, arises out of the depth of divine predestination. *Who has measured the depth of the abyss?* (Sir 1:2)

Thus **you may be able to comprehend**, in the sense of perfectly attaining to, **with all the saints, what is the breadth** with which your charity should extend even to enemies, and what is the **length** during which it never ceases, and its **height** in loving God for his own sake, and the **depth** of its predestination.

180. At this point it should be realized that it was within Christ's power to choose what type of death he wanted. And since he underwent death out of charity, he chose the death of the cross in which the aforesaid four dimensions are present. The cross-beam has **breadth** and to it his hands were nailed because through charity our good works ought to stretch out even to adversaries: *the Lord brought me forth into a broad place* (Ps 18:19). The trunk of the cross has **length** against which the whole body leans since charity ought to be enduring, thus sustaining and saving man: *he that shall persevere unto the end, he shall be saved* (Matt 10:22). The upper portion of wood, against which the head is thrown back, has **height** since our hope must rise toward the eternal and the divine: *the head of every man is Christ* (1 Cor 11:3). The cross is braced by its **depth** which lies concealed beneath the ground; it is not seen because the depth of the divine love which sustains us is not visible insofar as the plans of predestination, as was said above, are beyond our intelligence.

In this manner we should comprehend the power of our love, and of Christ's, realizing that his **surpasses** human **understanding**. For no one can know how much Christ has loved us; nor can one know the charity of the knowledge of Christ, which is possessed with knowledge of Christ. I hold that such a **charity** is one that **surpasses** a charity that is without knowledge.

181. Is it not correct that a charity with knowledge is more eminent than a charity without knowledge? It seems that it is not, for then a wicked theologian would have a charity of greater dignity than a holy old woman.

I reply that what is discussed here is an influential kind of knowledge. For the force of the knowledge stimulates one to love more since the more God is known, so much

magis diligitur. Propter quod petebat Augustinus: *noverim te, noverim me*. Vel hoc dicitur propter quosdam qui habent zelum Dei, sed non secundum scientiam. Talium enim caritati supereminet caritas, cum habetur praedicta scientia Christi.

182. Consequenter cum dicit **ut impleamini**, etc., ponit cognitionis divinae efficaciam, dicens **ut impleamini in omnem plenitudinem Dei**, id est ut habeatis perfectam participationem omnium donorum Dei, ut scilicet hic habeatis plenitudinem virtutum, et postea beatitudinis, quae quidem efficit caritas. Eccli. XXIV, 26: *transite ad me, omnes qui concupiscitis me*, et cetera.

183. Consequenter sequitur illa pars **ei autem qui potens**, et cetera. In qua Apostolus agit Deo gratias de suae petitionis exauditione.

Circa quod tria facit, quia

primo ponit potestatem Dei, qua postulata concedit;

secundo potestatis exemplum, ibi **secundum virtutem quae operatur in nobis**, etc.;

tertio materiam gratiarum actionis, ibi **ipsi gloria**, et cetera.

184. Potestatem autem Dei describit infinitam, dicens **ei autem**, scilicet Deo Christo et Deo Patri, **qui potens est omnia facere**, et cetera. Ex. XV, 3: *omnipotens nomen eius*. Rom. ult.: *ei autem qui potens est vos confirmare iuxta Evangelium*, et cetera. Et hoc **superabundanter** facere in nobis omnia quam sciamus petere per affectum, aut intelligere per intellectum, et hoc est quod dicit **quam petimus, aut intelligimus**.

185. Exemplum autem huiusmodi abundantiae in nobis exhibitae ostendit, dicens **secundum virtutem quam operatur in nobis**, quasi dicat: apparet si attendamus ea quae operatus est in nobis, scilicet hominibus. Nam nec affectus, nec intellectus humanus potuissent considerare, vel intelligere, vel petere a Deo quod fieret homo et homo efficeretur Deus et consors naturae divinae, quae tamen secundum virtutem operatur in nobis, et hoc in Incarnatione Filii sui. II Petr. I, 4: *ut per hoc efficiamini divinae consortes naturae*. Unde de his dicitur Eccli. XVIII, 2: *quis sufficiet enarrare opera illius? Quis enim investigabit magnalia illius, virtutem autem magnitudinis quis annuntiabit?*

Vel **operatus est in nobis**, scilicet apostolis, quibus dedit gratiam evangelizandi **investigabiles divitias Christi, et illuminare omnes quae sit dispensatio sacramenti absconditi a saeculis in Deo**, ut supra eodem cap. et ibi dictum est.

186. Materia autem gratiarum actionis dicitur esse duplex beneficium quod nobis contulit Deus. Primum est Ecclesiae institutio; secundum est Filii Incarnatio.

the more is he loved. For this reason Augustine used to ask: *that I may know you and know myself*. Or, this is stated here on account of some who possess zeal for God *but not according to knowledge* (Rom 10:2). A charity coupled with the above mentioned knowledge of Christ surpasses the love of such people.

182. Next he speaks of the efficacy of a knowledge of the divine. *That you may be filled unto all the fullness of God*, that is, that you might enjoy a perfect participation in all God's gifts. In other words, that you might possess the fullness of the virtues here, and beatitude in the next life; and charity accomplishes just that. *Come over to me, all that desire me, and be filled with my fruits* (Sir 24–26).

183. After this, the Apostle gives thanks to God for hearing his prayer, at **to him who is able**.

In reference to this he does three things:

first, he mentions the power of God with which he grants petitions;

second, he gives an example of that power, at **according to the power that works in us**;

third, he mentions what prompts his thanksgiving, at **to him be glory**.

184. He describes the infinite power of God, saying **now to him**, meaning to Christ as God and to God the Father, **who is able to do all things**: *almighty is his name* (Exod 15:3). *Now, to him that is able to establish you, according to my Gospel and the preaching of Jesus Christ* (Rom 16:25). He effects this within us **more abundantly than we** either would know how to ask for through **desire**, **or understand** with our intelligence.

185. He gives an example of this abundance within us, saying **according to the power that works in us**. As if he had stated: it becomes apparent once we consider what he has wrought in us men. For the human mind and will could never imagine, understand or ask that God become man, and that man become God and a sharer in the divine nature. But he has done this in us by his power, and it was accomplished in the Incarnation of his Son, *that through this you may be made partakers of the divine nature* (2 Pet 1:4). Concerning these matters it is written: *who is able to declare his works? For who shall search out his glorious acts? And who shall show forth the power of his majesty? Or, who shall be able to declare his mercy?* (Sir 18:2–4)

Or, *that works in us* apostles, to whom he gave the grace of proclaiming the good news of **the unsearchable riches of Christ; and to enlighten all men, that they may see what is the dispensation of the mystery which has been hidden from eternity in God** (Eph 3:8).

186. The subject matter of the thanksgiving is the twofold blessing God has bestowed upon us. The first is the institution of the Church, and the second the Incarnation of his Son.

Dicit ergo *ipsi*, scilicet Deo Patri, *gloria*, sit, supple, *in Ecclesia*, id est pro his quae fecit in Ecclesia, quam instituit: quo ad primum; *in Christo*, id est per Christum, vel pro Christo, quem nobis dedit.

Ipsi, inquam, sit *gloria*, ut gloriosus appareat, non solum in praesenti sed *in omnes generationes saeculi saeculorum*, id est saeculi omnia continentis. I Tim. I, 17: *Regi autem saeculorum immortali, invisibili, soli Deo honor et gloria in saecula saeculorum. Amen.*

Hence he says *to him*, God the Father, *be glory in the Church* for all he has done in the Church he established, and *in Christ*, that is, through Christ; or for Christ whom he gave to us.

To him, I repeat, *be glory* that his glory might shine forth, not only now, but *unto all generations world without end*, meaning in the age which embraces all things. *Now, to the King of ages, immortal, invisible, the only God, be honor and glory forever and ever. Amen* (1 Tim 1:17).

Chapter 4

Lecture 1

⁴:¹Obsecro itaque vos ego vinctus in Domino, ut digne ambuletis vocatione, qua vocati estis, [n. 188]

⁴:²cum omni humilitate, et mansuetudine, cum patientia, supportantes invicem in caritate, [n. 191]

⁴:³solliciti servare unitatem Spiritus in vinculo pacis. [n. 192]

⁴:⁴Unum corpus, et unus spiritus, sicut vocati estis in una spe vocationis vestrae. [n. 195]

⁴:¹Παρακαλῶ οὖν ὑμᾶς ἐγὼ ὁ δέσμιος ἐν κυρίῳ ἀξίως περιπατῆσαι τῆς κλήσεως ἧς ἐκλήθητε,

⁴:²μετὰ πάσης ταπεινοφροσύνης καὶ πραΰτητος, μετὰ μακροθυμίας, ἀνεχόμενοι ἀλλήλων ἐν ἀγάπῃ,

⁴:³σπουδάζοντες τηρεῖν τὴν ἑνότητα τοῦ πνεύματος ἐν τῷ συνδέσμῳ τῆς εἰρήνης:

⁴:⁴ἓν σῶμα καὶ ἓν πνεῦμα, καθὼς καὶ ἐκλήθητε ἐν μιᾷ ἐλπίδι τῆς κλήσεως ὑμῶν:

⁴:¹I therefore, a prisoner in the Lord, beseech you that you walk worthy of the vocation in which you are called: [n. 188]

⁴:²With all humility and mildness, with patience, supporting one another in charity, [n. 191]

⁴:³Careful to keep the unity of the Spirit in the bond of peace. [n. 192]

⁴:⁴One body and one spirit: as you are called in one hope of your calling. [n. 195]

---

187. Supra commemoravit Apostolus divina beneficia, per quae unitas Ecclesiae constituitur et conservatur, hic monet eos Apostolus ad permanendum in Ecclesiae unitate.

Circa quod duo facit, quia

primo monet eos ut in ipsa unitate perseverent;

secundo instruit eos quomodo in ea permaneant, ibi *hoc ergo dico et testificor in domino*, et cetera.

Item prima in duas, quia

primo monet eos ad servandam ecclesiasticam unitatem;

secundo proponit ipsius ecclesiasticae unitatis formam, ibi *unus Dominus, una fides*, et cetera.

Prima iterum in tres.

Primo praemittit quaedam inductiva ad servandam ecclesiasticam unitatem;

secundo ponit monitionem, ibi *cum omni humilitate*, etc.;

tertio ostendit monitionis finem, ibi *solliciti servare*, et cetera.

Inducit autem ex tribus ad servandam ecclesiasticam unitatem. Primo ex caritatis affectu; secundo ex commemoratione suorum vinculorum; tertio ex consideratione divinorum.

188. Caritatis autem affectum insinuat per obsecrationem. Unde dicit *itaque*, ex quo tot beneficia a Domino recepistis, *obsecro vos*, cum tamen imperare possem, sed propter humilitatem non impero, magis autem obsecro. Prov. XVIII, 23 dicitur: *cum obsecrationibus loquitur pauper*. Item propter caritatem, quae magis movet ad opus, quam timor. Phil. I, 8: *fiduciam multam habens in*

187. The Apostle recalled above the divine blessings through which the Church's unity has originated and been preserved. Now he admonishes the Ephesians to remain within this ecclesial unity.

Regarding this he does two things:

first, he cautions them to persevere in unity;

second, he instructs them how to remain in it, at **this then I say and testify in the Lord** (Eph 4:17).

The first section is again divided into two parts:

first, he cautions them to keep ecclesial unity;

second, he sets forth the pattern of this Church unity, at **one Lord, one faith** (Eph 4:5).

The first part has three divisions:

first, he offers certain incentives to maintain ecclesial unity;

second, he sets down an admonition, at **with all humility and mildness**;

third, he shows the purpose of his admonition, at **careful to keep**.

Three incentives are given for them to maintain the Church's unity. First is the affection of Paul's love, second is the remembrance of his chains, and third is the consideration of the divine favors.

188. The affection of his love is intimated by his entreaty. **Therefore** because you have obtained so many blessings from the Lord, **I beseech you**. I do not command you even though I could; on account of my lowliness I do not command but plead with you. *The poor will speak with supplications* (Prov 18:23). Charity is another reason, since it prompts men to action more than fear: *wherefore,*

Christo imperandi tibi quod ad rem pertinet, propter caritatem magis obsecro, et cetera.

189. Ex commemoratione vero suorum vinculorum inducit eos, dicens **ego vinctus in Domino**. Ex quibus inducit eos ad servandam sic unitatem, propter tria. Primo quia amicus magis compatitur amico afflicto, et nititur in pluribus facere voluntatem suam, ut vel sic eum consoletur. Eccli. XII, 8 s.: *non agnoscetur in bonis amicus, et non abscondetur in malis inimicus. In bonis viri, inimici illius in tristitia, et in malitia illius, amicus agnitus est.*

Secundo quia Apostolus ipse vincula patiebatur pro ipsorum utilitate, et ideo inducit eos ad memoriam, quasi volens eos obligare. II Cor. I, 6: *sive autem tribulamur pro vestra exhortatione et salute, sive consolamur pro vestra consolatione, sive exhortamur pro vestra exhortatione et salute; quae operatur tolerantiam earumdem passionum, quas et nos patimur.*

Tertio quia, ut supra dictum est cap. III in illa parte: *quae est gloria vestra*, huiusmodi erant eis ad magnam gloriam, dum Deus pro eis amicos et electos suos exposuit tribulationibus pro ipsorum salute. Et ideo addit **in Domino**, id est, propter Dominum. Vel ideo dicit hoc, quia erat ad gloriam Apostoli, quod non ut fur, aut homicida, sed ut Christianus et propter Dominum nostrum Iesum Christum vinculatus erat, iuxta illud Ezech. III, 25: *ecce data sunt super te vincula, et ligabunt te in eis*, et cetera.

190. Ex consideratione vero divinorum beneficiorum inducit eos, dicens **ut digne ambuletis vocatione qua vocati estis**, id est attendentes dignitatem ad quam vocati estis, ambuletis secundum quod ei convenit. Si enim quis vocatus esset ad nobile regnum, indignum esset quod faceret opera rusticana. Sic monet Ephesios Apostolus, quasi dicat: vocati estis ut sitis **cives sanctorum et domestici Dei**, ut dictum est supra cap. II, 19, non est ergo dignum ut faciatis opera terrena, nec ut de mundanis curetis. Ideo dicit **digne**, et cetera. Col. I, 10: *ambuletis digne, Deo per omnia placentes*. Phil. I, 27: *digne Evangelio Christi conversamini.* Et quare? Quia *vocavit vos de tenebris in admirabile lumen suum*, I Petr. II, 9.

191. Consequenter cum dicit **cum omni humilitate**, etc., ponit modum suae monitionis, docens quomodo digne poterunt ambulare.

Ponit ergo quatuor virtutes, et excludit quatuor vitia eis opposita. Primum autem vitium quod excludit est superbia. Dum enim unus superbiens vult alii praeesse

189. He stirs them by recalling his chains: *I, a prisoner in the Lord*. With these words he urges them to remain united, giving them three motives. First, a friend sympathizes with a suffering friend and more readily tries to fulfill his wishes so that he might thereby console him. *A friend shall not be known in prosperity, and an enemy shall not be hidden in adversity. In the prosperity of a man, his enemies are grieved; and a friend is known in his adversity* (Sir 12:8–9).

Second, the Apostle himself suffers imprisonment for their own utility. Hence he urges them to remember this, as though he wanted to put them under certain obligations. *Now, whether we be in tribulation, it is for your exhortation and salvation; or whether we be comforted, it is for your consolation; or whether we be exhorted, it is for your exhortation and salvation, which works the enduring of the same sufferings which we also suffer* (2 Cor 1:6).

Third, as was mentioned previously at *my tribulations for you, which is your glory* (Eph 3:13), these sufferings were for the Ephesians' own immense glory. For God exposed his own chosen friends to adversities in behalf of their salvation. Therefore he adds *in the Lord* which means, on account of the Lord. Or, he annexes *in the Lord* since it was the Apostle's glory to be imprisoned, not as a thief or murderer, but as a Christian and for the sake of our Lord Jesus Christ, in accordance with what is written: *and you, O son of man, behold, they shall put bands upon you, and they shall bind you with them: and you shall not go forth from the midst of them* (Ezek 3:25).

190. He also stimulates them by a consideration of the divine blessings: *that you walk worthy of the vocation in which you are called*. That is, you should be attentive to the dignity to which you are summoned, and you ought to behave in a way conformable to it. If someone had been chosen to a rank of nobility in a kingdom, it would be an indignity for him to perform peasant work. Hence the Apostle warns the Ephesians, as though he said: you are called to be *fellow citizens with the saints and domestics of God* (Eph 2:19); henceforth it is unworthy of you to engage in earthly affairs or worry about worldly matters, which is why he says *worthy of the vocation*. *You should walk worthy of God, in all things pleasing* (Col 1:10); *let your conversation be worthy of the Gospel of Christ* (Phil 1:27). And why? Because *he has called you out of darkness into his marvelous light* (1 Pet 2:9).

191. Subsequently, when he says *with all humility and mildness, with patience, supporting one another in charity*, he expresses the way to fulfill his admonition, teaching them how they can behave in a worthy manner.

Four virtues must be cultivated, and their four opposite vices shunned. The first vice which he rejects is pride. When one arrogant person decides to rule others, while the

et alius similiter superbus non vult subesse, causatur dissensio in societate et tollitur pax. Unde Prov. XIII, 10: *inter superbos semper iurgia sunt.* Ad quod excludendum dicit **cum omni humilitate**, scilicet interiori et exteriori. Eccli. III, 20: *quanto magnus es, humilia te in omnibus,* et cetera. Phil. II, 3: *in humilitate superiores invicem arbitrantes.* Iac. IV, 6: *Deus superbis resistit, humilibus autem dat gratiam.*

Secundum est ira. Iracundi enim sunt propinqui ad iniuriam inferendam verbis vel factis, ex quo turbationes oriuntur. Prov. XV, v. 18: *vir iracundus provocat rixas; qui patiens est, mitigat suscitatas.* Ad hoc excludendum dicit **et in mansuetudine**, quae mitigat rixas, et pacem conservat. Prov. III, 34: *mansuetis dabit gratiam.* Ps. XXXVI, 11: *mansueti autem haereditabunt terram.* Eccli. III, 19: *fili, in mansuetudine opera tua perfice, et super gloriam hominum diligeris.*

Tertium est impatientia. Quandoque enim aliquis humilis est et mansuetus in se, abstinens a molestiis inferendis, non tamen patienter sustinet molestias sibi illatas, vel attentatas. Ideo subdit **cum patientia**, scilicet adversorum. Iac. I, 4: *patientia autem opus perfectum habet.* Eccli. II, 4: *in humilitate tua patientiam habet.* Hebr. X, 36: *patientia vobis necessaria est, ut voluntatem Dei facientes,* et cetera.

Quartum inordinatus zelus. Cum enim inordinate zelantes, omnia quae vident iudicant, nec tempus, nec locum servantes, concitatur turbatio in societate. Gal. V, 15: *si mordetis invicem et comeditis, videte ne ab invicem consumamini.* Et ideo dicit **supportantes invicem in caritate**, scilicet mutuo sustinentes defectus aliorum, et hoc ex caritate. Quia quando deficit aliquis, non debet statim corrigi, nisi adsit locus et tempus, sed misericorditer expectari, quia *caritas omnia sustinet,* I Cor. XIII, 7. Non autem debent huiusmodi defectus supportari ex negligentia vel ex consensu et familiaritate, vel carnali amicitia, sed ex caritate. Gal. VI, 2: *alter alterius onera portate,* et cetera. Rom. XV, 1: *debemus nos firmiores imbecillitates infirmorum sustinere.*

192. Consequenter cum dicit **solliciti servare**, etc., ostendit monitionis finem, qui quidem est ut servetur unitas inter fideles.

Circa quod tria facit.

Primo ponit ipsam unitatem, quae est finis;

secundo describit modum unitatis, ibi **in vinculo pacis**;

tertio ponit rationem servandae unitatis, ibi **sicut vocati estis**, et cetera.

193. Dicit ergo primo: dico quod **digne ambuletis**, etc., et hoc faciatis **solliciti servare unitatem Spiritus**. Est autem duplex unitas. Una ad malefaciendum, quae

other proud individuals do not want to submit, dissension arises in the society and peace disappears: *among the proud there are always contentions* (Prov 13:10). To eliminate this he says **with all** interior and exterior **humility**. *The greater you are, humble yourself all the more in all things: and you shall find grace before God* (Sir 3:20); *let nothing be done through contention, neither by vainglory; but in humility, let each esteem others better than themselves* (Phil 2:3). *God resists the proud and gives grace to the humble* (Jas 4:6).

Anger is the second vice. For an angry person is inclined to inflict injury, whether verbal or physical, from which disturbances occur. *A passionate man stirs up strifes: he that is patient appeases those who are stirred up* (Prov 15:18). To discard it he says **and mildness**; this softens arguments and preserves peace. *To the meek he will give grace* (Prov 3:34); *the meek shall inherit the land* (Ps 36:11). *My son, do your works in mildness: and you shall be beloved above the glory of men* (Sir 3:19).

The third is impatience. Occasionally, someone who himself is humble and mild, refraining from causing trouble, nevertheless will not endure patiently the real or attempted wrongs done to himself. Therefore, he adds **with patience** in adversities. *Patience has a perfect work* (Jas 1:4), *in your humiliation keep patience* (Sir 2:4). *For patience is necessary for you; that, doing the will of God, you may receive the promise* (Heb 10: 36).

An inordinate zeal is the fourth vice. Inordinately zealous about everything, men will pass judgment on whatever they see, not waiting for the proper time and place; and a turmoil arises in society. *If you bite and devour one another, take heed that you be not consumed one of another* (Gal 5:15). Hence he says **supporting one another in charity**, mutually bearing with the defects of others out of charity. When someone falls he should not be immediately corrected—unless it is the time and the place for it. With mercy these should be waited for since *charity bears all things* (1 Cor 13:7). Not that these failings are tolerated out of negligence or consent, nor from familiarity or carnal friendship, but from charity. *Bear one another's burdens; and so you shall fulfill the law of Christ* (Gal 6:2). *Now, we that are stronger ought to bear the infirmities of the weak* (Rom 15:1).

192. After this, at **careful to keep**, he shows the purpose of his admonition which is to maintain unity among the faithful.

Concerning this he makes three points:

first, he sets forth the unity itself which is the goal;

second, he describes how the unity is kept, at **in the bond of peace**;

third, he expresses the reason for preserving this unity, at **as you are called**.

193. First of all he remarks: you ought to **walk worthy of your calling** and be **careful to keep the unity of the Spirit**. Two types of unity exist, one whose purpose is to commit

est mala, et potest dici unitas carnis. Eccli. XI, 34: *a scintilla una augetur ignis, et ab uno doloso augetur sanguis.* Alia est unitas spiritus, quae est bona ad faciendum bonum. Ps. CXXXII, 1: *ecce quam bonum et quam iucundum*, et cetera. Io. XVII, 11: *ut sint unum, sicut et nos unum sumus.*

194. Modus autem servandae unitatis est **in vinculo pacis**. Caritas enim est coniunctio animorum. Nulla autem rerum materialium coniunctio stare potest, nisi ligetur aliquo vinculo. Eodem modo nec coniunctio animorum per caritatem stare potest, nisi ligetur; huiusmodi autem verum ligamen est pax, quae, est, secundum Augustinum, tranquillitas modi, speciei et ordinis, quando scilicet unusquisque habet quod suum est. Propter quod dicit **in vinculo pacis**. Ps. CXLVII, v. 14: *qui posuit fines tuos pacem*, et cetera. Quae quidem pax servatur per iustitiam. Is. XXXII, v. 17: *opus iustitiae pax*. Eccli. VI, 26: *ne acedieris vinculis eius.* Et quare? Quia certe, ut dicitur ibidem, *vincula illius alligatura salutis.*

195. Nunc autem, quia in homine est duplex unitas, una scilicet membrorum ad invicem simul ordinatorum, alia corporis et animae tertium constituentium, Apostolus autem loquitur hic de unitate Ecclesiae ad modum unitatis quae est in homine, ideo subiungit **unum corpus**, quasi dicat: ligemini vinculo pacis, ut sitis unum corpus, quantum ad primam unitatem, ut scilicet omnes fideles sint ordinati ad invicem, sicut membra unum corpus constituentia. Rom. XII, 5: *multi unum corpus sumus in Christo*, et cetera. **Et unus spiritus**, quantum ad secundum, ut videlicet unum habeatis spiritualem consensum per unitatem fidei et caritatis.

Vel: **unum corpus** quoad proximum, et **unus spiritus** quoad Deum; quia *qui adhaeret Deo, unus spiritus est*, I Cor. VI, 17.

196. Deinde cum dicit **sicut vocati estis**, etc., subdit rationem huius unitatis. Quia, sicut videmus, quod quando aliqui sunt vocati simul ad aliquid pariter habendum et mutuo percipiendum, solent simul etiam manere et simul ire, ita spiritualiter dicit: quia vos estis vocati ad unum, scilicet finale praemium, ideo debetis simul cum unitate spiritus ambulare **in una spe vocationis vestrae**, id est in unam spem speratam, quae est effectus vocationis. Hebr. III, 1: *fratres, facti vocationis caelestis participes.* I Cor. I, 26: *videte vocationem vestram*, et cetera.

Sed posset aliquis dicere: *quis vocabit nos, et ad quid?* Respondetur I Petr. V, 10: *Deus autem omnis gratiae, qui vocavit nos in aeternam gloriam suam*, etc., ubi est beatitudo vestra. Apoc. XIX, 9: *beati qui ad coenam nuptiarum Agni vocati sunt.*

evil; it is wicked and might be called a unity of the flesh. Of one spark comes a great fire, and of one deceitful man much blood (Sir 11:34). The other is a unity of the spirit; it is good and its purpose is to do good. *Behold how good and how pleasant it is for brethren to dwell together in unity!* (Ps 133:1). *That they may be one, as we also are* (John 17:11).

194. The way to preserve this unity is through **the bond of peace**. For charity is a union of souls. Now the fusion of material objects cannot last unless it is held by some bond. Similarly, the union of souls through love will not endure unless it is bound. Peace proves to be a true bond; that peace which is, according to Augustine, tranquility among measure, form, and order. This is achieved when each possesses what is proper to himself. For this reason he says **in the bond of peace**. *God has placed peace in your borders* (Ps 147:14). Peace in its turn is maintained by justice: *and the work of justice shall be peace* (Isa 32:17). *Be not grieved with her bands* (Sir 6:26). Why? Because *in her is the beauty of life: and her bands are a healthful binding* (Sir 6:29).

195. Now in man there is a twofold unity. The first is the ordered structure of the organs among themselves, the second is the union of the body and the soul constituting a third substance. Because the Apostle speaks of the Church's unity after the fashion of the unity found in man, he adds **one body** as if to say: be united in the bond of peace that you may be one body—regarding the first type of unity, that all the faithful should be ordered among themselves as members making up a single body. *We, being many, are one body in Christ; and every one members one of another* (Rom 12:5). **And one spirit**—referring to the second type of unity, that you might possess a spiritual consensus through the unity of your faith and charity.

Or: **one body** designates a unity with other men, and **one spirit** union with God; because *he who is joined to the Lord is one spirit* (1 Cor 6:17).

196. Next, when he says **as you are called in one hope of your calling** he points out the reason for this unity. We notice that when persons are called together to possess something in common and mutually enjoy it, they usually remain or depart together. Thus, in a spiritual way he says: because you are called to one and the same reality, namely, the final reward, you ought to walk together with a unity of spirit **in the one hope of your calling**, tending toward the one reality you hope for as a result of your vocation. *Wherefore, holy brethren, partakers of the heavenly vocation* (Heb 3:1), *consider your vocation* (1 Cor 1:26).

Someone might ask: *who will call us? And to what?* The response is given: *the God of all grace, who has called us unto his eternal glory in Christ Jesus* (1 Pet 5:10) where your true happiness is. *Blessed are they that are called to the marriage supper of the Lamb* (Rev 19:9).

Lecture 2

^{4:5}Unus Dominus, una fides, unum baptisma. [n. 198]

^{4:6}Unus Deus et Pater omnium, qui est super omnes, et per omnia, et in omnibus nobis. [n. 201]

^{4:5}εἷς κύριος, μία πίστις, ἓν βάπτισμα:

^{4:6}εἷς θεὸς καὶ πατὴρ πάντων, ὁ ἐπὶ πάντων καὶ διὰ πάντων καὶ ἐν πᾶσιν.

^{4:5}One Lord, one faith, one baptism. [n. 198]

^{4:6}One God and Father of all, who is above all, and through all, and in us all. [n. 201]

---

197. Posita eorum exhortatione pro servanda ecclesiastica unitate, in hac parte Apostolus formam dictae unitatis ipsis Ephesiis insinuat. Ubi sciendum est, quod cum Ecclesia Dei sit sicut civitas, est aliquod unum et distinctum, cum non sit unum sicut simplex, sed sicut compositum ex diversis partibus. Et ideo Apostolus duo facit.

Primo ostendit id quod est commune Ecclesiae;

secundo ostendit id quod est distinctum in ipsa, ibi *unicuique autem nostrum data est gratia*, et cetera.

In qualibet autem civitate, ad hoc ut sit una, quatuor debent esse communia, scilicet unus gubernator, una lex, eadem insignia, et idem finis: haec autem quatuor dicit Apostolus esse in Ecclesia.

198. Dicit ergo: dico quod debetis habere *unum corpus et unum spiritum*, quia estis in unitate Ecclesiae, quae est una.

Primo, quia habet ducem unum, scilicet Christum, et quantum ad hoc dicit *unus Dominus*, non plures, pro quorum diversis voluntatibus oporteat vos discordare. Dicitur enim Hebr. III, 6: *Christus est tamquam Filius in domo sua*. Act. II, 36: *certissime ergo sciat omnis domus Israel, quia et Dominum eum et Christum Deus fecit hunc Iesum, quem vos crucifixistis*. I Cor. VIII, 6: *unus Dominus noster Iesus Christus*. Zach. c. XIV, 9: *in illa die erit Dominus unus, et nomen eius unum*.

199. Secundo quia lex eius est una. Lex enim Ecclesiae est lex fidei. Rom. III, v. 27: *ubi est ergo nunc gloriatio tua? Exclusa est. Per quam legem? Factorum? Non, sed per legem fidei*.

Sed *fides* quandoque sumitur pro ipsa re credita, secundum illud: *haec est fides Catholica*, etc., id est, ista debent credi. Quandoque vero sumitur pro habitu fidei, quo creditur in corde. Et de utroque hoc potest dici.

De primo, ut sit sensus *una est fides*, id est, idem iubemini credere et eodem modo operari, quia unum et idem est quod creditur a cunctis fidelibus, unde universalis seu Catholica dicitur. Unde I Cor. I, 10: *idipsum dicatis*, id est sentiatis, *omnes*, et cetera.

197. After he has exhorted them to secure ecclesial unity, the Apostle offers the Ephesians, in this section, a glimpse of this unity's pattern. Since the Church of God is likened to a city, it is one and distinct, although this unity is not uncomposed but composed of different parts. Thus the Apostle does two things:

first, he shows what is common in the Church;

second, he shows what is distinctive to each member in her, at *but to every one of us is given grace* (Eph 4:7).

The solidarity of any city demands the presence of four common elements: one governor, one law, the same symbols, and a common goal. The Apostle affirms that these are present in the Church also.

198. Hence, he says: you ought to have *one body and one spirit* (Eph 4:4) since you belong to the one unified Church.

First, she has one leader, Christ. Obeying *one Lord*, not many, conflicts do not arise from trying to comply with divergent commands. For it is written: *Christ is as the Son in his own house* (Heb 3:6). *Therefore let all the house of Israel know most certainly that God has made both Lord and Christ, this same Jesus, whom you have crucified* (Acts 2:36). *There are many lords; yet to us there is but one God, the Father, of whom are all things . . . and one Lord Jesus Christ, by whom are all things* (1 Cor 8:5–6). *And the Lord shall be king over all the earth. In that day there shall be one Lord, and his name shall be one* (Zech 14:9).

199. Second, her law is one. For the law of the Church is the law of faith: *where then is your boasting? It is excluded. By what law? Of works? No, but by the law of faith* (Rom 3:27).

Faith is sometimes applied to the reality believed in, as with *this is the Catholic faith*, meaning this is what must be believed. At other times, *faith* refers to the habit of faith by which a man believes what he must in his very heart. Faith in both these senses can be called one.

In the former, *one faith* would mean that you are bidden to believe in the same truths and in the same way of acting. For what is believed by all the faithful is one and the same reality, hence their faith is termed Catholic or universal. *Now I beseech you, brethren, by the name of our Lord Jesus Christ, that you all speak*, that is, think, *the same thing and that there be no schisms among you; but that you be perfect in the same mind and in the same judgment* (1 Cor 1:10).

Alio modo *una est fides*, id est unus habitus fidei quo creditur; una, inquam, non numero, sed specie, quia idem debet esse in corde omnium; et hoc modo idem volentium dicitur una voluntas.

200. Tertio eadem sunt insignia Ecclesiae, scilicet sacramenta Christi, inter quae primum baptisma, quod est ianua omnium aliorum. Et ideo dicit *unum baptisma*.

Dicitur autem unum triplici ratione. Primo quia Baptismata non differunt secundum baptizantes; quia a quocumque conferantur, uniformem virtutem habent, quia qui baptizat interius, unus est, scilicet Christus. Io. I, v. 33: *super quem videris Spiritum descendentem, et manentem super eum, hic est qui baptizat in Spiritu Sancto*.

Secundo dicitur unum, quia datur in nomine unius, scilicet Trinitatis. *Baptizantes eos in nomine Patris, et Filii, et Spiritus Sancti*.

Tertio quia iterari non potest. Poenitentia autem, matrimonium, Eucharistia, et extrema unctio, iterari possunt, non autem Baptismus. Hebr. VI, 4: *impossibile est eos qui semel sunt illuminati*, scilicet per baptismum, *gustaverunt autem donum caeleste, et participes facti sunt Spiritus Sancti, gustaverunt nihilominus bonum Dei verbum virtutesque saeculi venturi, et prolapsi sunt*, scilicet per peccatum, *renovari rursus ad poenitentiam*. Non iteratur autem vel propter characterem, vel quia causa eius non iteratur. Rom. VI, 4: *consepulti enim sumus cum illo per baptismum in mortem*, et cetera. Nunc autem *Christus semel pro peccatis mortuus est*, ut dicitur I Petr. III, 18.

201. Quarto in Ecclesia est idem finis, qui est Deus. Filius enim ducit nos ad Patrem. I Cor. XV, 24: *cum tradiderit regnum Deo et Patri, cum evacuaverit omnem principatum, et potestatem, et virtutem, oportet autem illum regnare*, et cetera. Et quantum ad hoc subiungit, dicens *unus Deus*, etc., ubi

primo, ponit apostolus eius unitatem;

secundo eius dignitatem, ibi *qui est super omnes*, et cetera.

202. Circa primum duo dicit: primum pertinet ad naturam divinam; unde dicit *unus Deus*. Deut. VI, 4: *audi, Israel, Dominus Deus tuus unus est*. Aliud pertinet ad eius benevolentiam ad nos et ad pietatem; unde dicit *et Pater omnium*. Is. LXIII, 16: *tu, Domine, Pater noster, et redemptor noster*. Mal. II, 10: *numquid non Pater unus omnium nostrum? Numquid non Deus creavit nos?*

203. Dignitatem autem eius commendat ex tribus. Ex altitudine divinitatis, cum dicit *qui est super omnes*. Ps. CXII, 4: *super omnes gentes Dominus*, et cetera. Ex amplitudine eius potestatis, cum dicit *per omnia*. Ier. c. XXXIII, 24: *caelum et terram ego impleo*, et

In the second way, *one faith* designates the unity of the habit of faith by which all believe. I mean that it is specifically one—not numerically one—since the same faith is present in each one's heart; just as when many persons want the same thing, they are said to be of one will.

200. Third, the Church shares the same symbols. They are Christ's sacraments, of which baptism is the first and the entrance to the rest. Hence he says *one baptism*.

Three reasons account for this unity. First, baptisms do not differ by reason of who administers them. No matter who performs the rites they possess an unvaried power because he who baptizes interiorly is one, namely, Christ. *He upon whom you shall see the Spirit descending and remaining upon him, he it is that baptizes with the Holy Spirit* (John 1:33).

Second, baptism is one since it is conferred in the name of the one Triune God: *baptizing them in the name of the Father and of the Son and of the Holy Spirit* (Matt 28:19).

The third reason is that it cannot be repeated. The sacraments of penance, matrimony, the Eucharist and last anointing may be repeated, but not baptism. *For it is impossible for those who were once illuminated*, by baptism, *have tasted also the heavenly gift and were made partakers of the Holy Spirit, have moreover tasted the good word of God and the powers of the world to come, and are fallen away*, through sins, *to be renewed again to penance* (Heb 6:4–6). It is not repeated, either by reason of the sacramental character it imparts, or because its cause is not repeated: *for we are buried together with him by baptism into death; that, as Christ is risen from the dead by the glory of the Father, so we also may walk in newness of life* (Rom 6:4). And *Christ also died for sins once for all* (1 Pet 3:18).

201. Fourth, the Church has the same goal, which is God. The Son leads us to the Father: *when he shall have delivered up the kingdom to God and the Father; when he shall have brought to naught all principality and power and virtue* (1 Cor 15:24). In reference to this the Apostle adds *one God and Father of all*:

first, he mentions his unity;

second, his dignity, at *who is above all*.

202. Regarding the first he has two remarks. One pertains to the divine nature; he says there is *one God*: *hear, O Israel: the Lord our God is one Lord* (Deut 6:4). The other has to do with his kindness to us and our piety; whence he says *Father of all*: *you, O Lord, are our Father, our redeemer: from everlasting is your name* (Isa 63:16); *Have we not all one Father? Has not one God created us?* (Mal 2:10).

203. He extols Gods dignity on three scores. The divine majesty *who is above all*: *the Lord is high above all nations; and his glory above the heavens* (Ps 113:4). His power which extends *through all*: *do I not fill heaven and earth? says the Lord* (Jer 23:24). *You have subjected all things under his feet*

cetera. Ps. VIII, 8: *omnia subiecisti sub pedibus*, et cetera. Lc. X, 22: *omnia mihi quippe tradita sunt*, quippe quia *omnia per ipsum facta sunt*, Io. I, 3. Sed modo quo dicitur Sap. XI, 21: *omnia in numero, et pondere, et mensura disposuisti*. Ex largitate gratiae, cum dicit **et in omnibus nobis**, scilicet per gratiam. Ier. XIV, 9: *tu autem in nobis es, Domine*, et cetera.

Sed primum appropriatur Patri, qui est fontale principium divinitatis et omnes creaturas excellit. Secundum Filio, qui est sapientia *attingens a fine usque ad finem fortiter*, Sap. VIII, 1. Tertium vero Spiritui Sancto, qui *replet orbem terrarum*, Sap. I, 7.

(Ps 8:8). *All things are delivered to me* (Luke 10:22) since *all things were made by him* (John 1:3). It is indicated how this is accomplished: *you have ordered all things in measure, and number, and weight. For great power always belonged to you alone: and who shall resist the strength of your arm?* (Wis 11:21) Finally, there is the abundance of his grace **in us all**: *you, O Lord, are among us, and your name is called upon by us* (Jer 14:9).

Majesty is appropriated to the Father who is the source and principle in the divinity, exceeding the whole of creation. Power is appropriated to the Son who is that wisdom which *reaches from end to end mightily* (Wis 8:1). Grace is appropriated to the Holy Spirit who *has filled the whole world* (Wis 1:7).

Lecture 3

⁴:⁷Unicuique autem nostrum data est gratia secundum mensuram donationis Christi. [n. 205]

⁴:⁸Propter quod dicit: *ascendens in altum, captivam duxit captivitatem: dedit dona hominibus.* [n. 206]

⁴:⁹Quod autem ascendit, quid est, nisi quia et descendit primum in inferiores partes terrae? [n. 207]

⁴:¹⁰Qui descendit, ipse est et qui ascendit super omnes caelos, ut impleret omnia. [n. 209]

⁴:⁷Ἑνὶ δὲ ἑκάστῳ ἡμῶν ἐδόθη ἡ χάρις κατὰ τὸ μέτρον τῆς δωρεᾶς τοῦ Χριστοῦ.

⁴:⁸διὸ λέγει, Ἀναβὰς εἰς ὕψος ᾐχμαλώτευσεν αἰχμαλωσίαν, ἔδωκεν δόματα τοῖς ἀνθρώποις.

⁴:⁹{τὸ δὲ Ἀνέβη τί ἐστιν εἰ μὴ ὅτι καὶ κατέβη εἰς τὰ κατώτερα [μέρη] τῆς γῆς;

⁴:¹⁰ὁ καταβὰς αὐτός ἐστιν καὶ ὁ ἀναβὰς ὑπεράνω πάντων τῶν οὐρανῶν, ἵνα πληρώσῃ τὰ πάντα.}

⁴:⁷But to every one of us is given grace, according to the measure of the giving of Christ. [n. 205]

⁴:⁸Wherefore he says: *ascending on high, he led captivity captive: he gave gifts to men.* [n. 206]

⁴:⁹Now, that he ascended, what is it, except that he also descended first into the lower parts of the earth? [n. 207]

⁴:¹⁰He that descended is the same also that ascended above all the heavens: that he might fill all things. [n. 209]

---

204. Supra ostendit Apostolus ecclesiasticam unitatem quantum ad id quod in Ecclesia est commune, hic idem ostendit quantum ad hoc quod singulis fidelibus membris Ecclesiae est proprium et speciale.

Circa quod tria facit:
primo proponit distinctionem;
secundo inducit ad hoc auctoritatem, ibi **propter quod dicit**, etc.;
tertio ponit auctoritatis expositionem, ibi **quod autem ascendit**, et cetera.

205. Dicit ergo: habemus in Ecclesia unum Deum, unam fidem, etc., sed tamen diversas gratias diversis particulariter collatas habemus, quia **unicuique nostrum data est gratia**, quasi dicat: nullus nostrum est qui non sit particeps divinae gratiae et communionis. Io. I, 16: *de plenitudine eius omnes accepimus gratiam pro gratia*.

Sed certe ista gratia non est data omnibus uniformiter seu aequaliter, sed **secundum mensuram donationis Christi**, id est secundum quod Christus est dator, et eam singulis mensuravit. Rom. XII, 6: *habentes donationes secundum gratiam quae data est nobis differentes*.

Haec differentia non est ex fato, nec a casu, nec ex merito, sed ex donatione Christi, id est secundum quod Christus nobis commensuravit. Ipse enim solus recepit Spiritum non ad mensuram, Io. III, 34, caeteri autem sancti ad mensuram recipiunt. Rom. XII, 3: *unicuique sicut Deus divisit mensuram fidei*. I Cor. III, 8: *unusquisque propriam mercedem accipiet*, et cetera. Matth. XXV, 15: *unicuique secundum propriam virtutem*, et cetera. Quia sicut in potestate Christi est dare vel non dare, ita dare tantum vel minus.

206. Sequitur **propter quod dicit**, et cetera. Hic ponit quamdam auctoritatem assumptam de Ps. LXVII, 19, et

204. Previously the Apostle dealt with ecclesial unity in the perspective of what is common within the Church, and now he manifests this same unity from the viewpoint of what is personal and specific to each of the faithful members of the Church.

Concerning this he makes three points:
first, he points out the fact of distinctions;
second, he introduces an authority for them, at **wherefore he says**;
third, he explains this authoritative quotation, at **now that he ascended**.

205. He states: we have in the Church one God, one faith, one baptism. Nonetheless, each of us has the diverse graces especially granted to him—**to every one of us is given grace**. As though he said: none of us lack a share in divine grace and communion, for *of his fullness we all have received; and grace for grace* (John 1:16).

This grace, however, is certainly not bestowed on everyone uniformly and equally but **according to the measure of the giving of Christ**. Christ is the donor who metes out the grace to each, who have *different gifts according to the grace that is given us* (Rom 12:6).

The variation does not spring from fate or chance, nor from merit, but from the giving of Christ; that is, according as Christ allots it to us. Only he has received the Spirit without measure (John 3:34); the rest of the saints obtain it in a limited degree, *according as God has divided to every one the measure of faith* (Rom 12:3). *And every man shall receive his own reward, according to his own labor* (1 Cor 3:8). Again, *to one he gave five talents, and to another two, and to another one, to every one according to his proper ability* (Matt 25:15). Just as it is in Christ's power to give or not, so he can grant more or less.

206. **Wherefore he says** introduces an authoritative text from Psalm 67:19 supporting **according to the measure of**

refertur ad hoc quod dixit **secundum mensuram donationis Christi**; ubi tria facit. Primo commemorat Christi ascensionem; secundo humani generis liberationem; tertio ponit donorum spiritualium collationem. Partes consequuntur se.

Ostendit ergo primum, dicens sic: **propter quod**, scilicet significandum, **dicit**, scilicet propheta David in Ps. LXVII, 19: *ascendens Christus in altum*, et cetera. Mich. II, 13: *ascendit ante eos pandens iter*, et cetera. Iob XXXIX, 18: *in altum alas erigit*, et cetera. Ascendens, inquam, sed non solus, quia **captivam duxit captivitatem**, eos scilicet quos diabolus captivaverat. Humanum enim genus captivatum erat, et sancti in caritate decedentes, qui meruerant gloriam, in captivitate diaboli detinebantur quasi captivi in Limbo. Is. V, 13: *ductus est captivus populus meus*, et cetera. Hanc ergo captivitatem Christus liberavit, et secum duxit in caelum. Is. XLIX, 24 s.: *numquid tolletur a forti praeda, aut quod captum fuerit a robusto salvabitur, ac salvum poterit esse? Quia haec dicit Dominus: equidem et captivitas a forti tolletur, et quod ablatum fuerit a robusto, salvabitur.*

Sed certe hoc non verificatur solum quantum ad iam mortuos, sed etiam quantum ad viventes, qui captivi tenebantur sub peccato, quos, a peccato liberans, *servos fecit iustitiae*, ut dicitur Rom. VI, 18, et sic quodammodo eos in captivitatem duxit, non ad perniciem sed ad salutem. Lc. V, 10: *ex hoc iam homines eris capiens.*

Non solum autem homines a diaboli captivitate eripuit, et suae servituti subiecit, sed etiam eos spiritualibus bonis dotavit. Unde subditur **dedit dona hominibus**, scilicet gratiae et gloriae. Ps. LXXXIII, 12: *gratiam et gloriam dabit Dominus.* II Petr. I, 4: *per quem et pretiosa nobis promissa donavit*, et cetera.

Nec est contrarium quod in littera praecedenti dicitur *accepit dona in hominibus*, quia certe ipse dedit ut Deus et accepit ut homo in fidelibus, sicut in membris suis. Dedit in caelo sicut Deus, et accepit in terra secundum modum loquendi quo dicitur Matth. c. XXV, 40: *quod uni ex minimis meis fecistis, mihi fecistis.*

207. Deinde cum dicit **quod autem ascendit**, etc., exponit propositam auctoritatem, et

primo quantum ad ascensionem;

secundo quantum ad materiam donationis, ibi **et ipse dedit**, et cetera.

Circa primum duo facit.

Primo ostendit quomodo descendit, ibi **qui descendit**;

secundo quomodo ascendit, ibi **qui ascendit**, et cetera.

208. Circa primum considerandum, quod cum Christus vere sit Deus, inconveniens videbatur quod sibi

the giving of Christ. Three points are made. First, it speaks of Christ's ascension; second, of mankind's liberation; third, of the bestowal of spiritual gifts. Each of these will follow in order.

He refers to the ascension saying: **wherefore** to signify this the prophet David **says: 'ascending on high'** (Ps 68:18). *For he shall go up that shall open the way before them.* (Mic 2:13). Christ *sets up his wings on high* (Job 39:18). He ascends, I say, but not alone because **he led captivity captive**, that is, those whom the devil had captured. For the human race was imprisoned; the saints who had died in love, and so merited eternal glory, were held like prisoners by the devil in limbo. *My people led away captive because they had not knowledge* (Isa 5:13). Christ liberated these prisoners and brought them with himself to heaven. *Shall the prey be taken from the strong? Or can that which was taken by the mighty be delivered? For thus says the Lord: yes truly. Even the captivity shall be taken away from the strong: and that which was taken by the mighty shall be delivered* (Isa 49:24–25).

Indeed, this is not only true of those already dead; it also applies to the living. Held under sin's bondage, Christ made men the *slaves of justice* (Rom 6:18) in delivering them from sin. Thus in some way he led men captive not unto destruction but salvation. *From henceforth you shall catch men* (Luke 5:10).

Besides rescuing men from a diabolical slavery and placing them in his own service, he has enriched them spiritually. Hence he adds **he gave gifts** of grace and glory **to men**. *For God loves mercy and truth; the Lord will give grace and glory* (Ps 84:11). *By whom he has given us most great and precious promises, that by these you may be made partakers of the divine nature* (2 Pet 1:4).

This version does not contradict the reading which has: *he received gifts in men.* Clearly, he as God bestows the gifts which he as man receives in the faithful who are his members. In heaven he gives, since he is God, while on earth he accepts what is given in the manner described: *as long as you did it to one of these my least brethren, you did it to me* (Matt 25:40).

207. Next, at **now, that he ascended**, he comments on the authority:

first, in reference to the ascension;

second, regarding what is given men, at **and he gave some** (Eph 4:11).

He does two things concerning the first:

first, he shows how he descended, at **he that descended**;

second, how he ascended, at **that ascended**.

208. In reflecting upon the first point, it appears improper for Christ, who is true God, to lower himself, since

conveniret descendere, quia nihil est Deo sublimius. Et ideo ad hanc dubitationem excludendam subdit Apostolus *quod autem ascendit quid est, nisi quia et descendit primum*, et cetera. Ac si diceret: ideo postea dixi quod ascendit, quia ipse primo descenderat, ut ascenderet: aliter enim ascendere non potuisset.

Quomodo autem descendit, subdit, dicens quia *in inferiores partes terrae*. Quod potest intelligi dupliciter. Uno modo ut per inferiores partes terrae intelligantur istae partes terrae, in quibus nos habitamus, quae dicuntur inferiores, eo quod sunt infra caelum et aerem. In has autem partes terrae dicitur descendisse Filius Dei, non motu locali, sed assumptione inferioris et terrenae naturae, secundum illud Phil. II, 7: *exinanivit semetipsum*, et cetera. Alio modo potest intelligi de Inferno, qui etiam infra nos est. Illuc enim descendit dominus secundum animam, ut inde sanctos liberaret. Et sic videtur hoc eis convenire quod dixerat: *captivam duxit captivitatem*. Zach. IX, 11: *tu quoque in sanguine testamenti tui eduxisti vinctos tuos de lacu, in quo non erat aqua*. Apoc. X, 1: *vidi alium angelum fortem descendentem de caelo*, et cetera. Ex. III, 7: *vidi afflictionem populi mei qui est in Aegypto*, etc.; et sequitur: *et descendi liberare eum*.

209. Deinde cum dicit *qui descendit*, etc., manifestat eius ascensionem quantum ad tria. Primo quantum ad personam ascendentis, cum dicit *qui descendit, ipse est qui ascendit*, et cetera. In quo designatur unitas personae Dei et hominis. Descendit enim, sicut dictum est, Filius Dei assumendo humanam naturam, ascendit autem Filius hominis secundum humanam naturam ad vitae immortalis sublimitatem. Et sic est idem Filius Dei qui descendit et Filius hominis qui ascendit. Io. c. III, 13: *nemo ascendit in caelum, nisi qui descendit de caelo Filius hominis, qui est in caelo*. Ubi notatur quod humiles, qui voluntarie descendunt, spiritualiter Deo sublimiter ascendunt, quia *qui se humiliat, exaltabitur*, Lc. XIV, 11.

Secundo ostendit terminum ascensionis, cum dicit *super omnes caelos*. Ps. LXVII, 34: *qui ascendit super omnes caelos ad orientem*. Nec solum intelligendum est quod ascenderit super omnes caelos corporales, sed etiam super omnem spiritualem creaturam. Supra c. I, 20: *constituens illum ad dexteram suam in caelestibus super omnem principatum, et potestatem, et virtutem, et dominationem, et omne nomen quod nominatur*, et cetera.

Tertio ponit ascensionis fructum, cum dicit *ut adimpleret omnia*, id est omne genus hominum spiritualibus donis repleret. Ps. LXIV, 5: *replebimur in bonis domus tuae*. Eccli. XXIV, 26: *a generationibus meis adimplemini*. Vel *adimpleret*, id est ut ad effectum perduceret, *omnia*

nothing is more eminent than God. To remove any doubts on this score the Apostle asserts, *now, that he ascended, what is it, except that he also descended first*. As if he would say: for this reason do I first mention that he ascended and only afterward that he descended; he descended in order that he might ascend. For otherwise he could not have ascended.

How he descended is shown in *into the lower parts of the earth*, which can be interpreted in two ways. In one, the lower regions are understood as those parts of the earth we inhabit. It is lower than the heavens and the atmosphere. The Son of God came down to these sections of the earth, not by any local movement, but by assuming a lowly, terrestrial nature; according to what is written: *he emptied himself, taking the form of a servant, being made in the likeness of men, and in habit found as a man* (Phil 2:7). In the second way it can be understood as referring to hell, which is even below us. He descended thither in his soul that he might free the saints from it. This seems to agree with what he said above: *he led captivity captive*. *You also, by the blood of your testament, have sent forth your prisoners out of the pit wherein is no water* (Zech 9:11). *I saw another mighty angel come down from heaven* (Rev 10:1). *I have seen the affliction of my people in Egypt, and I have heard their cry . . . and knowing their sorrow, I have come down to deliver them* (Exod 3:7–8).

209. Next, at *he that descended*, three aspects of the ascension are discussed. First, *he that descended is the same also that ascended* indicates the person who ascends. It affirms the unity of person, the divine and the human. For he who descended, as was said, is the Son of God taking on human nature. He who ascends is the Son of man, ascending in his human nature to the sublimity of immortal life. Thus the Son of God who descended and the Son of man who ascended are identical: *and no man has ascended into heaven, but he that descended from heaven, the Son of man who is in heaven* (John 3:13). Notice too how the humble who voluntarily lower themselves, spiritually ascend to the grandeur of God: *he that humbles himself shall be exalted* (Luke 14:11).

Second, *above all the heavens* denotes the destination of the ascension. *He ascends above the heaven of heavens, to the east* (Ps 68:33). This should not be understood simply in reference to an ascension above the physical heavens, but also above every spiritual creature. God has set Christ *on his right hand in the heavenly places. Above all principality and power and virtue and dominion and every name that is named, not only in this world, but also in that which is to come* (Eph 1:20–21).

Third, the fruitful outcome of the ascension is *that he might fill all things*, bestowing spiritual gifts on every race of men. *We shall be filled with the good things of your house* (Ps 65:4); *come over to me, all that desire me, and be filled with my fruits* (Sir 24:26). Or, *that he might fulfill*,

quae de ipso erant scripta. Lc. ult.: *oportet impleri omnia quae scripta sunt in lege et prophetis et psalmis de me.*

that is, put into effect **all things** written concerning himself: *all things need to be fulfilled which are written in the law of Moses and in the prophets and in the psalms, concerning me* (Luke 24:44).

Lecture 4

⁴:¹¹Et ipse dedit quosdam quidem apostolos, quosdam autem prophetas, alios vero evangelistas, alios autem pastores et doctores, [n. 211]	⁴:¹¹καὶ αὐτὸς ἔδωκεν τοὺς μὲν ἀποστόλους, τοὺς δὲ προφήτας, τοὺς δὲ εὐαγγελιστάς, τοὺς δὲ ποιμένας καὶ διδασκάλους,	⁴:¹¹And he gave some apostles, and some prophets, and others evangelists, and others pastors and doctors: [n. 211]
⁴:¹²ad consummationem sanctorum in opus ministerii, in aedificationem corporis Christi: [n. 213]	⁴:¹²πρὸς τὸν καταρτισμὸν τῶν ἁγίων εἰς ἔργον διακονίας, εἰς οἰκοδομὴν τοῦ σώματος τοῦ Χριστοῦ,	⁴:¹²For the perfecting of the saints, for the work of the ministry, for the edifying of the body of Christ: [n. 213]
⁴:¹³donec occurramus omnes in unitatem fidei, et agnitionis Filii Dei, in virum perfectum, in mensuram aetatis plenitudinis Christi: [n. 215]	⁴:¹³μέχρι καταντήσωμεν οἱ πάντες εἰς τὴν ἑνότητα τῆς πίστεως καὶ τῆς ἐπιγνώσεως τοῦ υἱοῦ τοῦ θεοῦ, εἰς ἄνδρα τέλειον, εἰς μέτρον ἡλικίας τοῦ πληρώματος τοῦ Χριστοῦ,	⁴:¹³Until we all meet into the unity of faith and of the knowledge of the Son of God, unto a perfect man, unto the measure of the age of the fullness of Christ: [n. 215]

210. Hic exponit Apostolus quod supra dixerat de donatione donorum.

Circa quod duo facit.

Primo ostendit quod Dominus singulis fidelibus dedit donorum diversitatem;

secundo ostendit illorum donorum fructum et utilitatem, ibi *ad consummationem sanctorum*, et cetera.

211. Et quia per dona Christi diversi status et munera in Ecclesia designantur, considerandum est quod, inter dona Christi, primo ponit apostolos. Unde dicit *et ipse dedit quosdam quidem apostolos*. Lc. VI, 13: *elegit ex ipsis quos et apostolos nominavit*. I Cor. XII, 28: *quosdam quidem posuit in Ecclesia: primum apostolos, secundo prophetas, tertio doctores, quarto virtutes*.

Apostoli primo loco ponuntur, quia ipsi privilegiati fuerunt in omnibus donis Christi. Habuerunt enim plenitudinem gratiae et sapientiae, quidam quantum ad revelationem divinorum mysteriorum. Lc. ult.: *aperuit eis sensum ut intelligerent*, et cetera. Mc. c. IV, 11: *vobis datum est nosse mysterium regni Dei*, et cetera. Io. XV, 15: *omnia quae audivi a Patre meo, nota feci vobis*. Habuerunt etiam copiam eloquentiae ad annuntiandum Evangelium. Lc. XXI, 15: *dabo vobis os et sapientiam, cui non poterunt resistere, et contradicere omnes adversarii vestri*. Mc. ult.: *euntes in mundum universum, praedicate*, et cetera. Habuerunt etiam praerogativam auctoritatis et potentiae quantum ad curam Dominici gregis. Io. ult.: *pasce oves meas*. I Cor. X: *de potestate nostra quam dedit nobis Deus in aedificationem, non in destructionem vestram*, et cetera.

212. Ideo Apostolus subiungit hic tres gradus ecclesiasticos secundum participationem singulorum praemissorum. Nam quantum ad revelationem divinorum mysteriorum, subdit *quosdam autem prophetas*, qui praenuntiatores fuerunt Incarnationis Christi, de quibus

210. Here the Apostle expounds what was mentioned earlier about the bestowal of gifts.

Concerning this he makes two points:

first, he shows that the Lord has imparted a variety of gifts on each of the faithful;

second, he indicates the utility and fruitfulness of these gifts, at *for the perfecting of the saints*.

211. The many different states and functions in the Church are designated as the gifts of Christ. Consider how, among the gifts of Christ, the apostles are conceded the first place: *and he gave some apostles*. And he chose twelve of them whom also he named apostles (Luke 6:13). *God indeed has set some in the Church; first apostles, second prophets, third doctors; after that miracles* (1 Cor 12:28).

Apostles are put first because they had a privileged share in all of Christ's gifts. They possessed a plenitude of grace and wisdom regarding the revelation of divine mysteries. Christ *opened their understanding that they might understand the Scriptures* (Luke 24:45). *To you it is given to know the mystery of the kingdom of God* (Mark 4:11). *Because all things, whatsoever I have heard of my Father, I have made known to you* (John 15:15). They also possessed an ample ability to speak convincingly in order to proclaim the Gospel. *I will give you a mouth and wisdom, which all your adversaries shall not be able to resist and gainsay* (Luke 21:15). *Go unto the whole world and preach the Gospel to every creature* (Mark 16:15). Moreover, they also had a privileged authority and power for looking after the Lord's flock. *Feed my sheep* (John 21:17). *For if also I should boast somewhat more of our power, which the Lord has given us unto edification and not for your destruction, I should not be ashamed* (2 Cor 10:8).

212. Therefore, the Apostle adds three ecclesiastical categories according as they share in each of the foregoing. Related to the revelation of divine mysteries he annexes *and some prophets* who foretold the Incarnation of Christ. Of them it is written: *of which salvation the prophets*

dicitur I Petr. I, 10: *prophetae qui de futura in vobis gloria prophetaverunt*. Matth. XI, 13: *omnes enim prophetae, et lex usque ad Ioannem prophetaverunt*. Sed Apostoli prophetantes fuerunt post adventum Christi gaudia vitae futurae. Apoc. I, 3: *beatus qui legit et qui audit verba prophetiae huius*, et cetera. Item fuerunt exponentes antiquorum prophetarum prophetias. I Cor. XIV, 1: *aemulamini spiritualia; magis autem ut prophetetis*. Matth. XXV: *ecce ego mitto ad vos prophetas et sapientes*, et cetera.

Quantum vero ad annuntiandum Evangelium, subdit *alios vero evangelistas*, qui scilicet habent officium praedicandi Evangelium, vel etiam conscribendi, quamvis non essent de principalibus apostolis. Rom. X, 15: *quam speciosi pedes evangelizantium pacem*, et cetera. Is. XLI, 27: *dabo Ierusalem evangelistam*.

Quantum vero ad curam Ecclesiae subdit *alios autem pastores*, curam scilicet Dominici gregis habentes. Et sub eodem addit *et doctores*, ad ostendendum quod proprium officium pastorum Ecclesiae est docere ea quae pertinent ad fidem et bonos mores. Dispensare autem temporalia non pertinet ad episcopos, qui sunt apostolorum successores, sed magis ad diaconos. Act. VI, 2: *non est aequum nos derelinquere verbum Dei, et ministrare mensis*. Tit. I, 9: *amplectentem eum qui secundum doctrinam est, fidelem sermonem*. Dicitur de episcopis Ier. III, 15: *dabo vobis pastores iuxta cor meum, et pascent vos scientia et doctrina*.

213. Deinde cum dicit *ad consummationem sanctorum*, etc., ostendit fructum praedictorum donorum seu officiorum. Et

circa hoc duo facit, quia

primo assignat fructum;

secundo ostendit qualiter fideles ad hunc fructum possent advenire, ibi *ut iam non simus parvuli*, et cetera.

Prima iterum in duas.

Primo proponit effectum proximum;

secundo ostendit fructum ultimum, ibi *donec occurramus omnes*, et cetera.

214. Effectus autem proximus praedictorum donorum seu officiorum, potest attendi quantum ad tria. Uno modo quantum ad ipsos qui sunt in officiis constituti, quibus ad hoc sunt collata dona spiritualia, ut ministrarent Deo et proximis. Et quantum ad hoc dicit *in opus ministerii*, per quod scilicet procuratur honor Dei, et salus proximorum. I Cor. IV, 1: *sic nos existimet homo ut ministros Christi*, et cetera. Is. LXI, 6: *ministri Dei, dicetur vobis*.

have inquired and diligently searched, who prophesied of the glory to come in you (1 Pet 1:10). *For all the prophets and the law prophesied until John* (Matt 11:13). But after Christ came, the apostles became the prophets of the joy of the life to come. *Blessed is he that reads and hears the words of this prophecy, and keeps those things which are written in it; for the time is at hand* (Rev 1:3). They also became the interpreters of what the ancient prophets had foretold. *Be zealous for spiritual gifts; but rather that you may prophesy* (1 Cor 14:1). *Behold I send to you prophets and wise men and scribes* (Matt 23:34).

Relative to the proclamation of the Gospel he adds *others evangelists*. They had the duty of preaching the good news, and even of writing it down although they were not among the principal apostles. *How beautiful are the feet of them that preach the Gospel of peace, of them that bring glad tidings of good things!* (Rom 10:15). *To Jerusalem I will give an evangelist* (Isa 41:27).

In reference to the care of the Church he says *and others pastors* who are responsible for the Lord's flock. Under the same heading he adds *and doctors* to bring out how the pastor's specific task in the Church is to instruct the people in what pertains to faith and good conduct. The administration of temporalities does not belong to bishops, who are the successors of the apostles, but rather to deacons. *It is not reasonable that we should leave the word of God, and serve tables* (Acts 6:2). *Embracing that faithful word which is according to doctrine, that he may be able to exhort in sound doctrine* (Titus 1:9). Concerning bishops it is written: *I will give you pastors according to my own heart, and they shall feed you with knowledge and doctrine* (Jer 3:15).

213. Next, at *for the perfecting of the saints*, he discloses the fruitful results of these gifts or functions.

Concerning this he does two things:

first, he speaks of their fruit;

second, he explains how the faithful may attain to this fruit, at *so that we may no longer be children*.

The first section has two divisions also:

first, he sets down their immediate result;

second, he indicates their ultimate fruit, at *until we all meet*.

214. The proximate effects of the above mentioned gifts or functions are threefold. The first is in reference to those who are placed in these functions; spiritual gifts are communicated to them that they might be at the service of God and their fellow man. Thus he states *for the work of the ministry* which offers honor to God and salvation to one's fellow men. *Let a man so account of us as of the ministers of Christ and the dispensers of the mysteries of God* (1 Cor 4:1). *You shall be called the priests of the Lord; to you it shall be said: you ministers of our God* (Isa 61:6).

The second is in reference to the perfection of those who already believe; so he says for **the perfecting of the saints**, that is, of those already sanctified through faith in Christ. Prelates must be especially anxious to lead those entrusted to them toward the state of perfection. This is why Dionysius claims, in his *Ecclesiastica Hierarchia*, that they are to be all the more perfect. *Wherefore, leaving the word of the beginning of Christ, let us go on to things more perfect; not laying again the foundation of penance from dead works and of faith towards God* (Heb 6:1). *The consumption abridged shall overflow with justice. For the Lord God of hosts shall make a consumption, and an abridgment in the midst of all the land* (Isa 10:22).

The third is in reference to the conversion of the unbelievers. About this he states **for the edifying of the body of Christ**. When the infidels are converted, Christ's Church—which is his body—is built up. Whoever preaches *speaks to men unto edification and exhortation and comfort* (1 Cor 14:3). *For greater is he that prophesies than he that speaks with tongues; unless perhaps he interpret, that the Church may receive edification . . . so you also, forasmuch as you are zealous of spirits, seek to abound unto the edifying of the Church* (1 Cor 14:5, 12).

215. At **until we all meet**, he goes on to discuss the ultimate fruit of the Church's preaching which can be understood in two ways.

One way is concerning the absolutely ultimate effect: the resurrection of the saints. In this perspective two facts are asserted. First is the spiritual and corporeal convergence of all who have risen. The physical convergence will consist in this, that all the saints will be drawn together toward Christ: *wheresoever the body shall be, there shall the eagles also be gathered together* (Matt 24:28). Concerning this he says **until we all meet**, as if to say: the above ministry, the perfecting of the saints, and the edifying of the Church will continue until we all meet Christ in the resurrection. *Behold, the bridegroom comes. Go forth to meet him* (Matt 25:6). *Be prepared to meet your God, O Israel* (Amos 4:12). We shall meet one another also: *we who are alive, who are left, shall be taken up together with them in the clouds to meet Christ* (1 Thess 4:16). *If by any means I may attain to the resurrection which is from the dead* (Phil 3: 11).

The spiritual convergence, however, is seen in relation to our merits, which is according to the same faith; regarding this he says **into the unity of faith**. There is only **one Lord, one faith** (Eph 4:5). Again he said earlier: **careful to keep the unity of the Spirit in the bond of peace** (Eph 4:3). **The knowledge of the Son of God** is the reward; it consists in the perfect vision and knowledge of God of which it is written: *then shall I know even as I am known* (1 Cor 13:12). *And they shall teach no more every man his neighbor, and every man his brother, saying: know the Lord; for all shall know me from the least of them even to the greatest* (Jer 31:34).

216. Secundo declarat praedictum fructum quantum ad perfectionem resurgentium.

Et primo ponit ipsam perfectionem, cum dicit *in virum perfectum*. Ubi non est intelligendum, sicut quidam intellexerunt, quod scilicet foeminae mutentur in sexum virilem in resurrectione, quia uterque sexus permanebit non quidem ad commixtionem sexuum, quae tunc de caetero non erit, secundum illud Matth. XXII, 30: *in resurrectione enim non nubent, neque nubentur, sed sunt sicut angeli*, sed ad perfectionem naturae et gloriae Dei, qui talem naturam condidit. Dicit ergo *virum perfectum*, ad designandum omnimodam perfectionem illius status. I Cor. XIII, 10: *cum venerit quod perfectum est, evacuabitur quod ex parte est*. Et propter hoc vir magis sumitur secundum quod dividitur contra puerum, quam secundum quod dividitur contra foeminam.

Secundo ostendit exemplar huius perfectionis, cum dicit *in mensuram aetatis plenitudinis Christi*. Ubi considerandum est, quod corpus Christi verum est exemplar corporis mystici: utrumque enim constat ex pluribus membris in unum collectis. Corpus autem Christi fuit perductum ad plenam aetatem virilem, scilicet triginta trium annorum, in qua mortuus fuit. Huiusmodi ergo aetatis plenitudini conformabitur aetas sanctorum resurgentium, in quibus nulla erit imperfectio, nec defectus senectutis. Phil. III, 21: *reformabit corpus humilitatis nostrae, configuratum corpori claritatis suae*.

217. Alio modo potest intelligi de fructu ultimo praesentis vitae, in qua quidem sibi occurrent omnes fideles ad unam fidem et agnitionem veritatis. Io. X, 16: *alias oves habeo, quae non sunt de hoc ovili*, et cetera. In qua perficitur etiam corpus Christi mysticum spirituali perfectione, ad similitudinem corporis Christi veri. Et secundum hoc totum corpus Ecclesiae dicitur corpus virile, secundum illam similitudinem qua utitur Apostolus Gal. IV, 1: *quanto tempore haeres parvulus est, nihil differt a servo*, et cetera.

216. Second, he discusses the aforementioned fruit in respect to the perfection of those who rise.

He relates first of all the perfection itself when he says *unto a perfect man*. This should not be understood as though women will be changed into men at the resurrection—some have misread it in such a fashion. Both sexes will remain, though sexual intercourse will no longer occur, as our Lord indicates: *for in the resurrection they shall neither marry nor be married, but shall be as the angels of God in heaven* (Matt 22:30). They will remain as a witness to the perfection of nature, and for the glory of God who created such a nature. The *perfect man* designates the complete and total perfection of that state. *When that which is perfect is come, that which is in part shall be done away* (1 Cor 13:10). Thus man is used here rather in contradistinction to boy than as the opposite of woman.

He describes, in the second place, the exemplar of this perfection when he says *unto the measure of the age of the fullness of Christ*. Consider how the true physical body of Christ is the exemplar of his mystical body. Both are made up of many members joined into a unified whole. Now the physical body of Christ grew to the mature and robust age of thirty-three years before he died. Therefore, the age of the risen saints, who will experience neither imperfection nor the failings of old age, will correspond to that mature age. *He will reform the body of our lowness, made like to the body of his glory* (Phil 3:21).

217. In another way, this passage can be understood as referring to the ultimate fruit of the Church's ministry in the present life. This will happen when all the faithful come to her in the unity of faith and the knowledge of the truth. *And other sheep I have that are not of this fold; them also I must bring. And they shall hear my voice; and there shall be one fold and one shepherd* (John 10:16). In this the mystical body is perfected spiritually in a manner similar to the physical perfection of Christ's natural body. In this perspective, the whole body of the Church is termed a manly body, following the metaphor used by the Apostle: *now, I say: as long as the heir is a child, he is no different than a servant, though he be lord of all* (Gal 4:1).

Lecture 5

⁴:¹⁴ut jam non simus parvuli fluctuantes, et circumferamur omni vento doctrinae in nequitia hominum, in astutia ad circumventionem erroris. [n. 219]

⁴:¹⁵Veritatem autem facientes in caritate, crescamus in illo per omnia, qui est caput Christus: [n. 221]

⁴:¹⁶ex quo totum corpus compactum et connexum per omnem juncturam subministrationis, secundum operationem in mensuram uniuscujusque membri, augmentum corporis facit in aedificationem sui in caritate. [n. 225]

⁴:¹⁴ἵνα μηκέτι ὦμεν νήπιοι, κλυδωνιζόμενοι καὶ περιφερόμενοι παντὶ ἀνέμῳ τῆς διδασκαλίας ἐν τῇ κυβείᾳ τῶν ἀνθρώπων ἐν πανουργίᾳ πρὸς τὴν μεθοδείαν τῆς πλάνης,

⁴:¹⁵ἀληθεύοντες δὲ ἐν ἀγάπῃ αὐξήσωμεν εἰς αὐτὸν τὰ πάντα, ὅς ἐστιν ἡ κεφαλή, Χριστός,

⁴:¹⁶ἐξ οὗ πᾶν τὸ σῶμα συναρμολογούμενον καὶ συμβιβαζόμενον διὰ πάσης ἁφῆς τῆς ἐπιχορηγίας κατ' ἐνέργειαν ἐν μέτρῳ ἑνὸς ἑκάστου μέρους τὴν αὔξησιν τοῦ σώματος ποιεῖται εἰς οἰκοδομὴν ἑαυτοῦ ἐν ἀγάπῃ.

⁴:¹⁴That henceforth we be no more children tossed to and fro and carried about with every wind of doctrine, by the wickedness of men, by cunning craftiness by which they lie in wait to deceive. [n. 219]

⁴:¹⁵But doing the truth in charity, we may in all things grow up in him who is the head, even Christ: [n. 221]

⁴:¹⁶From whom the whole body, being compacted and fitly joined together, by what every joint supplies, according to the operation in the measure of every part, makes increase of the body, unto the edifying of itself in charity. [n. 225]

---

218. Posita donorum spiritualium diversitate et fructu eorum, hic ostendit Apostolus quomodo ad fructum illum perveniamus.

Circa quod duo facit.

Primo duo impedimenta removet;

secundo modum veniendi docet, ibi *veritatem facientes*, et cetera.

219. Dicit ergo: bene dictum est, quod hic est fructus ultimus istorum donorum, quod scilicet occurramus Domino *in virum perfectum*, etc., ergo oportet nos videre *ut iam non simus parvuli*, sed certe viri perfecti; quia quamdiu aliquis est puer, non est perfectus vir. Oportet ergo quod deserat pueritiam, qui Domino debet occurrere. Sic faciebat Apostolus. I Cor. XIII, 11: *quando autem factus sum vir, evacuavi quae erant parvuli*.

Conditio autem pueri est, quod non est fixus vel determinatus in aliquo, sed credit omni verbo. Si ergo volumus exhibere nos ut viros perfectos, oportet quod deseramus cogitationem fluctuantem, id est instabilem. Et hoc est quod dicit *fluctuantes*. I Cor. XIV, v. 20: *nolite pueri effici sensibus, sed malitia parvuli estote*.

Dicuntur autem *fluctuantes* a fluctu, quia tales ad modum fluctus non sunt firmi in fide. Iac. I, 6: *qui enim haesitat, similis est fluctui maris, qui a vento movetur et circumfertur*. Nunc autem necesse est nos stabiles esse et non fluctuare.

220. Et quia ventus est prava doctrina, de qua merito dicitur Prov. XXV, 23: *ventus Aquilo dissipat pluvias*. Matth. VII, 25: *descendit pluvia, venerunt flumina, flaverunt venti, et irruerunt in domum illam, et cecidit, et fuit ruina eius magna* ideo dicit *et non circumferamur omni vento doctrinae*, etc.; quasi dicat: nulla doctrina perversa perflante ad commotionem cordis et ruinam spiritualis aedificii debemus moveri, quia non est bona doctrina;

218. Having spoken of the diversity of spiritual gifts and their fruit, now the Apostle describes how we attain to that fruit.

Concerning this he does two things:

first, he removes two obstacles;

second, he teaches the way of gaining access to them, at *doing the truth*.

219. It was well said, he says, that the ultimate fruit of these gifts is for us to meet the Lord as a ***perfect man unto the measure of the age of the fullness of Christ***. We are obliged ***henceforth*** to cease being ***children*** and become mature men; for as long as a person is a boy he is not a perfect man. Whoever is to meet the Lord must leave his childhood behind. The Apostle did just that: *when I became a man, I put away the things of a child* (1 Cor 13:11).

It is a quality of the child never to be fixed or determinate in anything; he rather believes whatever is told him. To act like grown men we have to abandon a fickle oscillation and instability in our judgments. That is why he says ***tossed to and fro***. *Do not become children mentally; in malice be children but in your mind be mature* (1 Cor 14:20).

Those who waver are called such from the word *wave*; like a wave ***tossed to and fro*** they are not firm in the faith. *He that wavers is like a wave of the sea, which is moved and carried about by the wind* (Jas 1:6). But now it is imperative for us to stand firm and not fluctuate.

220. Evil teachings are like the wind which is spoken of with merit: *the north wind brings forth rain* (Prov 25:23). *And the rain fell, and the floods came and the winds blew; and they beat upon that house. And it fell; and great was the fall thereof* (Matt 7:27). Hence he warns against being ***carried about with every wind of doctrine***. As though he said: we must not be shaken by these wicked doctrines that buff about seeking to agitate hearts and ruin spiritual

quod patet ex tribus. Primo ex eius principio, quod est *in nequitia hominum*; ideo non est bona doctrina, sed falsa et nequam, quam dogmatizat aliquis ad perditionem animarum, ut obtineat principatum, sicut doctrina Arii nequissimi, qui crepuit medius, ut de ipso possit exponi illud Eccli. XXXI, 29: *testimonium nequitiae eius verum est*. Item, talis doctrina perversa est quod patet.

Secundo, ex eius processu, qui est *astutia*, quia cum dolo, id est unum intendit et aliud simulat; propter quod Apostolus dicit II Cor. XI, 3: *timeo ne sicut serpens Evam seduxit astutia sua: ita ut corrumpantur sensus vestri et excidant a simplicitate, quae est in Christo Iesu*.

Tertio patet hoc idem ex effectu, quia effectus talis doctrinae est *ad circumventionem erroris*, non ad denarios vel alia temporalia acquirenda, sed ad seminandos errores seducunt et circumveniunt tales doctores; de quibus dicitur II Tim. III, 13: *mali homines et seductores proficient in peius errantes, et in errorem alios mittentes*.

221. Deinde cum dicit *veritatem autem facientes*, etc., ostensis impedimentis per quae a fructu donorum spiritualium impeditur quis, hic ostendit qualiter ad fructum debitum pervenitur. Et arguit sic: statim dictum est quod si volumus ad spiritualium donorum fructum pervenire, oportet ut iam non simus parvuli, et cetera. Sed tamdiu sumus parvuli, quamdiu virilem statum non attingimus, nec crescimus: ergo nobis necessarium est, ut crescamus. Et hoc est quod dicit *veritatem autem facientes*, et cetera.

Duo ergo facit.
Primo ostendit in quo debemus crescere;
secundo per quem, ibi *in illo per omnia*, et cetera.

222. Dicit ergo quantum ad primum *veritatem facientes crescamus*, et hoc in duobus, scilicet in bono opere et forma boni operis, quae duo sunt veritas et caritas.

Veritas autem quandoque dicitur omne opus bonum, ut Tob. I, 2: *in captivitate tamen positus viam veritatis non deseruit*. Faciamus ergo veritatem, scilicet omne opus bonum, vel veritatem doctrinae: quia non sufficere nobis debet audire vel docere veritatem, sed oportet facere; propter hoc dicebat Apostolus I Tim. IV, 16: *hoc enim faciens, et teipsum salvum facies, et eos qui te audiunt*. *Estote ergo factores*, etc., ut dicitur Iac. I, 22; quia *factores iustificabuntur*, ut habetur Rom. c. II, 13. Et hoc si fiat in caritate, quae est forma boni operis. I Cor. XVI, 13 s.: *viriliter agite, et confortetur cor vestrum, et omnia opera vestra in caritate fiant*: quia certe aliter nihil valerent. I Cor. XIII, 3: *si tradidero corpus meum, ita ut ardeam, caritatem autem non habuero, nihil mihi prodest*.

accomplishments. Three qualities demonstrate that it is not good doctrine. First, its source is **the wickedness of men**. Not being sound doctrine, but false and wicked, someone will concoct dogmas out of it in order to wield dominion over others, even though souls are lost. Such were the teachings of that most wicked Arius whose abdomen burst asunder. He could be made the subject of what is written: *the testimony of his wickedness is true* (Sir 31:29).

Second, its methods are by **cunning craftiness** to mean one thing and pretend to hold some other opinion. On this account the Apostle wrote: *I fear lest, as the serpent seduced Eve by his subtlety, so your minds should be corrupted and fall from the simplicity that is in Christ* (2 Cor 11:3).

Third, this is also evident from its effects, for such doctrine **lies in wait to deceive**. Its teachers seduce and lie in wait, not to rob money or temporal goods, but to spread errors. *Evil men and seducers shall grow worse and worse; erring, and driving into error* (2 Tim 3:13).

221. Next, when he says **doing the truth**, having pointed out the impediments which prevent one from acquiring the fruit of spiritual gifts, he discloses here how that fruit can be attained. He argues this way: it was said just now that to obtain the fruit of these spiritual gifts we must stop being children and grow up into mature adults. As long as we are childish we have not reached a mature state, neither do we grow. Hence, it is necessary for us to grow up. This is what he says about **doing the truth in charity**.

Hence he makes two points:
first, he shows in what areas we ought to grow up;
second, through whom we are to grow, at **into him who is the head**.

222. With respect to the first he states **doing the truth in charity, we may grow up** in good works and the form of good works, which two are truth and charity.

Any good work is at times referred to as truth: *even in his captivity he forsook not the way of truth* (Tob 1:2). Let us, therefore, do the truth, namely, every good work. Or, put true doctrine into practice since it is not enough simply to hear or teach the truth, it must be acted on as well. Thus the Apostle counsels Timothy: *take heed to yourself and to doctrine; be earnest in them. For in doing this you shall both save yourself and them that hear you* (1 Tim 4:16). *Be doers of the word and not hearers only* (Jas 1:22) since *doers shall be justified* (Rom 2:13), that is, if they act out of charity, the form of good works. *Do manfully and be strengthened. Let all your actions be done in charity* (1 Cor 16:13–14); otherwise they will be useless: *if I should distribute all my goods to feed the poor, and if I should deliver my body to be burned, and have not charity, it profits me nothing* (1 Cor 13:3).

223. Sed quia in via Dei non progredi, est regredi, ideo subdit Apostolus *ut crescamus in illo*, etc., ubi tria facit.

Primo ostendit auctorem nostri augmenti;

secundo eius veritatem;

tertio modum augmenti.

Secunda, ibi *ex quo totum corpus*. Tertia, ibi *secundum operationem in mensuram uniuscuiusque membri*.

224. Dicit ergo *crescamus in illo*, scilicet in Christo, de quo I Petr. II, 2: *in eo crescatis in salutem*. *In illo*, inquam, *qui est caput* nostrum *Christus* et in Ecclesia, quae est corpus ipsius, ut dicitur Col. I, 24. Crescamus, inquam, non in possessionibus, sicut dicitur Iob I, 10: *possessio eius crevit in terra*, sed in spiritualibus. Nec in uno tantum, sed *per omnia*, id est in omni bono, fructificantes et crescentes. I Cor. X, 31: *omnia in gloriam Dei facite*, et cetera. Et ibi sequitur: *sicut et ego per omnia omnibus placeo*. De hoc commendat Corinthios Apostolus, dicens I Cor. XI, 2: *laudo vos, fratres, quod per omnia mei memores estis, et sicut tradidi vobis, omnia praecepta mea tenetis*.

225. Consequenter cum dicit *ex quo totum corpus*, etc., ostendit veritatem Christi per quem crescere debeamus.

Ubi sciendum est, quod corpus naturale tria habet, scilicet compactionem membrorum ad invicem, ligationem per nervos et mutuam subministrationem. I Cor. XII, 16 s.: *si dixerit pes: quoniam non sum manus, non sum de corpore; num ideo non est de corpore? Et si dixerit auris: quoniam non sum oculus, non sum de corpore*, et cetera. *Si totum corpus est odoratus, ubi auditus?*

Spiritualiter ergo, sicut unum corpus efficitur ex multis his tribus modis, scilicet per compactionem seu adunationem, per ligationem et per mutuam operationem et subventionem: ita et omnia, quae sunt a capite corporali, scilicet compactio, nervorum ligatio, ad opus motio, fluunt a capite nostro Christo in corpore Ecclesiae.

226. Et, primo, compactio per fidem; unde dicit *ex quo*, scilicet Christo, qui est caput nostrum, ut modo dictum est, *totum corpus compactum est*, id est, coadunatum. Ps. CXLVI, 2: *dispersiones Israel congregabit*. Abac. II, 5: *congregabit ad se omnes gentes, et coacervabit ad se omnes populos*. De hoc dicitur Col. II, 19: *caput ex quo totum corpus per nexus et coniunctiones subministratum et constructum crescit in augmentum Dei*.

227. Secundo, fluit a Christo capite in corpus Ecclesiae suae mysticum connexio et colligatio, quia oportet

223. Because not to make progress in the approach to God is itself a retrogression, the Apostle adds that *we may grow up in him*, where he states three points by explaining:

first, the author of our development;

second, the truth about him;

third, the manner of the development.

He describes the second at *from whom the whole body*, and the third at *according to the operation in the measure of every part*.

224. He asks that *we may grow up in him*, namely, in Christ, of whom it is written: *in him may you grow unto salvation* (1 Pet 2:2). *In him*, I repeat, *who is the head, Christ*, and in the Church which is his body (Col 1:24). Let us increase, not in wealth as was said of Job that *his possession has increased on the earth* (Job 1:10), but in spiritual goods. Nor in one area only, but *in all things*, that is, being fruitful and increasing in every good. *Whatsoever else you do, do all to the glory of God . . . as I also in all things please all men* (1 Cor 10:31; 33). The Apostle commends the Corinthians on this score: *now, I praise you, brethren, that in all things you are mindful of me and keep my ordinances as I have delivered them to you* (1 Cor 11:2).

225. Next, when he says *from the whole body*, he speaks about the truth of Christ through whom we ought to grow.

Three points concerning an organic body are to be kept in mind: its organs are interrelated, they are bound together by tendons, and each member serves the rest. *If the foot should say: because I am not the hand, I am not of the body; is it therefore not of the body? And if the ear should say: because I am not the eye, I am not of the body; is it therefore not of the body? If the whole body were the eye, where would be the hearing? If the whole were hearing, where would be the smelling?* (1 Cor 12:15–17).

Therefore, one body is composed of many members in these three ways: through its structured whole or unity, through its connective bindings, and through its reciprocal actions and assistance, just as all these actions of interrelating organs, the connecting of tendons, and movements take their initiative from the body's head, so the spiritual counterparts of these flow from Christ, our head, into his body, the Church.

226. First, there is a structured unity through faith. Whence he says *from whom*, namely Christ, who is our head, as was already mentioned, *the whole body, being compacted* is joined together in a unity. *He will gather together the dispersed of Israel* (Ps 147:2). *He will gather together unto him all nations, and heap together unto him all people* (Hab 2:5). Christ is *the head, from which the whole body, by joints and bands, being supplied with nourishment and compacted, grows unto the increase of God* (Col 2:19).

227. Second, a connecting and binding force emanates from Christ, the head, into his body, the Church, since

adunata aliquo nexu vel vinculo necti, vel colligari. Et propter hoc dicit *et connexum per omnem iuncturam subministrationis*, id est per fidem et caritatem, quae connectunt et coniungunt membra corporis mystici ad mutuam subministrationem. Eccli. XXXIX, 39: *omnia opera Domini bona, et omne opus hora sua subministrabit.*

Unde ipse Apostolus, confidens de ista mutua subministratione quae est inter membra Ecclesiae per divinam coniunctionem, dicebat Phil. I, 19: *scio enim, quia hoc proveniet in salutem per vestram orationem et subministrationem Spiritus Iesu Christi.*

228. Tertio, a capite Christo in membris, ut augmententur spiritualiter, influitur virtus actualiter operandi. Unde dicit *secundum mensuram uniuscuiusque membri, augmentum corporis facit*; quasi dicat: non solum a capite nostro Christo est membrorum Ecclesiae compactio per fidem, nec sola connexio, vel colligatio per mutuam subministrationem caritatis, sed certe ab ipso est actualis membrorum operatio sive ad opus motio, secundum mensuram et competentiam cuiuslibet membri. Unde dicit, quod *facit augmentum corporis secundum operationem et mensuram uniuscuiusque membri*, debite mensurati; quia non solum per fidem corpus mysticum compaginatur, nec solum per caritatis subministrationem connectentem augetur corpus; sed per actualem compositionem ab unoquoque membro egredientem, secundum mensuram gratiae sibi datae, et actualem motionem ad operationem, quam Deus facit in nobis. Unde Is. XXVI, 12: *omnia opera nostra operatus es in nobis*. Idem vero Deus, *qui operatur omnia in omnibus*, ut dicitur I Cor. XII, 6.

Et haec expositio concordat glossatori.

229. Sed ad quid augmentat Deus unumquodque membrum? Ut corpus aedificet. Supra II, 21: *in quo omnis aedificatio constructa crescit in templum sanctum in Domino, in quo et vos coaedificamini*, et cetera. Unde I Cor. III, 9: *Dei aedificatio estis*. Et haec omnia fiunt **in caritate**, quia, ut dicitur I Cor. c. VIII, 1: *caritas aedificat.*

Vel *in caritate* facit Deus haec omnia, id est ex mera dilectione. Ier. XXXIII, 3: *in caritate perpetua dilexi te, ideo attraxi te miserans. Rursusque: aedificabo, et aedificaberis*. Hoc est ergo quod dicit *in aedificationem sui in caritate*.

whatever is united must be held together or bound by some nexus or bond. On this account he says *fitly joined together, by what every joint supplies*, that is, through the faith and charity which unite and knit the members of the mystical body to one another for their mutual support. *All the works of the Lord are good: and he will furnish every work in due time* (Sir 39:39).

Thus the Apostle himself, confident of this mutual being-of-service which reigns among the members of the Church due to the divine unifying action, had said: *I know that this shall happen to me unto salvation, through your prayer and the assistance of the Spirit of Jesus Christ* (Phil 1:19).

228. Third, from Christ the head there is infused into his members the power to act in order that they may grow spiritually. For this reason he states *according to the operation in the measure of every part, makes increase of the body*. As if he said: not only is the structured unity of the members of the Church through faith, and their connection or being joined together through the mutual service of charity, from Christ the head. Indeed, from him comes the actual operation or movements of the members needed for action, and this according to the measure and competency of each member. Thus he asserts that Christ accomplishes the *increase of the body according to the operation* and *in the* due *measure of every part*. Therefore, the body not only grows through the faith which compacts it into a structured whole and through charity's mutual assistance, but also through the actual binding force which flows out from each member according to the degree of grace given him; and also through the actual impulse to act which God effects in us. *You have wrought all our works for us* (Isa 26:12). He is the *same God who works all in all* (1 Cor 12:6).

This interpretation accords with that of the glossator.

229. But why does God make each member grow? To build up the body. *In whom all the building, being framed together, grows up into a holy temple in the Lord. In whom you also are built together into a habitation of God in the Spirit* (Eph 2:21–22). *You are God's building* (1 Cor 3:9). All this occurs *in* the *charity* of which it is said that *charity edifies* (1 Cor 8:1).

Or, God accomplishes all this *in charity*, that is, simply out of love. *Yea, I have loved you with an everlasting love: therefore have I drawn you, taking pity on you. And I will build you again, and you shall be built* (Jer 31:3–4). This is what he states in *unto the edifying of itself in charity*.

Lecture 6

⁴:¹⁷Hoc igitur dico, et testificor in Domino, ut jam non ambuletis, sicut et gentes ambulant in vanitate sensus sui, [n. 231]

⁴:¹⁸tenebris obscuratum habentes intellectum, alienati a vita Dei per ignorantiam, quae est in illis, propter caecitatem cordis ipsorum, [n. 233]

⁴:¹⁹qui desperantes, semetipsos tradiderunt impudicitiae, in operationem immunditiae omnis in avaritiam. [n. 235]

⁴:¹⁷Τοῦτο οὖν λέγω καὶ μαρτύρομαι ἐν κυρίῳ, μηκέτι ὑμᾶς περιπατεῖν καθὼς καὶ τὰ ἔθνη περιπατεῖ ἐν ματαιότητι τοῦ νοὸς αὐτῶν,

⁴:¹⁸ἐσκοτωμένοι τῇ διανοίᾳ ὄντες, ἀπηλλοτριωμένοι τῆς ζωῆς τοῦ θεοῦ, διὰ τὴν ἄγνοιαν τὴν οὖσαν ἐν αὐτοῖς, διὰ τὴν πώρωσιν τῆς καρδίας αὐτῶν,

⁴:¹⁹οἵτινες ἀπηλγηκότες ἑαυτοὺς παρέδωκαν τῇ ἀσελγείᾳ εἰς ἐργασίαν ἀκαθαρσίας πάσης ἐν πλεονεξίᾳ.

⁴:¹⁷This then I say and testify in the Lord: that henceforward you walk not as also the gentiles walk in the vanity of their mind: [n. 231]

⁴:¹⁸Having their understanding darkened: being alienated from the life of God through the ignorance that is in them, because of the blindness of their hearts. [n. 233]

⁴:¹⁹Who despairing have given themselves up to lasciviousness, unto the working of all uncleanness, unto covetousness. [n. 235]

---

230. Supra monuit Apostolus Ephesios ut manerent in ecclesiastica unitate, describendo modum eius et formam, in hac parte docet eos viam per quam possint manere in ecclesiastica unitate.

Et circa hoc duo facit.

Primo proponit praecepta, per quae possunt manere in ecclesiastica unitate;

secundo ostendit potestatem hanc ad implenda praecepta in fine epistolae, ibi *de caetero, fratres, confortamini*, et cetera.

Prima in duas.

Primo proponit praecepta ad omnes;

secundo pertinentia ad singulos gradus Ecclesiae, ibi *mulieres viris suis subditae sint*, et cetera.

Prima in duas.

Primo ponit quaedam praecepta generalia ad quae reducuntur omnia alia;

secundo ponit specialia, ibi *propter quod deponentes mendacium*, et cetera.

Prima iterum in duas, quia cum intentio Apostoli sit eos revocare a vetere consuetudine ad novam Christi doctrinam,

primo ostendit doctrinam Christi esse contrariam antiquae perversitati gentilitatis;

secundo inducit eos, ut eam deponant et eam, quae Christi est assumant, ibi *deponite vos secundum pristinam*, et cetera.

Prima in duas, quia primo describit conversationem gentilium;

secundo ostendit, quod ei contrariatur doctrina Christi, ibi *vos autem non ita*, et cetera.

Prima in tres.

Primo hortatur eos, ut declinent conversationem gentilium;

secundo describit eam quantum ad interiorem animum, ibi *tenebris obscuratum*, etc.;

230. The Apostle previously admonished the Ephesians to persevere in ecclesial unity by describing to them its quality and pattern. In the part that follows he teaches them the way to remain within the Church's unity.

Regarding this he does two things:

first, he gives them precepts by which they can remain in ecclesial unity;

second, near the end of the letter, at *finally, brethren, be strengthened* (Eph 6:10), he shows them the strength by which they can fulfill these commands.

The first section has two parts:

first, he sets down precepts for everyone;

second, he adds certain ones pertaining to particular classes within the Church, at *so also let wives be* (Eph 5:24).

The first contains two divisions:

first, he expresses certain general precepts to which all the others can be reduced;

second, he treats of particular ones, at *wherefore, putting away lying* (Eph 4:25).

Again, the first section has two parts. Since the Apostle's intention is to draw them away from their old customs to embrace Christ's new teaching:

first, he demonstrates how the doctrine of Christ is just the opposite of the old pagan perversity;

second, he offers them incentives to leave it behind and adopt the way of Christ, at *put off according to former* (Eph 4:22).

The first of these has two sections: first, he describes the pagans' way of life;

second, he shows that Christ's teaching is contrary to it, at *you have not so learned Christ* (Eph 4:20).

The first part has three divisions:

first, he exhorts them to reject the pagan way of life;

second, he describes it in reference to the pagan's inner mind, at *having their understanding darkened*;

tertio quantum ad exteriorem modum, ibi *qui desperantes*, et cetera.

231. Dicit ergo: ad hoc quod possitis implere ea, quae dicta sunt, *dico*, id est non obsecro, ut prius, sed dico, *et testificor*, hoc quod dixi. Gal. V, 3: *testificor autem omni homini rursum circumcidenti se, quoniam debitor est universae legis faciendae*. II Tim. IV, 1: *testificor coram Deo et Christo Iesu*, et cetera.

Et quid? *Ut iam*, scilicet tempore fidei et conversionis ad Christum, quia *iam vos mundi estis*, Io. XIII, 10, *non ambuletis*, id est vivatis. Gal. V, 25: *si Spiritu vivimus, Spiritu et ambulemus*, et cetera. Et hoc *sicut et gentes ambulant*. I Cor. XII, 2: *scitis, quoniam cum gentes essetis, ad simulacra muta prout ducebamini euntes*, et cetera. Non sic igitur ambuletis. Prov. I, 15: *fili mi, ne ambules cum eis, prohibe pedem tuum a semitis eorum*, et cetera.

232. Consequenter cum dicit *in vanitate sensus sui*, reddit causam huius prohibitionis.

Ubi notandum est, quod cum ambulare spiritualiter sit proficere, secundum illud Is. c. XXVI, 7: *rectus callis iusti ad ambulandum*, et cetera. Gen. XVII, 1: *ambula coram me, et esto perfectus*, dicitur Abrahae, ad hoc ergo ut homo iuste ambulet, id est spiritualiter proficiat, oportet tria, quae in ipso sunt, regulari et ordinari.

In homine enim est ratio iudicans de particularibus agendis; item, intellectus universalium principiorum, qui est synderesis; tertio, lex divina seu Deus. Quandocumque ergo aliquis secundum ista tria sibi invicem or dinata dirigitur, ita quod actio ordinetur secundum iudicium rationis, et haec, scilicet ratio, iudicet secundum intellectum rectum, vel synderesim, et haec, scilicet synderesis, ordinetur secundum legem divinam, tunc actio est bona et meritoria.

Sed vita gentilium non est talis, imo deficit in praedictis tribus; quia, primo, deficit a ratione iudicante, quia *ambulant in vanitate sensus sui*. *Sensus* autem est vis apprehensiva, per quam iudicamus singularia. Unde aliquis homo rectus dicitur quando bene iudicat de agendis.

Sed sensus iste quandoque est rectus, quandoque est vanus. Rectus dicitur, quando debita regula regitur, qua venit ad debitum finem; vanus autem quando, indebita regula ductus, non venit ad debitum finem. Sap. c. XIII, 1: *vani sunt omnes homines in quibus non subest scientia Dei*, et cetera. Rom. I, 21: *evanuerunt in cogitationibus suis*, et cetera. Ier. II, v. 5: *ambulaverunt post vanitates suas, et vani facti sunt*.

233. Quare? Quia certe ratio istorum in agendis non dirigebatur ab intellectu illuminato, sed erroneo. Et hoc est quod ait *tenebris obscuratum habentes*

third, he does so in reference to his external way of acting, at *who despairing*.

231. That you will be able to carry out, he says, what I have spoken of above, *I say*, not beseeching you as previously, rather I say *and testify* to what I have asserted. *I testify again to every man circumcising himself that he is a debtor to the whole law* (Gal 5:3). *I charge you, before God and Jesus Christ, who shall judge the living and the dead* (2 Tim 4:1).

And what does he bear witness to here? *That henceforward*, from the moment you believed and were converted to Christ, since *you are now clean* (John 13:10), *you walk not as also the gentiles walk*. To *walk* here means to live: *if we live in the Spirit, let us also walk in the Spirit* (Gal 5:25). This should not be *as the gentiles walk*: *you know that, when you were heathens, you went to dumb idols according as you were led* (1 Cor 12:2). You must not walk in such a manner: *my son, walk not with them: restrain your foot from their paths* (Prov 1:15).

232. Then, in saying *in the vanity of their mind*, he gives the reason for his prohibition.

Note that to walk spiritually is to make progress. *The path of the just is right to walk in* (Isa 26:27), and to Abraham it was said: *walk before me, and be perfect* (Gen 17:1). There are three norms immanent in man by which he must be guided and regulated if he is to walk justly and make spiritual progress.

In man, one of these is the reason which judges about what is to be done in particular circumstances. Another is the understanding of universal principles, called synderesis; and third, there is the divine law or God. Actions are good and meritorious when the person is guided by these three in their proper interrelations; namely, when the action is in accord with the judgment of reason, and this reason judges according to true understanding, or synderesis; and this synderesis is, in turn, directed by the divine law.

The life of the gentiles did not resemble this, but rather was lacking these three. First of all, rational judgment was missing since they *walked in the vanity of their mind*. *Mind* here is the power to apprehend, through which we judge about individual objects. Hence, a man is called upright when he judges correctly about what should be done.

But this mind is sometimes upright, and at other times vain. It is termed upright when, guided by appropriate norms, it attains to the proper end; it is vain when, led by the wrong norms, it does not achieve the proper end. *All men are vain, in whom there is not the knowledge of God* (Wis 13:1), *because they became vain in their thoughts* (Rom 1:21) *and walked after vanity and are become vain* (Jer 2:5).

233. Why? Obviously because in performing such acts their reason is not guided by an enlightened understanding, but an erroneous one. This is what he says about them

intellectum. Rom. I, 21: *obscuratum est insipiens cor eorum*. Ps. LXXXI, 5: *nescierunt, neque intellexerunt, in tenebris ambulant*.

Et ratio est, quia tales non sunt participes divini luminis, seu legis divinae illuminantis et regulantis; propter quod subdit **alienati a vita Dei**, id est a Deo, qui est vita animae. Io. XIV, 6: *ego sum via, veritas, et vita*.

Vel, **a vita Dei**, id est a caritate et gratia spirituali, qua anima vivit formaliter. Rom. VI, 23: *gratia autem Dei vita aeterna*. Isti autem erant sine spe vitae aeternae, quia ponebant mortalitatem animae contra fidem et spem. Sap. II, 22: *nescierunt sacramenta Dei, neque speraverunt mercedem iustitiae, neque iudicaverunt honorem animarum sanctarum*, et cetera.

Vel **a vita Dei**, id est a vita sancte vivendi, quae est per fidem. Gal. II, 20: *vivo ego, iam non ego*, et cetera. *Iustus autem ex fide vivit*, ut dicitur Rom. I, 17. Vel quae est per caritatem. I Io. III, 14: *nos scimus, quia translati sumus de morte ad vitam, quoniam diligimus fratres*, et cetera. Non sic autem isti, sed magis alienati.

234. Modum autem huius alienationis tangit, scilicet **per ignorantiam** non stellarum vel cursus siderum, sed naturae divinae, I Cor. c. XV, 33: *ignorantiam quidem Dei quidam habent*, quia certe tunc solum in Iudaea notus erat Deus, sed modo, ut dicitur Act. XVII, v. 30: *tempora huius ignorantiae despiciens Deus, nunc annuntiat hominibus, ut omnes ubique poenitentiam agant*, et cetera.

Huius autem ignorantiae Deus non erat causa quantum de se erat, ut dicitur Rom. I, v. 19: *Deus enim illis revelavit*, sed certe causa erat illis **propter caecitatem cordis ipsorum**. Et vere dicit **caecitatem** eo quod ex creaturis non poterant venire in notitiam Creatoris, quia, ut dicitur Sap. II, 21, *excaecavit eos malitia eorum*; et sequitur: *et nescierunt sacramenta Dei, neque mercedem speraverunt iustitiae*.

235. Et hoc est quod sequitur **qui desperantes**, etc., ubi ostendit Apostolus quales erant in exteriori conversatione, quoniam sine spe, et hoc quia alienati a vita. Iob VII, v. 16: *desperavi, nequaquam ultra iam vivam*, et cetera. Ier. XVIII, 12: *desperavimus, post cogitationes enim nostras ibimus, et unusquisque post pravitatem cordis sui malefaciemus*.

236. Et hoc est quod sequitur **tradiderunt semetipsos impudicitiae**, et cetera. Et hoc legi potest dupliciter, vel separatim, ut dicatur **in avaritia**, quia avari erant. Rom. I, 29: *repletos omni iniquitate et malitia, fornicatione, avaritia*. Hebr. XIII, 5: *sint mores sine avaritia*, etc., quia, ut dicitur Eccli. X, 9: *avaro nihil est scelestius*.

having their understanding darkened. *Their foolish heart was darkened* (Rom 1:21), and *they have not known nor understood: they walk on in darkness* (Ps 82:5).

This is traceable to their not sharing in the divine light, or not being enlightened and directed by the divine law. Thus he adds **alienated from the life of God**, from God who is the life of the soul. *I am the way, and the truth, and the life* (John 14:6).

Or, **from the life of God** may mean from charity and spiritual grace by which the soul lives formally. *The grace of God is life everlasting* (Rom 6:23). Existing without an expectation of eternal life, they held for a mortality of the soul contrary to faith and hope. *And they knew not the secrets of God, nor hoped for the wages of justice, nor esteemed the honor of holy souls* (Wis 2:22).

Or again, **from the life of God** might indicate an existence estranged from that holy living which comes through faith: *I live, now not I; but Christ lives in me* (Gal 2:20). *The just man lives by faith* (Rom 1:17). Or, the life which comes through charity: *we know that we have passed from death to life, because we love the brethren* (1 John 3:14). The pagans were not like this; instead, they were alienated.

234. He briefly discusses the quality of this alienation; it is **through the ignorance that is in them**, not of stars or the movement of the constellations, but of the divine nature. *Some have not the knowledge of God* (1 Cor 15:34), since in former times God was known only among the Jews. But *God, indeed having winked at the times of this ignorance, now declares unto men that all should everywhere do penance* (Acts 17:30).

God, insofar as he himself was concerned, was not the cause of this ignorance since *that which is known of God is manifest in them. For God has manifested it unto them* (Rom 1:19). Certainly the cause was themselves due to the **blindness of their hearts**. He describes it well as **blindness** since from created reality they could not attain to a knowledge of the Creator. *For their own malice blinded them. And they knew not the secrets of God, nor hoped for the wages of justice* (Wis 2:21–22).

235. Then the Apostle goes on, at **who despairing**, to portray how their exterior manner of life was once they lost hope, a loss due to their alienation from life. *I have done with hope. I shall now live no longer* (Job 7:16). *And they said: we have no hopes; for we will go after our own thoughts and we will do everyone according to the perverseness of his evil heart* (Jer 18:12).

236. This is what follows in that they have **given themselves up to lasciviousness unto the working of all uncleanness, unto covetousness**. The text can be read in two ways. **Unto covetousness** may be taken as a separate vice meaning they were avaricious: *being filled with all iniquity, malice, fornication, avarice* (Rom 1:29). *Let your manners be without covetousness, contented with such things as you have*

Propter quod Hab. c. II, 9: *vae qui congregat avaritiam malam domui suae*, et cetera.

Potest etiam legi coniunctim cum praecedentibus, ut dicatur **in avaritia**, id est avare, ita ut sit modificans praecedentia. Et secundum hoc aggravat eorum vitam tripliciter; quia, primo, peccaverunt non ex passione, sed potius ex electione, unde dicit **tradiderunt semetipsos impudicitiae**; quasi dicat: non passionibus, vel infirmitate peccaverunt, sed semetipsos tradiderunt, et cetera. Iudith VII, 15: *sponte tradamus nos omnes populo Holofernis*, et cetera. II Cor. XII, 21: *non egerunt poenitentiam super immunditia quam gesserunt*, et cetera.

Secundo, ex actuali effrenatione. II Petr. II, v. 10: *post carnem in concupiscentiam immunditiae ambulant*, et cetera. Et ideo dicit **in operationem omnis immunditiae**. Ez. XIV, 3: *isti posuerunt immunditias suas in cordibus suis*, et cetera.

Tertio, aggravatur eorum peccatum ex continuatione, quia incessanter peccabant. Os. IV, v. 10: *fornicati sunt, et non cessaverunt, quoniam Dominum reliquerunt*. Unde dicit **in avaritiam**, id est ardenter, et appetitu continuo, et insatiabili. II Petr. II, 14: *oculos habentes plenos adulterii et incessabilis delicti, pellicientes animas instabiles, cor exercitatum in avaritia habentes, maledictionis filii*, et cetera.

(Heb 13:5). For *nothing is more wicked than the covetous man* (Sir 10:9). Thus, *woe to him that gathers together an evil covetousness to his house that his nest may be on high, and thinks he may be delivered out of the hand of evil* (Hab 2:9).

Unto covetousness might also be joined with what goes before, meaning *covetously* and modifying the preceding. In that case their life was weighted down with a triple burden. First, they did not sin from passion but by choice, thus he says they **have given themselves up to lasciviousness**. As though he had said: instead of sinning through passion or weakness they just sold themselves over to it: *assemble all you that are in the city, that we may of our own accord yield ourselves all up to the people of Holofernes* (Jdt 7:15). *They have not done penance for the uncleanness, and fornication, and lasciviousness, that they have committed* (2 Cor 12:21).

Second, their sins were aggravated from the complete lack of restraint; they *walk after the flesh in the lust of uncleanness and despise government* (2 Pet 2:10). Therefore, he adds **unto the working of all uncleanness**; these men have placed their uncleannesses in their hearts, and have set up before their face the stumbling-block of their iniquity (Ezek 14:3).

Third, their sin was greater from its continuance, for they sinned incessantly. *They have committed fornication and have not ceased: because they have forsaken the Lord in not observing his law* (Hos 4:10). Whence he states **unto covetousness**, that is, they sinned ardently, with a constant and insatiable appetite for more. *Having eyes full of adultery and of sin that ceases not, alluring unstable souls, having their heart exercised with covetousness, children of malediction. Leaving the right way they have gone astray* (2 Pet 2:14–15).

Lecture 7

4:20Vos autem non ita didicistis Christum, [n. 238]

4:21si tamen illum audistis, et in ipso edocti estis, sicut est veritas in Jesu, [n. 239]

4:22deponere vos secundum pristinam conversationem veterem hominem, qui corrumpitur secundum desideria erroris. [n. 240]

4:23Renovamini autem spiritu mentis vestrae, [n. 242]

4:24et induite novum hominem, qui secundum Deum creatus est in justitia, et sanctitate veritatis. [n. 245]

4:20ὑμεῖς δὲ οὐχ οὕτως ἐμάθετε τὸν Χριστόν,

4:21εἴ γε αὐτὸν ἠκούσατε καὶ ἐν αὐτῷ ἐδιδάχθητε, καθώς ἐστιν ἀλήθεια ἐν τῷ Ἰησοῦ,

4:22ἀποθέσθαι ὑμᾶς κατὰ τὴν προτέραν ἀναστροφὴν τὸν παλαιὸν ἄνθρωπον τὸν φθειρόμενον κατὰ τὰς ἐπιθυμίας τῆς ἀπάτης,

4:23ἀνανεοῦσθαι δὲ τῷ πνεύματι τοῦ νοὸς ὑμῶν,

4:24καὶ ἐνδύσασθαι τὸν καινὸν ἄνθρωπον τὸν κατὰ θεὸν κτισθέντα ἐν δικαιοσύνῃ καὶ ὁσιότητι τῆς ἀληθείας.

4:20But you have not so learned Christ: [n. 238]

4:21Yet if you have heard him and have been taught in him, as the truth is in Jesus: [n. 239]

4:22To put off, according to former way of life, the old man, who is corrupted according to the desire of error. [n. 240]

4:23And be renewed in spirit of your mind: [n. 242]

4:24And put on the new man, who according to God is created in justice and holiness of truth. [n. 245]

---

237. Ostensa perversitate gentilis conversationis, hic ostendit Apostolus quod doctrina Christi totaliter contraria est isti conversationi et statui. Et quia pervertentes quidam doctrinam Christi dixerunt non esse aliam vitam post istam, sed animam mori cum corpore, ut animalia, ideo Apostolus ostendit,

primo doctrinam Christi contrariam esse vitae et statui praecedenti;

secundo ostendit conditiones debitas doctrinae Christi, ibi *deponite vos*, et cetera.

238. Dicit ergo: ita dictum est, quod illi *desperantes*, etc., *vos autem non ita didicistis Christum*, scilicet esse imitandum. Quomodo ergo? *Ipsi enim vos a Deo didicistis ut diligatis invicem*. II Thess. II, 15: *itaque, fratres, state et tenete traditiones quas credidistis*. Et quomodo tenebimus? I Thess. c. II, 13: *quoniam cum accepissetis a nobis verbum auditus Dei, accepistis illud non ut verbum hominum, sed sicut est vere, verbum Dei*, et cetera. Col. II, 7: *radicati et superaedificati in ipso, et confirmati in fide, sicut didicistis abundantes in illo in gratiarum actione*.

239. Et hoc certe, *si tamen illum audistis*, quia auditus deservit disciplinae. *Si*, pro quia. *Quia haec est Annuntiatio quam audistis*, ut dicitur I Io. I, 5. Et hoc quantum ad praedicationem fidei. Eccli. XXIV, 30: *qui audit me, non confundetur*. Prov. XV, 31: *auris quae audit increpationes vitae, in medio sapientium commorabitur*, et cetera. *Et in illo edocti estis*, scilicet quomodo pertinentia ad fidem sunt custodienda et adimplenda. Matth. ult.: *fecerunt sicut erant edocti*, et cetera. Et hoc *sicut est veritas in Iesu*, quasi dicat: si audivistis fidem Christi

237. Having shown the depravity of the gentile's conduct, the Apostle points out now that Christ's teaching is completely contrary to such a way of life and condition. Because some men who distorted Christian doctrine held there is no life after the present one, but that man's soul, like the rest of the animals, dies with his body, the Apostle makes clear:

first, that Christ's teaching is contrary to their former life and condition;

second, the requisites of Christ's teaching, at *to put off*.

238. Thus he affirms: it was said that they, *despairing, have given themselves up to lasciviousness* (Eph 4:19), *but you have not learned* that *Christ* is to be so imitated. How should he be imitated? *You yourselves have been taught by God that you must love one another* (1 Thess 4:9). *Therefore, brethren, stand fast; and hold the traditions which you have learned* (2 Thess 2:14). And how shall we retain them? *When you had received of us the word of the hearing of God, you received it not as the word of men, but, as it is indeed, the word of God, who works in you that have believed* (1 Thess 2:13). Therefore, *rooted and built up in him and confirmed in the faith, as also you have learned; abounding in him in thanksgiving* (Col 2:7).

239. This certainly will happen *if you have heard him*, for hearing is the servant of instruction. *If* here is the equivalent of *because*. *And this is the declaration which you have heard* (1 John 1:5); this is in reference to the proclamation of the faith. *He that harkens to me shall not be confounded* (Sir 24:30). And *the ear that hears the reproofs of life shall abide in the midst of the wise. He that rejects instruction despises his own soul: but he that yields to reproof possesses understanding* (Prov 15:31–32). If also *you have been taught in him* how what pertains to faith must be kept and

praedicari et quomodo praedicata debeant adimpleri, estis edocti, sicut Iesus, de quo praedicatur vobis, qui est veritas. Vos autem non ita, scilicet oportet ambulare, sicut aliqui desperantes.

240. Sed quomodo? Subdit **deponite vos**, et cetera. Quae quidem littera potest legi dupliciter. Uno modo, ut dicatur **deponere**, et tunc construitur cum praecedentibus sic: ita est veritas in qua edocti estis in Iesu, **deponere vos**, et cetera. Si autem dicatur **deponite**, quae littera communius habetur, dicemus quod quia contraria est et vita et doctrina gentilium, vitae et doctrinae Iesu, in qua edocti estis, restat ut deponatis, et cetera.

Duo ergo facit. Quia cum primo extirpanda sint vitia quam inserantur virtutes,

primo docet eos statum pristinae ac veteris conversationis deponere;

secundo novum statum Iesu assumere, ibi **renovamini autem spiritu**, et cetera.

241. Dicit ergo: **deponite**, et cetera. Ubi tria sunt consideranda. Primo quid intelligatur per **veterem hominem**.

Dicunt aliqui, quod hic homo vetus exterior, novus vero dicitur interior. Sed dicendum est quod homo vetus dicitur tam interior quam exterior, qui subiicitur vetustati quantum ad animam per peccatum et quantum ad corpus, quia membra corporis sunt arma peccati. Et sic, subiectus homo peccato secundum animam et corpus, dicitur vetus homo, secundum quod illa vetusta sunt, quae sunt in via corruptionis, vel in ipso corrumpi; quia *quod antiquatur et senescit, prope interitum est*, ut dicitur ad Hebr. VIII, 13. Et sic homo subiectus peccato dicitur vetus, quia est in via corruptionis; propter quod subdit **qui corrumpitur secundum desideria erroris**. Nam unumquodque corrumpitur, cum recedit ab ordine naturae suae. Natura autem hominis est, ut desiderium eius tendat ad id quod est secundum rationem. Perfectio autem et bonum rationis est veritas. Quando ergo ratio tendit ad errorem, et desiderium ex hoc errore corrumpitur, tunc vetus homo dicitur.

Dicit autem **secundum desideria**, scilicet mala. Rom. XIII, 14: *carnis curam ne feceritis in desideriis*. I Tim. VI, 9: *desideria multa, et nociva, et inutilia, quae mergunt hominem in interitum et perditionem*, et cetera. Quia autem haec desideria in quibusdam trahuntur ex infirmitate, in quibusdam vero ex malitia, sicut in illis qui dicunt Deum providentiam non habere, ideo dicit **erroris**; quia in talibus sic errantibus corrumpitur intellectus et affectus. Vel **secundum desideria erroris**, id est quae homines faciunt errare, secundum illud

fulfilled. *They did as they were taught* (Matt 28:15), **as the truth is in Jesus**. As though he said: if you have heard the faith of Christ preached and how this faith must be put into practice, you have been taught what Jesus is like, who is himself the truth which is imparted to you. You must not, therefore, behave as those who despair.

240. How should they live? He adds **to put off, according to the former way of life, the old man**. The passage has two variant readings. One is the infinitive, **to put off**; then it would be construed with what preceded to read: the truth about which you were instructed in Jesus was to **put off the old man**. The more common reading has an imperative, **put off**; in this case the signification is: since the life and teachings of the gentiles are contrary to those of Jesus, in which you have been taught, the only alternative is that you discard the old man.

Hence he makes two points here since vices must first be eradicated before virtues can be cultivated:

first, he instructs them to put aside their former condition, their old way of living;

second, how they must take on a new way of life characteristic of Jesus, at **and be renewed in the spirit**.

241. Hence, he says **put off, according to former way of life, the old man**; and three considerations follow. First, what does **the old man** mean?

Some hold that the old man is external and the new man interior. But it must be said that the old man is both interior and exterior; he is a person who is enslaved by a senility in his soul, due to sin, and in his body whose members provide the tools for sin. Thus a man enslaved to sin in soul and body is an old man. He is already on the way to corruption, or is actually beginning to decay since *that which decays and grows old is near its end* (Heb 8:13). And so a man subjected to sin is termed an old man because he is on the way to corruption. On this account he goes on, **corrupted according to the desire of error**. Anything will corrupt when it deviates from the order of its nature. Man's nature longs for what accords with reason; and truth is reason's perfection and good. Hence, when someone's reason sways toward error, and his desire is corrupted from this error, he is referred to as an old man.

This, he says, is **according to** evil **desire**. *Make not provision for the flesh in its concupiscences* (Rom 13:14); *many are the unprofitable and hurtful desires which drown men into destruction and perdition* (1 Tim 6:9). Some people are lured into these cravings through their own weakness. Malice will draw others to them, as it does those who say that God does not have a providential care. Therefore he adds **of error** because the mind and affections of those who maliciously err become corrupted. Possibly the **desire of error** refers to whatever makes men err, according to what is written: *these things they thought, and were deceived: for*

Sap. II, 21: *haec cogitaverunt et erraverunt*, et cetera. Prov. XIV, 8: *imprudentia stultorum errans*.

Sed quomodo deponendus sit, docet Apostolus, dicens Col. III, 9: *expoliantes vos veterem hominem cum actibus suis*, et cetera. Non ergo substantialiter debet deponi vel expoliari, sed solum quoad opera mala, vel conversationem. I Petr. II, 12: *conversationem vestram inter gentes habentes bonam*. I Tim. IV, 12: *exemplum esto fidelium in verbo et conversatione*.

242. Deinde cum dicit **renovamini**, etc., ostendit, quod debemus novum statum induere.

Circa quod tria facit.

Primo ostendit per quid consequi possumus hanc novitatem;

secundo in quo haec novitas consistat;

tertio quae sit.

243. Quantum ad primum dicit **renovamini spiritu**, et cetera.

Ubi notandum est quod licet **spiritus** multipliciter dicatur in homine, tamen triplex spiritus invenitur, scilicet Spiritus Sanctus, I Cor. c. III, 16: *nescitis quod templum Dei estis, et Spiritus Dei habitat in vobis?* Item, spiritus rationalis, Gal. V, 17: *caro concupiscit adversus spiritum*. Item, spiritus phantasticus. Os. IX, 7: *scitote Israel stultum prophetam, insanum virum, spiritualem*, id est phantasticum. Hoc ergo quod dicit **Spiritu mentis**, sumitur pro Spiritu Sancto. Dicit autem causam renovationis esse Spiritum Sanctum, qui habitat in mente nostra. Gal. IV, 6: *misit Deus Spiritum Filii sui in corda*, et cetera. Ps. CIII, v. 30: *emitte Spiritum tuum, et creabuntur*, et cetera.

Vel potest accipi **spiritus** pro spiritu rationali, et tunc spiritus idem est quod mens nostra, et est simile huic quod dicitur Col. II, v. 11: *in expoliatione corporis carnis*, id est corporis, quae est caro; ita hic **spiritu mentis**, id est spiritu, qui est mens; hoc autem dicit, quia in nobis est alius spiritus, qui non est mens, qui scilicet est communis nobis et brutis.

244. Dicit autem **renovamini spiritu mentis**, quia illud quod non est corruptum est novum, nec renovatione indiget. Nam si Adam corruptus non fuisset, renovatione non indiguisset, nec nos etiam. Sed quia corruptus fuit, renovatione indiguit et eius posteriores. Et ideo oportet renovari nos in praesenti secundum animam, et in futuro secundum corpus, quando *corruptibile hoc induet incorruptionem, et mortale immortalitatem*, ut dicitur I Cor. XV, 53. Dicit ergo **renovamini spiritu**, hic scilicet, quia nisi in praesenti spiritus renovetur, numquam corpus eius innovabitur.

their own malice blinded them (Wis 2:21); *the imprudence of fools errs* (Prov 14:8).

The Apostle indicates how to leave the old man behind: *stripping yourselves of the old man with his deeds* (Col 3:9). The substance of human nature is not to be rejected or despoiled, but only wicked actions and conduct. *Have your manner of life good among the gentiles* (1 Pet 2:12); *be an example of the faithful, in word, in conduct, in charity, in faith, in chastity* (1 Tim 4:12).

242. Next, when he says **be renewed**, he indicates the new condition they are to take on.

Concerning this, he shows three things:

first, through what means we can obtain this newness;

second, in whom this newness resides;

third, what the newness is.

243. Regarding the first he says **be renewed in the spirit of your mind**.

Notice that although **spirit** is frequently said to be in man, nevertheless three spirits are discernible in him. One is the Holy Spirit: *do you not know that you are the temple of God and that the Spirit of God dwells in you?* (1 Cor 3:16). Another is his spiritual reason: *for the flesh lusts against the spirit; and the spirit against the flesh* (Gal 5:17). Finally, there is man's imaginative spirit: *know, O Israel, that the prophet was foolish, the man was mad, and spiritual* (Hos 9:7), that is, his imagination went wild. Therefore, the **Spirit of your mind** may point to the Holy Spirit. He then states that the cause of renewal is the Holy Spirit who dwells in our mind: *God has sent the Spirit of his Son into your hearts* (Gal 4:6). *Send forth your Spirit, and they shall be created: and you shall renew the face of the earth* (Ps 104:30).

Or **spirit** could refer to the rational spirit and would be identical with our mind, similar to the expression: *in despoiling of the body of the flesh* (Col 2:11), that is, the body which the flesh is. Likewise here, **in the spirit of your mind** would refer to the spirit which the mind is. He would qualify it in this way since there is another spirit within us, differing from the mind, and which is common to both us and the beasts.

244. However, he states **be renewed in the spirit of your mind**; what is not spoiled is new and does not require a renewal. If Adam had not become tainted neither he nor ourselves would need a renovation. Yet, once he was corrupted, both he and his offspring are in need of a renovation. In the present life we must be renewed in soul; our body will be in the future when *this corruptible must put on incorruption, and this mortal must put on immortality* (1 Cor 15:52). Hence he says **be renewed in the spirit** since, unless the spirit is renewed in this life, the body will never be renewed.

Vel potest exponi *spiritu mentis*, id est mente vestra spirituali facta; et in idem redit.

245. In quo autem haec renovatio consistat, quantum ad secundum, subdit cum dicit *et induite novum hominem*, et cetera.

Hic advertendum est quod sicut uniuscuiusque rei primum vetustatis principium fuit Adam, per quem peccatum in omnes intravit, ita principium primum novitatis et renovationis Christus est; quia *sicut in Adam omnes moriuntur, ita et in Christo omnes vivificabuntur*. Unde Gal. ult.: *in Christo Iesu neque circumcisio, neque praeputium aliquid valet, sed nova creatura. Induimini ergo Dominum nostrum Iesum Christum*, Rom. c. XIII, 14.

246. Quae autem sit renovatio ostendit, cum dicit *qui secundum Deum creatus est*, et cetera. Hoc autem potest intelligi tripliciter. Uno modo sic, ut ly *qui*, referatur ad spiritum, id est: spiritus, qui est mens nostra, creatus est a Deo, scilicet in originali iustitia, scilicet in sui novitate; vel recreatus nova creatione, ut esset iustus. Supra II, 10: *creati in Christo Iesu in operibus bonis*.

Vel ly *qui*, potest referri ad novum hominem, scilicet Christum. Et tunc construetur sic: *qui creatus est*, id est formatus in utero Virginis *secundum Deum*, id est non semine humano, sed Spiritu Sancto. Vel *creatus est* secundum esse gratiae et plenitudinis, et hoc *in iustitia*, quoad homines, *et sanctitate*, quoad Deum, et hoc *veritatis*, non falsitatis. Lc. I, 75: *in sanctitate et iustitia*. Vel ut sanctitas sit in corde, veritas in ore, iustitia in opere.

Or, *in the spirit of your mind* can be interpreted as in your mind which was made spiritual and will return to the same.

245. *And put on the new man* discloses in whom this renewal takes place.

Here it is to be remembered that Adam introduced sin into all men, and thus became for everything the primary source of oldness. Likewise, the primary source of newness and renovation is Christ. *As in Adam all die, so also in Christ all shall be made alive* (1 Cor 15:22). *For in Christ Jesus neither circumcision avails any thing, nor uncircumcision; but a new creature* (Gal 6:15). Therefore, *put on the Lord Jesus Christ* (Rom 13:14).

246. *Who, according to God, is created in justice and holiness of truth* makes known what the renovation is. It admits of a triple explanation. If *who* refers to man's spirit, it would mean: the spirit, which our mind is, was created by God in the freshness of original justice; or, by a second creative act was renewed to be just again: *created in Christ Jesus in good works* (Eph 2:10).

Or, *who* might have reference to the new man, Christ. Then the text could be construed as: *who is created*, that is, formed in the Virgin's womb *according to God* by the Holy Spirit and not human seed. Or, he *was created* according to an existence of grace, as well as a fullness *in justice* toward men *and holiness* before God that was not fictitious but *of truth*: *in holiness and justice before him* (Luke 1:75). Or it could mean that holiness is in his heart, truth on his tongue, and justice in his actions.

Lecture 8

⁴:²⁵Propter quod deponentes mendacium, loquimini veritatem unusquisque cum proximo suo: quoniam sumus invicem membra. [n. 248]

⁴:²⁶Irascimini, et nolite peccare: sol non occidat super iracundiam vestram. [n. 249]

⁴:²⁷Nolite locum dare diabolo: [n. 252]

⁴:²⁵Διὸ ἀποθέμενοι τὸ ψεῦδος λαλεῖτε ἀλήθειαν ἕκαστος μετὰ τοῦ πλησίον αὐτοῦ, ὅτι ἐσμὲν ἀλλήλων μέλη.

⁴:²⁶ὀργίζεσθε καὶ μὴ ἁμαρτάνετε· ὁ ἥλιος μὴ ἐπιδυέτω ἐπὶ [τῷ] παροργισμῷ ὑμῶν,

⁴:²⁷μηδὲ δίδοτε τόπον τῷ διαβόλῳ.

⁴:²⁵Wherefore, putting away lying, speak the truth, every man with his neighbor. For we are members one of another. [n. 248]

⁴:²⁶Be angry: and do not sin. Do not let the sun go down upon your anger. [n. 249]

⁴:²⁷Do not give place to the devil. [n. 252]

---

247. Supra posita generali monitione, ut novitatem induerent, hic Apostolus ponit praecepta specialia.

Circa quod duo facit.

Primo inhibet eis peccata interiora corrumpentia spiritum;

secundo peccata exteriora, quae corrumpunt carnem, ibi *fornicatio autem*, et cetera.

Prima in duas.

Primo prohibet peccata, quae in deordinatione propria consistunt;

secundo peccata, quae consistunt in deordinatione alterius, ibi *omnis sermo malus*, et cetera.

Prima iterum in tres, quia

primo prohibet peccatum corrumpens rationalem;

secundo peccatum deordinans irascibilem, ibi *irascimini, et nolite peccare*, etc.;

tertio peccatum pertinens ad concupiscibilem, ibi *qui furabatur*, et cetera.

248. Circa primum tria facit. Primo quia unum istorum prohibet; secundo inducit ad aliud; tertio rationem assignat.

Prohibet ergo illud primo quod ad veterem hominem pertinet, ita ut ista littera sit expositiva huius, quod praedixerat: *induite novum hominem*, ad quem induendum primo prohibet mendacium, quia per hoc peccatum oris corrumpitur veritas rationis. Unde dicit *propter quod*, scilicet novum hominem induendum, sitis supple, *deponentes mendacium*, quia, ut dicitur in Ps. V, 7: *perdes omnes qui loquuntur mendacium*, scilicet perniciosum.

Et postea inducit ad novitatem, dicens Zac. c. VIII, 16: *loquimini veritatem unusquisque cum proximo suo*.

Et quare? *Quoniam sumus invicem membra*. Membra enim se invicem diligunt et se iuvant mutuo in veritate. Rom. XII, 5: *unum corpus sumus in Christo, singuli autem alter alterius membra*.

249. Sequitur *irascimini*, et cetera. Ubi prohibet peccatum, corrumpens irascibilem.

Circa quod tria facit.

247. Having set down above the general admonition to put on a newness of life, now the Apostle lays out the particular precepts.

Concerning this he does two things:

first, he restrains them from committing interior sins which corrupt the spirit;

second, he prohibits exterior sins which corrupt the flesh, at *but fornication* (Eph 5:3).

The first has two divisions:

first, he forbids sins which consist in one's personal disorder;

second, he forbids sins which consist in the disorder of others, at *let no evil speech* (Eph 4:29).

The first section again is divided into three parts since he forbids:

first, sin corrupting man's rational powers;

second, sin disordering his irascible emotions, at *be angry: and do not sin*;

third, sin pertaining to the concupiscible emotions, at *he that stole* (Eph 4:28).

248. Regarding the first of these he does three things. First, he forbids one of them; then he urges its opposite; third, he gives his reason.

Hence, he first prohibits what is characteristic of the old man, thereby expounding what he said above: *put on the new man* (Eph 4:24). To accomplish this he first bans lying because through this sin of the tongue the truth of reason is corrupted. *Wherefore* to put on the new man you should be *putting away lying*, for *you O Lord will destroy all that speak a lie* (Ps 5:7) maliciously.

Then he urges them on to newness of life. *Speak the truth, every man with his neighbor* (Zech 8:16).

And why? *For we are members one of another*. For members are to love and mutually assist one another in truth. *We, being many, are one body in Christ; and every one members one of another* (Rom 12:5).

249. Next, at *be angry: and do not sin*, he forbids sins destructive of the order in the irascible emotions.

Concerning this he makes three points:

Primo ponit monitionem;

secundo eam exponit, ibi *sol non occidat*, etc.;

tertio rationem reddit, ibi *nolite locum*, et cetera.

250. Monitionem autem ponit, cum dicit *irascimini*, et cetera. Quod potest exponi dupliciter, quia duplex est species irae, quaedam bona, quaedam mala. Mala quidem quando inordinate tendit in vindictam, scilicet contra iustitiam; bona vero quando in vindictam debitam, quando scilicet quis irascitur quando oportet, cum quibus, et quantum oportet. Et de utraque potest exponi.

Si de mala, sic est sensus: non praecipit, sed permittit; quasi dicat: si sic est, quod motus irae insurgat, quod humanum est, nolite peccare, id est nolite perducere ad effectum per consensum. I Cor. X, 13: *tentatio vos non apprehendat nisi humana*. Quia certe, qui aliter irascitur fratri suo, *reus erit iudicio*, ut dicitur Matth. V, 22. De hac ira monebat Ioseph fratres suos Gen. XLV, 24: *ne irascimini in via*.

Si autem exponatur de bona, sic tenetur non solum permissive, ut primo, sed imperative, *irascimini*, scilicet contra peccata vestra, quoniam duplex est vindicta, quam homo appetit. Una de seipso peccante, et sic poenitentia est quaedam vindicta, quam homo facit et capit de seipso. Et haec est bona ira, et de hac dicitur imperative *irascimini*, scilicet contra peccata vestra, *et nolite peccare*, scilicet de caetero, nec talia committere, contra quae iterum oporteat irasci.

Modo credunt aliqui quod homo secure possit sibi ipsi irasci propter peccata sua, sed non proximo suo propter sua; sed non est ita: sicut enim contra seipsum quis irascitur propter peccata propria, ita proximo suo propter sua; ergo *irascimini* contra vitia aliena, et hoc cum zelo. Num. XXV, 11: *Phinees avertit iram meam a filiis Israel, quia zelo meo commotus est contra eos*. Sic Helias III Reg. XIX, 10: *zelo zelatus sum pro Domino Deo exercituum, quia dereliquerunt pactum Domini filii Israel*, et cetera. *Et nolite peccare* praeveniendo rationem, sed potius sequendo. Iac. I, 19: *sit autem omnis homo velox ad audiendum, tardus autem ad loquendum, et tardus ad iram*, et cetera.

251. Sequitur *sol non occidat*, et cetera. Ubi exponit quod dixerat, et, secundum tres praedictas expositiones, potest tripliciter exponi, quia si de mala ira, tunc sic: *sol*, etc., id est: non persistatis in ira concepta sed ante solis occasum deponatis, quia licet permittatur motus, propter fragilitatem, non permittitur mora.

Si de bona, et hoc contra peccata propria, tunc sic: *sol*, id est Christus, Mal. IV, 2: *orietur vobis timentibus*

first, he gives a warning;

second, he explains what he means, at *do not let the sun go down*;

third, he gives the reason for his concern, at *give no place*.

250. He gives his warning when he says *be angry: and do not sin*. This is susceptible of two interpretations; for there are two types of anger, a good one and an evil one. Anger is evil when, contrary to justice, it strives inordinately for revenge. It is good when it seeks a just vindication, namely, when the person is vexed at the time, with whom, and to the degree that, he should be. The above warning is applicable to both.

If it concerns evil anger, the sense is that he does not command it but permits it. As though he said: should it happen that anger wells up within you—which is human—do not sin. You must not be led on to act upon it. *Let no temptation take hold on you, but such as is human* (1 Cor 10:13). For, without doubt, whoever is angered against his brother in any other way *shall be in danger of the judgment* (Matt 5:22). Joseph counseled his brothers against such anger: *be not angry on the way* (Gen 45:24).

If it is interpreted concerning righteous anger it is not simply permitted, like the first, but imperative. **Be angry** against your sins, for man desires a twofold vindication. One regarding himself when he sins, so that penance becomes a certain type of vindication which man inflicts and receives in himself. Such a wrath is good, and with respect to it the imperative is used: *be angry* against your sins, *and do not sin* any more, nor commit those types of sin by which you would again have to be angered.

Now, some are doubtless of the opinion that a man can be mad at himself for his own sins safely, but that this does not hold true concerning his neighbors and their sins. This is false; a man can be mad at himself for his own sins, and at his fellow man because of his sins. Therefore, zealously *be angry* at other people's offenses. *Phinees has turned away my wrath from the children of Israel because he was moved with my zeal against them* (Num 25:11). And Elias said: *with zeal have I been zealous for the Lord God of Hosts: for the children of Israel have forsaken your covenant* (1 Kgs 19:10). By following the dictates of reason, rather than acting before them, you *do not sin*. *Let every man be swift to hear, but slow to speak, and slow to anger* (Jas 1:19).

251. In *do not let the sun go down upon your anger* he explains what he had said, and the explanation can be interpreted according to the three above expositions. If it concerns evil anger, then he would be saying: do not persist in anger, but cast if off before sunset; for although the first impulses of temper are excusable, due to human frailty, it is illicit to dwell on them.

In reference to good anger, as it is directed against one's personal sins, the *sun* is Christ. *Unto you that fear my name*

nomen meum sol iustitiae, etc., **non occidat super iracundiam vestram**, id est super peccata vestra, pro quibus iterum oporteat vos irasci, et vosmetipsos punire.

Si contra peccata aliena, sic accipitur **sol**, scilicet rationis. Eccle. XII, 1: *memento Creatoris tui in diebus iuventutis tuae, antequam veniat tempus afflictionis, et appropinquent anni, de quibus dicas: non mihi placent, antequam tenebrescat sol, et cetera.* **Sol non occidat super iracundiam vestram**, id est non obtenebretur dictamen rationis. Iob V, 2: *virum stultum interficit iracundia*.

252. Sequitur **nolite locum dare diabolo**, ubi assignat rationem monitionis. Diabolus enim habet locum in nobis per peccatum, vel per consensum. Io. XIII, 2: *cum diabolus iam misisset in cor, ut traderet eum Iudas, et cetera*. Et sequitur ibid., quod *post buccellam introivit in eum Satanas*.

Nunc autem huiusmodi passiones multum inclinant ad consensum et maxime quando pervertunt iudicium rationis, et hoc specialiter facit ira, quae consistit in accensione sanguinis, quae quidem ratione velocitatis sui motus praecedit iudicium rationis. Et quia, sic nobis perturbatis, diabolus incipit locum habere in nobis, ideo dicit **nolite locum dare diabolo**, quasi dicat: non perseveretis in ira, quia per hoc datis locum diabolo, quia totus diabolus iracundus est. Ps. XVII, 48: *liberator meus de inimicis meis iracundis*. Intrat autem hominem cum furore et ira. Apoc. XII, 12: *descendit diabolus ad vos, habens iram magnam*. Hoc autem non potest facere saltem in anima, quamdiu homo iustus est. Haec autem iustitia per iram amittitur, quia *ira viri iustitiam Dei non operatur*, ut dicitur Iac. I, 20. Si ergo non vultis locum dare diabolo, saltem in anima, **sol non occidat super iracundiam vestram**. Eccle. XI, 10: *aufer iram a corde tuo*.

the sun of justice shall arise (Mal 4:2). **Do not let the sun go down upon your anger**, that is, on your sins, on account of which you must be angered again and punish yourselves.

When the sins of others are in question the **sun** refers to reason. *Remember your Creator in the days of your youth, before the time of affliction come, and the years draw nigh of which you shall say: they please me not; before the sun . . . is darkened* (Eccl 12:1). **Do not let the sun go down upon your anger**, that is, the dictates of reason must not be clouded over. *Anger indeed kills the foolish* (Job 5:2).

252. The reason for the warning is indicated in **do not give place to the devil**. The devil gains entrance to us either through sin or consent to it. *The devil having now put into the heart of Judas Iscariot, the son of Simon, to betray him* (John 13:2), after which it says: *after the morsel, Satan entered into him* (John 13:27).

Passions of this kind easily induce one's consent, especially when they have biased the judgment of reason. Anger particularly does this since it involves the rapid raising of blood, the speed of whose movement precedes any rational judgment. When we are excited like this, the devil wins a foothold within us; thus he says **do not give place to the devil**. You ought not to persist, he seems to say, in your ill temper, for you will only invite the demon who is himself continually angered. God is *my deliverer from my infuriated enemies* (Ps 18:48). The devil enters into man with rage and fury: *the devil is come down unto you, having great wrath* (Rev 12:12). He cannot accomplish this, at least not in the soul of a just man. But this justice is forfeited through anger: *for the anger of man does not work the justice of God* (Jas 1:20). If you do not want to give Satan a place, at least not in your soul, **do not let the sun go down upon your anger**. *Remove anger from your heart* (Eccl 11:10).

Lecture 9

4:28qui furabatur, jam non furetur: magis autem laboret, operando manibus suis, quod bonum est, ut habeat unde tribuat necessitatem patienti. [n. 254]

4:28ὁ κλέπτων μηκέτι κλεπτέτω, μᾶλλον δὲ κοπιάτω ἐργαζόμενος ταῖς [ἰδίαις] χερσὶν τὸ ἀγαθόν, ἵνα ἔχῃ μεταδιδόναι τῷ χρείαν ἔχοντι.

4:28He that stole, let him now steal no more: but rather let him labor, working with his hands the thing which is good, that he may have something to give to him who suffers need. [n. 254]

4:29Omnis sermo malus ex ore vestro non procedat: sed si quis bonus ad aedificationem fidei ut det gratiam audientibus. [n. 258]

4:29πᾶς λόγος σαπρὸς ἐκ τοῦ στόματος ὑμῶν μὴ ἐκπορευέσθω, ἀλλὰ εἴ τις ἀγαθὸς πρὸς οἰκοδομὴν τῆς χρείας, ἵνα δῷ χάριν τοῖς ἀκούουσιν.

4:29Let no evil speech proceed from your mouth: but that which is good, to the edification of faith: that it may administer grace to the hearers. [n. 258]

253. Exclusa supra vetustate hominis quantum ad vim rationalem et irascibilem, hic prohibet eam quantum ad concupiscibilem provenientem ex rerum inordinata concupiscentia.

Circa quod duo facit.

Primo prohibet concupiscibilis vetustatem;

secundo hortatur ad eius novitatem, ibi *magis autem laboret*, et cetera.

254. Ad vetustatem autem concupiscibilis pertinet furtum, quod provenit ex corrupto et inordinato appetitu rei temporalis. Ideo dicit *qui furabatur, iam non furetur*, etc., quasi dicat: qui habebat concupiscibilem corruptam et vetustam ex corrupto appetitu rerum temporalium, iam non furetur, scilicet si vult concupiscibilem renovare, quia, ut dicitur Eccli. V, 17: *super furem confusio*; propter hoc dicitur Ex. XX, 15: *non furtum facies*.

255. Et quia aliquis posset se excusare prae paupertate, ideo dicit *magis autem laboret*, et cetera. Sicut ipse fecit Apostolus, ut dicitur Act. XX, 33: *argentum et aurum nullius concupivi, aut vestem, vos ipsi scitis, quoniam ad ea quae mihi opus erant, et his qui mecum sunt, ministraverunt manus istae*. Item II Thess. III, 78: *ipsi enim scitis quemadmodum oporteat vos imitari nos, quoniam non inquieti fuimus inter vos, neque gratis panem manducavimus ab aliquo, sed in labore et fatigatione, nocte ac die laborantes, ne quem vestrum gravaremus*, et cetera.

256. Unde notandum est, quod opus manuale ad tria inducitur. Primo ad necessitatem victus acquirendam. Gen. III, 19: *in sudore vultus tui vesceris pane tuo*. Et ideo qui non habet unde licite vivat, tenetur manibus laborare. II Thess. III, 10: *si quis non vult operari, non manducet*; quasi dicat: sicut qui non comedit in necessitate peccat, ita et si non laborat. Et sic ponitur hic ad excludendum furtum.

Quandoque vero inducitur contra otium, quia *multa mala docuit otiositas*, Eccli. XXXIII, v. 29. Et ideo

253. Having banned the oldness of man in regard to his rational and irascible powers, here he proscribes it in regard to the concupiscible appetite when it desires temporal goods inordinately.

Concerning this he does two things:

first, he prohibits the old ways of the concupiscible appetite;

second, he encourages a renewal of it, at *rather let him labor*.

254. Stealing pertains to the concupiscible appetite's old ways; it arises from a corrupted and inordinate desire for a temporal object. Therefore he says *he that stole, let him now steal no more*, as if to say: whoever has an old and corrupted concupiscible appetite due to a contaminating desire for transitory goods, let him not steal any more if he wants to renew it. For *confusion is upon a thief* (Sir 5:17), so that it is written: *you shall not steal* (Exod 20:15).

255. Since someone might excuse himself by reason of his poverty, he says *rather let him labor, working with his hands*. The Apostle himself practiced this: *for such things as were needful for me and them that are with me, these hands have furnished* (Acts 20:34). *For you yourselves know how you ought to imitate us: for we were not disorderly among you; neither did we eat any man's bread for nothing, but in labor and in toil we worked night and day, lest we should be chargeable to any of you* (2 Thess 3:7–8).

256. Notice that three motives for manual labor are given. Primarily, it is to obtain necessary food: *in the sweat of your face shall you eat bread* (Gen 3:19). Therefore, anyone who does not lawfully have the where-with-all to live is bound to work with his hands. *If any man will not work, neither let him eat*, (2 Thess 3:10) seems to affirm: just as he who does not eat when necessity demands it sins, so likewise he who does not work when necessary. This is put here to exclude stealing.

Sometimes, however, work is urged in order to dispel idleness since *idleness has taught much evil* (Sir 33:29).

qui habent vitam otiosam, tenentur manibus laborare. II Thess. III, 11 s.: *audivimus quosdam inter vos ambulare in quiete nihil operantes, sed curiose agentes. His autem, qui huiusmodi sunt, denuntiamus et obsecramus in Domino Iesu Christo, ut cum silentio operantes suum panem manducent.*

Quandoque enim inducitur ad carnis macerationem et domationem. Unde ponitur inter alia opera continentiae II Cor. VI, 5: *in laboribus, in vigiliis, in ieiuniis,* et cetera.

Triplex ergo est ratio iniungendi laborem corporalem; sed prima omnibus necessaria est, et hoc de necessitate praecepti, quia aliis modis potest excludi otium, similiter et lascivia carnis potest alio modo domari et refrenari, et sufficit quomodocumque fiat.

257. Sequitur **quod bonum est**, quod dupliciter potest intelligi. Vel in vi accusativi, et sic construetur: **magis autem laboret operando manibus**, et quidem non illicita, sed **quod bonum est**. Gal. ult.: *bonum autem facientes, non deficiamus.* Is. I, 16 s.: *quiescite agere perverse, discite bene facere.*

Vel potest intelligi in vi nominativi: **laboret**, etc., **quod bonum est**, quasi haec sit ratio quare laborandum est; quasi dicat: non solum est necessarium laborare, immo etiam bonum est laborare, ut laborans possit vivere, et **ut habeat unde tribuat necessitatem patienti**. Eccli. XXIX, 2: *foenerare proximo tuo in tempore necessitatis illius,* et cetera.

258. Deinde cum dicit **omnis sermo malus**, etc., ponit pertinentia ad veterem hominem in deordinatione ad alium; et facit duo: quia

primo prohibet vetustatem, et inducit novitatem;

secundo inducit exemplum, in principio V cap., ibi **estote ergo**, et cetera.

Ad proximum autem potest quis male se habere dupliciter. Uno modo laedendo eum verbis malis; alio modo malis exemplis. Primo prohibet primum; secundo secundum, ibi **et nolite contristare**, et cetera.

Prima iterum in duas.

Primo prohibet vetustatem;

secundo inducit ad novitatem, ibi **sed si quis**, et cetera.

259. Dicit ergo **omnis sermo malus**, et cetera. Sermo oris praetendit et annuntiat quae sunt in anima, quia voces sunt earum, quae sunt in anima, passionum notae. Ille est bonus sermo, qui indicat bonam dispositionem interiorem, malus vero qui malam.

Tripliciter autem homo ordinatur interius, scilicet ad se, ut scilicet omnia sint rationi subiecta; ad Deum, ut ratio sit ei subdita; ad proximum, quando diligit eum ut

Hence, those who lead an idle life are bound to work with their hands: *for we have heard there are some among you who walk disorderly; working not at all, but curiously meddling. Now we charge them that are such and beseech them by the Lord Jesus Christ that, working with silence, they would eat their own bread* (2 Thess 3:11–12).

At other times work is recommended to discipline and subdue the flesh. In this sense it is included among the acts of continence: *in labors, in watchings, in fastings* (2 Cor 6:5).

Three reasons exist, therefore, for engaging in physical labor. The first is necessary for everyone, and is so by a necessity of precept, while idleness can be avoided in other ways and the immoral tendencies of the flesh can be controlled and checked by other means. It is sufficient if these latter are accomplished in some way.

257. Which is good follows and can be understood in two ways. If it has the accusative force it could be rendered: **rather let him labor, working with his hands**, not at what is unlawful, but at whatever is **good**. *And in doing good, let us not fail. For in due time we shall reap, not failing* (Gal 6:9). *Cease to do perversely. Learn to do well* (Isa 1:16–17).

Or it can be taken with a nominative force: **rather let him labor, working with his hands, which is good**. This is the reason why they should work, as though he said: not only is it necessary to work, it is even good to work that he who does can live and **that he may have something to give to him who suffers need**. *Lend to your neighbor in the time of his need* (Sir 29:2).

258. When he states **let no evil speech proceed from your mouth**, he begins to discuss what the old man does in relation to other men. He makes two points:

first, he prohibits the old and encourages the new;

second, he provides an example for imitation at the beginning of chapter five, at **be therefore followers** (Eph 5:1).

A person may be wrongly disposed toward his neighbor in two ways. In one way, he may hurt him through evil words; in another, he may harm him through bad example. First he forbids the former; second the latter, at **do not grieve** (Eph 4:30).

The first of these also has two sections:

first, he bans the old;

second, he urges them toward the new, at **but only that which is good**.

259. Thus he says **let no evil speech proceed from your mouth**. A word from the mouth exteriorizes or expresses whatever is on the mind since spoken words are signs of what occurs in the soul. A good word is one which indicates good interior dispositions, while an evil word externalizes evil dispositions.

Man should possess a threefold inner relationship; namely, to himself, that all his powers are subject to reason; to God, so that his reason submits to him; and to his

seipsum. Est ergo quandoque sermo malus, quando indicat hominem inordinatum in se, et hic est sermo falsus eius, qui aliud loquitur et aliud intendit: et similiter sermo inutilis et vanus. Item, est sermo malus qui indicat hominem inordinatum contra Deum: sicut periuria, blasphemiae, et huiusmodi. Item, etiam est sermo malus, quando est contra proximum suum: sicut iniuriae, doli, et fallaciae. Et ideo dicit **omnis sermo malus ex ore vestro non procedat**. **Omnis non** vero aequipollet huic signo, nullus. Sap. I, 11: *custodite ergo vos a murmuratione, quae nihil prodest, et a detractione parcite linguae, quia sermo obscurus in vacuum non ibit*; quia certe Deum *non praeterit omnis cogitatus et non abscondit se ab eo ullus sermo*, ut dicitur Eccli. XLII, 20. *Nunc autem deponite et vos omnia, iram, indignationem, malitiam, blasphemiam, turpem sermonem de ore vestro*, Col. III.

260. Sequitur **sed si quis bonus est**, et cetera. Inducit ad novitatem, quia sermo bonus benedicendus est pro loco et tempore. Prov. c. XV, 23: *sermo opportunus est optimus. Si quis ergo loquitur, quasi sermones Dei*, I Petr. c. IV, 11.

261. Et ad quid? Subdit **ad aedificationem fidei**, id est ut corroboretur fides in cordibus infirmorum. I Cor. XIV, 26: *omnia ad aedificationem fiant*.

Et hoc **ut det gratiam audientibus**, scilicet si talis bonus sermo sit probatus, vel talis sermo est conferens: quia frequenter homo ex bono sermone et per virtutem boni sermonis auditi, compunctus disponitur ad gratiam. Act. X, 44: *adhuc loquente Petro verba haec, cecidit Spiritus Sanctus super omnes qui audiebant verbum*. Sic loquebatur Dominus, de quo dicitur Lc. IV, 22: *mirabantur ex verbis gratiae, quae procedebant de ore ipsius*. Eccle. X, 12: *verba oris sapientis gratia*.

fellow man when he loves him as himself. Hence a word is evil when it shows that a man is not properly related within himself. This is the false word by which he means one thing and says another; futile and vain talk also belong to this category. Again, there are wicked words which indicate that a man is not related properly to God, such as perjury, blasphemy and the like. Finally, there is also evil talk which is against one's neighbor, such as injurious, deceitful, and fraudulent words. Therefore does he say **let no evil speech proceed from your mouth**. **No** is equivalent to *none*. *Keep yourselves therefore from murmuring which profits nothing, and refrain your tongue from detraction: for an obscure speech shall not go for naught* (Wis 1:11). For it is certainly true of God that *no thought escapes him and no word can hide itself from him* (Sir 42:20). *But now put away also any anger, indignation, malice, blasphemy, or filthy speech out of your mouth* (Col 3:8).

260. With **that which is good** he encourages them on toward newness because a good word, spoken at the right time and place, is blessed. *A word in due time is best* (Prov 15:23). *If any man speak, let him speak as the words of God* (1 Pet 4:11).

261. And what for? He adds **to the edification of faith** in order, that is, for faith to be strengthened in the hearts of the weak: *let all things be done to edification* (1 Cor 14:26).

If **it may administer grace to the hearers** such a word is proven good and it is profitable. For frequently a man repents and is disposed for grace from hearing a good sermon and through the power it conveys. *While Peter was yet speaking these words, the Holy Spirit fell on all them that heard the word* (Acts 10:44). Our Lord spoke in this fashion: *they wondered at the words of grace that proceeded from his mouth* (Luke 4:22). *The words of the mouth of a wise man are grace* (Eccl 10:12).

Lecture 10

4:30Et nolite contristare Spiritum Sanctum Dei: in quo signati estis in diem redemptionis. [n. 263]

4:31Omnis amaritudo, et ira, et indignatio, et clamor, et blasphemia tollatur a vobis cum omni malitia. [n. 264]

4:32Estote autem invicem benigni, misericordes, donantes invicem sicut et Deus in Christo donavit vobis. [n. 265]

4:30καὶ μὴ λυπεῖτε τὸ πνεῦμα τὸ ἅγιον τοῦ θεοῦ, ἐν ᾧ ἐσφραγίσθητε εἰς ἡμέραν ἀπολυτρώσεως.

4:31πᾶσα πικρία καὶ θυμὸς καὶ ὀργὴ καὶ κραυγὴ καὶ βλασφημία ἀρθήτω ἀφ' ὑμῶν σὺν πάσῃ κακίᾳ.

4:32γίνεσθε [δὲ] εἰς ἀλλήλους χρηστοί, εὔσπλαγχνοι, χαριζόμενοι ἑαυτοῖς καθὼς καὶ ὁ θεὸς ἐν Χριστῷ ἐχαρίσατο ὑμῖν.

4:30And do not grieve the Holy Spirit of God: whereby you are sealed unto the day of redemption. [n. 263]

4:31Let all bitterness and anger and indignation and clamor and blasphemy be put away from you, with all malice. [n. 264]

4:32And be kind one to another: merciful, forgiving one another, even as God has forgiven you in Christ. [n. 265]

---

262. Supra monuit Apostolus abstinere a verbis malis et nocivis, hic monet abstinere a verbis et factis turbativis seu contristativis proximorum.

Circa quod duo facit.
Primo prohibet quod pertinet ad vetustatem;
secundo persuadet quod pertinet ad novitatem, ibi *estote autem invicem benigni*, et cetera.
Prima iterum in duas, quia
primo prohibet quod ad vetustatem pertinet in generali;
secundo in speciali, ibi *omnis amaritudo*, et cetera.

263. Dicit ergo *nolite contristare Spiritum*, et cetera. Contra: Spiritus Sanctus est Deus, in quo non cadit passio aliqua, nec tristitia.

Respondeo. Spiritus Sanctus dicitur contristari, quando contristatur ille, in quo est Spiritus Sanctus. Lc. X, 16: *qui vos spernit, me spernit*. Is. LXIII, 10: *ipsi autem ad iracundiam provocaverunt eum, et afflixerunt Spiritum Sanctum eius, et conversus est eis in inimicum*.

Vel dicendum est quod est metaphorica locutio. Sicut enim Deus dicitur irasci propter similitudinem effectus, ita etiam dicitur contristari; quia sicut quando aliquis contristatur recedit a contristante, ita Spiritus Sanctus a peccante. Et sic est sensus *nolite contristare Spiritum Sanctum Dei*, id est nolite eum fugare, vel expellere per peccatum. Sap. I, 5: *Spiritus Sanctus enim disciplinae effugiet fictum, et auferet se a cogitationibus, quae sunt sine intellectu, et corripietur a superveniente iniquitate*.

Igitur non est contristandus Spiritus Sanctus, et hoc propter beneficium signi salutaris. Ideo subiungit *in quo signati estis*, id est reformati estis, et ab aliis distincti. Qui autem habebit hoc signum secum, habebit vitam aeternam. Ideo ergo est custodiendus et nullo

262. Previously the Apostle warned the Ephesians to abstain from wicked and injurious words. Here he advises them against words or actions which would upset or sadden other men.

Regarding this he does two things:
first, he prohibits what pertains to the old;
second, he encourages what pertains to the new, at *be kind to one another*.
Again the first part has two subdivisions:
first, he forbids what pertains to the old in a general way;
second, in a specific way, at *let all bitterness*.

263. There might be an objection to his saying *do not grieve the Holy Spirit of God*. The Holy Spirit is God in whom there can be no emotion or sorrow.

I reply that the Holy Spirit is said to be grieved when that person is saddened in whom the Holy Spirit dwells. *He that despises you, despises me* (Luke 10:16). *But they provoked to wrath and afflicted the Spirit of his Holy One: and he was turned to be their enemy* (Isa 63:10).

Or, it could be called a metaphorical expression. Just as God is said to be angry on account of the similarity of what he does to the results of human anger, so he could also be said to be grieved. When some person is saddened he withdraws from whoever is depressing him, likewise does the Holy Spirit withdraw from one who is sinning. Thus the meaning of *do not grieve the Holy Spirit* is: do not chase him away or reject him through sin. *For the Holy Spirit of discipline will flee from the deceitful, and will withdraw himself from thoughts that are without understanding: and he shall not abide when iniquity comes in* (Wis 1:5).

Therefore, the Holy Spirit must not be saddened, and this on account of the blessing of his saving seal. Thus he adds *whereby you are sealed*, that is, you are reformed and set apart from others. Whoever possesses this seal shall enjoy eternal life. For this reason he must be held on to and in

modo contristandus, quia sine eo non est vita aeterna. II Cor. I, 22: *qui signavit nos Deus, et dedit nobis pignus Spiritus.*

Et quando? **In die redemptionis**, id est baptismi. Io. III, 5: *nisi quis renatus fuerit ex aqua et Spiritu Sancto, et cetera.* Act. I, 5: *vos autem baptizabimini Spiritu Sancto, non post multos hos dies.* Dicit autem **redemptionis**, quia in baptismo fit homo particeps redemptionis factae per Christum.

264. Sequitur **omnis amaritudo**, et cetera. Ubi ostendit in speciali quae pertinent ad vetustatem.

Quandoque enim homo contristat amicum suum ex ira, aliquando ex industria. Sed in ira est triplex gradus, quia aliquando retinetur et manet solum in corde, sicut qui tantum interius irascitur. Aliquando vero exprimitur in voce, sine tamen contumeliae prolatione, sicut qui dicit racha. Aliquando fit etiam addita contumeliae prolatione, sicut qui dicit fatue. Primo ergo ponit quod pertinet ad iram cordis; secundo quod pertinet ad inordinatam prolationem; tertio quod pertinet ad contumeliam.

In ira autem cordis ista se consequuntur. Primo, quod ira est effectus tristitiae, et haec in Sacra Scriptura dicitur amaritudo. I Reg. c. I, 10: *cum esset Anna amaro animo, et oraret Deum flens, et cetera.* Et ideo dicit **omnis amaritudo**, etc., quae est per memoriam iniuriae praeteritae. Eccli. XXI, 15: *non est sensus ubi abundat amaritudo.* Secundo, quod statim appetit vindictam; ideo dicit **et ira**, quae est appetitus vindictae. Iac. I, 20: *ira enim viri Dei iustitiam non operatur.* Tertio, quod iratus indignum reputat, quod ei parcat, et indignum esse, quod sine punitione transeat; ideo sequitur **et indignatio**.

Sed quantum ad inordinatam prolationem sic est clamor. Is. V, 7: *expectavi ut faceret iudicium, et ecce iniquitas, et iustitiam, et ecce clamor.* Ideo dicit **et clamor**. Similiter et blasphemia est vel contra Deum, vel contra sanctos. Lev. XXIV, 16: *quicumque blasphemaverit nomen Domini, morte moriatur.* Ideo dicit **et blasphemia**. Et addit **tollatur a vobis cum omni malitia**, scilicet operis. I Petr. c. II, 2: *deponentes omnem malitiam, et omnem dolum et simulationem.*

265. Deinde cum dicit **estote autem**, etc., ponit pertinentia ad novitatem contrariam passionibus praemissis: contra amaritudinem, benignitatem. Unde dicit **estote autem invicem benigni**. Quia *benignus est spiritus sapientiae, et cetera.* Contra iram, misericordiam; unde dicit **misericordes**. Lc. VI, 36: *estote ergo misericordes, sicut et Pater vester misericors est.* Contra indignationem, condonationem; unde dicit **donantes invicem**, et cetera. Col. III, 13: *donantes vobismetipsis si quis adversus aliquem habet querelam, sicut et Dominus donavit nobis, ita*

no way grieved since without him there is no life everlasting. *God also has sealed us and given the pledge of the Spirit in our hearts* (2 Cor 1:22).

When did this happen? On **the day of redemption**, that is, of baptism. *Unless a man be born again of water and the Holy Spirit, he cannot enter into the kingdom of God* (John 3:5). *You shall be baptized with the Holy Spirit not many days hence* (Acts 1:5). He says **redemption** since in baptism a man becomes a sharer in the redemption accomplished by Christ.

264. In what follows, at **let all bitterness**, he discloses what specifically belongs to the old man.

For at times a man will sadden his friend out of anger, at other times on set purpose. Anger, however, has three degrees. Sometimes it is constrained and remains within the heart, as when someone is only inwardly angry. On other occasions it is expressed verbally, although not in a contemptuous way, as when someone says *raca* (Matt 5:22). At still another time contempt may be present in the verbal expression as in *you cursed fool!* Hence he first writes down what pertains to anger of the heart; second what is proper to its inordinate expression; and third what has reference to contempt.

In anger of the heart the following succeed one another. First, anger is the result of sorrow, which Sacred Scripture refers to as bitterness: *as Hannah had her heart full of bitterness, she prayed to the Lord, shedding many tears* (1 Sam 1:10). Thus he says **all bitterness** which arises from the memory of past injuries. For *there is no understanding where there is bitterness* (Sir 21:15). Second, it immediately desires revenge; hence he says **and anger** which is a craving for revenge. *For the anger of man does not work the justice of God* (Jas 1:20). Third, an angered person imagines whatever offends him is an insult, and he is indignant if it passes without punishment. Therefore, **and indignation** follows.

Noise has to do with the inordinate expression of anger. *And I looked that he should do judgment, and behold, iniquity: and do justice, and behold, a cry* (Isa 5:7). Hence he says **and clamor**. In a similar way, blasphemy is either against God or against his saints. Yet *he that blasphemes the name of the Lord, dying let him die* (Lev 24:16). Thus he says **and blasphemy**. And he adds that these **be put away from you, with all malice** of action. *Reject all malice and all guile and dissimulations* (1 Pet 2:1).

265. Next, when he says **be kind one to another** he determines what pertains to the new man which is contrary to the above mentioned passions. Opposed to bitterness is kindness; so he says **be kind one to another** since *the spirit of wisdom is benevolent* (Wis 1:6). Mercy is contrary to anger, thus he mentions **merciful**: *be therefore merciful, as your Father also is merciful* (Luke 6:36). Opposed to indignation is a pardoning attitude; whence he says **forgiving one another even as God has forgiven you in Christ**. *Forgiving one another, if any have a complaint against another. Even as*

et vos. Rom. c. VIII, 32: *qui etiam proprio Filio suo non pepercit*; et paulo post sequitur: *quomodo non etiam cum illo nobis omnia donavit?*

the Lord has forgiven you, so do you also (Col 3:13). *He that spared not even his own Son*, and shortly afterwards, *how has he not also, with him, given us all things?* (Rom 8:32).

Chapter 5

Lecture 1

⁵:¹Estote ergo imitatores Dei, sicut filii carissimi, [n. 267]

⁵:²et ambulate in dilectione, sicut et Christus dilexit nos, et tradidit semetipsum pro nobis, oblationem et hostiam Deo in odorem suavitatis. [n. 268]

⁵:¹γίνεσθε οὖν μιμηταὶ τοῦ θεοῦ, ὡς τέκνα ἀγαπητά,

⁵:²καὶ περιπατεῖτε ἐν ἀγάπῃ, καθὼς καὶ ὁ Χριστὸς ἠγάπησεν ἡμᾶς καὶ παρέδωκεν ἑαυτὸν ὑπὲρ ἡμῶν προσφορὰν καὶ θυσίαν τῷ θεῷ εἰς ὀσμὴν εὐωδίας.

⁵:¹Be therefore followers of God, as most dear children: [n. 267]

⁵:²And walk in love, as Christ also has loved us and has delivered himself for us, an oblation and a sacrifice to God for an odor of sweetness. [n. 268]

---

266. Posita exhortatione ad benignitatem et misericordiam, quae sunt effectus caritatis, hic ostendit eis exemplum.

Circa quod duo facit.

Primo inducit eos ad imitationem exemplaris, scilicet Dei;

secundo ostendit in quo debent ipsum imitari, ibi *et ambulate*, et cetera.

267. Dicit ergo: dixi quod debetis donare invicem, *sicut et Deus in Christo donavit vobis, ergo estote imitatores Dei*, quia hoc necessarium est, licet difficile sit. Eccle. II, v. 12: *quid est, inquam, homo, ut possit sequi Regem factorem suum?* Numquam tamen perficietur natura humana, nisi in coniunctione ad Deum. Unde Iob XXIII, 11: *vestigia eius secutus est pes meus*. Ergo imitandus est, taliter quomodo habemus possibilitatem, quia ad filium pertinet patrem imitari. Et ideo subdit *sicut filii*, Patrem scilicet per creationem. Deut. XXXII, 6: *nonne ipse est Pater tuus qui possedit, et fecit, et creavit te?* Et addit *charissimi*, quos scilicet elegit ad participationem sui ipsius.

268. Sequitur *et ambulate*, et cetera. Ubi

primo ponit imitandi modum, quia in caritate;

secundo ostendit immensae caritatis signum, ibi *et tradidit*, et cetera.

269. Quod ergo simus *filii charissimi*, hoc facit caritas Dei. Rom. VIII, 15: *non enim accepistis spiritum servitutis iterum in timore, sed accepistis Spiritum adoptionis filiorum, in quo clamamus: Abba, Pater. Ipse enim Spiritus testimonium reddit spiritui nostro, quod sumus filii Dei*.

Debemus ergo ipsum in dilectione imitari. Et dicit *ambulate*, id est semper proficite. Gen. XV: *ambula coram me, et esto perfectus*. Et hoc *in dilectione*, quia dilectio est tale bonum in quo debet homo proficere, et tale debitum quod debet homo semper solvere. Rom. XIII, 8: *nemini quidquam debeatis, nisi ut invicem diligatis*. Vel

266. Once he has exhorted them to kindness and mercy, which are the effects of charity, he gives them a model to imitate.

In reference to this he does two things:

first, he urges them to imitate the exemplar, namely, God;

second, he lets them know in what they should imitate him, at *and walk in love*.

267. I have affirmed, he says, that you ought to forgive one another *as God has forgiven you in Christ* (Eph 4:32). *Be therefore followers of God* because this is indispensable even if it is difficult. *What is man, said I, that he can follow the King his maker?* (Eccl 2:12). Nonetheless, human nature would never achieve its end except in union with God. *My foot has followed his steps: I have kept his way, and have not declined from it* (Job 23:11). He must be imitated insofar as it is possible for us to do so, since a son must imitate his father. Thus he adds *as children* since he is our Father through creation: *is he not your Father, who possessed you, and made you, and created you?* (Deut 32:6) He puts in *most dear* because God chose us to share in what is his very own.

268. *And walk in love* comes next, and here:

first, he maintains that the way to imitate God is in charity;

second, he speaks of the tremendous sign of charity, at *and has delivered himself*.

269. The charity of God has made us his *most dear children*: *for you have not received the spirit of bondage again in fear; but you have received the Spirit of adoption of sons, whereby we cry: Abba, Father. For the Spirit himself gives testimony to our spirit that we are the sons of God* (Rom 8:15–16).

Certainly we ought to follow him in love. He says *walk* to signify you must always advance: *walk before me and be perfect* (Gen 17:1). This should be *in love* since love is so good that man ought always to make further progress in it, and is that kind of a debt which man always has to pay. *Owe no man any thing, but to love one another* (Rom 13:8). Or

in dilectione, quae est via sequendi Deum magis de propinquo. I Cor. XII, 31: *adhuc excellentiorem viam vobis demonstro*. I Cor. XIII, v. 1: *si linguis hominum loquar et angelorum*, et cetera. Col. III, 4: *super omnia haec caritatem habentes*, et cetera. Et hoc exemplo Christi. Unde subdit **sicut et Christus dilexit nos**. Io. XIII, 1: *cum dilexisset suos, qui erant in mundo, in finem dilexit eos*.

270. Et quia, secundum Gregorium, *probatio dilectionis, exhibitio est operis*, ideo subdit **et tradidit semetipsum pro nobis**. Apoc. I, 5: *dilexit nos, et lavit nos a peccatis nostris*. Gal. II, 20: *in fide vivo Filii Dei, qui dilexit me et tradidit in mortem seipsum pro me*. Is. LIII, 12: *tradidit in mortem animam suam*, et cetera.

Haec autem mors fuit nobis utilis et necessaria, ideo subdit **oblationem et hostiam**, et cetera. Loquitur autem hic Apostolus more veteris legis, in qua, ut dicitur Lev. IV, 25 ss., quando quis peccaverat, offerri debebat pro eo hostia et oblatio, quae dicitur pro peccato. Item, quando quis agebat gratias Deo, vel aliquid consequi volebat, oportebat offerri *hostiam pacificam*, ut dicitur Lev. III, 9, quae quidem erat in oblationem *suavissimi odoris* Domino, ut dicitur ibidem. Haec autem facta sunt per Christum, quia, ut a peccatis mundaremur et gloriam consequeremur, **tradidit semetipsum pro nobis in oblationem** per ea quae in vita gessit. Is. LIII, 7: *oblatus est, quia ipse voluit*, et cetera. **Et hostiam Deo** pro peccato.

Et hoc **in odorem suavitatis**. Alludit autem hic, quod dicitur Lev. III, 5 s. Sed certe ille odor non erat tunc Deo acceptus secundum se, sed secundum suam significationem, inquantum significabat oblationem odoriferam corporis Christi Filii Dei. Gen. II: *ecce odor filii mei, sicut odor agri pleni*. Cant. I, 3: *trahe me post te, curremus in odorem unguentorum tuorum*. Sic autem debemus nos sacrificare Deo spiritualiter. Ps. l, v. 19: *sacrificium Deo spiritus*, et cetera.

in love may mean the way in which God is followed more closely: *and I show you yet a more excellent way. If I speak with the tongues of men, and of angels, and have not charity, I am become as sounding brass, or a tinkling symbol* (1 Cor 12:31–13:1). *Above all these things have charity, which is the bond of perfection* (Col 3:14). This must be done according to Christ's example, whence he adds **as Christ also has loved us**. Jesus *having loved his own who were in the world, he loved them unto the end* (John 13:1).

270. According to Gregory, *love is verified when it is expressed in action*. Therefore he adds **and delivered himself for us**. *He has loved us, and washed us from our sins in his own blood* (Rev 1:5). *I live in the faith of the Son of God, who loved me and delivered himself for me* (Gal 2:20). *He has delivered his soul unto death and was reputed with the wicked* (Isa 53:12).

This death was both advantageous and necessary for us, thus he says an **oblation and a sacrifice**. Here the Apostle is speaking in the way the old law does. In it, as Leviticus 4 indicates, when someone sinned he was obliged to offer, because of it, the sacrifice and oblation which was designated for the sin. Then too, when someone gave thanks to God, or wished to obtain some favor, he had to offer a *victim of peace* (Lev 3:9), which was *of a most sweet savor* (Lev 3:16) to the Lord. These, however, are all accomplished through Christ who, in order that we might be cleansed from sin and attain to glory, **delivered himself for us, an oblation** through the actions he performed during his life: *he was offered because it was his own will, and he opened not his mouth* (Isa 53:7); and he delivered himself as **a sacrifice to God** for sin.

This was **for an odor of sweetness**, hinting at what is said in Leviticus 3:5 ff. But certainly the odor described there was not pleasing to God in itself but according to its signification, inasmuch as it symbolized the sweet-smelling oblation of the body of Christ, the Son of God. *Behold, the smell of my son is as the smell of a plentiful field* (Gen 27:27). *Draw me, we will run after you to the odor of your ointments* (Song 1:3). In this way also we ought to offer spiritual sacrifices to God: *a sacrifice to God is an afflicted spirit* (Ps 51:19).

Lecture 2

5:3Fornicatio autem, et omnis immunditia, aut avaritia, nec nominetur in vobis, sicut decet sanctos: [n. 272]

5:4aut turpitudo, aut stultiloquium, aut scurrilitas, quae ad rem non pertinet: sed magis gratiarum actio. [n. 275]

5:3πορνεία δὲ καὶ ἀκαθαρσία πᾶσα ἢ πλεονεξία μηδὲ ὀνομαζέσθω ἐν ὑμῖν, καθὼς πρέπει ἁγίοις,

5:4καὶ αἰσχρότης καὶ μωρολογία ἢ εὐτραπελία, ἃ οὐκ ἀνῆκεν, ἀλλὰ μᾶλλον εὐχαριστία.

5:3But fornication and all uncleanness or covetousness, let it not so much as be named among you, as becomes saints: [n. 272]

5:4Or obscenity or foolish talking or scurrility, which is to no purpose: but rather giving of thanks. [n. 275]

271. Supra, posita monitione, Apostolus docuit ut deposita vetustate Ephesii novitatem assumerent prohibendo vitia spiritualia, hic prohibet eisdem vitia etiam carnalia.

Dividitur autem in duas.

Primo enim prohibet vetustatem vitiorum carnalium;

secundo inducit ad novitatem, ibi *videte itaque, fratres*, et cetera.

Prima iterum dividitur in tres.

Primo excludit vetustatem vitiorum;

secundo proponit poenam eorum, ibi *hoc autem scitote*, etc.;

tertio excludit fallaciam, ibi *nemo vos seducat*, et cetera.

Prima iterum in duas.

Primo excludit quaedam vitia principalia;

secundo excludit quaedam adiuncta, ibi *aut turpitudo*, et cetera.

272. Excludit autem tria vitia, scilicet luxuriam naturalem, quae est cum non sua, unde dicit *fornicatio*. Os. IV, 12: *spiritus enim fornicationum decepit eos*. I Cor. VI, v. 18: *fugite fornicationem*. Sic faciebat Iob c. XXXI, 1: *pepigi foedus cum oculis meis, ut nec cogitarem de virgine*. Dicitur autem fornicatio a fornice, id est arcu triumphali, iuxta quem erant lupanaria. Prov. XX: *intravit super eos fornicatio*, et cetera.

Et omnis immunditia, id est omnis pollutio contra naturam, scilicet quae non ordinatur ad generationem. Gal. V, 12: *manifesta sunt opera carnis, quae sunt fornicatio, immunditia, luxuria*, et cetera.

Tertio excludit avaritiam, dicendo *aut avaritia*.

273. Sed quare hoc? Numquid est idem cum peccatis carnalibus?

Respondeo. Dicendum est quod non, nec totaliter est divisa, sed medium inter spiritualia et carnalia peccata: quod patet sic. In peccato sunt duo, scilicet obiectum peccati, et delectatio in obiecto. Quaedam ergo sunt peccata quorum obiectum et delectatio est spiritualis, sicut ira. Nam vindicta, quae est obiectum irae, et delectatio

271. Having previously cautioned them, the Apostle taught the Ephesians to put off the old man and put on the new by forbidding spiritual vices. Now he also bans carnal sins.

It is divided into two parts:

first, he prohibits the old way of carnal sins;

second, he stimulates them on to the new life, at *see therefore, brethren* (Eph 5:15).

The first part has three subdivisions:

first, he rejects the old sins;

second, he sets forth their punishment, at *for know this* (Eph 5:5);

third, he precludes a fallacy, at *let no man deceive you* (Eph 5:6).

The first section has two parts:

first, he bars certain principal vices;

second, he rejects some vices associated with them, at *or obscenity*.

272. He eliminates three vices. There is a natural voluptuousness committed with another outside of wedlock; whence he says *fornication*. *For the spirit of fornication has deceived them* (Hos 4:12); *flee from fornication* (1 Cor 6:18). Job did this: *I made a covenant with my eyes, that I would not so much as think upon a virgin* (Job 31:1). This is called *fornication* from the word 'fornix,' that is, the triumphal arch near which brothels were situated. *Fornication came in upon them* (Prov 20).

And all uncleanness designates every impurity against nature, namely, when the act is not ordered toward the generation of offspring. *Now the works of the flesh are manifest, which are: fornication, uncleanness, immodesty, luxury* (Gal 5:19).

Third, he bans avarice in mentioning *covetousness*.

273. But why this? Is it to be classed with carnal sins?

I reply that it is neither identified with, nor completely separate from, carnal sin but midway between the spiritual and carnal sins. It can be explained this way. Sin contains two elements, the object of the sin and the gratification the object affords. Thus with certain sins both the object and the gratification are spiritual, such as anger. Both revenge,

eius, est quid spirituale, et similiter inanis gloria. Quaedam vero sunt omnino carnalia et obiectum et delectatio; sicut gula et luxuria. Sed avaritia tenet medium, quia eius obiectum est carnale, scilicet pecunia, sed delectatio est spiritualis, quia animo quiescit quis in pecunia. Et ideo connumeratur avaritia cum peccatis carnalibus ratione obiecti, cum spiritualibus vero ratione delectationis. Heb. ult.: *sint mores sine avaritia*.

Vel dicendum est, quod *avaritia* opponitur iustitiae, unde ponitur pro specie luxuriae, quae est adulterium, quod est iniustus usus mulieris alterius: sicut avaritia iniustus usus pecuniae.

274. Sed supra dixit: *qui furabatur*, etc., hic autem dicit quod *nec nominetur*, etc., quia in pugna spirituali vitia carnalia primo occurrunt vincenda: quia frustra pugnat quis contra intrinseca, nisi primo vincat extrinseca, scilicet carnalia, contra quae semper remanet bellum. Et ideo dicit *nec nominetur in vobis, sicut decet sanctos*, scilicet abstinere a factis, a cogitationibus, et a dictis. Is. XIV: *perdam Babylonis nomen, et reliquias, et progeniem et germen*. Eccli. c. XLI, 15: *curam habe de bono nomine, quia hoc decet sanctos*. II Cor. VI, 4: *in omnibus exhibeamus nosmetipsos sicut Dei ministros*, et cetera.

275. Sequitur *aut turpitudo*, et cetera. Ubi ponit quaedam vitia adiuncta. Circa quod duo facit. Primo adiuncta vitia excludit; secundo ad contraria eorum inducit, ibi *sed magis gratiarum actio*, et cetera.

Tria ergo vitia excludit, scilicet *turpitudinem*, quae est in tactibus turpibus et amplexibus et osculis libidinosis. Prov. VI, 32: *qui autem adulter est, propter cordis inopiam, perdet animam suam, et turpitudinem, et ignominiam congregat sibi*. Item, *stultiloquium*, id est verba provocantia ad malum. Eccli. IX, 11: *colloquium illius quasi ignis exardescit*, scilicet malae mulieris. Et *scurrilitatem*, id est verbum ioculatorium, per quod aliqui volunt inde placere aliis. Matth. XII, v. 36: *de omni verbo otioso quod locuti fuerint homines, reddent rationem de eo in die iudicii*. Et haec omnia sunt mortalia, inquantum ad mortalia peccata ordinantur, quia aliquid etiam si bonum sit ex genere, inquantum ad mortale ordinatur, est mortale.

Deinde inducit ad contraria, scilicet gratiarum actiones. Unde dicit *sed magis gratiarum actio*. Is. LI, 3: *gaudium, et laetitia invenietur in ea, gratiarum actio, et vox laudis*.

which is the objective of anger, and its gratification, are spiritual; the same holds true for vainglory. Other sins, however, are completely carnal both in their objects and their gratification; such as gluttony and voluptuousness. But covetousness is between each of these because its object is carnal, namely money, whereas its gratification is spiritual inasmuch as the mind finds rest in the possession of money. Therefore, covetousness is enumerated among the carnal sins by reason of its object, and among the spiritual ones by reason of the gratification it affords. *Let your manners be without covetousness* (Heb 13:5).

Or it might be answered that *covetousness* is opposed to justice and thus is classed with the kind of sensuality known as adultery. The latter is the unjust use of another man's woman and covetousness is the unjust use of money.

274. Above he said, **he who stole, let him now steal no more** (Eph 4:28). But here he says **let it not so much as be named among you** because in the spiritual battle carnal sins must first be conquered. In vain would anyone struggle against internal sins unless he had first overcome external, carnal ones—against which there will always be a struggle. Therefore he says **let it not so much as be named among you, as becomes saints** who refrain from such actions, thoughts and words. *I will destroy the name of Babylon, and the remains, and the bud, and the offspring* (Isa 14:22). *Take care of a good name* (Sir 41:15) since this is fitting for saints. *In all things let us exhibit ourselves as the ministers of God* (2 Cor 6:4).

275. Next, at **or obscenity**, he sets down some vices associated with the aforementioned. Regarding them he makes two points: first, he rejects these vices; second, he encourages them to practice the contrary virtue, at **but rather giving of thanks**.

Hence he bans three vices, namely, **obscenity** which consists in impure touches, embraces and lustful kisses. *But he who is an adulterer, for the folly of his heart shall destroy his own soul. He gathers to himself shame and dishonor* (Prov 6:32–33). Then there is **foolish talking** which is words provocative of evil. *For her conversation*, that is, of an evil woman, *burns as fire* (Sir 9:11). Finally there is **scurrility** consisting in jocose words with which some attempt to please others. *But I say to you that for every idle word that men shall speak, they shall render an account on the day of judgment* (Matt 12:36). All of these are grave insofar as they are ordered towards mortal sins; for anything, even if it is generally good, becomes mortal to the degree that it is ordered toward mortal sins.

Then he introduces them to the opposite, namely, thanksgiving. Whence he says **but rather giving of thanks**. *Joy and gladness shall be found therein, thanksgiving and the voice of praise* (Isa 51:3).

Lecture 3

⁵:⁵Hoc enim scitote intelligentes: quod omnis fornicator, aut immundus, aut avarus, quod est idolorum servitus, non habet haereditatem in regno Christi et Dei. [n. 277]

⁵:⁶Nemo vos seducat inanibus verbis: propter haec enim venit ira Dei in filios diffidentiae. [n. 281]

⁵:⁷Nolite ergo effici participes eorum. [n. 284]

⁵:⁵τοῦτο γὰρ ἴστε γινώσκοντες ὅτι πᾶς πόρνος ἢ ἀκάθαρτος ἢ πλεονέκτης, ὅ ἐστιν εἰδωλολάτρης, οὐκ ἔχει κληρονομίαν ἐν τῇ βασιλείᾳ τοῦ Χριστοῦ καὶ θεοῦ.

⁵:⁶Μηδεὶς ὑμᾶς ἀπατάτω κενοῖς λόγοις, διὰ ταῦτα γὰρ ἔρχεται ἡ ὀργὴ τοῦ θεοῦ ἐπὶ τοὺς υἱοὺς τῆς ἀπειθείας.

⁵:⁷μὴ οὖν γίνεσθε συμμέτοχοι αὐτῶν·

⁵:⁵For know this and understand: that no fornicator or unclean or covetous person (which is a serving of idols) has inheritance in the kingdom of Christ and of God. [n. 277]

⁵:⁶Let no man deceive you with vain words. For because of these things comes the anger of God upon the children of unbelief. [n. 281]

⁵:⁷Therefore do not be partakers with them. [n. 284]

---

276. Supra prohibuit Apostolus peccata carnalia, hic comminatur poenam damnationis, quae peccatoribus infligitur.

Circa quod duo facit. Primo enim de hoc eos certificat; secundo sigillatim peccata recitat, ibi *quod omnis fornicator*, et cetera.

277. Dicit ergo *hoc scitote intelligentes*, id est actualiter, non solum habitualiter, pro certo habete. I Io. III: *haec scripsi vobis, ut sciatis*, et cetera.

278. Et quid? *Quod omnis fornicator, aut immundus, aut avarus, quod est idolorum servitus, non habet haereditatem in regno Christi et Dei*.

Nota quod vocat hic avaritiam idolatriam, quoniam idololatria est, quando honor soli Deo debitus, impenditur creaturae. Nunc autem Deo dupliciter honor debetur, scilicet ut in eo finem nostrum constituamus, et ut in eo fiduciam nostram finaliter ponamus; ergo qui hoc in creaturis ponit, reus est idololatriae. Hoc autem facit avarus, qui finem suum in re creata ponit, et etiam totam suam fiduciam. Os. VIII, 4: *argentum suum et aurum suum fecerunt sibi idola, ut interirent*. Et hoc, quia, ut dicitur Prov. XI, 28: *qui confidit in divitiis suis, corruet*.

279. Sed cum in aliis peccatis ponat homo finem suum in creatura, cui amore inhaeret, quare etiam in illis non dicitur peccator idololatra?

Respondeo. Idololatrare est aliquid exterius indebite colere. Nunc autem in aliis peccatis ponitur finis in interioribus quasi in propria exaltatione. Sed qui ponit finem in divitiis, ponit in eis finem ut in re exteriori, sicut idololatra.

Sed numquid avari honorem Deo debitum exhibentes creaturae, realiter sunt idololatrae, et per se? Dico quod non, quia in moralibus actus seu opera iudicantur ex fine. Ille ergo per se est idololatra, qui intendit per se cultum exhibere creaturae. Hoc autem non intendit

276. The Apostle above forbade carnal sins, and here he threatens them with the penalty of damnation that is inflicted on sinners.

In reference to this he does two things: first, he assures them of it; second, he mentions the sins one by one, at *that no fornicator*.

277. He states *for know this and understand*, that is, be actually certain of it and not just habitually. *These things I write to you that you may know that you have eternal life; you who believe in the name of the Son of God* (1 John 5:13).

278. And what does he write? *That no fornicator or unclean or covetous person, which is a serving of idols, has inheritance in the kingdom of Christ and of God*.

Notice that he calls covetousness idolatry, for idolatry happens when the honor due God alone is given to creatures. Now there is a twofold honor due God; we must establish him as the goal of our life and we must put our trust of reaching the goal in him. Hence, whoever places these in creatures is guilty of idolatry. A covetous person commits this when he fixes his end in a created reality as well as putting all his trust in it. *Of their silver and their gold they have made idols to themselves, that they might perish* (Hos 8:4). This happens because *he that trusts in his riches shall fall* (Prov 11:28).

279. However, since in the other sins a man also puts his goal in a creature, clinging to it by love, why are they not termed idolatry too?

I reply that idolatry consists in giving an illegitimate worship to some external object, whereas in the other sins one fixes one's end on interior things, as though it consisted in one's own exaltation. Whoever places his end in riches, on the other hand, fixes it in an external object as an idol.

Does that mean that covetous persons, giving the honor due God to creatures, are really and essentially idolaters? I hold that they are not, because in moral issues acts or deeds are judged by their end. Therefore, only those are essentially idolaters who intend to really offer worship

avarus per se, sed per accidens hoc facit, inquantum superflue et inordinate diligit.

280. Et quid de tali? ***Non habebit haereditatem***, quippe quia filii et haeredes, ut dicitur Rom. VIII, 17. Nunc autem tales non sunt filii, qui sic carnales sunt; ergo haereditatem non habent, quia, ut dicitur I Cor. c. XV, 50: *caro et sanguis regnum Dei non possidebunt*, id est Deum, qui dicit Ez. XLIV, v. 28: *ego haereditas eorum*.

Sed posset quaeri: si haereditas ista est ipse Deus, cum sit indivisibilis et impartibilis, quare dicit ***in regno Christi et Dei*** divisive, ac si haereditas ista sit divisibilis?

Respondeo. Haereditas nostra consistit in fruitione Dei, nunc autem Deus aliter se fruitur, et nos eo; quia Deus seipso perfecte fruitur, quia seipsum perfecte cognoscit et totaliter diligit quantum cognoscibilis et diligibilis est. Non autem sic nos, quia licet ipsum perfecte cognoscamus in patria, et per consequens diligamus, quia qui aliquid simplex attingit, ipsum totum cognoscit, etsi non totaliter, sicut lux solis si esset punctalis, humanus oculus ipsam totam apprehenderet, non totaliter, oculus vero aquilae ipsam totaliter comprehenderet. Sic et si Deum perfecte cognoscimus in patria et perfecte diligimus, sed ipsum totaliter non comprehendimus, ideo videtur ibi esse quaedam imperfectio et particularitas.

Et ideo dicit ***Christi et Dei*** coniunctim, quasi partem cum parte ponendo, id est quia per Christum et non per alium habetur haereditas.

281. Deinde cum dicit ***nemo vos seducat***, hic excludit fallaciam seductorum.

Et circa hoc duo facit.

Primo enim ponit admonitionem;

secundo subiungit ipsius rationem, ibi ***eratis enim aliquando tenebrae***, et cetera.

Prima iterum in duas, quia

primo monet eos, ut non seducantur verbis, eis credendo;

secundo ut non communicent eis mala faciendo, ibi ***nolite ergo effici***, et cetera.

Prima adhuc in duas, quia

primo removet seductiones;

secundo ostendit seductionis signum, ibi ***propter hoc enim venit ira***, et cetera.

282. Notandum est ergo quod in vitiis carnalibus solum docuit cavere seductionem, quia a principio, ut homines possent libere frui concupiscentiis, cogitaverunt invenire rationes, quod fornicationes et huiusmodi venerea non essent peccata. Et ideo dicit ***inanibus verbis***, quia sine ratione sunt talia verba, quae dicunt quod

to a creature. A covetous person does not really intend to do this, but only happens to do it in his excessive and inordinate love for riches.

280. What happens to such people? They do not possess the ***inheritance*** since heirs are sons, as Romans states (Rom 8:17). But these persons are not sons because they are carnal, therefore they do not enjoy the inheritance. *Now this I say, brethren, that flesh and blood cannot possess the kingdom of God* (1 Cor 15:50), that is, God himself, who said: *I am their inheritance* (Ezek 44:28).

It might be asked: if the inheritance is God himself who is indivisible and inseparable, why does he say ***in the kingdom of Christ and of God***, dividing the two as if the inheritance could be divided?

I reply. Our inheritance consists in the enjoyment of God. But God enjoys himself in a way different from that in which we shall enjoy him. God perfectly delights in himself since he perfectly knows and totally loves himself inasmuch as he is knowable and lovable. Not so with us, even though we shall perfectly know him in heaven and, as a consequence, love him. For someone may indeed grasp a simple reality and know the whole of it, yet not totally. For example, if the light of the sun were as small as a point, the human eye could perceive the whole of it, although not fully, whereas the eagle's eye would grasp it totally. Similarly, even if we know God perfectly in heaven and love him perfectly, nevertheless we do not totally comprehend him. Hence it seems that there is a certain imperfection and individuality there.

Therefore he says ***of Christ and of God*** conjointly, as though setting one part with another part, since it is through Christ and none other that the inheritance is had.

281. Next he says ***let no man deceive you***, thereby rejecting a fallacy of those who would mislead them.

Regarding this he makes two points:

first, he sets down a warning;

second, he adds the reason for it, at ***for heretofore you were darkness*** (Eph 5:8).

The first has two more parts:

first, he warns them not to be deceived into believing what is told them;

second, that they should not associate with those liars by doing evil, at ***therefore do not be partakers***.

The first section still has two parts:

first, he puts an end to the deception;

second, he shows them a sign of the deceit, at ***for because of these things comes the anger***.

282. Notice that only in reference to carnal vices does he teach them to avoid being deceived. For from the beginning men have rationalized to find reasons why fornication and other venereal sins were not really sins so that they might indulge their cupidity without restraint. Hence he states ***vain words*** since words that claim that these are

huiusmodi non sint peccata, nec excludant a regno Dei et Christi. Col. II, 8: *videte ne quis vos seducat per prophetiam et inanem fallaciam.*

283. Et quod tales sint seductores et talia verba seducentia, ostendit, quia nisi peccata carnalia essent peccata, non punirentur a Deo, quia cum Deus sit iustus, non infligit poenam sine culpa. Nunc autem talia puniuntur a Deo, ergo peccata sunt.

Minorem probat, cum dicit *propter haec enim venit ira Dei*, scilicet propter peccata carnalia, *in filios diffidentiae*, ut patuit in diluvio; item in Sodomitis; item tribus Beniamin fere tota consumpta fuit propter haec.

Dicit autem *filios diffidentiae*, quia sic peccantes diffidunt de vita aeterna; quia si sic faciens speraret vitam aeternam, magis esset praesumptio, quam spes, quae est certa expectatio futurae beatitudinis ex meritis, et cetera. Unde supra IV, 19: *qui desperantes semetipsos tradiderunt impudicitiae in operationem immunditiae omnis, in avaritiam.* Sap. VII: *nullum pratum sit quod non pertranseat luxuria nostra*, et cetera. Et sequitur in fine capitis: *quia tales non speraverunt mercedem iustitiae*, et cetera.

Dicit ergo, quod *in filios diffidentiae*, id est qui non confidunt de gaudiis aeternis, *venit ira Dei*, scilicet propter peccata. Vel *diffidentiae*, id est de quibus non est confidendum, quantum est ex parte meritorum.

284. Et ideo concludit *nolite ergo effici participes eorum*, communicando scilicet eis in talibus operibus. II Cor. VI, 14 s.: *quae enim participatio iustitiae cum iniquitate, aut quae societas lucis ad tenebras, aut quae communicatio Christi ad Belial, aut quae pars fidelis cum infideli?*

not sins and do not exclude one from the kingdom of God and of Christ are irrational. *Beware lest any man cheat you by prophecy and vain deceit* (Col 2:8).

283. He demonstrates that such men are deceivers and their words fallacious since, if carnal sins were not sins, they would not be punished by God; God is just and does not impose a penalty where there is no offense. But such acts are punished by God and therefore are sins.

He proves the minor when he says *for because of these things comes the anger of God*, namely, on account of carnal sins, *upon the children of unbelief*. This is evident in the flood (Gen 7), in what happened to the Sodomites (Gen 19); and again, almost the whole tribe of Benjamin was destroyed on account of this (Judg 19, 20).

He says the *children of unbelief* because those who sin in this way despair of eternal life. If they acted this way and still hoped for eternal life, it would rather be presumption than hope, which is the certain expectation of obtaining future beatitude meritoriously. So he mentioned previously: *who, despairing, have given themselves up to lasciviousness unto the working of all uncleanness, unto covetousness* (Eph 4:19). *Let no meadow escape our riot. Let none of us go without his part in luxury*, and near the end of the same chapter, *for they hoped not for the wages of justice, nor esteemed the honor of holy souls* (Wis 2:8; 22).

Hence he states that *upon the children of unbelief* who do not hope for eternal joys, *comes the anger of God* on account of their sins. Or, *of unbelief* signifies those of whom we cannot be confident of as far as their merits are concerned.

284. He concludes, *therefore do not be partakers with them* by associating with them in such actions. *For what participation does justice have with injustice? Or what fellowship does light have with darkness? And what concord does Christ have with Belial? Or what part hath the faithful with the unbeliever?* (2 Cor 6:14–15).

Lecture 4

⁵:⁸Eratis enim aliquando tenebrae: nunc autem lux in Domino. [n. 286] Ut filii lucis ambulate: [n. 288]	⁵:⁸ἦτε γάρ ποτε σκότος, νῦν δὲ φῶς ἐν κυρίῳ· ὡς τέκνα φωτὸς περιπατεῖτε	⁵:⁸For you were heretofore darkness, but now light in the Lord. [n. 286] Walk then as children of the light. [n. 288]
⁵:⁹fructus enim lucis est in omni bonitate, et justitia, et veritate: [n. 290]	⁵:⁹ὁ γὰρ καρπὸς τοῦ φωτὸς ἐν πάσῃ ἀγαθωσύνῃ καὶ δικαιοσύνῃ καὶ ἀληθείᾳ	⁵:⁹For the fruit of the light is in all goodness and justice and truth: [n. 290]
⁵:¹⁰probantes quid sit beneplacitum Deo: [n. 292]	⁵:¹⁰δοκιμάζοντες τί ἐστιν εὐάρεστον τῷ κυρίῳ·	⁵:¹⁰Proving what is well pleasing to God. [n. 292]
⁵:¹¹et nolite communicare operibus infructuosis tenebrarum, magis autem redarguite. [n. 293]	⁵:¹¹καὶ μὴ συγκοινωνεῖτε τοῖς ἔργοις τοῖς ἀκάρποις τοῦ σκότους, μᾶλλον δὲ καὶ ἐλέγχετε,	⁵:¹¹And have no fellowship with the unfruitful works of darkness: but rather reprove them. [n. 293]

285. Supra prohibuit Apostolus peccata carnalia, comminando poenam et removendo fallaciam, hic assignat rationem sumptam ex eorum conditione, et duo facit.

Proponit enim primo eorum conditionem;

secundo ex eis duas conclusiones inducit, ibi *ut filii lucis sitis*, et cetera.

Ponit autem duas conditiones:

primo praeteritam,

secundo conditionem praesentem, ibi *nunc autem lux*, et cetera.

286. Dicit ergo *eratis aliquando tenebrae*, id est excaecati ignorantia et errore. Supra IV, 18: *tenebris obscuratum habentes intellectum*. Ps. LXXXI, 5: *nescierunt, neque intellexerunt, in tenebris ambulant*. Item, tenebrosi per peccatum. Prov. IV, 12: *via impiorum tenebrosa, nesciunt ubi corruant*.

Sed notandum est, quod indeterminate non dicit tenebrosi, sed *tenebrae*, quia sicut quilibet videtur esse quod principaliter est in eo, sicut tota civitas videtur esse rex et quod rex facit, civitas dicitur facere: ita quando peccatum regnat in homine, tunc totus homo dicitur peccatum et tenebrae.

287. Sequitur *nunc autem lux*, et cetera. Ubi ponit conditionem praesentem; quasi dicat: nunc autem habetis lucem fidei. Phil. II, 15: *inter quos lucetis sicut luminaria in mundo*. Matth. V, 14: *vos estis lux mundi*.

Sed contra dicitur de Ioanne Baptista: *non erat ille lux*; quomodo ergo fideles alii lux dicuntur? Respondeo. Non dicuntur lux per essentiam, sed per participationem.

288. Deinde cum dicit *ut filii lucis ambulate*, etc., concludit duas conclusiones.

Dixerat enim, quod tenebrae fuerunt et quod nunc sunt lux. Et ideo

primo concludit, ut se conforment ei, quod nunc sunt;

285. Previously the Apostle had banned carnal sins by threatening punishment and rejecting a fallacy. Here he gives the reason, which is taken from their situation. He does two things:

first, he describes their situation;

second, he deduces two conclusions from it, at *as children of the light*.

Their situation, however, is described as twofold:

first, their past;

second, their present situation, at *but now light*.

286. Thus he remarks *you were heretofore darkness* blinded by ignorance and error: *having their understanding darkened* (Eph 4:18). *They have not known nor have they understood; they walk on in darkness* (Ps 82:5). The darkness also comes from sin: *the way of the wicked is darksome; they know not where they fall* (Prov 4:19).

But observe that he does not vaguely call them *darksome* but *darkness*. For anyone appears to be whatever is predominant in him; thus the whole state appears to be the king and whatever the king does is said to be done by the state, likewise when sin dominates a man the entire person is referred to as sin and darkness.

287. Next, at *but now light*, he describes their present condition, as though he said: but now you enjoy the light of faith: *among whom you shine as lights in the world* (Phil 2:15), for *you are the light of the world* (Matt 5:14).

But this contradicts what was said of John the Baptist: *he was not the light* (John 1:8). How then can other believers be called the light? I reply. They are not referred to as the light in essence but through participation.

288. Afterward, at *as children of the light*, he derives two conclusions.

He had said that they had been darkness but now are light. Therefore:

first, he concludes that they should conform themselves to what they now are;

secundo ut vitent ea quae prius fuerunt, ibi *et nolite communicare*.

Prima in duas.

Primo ponit admonitionem;

secundo eam exponit, ibi *fructus enim lucis*, et cetera.

289. Dicit ergo: quia nunc lux estis, faciatis opera lucis, ergo *ut filii lucis ambulate*. Io. XII, 35: *ambulate dum lucem habetis*, et cetera.

290. Hoc autem exponit, cum dicit *fructus enim*, et cetera. Ambulat autem quis ut filius lucis dupliciter. Primo quantum ad substantiam, vel genus operis; secundo quantum ad modum, vel intentionem facientis.

Primo ergo ponit opera, quae oportet facere;

secundo qua debent fieri intentione, ibi *probantes*, et cetera.

291. Dicit ergo: dixi ut ambuletis ut filii lucis, *fructus autem lucis* sunt opera fructifera et clara. Eccli. XXIV, 23: *flores mei fructus honoris*, et cetera.

Et hoc *in omni bonitate*, et cetera. Ubi advertendum est, quod omnis actus virtutis ad tria reducitur. Nam oportet, quod agens ordinetur in se, ad proximum, et ad Deum. In se, ut sit bonus in seipso et propter hoc dicit *in omni bonitate*. Ps. CXVIII, 66: *bonitatem et disciplinam et scientiam doce me*, et cetera. Item, ad proximum per iustitiam. Ideo dicit *in iustitia*. Ps. CXVIII, 121: *feci iudicium et iustitiam*, et cetera. Ad Deum per cognitionem et confessionem veritatis. Et ideo dicit *et veritate*. Zach. VIII, 19: *veritatem enim et pacem diligite*.

Vel aliter, ut bonitas referatur ad cor, iustitia ad opus, veritas ad os. Supra IV, 25 et Zach. VIII, 16: *loquimini veritatem unusquisque cum proximo suo*.

292. Deinde cum dicit *probantes*, etc., ostendit qua intentione debeant operari, quia non ex abrupto, sed *probantes*, id est, ratione discernentes. *Opus suum probet unusquisque*, ut dicitur Gal. VI, 4. Et hoc *quid sit beneplacitum Deo*, id est ut intendatis facere, quod placet Deo. Rom. XV: *probetis quae sit voluntas Dei bona, et beneplacens et perfecta*.

293. Deinde cum dicit *et nolite communicare*, etc., hortatur eos ne redeant ad statum quem reliquerunt, quia, ut dicitur Gal. c. II, 18: *si enim, quae destruxi, haec iterum reaedifico, praevaricatorem me constituo*; II Petr. II, 22: *canis reversus ad suum vomitum, et sus lota in volutabro luti*.

second, that they should avoid what they previously were, at *and have no fellowship with*.

The first has two sections:

first, he writes down an admonition;

second, he explains it, at *for the fruit of the light*.

289. He affirms: since you are now light, perform the deeds of light—*walk as children of the light*. *Walk while you have the light, that the darkness does not overtake you* (John 12:35).

290. He interprets this when he says *for the fruit of the light is in all goodness*. However, a person behaves as a child of the light in two ways; first in reference to the substance or kind of actions he performs, then in reference to the manner or intention he does them with.

Thus: first, he determines the actions which should be performed;

second, with what intention they should be done, at *proving*.

291. Therefore he remarks: I have said that you should walk as children of the light, *but the fruit of the light* is actions which are fruitful and resplendent. *And my flowers are the fruit of honor and riches* (Sir 24:23).

This is *in all goodness*. Whence it must be recalled that every act of virtue is reduced to three relationships. For it is necessary that the agent be ordered within himself, to his neighbor, and to God. Within himself, that he be good in himself; and on this account he says *in all goodness*. *Teach me goodness and discipline and knowledge* (Ps 119:66). He must be ordered to his fellow man by justice; whence he says *and justice*. *I have done judgment and justice* (Ps 119:121). While he is ordered to God through knowledge and a confession of the truth; so he adds *and truth*. *Only love truth and peace* (Zech 8:19).

Another interpretation is that goodness refers to the heart, justice to one's actions, and truth to the tongue. This was mentioned above (Eph 4:25) as well as elsewhere: *speak truth every one with his neighbor* (Zech 8:16).

292. Then, when he says *proving*, he discloses with what intention the actions should be performed. For they should not be done abruptly but with *proving*, that is, discerning with one's mind—*let everyone prove his own work* (Gal 6:4)—*what is well pleasing to God*, that is, you ought to have the intention of doing whatever pleases God. *Be reformed in the newness of your mind, that you may prove what is the good and the acceptable and the perfect will of God* (Rom 12:2).

293. After this, at *have no fellowship with*, he exhorts them not to return to the state they have left behind because, *if I build up again the things which I have destroyed, I make myself a prevaricator* (Gal 2:18). Lest *the dog is returned to his vomit; and, the sow that was washed, to her wallowing in the mire* (2 Pet 2:22).

Dividitur autem ista pars in duas.

Primo ponit monitionem;

secundo assignat rationem, ibi *quae autem in occulto*, et cetera.

Prima iterum in duas.

Primo monet eos ne malefaciant;

secundo ut mala reprehendant, ibi *magis autem redarguite*, et cetera.

294. Dicit ergo *probantes quid sit beneplacitum Deo, et nolite communicare operibus infructuosis tenebrarum*, id est operibus carnalibus ducentibus ad tenebras perpetuas: quae quidem sunt infructuosa, quia non habent nisi momentaneam delectationem citissime transeuntem. Rom. VI, 21: *quem ergo fructum habuistis tunc in illis, in quibus nunc erubescitis?* Iud. I, 12: *arbores autumnales infructuosae, bis mortuae, eradicatae, fluctus feri maris, despumantes suas confusiones*, et cetera.

Item, tenebrosa loca quaerunt propter turpitudinem, quia communicant in eis cum brutis. Iob XXIV, 15: *oculus adulteri observat caliginem, dicens: non me videbit oculus, et operiet vultum suum, perfodit in tenebris domos*, et cetera.

Istis ergo *nolite communicare*, imitando, coadiuvando, consentiendo. Eccli. XIII, 22: *quae communicatio homini sancto ad canem?*

295. Sed certe hoc non sufficit, nisi etiam eos reprehendatis, quia, ut dicit Augustinus, aliquando Deus punit communicantes insontes, quia aliqui boni non reprehendunt malos. Eccli. XVII, 12: *mandavit autem unicuique de proximo suo*. Et ideo dicit *magis autem autem redarguite*. II Tim. IV, 2: *argue, obsecra, increpa*, et cetera.

Sed numquid semper peccamus si non reprehendimus? Respondet Augustinus: quod enim non reprehendis ex timore caritatis, ne scilicet peior efficiatur et scandalizatus affligat bonos, non peccas. Si autem ex timore cupiditatis, ne scilicet indignetur et perdas beneficia tua, sic peccas.

This section is divided into two parts:

first, he gives the caution;

second, he tells them his reason, at *for the things that are done* (Eph 5:12).

The first is again divided into two sections:

first, he warns them not to do evil;

second, he tells them to reprehend wickedness, at *but rather reprove them*.

294. He stated *proving what is well pleasing to God. And have no fellowship with the unfruitful works of darkness* which are sensuous actions leading to an everlasting darkness. They are unfruitful since they only possess a momentary delight which disappears very quickly. *What fruit therefore had you then in those things of which you are now ashamed?* (Rom 6:21). *Trees of the autumn, unfruitful, twice dead, plucked up by the roots, raging waves of the sea, foaming out their own confusion; wandering stars, to whom the storm of darkness is reserved for ever* (Jude 1:12).

Moreover, they seek out places of darkness for their depravity where they have the companionship of beasts. *The eye of the adulterer observes darkness, saying: no eye shall see me. And he will cover his face. He digs through houses in the dark, as in the day they had appointed for themselves; and they have not known the light* (Job 24:15–16).

With these, therefore, *have no fellowship*, neither by imitating, nor assisting, nor consenting to them. *What fellowship does a holy man have with a dog?* (Sir 13:22)

295. But clearly this is not enough; you must also reprehend them since, as Augustine remarks, God sometimes punishes innocent companions because those who are good do not reprimand the evil ones. *And he gave every one of them commandment concerning his neighbor* (Sir 17:12). Hence he says *but rather reprove them*. *Reprove, entreat, rebuke in all patience and doctrine* (2 Tim 4:2).

But do we always sin if we do not reprove those who sin? Augustine replies: should you refrain from reprimanding out of a fear of charity, namely, lest the sinner fall into greater evil and begin to afflict those who are good, you shall not sin. But if you do this from a fear that has its source in greed, lest the sinner grow indignant and you lose your benefices, then you do sin.

Lecture 5

5:12 Quae enim in occulto fiunt ab ipsis, turpe est et dicere. [n. 297]

5:13 Omnia autem, quae arguuntur, a lumine manifestantur: [n. 298]

5:14 omne enim, quod manifestatur, lumen est. Propter quod dicit: *surge qui dormis, et exsurge a mortuis, et illuminabit te Christus*. [n. 300]

5:12 τὰ γὰρ κρυφῇ γινόμενα ὑπ' αὐτῶν αἰσχρόν ἐστιν καὶ λέγειν·

5:13 τὰ δὲ πάντα ἐλεγχόμενα ὑπὸ τοῦ φωτὸς φανεροῦται,

5:14 πᾶν γὰρ τὸ φανερούμενον φῶς ἐστιν. διὸ λέγει, Ἔγειρε, ὁ καθεύδων, καὶ ἀνάστα ἐκ τῶν νεκρῶν, καὶ ἐπιφαύσει σοι ὁ Χριστός.

5:12 For the things that are done by them in secret, it is a shame even to speak of. [n. 297]

5:13 But all things that are reproved are made manifest by the light: [n. 298]

5:14 For all that is made manifest is light. Wherefore he says: *rise, you who sleep, and arise from the dead: and Christ shall enlighten you*. [n. 300]

---

296. Supra posuit Apostolus monitiones, hic assignat rationes earum. Duas autem monitiones posuit. Prima ut non communicarent operibus tenebrarum; secunda ut redarguerent peccatores. Secundum hoc ergo duo facit.

Primo ponit rationem primae monitionis;

secundo rationem secundae, ibi *omnia enim quae arguuntur*, et cetera.

297. Dicit ergo: bene dixi: nolite communicare, immo debetis et tales increpare et redarguere. Quare? Quia *quae in occulto fiunt ab ipsis, turpe est dicere*. Hoc autem est de vitiis carnalibus in quibus est turpitudo magna, quia minimum est ibi de bonis rationis, cum huiusmodi actus communes sint nobis et brutis.

298. Sequitur *omnia quae arguuntur*, et cetera. Hic ponit Apostolus rationem secundae monitionis, et facit duo.

Primo enim ponit rationem;

secundo assignat confirmationem, ibi *propter quod dicit*, et cetera.

299. Quantum ergo ad primum, vult probare quod eos deceat delinquentes arguere, et hoc probat sic: quidquid ostenditur malum esse redarguitur, omnis enim redargutio manifestatio quaedam est; sed omnis manifestatio fit per lumen, vos autem estis lux; ergo decet vos arguere et eos manifestare.

Ponit autem huius rationis maiorem, ibi *omnia autem quae arguuntur*, et cetera. Minorem autem ponit, ibi *omne quod*, et cetera. Quasi dicat: ideo decet eos arguere, quia, ut dicitur I Cor. II, 15: *spiritualis iudicat omnia, et ipse a nemine iudicatur*. Unde Glossa sic exponit: *omnia*, scilicet peccata *quae arguuntur a lumine*, id est, a bonis et sanctis hominibus, qui sunt filii lucis, *manifestantur*, scilicet per confessionem. Prov. XXVIII, 13: *qui autem confessus fuerit et reliquerit ea, misericordiam consequetur. Omne autem*, scilicet malum, *quod*

296. The Apostle explained his warnings above, and now he gives the reasons for them. He had given two warnings: the first was that they should not associate in the works of darkness, the second that they should reprove sinners. Hence he does two things:

first, he gives the reason for the first warning;

second, the reason for the second, at *but all things that are reproved*.

297. Thus he asserts: I said well that you ought not to have fellowship but rather reprimand and refute such as these. Why? Because *the things that are done by them in secret, it is a shame even to speak of*. This is characteristic of carnal vices which possess a great depravity; they have the least amount of rational good since actions of this type are common to us and the beasts.

298. After this, at *but all things that are reproved*, the Apostle gives the reason for the second warning, and he makes two points:

first, he sets down the reason;

second, he produces a confirmation of it, at *wherefore he says*.

299. Regarding the first, he wants to prove that it is fitting for them to refute delinquents. He proves it this way: whatever is shown to be evil is to be refuted, for every refutation is a certain manifestation; but every manifestation occurs through the light, and you are the light; hence it is fitting for you to refute and reveal those who are evil.

He expresses the major of this reasoning at *but all things that are reproved are made manifest by the light*. And the minor is expressed in *for all that is made manifest is light*. As though he said: for this reason it is fitting for you to refute them because, *the spiritual man judges all things; and he himself is judged of no man* (1 Cor 2:15). Thus a Gloss offers the following interpretation: *all* sins *that are reproved by the light* that is, by the good and holy men who are the children of the light, *are made manifest* through a confession. *But he that shall confess and forsake them shall obtain mercy*

manifestatur per confessionem, **lumen est**, id est in lumine vertitur.

300. Deinde confirmat hoc per auctoritatem, dicens **propter quod dicit: surge**, et cetera. Glossa sic exponit: propter hoc quod sit lumen, dicit, scilicet Spiritus Sanctus: o tu **qui dormis, surge**, et cetera.

Sed haec non est consuetudo Pauli. Et ideo dicendum est, quod Apostolus introducit figuram positam Is. LX, 1: *surge, illuminare, Ierusalem*, etc., dicens **propter quod dicit**, scilicet Scriptura, **surge** a negligentia boni operis, tu scilicet **qui dormis**. Prov. VI, 9: *usquequo, piger, dormies?* Ps. XL, 9: *numquid qui dormit, non adiiciet, ut resurgat?* **Et exurge a mortuis**, id est, ab operibus mortuis, seu mortificantibus. Hebr. IX, 14: *emundabit conscientiam nostram ab operibus mortuis*, et cetera. Is. XXVI, 19: *vivent mortui tui, interfecti mei resurgent*. **Exurge** ergo, **et illuminabit te Christus**. Ps. XXVI, 1: *Dominus illuminatio mea*, et cetera. Idem XII, 4: *illumina oculos meos, ne unquam obdormiam in morte*.

Sed numquid possumus per nos resurgere a peccato, quia dicit: **surge, et illuminabit te Christus**? Respondeo. Dicendum est, quod ad iustificationem impii duo requiruntur, scilicet liberum arbitrium cooperans ad resurgendum et ipsa gratia. Et certe hoc ipsum habet liberum arbitrium a gratia praeveniente, et postea meritorie operari a gratia subsequente. Unde dicitur Thren. ult.: *converte nos, Deus, et convertemur*.

(Prov 28:13). **For all** evil **that is made manifest** through confession, **is light**, that is, is turned into light.

300. Next, he verifies this by an authority, at **wherefore he says: 'rise'**, which a Gloss interprets: in order that light might prevail he—the Holy Spirit—says: **rise, you who sleep, and arise from the dead and Christ shall enlighten you.**

But this is not customary for Paul. Hence it must be said that the Apostle is introducing the image found elsewhere: *arise, be enlightened, O Jerusalem; for your light has come, and the glory of the Lord has risen upon you* (Isa 60:1). Thus **wherefore it says** refers to Scripture. **Rise** from a neglect of good works, **you who sleep**. *How long will you sleep, O sluggard?* (Prov 6:9) *Shall he that sleeps rise again no more?* (Ps 41:8) **And arise from the dead**, that is, from dead or destructive actions. Christ *will cleanse our conscience from dead works* (Heb 9:14). *Your dead men shall live, my slain shall rise again* (Isa 26:19). **Rise** therefore **and Christ shall enlighten you**. *The Lord is my light and my salvation; whom shall I fear?* (Ps 27:1) *Enlighten my eyes that I never sleep in death* (Ps 13:3).

Yet are we capable of rising from sin ourselves since it says: **rise . . . and Christ shall enlighten you**? I reply. Two things are requisite for the justification of a sinner, namely, a free decision cooperating in the act of rising from sin, and grace itself. And certainly the free decision itself is had from prevenient grace, while the meritorious actions that follow are from subsequent grace. *Convert us, O Lord, to you, and we shall be converted* (Lam 5:21).

Lecture 6

⁵:¹⁵Videte itaque, fratres, quomodo caute ambuletis: non quasi insipientes, sed ut sapientes: [n. 302]

⁵:¹⁶redimentes tempus, quoniam dies mali sunt. [n. 303]

⁵:¹⁷Propterea nolite fieri imprudentes, sed intelligentes quae sit voluntas Dei. [n. 305]

⁵:¹⁵Βλέπετε οὖν ἀκριβῶς πῶς περιπατεῖτε, μὴ ὡς ἄσοφοι ἀλλ' ὡς σοφοί,

⁵:¹⁶ἐξαγοραζόμενοι τὸν καιρόν, ὅτι αἱ ἡμέραι πονηραί εἰσιν.

⁵:¹⁷διὰ τοῦτο μὴ γίνεσθε ἄφρονες, ἀλλὰ συνίετε τί τὸ θέλημα τοῦ κυρίου.

⁵:¹⁵See therefore, brethren, how you walk circumspectly: not as unwise, but as wise: [n. 302]

⁵:¹⁶Redeeming the time, because the days are evil. [n. 303]

⁵:¹⁷Wherefore, do not become imprudent: but understanding what is the will of God. [n. 305]

301. Supra prohibuit fallaciarum carnalium vetustatem, hic hortatur ad contrariam novitatem. Et

primo hortatur ad novitatem contrariam fallaciae;
secundo ad novitatem contrariam luxuriae, ibi *et nolite inebriari*, et cetera.

Prima in tres.

Primo inducit ad cautelam contrariam fallaciae;
secundo ostendit novitatem cautelae, ibi *redimentes tempus*, etc.;
tertio docet modum cautelae, ibi *propterea nolite fieri*, et cetera.

302. Dicit ergo *itaque*, scilicet ex praemissis, *videte quomodo caute ambuletis*. Cautio est quaedam conditio prudentiae, per quam aliquis vitat impedimenta agendorum, et hanc cautelam debent omnes habere. Prov. c. IV, 23: *oculi tui videant recta, et palpebrae tuae praecedant gressus tuos*.

Hoc autem pertinet ad sapientes, et ideo dicit *non quasi insipientes*, qui scilicet nesciunt vitare impedimenta. Ps. LXXV, 6: *turbati sunt omnes insipientes corde*. *Sed ut sapientes*. Eccle. II, 14: *sapientis oculi in capite eius: stultus in tenebris ambulat*. Quidam dicunt: si non caste, tamen caute. Sed sic non accipit Apostolus, sed dicit *caute*, ac si diceret: cavete ab hominibus contrariis castitati.

303. Necessitatem autem huius cautelae ostendit, cum dicit *redimentes tempus*, etc.; quod potest exponi dupliciter.

Redimit enim aliquis quandoque rem suam, dando enxenia vel aliquid pro ea, sicut dicitur aliquis redimere vexationem suam dando enxenia, vel pecuniam, vel quando dimittit de iure suo. Dicit ergo: totum tempus hoc est tempus calumniae, et ideo sitis *redimentes tempus, quoniam dies mali sunt*. Ex quo peccavit Adam, ex tunc semper paratae sunt insidiae impellentes ad peccatum. Non sic autem in statu innocentiae, in quo non oportebat hominem ab aliquo licito abstinere, quia in eius voluntate non erat impellens aliquid ad peccatum. Modo autem oportet nos tempus redimere, *quoniam dies mali sunt*, id est debemus malitiam dierum

301. Above he forbade the old ways of carnal illusions, and now he exhorts them to the contrary newness. He encourages them:

first, toward a newness opposed to the former illusions;
second, toward a newness opposed to voluptuousness, at *and do not be drunk* (Eph 5:18).

The first section contains three parts:
first, he gives them a caution against the fallacy;
second, he shows them the newness of this precaution, at *redeeming the time*;
third, he teaches them how to act according to it, at *wherefore, do not become imprudent*.

302. Whence he states *therefore* from the preceding *see how you walk circumspectly*. Caution is one of the conditions of prudence by which a person avoids hindrances in accomplishing what he has to do. Everyone ought to possess this caution. *Let your eyes look straight on and let your eyelids go before your steps* (Prov 4:25).

This is a characteristic of wise men, thus he adds *not as unwise* who do not know how to avoid the obstacles. *All the foolish of heart were troubled* (Ps 76:5). *But as wise*: the eyes of a wise man are in his head: the fool walks in darkness (Eccl 2:14). Some say: if you do not act chastely, nonetheless act cautiously. The Apostle does not take it in such a sense; when he says *circumspectly* it is as though he said: beware of men who thwart chastity.

303. He explains the necessity of this precaution when he says *redeeming the time*, which can be interpreted in two ways.

On certain occasions a man redeems his property by offering a gift or something else for it; for instance, someone is said to compensate for a grievance he caused by offering a gift or money, or by renouncing something which is rightfully his. In this sense he would be saying: the whole of time is now a time of deception, hence you should be *redeeming the time, because the days are evil*. At the time Adam sinned, and from then on, snares have always been set to thrust men into sin. It was not that way in the state of innocence when it was unnecessary for a man to abstain from anything which was licit, since there was nothing in his will driving him to sin. But now we have to redeem the time,

vitare, *diem malum praecavere*, ut dicitur Ecce. VII, 15, et etiam a quibusdam licitis abstinere. I Cor. c. X, 23: *omnia mihi licent, sed non omnia aedificant*. In hunc autem modum dicitur aliquis vexationem suam redimere, quia dimittit aliquid de iure suo perire.

304. Vel aliter: *redimentes tempus*, et cetera. Contingit quandoque quod aliquis per magnum tempus vitae vivit in peccato, et hoc est tempus perditum.

Sed quomodo redimet, cum homo non sufficiat ad debita persolvenda? Respondeo. Dicendum est quod tanto magis debet vacare operibus bonis, quanto prius instetit malis. I Petr. I: *sufficit enim praeteritum tempus ad voluntatem gentium consumendam his, qui ambulaverunt in luxuriis, vinolentiis, desideriis*, et cetera. Sed prima expositio est melior.

305. Deinde cum dicit *propterea nolite fieri*, etc., docet modum cautelae, dicens: *propterea*, scilicet ut possitis tempus redimere, *nolite fieri imprudentes*.

Nota quod differentia est inter sapientiam et prudentiam. Prudentia enim est quaedam sapientia, sed non universalis sapientia. Prov. c. X, 23: *sapientia autem est viro prudentia*. Sapiens enim simpliciter dicitur, qui habet de omnibus ordinare: sapiens autem secundum quid dicitur, qui habet ordinare de his de quibus est sapiens. I Cor. III, 10: *ut sapiens architectus fundamentum posui*. Quia sapientis est ordinare, ut dicitur I *Methaphysicae*.

Omnis autem ordinator respicit finem; ille ergo simpliciter est sapiens, qui cognoscit finem, vel qui agit propter finem universalem, scilicet Deum. Deut. IV, 6: *haec est enim sapientia vestra*, et cetera. Sapientia enim est divinarum rerum cognitio, ut dicit Augustinus, IV *de Trinitate*. Prudentia vero est particularis rei providentia, quando scilicet quis ordinat facta sua. Et ideo *sapientia est viro prudentia*. Propter hoc ergo dicit: *nolite fieri imprudentes, sed intelligentes*, et cetera. Sicut ratio speculativa ordinat de agendis et iudicat: oportet autem conclusiones habere et iudicare per principia, et similiter in operabilibus. Istud autem primum principium, per quod debemus iudicare omnia et regulare, est voluntas Dei; et ideo intellectus in moralibus et divinis debet habere pro principio voluntatem Dei, quia, si hanc habeat pro principio, fit prudens intellectus. Deut. c. XXXII, 29: *utinam saperent et intelligerent*, et cetera. Hoc autem docuit Dominus, Matth. c. XXVI, 42: *fiat voluntas tua*.

because the days are evil; we must avoid the depravity of the days, and *beware beforehand of the evil day* (Eccl 7:15). To do this we must renounce even certain things which are lawful: *all things are lawful for me; but all things do not edify* (1 Cor 10:23). In this way a person is said to redeem a grievance he caused since he permits something that is rightfully his to be forfeited.

304. There is another interpretation of *redeeming the time*. For it sometimes happens that a person lives a great part of his life in sin, and this is time lost.

But how is he to redeem it when man is incapable of paying his debts? I reply that he ought to devote himself to good works to an even greater degree than he had previously pursued sinful ones. *For the time past is sufficient to have fulfilled the will of the gentiles, for them who have walked in riotousness, lusts, excesses of wine, revellings, banquetings, and unlawful worshipping of idols* (1 Pet 4:3). The first interpretation, however, is better.

305. Then, when he says *wherefore, do not become imprudent*, he goes on to teach them how to abide by the precaution, saying: *wherefore* that you may be able to redeem the time, *do not become imprudent*.

Notice that there is a difference between wisdom and prudence. For prudence is a certain type of wisdom, but not the whole of wisdom. *Wisdom is prudence to a man* (Prov 10:23). That man is called wise in an absolute sense who puts everything into perspective; but a man is wise only in a certain respect when he puts in order only those things about which he is well informed. *As a wise architect I have laid the foundation* (1 Cor 3:10). For the role of the wise man is to put things in order, as the *Metaphysics* I states.

Everyone who sets things in perspective considers their end; hence he is wise in an absolute sense who knows and acts for the universal end, God. *For this is your wisdom, and understanding in the sight of nations* (Deut 4:6). For wisdom, as Augustine mentions in the fourth book of *On the Trinity*, is the knowledge of divine realities. Prudence, on the other hand, is the directive care of particular things, as when a person regulates his actions. Thus, *wisdom is prudence to man* (Prov 10:23). For this reason he says **do not become imprudent, but understanding what is the will of God**. For just as speculative reason puts whatever is to be done in perspective and judges it—it is necessary to have conclusions and to judge them by principles—so likewise in the field of performance. Now the first principle through which we ought to judge and regulate everything is the will of God. Hence the intellect, in moral matters and those which lead to God, must have the will of God for its principle. If it does, then the intellect becomes prudent. *O that they would be wise and would understand, and would provide for their last end* (Deut 32:29). Our Lord taught this: *your will be done* (Matt 26:42).

Lecture 7

5:18Et nolite inebriari vino, in quo est luxuria, sed implemini Spiritu Sancto, [n. 307]

5:19loquentes vobismetipsis in psalmis, et hymnis, et canticis spiritualibus, cantantes et psallentes in cordibus vestris Domino, [n. 310]

5:20gratias agentes semper pro omnibus in nomine Domini nostri Jesu Christi Deo et Patri, [n. 314]

5:21subjecti invicem in timore Christi. [n. 315]

5:18καὶ μὴ μεθύσκεσθε οἴνῳ, ἐν ᾧ ἐστιν ἀσωτία, ἀλλὰ πληροῦσθε ἐν πνεύματι,

5:19λαλοῦντες ἑαυτοῖς [ἐν] ψαλμοῖς καὶ ὕμνοις καὶ ᾠδαῖς πνευματικαῖς, ᾄδοντες καὶ ψάλλοντες τῇ καρδίᾳ ὑμῶν τῷ κυρίῳ,

5:20εὐχαριστοῦντες πάντοτε ὑπὲρ πάντων ἐν ὀνόματι τοῦ κυρίου ἡμῶν Ἰησοῦ Χριστοῦ τῷ θεῷ καὶ πατρί,

5:21ὑποτασσόμενοι ἀλλήλοις ἐν φόβῳ Χριστοῦ.

5:18And do not be drunk with wine, wherein is luxury: but be filled with the Holy Spirit, [n. 307]

5:19Speaking to yourselves in psalms and hymns and spiritual canticles, singing and making melody in your hearts to the Lord: [n. 310]

5:20Giving thanks always for all things, in the name of our Lord Jesus Christ, to God and the Father: [n. 314]

5:21Being subject one to another, in the fear of Christ. [n. 315]

---

306. Supra induxit ad novitatem contra vetustatem fallaciae, hic hoc idem facit contra vetustatem vitiorum carnalium. Vel dicamus quod prius reprehenderit peccata carnalia quantum ad luxuriam, hic autem quantum ad gulam.

Duo autem facit. Primo enim prohibet vetustatem; secundo inducit statum ad novitatem, ibi **sed impleamini**, et cetera.

307. Dicit ergo: dixi quod *fornicatio et omnis immunditia non nominetur in vobis*; sed ad hoc cavendum debetis a vino superfluo abstinere, quia cibus et potus superfluus est causa luxuriae, et praecipue vinum, quod calefacit et movet. Prov. XX, 1: *luxuriosa res vinum, et tumultuosa ebrietas*. Esth. c. I, 10: *cum esset rex hilarior, et post nimiam potationem incaluisset mero*, et cetera. Os. c. IV, 11: *fornicatio, et vinum, et ebrietas auferunt cor*. Unde Hieronymus: *quem Sodoma non vicit, vina vicerunt Lot*. **Nolite ergo**, et cetera.

308. Sed impleamini Spiritu Sancto. Inter omnia quae multos spiritus generant est vinum, unde generat animositatem et facit homines *per talenta loqui*, ut dicitur III Esd. III, 21. Et ideo convenienter docet eos contra hoc repleri Spiritu Sancto, qui generat fervorem devotionis. Rom. XII, 11: *spiritu ferventes*. Item, etiam generat gaudium et laetitiam spiritualem. Rom. XIV, 17: *iustitia, et pax, et gaudium in Spiritu Sancto*. Item, facit audacter loqui. Act. II, 4: *repleti sunt omnes Spiritu Sancto, et coeperunt loqui*, etc., et ideo qui eos loquentes audiebant, credebant eos ebrios.

309. Sed numquid habemus Spiritum Sanctum in nostra potestate?

306. He urged them before to that newness which is in opposition to the old illusion, and now he does the same in reference to the old ways of carnal sins. Or, we might say that he previously reprimanded carnal sins in regard to voluptuousness, and here does it concerning gluttony.

He makes two points: first, he forbids the old way; second, he introduces them to the new condition, at **but be filled**.

307. Thus he says: I have stated that *fornication and all uncleanness* should *not so much as be named among you* (Eph 5:23). Yet you ought also be careful to abstain from superfluous wine since excessive food and drink is a cause of sensuality; and especially wine which warms and excites a man. *Wine is a luxurious thing, and drunkenness riotous* (Prov 20:1). *When the king was merry, and after very much drinking was well warmed with wine, he commanded . . . to bring in queen Vasthi before the king* (Esth 1:10–11). *Fornication and wine and drunkenness take away the understanding* (Hos 4:11). Whence Jerome remarks: *a man over whom Sodom could not prevail was conquered by wine—Lot*. Therefore **do not be drunk with wine, wherein is luxury**.

308. But be filled with the Holy Spirit. Among all those things which breed a variety of moods is wine; thus it begets animosity and makes men *talk in thousands* (3 Esd 3:21). Appropriately therefore does he teach them the opposite, to be filled with the Holy Spirit who engenders an intensity of devotion: *in spirit fervent* (Rom 12:11). Who also spreads joy and spiritual happiness: *justice, and peace, and joy in the Holy Spirit* (Rom 14:17). Who, moreover, makes men speak out boldly: *and they were all filled with the Holy Spirit; and they began to speak with diverse tongues, according as the Holy Spirit gave them to speak* (Acts 2:4), so that those who heard them thought they were drunk (Acts 2:13).

309. But do we possess the Holy Spirit by our own power?

Respondeo et dico quod habere Spiritum Sanctum est dupliciter: vel receptive, et sic non est in nostra potestate eum recipere, sed ex dono Dei eum recipimus. Rom. V, 5: *caritas Dei diffusa est in cordibus nostris, et cetera.* Vel dispositive, et sic adhuc non sumus sufficientes eum recipere, id est nos disponere sine gratia Dei. II Cor. III, 5: *non sumus sufficientes cogitare aliquid a nobis quasi ex nobis, sed sufficientia nostra ex Deo est.*

Vel aliquis dicitur recipere Spiritum Sanctum, non tamen plenus esse Spiritu Sancto, quando scilicet habet gratiam Spiritus Sancti quantum ad aliquam et non quantum ad omnem hominis operationem. Tunc autem dicitur plenus Spiritu Sancto, quando eo utitur generaliter.

310. Modus autem repletionis est in dilectione Dei et proximi. Et ideo cum dicit **loquentes**, etc.,

primo tangit modum repletionis ex parte Dei;

secundo ex parte proximi, ibi **subiecti invicem**, et cetera.

Circa primum tria facit.
Primo ponitur spiritualis meditatio;
secundo spiritualis exultatio, ibi **cantantes**, etc.;
tertio gratiarum actio, ibi **gratias agentes**, et cetera.
Prima in duas, quia
primo ponit modum meditationis,
secundo materiam eius, ibi **in psalmis**, et cetera.

311. Dicit ergo **loquentes vobis**, et cetera. Est autem duplex locutio. Una exterior, hominis ad homines; alia interior, hominis ad seipsum. Talis autem debet esse compunctiva. Iob X, 1: *loquar in amaritudine animae meae.* Item, debet fieri in secreto. Matth. VI, v. 6: *tu autem cum oraveris, intra in cubiculum tuum, et clauso ostio, ora Patrem tuum.* Et Sap. VIII, 16: *intrans in domum meam, conquiescam cum illa.*

312. Materiam vero meditationis tangit, cum dicit **in psalmis**, et cetera. Psallere est uti Psalterio. Et sic **in psalmis**, id est bonis operationibus. Ps. LXXX, 3: *sumite Psalmum, et date tympanum, Psalterium iucundum*, et cetera. **Et hymnis**, id est laudibus divinis. Ps. CXLVIII, 14: *hymnus omnibus sanctis eius*, et cetera. **Et canticis spiritualibus**, scilicet de spe aeternorum. Rom. XII, 12: *spe gaudentes.* Ps. XCI, 4: *in decachordo Psalterio cum cantico in cithara.* Ps. XCVII, 1: *cantate Domino canticum novum*, et cetera.

Meditemur ergo de recta operatione quid faciendum, de divina laudatione quid imitandum, de caelesti iucundatione quid et quomodo serviendum.

I reply and say that the Holy Spirit is possessed in two ways. Either he is had receptively, and it is not in our power to receive him, rather we accept him as a gift from God: *the charity of God is poured forth in our hearts, by the Holy Spirit, who is given to us* (Rom 5:5). Or he is possessed dispositively, and even here we are not capable of receiving him since we cannot dispose ourselves without the grace of God: *not that we are sufficient to think any thing of ourselves, as of ourselves; but our sufficiency is from God* (2 Cor 3:5).

Or, someone may be said to receive the Holy Spirit, and nonetheless not be full of the Holy Spirit. He has the grace of the Holy Spirit in reference to certain aspects of his life, but not in reference to every one of his actions. Then is he said to be full of the Holy Spirit when he avails himself of the Spirit in all he does.

310. The way to be filled is found in the love of God and one's fellow men. Thus when he says **speaking to yourselves in psalms**:

first, he touches on the way of being filled in relation to God;

second, in relation to one's fellow man, at **being subject to one another**.

Concerning the first of these he does three things:
first, he prescribes spiritual meditation;
second, he speaks of spiritual exultation, at **singing**;
third, he mentions the thanksgiving, at **giving thanks**.
The first has two parts:
first, he writes of the manner of the meditation;
second, its subject matter, at **in psalms**.

311. Thus he says **speaking to yourselves**. But there are two ways of speaking to yourselves. One is external, of a man talking to other men; another is interior, of a man speaking to himself. This latter ought to be repentant: *I will speak in the bitterness of my soul* (Job 10:1). And it ought to be done in secret: *when you pray, enter your chamber and, having shut the door, pray to your Father in secret* (Matt 6:6). *When I go into my house, I shall repose myself with her* (Wis 8:16).

312. He then touches on the subject-matter of meditative prayer when he says **in psalms and hymns and spiritual canticles**. To sing is to make use of the psaltery; and thus in psalms, that is, in good works. *Take a psalm, and bring hither the timbrel: the pleasant psaltery with the harp* (Ps 81:2). **And hymns**, that is, by the divine praises: *a hymn to all his saints* (Ps 148:14); and **spiritual canticles** concerning the hope of eternal realities: *rejoicing in hope* (Rom 12:12); *upon the ten stringed psaltery, with a canticle upon the harp* (Ps 92:3); *sing to the Lord a new canticle, because he has done wonderful things* (Ps 98:1).

Hence we meditate on honest actions that we should do; on the divine praise and what we should imitate; and on the joy of heaven and what we should render homage to, and how.

313. Sic ergo effectus Spiritus Sancti primus est sacra meditatio, secundus spiritualis exultatio, quia ex frequenti meditatione ignis caritatis in corde accenditur. Ps. XXXVIII, 4: *concaluit cor meum intra me, et in meditatione mea exardescet ignis*, et cetera. Et hinc generatur laetitia spiritualis in corde. Et ideo dicit **cantantes et psallentes**, id est ut affectus nostri afficiantur gaudio spirituali ad operanda bona. I Cor. XIV, 15: *psallam spiritu, psallam et mente*. Col. III, 16: *in omni sapientia docentes et commonentes vosmetipsos in psalmis et hymnis et canticis spiritualibus, in gratia cantantes et psallentes in cordibus vestris domino.*

Ex hoc error haereticorum confunditur dicentium quod vanum est cantare Domino cantica vocalia sed spiritualia tantum. Nam in laudibus Ecclesiae est aliquid per se considerandum, et hoc est quod Apostolus dicit **in cordibus**. Aliquid vero propter duo, scilicet propter nos, ut mens nostra incitetur ad devotionem interiorem; sed si ex hoc aliquis commoveatur ad dissolutionem, vel in gloriam inanem, hoc est contra intentionem Ecclesiae. Item, propter alios, quia per hoc rudes efficiuntur devotiores. IV Reg. III, 15: *cumque caneret psaltes, facta est super eum manus Domini.*

314. Tertius effectus est gratiarum actio: quia ex hoc quod aliquis sic affectus est ad Deum, recognoscit se omnia habere a Deo.

Quanto enim aliquis magis afficitur ad Deum, et ipsum cognoscit, tanto videt eum maiorem et se minorem; imo prope nihil, in comparatione ad Deum. Iob XLII, 5: *oculus meus videt te, idcirco me reprehendo*, et cetera. Et ideo dicit **gratias agentes semper pro omnibus**, scilicet donis, vel prosperis, vel adversis. Ps. XXXIII, 1: *benedicam Dominum in omni tempore*, et cetera. Quia haec etiam sunt nobis dona in via. Iac. I, 2: *omne gaudium existimate*, etc., Act. V, 41: *ibant apostoli gaudentes*, et cetera. I Thess. V, 18: *in omnibus gratias agite*.

Sed hoc **in nomine Domini nostri Iesu Christi**, quia omnia bona proveniunt per eum. Rom. V, 1: *pacem habemus ad Deum per Dominum nostrum Iesum Christum, per quem accessum*, et cetera. Sed addit **Deo**, inquantum actor noster est per creationem, **et Patri**, inquantum misit nobis Christum, per quem regeneravit nos. Et sic gratias Deo, quantum ad bona naturae; Patri, quantum ad bona gratiae.

315. Sed quantum ad proximum, ponit modum repletionis, dicens **subiecti invicem in timore Christi**, id est non propter timorem humanum, sed Christi.

313. The first effect of the Holy Spirit is a holy meditation, and the second is a spiritual exultation; from frequent meditation the fire of charity is enkindled in the heart. *My heart grew hot within me: and in my meditation a fire shall flame out* (Ps 39:3). And from this a spiritual joy is born within the heart; thus he mentions **singing and making melody** so that our affections would be stirred by spiritual joys towards good works. *I will sing with the spirit, I will sing also with the understanding* (1 Cor 14:15). *In all wisdom teaching and admonishing one another in psalms, hymns, and spiritual canticles, singing in grace in your hearts to God* (Col 3:16).

This refutes the error of those heretics who claim that it is useless to sing vocal canticles to the Lord; that only spiritual ones matter. In the praises of the Church there is an essential element to consider, what the Apostle refers to as **in your hearts**. Yet there is another element, external song, which has a twofold purpose. One is that it is for us, to stimulate our minds to an interior devotion. If someone is rather moved to frivolity or vain glory by it, this is contrary to the Church's intention. Its second purpose is for others, since by it the illiterate become more devout: *and when the minstrel played, the hand of the Lord came upon him* (2 Kgs 3:15).

314. The third effect is thanksgiving because, when someone is influenced in these ways toward God, he recognizes that everything he has is from God.

For the more a person is influenced by his relation to God and knows him, the more does he see God as greater and himself as smaller, indeed almost nothing, in comparison with God. *Now my eye sees you. Therefore do I reprehend myself, and do penance in dust and ashes* (Job 42:5–6). So he declares **giving thanks always for all things**, for all his gifts, whether of prosperity or adversity. *I will bless the Lord at all times; his praise shall be always in my mouth* (Ps 34:1). For adversities are also gifts to us on the way: *count it all joy when you shall fall into diverse temptations* (Jas 1:2). And the apostles *indeed went from the presence of the council, rejoicing that they were accounted worthy to suffer reproach for the name of Jesus* (Acts 5:41). *In all things give thanks* (1 Thess 5:18).

This is **in the name of our Lord Jesus Christ** since all blessings come through him. *Let us have peace with God, through our Lord Jesus Christ; by whom also we have access through faith into this grace* (Rom 5:1–2). Yet he adds **to God** inasmuch as he is our maker through creation, **and the Father** since he sent Christ to us through whom he regenerated us. Thus we give thanks to him as God regarding the goods of nature, and to him as Father in reference to the goods of grace.

315. He sets down the way of being filled by the Spirit in relation to one's fellow men by saying **being subject one to another, in the fear of Christ**, that is, not out of a human fear but from a reverence for Christ.

Lecture 8

⁵:²²Mulieres viris suis subditae sint, sicut Domino: [n. 317]

⁵:²³quoniam vir caput est mulieris, sicut Christus caput est Ecclesiae: ipse, salvator corporis ejus. [n. 318]

⁵:²⁴Sed sicut Ecclesia subjecta est Christo, ita et mulieres viris suis in omnibus.

⁵:²⁵Viri, diligite uxores vestras, sicut et Christus dilexit Ecclesiam, et seipsum tradidit pro ea, [n. 319]

⁵:²⁶ut illam sanctificaret, mundans lavacro aquae in Verbo vitae, [n. 323]

⁵:²⁷ut exhiberet ipse sibi gloriosam Ecclesiam, non habentem maculam, aut rugam, aut aliquid hujusmodi, sed ut sit sancta et immaculata. [n. 324]

⁵:²²Αἱ γυναῖκες τοῖς ἰδίοις ἀνδράσιν ὡς τῷ κυρίῳ,

⁵:²³ὅτι ἀνήρ ἐστιν κεφαλὴ τῆς γυναικὸς ὡς καὶ ὁ Χριστὸς κεφαλὴ τῆς ἐκκλησίας, αὐτὸς σωτὴρ τοῦ σώματος.

⁵:²⁴ἀλλὰ ὡς ἡ ἐκκλησία ὑποτάσσεται τῷ Χριστῷ, οὕτως καὶ αἱ γυναῖκες τοῖς ἀνδράσιν ἐν παντί.

⁵:²⁵Οἱ ἄνδρες, ἀγαπᾶτε τὰς γυναῖκας, καθὼς καὶ ὁ Χριστὸς ἠγάπησεν τὴν ἐκκλησίαν καὶ ἑαυτὸν παρέδωκεν ὑπὲρ αὐτῆς,

⁵:²⁶ἵνα αὐτὴν ἁγιάσῃ καθαρίσας τῷ λουτρῷ τοῦ ὕδατος ἐν ῥήματι,

⁵:²⁷ἵνα παραστήσῃ αὐτὸς ἑαυτῷ ἔνδοξον τὴν ἐκκλησίαν, μὴ ἔχουσαν σπίλον ἢ ῥυτίδα ἤ τι τῶν τοιούτων, ἀλλ' ἵνα ᾖ ἁγία καὶ ἄμωμος.

⁵:²²Let women be subject to their husbands, as to the Lord: [n. 317]

⁵:²³Because the husband is the head of the wife, as Christ is the head of the Church. He is the savior of his body. [n. 318]

⁵:²⁴Therefore as the Church is subject to Christ: so also let the wives be to their husbands in all things.

⁵:²⁵Husbands, love your wives, as Christ also loved the Church and delivered himself up for it: [n. 319]

⁵:²⁶That he might sanctify it, cleansing it by the laver of water in the Word of life: [n. 323]

⁵:²⁷That he might present it to himself, a glorious Church, not having spot or wrinkle or any such thing; but that it should be holy and without blemish. [n. 324]

---

316. Supra Apostolus posuit praecepta generalia ad omnes, hic ponit ea quae pertinent ad speciales quasdam personas et status. Et quia secundum Philosophum in *Politicis* domus habet tres connexiones, sine quibus non est perfecta, scilicet viri et mulieris, patris et filii, domini et servi; ideo, haec tria prosequens, instruit:

primo mulierem et virum;

secundo patrem et filium, cap. VI, ibi *filii, obedite*, etc.;

tertio servos et dominos, ibi *servi, obedite*, et cetera.

Prima in duas.

Primo enim monet mulieres de subiectione;

secundo viros de dilectione, ibi *viri, diligite*, et cetera.

Prima in duas.

Primo ponit admonitionem;

secundo eius rationem, ibi *quoniam vir caput est*, et cetera.

317. Dicit ergo *mulieres viris suis subditae sint*, quia certe mulier, si primatum habeat, contraria est viro suo, ut dicitur Eccli. c. XXV, 30. Et ideo specialiter monet eas de subiectione. Et hoc *sicut domino*, quia proportio viri ad uxorem quodammodo est sicut servi ad dominum, quantum debet regi mandato domini; sed differentia est in hoc, quod dominus utitur servis suis quo ad id quod

316. Up until now the Apostle has set down general precepts applicable to everyone, and at this point he expresses those which pertain to particular persons or classes. According to the Philosopher in his *Politics*, a home must possess three relationships if it is to be complete, namely, that of the husband and wife, of the father and the children, and that between the master and his servants. Hence these three are dealt with when the Apostle instructs:

first, the husband and wife;

second, the father and child, at *children, obey* (Eph 6:1);

third, the servants and masters, at *slaves, be obedient* (Eph 6:5).

The first has two divisions:

first, he cautions the women to be subject;

second, he admonishes the men to love, at *husbands, love*.

The first is again twofold:

first, he gives an admonition;

second, he explains the reason for it, at *because the husband is the head*.

317. Hence he states: *let women be subject to their husbands* because *a woman, if she have superiority, is contrary to her husband* (Sir 25:30). So he especially warns them about subjection. This is *as to a lord* since the relation of a husband to his wife is, in a certain way, like that of a master to his servant, insofar as the latter ought to be governed by the commands of his master. The difference

est sibi utile: sed vir utitur uxore et liberis ad utilitatem communem. Et ideo dicit **sicut domino**; non quod vere sit dominus, sed sicut dominus. I Petr. III, 1: *mulieres subditae sint viris suis*, et cetera.

318. Deinde subdit rationem suam. Circa quod tria facit. Primo eam proponit; secundo exemplum inducit, ibi **sicut Christus**, etc.; tertio ex exemplo intentum concludit, ibi **sed sicut**, et cetera.

Ratio autem haec est, quoniam vir est caput mulieris, in capite autem viget sensus visus, Eccle. II, 14: *sapientis oculi in capite eius*, et ideo vir debet gubernare mulierem ut caput eius. I Cor. XI, 3: *caput quidem mulieris vir*.

Deinde ponit exemplum, cum dicit **sicut Christus caput est Ecclesiae**. Supra I, 22 s.: **ipsum dedit caput supra omnem Ecclesiam, quae est corpus ipsius**, et hoc non ad utilitatem suam, sed Ecclesiae, **quia ipse est salvator corporis eius**. Act. IV, 12: *non est enim aliud nomen sub caelo datum hominibus, in quo oporteat nos salvos fieri*. Is. c. XII, 2: *ecce Deus salvator meus*, et cetera. Ex hoc autem concludit intentionem, cum dicit **sed sicut**, et cetera. Quasi dicat: non est conveniens, quod membrum repugnet ipsi capiti in aliquo; nunc autem, sicut Christus caput est Ecclesiae, suo modo, ita vir est caput mulieris: non debet ergo mulier inobediens esse viro, **sed sicut Ecclesia subiecta est Christo**, Ps. LXI, 2: *nonne Deo subiecta erit anima mea*, etc., **ita et mulieres viris suis**. Gen. III, v. 16: *sub viri potestate eris*. Et hoc **in omnibus**, scilicet quae non sunt contra Deum; quia dicitur Act. V, 29: *obedire oportet Deo magis, quam hominibus*.

319. Deinde cum dicit **viri, diligite uxores vestras**, etc., monet viros ad dilectionem uxorum. Et

primo facit hoc,

secundo assignat rationem huius, ibi **sicut Christus**, et cetera.

320. Dicit ergo **viri, diligite uxores vestras**, quia certe ex amore, quem habet vir ad uxorem, magis caste vivit et pacifice uterque se habet. Si autem vir aliam magis diligit, quam suam, se et suam discrimini exponit. Col. III, 19: *viri, diligite uxores vestras, et nolite amari esse ad illas*.

321. Tangit autem rationem huius triplicem.

Primam sumit ex exemplo Christi, cum dicit **sicut et Christus**, etc.;

secundam ex parte viri, ibi **qui suam uxorem diligit**, etc.;

tertiam ex parte mandati divini, ibi **propter hoc relinquet**, et cetera.

Circa primum tria facit.

322. Primo proponit exemplum dilectionis Christi;

between these two relationships is that the master employs his servants in whatever is profitable to himself; but a husband treats his wife and children in reference to the common good. Thus he mentions **as to a lord**; the husband is not really a lord, but is as a lord. *Let wives be subject to their husbands* (1 Pet 3:1).

318. Next, he adds his reason; regarding it he makes three points: first, he offers it for consideration; second, he introduces an example, at **as Christ**; third, from the example he draws his conclusion, at **as the Church**.

The reason for this subjection is that the husband is the head of the wife, and the sense of sight is localized in the head—*the eyes of a wise man are in his head* (Eccl 2:14)—and hence a husband ought to govern his wife as her head. *The head of the woman is the man* (1 Cor 11:3).

Then he brings in his example when he says: **as Christ is the head of the Church**. God **has made him head over all the Church, which is his body** (Eph 1:22–23). This is not for his own utility, but for that of the Church since **he is the savior of his body**. *For there is no other name under heaven given to men, whereby we must be saved* (Acts 4:12). *Behold, God is my savior; I will deal confidently and will not fear* (Isa 12:2). From this he draws the conclusion he intended, saying **therefore, as the Church is subject to Christ**. As though he said: it is not proper for an organ to rebel against its head in any situation; but as Christ is head of the Church in his own way, so a husband is the head of his wife; therefore the wife must be obedient to her husband **as the Church is subject to Christ**. *Shall not my soul be subject to God?* (Ps 62:1), **so also let the wives be to their husbands**. *And you shall be under your husband's power* (Gen 3:16), **in all things** which are not contrary to God, since *we ought to obey God rather than men* (Acts 5:29).

319. After this, at **husbands, love your wives**, he admonishes the husbands that they are to love their wives.

First, he does this.

Second, he gives his reason, at **as Christ**.

320. He states: **husbands, love your wives**. For certainly it is from the love he has for his wife that he will live more chastely and both of them will enjoy a peaceful relationship. If he should love another more than his own wife, he exposes himself and his wife to division. *Husbands, love your wives and be not bitter towards them* (Col 3:19).

321. He then treats of the threefold reason for this.

First, he draws one reason from the example of Christ, at **as Christ**;

second, another one from the husband himself, at **he who loves his wife** (Eph 5:28);

third, another from a divine commandment, at **for this cause shall a man should leave** (Eph 5:31).

Concerning the first he does three things:

322. first, he offers the example of Christ's love;

323. secundo signum, ibi *et tradidit*, etc.;

tertio concludit intentum *ita et viri*, et cetera.

322. Dicit ergo: *sicut et Christus dilexit Ecclesiam*. Supra eodem: *estote imitatores Dei sicut filii charissimi*, et cetera.

323. Signum autem dilectionis Christi ad Ecclesiam ostenditur, quia *tradidit semetipsum pro ea*. Gal. II, 20: *dilexit me, et tradidit semetipsum pro me*, et cetera. Is. LIII, 12: *tradidit in mortem animam suam*, et cetera.

Sed ad quid? *Ut illam sanctificaret*. Hebr. c. ult.: *Iesus ut sanctificaret per suum sanguinem populum*, et cetera. Io. XVII, 17: *sanctifica eos in veritate*. Iste est effectus mortis Christi.

324. Effectus autem sanctificationis est mundatio eius a maculis peccatorum. Ideo subdit dicens *mundans eam lavacro aquae*. Quod quidem lavacrum habet virtutem a passione Christi. Rom. VI, 3: *quicumque baptizati sumus in Christo Iesu, in morte ipsius baptizati sumus, consepulti enim sumus cum illo per baptismum in mortem*. Ez. XXXIX: *effundam super vos aquam mundam*, et cetera. Zac. XIII, 1: *erit fons patens domui David*, et cetera. Et hoc *in Verbo vitae*, quod adveniens aquae dat ei virtutem abluendi. Matth. c. ult.: *euntes ergo docete omnes gentes, baptizantes eos in nomine Patris, et Filii, et Spiritus Sancti*.

Finis autem sanctificationis est puritas Ecclesiae. Ideo dicit *ut exhiberet sibi gloriosam Ecclesiam*; quasi dicat Apostolus: indecens est quod immaculatus sponsus sponsam duceret maculatam. Et ideo sibi exhibet eam immaculatam: hic per gratiam sed in futuro per gloriam. Unde dicit *gloriosam*, scilicet per claritatem animae et corporis. Phil. III, v. 21: *reformabit corpus humilitatis nostrae*, et cetera. Et ideo addit *non habentem maculam*. Ps. c, 6: *ambulans in via immaculata*, et cetera. Ps. CXVIII, 1: *beati immaculati in via*, et cetera. *Neque rugam*, id est, sine defectu passibilitatis; quia, ut dicitur Apoc. VII, 16: *non esurient, neque sitient amplius*. *Aut aliquid huiusmodi, sed ut sit sancta*, per confirmationem gratiae, *et immaculata* ab omni immunditia.

Et haec omnia intelligi possunt de exhibitione, quae erit in futuro per gloriam. Si autem de exhibitione per fidem, tunc diceretur: *ut exhiberet sibi*, scilicet per fidem, *Ecclesiam gloriosam*, quia *gloria magna est sequi Dominum*, ut dicitur Eccli. XXIII, 38, *non habentem maculam*, scilicet criminis mortalis. *Maculata es in iniquitate tua*, Ier. II, v. 22. *Neque rugam*, id est duplicitatem

323. second, he shows the sign of that love, at *and delivered himself up*;

third, finally he deduces his intended conclusion, at *so also ought men* (Eph 5:28).

322. Thus he says: *as Christ also loved the Church*; *be therefore followers of God, as most dear children; and walk in love, as Christ also has loved us and has delivered himself for us* (Eph 5:1–2).

323. The sign of Christ's love for the Church is that *he delivered himself up for it*. *The Son of God who loved me and delivered himself for me* (Gal 2:20). *He has delivered his soul unto death* (Isa 53:12).

And for what? *That he might sanctify it*: wherefore *Jesus also, that he might sanctify the people by his own blood, suffered without the gate* (Heb 13:12). *Sanctify them in truth* (John 17:17). That is the effect of Christ's death.

324. As a result of this sanctification he cleanses it from the stains of sin. Hence he adds *cleansing it by the laver of water*. This washing has a power from the passion of Christ. *All we who are baptized in Christ Jesus are baptized in his death; for we are buried together with him by baptism into death* (Rom 6:3–4). *And I will pour upon you clean water and you shall be cleansed from all your filthiness* (Ezek 36:25). *There shall be a fountain open to the house of David and to the inhabitants of Jerusalem; for the washing of the sinner and of the unclean woman* (Zech 13:1). This occurs *in the Word of life* which, coming upon the water, gives it the power to cleanse: *going, therefore, teach all nations; baptizing them in the name of the Father and of the Son and of the Holy Spirit* (Matt 28:19).

The goal of this sanctifying action is the Church's purity. Thus he states *that he might present it to himself, a glorious Church*; as if the Apostle said: it would be highly improper for the immaculate bridegroom to wed a soiled bride. This is why he presents her to himself in an immaculate state, now through grace and in the future through glory. Regarding the latter, he says *glorious* by the clarity of both body and soul. For *he will reform the body of our lowness, made like to the body of his glory* (Phil 3:21). Hence he adds *not having spot*: *the man that walked in the perfect way, he served me* (Ps 101:6); *blessed are the undefiled in the way: who walk in the law of the Lord* (Ps 119:1). *Or wrinkle* refers to the lack of suffering since, as it is written: *they shall no more hunger nor thirst* (Rev 7:16), *or any such thing, but that it should be holy* through its confirmation in grace, *and without* the *blemish* of any defilement.

Thus all of these characteristics can be understood of the appearance of the Church in the future through glory. But if they are taken to refer to her appearance through faith, then he would be saying: *that he might present to himself*, through faith, *a glorious Church*, since *it is a great glory to follow the Lord* (Sir 23:38), *not having* a *spot* of mortal sin. *You are stained in your iniquity* (Jer 2:22). Nor

intentionis, quam non habent qui recte coniuncti sunt Christo et Ecclesiae. Iob XVI, 9: *rugae meae testimonium dicunt contra me*, et cetera. **Sed** magis **sanctam** per intentionem, **et immaculatam** per omnimodam puritatem.

does it have a **wrinkle**, that is, a duplicity of purpose which those who are rightly united with Christ and the Church do not have. *My wrinkles bear witness against me* (Job 16:9). **But** rather **that it should be holy** through its intention and **without blemish** through every kind of purity.

324. Ex hoc tertio concludit intentum, dicens ***ita et viri debent diligere uxores suas, ut corpora sua***.

324. From the above he, in the third place, draws the conclusion he intended by affirming: ***so also ought men to love their wives as their own bodies*** (Eph 5:28).

Lecture 9

⁵:²⁸Ita et viri debent diligere uxores suas ut corpora sua. Qui suam uxorem diligit, seipsum diligit. [n. 326]

⁵:²⁹Nemo enim umquam carnem suam odio habuit: sed nutrit et fovet eam, sicut et Christus Ecclesiam: [n. 327]

⁵:³⁰quia membra sumus corporis ejus, de carne ejus et de ossibus ejus.

⁵:²⁸οὕτως ὀφείλουσιν [καὶ] οἱ ἄνδρες ἀγαπᾶν τὰς ἑαυτῶν γυναῖκας ὡς τὰ ἑαυτῶν σώματα. ὁ ἀγαπῶν τὴν ἑαυτοῦ γυναῖκα ἑαυτὸν ἀγαπᾷ,

⁵:²⁹οὐδεὶς γάρ ποτε τὴν ἑαυτοῦ σάρκα ἐμίσησεν, ἀλλὰ ἐκτρέφει καὶ θάλπει αὐτήν, καθὼς καὶ ὁ Χριστὸς τὴν ἐκκλησίαν,

⁵:³⁰ὅτι μέλη ἐσμὲν τοῦ σώματος αὐτοῦ.

⁵:²⁸So also ought men to love their wives as their own bodies. He who loves his wife loves himself. [n. 326]

⁵:²⁹For no man ever hated his own flesh, but nourishes and cherishes it, as also Christ does the Church: [n. 327]

⁵:³⁰Because we are members of his body, of his flesh and of his bones.

---

325. Supra induxit viros ad dilectionem uxorum, ex parte Christi, vel exemplo dilectionis quam habet Christus ad Ecclesiam, hic ostendit idem ex parte ipsiusmet viri. Et facit duo:

primo ponit rationem;

secundo confirmat eam per exemplum, ibi *sicut et Christus*, et cetera.

326. Ratio est talis: vir et mulier sunt quodammodo unum; unde sicut caro subditur animae, ita mulier viro; sed nullus unquam habuit carnem suam odio: ergo nec uxorem. Dicit ergo **qui suam uxorem diligit, seipsum diligit**. Matth. XIX, 6: *itaque non sunt duo, sed una caro*. Et ideo sicut peccaret contra naturam qui seipsum odio haberet, ita qui uxorem. Eccli. XXV, 1 s.: *in tribus beneplacitum est spiritui meo, quae sunt probata coram Deo et hominibus: concordia fratrum, amor proximorum, et vir et mulier bene sibi consentientes*.

327. Quod autem sic debeant se diligere, probat dicens **nemo enim carnem suam unquam odio habuit**; quod patet per effectum, quia probatio dilectionis exhibitio est operis. Nam id quod pro viribus conservamus, diligimus. **Sed** quilibet **nutrit et fovet carnem suam** propter conservationem. I Tim. ult.: *habentes autem alimenta et quibus tegamur*, et cetera.

328. Sed contra Lc. XIV, 26: *qui non odit uxorem*, etc., *non potest esse meus discipulus*.

Respondeo. Dicendum est quod, ut Apostolus dicit, sic homo uxorem debet diligere sicut se; se autem debet homo diligere infra Deum; sic ergo uxorem debet diligere, scilicet infra Deum. Dicit autem *qui non odit uxorem*, non quia praecipiat eam odire, quod esset peccatum mortale praecipere, sed praecipit eam ita ut se diligere; nunc autem minor dilectio est quasi quoddam odium respectu eius quod summe et plus diligitur, scilicet respectu Dei; ita **nemo carnem suam odit**, et cetera.

325. Above he urged husbands to love their wives, he appealed to Christ and to the example of Christ's love for the Church. Here he demonstrates the same thing from the point of view of the husband himself. He makes two points:

first, he gives the reason;

second, he verifies it through an example, at *as Christ*.

326. The reason is as follows. A husband and wife are somehow one; hence, as the flesh is subject to the soul, so is the wife to the husband; but no one ever held his own flesh in contempt, therefore neither should anyone his wife. Whence he states: *he who loves his wife loves himself*. *Therefore, now they are not two, but one flesh* (Matt 19:6). Just as a man sins against nature in hating himself, so does he who hates his wife. *With three things my spirit is pleased, which are approved before God and men: the concord of brethren, and the love of neighbors, and man and wife that agree well together* (Sir 25:1–2).

327. He proves that they ought to love one another in saying *for no man ever hated his own flesh*. This love is evident in what happens since love is verified when it is expressed in action. For we love anything whose powers we sustain. *But* everyone *nourishes and cherishes his own flesh* in order to sustain it. *But, having food and wherewith to be covered, with these we are content* (1 Tim 6:8).

328. But is not this contrary to what is written: *if any man come to me, and hate not his father and mother and wife and children and brethren and sisters, yes and his own life also, he cannot be my disciple* (Luke 14:26)?

I reply. The Apostle affirms that a man ought to love his wife as he does himself; but he must love himself less than God; hence he should also love his wife less than God. In stating *he who does not hate his wife*, he is not commanding that she be hated—which would be to command a mortal sin—but that she be loved as the man loves himself. Now love in a lesser degree is like a certain hatred in comparison with whatever is loved most or to a greater degree, in this case, God. Likewise, *no man ever hated his own flesh, but nourishes and cherishes it*.

329. Sed contra: qui diligit aliquem, non vult, nec appetit ab eo separari; sed sancti volunt a carne separari. Rom. VII, 24: *infelix ego homo, quis me liberabit de corpore mortis huius?* Phil. I, 23: *desiderium habens dissolvi*, et cetera.

Praeterea, nullus affligit quod diligit, sed sancti affligunt carnem suam in hoc mundo. I Cor. IX, 27: *castigo corpus meum*, et cetera.

Praeterea, quidam occidunt se, sicut auditum est frequenter. Item de Iuda.

Respondeo. Caro potest considerari in se: et sic non habetur odio, sed naturaliter quilibet appetit eam esse et fovet eam ut sit. Vel potest considerari caro inquantum est alicuius impeditiva quod volumus, et sic odio quodammodo habetur per accidens. Nam omne quod volumus, aut est bonum, aut malum: si bonum, vel est ut finis ultimus, scilicet vita aeterna, a qua impedimur per carnem. II Cor. V, 6: *quamdiu sumus in hoc corpore, peregrinamur a Domino*. Et quia naturaliter appetimus finem nostrum et bene esse, nec hoc possumus quamdiu in hac carne sumus, ideo vellemus eam abiicere; non sicut malum odio habitum sed sicut bonum minus dilectum, impediens maius bonum.

Et sic exponendae sunt auctoritates supra inductae: *infelix*, et cetera. Item: *desiderium habens*, etc.; vel consimiles.

Vel illud quod volumus est bonum non ut finis sed disponens ad finem, sicut sunt habitus virtutum; hoc autem bonum impeditur per carnis lasciviam. Et ideo sancti affligunt et macerant carnem suam, ut subdatur spiritui ad repressionem concupiscentiarum, quia caro concupiscit impediens acquisitionem virtutum nos disponentium ad bonum ultimum. Et ideo qui sic affligit carnem suam, ut subdatur spiritui, non odit eam, sed procurat bonum eius, quia bonum eius est quod subiiciatur spiritui, sicut bonum hominis est quod subiiciatur Deo. Ps. LXXII, 28: *mihi autem adhaerere Deo bonum est*.

Et sic intelligitur: *castigo corpus meum*, etc., et consimiles. Unde hoc non oportebat fieri in statu innocentiae, quamdiu homo subditus fuit Deo, et caro totaliter subdita fuit spiritui, in qua quidem mutua subiectione consistebat donum originalis iustitiae.

Sed aliquando illud quod volumus est malum, et ideo, sicut boni carnem affligunt vel deponere volunt, inquantum impeditiva est boni quod appetunt, ita mali, inquantum caro est impeditiva mali quod appetunt, eam occidunt et se suspendunt, sicut Iudas.

330. Deinde ostendit quod virum oportet uxorem diligere, et hoc per exemplum. Unde dicit **sicut et Christus Ecclesiam**, scilicet dilexit, sicut aliquid sui, **quia**

329. But there are objections to this. When anyone loves something he never wants nor desires to be separated from it. Yet the saints wanted to be separated from the flesh. *Unhappy man that I am, who shall deliver me from the body of this death?* (Rom 7:24) *having a desire to be dissolved and to be with Christ* (Phil 1:23).

Besides, nobody afflicts what he loves, but the saints punished their flesh while they were in this world. *I chastise my body and bring it into subjection* (1 Cor 9:27).

Moreover, some people even kill themselves, as is frequently heard of. Judas did this.

I reply. The flesh, when considered in itself, is not held in contempt, but everyone naturally wants it to exist and nourishes it for this end. On the other hand, the flesh can be considered as an obstacle to what we will, and thus, through circumstance, it can be detested in a certain way. For everything that we will is either good or evil. If good, it may be the ultimate end, eternal life, from which we are held back by the flesh. *While we are in the body we are absent from the Lord* (2 Cor 5:6). And since we naturally desire our fulfillment and well-being—nor can we enjoy these while we are in the flesh—we will to discard it, not as an evil held in contempt, but as a good we love less than the greater good it impedes.

The authoritative texts quoted above—*unhappy man that I am* (Rom 7:24) and *having a desire to be dissolved* (Phil 1:23)—and others like them, are to be explained in this way.

Or, we may will a good that is not the end, but disposes for the end; for example, virtuous habits. But this type of good is opposed by the immoral tendencies of the flesh. On this account do the saints discipline and punish their flesh in order that it might submit to the spirit for the curbing of sensual desires. For, in desiring such, the flesh blocks our acquisition of the virtues which dispose us for the ultimate good. Therefore, whoever punishes his flesh that it might submit to his spirit does not hate it, but rather obtains its own good which is that it be subject to the spirit—just as the good of man is to be subject to God: *it is good for me to adhere to my God* (Ps 73:28).

I chastise my body (1 Cor 9:27) and similar passages are to be understood in this way. This would not have been necessary in the state of innocence as long as man was subject to God, and the flesh totally submissive to the spirit; the gift of original justice consisted precisely in this mutual submission.

On the other hand we sometimes will what is evil. Hence, just as holy persons discipline, or wish to discard, their flesh inasmuch as it is an obstacle to the good they desire, so also the wicked, insofar as the flesh blocks the evil they desire, will kill it and commit suicide, as Judas did.

330. Then he indicates that a man must love his wife through an example. Thus he says, **Christ also** loved **the Church** as something of his very self **because we are**

membra sumus corporis. Supra IV, 25: *sumus enim invicem membra*. Dicit autem *de carne eius* propter eamdem participationem naturae. Lc. ult.: *spiritus autem carnem et ossa non habet*, et cetera.

Vel dicit *de carne*, mystice, quantum ad debiles qui sunt carnei, et *de ossibus eius*, quantum ad fortes qui sunt ossei.

members of his body. For we are members one of another (Eph 4:25). He mentions *of his flesh* on account of his sharing the same nature with us. *For a spirit does not have flesh and bones, as you see me to have* (Luke 24:39).

Or, he says this mystically so that *of his flesh* refers to the weak who are of the flesh, and *of his bones* would refer to the strong who are hard as bone.

Lecture 10

5:31 Propter hoc relinquet homo patrem et matrem suam, et adhaerebit uxori suae, et erunt duo in carne una. [n. 333]

5:32 Sacramentum hoc magnum est, ego autem dico in Christo et in Ecclesia. [n. 334]

5:33 Verumtamen et vos singuli, unusquisque uxorem suam sicut seipsum diligat: uxor autem timeat virum suum. [n. 335]

5:31 ἀντὶ τούτου καταλείψει ἄνθρωπος [τὸν] πατέρα καὶ [τὴν] μητέρα καὶ προσκολληθήσεται πρὸς τὴν γυναῖκα αὐτοῦ, καὶ ἔσονται οἱ δύο εἰς σάρκα μίαν.

5:32 τὸ μυστήριον τοῦτο μέγα ἐστίν, ἐγὼ δὲ λέγω εἰς Χριστὸν καὶ εἰς τὴν ἐκκλησίαν.

5:33 πλὴν καὶ ὑμεῖς οἱ καθ' ἕνα ἕκαστος τὴν ἑαυτοῦ γυναῖκα οὕτως ἀγαπάτω ὡς ἑαυτόν, ἡ δὲ γυνὴ ἵνα φοβῆται τὸν ἄνδρα.

5:31 For this cause shall a man leave his father and mother: and shall cleave to his wife. And they shall be two in one flesh. [n. 333]

5:32 This is a great sacrament: but I speak in Christ and in the Church. [n. 334]

5:33 Nevertheless, let every one of you in particular love his wife as himself: and let the wife fear her husband. [n. 335]

331. Supra exhortatus est Apostolus Ephesios ad amorem uxorum dupliciter, scilicet exemplo dilectionis Christi ad Ecclesiam, item ex amore hominis ad seipsum, hic tertio hortatur eos per auctoritatem Scripturae.

Et circa hoc tria facit:
primo auctoritatem inducit;
secundo eam mystice exponit, ibi *sacramentum hoc*, etc.;
tertio adaptat eam secundum litteralem sensum ad propositum suum, ibi *verumtamen et vos*, et cetera.

332. Auctoritas haec dicitur Gen. II, 24 dicta est ab Adam vidente uxorem, scilicet de costa sua formatam.

332. Sed contra dicitur Matth. XIX, 4 s. quod Deus hoc dixit.

Respondeo: Adam ut a Deo inspiratus hoc dixit; Deus autem ut Adam inspirans et docens. Nos autem hoc idem dicimus et multa alia, quae dixit Dominus, Spiritu Dei docente; unde dicitur Matth. X, 20: *non enim vos estis qui loquimini*, et cetera.

333. Notandum hic est quod in praedicta auctoritate triplex coniunctio viri ad mulierem designatur. Prima per affectum dilectionis, quia est tantus affectus utriusque ut patres relinquant. II Esdr. IV, 25: *diligit homo uxorem suam magis quam patrem, et multi dementes facti sunt propter uxores suas*, et cetera. Ibi multa. Hoc autem naturale est, quia appetitus naturalis est concors debitae actioni. Constat autem, quod omnibus agentibus superioribus inest appetitus ut propinent et communicent inferioribus, et ideo amor naturalis inest eis versus inferiora. Et quia homo respectu patris et matris est inferior, non superior, ideo ad uxorem, cuius est superior,

331. The Apostle exhorted the Ephesians above to love their wives. He did this in two ways: both by offering the example of Christ's love for the Church, and by the love a man has for himself. Now he gives a third encouragement drawn from the authority of Scripture.

Regarding this he does three things:
first, he brings in the authoritative text;
second, he explains it mystically, at *this is a great sacrament*;
third, he adapts it according to its literal meaning to the case in question, at *however, let every one of you*.

332. The authoritative text is Genesis, words spoken by Adam when he saw his wife who had been formed from his rib (Gen 2:24).

332. Yet does not this contradict Matthew which states that God himself spoke these words? (Matt 19:4-5)

I reply that Adam spoke them as inspired by God, and God spoke them insofar as he was inspiring and teaching Adam. We use the same expressions; there are many words which the Lord spoke by those whom the Spirit of God instructed. *For it is not you who speak, but the Spirit of your Father speaks in you* (Matt 10:20).

333. It should be noted that in the above mentioned authority a threefold union of a man and wife is designated. The first union is through the devotion of their love, for it is strong enough in each that they both left their fathers behind. *So a man loves his wife better than his father or mother. Many have lost their heads completely for their wives* (3 Esd 4:25-26), and much more concerning this is stated there (3 Esd 4). But this is natural, for natural desires are harmonious with actions that must be performed. It is evident that a desire exists in all higher agents that they administer to, and communicate with, lower agents. Thus a natural love for the lower is present in them. Now a man is an

333. Secunda coniunctio est per conversationem. Unde dicit: *et adhaerebit uxori suae*, et cetera. Eccli. XXV, 1: *in tribus beneplacitum est spiritui meo*, et cetera.

Tertia est per carnalem coniunctionem, ibi: *et erunt duo in carne una*, id est in carnali opere. In qualibet enim generatione est virtus activa et passiva; sed in plantis utraque est in eodem, in perfectis autem animalibus distinguuntur. Et ideo in actu generationis ita se habent masculus et foemina in animalibus sicut in plantis solo eodem uno corpore fit.

334. Consequenter exponit eam mystice, et dicit *sacramentum hoc magnum est*, idest sacrae rei signum, scilicet coniunctionis Christi et Ecclesiae. Sap. VI, 24: *non abscondam a vobis sacramentum Dei*.

Notandum est hic, quod quatuor sacramenta dicuntur magna, scilicet baptismus ratione effectus, quia delet culpam et aperit ianuam paradisi; confirmatio ratione ministri, quia solum a pontificibus et non ab aliis confertur; Eucharistia ratione continentiae, quia totum Christum continet; item matrimonium ratione significationis, quia significat coniunctionem Christi et Ecclesiae.

Et ideo si mystice exponatur, debet sic exponi littera praecedens: *propter hoc relinquet homo*, scilicet Christus, *patrem et matrem*. Reliquit, inquam, *patrem*, inquantum est missus in mundum et incarnatus. Io. XVI, v. 28: *exivi a Patre, et veni in mundum*, et cetera. *Et matrem*, scilicet synagogam. Ier. XII, 7: *reliqui domum meam, et dimisi haereditatem meam*, et cetera. *Et adhaerebit uxori suae*, Ecclesiae. Matth. ult.: *ecce vobiscum sum omnibus diebus*, et cetera.

335. Consequenter argumentatur secundum sensum litteralem exponendo praedictum exemplum. Quaedam enim sunt in Sacra Scriptura Veteris Testamenti, quae tantum dicuntur de Christo, sicut illud Ps. XXI, 17: *foderunt manus meas*, etc.; et illud Is. VII, 14: *ecce virgo concipiet*, et cetera. Quaedam vero de Christo et aliis exponi possunt, sed de Christo principaliter, de aliis vero in figura Christi, sicut praedictum exemplum.

Et ideo primo exponendum est de Christo et postea de aliis. Et ideo dicit *verumtamen et vos singuli, unusquisque uxorem suam diligat*, quasi dicat: de Christo dicitur principaliter et si non singulariter, quia exponendum et implendum est in aliis in figura Christi. Dicit

inferior in relation to his father and mother, not a superior; hence he is naturally more drawn towards his wife and children, to whom he is superior, than to his parents. And also because his wife is intimately united to him in the act of procreation.

333. The second union is through living together. Thus he says *and he shall cleave to his wife*. *With three things my spirit is pleased, which are approved before God and men: the concord of brethren, and the love of neighbors, and man and wife that agree well together* (Sir 25:1–2).

The third is their carnal union: *and they shall be two in one flesh*, that is, in their carnal intercourse. For in any act of generation there is an active and a passive power. In plants both powers are in the same plant, but in the perfect animals they are distinguished. And hence in the act of generation among animals the male and female become, as in plants, only one and the same body.

334. He goes on to interpret this mystically, and he says *this is a great sacrament*, it is the symbol of a sacred reality, namely, the union of Christ and the Church. *I will not hide from you the mysteries of God* (Wis 6:24).

Notice here that four sacraments are termed great: baptism by reason of its effect, since it blots out sin and opens the gate of paradise; confirmation by reason of its minister, since it is conferred only by bishops and not by others; the Eucharist because of what it contains, the whole Christ; and matrimony by reason of its signification, for it symbolizes the union of Christ and the Church.

If, therefore, the text is mystically interpreted, the preceding passage should be explained as follows: *for this cause shall a man*, namely, Christ, *leave his father and mother*. I say *leave his father*, because he was sent into the world and became incarnate—*I came forth from the Father and am come into the world* (John 16:28)—*and his mother* who was the synagogue—*I have forsaken my house, I have left my inheritance, I have given my dear soul into the hand of her enemies* (Jer 12:7). *And he shall cleave to his wife*, the Church. *Behold, I am with you all days, even to the consummation of the world* (Matt 28:20).

335. Next, the point is argued by interpreting the above example according to its literal meaning. For there are certain passages in the Old Testament which can be said only of Christ. For instance: *they have dug my hands and feet: they have numbered all my bones* (Ps 22:16); or *behold, a virgin shall conceive, and bear a son; and his name shall be called Emmanuel* (Isa 7:14). Other passages, however, can be explained as referring to Christ and others; to Christ principally, and to others as they were types of Christ. The above example (Gen 2:24) is of this category.

Thus it must first be interpreted in reference to Christ, and afterwards concerning others. Hence he says *nevertheless, let every one of you in particular love his wife*, as though he asserted: the above example is principally related of Christ, but not only about him since it must be

autem *sicut semetipsum*, quia sicut unusquisque se diligit in ordine ad Deum, ita debet uxorem diligere, non inquantum trahit ad peccatum. Lc. XIV, 26: *si quis venit ad me, et non odit patrem et matrem, et uxorem suam*, etc., sequitur: *non potest meus esse discipulus*.

Sed quid de uxore? ***Uxor autem virum suum timeat***, scilicet timore reverentiae et subiectionis, quia debet ei esse subiecta.

interpreted and fulfilled in other persons as types of Christ. He states **as himself** because, just as everyone loves himself in relation to God, so he ought to love his wife in this way, and not inasmuch as she draws him into sin. *If any man come to me, and hate not his father and mother and wife . . . he cannot be my disciple* (Luke 14:26).

But what about the wife? **And let the wife fear her husband**, with the fear of reverence and submission since she must be subject to him.

Chapter 6

Lecture 1

⁶:¹*Filii, obedite parentibus vestris in Domino: hoc enim justum est.* [n. 337]

⁶:²*Honora patrem tuum, et matrem tuam, quod est mandatum primum in promissione:* [n. 338]

⁶:³*ut bene sit tibi, et sis longaevus super terram.* [n. 340]

⁶:⁴*Et vos patres, nolite ad iracundiam provocare filios vestros: sed educate illos in disciplina et correptione Domini.* [n. 342]

⁶:¹Τὰ τέκνα, ὑπακούετε τοῖς γονεῦσιν ὑμῶν [ἐν κυρίῳ], τοῦτο γάρ ἐστιν δίκαιον.

⁶:²τίμα τὸν πατέρα σου καὶ τὴν μητέρα, ἥτις ἐστὶν ἐντολὴ πρώτη ἐν ἐπαγγελίᾳ,

⁶:³ἵνα εὖ σοι γένηται καὶ ἔσῃ μακροχρόνιος ἐπὶ τῆς γῆς.

⁶:⁴Καὶ οἱ πατέρες, μὴ παροργίζετε τὰ τέκνα ὑμῶν, ἀλλὰ ἐκτρέφετε αὐτὰ ἐν παιδείᾳ καὶ νουθεσίᾳ κυρίου.

⁶:¹**Children, obey your parents in the Lord: for this is just.** [n. 337]

⁶:²**Honor your father and your mother, which is the first commandment with a promise:** [n. 338]

⁶:³**That it may be well with you, and you may live long upon the earth.** [n. 340]

⁶:⁴**And you, fathers, do not provoke your children to anger: but bring them up in the discipline and correction of the Lord.** [n. 342]

---

336. Supra monuit virum et uxorem, quae est una connexio familiae, hic monet patrem et filios, quae est secunda connexio domus. Et

primo facit mentionem, quomodo filii se debeant habere ad parentes;

secundo quomodo, e converso, patres ad filios, ibi ***nolite***, et cetera.

Prima in duas. Primo proponit monitionem;

secundo ostendit rationem, ibi ***hoc enim est iustum***, et cetera.

337. Dicit ergo ***filii, obedite***, et cetera. Notandum est hic quod patres debent naturaliter instruere filios moribus, filii autem, instruentibus parentibus, naturaliter debent eis obedire, sicut infirmi obediunt medicis. Unde proprium filiorum est obedientia. Col. III, v. 20: *filii, obedite*, scilicet patribus, *per omnia, hoc est enim beneplacitum Domino*, et cetera. Dicit autem ***in Domino***, quia non est obediendum parentibus, nec alicui in his quae sunt contra Deum. Act. V, 29: *obedire oportet Deo magis quam hominibus*.

Et per hoc solvitur auctoritas modo allegata: *si quis venit ad me, et non odit patrem*, etc.; quia hoc intelligitur inquantum sunt contra Deum.

338. Rationem autem assignat ex duobus, scilicet ex iustitia, et utilitate: quod autem sit iustum patet ac probatur, quia lex divina nihil mandat nisi iustum.

336. He had previously given advice to husband and wife which is one relationship in the family. Now he cautions the fathers and children, which is the home's second relationship:

first, he mentions how the children should behave toward their parents;

second, how, conversely, fathers should be related to their children, at ***do not provoke***.

The first has two sections: first, he sets down the warning;

second, he gives the reason, at ***for this is just***.

337. He begins, ***children, obey your parents***. Note here that fathers have a natural duty to instruct their children in moral conduct. The children, on the other hand, have a natural duty, while their parents are instructing them, to be obedient to them—as the sick are to obey doctors. Hence the proper characteristic of children is obedience. *Children, obey your parents in all things; for this is well pleasing to the Lord* (Col 3:20). He says ***in the Lord*** because neither parents, nor anyone else, ought to be obeyed in what is contrary to God. *It is necessary to obey God rather than men* (Acts 5:29).

The authoritative text previously brought forward is to be explained in this way also. *If any man come to me, and hate not his father and mother . . . he cannot be my disciple* (Luke 14:26) is to be understood insofar as they are against God.

338. The reason he gives for this arises from two sources: from justice and from a utility. That it is just is evident and proved from the fact that the divine law commands

only what is just. *The justices of the Lord are right* (Ps 19:8). And the divine law commands: *honor your father and mother, as the Lord your God has commanded you* (Exod 20:12; Deut 5:16). *He who fears the Lord honors his parents and will serve them as his masters that brought him into the world* (Sir 3:8). Honor implies a manifestation of reverence to those who are over us; and since we have parents over us, the word 'honor' is used. Hence he affirms: **for this is just, honor your father and your mother**. *He who honors his father shall enjoy a long life; and he who obeys his father shall be a comfort to his mother* (Sir 3:7). That children ought to honor their parents is to be understood in three ways. They must venerate them as elders; show obedience to them as teachers; and give them sustenance as the ones who had nourished them when they were strong.

339. He goes on to indicate the dignity of this precept, saying **which is the first commandment**. On the contrary, the first commandment is that the one God must be worshipped.

I reply. The commandments were contained on two tablets. The first contained those whose reference was to God; the second those which referred to one's neighbors. On this second tablet the first commandment is to honor one's parents. And this is for two reasons. First, it is the only affirmative precept on the second tablet since it is natural for us to serve our parents, which is not true of our other fellow men, and hence there is no other affirmative command. Rather, nature dictates that a man should not harm his neighbors, and hence this is forbidden. Therefore, the first possesses a prior and greater obligation and so is the first.

The second reason is that God must be honored as the source of our existence, and our parents also as the source of our existence. The sixth book of the *Ethics* points out that we have three things from our parents: existence, life and education. Thus it is fitting that after the commandments related to God, the first would be in reference to our parents.

340. Or, **first** may refer to the promise which is annexed to this one only. There are two reasons for this. One is that men, in doing things for others, seek their own good; and they can expect no advantage from parents who have already grown old, unless a reward come from God.

The second reason is lest anyone imagine that honoring one's parents was not meritorious because it is natural; on this account he adds **that you may live long upon the earth**. In the Old Testament temporal promises were pledged because the people then were immature and hence were graciously taught as children under a pedagogue. Nevertheless, in those little gifts which were suited to a young people, great spiritual favors were symbolized. Therefore this text can refer, according to its literal meaning, to temporal goods; which is why he says **with a promise, that it may be well with you**, that is, that you may abound in the

minoribus beneficiis, meretur maiora recipere; maxima autem beneficia habemus a parentibus, scilicet esse, nutrimentum et disciplinam. Quando ergo quis gratus est his, fit dignus ut maiora recipiat. Et ideo dicit **ut bene sit tibi**; quia, ut dicitur I Tim. IV, 8: *pietas ad omnia utilis est, promissionem habens vitae, quae nunc est, et futurae*. Et ideo addit **et sis longaevus super terram**, quasi super gratiam et beneficium vitae, quam habes a parentibus. Prov. III, 16: *longitudo dierum in dextera eius, et in sinistra illius divitiae et gloria*.

341. Sed contra. Multi devoti parentibus cito moriuntur.

Et ideo sciendum quod haec temporalia non sunt bona absolute, nisi inquantum ordinata ad spiritualia, et ideo intantum homini bona, inquantum per ea iuvatur ad spiritualia. Unde fortuna non est dicenda bona, si est impediens a virtute. Et ideo longitudo vitae intantum est bona, inquantum ad servitia Dei est ordinata. Et ideo quandoque subtrahitur ne impediat. Sap. IV, 11: *raptus est, ne malitia mutaret intellectum eius*.

Vel potest referri ad sensum spiritualem, **ut sis longaevus** in terra viventium. Ps. CXLII, v. 10 s.: *Spiritus tuus bonus deducet me in terram rectam; propter nomen tuum, Domine, vivificabis me*.

342. Consequenter instructis filiis, instruuntur parentes. Circa quod duo facit: primo ponit unum prohibitivum; secundo aliud inductivum, ibi **sed educate eos**, et cetera.

Dicit ergo: **et vos, patres, nolite provocare filios vestros ad iracundiam**, non quod in omnibus assentiatis voluntati eorum.

Ubi notandum est quod alius est principatus patris ad filium, et domini ad servum, quia dominus utitur servo suo ad utilitatem propriam, sed pater utitur filio ad utilitatem filii. Et ideo est necesse quod patres instruant filios propter utilitatem suam, non tamen minis arcendo aut subiiciendo. Et ideo dicitur Col. III, 21: *patres, nolite ad indignationem provocare filios vestros, ut* scilicet *non pusillo animo fiant*, quia talis provocatio non animat ad bonum.

Quomodo ergo? Subdit **sed educate illos in disciplina**, scilicet verberum, **et correctione**, scilicet verborum, id est corripite eos et educate, ut serviant Domino. Vel: **in disciplina**, eos ad bonum inducendo, **et correctione** a malis retrahendo.

promised benefits. For he who is grateful in receiving lesser favors deserves to receive greater ones. Now we have the greatest of benefits from our parents: existence, nourishment, and education. Therefore, when anyone is grateful for these, he becomes worthy to receive greater. Thus he remarks **that it may be well with you**. For, *godliness is profitable to all things, having promise of the life that now is and of that which is to come* (1 Tim 4:8). He joins **and you may live long upon the earth** as though in addition to the grace and favor of life which you enjoy from your parents. *Length of days is in her right hand: and in her left hand riches and glory* (Prov 3:16).

341. Yet it is objected: many who are devoted to their parents die quickly.

Therefore it must be realized that these temporal goods are not absolute except insofar as they are related to spiritual benefits. They are good for a man to the degree that he is aided by them towards spiritual realities. If it is an obstacle to virtue, fortune must not be termed good. Hence, a long life is good in the measure that it is related to the service of God. It is sometimes not given lest it thwart this service. *He was taken away lest wickedness should alter his understanding, or deceit beguile his soul* (Wis 4:11).

Or, he could be referring to a spiritual meaning, **that you may live long** in the land of the living. *Your good Spirit shall lead me into the right land; for your name's sake, O Lord, quicken me* (Ps 143:10–11).

342. After he has instructed the children, he counsels the parents. Regarding which he makes two points: first, he places one restriction; second, he gives an incentive, at **but bring them up**.

When he says **and you, fathers, do not provoke your children to anger**, it is not that the fathers must give in to their will in all matters.

Here it must be noted that the authority of a father with respect to his child is different from that of a master with respect to his servant. For the master employs his servant to his own advantage, but the father manages his child for the child's advantage. It is necessary that fathers educate their children for the children's own good; not, however, by excessively restricting or subjecting them. *Fathers, provoke not your children to indignation, lest they be discouraged* (Col 3:21). Because such provocation does not inspire them to good.

How then should they? He adds **but bring them up in the discipline** of spankings **and the correction** of words. That is, correct and educate them that they might be of service to the Lord. Or, **in the discipline** may designate that they should encourage them to do good, **and correction** to restrain them from evils.

Lecture 2

6:5Servi, obedite dominis carnalibus cum timore et tremore, in simplicitate cordis vestri, sicut Christo: [n. 344]

6:6non ad oculum servientes, quasi hominibus placentes, sed ut servi Christi, facientes voluntatem Dei ex animo, [n. 345]

6:7cum bona voluntate servientes, sicut Domino, et non hominibus: [n. 348]

6:8scientes quoniam unusquisque quodcumque fecerit bonum, hoc recipiet a Domino, sive servus, sive liber. [n. 349]

6:9Et vos domini, eadem facite illis, remittentes minas: scientes quia et illorum et vester Dominus est in caelis: et personarum acceptio non est apud eum. [n. 350]

6:5Οἱ δοῦλοι, ὑπακούετε τοῖς κατὰ σάρκα κυρίοις μετὰ φόβου καὶ τρόμου ἐν ἁπλότητι τῆς καρδίας ὑμῶν ὡς τῷ Χριστῷ,

6:6μὴ κατ' ὀφθαλμοδουλίαν ὡς ἀνθρωπάρεσκοι ἀλλ' ὡς δοῦλοι Χριστοῦ ποιοῦντες τὸ θέλημα τοῦ θεοῦ ἐκ ψυχῆς,

6:7μετ' εὐνοίας δουλεύοντες, ὡς τῷ κυρίῳ καὶ οὐκ ἀνθρώποις,

6:8εἰδότες ὅτι ἕκαστος, ἐάν τι ποιήσῃ ἀγαθόν, τοῦτο κομίσεται παρὰ κυρίου, εἴτε δοῦλος εἴτε ἐλεύθερος.

6:9Καὶ οἱ κύριοι, τὰ αὐτὰ ποιεῖτε πρὸς αὐτούς, ἀνιέντες τὴν ἀπειλήν, εἰδότες ὅτι καὶ αὐτῶν καὶ ὑμῶν ὁ κύριός ἐστιν ἐν οὐρανοῖς, καὶ προσωπολημψία οὐκ ἔστιν παρ' αὐτῷ.

6:5Servants, be obedient to those who are your lords according to the flesh, with fear and trembling, in the simplicity of your heart, as to Christ. [n. 344]

6:6Not serving to the eye, as it were pleasing men: but, as the servants of Christ, doing the will of God from the heart. [n. 345]

6:7With a good will serving, as to the Lord, and not to men. [n. 348]

6:8Knowing that whatsoever good thing any man shall do, the same shall he receive from the Lord, whether he be bond or free. [n. 349]

6:9And you, masters, do the same things to them, forbearing threatenings: knowing that the Lord both of them and you is in heaven. And there is no respect of persons with him. [n. 350]

---

343. Instructis duabus connexionibus, scilicet viri et mulieris, patris et filii, hic instruit connexionem servi ad dominum. Et

circa hoc facit duo.

Primo instruit servum;

secundo dominum, ibi *et vos, domini*, et cetera.

Iterum prima in tres.

Primo enim ponit monitionem;

secundo exponit, ibi **non ad oculum servientes**, etc.;

tertio ostendit retributionem, ibi **scientes quoniam unusquisque**, et cetera.

344. Iterum prima in tres. Quia primo monet ad obedientiam; secundo ad reverentiam; tertio ad cordis simplicitatem.

Secunda, ibi *cum omni timore*, et cetera. Tertia, ibi *in simplicitate*, et cetera.

Monet enim eos ad obedientiam ex imperio Domini. Unde dicit **servi, obedite dominis carnalibus**.

Monet eos ad reverentiam, dicens **cum timore**, interius. Mal. I, 6: *si ego dominus, ubi est timor meus? Et tremore*, exterius. Ps. II, 11: *servite Domino in timore*, et cetera.

Et **in simplicitate cordis**. Sap. I, 1: *in simplicitate cordis quaerite illum*. Lc. XII, v. 42: *fidelis servus*, et cetera. Iob I, 8: *numquid considerasti servum meum Iob*, etc., et, paulo post: *vir simplex*, et cetera.

343. Once he has given advice concerning the two relationships of husband to wife, and father to children, he now instructs them regarding the relation of servant to master.

In reference to this he does two things:

first, he instructs the servant;

second, the master, at **masters, do the same**.

The first has three parts:

first, he sets down the admonition;

second, he explains it, at **not serving to the eye**;

third, he indicates the reward, at **knowing that**.

344. Again, the first part has three subdivisions; he admonishes them: first, to obedience; second, to reverence; third, to simplicity of heart.

The second he does at **with fear**; the third at **in simplicity**.

For he instructs them to obey as by a command of the Lord. Hence he states **servants, be obedient to those who are your lords according to the flesh**.

He cautions them regarding reverence, saying **with** interior **fear**: *if I be a master, where is my fear?* (Mal 1:6) **And** exterior **trembling**: *serve the Lord with fear; and rejoice unto him with trembling* (Ps 2:11).

And this must be **in the simplicity of your heart**: *seek him in simplicity of heart* (Wis 1:1); *have you considered my servant Job, a simple and upright man, and fearing God, and avoiding evil?* (Job 1:8)

Sic enim serviendum est Christo. Unde dicit *sicut Christo*. Sap. I, 1: *in simplicitate cordis quaerite illum*. I Par. XXIX, 17: *Domine Deus, in simplicitate cordis mei laetus obtuli universa*. Dicit etiam *sicut Christo*, quia a Domino Christo est quod dominus aliquid possit. Rom. XIII, 2: *qui potestati resistit, Dei ordinationi resistit*. Et ideo serviendum est eis sicut Christo, in his quae non sunt contra fidem, nec contra ipsum.

345. Exponit autem *in simplicitate*, et

primo removet quod simplicitati contrariatur;

secundo docet modum convenientem, ibi *facientes voluntatem Dei*, et cetera.

346. Contrarium autem simplicitatis est, quod servus habeat respectum ad oculum et non ad complacentiam domini. Talis enim servus non habet simplicitatem et rectam intentionem. Et ideo hoc prohibet, dicens **non ad oculum servientes**, scilicet domino propter lucrum temporale tantum, **quasi hominibus placentes**, id est complacere volentes. Gal. I, 10: *si adhuc hominibus placerem, Christi servus non essem*. **Sed ut servi Christi**. Col. III, 24: *Domino Christo servite*.

347. Et quomodo? *Facientes voluntatem Dei*, scilicet implendo mandata eius opere. Ps. CII, 20: *facientes verbum illius*, sicut Christus Io. VI, 38, *descendi de caelo, non ut facerem voluntatem meam, sed voluntatem eius, qui misit me. Haec est enim voluntas eius qui misit me*, scilicet ut obediam hominibus propter Deum. Et ideo dicit **sicut servi Christi**, et sicut servientes Domino, non hominibus, scilicet non propter se, sed propter Dominum.

348. Quomodo? **Ex animo**. Col. III, v. 23: *quodcumque facitis, ex animo operamini, sicut Domino, et non hominibus*. Item, idem subiungit hic dicens **sicut Domino et non hominibus**. **Cum bona voluntate**, id est recta intentione. Col. IV, 12: *stetis perfecti et pleni in omni voluntate Dei*.

349. Deinde subiungit remunerationem, dicens **scientes**. I Io. V, 13: *scripsi vobis ut sciatis*, et cetera. **Quoniam unusquisque, (…) sive servus sive liber**. Sine personarum acceptione. Non enim est personarum acceptio apud Deum. Gal. III, 28: *non est servus neque liber, non est masculus neque foemina, omnes enim vos unum estis in Christo Iesu*. Act. X, v. 34 s.: *in veritate comperi quoniam non est personarum acceptor Deus, sed in omni gente, qui timet Deum et operatur iustitiam*, et cetera. Eccle. IX, 10: *quodcumque potest facere manus tua, instanter operare*, et cetera. **Recipiet a Domino** pro remuneratione. Col. III, 24: *scientes quod a Domino accipient retributionem haereditatis*.

In this way is Christ to be served; thus he says **as to Christ**. *Seek him in simplicity of heart* (Wis 1:1); *O Lord God, I also in the simplicity of my heart have joyfully offered all these things* (1 Chr 29:17). He also mentions **as to Christ** since whatever power a master has comes from Christ the Lord. *Therefore, he who resists the power resists the ordinance of God* (Rom 13:2). They must be served as Christ is in whatever is not contrary to faith nor contrary to Christ himself.

345. He explains **in simplicity of heart**:

first, he repudiates what is against simplicity;

second, he teaches the appropriate way of acting, at **doing the will of God**.

346. It is against simplicity that a servant be concerned with what the eye sees instead of what pleases his lord. For such a servant does not possess simplicity and rectitude of intention. Hence he forbids this saying **not serving to the eye**, namely, the master, on account of a temporal advantage only, **as it were pleasing men**. *If I yet pleased men, I should not be the servant of Christ* (Gal 1:10). **But, as the servants of Christ**; *serve the Lord Christ* (Col 3:24).

347. And how? **Doing the will of God**, by carrying his commands into action. *Carry out his word* (Ps 103:20), just as Christ did: *I came down from heaven, not to do my own will but the will of him that sent me. Now this is the will of the Father who sent me* (John 6:38–39), that I obey men for the sake of God. And thus he states **as servants of Christ**, being of service to the Lord and not to men; that is, not for their own sakes but for that of the Lord.

348. How should this be done? **From the heart**. *Whatsoever you do, do it from the heart, as to the Lord, and not to men* (Col 3:23); he says the same here: **as to the Lord, and not to men**; and do it **with a good will**, that is, with the right intention; *that you may stand perfect and full in all the will of God* (Col 4:12).

349. Next, he mentions the reward, saying **knowing**—*these things I write to you that you may know* (1 John 5:13)—**that any man … whether he be bond or free** is without acknowledgment of personage. For there is no respect of persons with God. *There is neither Jew nor Greek; there is neither bond nor free; there is neither male or female. For you are all one in Christ Jesus* (Gal 3:28). *In very deed I perceive that God is not a respecter of persons. But, in every nation, he that fears him and works justice is acceptable to him* (Acts 10:34–35). *Whatever your hand is able to do, do it earnestly: for neither work, nor reason, nor wisdom, nor knowledge, shall be in hell, whither you are hastening* (Eccl 9:10). What he does **the same shall he receive from the Lord**, as a recompense. *Knowing that you shall receive of the Lord the reward of inheritance* (Col 3:24).

350. Deinde cum dicit *et vos, domini*, etc., instruit dominos, et facit duo. Primo ponit monitionem; secundo subdit rationem, ibi *scientes quia et illorum*, et cetera.

Dicit ergo *et vos, domini, eadem faciatis*, eadem scilicet identitate proportionis, ut sicut illi *ex animo* et *bona voluntate*, ita et vos faciatis. Eccli. XXXIII, 31: *si est tibi aliquis servus fidelis, sit tibi sicut anima tua*. *Remittentes minas*, non solum verba, vel flagella.

Et quare? Rationem subdit, dicens *scientes quia et illorum et vester Dominus est in caelis*. *Nam idem Dominus omnium*, Rom. X, v. 12. Quasi dicat: conservi estis, et ideo debetis vos bene habere ad eos. Matth. XVIII, v. 33: *oportuit et te misereri conservi tui. Et personarum acceptio non est apud Deum*. Rom. II, 11 idem dicitur; Lc. XX, 21: *non accipis personam hominum*; Act. X, 34 idem.

350. Then he goes on to give advice to masters, and he makes two points: first, he sets down a warning, at *masters, do the same*; second, he adds the reason, at *knowing that the Lord*.

He states, therefore, *and you, masters, do the same*, namely, with a proportional identity: as servants act *from the heart* and *with a good will*, so also should you act. *If you have a faithful servant, let him be to you as your own soul* (Sir 33:31)—*forbearing threatenings*, and not only blows and whippings.

Why? He gives the reason when he says *knowing that the Lord both of them and you is in heaven*. *For the same is Lord over all* (Rom 10:12). It is as though he were saying: you are fellow servants, and hence you ought to behave well towards them. *Should not you then have had compassion also on your fellow servant?* (Matt 18:33). *And there is no respect of persons with him* (Rom 2:11). *You do not respect any person* (Luke 20:21). And Acts also says the same (Acts 10:34).

Lecture 3

6:10 De cetero, fratres, confortamini in Domino, et in potentia virtutis ejus. [n. 352]

6:11 Induite vos armaturam Dei, ut possitis stare adversus insidias diaboli: [n. 353]

6:12 quoniam non est nobis colluctatio adversus carnem et sanguinem, sed adversus principes, et potestates, adversus mundi rectores tenebrarum harum, contra spiritualia nequitiae, in caelestibus. [n. 354]

6:10 Τοῦ λοιποῦ ἐνδυναμοῦσθε ἐν κυρίῳ καὶ ἐν τῷ κράτει τῆς ἰσχύος αὐτοῦ.

6:11 ἐνδύσασθε τὴν πανοπλίαν τοῦ θεοῦ πρὸς τὸ δύνασθαι ὑμᾶς στῆναι πρὸς τὰς μεθοδείας τοῦ διαβόλου·

6:12 ὅτι οὐκ ἔστιν ἡμῖν ἡ πάλη πρὸς αἷμα καὶ σάρκα, ἀλλὰ πρὸς τὰς ἀρχάς, πρὸς τὰς ἐξουσίας, πρὸς τοὺς κοσμοκράτορας τοῦ σκότους τούτου, πρὸς τὰ πνευματικὰ τῆς πονηρίας ἐν τοῖς ἐπουρανίοις.

6:10 Finally, brethren, be strengthened in the Lord and in the power of his virtue. [n. 352]

6:11 Put on the armor of God, that you may be able to stand against the deceits of the devil. [n. 353]

6:12 For our wrestling is not against flesh and blood; but against principalities and powers, against the rulers of the world of this darkness, against the spirits of wickedness in the high places. [n. 354]

---

351. Supra posuit Apostolus multa praecepta generalia, et specialia ad destruendam vetustatem peccati, et inducendam novitatem gratiae, hic ostendit qua virtute debent uti ad praecepta haec implenda, quia fiducia auxilii divini.

Circa quod duo facit.

Primo, ponit monitionem;

secundo, in speciali explicat eam, ibi *quoniam non est nobis colluctatio*, et cetera.

Prima in duas, quia

primo ostendit, de quo debemus confidere, sicut de interiori;

secundo ostendit de quo debemus confidere sicut de exteriori, ibi *induite vos*, et cetera.

352. Illud autem interius, de quo debemus confidere, est auxilium divinum, et ideo dicit *de caetero, fratres, confortamini*. Ier. XVII, 7: *benedictus vir, qui confidit in Domino, et erit Dominus fiducia eius*, et cetera.

Duplici autem ratione confidit quis de aliquo. Una est, quia ad eum pertinet sua defensio; alia est, quia potens est, et paratus est eum defendere. Et haec duo sunt in Deo respectu creaturae suae, quia cura est Deo de vobis, ut dicitur I Petr. ult.: *omnem sollicitudinem vestram proiicientes in eum, quoniam ipsi cura est de vobis*. Item, ipse potens est, et promptus auxiliari.

Et ideo dicit *de caetero, fratres*, etc., quasi dicat: postquam vos instruxi supra de praeceptis implendis, iam *confortamini*, non in vobis, sed *in Domino*, qui curam habet de vobis. Ps. LXXII, 28: *mihi autem adhaerere Deo bonum est*, et cetera. Is. XXXV, 4: *dicite pusillanimis: confortamini*, et cetera. Ier. XX, 11: *Dominus mecum est tamquam bellator fortis, idcirco qui me persequuntur, cadent*, et cetera.

Et in potentia, et cetera. Lc. I, 49: *qui potens est*. Et licet in Deo virtus et potentia sint idem, tamen, quia virtus est ultimum de potentia, et, quasi perfectio potentiae,

351. The Apostle has previously written down many general and particular instructions aimed at destroying the old man of sin and encouraging the newness of grace. Now he speaks of the power by which we must carry out these precepts, for we must trust in divine assistance.

Concerning this he does two things:

first, he sets down the advice;

second, he explains it in detail, at *for our wrestling is not against*.

The first has two sections:

first, he shows what interior reality we ought to trust in;

second, then he shows what exterior reality we must trust in, at *put on the armor*.

352. The inner reality we should have confidence in is the divine help, thus he states *finally, brethren, be strengthened. Blessed is the man that trusts in the Lord, and the Lord shall be his confidence* (Jer 17:7).

There are two reasons why anyone would trust in another person. One is that this person is charged with protecting him; and the other reason is that he is strong and prepared to defend him. These two are realized in God with respect to his creatures; for God is concerned with you: *casting all your care upon him, for he has care of you* (1 Pet 5:7). Moreover, he is powerful and prompt to grant assistance.

Therefore he asserts *finally brethren*, as if to say: now that I have advised you above concerning the fulfillment of the precepts, *be strengthened*, not in yourselves, but *in the Lord* who has care of you. *It is good for me to adhere to my God, to put my hope in the Lord God* (Ps 73:28). *Say to the fainthearted, take courage, and fear not . . . God himself will come and will save you* (Isa 35:4). *The Lord is with me as a strong warrior: therefore they that persecute me shall fall and shall be weak* (Jer 20:11).

And in the power: *for he is mighty* (Luke 1:49). Although in God virtue and power are identical, nonetheless, since virtue is the ultimate of power, and as it were the perfection

ideo dicit **in potentia virtutis eius**, id est, in potentia virtuosa. Phil. IV, 13: *omnia possum in eo, qui me confortat.* Iob XVII, 3: *pone me iuxta te, et cuiusvis manus pugnet contra me.*

353. Sed posset dici: si Deus potest et vult, debemus esse securi. Ideo respondens, dicit quod non, imo debet quilibet facere quod in se est, quia si inermis iret ad bellum, quantumcumque rex protegeret eum, esset in periculo. Et ideo dicit **induite vos armaturam Dei**, id est dona et virtutes. Rom. c. XIII, 12: *abiiciamus ergo opera tenebrarum, et induamur arma lucis,* et cetera. Col. III, v. 12: *induite vos ergo sicut electi Dei sancti et dilecti viscera misericordiae, benignitatem, humilitatem, modestiam,* et cetera. Quia per virtutes homo protegitur contra vitia.

Sed contra: Dominus est rex ita potens, quod nullus potest eum impugnare.

Respondeo. Verum est per violentiam, sed per insidias et fallaciam impugnat eum diabolus in membris suis, non in se, quia, ut dicitur Eccli. XI, 31: *multae sunt insidiae dolosi,* et cetera. Et ideo subdit **ut possitis stare contra insidias diaboli**. I Petr. V, 8: *sobrii estote, et vigilate,* et cetera. Ps. IX, 30: *insidiatur in abscondito, quasi leo,* et cetera.

354. Consequenter cum dicit **quia non est nobis colluctatio**, etc., explicat in speciali monitionem. Et

primo de insidiis inimicorum;

secundo de armatura sumenda, ibi **propterea accipite**, etc.;

tertio de fiducia Christi habenda ibi **per omnium orationem**, et cetera.

355. Describit autem insidias, quia quando aliquis hostis imminet, si sit debilis, stultus et huiusmodi, non est multum cavendum nec timendum de eo; sed quando est potens, nequam et callidus, tunc est timendus. Haec tria sunt in diabolo.

Primo quia non est debilis. Et propter hoc dicit, quod **non est nobis colluctatio adversus carnem et sanguinem**, et cetera. Per **carnem et sanguinem** intelliguntur vitia carnis, I Cor. c. XV, 50: *caro et sanguis regnum Dei non possidebunt,* et homines carnales. Gal. I, 16: *continuo non acquievi carni et sanguini,* id est, hominibus carnalibus. Dicit ergo **non est nobis colluctatio**, et cetera.

Quod videtur esse falsum qualitercumque accipiatur; quia, ut dicitur Gal. V, 17: *caro concupiscit adversus spiritum,* et cetera. Ps. CXVIII, v. 157: *multi qui persequuntur me.*

Respondeo dupliciter. Primo ut dicamus **non est nobis colluctatio adversus**, etc., supple tantum, quin etiam adversus diabolum. Vel aliter, quia actio quae instrumento attribuitur, est principaliter agentis, sicut accipitur illud Rom. IX, 16: *non est volentis, neque currentis,*

of power, on this account he says **in the power of his virtue**, that is, in his virtuous power. *I can do all things in him who strengthens me* (Phil 4:13). *O Lord, set me beside you; and let any man's hand fight against me* (Job 17:3).

353. Someone might say: if God is powerful and wills to protect us, we ought to be unconcerned. He replies that this is not so; indeed, everyone must do what he can since, if an unarmed man went into battle, no matter how much the king protected him he would still be in danger. Hence he says **put on the armor of God**, that is, the gifts and virtues. *Let us therefore cast off the works of darkness and put on the armor of light* (Rom 13:12). *Put on therefore, as the elect of God, holy and beloved, the bowels of mercy, benignity, humility, modesty, patience* (Col 3:12). For the virtues protect man from vices.

An objection: the Lord is so powerful a king that no one can attack him.

I reply. This is true concerning violence; yet the devil does attack him, not in himself, but in his members through deceit and illusions. *For many are the snares of the deceitful* (Sir 11:31). Thus he adds **that you may be able to stand against the deceits of the devil**. *Be sober and watch; because your adversary the devil, as a roaring lion, goes about seeking whom he may devour* (1 Pet 5:8). *He lies in wait in secret like a lion in his den* (Ps 10:8).

354. At **for our wrestling is not against**, he then goes on to explain this warning in detail:

first, concerning the snares of the enemies;

second, what arms should be taken up, at **therefore take unto you** (Eph 6:13);

third, the confidence which must be had in Christ, at **by all prayer** (Eph 6:18).

355. He describes the snares because, when an enemy is near at hand, there is not much reason to be on one's guard or fear him if he is weak, stupid and the like. But when he is strong, evil and shrewd, then he ought to be dreaded. These latter three are found in the devil.

First, he is not weak. For this reason he states that **our wrestling is not against flesh and blood**. By **flesh and blood** sins of the flesh are to be understood: *flesh and blood cannot possess the kingdom of God* (1 Cor 15:50), nor can carnal men. *Immediately I condescended not to flesh and blood* (Gal 1:16), that is, to carnal men. Therefore he says **our wrestling is not against flesh and blood**.

But, this saying seems to be false no matter how it is understood since, *for the flesh lusts against the spirit; and the spirit against the flesh* (Gal 5:17). *Many are they that persecute me and afflict me* (Ps 119:157).

I reply in two ways. First, supply *only* so that we could say our **wrestling is not** only **against flesh and blood** without it also being against the devil. A second answer is that an action which is attributed to an instrument is principally of the agent. *It is not of him who wills, nor of him who runs,*

sed miserentis Dei, quasi dicat: quod vultis aliquid, vel facitis, a vobis non est, sed aliunde, scilicet a Deo; sic hic **non est nobis colluctatio**, etc., exponatur, id est quod nos impugnent, scilicet caro et sanguis, hoc non est eorum principaliter, sed a superiore movente, scilicet a diabolo.

356. Consequenter describitur a potentia, quia **adversus principes et potestates tenebrarum harum**. Io. XIV, 30: *venit enim princeps huius mundi*, et cetera.

Dicitur autem princeps mundi, non creatione sed imitatione mundanorum. Io. I, 10: *et mundus eum non cognovit*, id est principes mundani. Vel dicitur princeps, quasi primatum capiens. Unde principes quasi primi duces ad aliquid. Ps. LXVII, 26: *principes coniuncti psallentibus*. Gen. XXIII, 6: *princeps Dei es apud nos*.

Ad potestatem autem pertinet iustitiam exercere. Inquantum ergo aliqui daemones inducunt aliquos ad rebellandum Deo, dicuntur principes, inquantum vero habent potestatem puniendi illos, qui eis subiiciuntur, dicuntur potestates. Lc. XXII, 53: *haec est hora vestra, et potestas tenebrarum*, et cetera.

357. Sed cum ex ordinibus omnibus ceciderint aliqui, quare mentionem facit Apostolus de illis duobus ordinibus, denominans daemones?

Respondeo. In nominibus ordinum sunt tria in quibusdam enim importatur ordo ad Deum, in quibusdam vero potestas, in quibusdam vero Dei ministerium. In nominibus enim cherubim et seraphim et thronorum, importatur conversio ad Deum. Daemones autem adversi sunt Deo, et ideo eis non competunt haec nomina. Item quaedam nomina important ordinem ad ministerium Dei, sicut angeli et archangeli: et ista etiam nomina non competunt daemonibus, nisi cum adiuncto scilicet *Satanae*. Tertio etiam, quia virtutes et dominationes important ordinem ad servitium Dei: ideo eis non conveniunt haec nomina, sed tantum ista duo, quae communia sunt bonis et malis, scilicet principatus et potestates.

Sunt ergo et potentes et magni, ideo habent magnum exercitum, contra quem habemus pugnare **adversus mundi rectores tenebrarum harum**, scilicet peccatorum. Supra V, v. 8: **eratis enim aliquando tenebrae**, et cetera. Quia quidquid est tenebrosum, totum est de ordine istorum, et subiectum eis. Glossa: *mali homines sunt equi, diaboli equites, ergo occidamus equites, et equos possideamus*. Io. I, 5: *et tenebrae eum non comprehenderunt*.

358. Sunt etiam astuti, quia **contra spiritualia nequitiae**, id est contra spirituales nequitias, emphatice loquendo, per quod intelligitur plenitudo nequitiae.

Dicit autem **spiritualia nequitiae**, quia quanto est altior secundum naturam, tanto, quando convertitur ad malum, est peior et nequior. Unde Philosophus dicit,

but of God who shows mercy (Rom 9:16). He seems to say: when you will or do anything, it is not from yourself, but from another, namely God. Thus here, **our wrestling is not against flesh and blood** would be interpreted: when flesh and blood attack us, it is not of themselves principally but from a higher moving force, namely, from the devil.

356. Next, the devil's power is described, for we fight **against principalities and powers . . . of this darkness**. *The prince of this world comes, and in me he does not have anything* (John 14:30).

He is called the prince of the world, not by reason of creation, but because the worldly minded imitate him. *And the world knew him not* (John 1:10), that is, the worldly princes. Or, he is called the prince as though he had captured the primacy. Hence princes are, as it were, the first leaders in something. *Princes went before joined with singers* (Ps 68:25). *You are a prince of God among us* (Gen 23:6).

The exercise of justice pertains to power. Hence, insofar as some demons incite others to rebel against God, they are called principalities; insofar as they have the power to punish those who are subjected to them, they are called powers. *But this is your hour and the power of darkness* (Luke 22:53).

357. But since some angels fell from every one of the ranks, why does the Apostle only mention those two ranks, calling them demons?

I reply. There are three characteristics in the names of the ranks. For in some is implied a relation to God, in others power, in still others the service of God. In the names cherubim, seraphim and thrones, a turning toward God is connoted. The devils, on the other hand, are turned away from God, and hence these names do not apply to them. Again, certain names imply an ordination to the service of God, as the angels and archangels; these also are not applicable to the demons, unless one joins *of Satan* to the names. Third, since virtues and dominations also imply an ordering toward God's worship these names cannot be applicable to the demons. Only those two, principalities and powers, are common to the good and bad angels.

Hence, they are powerful and great, possessing an immense army against which we must fight as **against the rulers of the world of this darkness** of sin. **For you were heretofore darkness, but now light in the Lord** (Eph 5:8). Whatever is darksome is wholly of their rank and subject to them. As a Gloss comments: *evil men are horses, and the demons the riders; hence, if we kill the riders, the horses will be ours*. *And the darkness did not comprehend it* (John 1:5).

358. They are also cunning, for we must fight **against the spirits of wickedness**; this is an emphatic way of saying *spiritual wickedness*, by which is understood the fullness of evil.

He affirms **the spirits of wickedness** because the higher one's nature is, the more terrible and pernicious it is when one turns to evil. Whence the Philosopher states that an evil

quod homo malus est pessimus omnium animalium. Et ideo dicit *spiritualia nequitiae*, quia spirituales et nequissimi sunt.

Et dicit *in caelestibus*, duplici de causa. Vel ut ostendat virtutem et avantagium, ad superandum nos: quia nos in terra, ipsi autem in alto, scilicet in aere caliginoso, et ideo habent partem meliorem. Lc. VIII, 5: *volucres caeli comederunt illud*. Vel dicit *in caelestibus*, quia pro caelestibus est ista pugna: et hoc debet animare nos ad pugnam.

man is worse than all the animals. Thus he says *the spirits of wickedness* since they are spiritual and most wicked.

He mentions *in the high places* for two possible reasons. Either to show the strength and advantage they possess to overcome us; we are on the earth, but they are on high in the dusky atmosphere so that they have the better position. *And the fowls of the air devoured it* (Luke 8:5). Or, he says *in the high places* because this struggle is for heaven, and this should urge us on to fight.

Lecture 4

⁶:¹³Propterea accipite armaturam Dei, ut possitis resistere in die malo, et in omnibus perfecti stare. [n. 360]

⁶:¹⁴State ergo succincti lumbos vestros in veritate, et induti loricam justitiae, [n. 362]

⁶:¹⁵et calceati pedes in praeparatione Evangelii pacis, [n. 364]

⁶:¹⁶in omnibus sumentes scutum fidei, in quo possitis omnia tela nequissimi ignea extinguere: [n. 365]

⁶:¹⁷et galeam salutis assumite, et gladium Spiritus (quod est verbum Dei), [n. 366]

⁶:¹³διὰ τοῦτο ἀναλάβετε τὴν πανοπλίαν τοῦ θεοῦ, ἵνα δυνηθῆτε ἀντιστῆναι ἐν τῇ ἡμέρᾳ τῇ πονηρᾷ καὶ ἅπαντα κατεργασάμενοι στῆναι.

⁶:¹⁴στῆτε οὖν περιζωσάμενοι τὴν ὀσφὺν ὑμῶν ἐν ἀληθείᾳ, καὶ ἐνδυσάμενοι τὸν θώρακα τῆς δικαιοσύνης,

⁶:¹⁵καὶ ὑποδησάμενοι τοὺς πόδας ἐν ἑτοιμασίᾳ τοῦ εὐαγγελίου τῆς εἰρήνης,

⁶:¹⁶ἐν πᾶσιν ἀναλαβόντες τὸν θυρεὸν τῆς πίστεως, ἐν ᾧ δυνήσεσθε πάντα τὰ βέλη τοῦ πονηροῦ [τὰ] πεπυρωμένα σβέσαι:

⁶:¹⁷καὶ τὴν περικεφαλαίαν τοῦ σωτηρίου δέξασθε, καὶ τὴν μάχαιραν τοῦ πνεύματος, ὅ ἐστιν ῥῆμα θεοῦ,

⁶:¹³Therefore, take unto you the armor of God, that you may be able to resist in the evil day and to stand in all things perfect. [n. 360]

⁶:¹⁴Stand therefore, having your loins girt about with truth and having on the breastplate of justice: [n. 362]

⁶:¹⁵And your feet shod with the preparation of the Gospel of peace. [n. 364]

⁶:¹⁶In all things taking the shield of faith, wherewith you may be able to extinguish all the fiery darts of the most wicked one. [n. 365]

⁶:¹⁷And take unto you the helmet of salvation and the sword of the Spirit (which is the word of God). [n. 366]

359. Supra exposuit Apostolus, quod dictum est de insidiis diaboli, hic monet nos de armatura sumenda. Et circa hoc facit duo.

Primo concludit ex praemissis armaturae necessitatem;

secundo, armorum diversitatem describit, ibi **state ergo**, et cetera.

360. Dicit ergo: habetis hostes malos, nequissimos et potentes, et pro re ardua pugnantes, quia pro caelestibus, **propterea accipite armaturam Dei**, id est armamini spiritualibus armis. II Cor. X, 4: *arma militiae nostrae non sunt carnalia, sed potentia Deo ad destructionem munitionum*, et cetera. Et hoc **ut possitis resistere**. I Petr. V, 9: *cui resistite fortes in fide*, et cetera. Iac. IV, 7: *resistite diabolo, et fugiet a vobis*. Quanto magis enim ei ceditur, tanto plus insequitur. **In die malo**, et hoc propter mala, quae in die fiunt. Supra V, 16: **redimentes tempus, quoniam dies mali sunt**. Eccle. VII, 15: *diem malam praecave*, et cetera.

Item accipite non solum ad resistendum, sed etiam ad proficiendum, **et in omnibus perfecti state**, id est in adversis et prosperis immobiliter state. Iac. I, 4: *sitis perfecti, in nullo deficientes*. De hoc I Petr. I, 13: *perfecti, sperate in eam, quae offertur vobis, gratiam*, et cetera.

361. Sed numquid omnes debent perfecti esse?

Respondeo. Triplex est perfectio. Una sufficientiae, quam habet homo, secundum quod habet quod sibi est necessarium ad salutem, sicut illud: *diliges Dominum Deum tuum ex toto corde tuo*; quasi dicat: ut nihil sit in

359. The Apostle explained the devil's snares previously, and here he advises us to take up arms.

In reference to this he does two things:

first, he concludes from the foregoing that arms are necessary;

second, he describes the variety of weapons, at **stand therefore**.

360. Thus he says: you have evil enemies who are powerful and most wicked, and the struggle is for an exacting object since it is for heaven. **Therefore, take unto you the armor of God**, that is, be armed with spiritual weapons. *For the weapons of our warfare are not carnal, but mighty to God unto the pulling down of fortifications, destroying counsels* (2 Cor 10:4). And this **that you may be able to resist**. *Resist him, strong in faith* (1 Pet 5:9). *Resist the devil; and he will fly from you* (Jas 4:7). For the more is conceded to him, the more will he press in upon you. **In the evil day** indicates that a day is evil from what occurs in it. **Redeeming the time, because the days are evil** (Eph 5:16). *Beware beforehand of the evil day* (Eccl 7:15).

Take up these weapons not only for defense, but also to make progress: **and to stand in all things perfect**, that is, stand firm in both adversity and prosperity. *That you may be perfect and entire, failing in nothing* (Jas 1:4). *Trust perfectly in the grace which is offered you in the revelation of Jesus Christ* (1 Pet 1:13).

361. However, must everyone be perfect?

I reply that there are three types of perfection. There is one of sufficiency when a man has what is necessary for his salvation; for instance, *you shall love the Lord your God with your whole heart*, as if to say: let there be nothing in your

corde tuo, quod sit contra Deum. Et hoc est de necessitate salutis. Iac. I, 4: *ut sitis perfecti et integri in nullo deficientes*, et cetera.

Alia est perfectio totalis abundantiae, quae est perfectio patriae, quae est consummata gloria, in hoc quod perfectus totaliter inhaereat Deo. Matth. XXII, 30: *in resurrectione neque nubent, neque nubentur, sed sunt sicut angeli Dei in caelo*. Et de hac loquebatur Apostolus Phil. III, 12: *non quod iam acceperim, aut quod iam perfectus sim*. Et paulo post: *fratres, ego non arbitror me comprehendisse*.

Alia est media, scilicet consilii, qua homo nititur se abstrahere ab his, et ire ad illas.

362. Deinde cum dicit **state ergo**, etc., describit diversitatem armorum. Est autem triplex genus spiritualium armorum, ad similitudinem corporalium: quorum quaedam sunt similia indumento ad tegendum, quaedam vero ad protegendum, et quaedam ad impugnandum.

363. Indumento autem tria sunt necessaria. Primo quod cingatur; et quantum ad hoc dicit **state ergo succincti lumbos vestros**, et cetera.

Sed prius induit se homo quam se cingat. Apostolus autem accipit haec secundum ordinem armaturae spiritualis. In bello autem spirituali prius est necesse concupiscentias carnis restringere, sicut vicinus hostis est prius vincendus: hoc autem fit per restrictionem lumborum, in quibus viget luxuria, quod fit per temperantiam, quae gulae et luxuriae contrariatur. Lc. XII, 35: *sint lumbi vestri praecincti*, et cetera. Iob XXXVIII, 3: *accinge sicut vir lumbos*, et cetera.

Sed **in veritate**, id est in rectitudine intentionis, et non simulate. Alia littera habet: **in caritate**. I Cor. ult.: *omnia vestra in caritate fiant*.

364. Secundo monet vincere cupiditates rerum. Duplex autem invenitur armatura contra eas, scilicet iustitia, et abrenuntiatio rerum temporalium. Et ideo primo praecipit ut eas non iniuste usurpemus, quod facit iustitia. Et ideo dicit **induti loricam iustitiae**, scilicet propter quam homo abstinet a rebus alienis. Dicitur autem iustitia lorica, quia sicut lorica tegit membra, ita iustitia virtutes omnes. Sap. V, 19: *induet pro thorace iustitiam, et accipiet pro galea iudicium certum*.

Secundo praecipit ut rerum temporalium curam superfluam deponamus, quia dum his nimis intendimus, non habemus pedes paratos ad divina negotia et mysteria annuntianda. Et propter hoc dicit **et calceati pedes**, id est affectus dispositi sint supple, **in praeparatione Evangelii pacis**. In signum huius misit apostolos Dominus,

heart which is contrary to God. This much is necessary for salvation. *That you may be perfect and entire, failing in nothing* (Jas 1:4).

Another is the total and overflowing perfection proper to the fatherland; there glory is consummated in this, that the perfect totally inhere in God. *For in the resurrection they shall neither marry nor be married; but shall be as the angels of God in heaven* (Matt 22:30). The Apostle speaks of this elsewhere: *not as though I had already attained, or were already perfect . . . brethren, I do not count myself to have apprehended* (Phil 3:12–13).

The third perfection is between the above two, which is that of the counsels by which a man strives to withdraw himself from the things of this life and make progress towards those of the next.

362. Then, at **stand therefore**, he goes on to describe the variety of weapons. There are three kinds of spiritual armor, paralleling bodily arms. Some are like clothes and are meant to cover one; others are to protect him; and still others are for fighting.

363. Three things are necessary for clothing. First, it must be bound with a belt; regarding this he says **stand therefore, having your loins girt about**.

However, a man clothes himself before he puts his belt on. Here the Apostle follows the order of spiritual armor. In spiritual warfare it is first necessary to check carnal desires, just as the nearest enemy must be conquered first. This is done by bridling the loins in which sensuality thrives; such girding is done through temperance which is opposed to gluttony and sensuality. *Let your loins be girt* (Luke 12:35); *gird up your loins like a man* (Job 38:3).

But this must be done **with truth**, that is, with the right intention and not with pretense. A variant reading gives **with charity**. *Let all that you do be done in charity* (1 Cor 6:14).

364. Second, he warns them to overcome greed for created things. Two weapons can be found against it: justice and the renunciation of temporalities. First, he commands us not to usurp these unjustly; justice will look after this. Thus he says **and having on the breastplate of justice**, on account of which a man keeps out of other people's property. Justice is referred to as a breastplate because it covers all the virtues just as a breastplate does the members of the body. *He will put on justice as a breastplate, and will take true judgment instead of a helmet* (Wis 5:19).

Second, he commands us to get rid of an excessive care about temporal realities. When we are too caught up in these, our feet are not ready to carry out divine pursuits and proclaim its mysteries. For this reason he says **and your feet shod**—understand by this that one's inclinations should be determined—**with the preparation of the Gospel of peace**.

Mc. VI, 9, *calceatos sandaliis, quae habent subtus soleas, per quod significatur elevatio mentis a terrenis: et aperta sunt superius, per quod significatur promptitudo ad divinam sapientiam.* Dicit autem *pacis,* quia per Evangelium pax nobis annuntiatur. Matth. X, 12: *in quamcumque domum intraveritis, dicite: pax huic domui.*

365. Item secundo, sunt arma ad protegendum. Duo autem in nobis sunt protegenda, quae sunt principia vitae, scilicet pectus in quo est cor et caput in quo est cerebrum. Pro pectore autem est scutum. Et ideo dicit *in omnibus sumentes scutum fidei,* quia sicut scutum supponitur omnibus armis, ita fides omnibus aliis virtutibus.

Alia sunt enim arma virtutum moralium, scilicet temperantiae, id est succinctio lumborum, et iustitiae, id est induitio loricae: et hoc genus armorum, scilicet scutum, est virtutis theologicae, scilicet fidei: quia sicut per scutum repelluntur tela, ita per fidem omnia contraria et habetur victoria. Hebr. XI, v. 33: *sancti per fidem vicerunt regna,* sicut per virtutes morales vincimus potestates terrenas. Et ideo ait *in quo possitis omnia tela ignea nequissimi extinguere,* scilicet diaboli, cuius tela sunt quaedam immissiones per angelos malos. Ignea sunt, quia adurentia pravis concupiscentiis. Ps. LVII, 9: *supercecidit ignis,* et cetera. Haec autem per fidem extinguuntur: quae tentationes praesentes et transitorias extinguit per bona spiritualia et aeterna, quae promittit Sacra Scriptura. Unde Dominus diabolo tentanti producebat et opponebat auctoritates Sacrae Scripturae. Et sic debemus facere, si tentat de gula, secundum illud Deut. VIII, 3: *non in solo pane vivit homo,* vel illud: *non est regnum Dei, esca et potus.* Si de luxuria: *non moechaberis.* Si de furto: *non furtum facies*; et sic de aliis.

Dicitur autem *scutum fidei,* quia sicut scutum protegit totum pectus, ita fides debet esse in pectore. Spes autem dicitur galea, quia sicut galea est in capite, ita caput virtutum moralium est finis; et de hoc est spes, scilicet de fine. Et ideo dicitur *et galeam salutis assumite.*

366. Item tertio, sunt arma ad impugnandum, quia non solum sufficit se defendere, sed etiam oportet adversarium impugnare. Hoc autem sicut fit per gladium materialem corporaliter, ita per verbum Dei, quod est Spiritus Sancti gladius, spiritualiter. Et propter hoc dicit *et gladium Spiritus, quod est verbum Dei,* scilicet assumite. Hebr. c. IV, 12: *vivus est sermo Dei et efficax, et penetrabilior omni gladio ancipiti, pertingens usque ad divisionem animae et spiritus.* Et praedicatio dicitur gladius Spiritus, quia non penetrat usque ad spiritum, nisi ducatur a Spiritu Sancto. Matth. X, 20: *non enim vos*

As a symbol of this the Lord sent the apostles (Mark 6:9) shod with sandals. These have soles underneath, by which the raising of the mind from earthly matters is signified; and they are open above, in which an eagerness for divine wisdom is signified. He adds *of peace* since through the Gospel peace is proclaimed to us. *When you come into the house, salute it, saying: peace be to this house* (Matt 10:12).

365. The second function of weapons is to protect. Two areas which contain the mainsprings of our life must be guarded: the chest in which the heart is situated, and the head which contains the brain. The chest is protected by a shield; thus he states *in all things taking the shield of faith* because faith is presupposed to all the other virtues just as a shield is basic to all weapons.

For there is a difference between the armor of the moral virtues, such as temperance which is to gird one's loins and justice which is to put on a breastplate, and this type of armament—the shield—which consists of the theological virtue of faith. Just as a shield wards off the arrows, so faith repels what is aimed against it and gains the victory. The saints *by faith conquered kingdoms* (Heb 11:33), whereas we conquer the powers of darkness by the moral virtues. Thus he says *wherewith you may be able to extinguish all the fiery darts of the most wicked one,* the devil, whose arrows are certain interferences from evil angels (Ps 78:49). They are fiery since evil desires burn: *fire has fallen on them, and they shall not see the sun* (Ps 58:9). These are extinguished through faith; it quenches present and transitory temptations with the eternal and spiritual blessings promised in Holy Scripture. Thus the Lord brought forward authoritative texts of Holy Scripture to oppose the devil's temptations. We ought to do the same; if tempted to gluttony, counter it with: *not in bread alone does man live* (Deut 8:3), or *the kingdom of God is not meat and drink* (Rom 14:17). If tempted to sensuality, *you shall not commit adultery* (Exod 20:14); if to theft, *you shall not steal* (Exod 20:15) and so on with any others.

Faith is called a *shield* since, as a shield protects the entire chest, so faith must be in our heart. Hope, on the other hand, is referred to as a helmet because, as a helmet is on the head, so the head of the moral virtues is the end, and hope is concerned with this end. Hence he states: *and take unto you the helmet of salvation.*

366. Finally, the third function of weapons is for attack. It is not enough to simply defend one's self, it is also necessary to assault the enemy. Physically, this is done with a material sword; it is done spiritually through the word of God which is the sword of the Holy Spirit. On this account he affirms and take up *the sword of the Spirit, which is the word of God. For the word of God is living and effectual and more piercing than any two-edged sword and reaching unto the division of the soul and the spirit* (Heb 4:12). Preaching is called the sword of the Spirit because it will not penetrate to the spirit unless it is disposed by the Holy Spirit. *For it is*

estis, qui loquimini, sed Spiritus Patris vestri, qui loquitur in vobis.

367. Sic ergo habemus arma quibus defendamur a carnalibus hostibus, scilicet a gula et luxuria, quod fit per temperantiam, ibi **state ergo succincti lumbos vestros**, et cetera.

Item, quibus vincamus cupiditates terrenas, scilicet arma iustitiae, quae abstinere nos faciunt ab illicitis, ibi **induti loricam iustitiae**. Et puritatem affectus seu paupertatem, quae nos retrahit etiam a licitis, ibi **calceati pedes**, et cetera.

Item, habemus arma quibus protegamur ab erroribus, scilicet arma fidei, ibi **in omnibus sumentes scutum fidei**, et etiam ab hostibus generis humani, ibi **quo**, scilicet scuto fidei, **possitis omnia tela nequissimi ignea extinguere**.

Item, habemus arma quibus in bonis spiritualibus confirmamur, scilicet arma spei, ibi **et galeam salutis assumite**. Galea ponitur in capite, sic spes in fine. Nunc autem caput virtutum moralium est ipse finis, de quo est spes. Unde nihil est aliud galeam salutis assumere, quam spem de ultimo fine habere.

Item, habemus arma ad impugnandum ipsos daemones, scilicet **gladium Spiritus, quod est verbum Dei**: quod fit frequenter in sermonibus, in quibus verbum Dei penetrans corda peccatorum expellit congeriem peccatorum et daemonum.

not you who speak, but the Spirit of your Father that speaks in you (Matt 10:20).

367. Therefore, we possess weapons to defend ourselves against carnal adversaries, namely, gluttony and sensuality, through temperance: **stand therefore, having your loins girt about with truth**.

By the arms of justice, which make us refrain from what is unlawful, we can conquer also earthly greed: **and having on the breastplate of justice**. This is aided by purity of heart or poverty which withdraw us even from things which are lawful: **and your feet shod with the preparation of the Gospel of peace**.

Moreover, we have weapons by which we are guarded from error, the armor of faith: **in all things taking the shield of faith**; and also protected from the enemies of the human race: **wherewith**, meaning the shield of faith, **you may be able to extinguish all the fiery darts of the most wicked one**.

We likewise possess armor by which we are strengthened in spiritual blessings, the armor of hope: **and take unto you the helmet of salvation**. A helmet rests on the head, and so does hope in its end. Now the head of the moral virtues is the very end with which hope is concerned. Thus, to take up the helmet of salvation is nothing other than to have hope in the ultimate end.

Finally, we have weapons to assault the demons themselves: **the sword of the Spirit, which is the word of God**. This happens frequently during sermons when the word of God, penetrating into the hearts of sinners, thrusts out the chaos of sins and demons.

⁶:¹⁸per omnem orationem et obsecrationem orantes omni tempore in Spiritu: et in ipso vigilantes in omni instantia et obsecratione pro omnibus sanctis: [n. 369]

⁶:¹⁹et pro me, ut detur mihi sermo in apertione oris mei [n. 370] cum fiducia, notum facere mysterium Evangelii: [n. 371]

⁶:²⁰pro quo legatione fungor in catena, ita ut in ipso audeam, prout oportet me loqui. [n. 372]

⁶:²¹Ut autem et vos sciatis quae circa me sunt, quid agam, omnia vobis nota faciet Tychicus, carissimus frater, et fidelis minister in Domino: [n. 373]

⁶:²²quem misi ad vos in hoc ipsum, ut cognoscatis quae circa nos sunt, et consoletur corda vestra. [n. 375]

⁶:²³Pax fratribus, et caritas cum fide a Deo Patre et Domino Jesu Christo. [n. 377]

⁶:²⁴Gratia cum omnibus qui diligunt Dominum nostrum Jesum Christum in incorruptione. Amen.

⁶:¹⁸διὰ πάσης προσευχῆς καὶ δεήσεως προσευχόμενοι ἐν παντὶ καιρῷ ἐν πνεύματι, καὶ εἰς αὐτὸ ἀγρυπνοῦντες ἐν πάσῃ προσκαρτερήσει καὶ δεήσει περὶ πάντων τῶν ἁγίων,

⁶:¹⁹καὶ ὑπὲρ ἐμοῦ, ἵνα μοι δοθῇ λόγος ἐν ἀνοίξει τοῦ στόματός μου, ἐν παρρησίᾳ γνωρίσαι τὸ μυστήριον τοῦ εὐαγγελίου

⁶:²⁰ὑπὲρ οὗ πρεσβεύω ἐν ἁλύσει, ἵνα ἐν αὐτῷ παρρησιάσωμαι ὡς δεῖ με λαλῆσαι.

⁶:²¹Ἵνα δὲ εἰδῆτε καὶ ὑμεῖς τὰ κατ' ἐμέ, τί πράσσω, πάντα γνωρίσει ὑμῖν Τυχικὸς ὁ ἀγαπητὸς ἀδελφὸς καὶ πιστὸς διάκονος ἐν κυρίῳ,

⁶:²²ὃν ἔπεμψα πρὸς ὑμᾶς εἰς αὐτὸ τοῦτο ἵνα γνῶτε τὰ περὶ ἡμῶν καὶ παρακαλέσῃ τὰς καρδίας ὑμῶν.

⁶:²³Εἰρήνη τοῖς ἀδελφοῖς καὶ ἀγάπη μετὰ πίστεως ἀπὸ θεοῦ πατρὸς καὶ κυρίου Ἰησοῦ Χριστοῦ.

⁶:²⁴ἡ χάρις μετὰ πάντων τῶν ἀγαπώντων τὸν κύριον ἡμῶν Ἰησοῦν Χριστὸν ἐν ἀφθαρσίᾳ.

⁶:¹⁸By all prayer and supplication praying at all times in the Spirit: and in the same watching with all instance and supplication for all the saints: [n. 369]

⁶:¹⁹And for me, that speech may be given me, that I may open my mouth [n. 370] with confidence, to make known the mystery of the Gospel, [n. 371]

⁶:²⁰For which I am an ambassador in a chain: so that therein I may be bold to speak according as I ought. [n. 372]

⁶:²¹But that you also may know the things that concern me and what I am doing, Tychicus, my dearest brother and faithful minister in the Lord, will make known to you all things: [n. 373]

⁶:²²Whom I have sent to you for this same purpose: that you may know the things concerning us, and that he may comfort your hearts. [n. 375]

⁶:²³Peace be to the brethren and charity with faith, from God the Father and the Lord Jesus Christ. [n. 377]

⁶:²⁴Grace be with all them that love our Lord Jesus Christ in incorruption. Amen.

---

368. Supra posuit Apostolus quae dixerat de insidiis et armaturis, hic exponit illud quod etiam dixerat de confirmatione et confortatione in potentia Dei: et hoc fit per orationem ad Deum super auxilio divino.

Facit autem tria. Primo monet eos ad orandum pro seipsis, secundo pro aliis, tertio pro ipsomet Apostolo.

369. Circa primum ponit septem conditiones orationis. Primo quod debet esse perfecta. Unde dicit **omnem orationem**, quod fit cum in omnibus recurrit quis ad orationem, vel orat pro omni bono.

Secundo quod sit humilis, non praesumptuosa. Ps. ci, 18: *respexit in orationem humilium*, et cetera. Quod fit quando homo non putat se exaudiri propter merita sua, sed propter misericordiam divinam. Et ideo dicit **obsecrationem**, id est per sacrae rei acceptionem. Phil. IV, 6:

368. Previously the Apostle set down what he had to say about snares and weapons, and now he explains what he had also said concerning a confirmation and strengthening in the power of God. He does this through a prayer to God for divine assistance.

He does three things: first, he cautions them to pray for themselves; second, for others; third, for the Apostle himself.

369. In reference to the first he determines seven conditions for prayer. First, it must be complete. Whence he says **by all prayer**; this occurs when someone has recourse to prayer in everything, or prays for every good.

Second, it must be humble and not presumptuous. *He has had regard to the prayer of the humble: and he has not despised their petition* (Ps 102:17). This happens when a man does not suppose that he is heard on account of his own merits, but on account of the divine mercy. And

in omni oratione et obsecratione, cum gratiarum actione petitiones vestrae innotescant apud Deum.

Tertio quod sit continua, ibi **omni tempore**. I Thess. V, 17: *sine intermissione orate, in omnibus gratias agite*. Ps. XXXIII, 2: *benedicam Dominum in omni tempore*, scilicet statuto.

Quarto quod sit devota, quia **in spiritu**. I Cor. XIV, 15: *psallam spiritu, psallam et mente*, id est, non ut vagus.

Quinto quod sit vigilans, ibi **vigilantes**. I Petr. IV, 7: *estote prudentes, et vigilate in orationibus*.

Sexto quod sit instans, ibi **in omni instantia**. Rom. XII, 12: *orationi instantes*, et cetera.

Septimo caritativa, ut scilicet fiat pro omnibus aliis sanctis, ibi **et obsecratione pro omnibus sanctis**. I Tim. II, 1: *obsecro enim primum omnium fieri obsecrationes, orationes, postulationes, gratiarum actiones pro omnibus hominibus*, et cetera.

370. Deinde, ultimo, pro se petit orationes fieri, ibi **et pro me**. Ubi tria petit pro se, quae cuilibet praedicatori sunt necessaria, scilicet quod os aperiat, et ad praedicandum se praeparet quantum in se est, et detur sibi gratia.

Et ut haec tria sibi dentur, petit ut oretur pro se, dicens **ut detur mihi sermo in apertione oris mei**. Non enim potero loqui, nisi quod dederit mihi Dominus, dicebat ille Balaam, Num. XXII, 18. Unde Dominus, Matth. c. X, 20: *non enim vos estis qui loquimini, sed Spiritus*, et cetera. Unde dicitur ibidem 19: *dabitur enim vobis in illa hora quid loquamini*. Hoc autem dictum primo ponit Apostolus. **Ut detur**, inquit, **mihi sermo in apertione oris mei**. Col. ult.: *orantes simul et pro nobis, ut Deus aperiat nobis ostium sermonis*.

371. Et ad quid, Paule? Respondet, ut scilicet possim **cum fiducia notum facere Evangelii mysterium, pro quo legatione fungor in catena**. Et hoc est secundum quod petit, quia non solum est necessarium praedicatori ut detur ei sermo in apertione oris, seu scientiae, sed ut sermonem sibi datum praedicet audacter et cum fiducia. Et hoc est quod dicit **cum fiducia**, et cetera. Et sic praedicabant apostoli, de quibus Act. IV, 31, quod *loquebantur cum fiducia verbum Dei*.

Commendat autem Apostolus officium praedicationis ab excellentia et altitudine. Unde dicit **mysterium Evangelii**. Secundo ostendit, quod pro ipso libenter sustinuit tribulationem et ignominiam. Unde dicit **pro quo legatione fungor in catena**. De his duobus simul Col. ult.: *Deus aperiat nobis ostium sermonis ad loquendum mysterium Christi, propter quod et vinctus sum*.

so he adds **and supplication**, that is, through an accepting of a sacred reality. *In every thing, by prayer and supplication, with thanksgiving, let your petitions be made known to God* (Phil 4:6).

Third, prayer must be continual, **at all times**. *Pray without ceasing, in all things give thanks* (1 Thess 5:17–18). *I will bless the Lord at all times* (Ps 34:1), that is, the established times.

Fourth, it should be devout since it is **in the spirit**. *I will sing with the spirit, I will sing also with the understanding* (1 Cor 14:15), that is, not in a distracted manner.

Fifth, it should be vigilant: **and in the same watching**. *Be prudent therefore and watch in prayers* (1 Pet 4:7).

Sixth, it must be in earnest: **with all instance**. *Instant in prayer* (Rom 12:12).

Seventh, it should be charitable, done for all the other saints: **and supplication for all the saints**. *I desire, therefore, first of all, that supplications, prayers, intercessions and thanksgivings be made for all men* (1 Tim 2:1).

370. Lastly, he asks prayers for himself: **and for me**. He asks three things for himself which are necessary for any preacher: that his mouth would be opened, that he might prepare himself as much as he can for preaching, and that grace be given him.

In order for these to be granted to him he begs them to pray for him, saying **that speech may be given me that I may open my mouth**. I cannot speak anything else but what the Lord gives me, as Balaam expressed it (Num 22:38). Hence our Lord affirmed: *for it is not you that speak, but the Spirit of your Father who speaks in you* (Matt 10:20). He also states there: *for it shall be given you in that hour what to speak* (Matt 10:19). The Apostle places this petition first, **that speech may be given me that I may open my mouth**. *Praying withal for us also, that God may open unto us a door of speech* (Col 4:3).

371. And for what, Paul? He answers, that I may **with confidence make known the mystery of the Gospel, for which I am an ambassador in a chain**. This is his second petition. For it is not only necessary for a preacher that the word or knowledge be given him when he talks, but also that he preach the word given him boldly and with assurance. This is what he means by **with confidence**. This is how the apostles preached, *they spoke the word of God with confidence* (Acts 4:31).

The Apostle praises the duty of preaching for its prominence and grandeur. Thus he says **the mystery of the Gospel**. Then he discloses how he willingly undergoes suffering and ignominy for it, **for which I am an ambassador in a chain**. These two are spoken of together elsewhere: *that God may open unto us a door of speech to speak the mystery of Christ, for which also I am bound* (Col 4:3).

372. Et quia dicitur Eccli. XX, 22: *ex ore fatui reprobatur parabola, non enim dicit eam tempore suo*, ideo Apostolus non solum petit, quod detur sibi sermo, seu praedicandi scientia, sed gratia loquendi cum fiducia, ut scilicet non desisteret ab incepto pro catenis, quibus catenatus erat ab incepto et commisso sibi officio fiducialiter et fideliter prosequendo. Tertio petit, ut detur sibi temporis seu modi congruentia, quia *tempus loquendi et tempus tacendi*, ut dicitur Eccle. III, 7. Et ideo dicit **ut in ipso audeam, prout oportet me loqui**. Et certe in omnibus modus et qualitas facit gratum. Et hoc idem petebat Apostolus Col. ult.: *ut manifestem illud, ita ut oportet me loqui*: quia, ut dicitur Prov. c. XV, 23: *sermo opportunus, optimus*.

373. In fine autem huius epistolae Apostolus statum suum Ephesiis manifestat, cum dicit **ut autem et vos sciatis**, et cetera. Ubi

primo facit quod dictum est;

secundo eos more solito salutat, ibi **pax fratribus**, et cetera.

In prima parte tria facit.

Primo ponitur status sui manifestatio, ibi **ut autem et vos sciatis**, etc.;

secundo discipuli nuntiantis multiplex commendatio, ibi **Tychicus frater meus charissimus et fidelis**, etc.;

tertio ostendit finem, pro quo eis manifestat statum suum, quia scilicet est ipsorum consolatio, ibi **et consolentur corda vestra**.

374. Dicit ergo: **ut autem vos sciatis quae circa me sunt, quid agam, omnia nota vobis faciet**, et cetera. Quasi dicat Apostolus: pro mysterio Evangelii, pro quo catenatus sum, volo quod sciatis quod catena et omnes tribulationes et omnia supplicia, quae in credito officio inferuntur, non me angunt, nec cor mutant, nec pervertunt interius, nec attingunt; sed certe sic angor de istis, quod omnia circa me sunt, non intra.

375. Et quia non possum ire ad annuntiandum vobis, utpote catenatus, **omnia nota faciet vobis Tychicus frater meus charissimus et fidelis minister in Domino**. Et ideo secure credatis ei de omnibus. Lc. XII, 42: *quis, putas, est fidelis servus et prudens*, et cetera. Et iste certe est talis, **quem misi ad vos in hoc ipsum, ut cognoscatis quae circa nos sunt**. Et haec est discipuli commendatio.

376. Et ad quid? **Ut consoletur corda vestra**.

377. Deinde cum dicit **pax fratribus**, etc., ponit Apostolus consuetam salutationem. Et advertendum est, quod licet gratia praecedat pacem et caritatem mutuam hominum ad se invicem, et ad Deum quo ad collationem

372. And because *a parable coming out of a fool's mouth shall be rejected; for he does not speak it in due season* (Sir 20:22). The Apostle does not merely ask that the word or knowledge of preaching be given him. He also prays for the grace of speaking with confidence so that he would not stop what he began on account of the chains by which he was bound; that he might fulfill confidently and faithfully the duty entrusted to him and begun by him. In the third place, he asks that the appropriate time and manner be granted him because there is *a time to keep silence, and a time to speak* (Eccl 3:7). Therefore he asks **that therein I may be bold to speak according as I ought**. Certainly among all people it is one's manner and quality of speaking which makes it acceptable. The Apostle also asked for this elsewhere: *that I may make it manifest as I ought to speak* (Col 4:4), since *a word in due time is best* (Prov 15:23).

373. At the end of this letter the Apostle reveals his condition to the Ephesians, at **but that you also may know**.

first, he does this;

second, greets them in the customary way, at **peace be to the brethren**.

In the first part he makes three points:

first, he makes known his condition, at **but that you also may know**;

second, he recommends, on several accounts, the disciple who brings the news, at **Tychichus, my dearest brother and faithful minister**;

third, he gives the purpose why he makes his condition known to them, namely, for their consolation, at **that he may comfort your hearts**.

374. **But that you also may know the things that concern me and what I am doing**. As though the Apostle said: for the sake of the mystery of the Gospel, on account of which I am imprisoned, I want you to know that chains and all tribulations and all torments, inflicted while discharging the duty entrusted to me, do not cause me anxiety. Neither do they change my heart or ruin me interiorly, nor do they even touch me; but, of course, I am disturbed by what goes on around me, not about what is within me.

375. Since I am not able to leave, chained as I am, to tell you, **Tychicus, my dearest brother and faithful minister in the Lord, will make known to you all things**. Thus you can safely believe him about all these matters. *Who do you think is the faithful and wise steward?* (Luke 12:42). He surely is such **whom I have sent to you for this same purpose, that you may know the things concerning us**. This is the disciple's recommendation.

376. And what for? **That he may comfort your hearts**.

377. Next, when he says **peace be to the brethren** the Apostle writes his usual greeting. And notice that although the bestowal of grace precedes peace and the mutual love of men among themselves and with God since *there is no*

(quia *non est pax impiis, dicit Dominus*), tamen quo ad executionem gratiae et veritatis et caritatis conservationem, pax praecedit suo modo. Et ideo primo optat eis pacem ad se invicem et caritatem ad Deum, dicens: ***pax fratribus, et caritas cum fide***.

Et quia licet pax et caritas multum faciant ad gratiae conservationem, tamen quia semper supponunt ipsam gratiam, sine qua haberi non possunt, ideo optat eis gratiam. Unde dicit: ***gratia cum omnibus, qui diligunt Dominum nostrum Iesum Christum in incorruptione. Amen***.

peace to the wicked, says the Lord (Isa 57:21), nevertheless, in its own way peace does precede the putting of grace into practice and the preservation of truth and charity. Hence, he first wishes that they have peace with one another and charity toward God—***peace be to the brethren and charity with faith***.

Peace and charity contribute greatly toward the preservation of grace; yet, since they always presuppose grace—they could not be had without it—on this account he prays that they receive grace. ***Grace be with all them that love our Lord Jesus Christ in incorruption. Amen***.